MAKING ANCIENT CITIES

This volume investigates how the structure and use of space developed and changed in cities and examines the role of different societal groups in shaping urbanism. Culturally and chronologically diverse case studies provide a basis for examining recent theoretical and methodological shifts in the archaeology of ancient cities. The book's primary goal is to examine how ancient cities were made by the people who lived in them. The authors argue that there is a mutually constituting relationship between urban form and the actions and interactions of a plurality of individuals, groups, and institutions, each with its own motivations and identities. Space is therefore socially produced as these agents operate in multiple spheres.

Andrew T. Creekmore III is Assistant Professor of Anthropology at the University of Northern Colorado. As part of his graduate work, he completed a Fulbright Fellowship in Turkey from 2002 to 2003. Creekmore's research areas include Near Eastern archaeology, High Plains archaeology, and archaeogeophysics. He is especially interested in how people organize themselves in space, in contexts ranging from Native American mobile forager campsites in the Rocky Mountains and Front Range of Colorado to Bronze Age cities of the Near East. Creekmore has conducted research in Turkey, Israel, Syria, Iraq, the eastern United States, and the plains of Colorado. His most recent publication in the area of urbanism and geophysics is in *Archaeological Prospection*.

Kevin D. Fisher is Assistant Professor of Eastern Mediterranean Archaeology at the University of British Columbia. He has been involved in archaeological research projects in Cyprus, Greece, Jordan, Guatemala, Peru, Canada, and the United States. Since 2008, he has been codirector of the Kalavasos and Maroni Built Environments (KAMBE) Project, a National Science Foundation–funded effort to explore the relationship between Late Bronze Age urbanism and social change on the island of Cyprus. Fisher's research interests include the social dynamics of built environments, urbanism, the origins and development of complex societies in the Eastern Mediterranean and Near East, and the application of geospatial and digital technologies in archaeological research. He has published widely on these topics in journals including the *Journal of Mediterranean Archaeology* and *Journal of Anthropological Archaeology*.

Making Ancient Cities

SPACE AND PLACE IN EARLY URBAN SOCIETIES

Edited by

Andrew T. Creekmore III
University of Northern Colorado

Kevin D. Fisher
The University of British Columbia

CAMBRIDGE
UNIVERSITY PRESS

CAMBRIDGE
UNIVERSITY PRESS

32 Avenue of the Americas, New York, NY 10013-2473, USA

Cambridge University Press is part of the University of Cambridge.

It furthers the University's mission by disseminating knowledge in the pursuit of education, learning, and research at the highest international levels of excellence.

www.cambridge.org
Information on this title: www.cambridge.org/9781107046528

© Cambridge University Press 2014

First published 2014

Printed in the United States of America

A catalog record for this publication is available from the British Library.

Library of Congress Cataloging in Publication data
Creekmore, Andrew.
Making ancient cities : space and place in early urban societies /
Andrew T. Creekmore III, University of Northern Colorado, Kevin D. Fisher,
University of British Columbia.
    pages   cm
Includes bibliographical references and index.
ISBN 978-1-107-04652-8 (hardback)
1. Cities and towns – History – To 1500.   2. City planning – History – To
1500.   3. Public spaces – History – To 1500.   I. Fisher, Kevin D., 1968–   II. Title.
HT114.C74   2014
307.7′16–dc23   2013040412

ISBN 978-1-107-04652-8 Hardback

Andrew Creekmore dedicates this volume to his parents, Ted and Carol Creekmore; his grandmother Sarah Roberts; and his wife Eleanor Moseman. Their love, support, and self-sacrifice made possible his career in archaeology.

Kevin Fisher dedicates this volume to the memory of Todd Michael Fisher (1973–2010), his little brother.

Contents

Figures

Tables

Contributors

Traci Ardren is Associate Professor of Anthropology at the University of Miami. She was codirector of the Pakbeh Regional Economy Project at Chunchucmil, Yucatán, from 1998 to 2002, and currently codirects the Xuenkal Archaeological Project. Her research interests include issues of social identity and other forms of symbolic representation in the archaeological record of New World prehistoric cultures and related aspects of contemporary heritage management.

James A. Brown, Professor Emeritus of Anthropology, Northwestern University, seeks to find in the archaeological record of the Eastern Woodlands of North America the social processes that contribute to a cross-cultural reading of cultural evolution. This focus has led to a reexamination of interpretations of the Mississippian period sites of Cahokia (Illinois) and Spiro (Oklahoma), and the Hopewellian site of Mound City (Ohio). An important part of his recent research is the incorporation of a perspective that draws on religious ritual, as represented by his reinterpretation of the main mound at Spiro. His concern with ritual extends to mortuary practices, which have received extended treatment in his rethinking of the Spiro and Mound City burial programs.

D. Matthew Buell recently completed his PhD in the Department of Classics at the University at Buffalo, State University of New York. He specializes in the archaeology of the Bronze Age Aegean and Near East, with a particular focus on state formation, urban planning, landscape, and settlement patterns. He has participated in a number of archaeological projects in North America, Cyprus, and Greece, and he currently serves as the field director for the Gournia Excavation Project in Gournia, Crete, Greece.

Andrew T. Creekmore III is Assistant Professor of Anthropology at the University of Northern Colorado. His research interests include spatial organization of human settlements ranging from mobile forager campsites in the High Plains of the United States to Bronze Age cities of Mesopotamia. His current research involves the application of multiple archaeological geophysics methods to these kinds of sites in order to investigate their structure and life history.

Bruce Dahlin retired from Howard University as Associate Professor of Anthropology. He initiated and codirected the Pakbeh Regional Economy Project at Chunchucmil, Yucatán, from 1993 to 2006. His research interests included ancient marketplaces, economic systems, settlement patterns, political organization, ancient agricultural systems, and paleoclimatic reconstruction.

Kevin D. Fisher is Assistant Professor of eastern Mediterranean Archaeology in the Department of Classical, Near Eastern, and Religious Studies at The University of British Columbia. His research focuses on the social dynamics of built environments, urbanism, the origins and development of complex societies in the eastern Mediterranean and Near East, and the application of geospatial and digital technologies in archaeological research. He has worked on archaeological projects in Cyprus, Greece, Jordan, Peru, Guatemala, the United States, and Canada and is currently codirector of the Kalavasos and Maroni Built Environments Project, Cyprus.

Rodney D. Fitzsimons is Associate Professor in the Department of Ancient History & Classics at Trent University. He specializes in the archaeology of the Bronze Age Aegean and Early Iron Age Greece, with a particular focus on early state formation, sociopolitical identity, monumental architecture, and funerary practices. He has participated in a number of archaeological projects in Greece and Albania, and he currently serves as the site architect for the Azoria Project, Azoria, Crete, Greece, and the codirector of the Ayia Irini Northern Sector Archaeological Project, Ayia Irini, Kea, Greece.

Jeffrey Fleisher is Assistant Professor of Anthropology at Rice University, Houston, Texas. His research on the ancient Swahili has focused on the role of rural and nonelite people in the context of urban development and the use of material culture in the construction of power and authority. His current research at Songo Mnara focuses on the social uses of open space.

Scott R. Hutson is Associate Professor of Anthropology at the University of Kentucky. He was codirector of the Pakbeh Regional Economy Project at Chunchucmil, Yucatán, from 2004 to 2006. He currently directs the Uci-Cansahcab Regional Integration Project in Yucatán, Mexico, and is interested in a broad range of topics including, but not limited to, settlement patterns, household archaeology, and political organization.

John E. Kelly is a Senior Lecturer in Archaeology in the Department of Anthropology at Washington University. He has served as codirector, with James A. Brown, of the Mound 34 Project at Cahokia since 1998, and as the coordinator of the Cahokia Mounds Museum Society's Central Palisade Project. In 2011, together with University of Bologna colleagues Maurizio Tosi, Davide Domenici, and Maurizio Cattani, he initiated the Cahokia Epicenter project that is currently focused on the architecture of the West Plaza. His interests also include the role and contextualization of ritual in Cahokian society, as well as efforts of preservation in the greater St. Louis region, including the ancient town of East St. Louis, which he rediscovered more than twenty years ago.

Aline Magnoni is Adjunct Assistant Professor of Anthropology at Tulane University. She was assistant director of the Pakbeh Regional Economy Project at Chunchucmil, Yucatán, from 1998 to 2006. She currently codirects the Proyecto de Interacción Politica en el Centro de Yucatán, which investigates diachronic regional patterns of political consolidation and dissolution in central Yucatán. Her research interests include landscape and household archaeology, political organization, urbanism and complex societies, public archaeology, and collaboration and engagement with communities.

Yoko Nishimura is a Postdoctoral Researcher in the Department of Anthropology at the University of Pennsylvania. Her research centers on the household archaeology and urban layout of third-millennium BC city-states in northern Mesopotamia. She is particularly interested in the ways ordinary city inhabitants organized their domestic space and activities within the context of a much larger, urban spatial configuration. By examining ancient burials made beneath house floors, she is also investigating the complex relationship between the quotidian activities and intra-mural mortuary practices of ordinary city inhabitants in the past.

Anna Razeto is a Postdoctoral Fellow in the Department of Cross-cultural and Regional Studies of the University of Copenhagen.

Her main field of research is comparative archaeology, particularly focused on aspects of urbanism in the Roman and Han empires. She is currently working on a volume on the comparison between the Han and Roman capitals. Her current project looks at modern interpretation techniques for the public of urban archaeological sites in a cross-cultural perspective.

Barbara L. Stark is Professor Emerita of Anthropology at Arizona State University. She is an archaeologist specializing in Mesoamerican civilizations, especially the Gulf lowlands. Her recent publications include (with coauthors) *Ethnic Identity in Nahua Mesoamerica: The View from Archaeology, Art History, Ethnohistory, and Contemporary Ethnography* (2008) and, coedited with C. P. Garraty, *Archaeological Approaches to Market Exchange in Ancient Societies* (2010).

Stephanie Wynne-Jones is Lecturer in Archaeology, Department of Archaeology, University of York, specializing in the archaeology of the Eastern African Swahili coast and its links with the wider Indian Ocean world, AD 600–1500. Her interests include urbanism, social space, and identity; in particular she has developed projects revolving around the ways that objects move and act within global and local networks. Wynne-Jones has directed projects at Vumba Kuu in Kenya and at Uvinza, Ujiji, Mafia Island, Kilwa, and Songo Mnara in Tanzania. Her current fieldwork is at the fourteenth- to fifteenth-century stonetown of Songo Mnara. In addition, she is working on a project exploring the movement of objects in the Indian Ocean in the early Islamic period of the seventh to tenth centuries AD.

Norman Yoffee is Senior Fellow in the Institute for the Study of the Ancient World, New York University, and professor emeritus in the Department of Near Eastern Studies and the Department of Anthropology at the University of Michigan. His most recent books are *Myths of the Archaic State: Evolution of Cities, States, and Civilizations* and *Questioning Collapse: Human Resilience, Ecological Vulnerability, and the Aftermath of Empire*, the latter co-edited with Patricia McAnany.

Preface

This volume owes its origins to a round-table discussion on ancient cities organized by Michael Smith at the 2008 Society for American Archaeology (SAA) annual meeting in Vancouver, British Columbia. The round table was attended by both editors of this volume and a number of other archaeologists interested in furthering the analysis of urban form across ancient cultures. The stimulating discussions that arose during the round table prompted us to organize a more formal symposium that would explore how urban space was produced through social action and interaction, using case studies from around the world. The chapters in this volume are expanded and updated versions of papers presented at the "Studies of the Production of Space in Ancient Cities" symposium at the 2009 SAA annual meeting held in Atlanta, Georgia. George Cowgill, who kindly served as discussant for the symposium, was unable to participate in this volume, and we are fortunate that Norman Yoffee was able to assume this role. Our work as editors was made easier by the patience and hard work of the volume contributors, and we thank them profusely for all their efforts. We are grateful to Michael Smith and an anonymous reviewer for their thoughtful comments on both the individual chapters and the volume as a whole. We also thank Virginia Ogg, who served as Assistant Editor, for her attention to detail through the final stages of the volume. As editors, we bear responsibility for any remaining errors or omissions.

Andrew T. Creekmore III and Kevin D. Fisher, June 2013

1

Making Ancient Cities: New Perspectives on the Production of Urban Places

Kevin D. Fisher and Andrew T. Creekmore III

Recent theoretical and methodological shifts in approaches to the built environment have reoriented how and why archaeologists investigate ancient cities. This volume examines these developments and their implications through culturally and chronologically diverse case studies. Its primary goal is to examine how ancient cities were made by the people who lived in them. It takes the view that there is a mutually constituting relationship between urban form and the actions and interactions of a plurality of individuals, groups, and institutions, each with their own motivations and identities. Space is therefore socially produced as these agents operate in multiple spheres. The volume provides examples of top-down actions by political authorities, often manifested in varying degrees of urban planning achieved through the exercise of structural power (Wolf 1990, 1999), mid-level actions of particular socioeconomic groups or neighborhoods and districts, and grassroots actions seen in the daily practice of households and individuals. It is clear that these processes operated simultaneously in ancient cities, although there is an ebb and flow as to when and where any of these spheres of agency might have had the greatest effect on particular urban landscapes. It is also apparent that these spheres had competing or conflicting interests that materialized in changing patterns of public and private space through time. This is manifested in the concept of heterarchy and multifocal distributions of power discussed in several chapters of this volume.

Tremendous variability is evident in the development and layout of ancient cities, not only between regions, but also within

KEVIN D. FISHER
AND ANDREW T.
CREEKMORE III

them. Detailed analyses of individual urban centers and their life histories, as well as comparative analyses within and between regions, are crucial to understanding this diversity. This volume includes both types of studies, bringing together a number of experts in the social aspects of ancient urbanism who represent a wide variety of regional and chronological specializations. This book is therefore global in scope, and the case studies address the social production of city space in both Old and New World regions, including Mesopotamia, the eastern Mediterranean, the Roman Empire, China, eastern Africa, North America, and Mesoamerica. Individual essays address both theoretical and methodological approaches to ancient cities, urbanism, and urban form in each of these geographical areas and, in many cases, make comparisons between urban sites within and between regions. The thread that links these diverse case studies is their emphasis on city space and how it articulates with the social processes that produce, transform, reproduce, or destroy the built environment. Although many chapters address top-down, mid-level, and bottom-up processes, the chapters are organized by which level is emphasized. The opening chapters (Creekmore, Nishimura, Wynne-Jones and Fleisher, Magnoni et al.) focus on household and mid-level actions, whereas the middle chapters (Fisher, Fitzsimons) address the tension between high- and mid- or low-level actions, and the remaining contributions (Buell, Kelly and Brown, Razeto, Stark) address mainly top-down planning by elites and state institutions, or the role of cosmology in shaping the city.

The cities explored in this volume are, in many cases, not the usual suspects that populate textbooks and edited volumes. And yet, most are not unusual examples for their respective regions. Too often a single, earlier-discovered, better-known, or exceptional city or subregion stands as the type-city for a given area, and cities that do not fit that mold are given less consideration in discussions of urban space. Our volume addresses this issue by introducing cities that receive less attention in the general literature, alongside some of the best-known cases, and investigating each with new approaches that, while grounded in the empirical analysis of archaeological remains, engage issues of power, materiality, agency, meaning, and identity. These diverse cases and approaches encourage readers to consider regions and perspectives with which they are less familiar, and to look at familiar regions or cases in a new light.

In what follows, we place our volume in context with a discussion of changing archaeological perspectives on ancient cities, including a brief review of other current offerings on the subject. This is followed by an introduction to the regions covered in the volume and a review of the major themes addressed by its contributors, focusing on the production of urban space at various socio-spatial scales, its intersection with the encoding and communication of meaning in urban environments, and the role of these processes in sociopolitical transformation. Finally, we conclude by outlining some of the challenges and prospects for further study of the social production of space in ancient cities.

ARCHAEOLOGICAL PERSPECTIVES ON ANCIENT CITIES

By the time V. Gordon Childe (1936) coined the term "urban revolution" to describe the momentous economic and sociopolitical transformations that accompanied their rise, ancient cities had long been a focus of scholarly inquiry (e.g., Fustel de Coulanges 1963 [1864]). Despite this, the systematic investigation of the remains of early cities by archaeologists to explain these changes is a comparatively recent phenomenon, spurred on by the emergence of New Archaeology in the 1960s and early 1970s and, later, processual archaeology. The goal of such investigations has typically been to reveal the origins, form, and function of ancient cities as a reflection of broad social evolutionary trends and regional patterns associated with the rise of state-level societies (Adams 1966; Ferguson 1991; Redman 1978; Sjoberg 1960). As a result, the emergence of urbanism has usually been viewed as the inexorable result of processes of demographic growth, nucleation, and politico-economic development. Such approaches tend to emphasize the function of cities within settlement hierarchies, catchment areas, and regional systems of production and exchange. Within these patterns and processes, the recursive relationship between cities and the social lives of their inhabitants has rarely been considered.

The rise of postprocessual critiques in the 1980s and 1990s brought with it two interrelated developments that have changed how archaeologists look at past built environments and the people who lived in them. The first is the recognition of the agency of people of the past, which has come to occupy an important, if not central, role in archaeological discourse (see reviews by Dobres and Robb

KEVIN D. FISHER
AND ANDREW T.
CREEKMORE III

2000; Dornan 2002; Gardner 2007). Agency theory is informed by the works of Anthony Giddens (1979, 1984), Pierre Bourdieu (1977), and others who argue for a mutually constituting relationship between human action and social structure. Bourdieu sees this relationship as enacted through *habitus*, an individually unique set of unconsciously internalized dispositions and categories that largely determines individual action and perception of the world. Giddens's structuration theory retains the linkage between routine actions and social reproduction, but is instead based on the assumption that human beings are knowledgeable agents who are largely conscious of the conditions and consequences of their actions. Through the "duality of structure," agents are at once constrained by the rules and resources of structure (thus ensuring social reproduction through the routinization of action) and yet able to make conscious choices in their social actions, opening the potential for social change. While agents act with intention, their knowledge is not perfect and their actions can also result in unintended consequences (e.g., Joyce 2004).

A second important development that arose out of the postprocessual critique is the "spatial turn" seen in archaeological inquiry and the social sciences more generally (see Blake 2003), also influenced by Giddens and Bourdieu, as well as other prominent social theorists who privilege the spatial dimensions of social life (e.g., Foucault 1977 [1975]; Lefebvre 1991 [1974]). This has led to a growing recognition that cities and other built environments, as spatial contexts in which human interaction takes place, play an active and central role in social production and reproduction (de Certeau 1988:98–99; 1998:142; Low 2000; Soja 1989:14, 2000:11). Agency and the social dimensions of space are interrelated through the concept of *place*. Whereas space might be seen as the passive, neutral physical location in which social action occurs, a place is "lived space" imbued with meanings, identities, and memories that actively shape, and are shaped by, the daily practice and experiences of its inhabitants and historically contingent social processes (Low and Lawrence-Zúñiga 2003; Mumford 2003 [1937]; Preucel and Meskell 2004; Rodman 1992). Cities, therefore, are made. They are at once products and facilitators of social life. As the studies in this volume demonstrate, they are created in the place-making of multiple agents or stakeholders, often with competing interests, from the top-down planning of ruling elites through the bottom-up actions of households. As Soja (2000:6–7) argues,

[O]ur "performance" as spatial beings takes place at many different scales, from the body ... to a whole series of more distant geographies ranging from rooms and buildings, homes and neighborhoods, to cities and regions, states and nations.... [A]lthough there is some "distance decay" out from the body in the degree to which we individually influence and are influenced by these larger spaces, every one of them must be recognized as products of collective human action and intention, and therefore susceptible to being modified or changed.

In this way the production of space in cities is actively implicated in processes of sociopolitical transformation (e.g., Fisher, Chapter 6; Fitzsimons, Chapter 7; Wynne-Jones and Fleisher, Chapter 4, all in this volume).

Seeing built environments as places acknowledges not only the agency of the people who create them, but also the agency of the buildings themselves. Ian Hodder (1982, 1992) has long maintained the need for archaeologists to see material culture as actively engaged in the production of social life, rather than as the passive by-product of human behavior. There has been a growing acknowledgment of the agency of things in the social sciences in general and in archaeology more specifically (e.g., Gosden 2005; Hodder 2012; Knappett and Malafouris 2008). George Mead's (1934) work has been particularly influential in this regard, emphasizing the central role of the physical world in the constitution and maintenance of the self and social identity and suggesting that relations between humans and objects are social relations (see also Gell 1998; McCarthy 1984). Actor-Network Theory situates agency in the relationships that people have with other people and objects, and proponents such as Latour (2005:71–72) contend that anything that modifies a state of affairs by making a difference is an actor. Like other human and material actors, cities and their individual buildings have biographies (Kopytoff 1986) or "life histories" constituted in the meanings accumulated over the duration of their existence and that of their "ancestors" and "descendants," as well as the memories of them held by their human occupants (Düring 2005; Hendon 2004:276, 2010; Pred 1984, 1990; Tringham 1995).

The affective relationships that people often form with the places in which they live further blur the distinction between human and material agents. Often expressed in terms of *place attachment* or

KEVIN D. FISHER
AND ANDREW T.
CREEKMORE III

place identity, these emotive aspects play an important role in the development of individual and group identities at various socio-spatial scales (Altman and Low 1992; Proshansky et al. 1983; Russell and Snodgrass 1987; Tuan 1977; see Fisher, Chapter 6 and Magnoni et al., Chapter 5, both in this volume). Research in environmental psychology has demonstrated that people often develop identities associated not only with their home and neighborhood, but also at the level of the city itself, whether a particular city or the "urban experience" in general – what Proshansky et al. (1983:78) refer to as "urban identity" (Graumann and Kruse 1993; Hummon 1986; Lalli 1992; Twigger-Ross and Uzzell 1996). The unique aspects of urban life are produced through a range of phenomena and their meanings, from the physical elements of the built environment and complexity and variability of the visual and aural scene, to the "epochs and anecdotes" of individual biographies and the "little pleasures and annoyances" of daily practice in urban environments (Graumann 2002:109; Proshansky et al. 1983). The critical mass of people and the creative synergies and opportunities for social (and economic) interaction that it generates were likely as important to the urban lifestyle in the past as they are today. It is this urban experience and people's identification with it that Cowgill (2004:526) sees as an important part of what defines a city.

Studies of city space often emphasize aspects that correspond to Rapoport's high- or mid-level meanings, including cosmologies, philosophy, and worldview (high-level), as well as notions of identity, status, wealth, and power (mid-level) (Rapoport 1988:325, 1990). These meanings are most often discussed in terms of monumental architecture, tombs, and formal planning of infrastructure. Less apparent, and more often neglected in studies of city space, are low-level meanings, including implicit messages about expected behavior embodied in architecture and the articulation of space (Rapoport 1988:325). Rapoport (1988:325) makes it clear that these are not discrete categories, but rather ideal types that structure a continuum. While these levels of meaning serve as a useful heuristic tool for thinking about how meanings are materialized in past built environments, it is important to emphasize that meanings often defy easy categorization and frequently cross-cut levels. Furthermore, these levels of meaning are not exclusive to particular scales of spatial production. For example, Bourdieu (1973) and others have demonstrated that high-level meanings were an important element in the construction of houses, where they play an important role in shaping daily practice. At the same time, mid-level meanings associated with status and power are in evidence at all spatial scales, from the coordination of monumental buildings and processional routes in a city to the "indexical" meanings communicated by individual houses (Blanton 1994).

Each level of meaning described by Rapoport (1988, 1990) is found throughout cities, meshed with different scales of spatial production, including the cityscape itself, which might be characterized by large-scale planning of infrastructure and public buildings; an intermediate/supra-household scale that includes districts and neighborhoods, or at least coordination among groups of neighbors; and the scale of individual households and their constituent spaces. Recognition of these multiple scales of socio-spatial production and levels of meaning encourages us to examine more closely the agents that produce city space. These agents are found in a complex web of social relations that combine both heterarchical (Crumley 1995) and hierarchical relationships. Although data to examine equally each of these levels and relationships are not always available, when possible, a multilevel analysis will provide a more complete understanding of the production of urban space.

The changing perceptions discussed here have resulted in the asking of new questions about the materiality and social production of ancient cities, as well as new approaches to old questions of urban origins, form, and change over time. Several studies challenge long-held assumptions about the kinds of spaces and social relationships that constitute a city (Hirth 2008; McIntosh 2005; A. Smith 2003; M. L. Smith 2003a; Soja 2000). Even cities that, on their surface, fit classical models of urban space are shown to have complex and often unique histories that emerge upon closer examination (e.g., Laurence 1994). In a series of recent articles, Michael Smith (2007, 2010a, 2010b, 2011) reinvigorates an empirical and comparative perspective by applying interdisciplinary theoretical and methodological approaches to the analysis of ancient and modern cities. Although Smith (2011:2) criticizes some of the theoretical ideas expressed in this volume and focuses on mid-level "empirical urban theory," by improving the linkage between low- and high-level theory, his work pushes researchers to pursue difficult questions about cities. Smith's efforts to articulate a more rigorous and comparative approach to urban structure and planning are adopted to varying degrees in several of this volume's chapters.

The study of ancient cities has been further transformed by recent methodological advances. On one level, there are analytical techniques applied to ancient city plans, such as space syntax analysis, that provide insight into patterns of movement, visibility, and social interaction (Ferguson 1996; Fisher 2009; Grahame 2000; Laurence 1994; A. Smith 2003). In addition, recent advances in archaeological geophysics, including the use of ground-penetrating radar, resistivity, and magnetometry, allow ancient urban areas to be investigated for archaeological features at a relatively low cost and time investment when compared to excavation (Aspinall et al. 2008:144–155; Gaffney and Gater 2003). These methods meet the need for a greater number of relatively complete city plans for both comparative research and intrasite spatial analysis (Marcus and Sabloff 2008b:19; 2008c:324), without resorting to prohibitively expensive and time-consuming extensive excavations (see Creekmore, Chapter 2, Fisher, Chapter 6, and Nishimura, Chapter 3, all in this volume). This advantage is tempered by the extent to which these plans compress life histories into a snapshot of an apparently fully formed, static city. When archaeological data are available, these snapshots can be complemented by life history and microscale studies of the development of individual structures or portions of the city (e.g., Benech 2007; Nishimura, Chapter 3 in this volume). In addition to these theoretical and methodological advances, the database of ancient cities has been growing as a result of ongoing survey and excavation throughout many regions of the world (Marcus and Sabloff 2008b:3), meaning that we have never been a better position to compare ancient urban form and development on a global scale.

Our challenge is to apply these new ways of looking at ancient cities to understand better the complex interrelationship between urban form and social life. As these theoretical and methodological developments take hold in the study of ancient cities, we are now at a point where we can assess their impact and examine the results obtained from regional or site-specific studies as well as cross-regional comparative studies. *Making Ancient Cities* is a response to this challenge.

THIS VOLUME IN CONTEXT

This volume follows in a long tradition of archaeological studies of cities. In addition to current texts devoted to particular cities, regions, or concepts (e.g., Algaze 2008; Arnauld et al. 2012; Aufrecht et al. 1997; Coulston and Dodge 2000; Gates 2003; Fash 2009; Hansen 2000, 2006; Kenoyer 1998; McIntosh 2005; Nichols 1997; Osborne and Cunliffe 2005; M. E. Smith 2008; Van de Mieroop 1999), there have been a few recent edited volumes that explore various aspects of past urban environments in multiple world regions (Marcus and Sabloff 2008a; M. L. Smith 2003a; Storey 2006). These volumes demonstrate the continued relevance and vitality of ancient cities as an area of archaeological inquiry. Of these, Monica Smith's approach has the most in common with the present volume and represents one of the more recent attempts to see ancient cities as a new social order in which numerous groups, both nonelite and elite, had to coexist. Some contributors to Smith's volume examine the role that these various groups played in the formation and development of particular cities.

In contrast to Smith's (2003a) emphasis on social processes in cities, Storey's (2006) volume focuses primarily on the demography of preindustrial urban populations and largely declines to place these populations in the contexts of the specific urban built environments they might have inhabited. Marcus and Sabloff's (2008a) volume shares the global perspective of the present volume and of Smith's (2003a) book. In addition to regional studies, there are introductory, concluding, overview, and response essays that focus on issues such as how to define "the city" and how scholars have studied ancient cities. Although the editors (Marcus and Sabloff 2008c:325) acknowledge in the conclusions that the process of urbanism can involve both top-down decision making directed by elites and bottom-up decisions made by commoners, this theme is touched on in only a few essays. By contrast, the present volume is less concerned with the definitions and trajectories of urbanism, focusing instead specifically on how particular ancient cities, or their constituent parts, were produced by the social actions and interactions of their inhabitants.

This volume avoids restrictive definitions of "city" or "urban" based solely on population size or density – factors that are notoriously difficult to substantiate in archaeological contexts (Trigger 2003:120–121; see also M. L. Smith 2003b:8). Instead, we take a broad view of cities, which recognizes the differentiation or specialization of roles evident in urban environments vis-à-vis their hinterlands (Trigger 1972; Southall 1973:6), as well as the unique opportunities for social interaction and information production and exchange that are a vital part of the urban experience (Knox 1995; M. L. Smith 2003b). This approach encompasses highly nucleated, high-density cities, such as Rome or the cities of China, the eastern Mediterranean, or Mesopotamia, as well as settlements that resemble McIntosh's "clustered" cities (McIntosh 2005:185), and low-density (Fletcher 2010, 2012), dispersed or multicentric urbanism, including cities of Mesoamerica, the east coast of Africa, and the Native American site of Cahokia, which is often ignored in more traditional considerations of ancient urbanism. Many of this volume's chapters emphasize the functions that define cities, and residents are viewed as active participants in the activities that generate and give meaning to cities and urban space. There are significant political and economic differences between a city the size of Rome and a 10–40 ha city elsewhere, but we contend that the processes that produce urban built environments are similar in each case. Although the chapters address different times and places, and range from regional analyses to case studies of single sites, macroscale to microscale, and synchronic to diachronic, they are linked by the application of the theoretical perspectives discussed here, as well as an emphasis on the importance of cities as generators of sociopolitical change. In the following section we introduce the world regions and cases covered in this volume, highlighting their contributions to these topics.

MAKING ANCIENT CITIES IN GLOBAL PERSPECTIVE

Mesopotamia

Mesopotamia is well known as the location of what is often touted as the first city in the world – Uruk – that emerged in the mid-fourth millennium BC as part of a process of urbanization that saw the subsequent spread of city-states across the arid but irrigated zone in and around the Tigris and Euphrates Rivers in southern Iraq (Algaze 2008; Nissen 1988; Pollock 1999). Less well known is that cities also developed in Upper Mesopotamia around the same time as Uruk, in areas mostly devoted to dry farming. This process is brought to light by recent excavations at the sites of Tell Brak and Tell Hamoukar (Emberling and McDonald 2003; Gibson et al. 2002; Oates et al. 2007; Ur 2010; Ur et al. 2007). These early cities do not seem to have had many contemporary peers in the region, although urbanism was widespread by the third millennium (Akkermans and Schwartz 2003). Much debate centers on whether the cities of Upper Mesopotamia were independent, indigenous formations, or if their development was heavily influenced by the cities of Lower Mesopotamia (Algaze 2008). Regardless of one's position on this debate, the emergence of cities in Upper Mesopotamia was a critical juncture in the prehistory of the region.

The structure of Upper Mesopotamian cities has much in common with the cities of Lower Mesopotamia, but there are also significant differences, discussed in this volume by Andrew Creekmore (Chapter 2) and Yoko Nishimura (Chapter 3). In each region, large cities are best characterized as city-states, in which a large urban center hosts a state government that rules a relatively small territory radiating from the capital city. Smaller cities had urban characteristics, but were linked politically and economically to a nuclear center in the region. Both small and large cities generally consisted of densely packed architecture – including residences, palaces, temples, and workshops – protected by fortification walls, with limited extramural settlement.

Creekmore's survey of patterns in the production of space in Upper Mesopotamian cities emphasizes the degree to which household- and neighborhood-level actions structure city space. He investigates several characteristics shared by these cities, including multiple centers of economic, political, and religious power; highly nucleated population; armature systems that link key monuments or routes through cities; conservative or enduring use of space; and defensible spaces, such as culs-de-sac that appear "organic" or "emergent," but may instead represent careful planning to meet residents' needs. Although Creekmore argues that general patterns in the production of space in these cities reflect a heterarchical process, he notes significant differences in the life history of some cities, which indicate that the degree of power-sharing and its role in the production of city space varied.

Nishimura identifies a similar interplay of bottom-up and top-down actions in the production of city space in her detailed case study of neighborhoods in the Upper Mesopotamian city of Titriş. Nishimura considers multiple levels of spatial production, including analysis of household activities, architecture, neighborhoods, street patterns, and special-use buildings. Her study ranges from a microscale, room-by-room and house-by-house analysis of patterns of artifact distribution at Titriş to a consideration of entire neighborhoods and their place within the city's structure. She finds that two widely separated neighborhoods in the city demonstrate high-density housing, homogeneous lifeways, a high standard of living, and standardized house plans that emphasize privacy. In concert with Creekmore's discussion of multiple nuclei of power in Upper Mesopotamian cities, Nishimura finds that public buildings are distributed throughout Titriş – often built at strategic locations including city gates, elevated spaces, and next to the mound that presumably functioned as a citadel.

The Eastern Mediterranean

The focus on Mesopotamia as progenitor of urban society in this general region and the long shadow cast by the famous cities of the Greek mainland and Ionia from the Classical and Hellenistic periods (ca. 480–30 BC) has meant that the prehistoric eastern Mediterranean has rarely been seen as important in the study of urban origins and development (cf. Branigan 2001). For the Bronze Age Aegean, the pre-occupation with palaces – that first appear in the late third through early second millennium BC – in both excavations and discussions of sociopolitical change, has meant that the urban environments within which most of these monumental buildings were situated have received scant attention. The situation is exacerbated by published reconstructions of palaces such as Knossos that show them sitting in splendid isolation in park-like settings (e.g., Klynne 1998). Matt Buell's discussion (Chapter 8 in this volume) on the important and only recently discovered Minoan site of Galatas counters such a view by situating its palace within an urban-built environment designed to promote both sociopolitical differentiation and community cohesion.

The development of palatial centers on Crete marked the earliest emergence of state-level societies in the Aegean region (see Manning 2008 for one account of this process). By the Neopalatial period (ca. 1750–1460 BC), Knossos had risen to prominence, and may have exercised hegemony over some or all of the island's other polities at this time (Knappett and Schoep 2000). Buell suggests the possibility that Knossos's expansion might explain the planning and development of a new palatial urban center at Galatas. Buell applies Michael Smith's (2007) criteria for analyzing planning in ancient cities, combined with Rapoport's levels of meaning (1988, 1990), and finds a high degree of planning at Galatas. This, combined with a reordering of local settlement patterns at the time of Galatas's development, demonstrates the emergence of an urban center that reoriented local systems of food and craft production.

Cyprus – in the midst of its more famous Aegean neighbors and the long-lived urban traditions of Anatolia, Syria-Palestine, Mesopotamia, and Egypt – has been similarly overlooked in discussions of ancient cities (cf. Gates 2003:154–158). Yet Kevin Fisher's study of the island's first cities, which emerge during the Late Bronze Age (c. 1700–1100 BC), demonstrates their vital and active role in the profound social transformations of this period. Through the production of space at various scales and the structuring of new patterns of social interaction, the new cityscapes were a driving force in the rapid sociopolitical change that saw the island shift from a relatively egalitarian, village-based society to one with hierarchical and heterarchical social structures. Fisher details city-scale – that is, centralized planning evidenced by gridded streets and spatially coordinated monumental buildings – but also reveals how neighborhoods and households modified city space and, in some cases, undermined the spatial control of the central authorities. These cities do not adhere rigidly to a single, ideal urban form, but each was constructed within the context of local history and decision making. The novel forms of monumental, domestic, and mortuary architecture in these urban environments provided various contexts for social action and interaction through which new statuses, roles, and identities were negotiated, established, and displayed.

Following the collapse of the Bronze Age palatial system ca. 1200 BC, the so-called Dark Age marked the beginning of various social, political, ideological, and economic developments that culminated in the emergence of the Greek city-state, or *polis*, in the ninth and eighth centuries BC (Osborne 1996; Thomas and Conant 2003). This process is still poorly understood and much of the archaeological evidence for the formative stages of many cities has been obscured, and often destroyed, by constructions of the Classical and later periods. Rodney Fitzsimons's chapter on the results of recent excavations at Azoria (Chapter 7 in this volume), on the island of Crete, offers us a rare glimpse of a *polis* in the making and the recursive relationship between the urban environment and the development of new sociopolitical institutions. Fitzsimons's study identifies an interplay between household-level spatial production and mid- or high-level, civic spatial production, implicating it in the far-reaching socio-political changes that characterized this period. In the building of houses, retaining walls, and public buildings – and the hosting of festivities in houses and communal structures – residents and rulers express spatially an ongoing negotiation of evolving social roles and institutions in a new kind of society. Fitzsimons argues that urban space in Azoria was designed at both the household and the civic levels to negotiate newly emerging social relationships in which civic identity competed with kinship to mark social allegiance and meaning. In the process of building a city, the residents of Azoria intentionally deviated from the spatial principles of past settlement at the site, a decision Fitzsimons argues was motivated by the need to supersede past sociopolitical relationships while building a new civic identity. In this way, the production of urban space was central to the emergence of the *polis* as the socio-spatial and political institution that came to define the reemergence of the state in the Late Geometric through Classical Greek world.

Africa

Ancient African cities receive less attention in the general literature than cities in other world regions, in part because of the legacy of racism and the view that Africa's climate and culture impeded urbanization. This lack of attention creates the perception that, outside of Egypt, cities in Africa are comparatively recent or developed only under the influence of external forces, including traders and colonizing populations (Kusimba 2008; McIntosh and McIntosh 2003). Even Egypt was once considered to lack cities, owing to issues of preservation and its character as a territorial state in contrast to the city-states of Mesopotamia (Bard 2008). Current concerns in the study of ancient African cities include examining their indigenous roots, relationship to hinterlands, influence of foreign trading partners, and connections between ancient and historical cases. McIntosh and his colleagues argue for the recognition of polities of the Niger River Valley in West Africa, such as Jenne-jeno, as representative of a different and therefore previously unacknowledged form of urbanism in which the dispersed settlement of corporate groups in separate but closely spaced sites within a given region functioned as a "clustered" city that developed 250 BC–AD 1400 in the absence of the state (McIntosh and McIntosh 1993, 2003; McIntosh 1991, 2005).

The dispersed nature of these and other African cities contrasts with highly nucleated, walled cities such as those of the Swahili and Yoruba (Kusimba 2008). Swahili cities, discussed in Chapter 4 of this volume by Stephanie Wynne-Jones and Jeff Fleisher, are city-states that formed in AD 800–1300 in eastern Africa, from southern Somalia to Mozambique, in the context of complex trading relationships with Muslim merchants plying the Arabian Sea. Distinctive for their use of coral as an architectural material, these cities are important examples of indigenous African urbanism because they highlight how social structure, daily practice, and economic activities influenced the development of the built environment.

In their analysis of Swahili cities, Wynne-Jones and Fleisher find that unifying models that emphasize the role of elite agency and high-level meaning in structuring and planning cities, such as that offered by Mark Horton (1994, 1996), cobble together features of different cities over time, presenting a useful – but ultimately inaccurate – picture of urban space that fails to explain the development of many cities. As a result, the diversity of cities is neglected because only a few cases fit the prevailing models. Wynne-Jones and Fleisher argue that this problem is best solved by examining low levels of meaning (after Rapoport 1988; 1990) and household activities, which reveal common engines of spatial production in these diverse cities. These authors explore the role of Rapoport's high- and mid-level meanings, for example, in the centrality of the main mosque, but they argue that household-level spatial production and low-level meanings are the driving forces that structure city space. Their approach, which they connect to practice theory, emphasizes the coordination of house construction among neighbors with shared walls, and the maintenance of open space around houses, which provides room to expand the house and space for common outdoor activities. These everyday practices generate low-level meanings that are perpetuated through the lifecycle of houses. In this way, sociopolitical processes are enacted within a changing urban landscape that both shapes and is shaped by urban residents and visitors alike.

Mesoamerica

Mesoamerican cities are usually divided into highland versus lowland examples, with the former in the hills of southern Mexico, and the latter in the tropics of southern Mexico, Guatemala, Belize,

KEVIN D. FISHER
AND ANDREW T.
CREEKMORE III

El Salvador, Honduras, and Nicaragua. In both areas, the earliest cities developed in the period between 650 BC–AD 500 (Trigger 2003:97). Highland polities include very large cities with nucleated populations, such as Teotihuacán, Tenochtitlán, and Monte Albán, which were the centers of regional states. In contrast, lowland cities – such as Copán, Palenque, and Tikal – tend to be smaller city-states, have more dispersed populations, and command smaller territories (Coe 2005). In these areas, there are different types of cities in terms of their economic, political, and ideological roles within subregions (Pyburn 2008:249). Interactions between these polities were complex and changed over time, as indicated by settlement pattern studies and world systems models (Balkansky 2006; Blanton et al. 1992; Smith and Berdan 2000).

The contrast between highly nucleated cities and cities characterized by a dispersed population centered on a ceremonial core presents challenges for scholars of Mesoamerican cities. In an attempt to make sense of this diversity, Marcus (1983) examined the structure of Mesoamerican cities in light of the models of modern urban planners. Later, Sanders and Webster (1988) applied Fox's (1977) typological approach in order to sort Mesoamerican cities into categories based on the size of the population, degree to which power is centralized, complexity of economic institutions, and importance of ritual functions. This approach was very influential in studies of these cities, but more recently, some scholars have argued for the importance of agency, identity, and meaning in the development and definition of Mesoamerican cities (Houston et al. 2003; Yaeger 2003). In his review of urbanism in Mesoamerica, Joyce calls for studies of urbanism to "focus on practice, social negotiation, identity, and materiality" in a manner that includes the agency of the entire range of persons in society, including everyday people of every age, occupation, and social status (Joyce 2009: 195). In contrast to Joyce's inclusiveness, to solve the problem of defining Aztec cities, Michael Smith focuses on the actions of political leaders in his study of Aztec city states (2008). Smith argues that the administrative, economic, and religious influences of cities mark them as urban regardless of population size. Like Joyce (2009), Hirth is critical of functional approaches like that of Smith and others, including Blanton (1976) and Marcus (1983). He argues that Central Mexican cities were "incidental" and "secondary" developments that derived from the "segmentary community structure" of the *altepetel* or "royal household and the land and people of the ruler" (Hirth 2008:277–278). Hirth's approach, which shifts the focus from specific urban centers to the rural and urban aspects of social structure at the regional level, incorporates ethnohistoric and archaeological data in an attempt to understand these cities from an emic perspective, rather than imposing formal models based on central-place theory or other products of western scholarship. A recent volume focuses specifically on the role of neighborhoods in Mesoamerican cities (Arnauld et al. 2012), further highlighting the importance of mid-level social structure in defining urban spaces.

In this volume, Aline Magnoni, Traci Ardren, Scott Hutson, and Bruce Dahlin (see Chapter 5) examine Chunchucmil – a Classic Maya city in Yucatán – and Barbara Stark (Chapter 11) focuses on Cerro de las Mesas, a lowland city in Veracruz, Mexico. Both chapters address aspects of the issues outlined earlier, including the contrast between nucleated and dispersed cities, agency in urbanization, political authority, meaning, and urban identity. Magnoni et al. emphasize household and neighborhood patterns as indicative of larger social processes at Chunchucmil. This city differs from its regional peers in terms of its relatively high-density settlement, lack of a single monumental core, and low walls that incorporate copious open space into specific household compounds. In light of the absence of a single ruling or administrative center in the city, and the wide distribution of trade goods among households, the authors argue that power was more widely distributed at Chunchucmil than at other cities in the region. This power-sharing is manifested in the dearth of evidence for centralized city planning as residents were left to coordinate the construction of household-lot boundary walls and narrow residential streets that characterize much of the city. The authors suggest that the commerce that drew people to settle in an otherwise less-than-ideal part of the landscape provided an opportunity for place-making that generated a unique version of the characteristic dispersed structure of Mesoamerican cities.

Stark's analysis of open spaces in Mesoamerican cities includes households, residential areas, and elite or institutional complexes, although the latter command more open space and thus are the major focus of her attention. Open spaces generally receive less study than built-up spaces because these "empty" spaces provide less tangible evidence for the activities they hosted, and they may be perceived as the accidental by-product of the production of other urban spaces (see also M. L. Smith 2008). Stark gives new life to the gardens, parks, plazas, and other delimited spaces that are particularly characteristic of Mesoamerican cities and that provide clues to the production of urban space. As Stark argues, leap-frogging the urban fringe belts of open space may be responsible for some of the copious open space in these dispersed or low-density cities, and open space may mark settlement boundaries. Open spaces also hold the key to measuring settlement nucleation in order to compare cities both intra- and inter-regionally. In her analysis, Stark emphasizes the role played by open space in negotiating social relationships, aesthetics, and symbolism. Elaborate gardens may serve as class markers, marking social distinctions on the landscape.

North America

In spite of a tradition of monumental construction among various Native American groups dating as far back as the mid-fourth millennium BC, there are few, if any, widely accepted examples of pre-Columbian cities in North America. While some scholars have characterized certain Puebloan sites in the Southwest as cities or at least near-urban (e.g., Lekson's [1999] discussion of Chaco Canyon, Aztec, and Paquimé [Casas Grandes]), North America is rarely included in studies of ancient cities. A key exception is the well-known Mississippian site of Cahokia, which emerged in the American Bottom outside of what is today St. Louis, reaching its zenith in the twelfth through thirteenth centuries AD. At five times the size of the next-largest such site, Pauketat (1998:45) describes Cahokia as an "archaeological behemoth," emphasizing that its effects on other cultural complexes of the time were "both apparent and, arguably, profound." Debate continues regarding the nature of Cahokia's sociopolitical organization, with divergent opinions as to whether it was some form of chiefdom (e.g., Pauketat 1994; Milner 1998) or rather a state (Gibbon 1974; O'Brien 1989), or whether we should jettison these evolutionary terms all together as Pauketat (2007) has more recently argued; nor is there agreement on the nature and extent of the site's hegemony over the surrounding region (see Holt 2009:232–235 for a recent summary; also Cobb 2003).

As John Kelly and Jim Brown – two scholars long associated with the famous site – discuss in their contribution to this volume (see Chapter 9), the idea of Cahokia as a city has proved equally contentious. They argue that although it does not conform in all aspects to the litmus tests for urbanism established on the basis of Near Eastern and other "classic" cities, Cahokia was indeed a city in the context of Mississippian culture. Kelly and Brown take a close look at the city's structure, interpreting its form in light of ethnographic and ethnohistoric studies of descendant populations in the region. They explore the complex structure of Cahokia's many plazas and mound groups, and argue that the overall structure of Cahokia was driven by local elites with a view toward mirroring cosmic structure, and corporate groups moving to the site established new monuments within this overall scheme. Some newcomers resisted the control of Cahokian elites by starting competing settlements nearby. As described by Kelly and Brown, in the structure of Cahokia there is a fundamental tension between social integration via corporate, reciprocal relationships, as expressed through positioning within both the imagined cosmos that structures the site and the tangible monuments of the city, and the enforcement of a hierarchical cosmos and society in the form of higher- or lower-ranking monument groups and competition for space. Thus, the plazas and monuments are built by corporate groups, but adhere to an elite-driven scheme that emphasizes the ranking of both the cosmos and the residents of Cahokia, as expressed in the relative size and importance of mound and plaza groups. Although this view of Cahokia de-emphasizes the construction of housing, and low-level meanings emphasized by other chapters, it highlights the complexity of the urban process in a settlement not often considered in discussions of ancient cities.

Rome and China

Rome stands out among the cities addressed in this volume as a well-documented and much-studied imperial capital. Chang'an, although less-well known in western scholarship, also served as the center of a vast empire – the Han Dynasty, which ruled much of China until the early twentieth century. In her contribution to this volume (Chapter 10), Anna Razeto examines these two cities in comparative perspective from the second century BC through the second century AD using the lens of facilities for craft production and retail. This period witnessed the transition of Rome from republic to far-flung empire. Under Augustus and his successors, the city was remade through various monumental building projects that glorified the imperial family, providing a conceptual model for the types of monuments and urban developments that should be given priority in cities throughout the empire (e.g., DeLaine 2008:108). These projects included new market and retail spaces needed to accommodate the demands of Rome's burgeoning population.

Sophisticated state-level sociopolitical organization existed in China at least since the Xia and Shang civilizations of the Bronze Age. A recent assessment of urbanism in pre-Imperial China suggests, however, that the spatial environment lacked many crucial features of urbanism seen elsewhere and that true cities did not emerge until the period of the Warring States capitals (481–221 BC; part of the Eastern Zhou Dynasty) – only then did cities become a "defining ingredient of Chinese civilization" (von Falkenhausen 2008:227; also Chang 1974). This period saw the rise of a substantial population of commoners in the capital cities who were not direct dependents of the rulers' courts and who pursued commerce and craft production (von Falkenhausen 2008:226). Urban form and function changed as cities expanded to accommodate specialized crafts and designated residential areas, resulting in the integration of royal administration with production and market exchanges (Shen 2003). This process of urbanization brought together a large number of residents with a wide variety of skills who contributed to the transformation of purely royal cities into the commercial-based urban centers of the Imperial period (Shen 1994, 2003).

Razeto compares and contrasts Chang'an and Rome in order to discern how state power and ideology structured city space. Instead of looking at the palaces, the traditional foci of imperial power, Razeto examines how the state determined the location, form, and function of markets and facilities for specialized production. She argues that although practical considerations – including ease of access, transport, and proximity to raw materials – contributed significantly to the form and placement of markets and manufacturing facilities for brick, metals, and other goods in Rome and China, state ideology, political interests, and elite consumption also played key roles. To control and protect commerce, Rome and China built elaborate markets that not only trumpeted state power and served as symbols of the city, but that also provided important foci of social interaction. In a nod to low-level spatial production, Razeto notes that despite state intervention in the structuring of market and manufacturing space, the workers in these professions were often independent producers with a hand in structuring their work space within the imperial edifice or city plan.

Razeto believes that the lack of civil rights for commoners in Chinese cities limited their agency in structuring city space, but surely their daily activities modified the spaces in which they lived worked.

FUTURE DIRECTIONS IN THE STUDY OF ANCIENT CITIES

We hope these case studies will challenge specialists to look outside their regions for inspiration in analyzing and interpreting the production of urban space. We also hope that readers will be inspired to apply the insights of this volume to the problems of the contemporary world. The year 2009 brought a significant milestone in human existence when, for the first time, the majority of the earth's population (50.1%) was living in urban environments; by 2050, that figure is predicted to rise to 68.7% (United Nations Department of Economic and Social Affairs 2012). Given the challenges faced by researchers in a number of disciplines in trying to understand the profound behavioral, social, and ecological effects of urban life, archaeology is in a unique position to provide much-needed time depth to these issues, offering insight into urbanism's origins and contributing to a diachronic perspective concerning the relationship between people and cities and the sustainability of urban systems (e.g., M. E. Smith 2010b). Many of the great urban theorists have recognized the need to understand the ancient roots of urbanism as a way to observe long-term social dynamics relevant to the cities in which we live today (Jacobs 1969; Mumford 1961; Soja 2000).

Going forward, the study of ancient cities must consider the agency of people at multiple social scales in the production of space, in addition to the standard attention to macro-level processes of population growth, environmental change, and international relations. A special challenge in most world regions is gaining a more representative view of the development of city space over time through examination of stratified and well-contextualized changes in the built environment. In this regard, the impact of geophysics and remote-sensing methods will continue to be significant as improvements in technology and analysis bring more data to bear on large-scale studies of the built environment of cities. Another challenge is weighing the diversity of urban form, both within and between world regions, and forging a way for comparative analysis while maintaining the richness of specific cases. A fruitful approach to this problem is to identify comparable features among cities and subject them to contextualized analysis. For example, in this volume Creekmore (Chapter 2) identifies several key features of Mesopotamian cities and discusses them as discrete categories that demonstrate both similarities and differences among cities in this region. These categories could be extended to other world regions for both intra- and interregional comparative studies, with the goal of making sense of diversity without losing sight of culturally specific developments (cf. Arnauld et al. 2012).

To access the making of cities, as described here, future studies would benefit from greater consideration of how cities form and change, rather than just their origins, demise, or snapshot-form in a given time period. Meeting this challenge requires attention to general laws and processes as well as the daily actions of residents. Comparative studies offer great promise in this regard, but rich case studies provide necessary material for comparison. If we really care about "what life was like" in ancient times, then we need more of the kinds of studies that we have in this volume: cross-regional comparative studies, as in Razeto's Chapter 10; intra-regional studies, as seen in chapters by Creekmore (Chapter 2), Fisher (Chapter 6), Stark (Chapter 11), and Wynne-Jones and Fleisher (Chapter 4); and individual case studies, as seen in chapters by Nishimura (Chapter 3); Magnoni et al. (Chapter 5); Buell (Chapter 8); Fitzsimons (Chapter 7); and Kelly and Brown (Chapter 9).

Ideally, studies of ancient cities should blend macroscale and microscale data, as demonstrated by Nishimura's Chapter 3 of this volume, which incorporates both piece-plotted household artifacts and city-wide house and street patterns identified in geophysical data. This approach is only possible in the context of long-term projects, a task made increasingly difficult by short-term grants and the ebb and flow of international politics. One solution to this challenge is increased collaboration between archaeologists, both local and international, to work together on megaprojects – by which we mean large, long-term research staffed by multiple specialists working with great numbers of scholars. These kinds of projects present substantial logistical and political challenges, but can yield a more complete picture of urban form and change over time than small-scale, short-duration projects, especially in cases where geophysical data are less revealing owing to local characteristics of geology and archaeological features.

Studies of ancient cities would also benefit from more attention to open spaces in the built environment, both theoretically and archaeologically. These spaces can often be identified in plans derived from geophysics, while the interpretation of their use must incorporate both archaeological data and ethnohistoric or ethnographic analogy. Stark's Chapter 11 in this volume serves as a benchmark in the study of open spaces in ancient cities, especially for Mesoamerica, but she also identifies parallel developments in other world regions. Many other chapters in this volume recognize the importance of open spaces, including Kelly and Brown's study (Chapter 9) of Cahokia, where open spaces served as focal points for various plaza groups across this North American city.

Finally, future studies of ancient cities would do well to include both well-known "type" sites that exemplify key features of cities in a given region, as well as lesser-known, but equally important, newly studied cities – cities of different sizes, and cities with features that do not align perfectly with the standard-setting cases. Attention to the full range of cities in regions around the world enriches our understanding of ancient cities, modifies our models of urban form and change, and enhances the potential for comparative analysis within and between regions. The studies in this volume indicate the strength of this approach, bringing new light to well-known cases such as Rome, Chang'an, and Monte Albán, as well as lesser-known cases, or cases overshadowed by earlier or contemporary cities in the same or nearby regions, such as Kazane Höyük and Titriş Höyük in Upper Mesopotamia, Chunchucmil in the Maya Lowlands, and cities of Swahili eastern Africa, Crete, and Cyprus. This volume also addresses cases for which not all scholars would apply the term "city," such as Cahokia or Galatas.

Despite the longstanding interest in ancient cities, it is clear that there is still a great deal of work to be done in understanding the recursive relationship between urban environments and the social lives of their inhabitants. Yet, as the contributions to this volume demonstrate, we have never been in a better position to take up this challenge as new theoretical frameworks, analytical approaches, and methodological innovations provide the impetus for what promises to be an exciting new chapter in the investigation of ancient cities.

REFERENCES CITED

Adams, Robert McC. 1966 *The Evolution of Urban Society: Early Mesopotamia and Prehispanic Mexico.* Aldine, Chicago.

Akkermans, Peter M. M. G., and Glenn M. Schwartz 2003 *The Archaeology of Syria from Complex Hunter-Gatherers to Early Urban Societies (ca. 16,000–300 BC)*. Cambridge University Press, Cambridge.

Algaze, Guillermo 2008 *Ancient Mesopotamia at the Dawn of Civilization: The Evolution of an Urban Landscape*. University of Chicago Press, Chicago.

Altman, Irwin and Setha M. Low (editors) 1992 *Place Attachment*. Plenum Press, New York.

Arnauld, M. Charlotte, Linda R. Manzanilla, and Michael E. Smith (editors) 2012 *The Neighborhood as a Social and Spatial Unit in Mesoamerican Cities*. University of Arizona Press, Tucson.

Aspinall Arnold, Chris Gaffney, and Armin Schmidt 2008 *Magnetometry for Archaeologists*. Altamira, Lanham, MD.

Aufrecht, Walter E., Neil A. Mirau, and Steven W. Gauley 1997 *Urbanism in Antiquity: From Mesopotamia to Crete*. Sheffield Academic Press, Sheffield, UK.

Balkansky, Andrew K. 2006 Surveys and Mesoamerican Archaeology: The Emerging Macroregional Paradigm. *Journal of Archaeological Research* 14(1):53–95.

Bard, Kathryn A. 2008 Royal Cities and Cult Centers, Administrative Towns, and Workmen's Settlements in Ancient Egypt. In *The Ancient City: New Perspectives on Urbanism in the Old and New World*, edited by Joyce R. Marcus and Jeremy A. Sabloff, pp. 165–182. School for Advanced Research Resident Scholar Book, Santa Fe, NM.

Benech, Christophe 2007 New Approach to the Study of City Planning and Domestic Dwellings in the Ancient Near East. *Archaeological Prospection* 14(2):87–103.

Blake, Emma 2003 Space, Spatiality, and Archaeology. In *A Companion to Social Archaeology*, edited by L. Meskell and W. Preucel, pp. 230–254. Blackwell, Malden, MA.

Blanton, Richard E. 1976 Anthropological Studies of Cities. *Annual Review of Anthropology* 5:249–264.

1994 *Houses and Households: A Comparative Study*. Plenum Press, New York.

Blanton, Richard E., Stephen A. Kowalewski, and Gary M. Feinman 1992 The Mesoamerican World System. *Review* 15(3):419–426.

Bourdieu, Pierre 1973 The Berber House. In *Rules and Meanings*, edited by M. Douglas, pp. 98–110. Penguin, Harmondsworth, UK.

1977 *Outline of a Theory of Practice*. Translated by R. Nice. Cambridge University Press, Cambridge.

Branigan, Keith 2001 Aspects of Minoan Urbanism. In *Urbanism in the Aegean Bronze Age*, edited by Keith Branigan, pp. 38–50. Sheffield Academic Press, London.

Chang, K. C. 1974 Urbanism and the King in Ancient China. *World Archaeology* 6:1–14.

Childe, V. Gordon 1936 *Man Makes Himself*. The New American Library, New York.

Cobb, Charles R. 2003 Mississippian Chiefdoms: How Complex? *Annual Review of Anthropology* 32:63–84.

Coe, Michael D. 2005 *The Maya*. Thames and Hudson, New York.

Coulston, Jon and Hazel Dodge (editors) 2000 *Ancient Rome: The Archaeology of the Eternal City*. Oxford University School of Archaeology, Oxford.

Cowgill, George L. 2004 Origins and Development of Urbanism: Archaeological Perspectives. *Annual Review of Anthropology* 33:525–549.

Creekmore III, Andrew T. 2010 The Structure of Upper Mesopotamian Cities: Insight from Fluxgate Gradiometer Survey at Kazane Höyük, Southeastern Turkey. *Archaeological Prospection* 17(2):73–88.

Crumley Carole L. 1995 Heterarchy and the Analysis of Complex Societies. In *Heterarchy and the Analysis of Complex Societies*, edited by R. M. Ehrenreich, Carole L. Crumley, and J. E. Levy, pp. 1–6. Archaeological Papers, No. 6. American Anthropological Association, Washington, DC.

de Certeau, Michel 1988 *The Practice of Everyday Life*. Translated by Steven Rendall. University of California Press, Berkeley.

   1998 *The Practice of Everyday Life, Volume 2: Living and Cooking*, edited by Luce Giard. Translated by Timothy J. Tomasik. University of Minnesota Press, Minneapolis.

DeLaine, Janet 2008 Between Concept and Reality: Case Studies in the Development of Roman Cities in the Mediterranean. In *The Ancient City: New Perspectives on Urbanism in the Old and New World*, edited by J. Marcus and J. A. Sabloff, pp. 95–116. School for Advanced Research Resident Scholar Book, Santa Fe, NM.

Dobres, Marcia-Anne and John E. Robb 2000 Agency in Archaeology: Paradigm or Platitude? In *Agency in Archaeology*, edited by Marcia-Anne Dobres and John E. Robb, pp. 3–17. Routledge, New York.

Dornan, Jennifer L. 2002 Archaeology and Agency: Past, Present, and Future Directions. *Journal of Archaeological Method and Theory* 9:303–329.

Düring, Bleda S. 2005 Building Continuity in the Central Anatolian Neolithic: Exploring the Meaning of Buildings at Aşıklı Höyük and Çatalhöyük. *Journal of Mediterranean Archaeology* 18(1):3–29.

Emberling, Geoff and Helen McDonald 2003 Excavations at Tell Brak 2001–2002: Preliminary Report. *Iraq* 65:1–75.

Fash, William Leonard and Leonardo López Luján 2009 *The Art of Urbanism: How Mesoamerican Kingdoms Represented Themselves in Architecture and Imagery*. Harvard University Press, Cambridge, MA.

Ferguson, T. J. 1996 *Historic Zuni Architecture and Society: An Archaeological Application of Space Syntax*. Anthropological Papers of the University of Arizona No. 60. University of Arizona Press, Tucson.

Ferguson, Yale 1991 Chiefdoms to City-States: The Greek Experience. In *Chiefdoms: Power, Economy, Ideology*, edited by Tim Earle, pp. 169–191. Cambridge University Press, Cambridge.

Fisher, Kevin D. 2009 Placing Social Interaction: An Integrative Approach to Analyzing Past Built Environments. *Journal of Anthropological Archaeology* 28(4):439–457.

Fletcher, Roland J. 2010 Shining Stars and Black Holes: Urbanism, Comparison, and Comparability. *Journal of Urban History* 36(2):251–256.

   2012 Low-Density, Agrarian-Based Urbanism. In *The Comparative Archaeology of Complex Societies*, edited by Michael E. Smith, pp. 285–320. Cambridge University Press, Cambridge.

Foucault, Michel 1977 [1975] *Discipline and Punish: The Birth of the Prison*. Translated by A. Sheridan. Vintage Books, New York.

Fox, Richard G. 1977 *Urban Anthropology: Cities in Their Cultural Settings.* Prentice-Hall, Englewood Cliffs, NJ.

Fustel de Coulanges, Numa Denis 1963 [1864] *The Ancient City.* Doubleday, New York.

Gaffney Chris and John A. Gater 2003 *Revealing the Buried Past: Geophysics for Archaeologists.* Stroud, Tempus, Gloucestershire, UK.

Gardner, Andrew 2007 Introduction: Social Agency, Power, and Being Human. In *Agency Uncovered. Archaeological Perspectives on Social Agency, Power, and Being Human,* edited by Andrew Gardner, pp. 1–18. Left Coast Press, Walnut Creek, CA.

Gates, Charles 2003 *Ancient Cities: The Archaeology of Urban Life in the Ancient Near East and Egypt, Greece and Rome.* Routledge, New York.

Gell, Alfred 1998 *Art and Agency: An Anthropological Theory.* Clarendon Press, Oxford.

Gibbon, Guy E. 1974 A Model of Mississippian Development and its Implications for the Red Wing Area, Minnesota. In *Aspects of Upper Great Lakes Anthropology,* edited by Eiden Johnson, pp. 129–137. Minnesota Historical Society, St. Paul.

Gibson, McGuire, Amr al-Azm, Clemens Reichel, Salam Quntar, Judith A. Franke, Lamya Khalidi, Carrie Hritz, Mark Altaweel, Colleen Coyle, Carlo Colantoni, Jonathan Tenney, Ghassan Abdul Aziz, and Tobin Hartnell 2002 Hamoukar: A Summary of Three Seasons of Excavation. *Akkadika* 123:11–34.

Giddens, Anthony 1979 *Central Problems in Social Theory.* University of California Press, Berkeley and Los Angeles.

1984 *The Constitution of Society: Outline of the Theory of Structuration.* University of California Press, Berkeley.

Gosden, Chris 2005 What Do Objects Want? *Journal of Archaeological Method and Theory* 12(3):193–211.

Grahame, Mark 2000 *Reading Space: Social Interaction and Identity in the Houses of Roman Pompeii. A Syntactical Approach to the Analysis and Interpretation of Built Space.* BAR International Series 886. Archaeopress, Oxford.

Graumann, Carl F. 2002 The Phenomenological Approach to People-Environment Relations. In *The Handbook of Environmental Psychology,* edited by Robert B. Bechtel and Arza Churchman, pp. 95–113. John Wiley and Sons, New York.

Graumann, Carl F. and Kruse, Lenelis 1993 Place Identity and the Physical Structure of the City. In *Perception and Evaluation of Urban Environment Quality. A Pluridisciplinary Approach in the European Context,* edited by Mirilia Bonnes, pp. 155–163. Proceedings of the UNESCO Programme on Man and Biosphere International Symposium, Rome, 1991. UNESCO-ENEL, Rome.

Hansen, Mogens Herman (editor) 2000 *A Comparative Study of Thirty City-State Cultures.* C. A. Reitzels Forlag, Copenhagen.

2006 *Polis.* Oxford University Press, Oxford.

Hendon, Julia M. 2004 Living and Working at Home: The Social Archaeology of Household Production and Social Relations. In *A Companion to Social Archaeology,* edited by Lynn Meskell and Robert W. Preucel, pp. 272–286. Blackwell, Malden, MA.

2010 *Houses in a Landscape: Memory and Everyday Life in Mesoamerica*. Duke University Press, Durham, NC.

Hirth, Kenneth G. 2008 The Altepetl and Urban Structure in Prehispanic Mesoamerica. In *Urbanism in Mesoamerica*, edited by William T. Sanders, Alba Guadalupe Mastache, and Robert H. Cobean, pp. 57–84. The Pennsylvania State University, State College.

Hodder, Ian 1982 *Symbols in Action*. Cambridge University Press, Cambridge.

1992 *Theory and Practice in Archaeology*. Routledge, London and New York.

2012 *Entangled: An Archaeology of the Relationships between Humans and Things*. Wiley-Blackwell, Malden, MA.

Holt, Julie Z. 2009. Rethinking the Ramey State: Was Cahokia the Center of a Theater State? *American Antiquity* 74:231–254.

Horton, Mark C. 1994 Swahili Architecture, Space and Social Structure. In *Architecture and Order*, edited by Michael Parker-Pearson and Colin Richards, pp. 132–152. Routledge, London.

1996 *Shanga: The Archaeology of a Muslim Trading Community on the Coast of East Africa*. British Institute in Eastern Africa, Nairobi.

Houston, Stephen D., Héctor Escobedo, Mark Child, Charles Goldon, and René Muñoz 2003 The Moral Community. Maya Settlement Transformationat Piedras Negras, Guatemala. In *The Social Construction of Ancient Cities*, edited by Monica L. Smith, pp. 212–253. The Smithsonian Institution, Washington, DC.

Hummon, David M. 1986 City Mouse, Country Mouse: The Persistence of Community Identity. *Qualitative Sociology* 9:3–25.

Jacobs, Jane 1969 *The Economy of Cities*. Random House, New York.

Joyce, Arthur A. 2009. Theorizing Urbanism in Ancient Mesoamerica. *Ancient Mesoamerica* 20 (2): 189 – 196.

Joyce, Rosemary A. 2004 Unintended Consequences? Monumentality as a Novel Experience in Formative Mesoamerica. *Journal of Archaeological Method and Theory* 11:4–29.

Kenoyer, Jonathan Mark 1998 *Ancient Cities of the Indus Valley Civilization*. Oxford University Press, Oxford.

Klynne, Allan 1998 Reconstructions of Knossos: Artists' Impressions, Archaeological Evidence and Wishful Thinking. *Journal of Mediterranean Archaeology* 11(2):206–229.

Knappett, Carl and Ilse Schoep 2000 Continuity and Change in Minoan Palatial Power. *Antiquity* 74: 365–371.

Knappett, Carl and L. Malafouris (editors) 2008 *Material Agency: Towards a Non-Anthropocentric Approach*. Springer, New York.

Knox, Paul L. 1995 World Cities in a World-System. In *World Cities in a World-System*, edited by Paul L. Knox and Peter J. Taylor, pp. 3–20. Cambridge University Press, Cambridge.

Kopytoff, Igor 1986 The Cultural Biography of Things: Commoditization as Process. In *The Social Life of Things: Commodities in Cultural Perspective*, edited by Arjun Appadurai, pp. 64–94. Cambridge University Press, Cambridge.

Kusimba, Chap M. 2008 Early African Cities: Their Role in the Shaping of Urban and Rural Interaction Spheres. In *The Ancient City: New Perspectives on Urbanism in the Old and New World*, edited by Joyce R. Marcus and Jeremy A. Sabloff, pp. 229–246. School for Advanced Research Resident Scholar Book, Santa Fe, NM.

Lalli, Marco 1992 Urban-Related Identity: Theory, Measurement and Empirical Findings. *Journal of Environmental Psychology* 12:285–303.

Latour, Bruno 2005 *Reassembling the Social: An Introduction to Actor Network Theory*. Oxford University Press, Oxford.

Laurence, Ray 1994 *Roman Pompeii: Space and Society*. Routledge, London.

Lefebvre, Henri 1991 *The Production of Space*. Translated by Donald Nicholson-Smith. Blackwell, Oxford.

Lekson, Stephen 1999 *The Chaco Meridian: Centers of Political Power in the Ancient Southwest*. Altamira Press, Walnut Creek, CA.

Low, Setha M. 2000 *On the Plaza*. University of Texas Press, Austin.

Low, Setha M. and Denise Lawrence-Zúñiga (editors) 2003 *The Anthropology of Space and Place: Locating Culture*. Blackwell, Malden, MA.

Manning, Sturt W. 2008 Formation of the Palaces. In *The Cambridge Companion to the Aegean Bronze Age*, edited by Cynthia Shelmerdine, pp. 105–120. Cambridge University Press, Cambridge.

Marcus, Joyce R. 1983 On the Nature of the Mesoamerican City. In *Prehistoric Settlement Patterns: Essays in Honor of Gordon R. Willey*, edited by Evon Zartman Vogt and Richard M. Leventhal, pp. 195–242. University of New Mexico Press, Albuquerque.

Marcus, Joyce R. and Jeremy A. Sabloff (editors) 2008a *The Ancient City: New Perspectives on Urbanism in the Old and New World*. School for Advanced Research Resident Scholar Book, Santa Fe, NM.

    2008b Introduction. In *The Ancient City: New Perspectives on Urbanism in the Old and New World*, edited by Joyce R. Marcus and Jeremy A. Sabloff, pp. 3–28. School for Advanced Research Resident Scholar Book, Santa Fe, NM.

    2008c Cities and Urbanism: Central Themes and Future Directions. In *The Ancient City: New Perspectives on Urbanism in the Old and New World*, edited by Joyce R. Marcus and Jeremy A. Sabloff, pp. 323–336. School for Advanced Research Resident Scholar Book, Santa Fe, NM.

McCarthy, E. Doyle 1984 Toward a Sociology of the Physical World: George Herbert Mead on Physical Objects. *Studies in Symbolic Interaction* 5:105–121.

McIntosh, Roderick J. 1991 Early Urban Clusters in China and Africa: The Arbitration of Social Ambiguity. *Journal of Field Archaeology* 18:199–212.

    2005 *Ancient Middle Niger. Urbanism and the Self-Organizing Landscape*. Cambridge University Press, Cambridge.

McIntosh, Roderick J. and Susan Keech McIntosh 1993 Cities without Citadels: Understanding Urban Origins along the Middle Niger. In *The Archaeology of Africa: Food, Metals and Towns*, edited by Thurstan Shaw, Paul Sinclair, Bassey Andah, and Alex Okpoko, pp. 622–641. Routledge, London and New York.

    2003 Early Urban Configurations on the Middle Niger: Clustered Cities and Landscapes of Power. In *The Social Construction of Ancient Cities*, edited by Monica L. Smith, pp. 103–120. The Smithsonian Institution, Washington, DC.

Mead, George H. 1934 *Mind, Self, and Society*, edited by Charles Morris. University of Chicago Press, Chicago.

Milner, George R. 1998 *The Cahokia Chiefdom*. Smithsonian Press, Washington, DC.

Mumford, Lewis 1961 *The City in History*. Harcourt, Brace and World, New York.

2003 [1937] What Is a City? In *The City Reader*, edited by Richard T. LeGates and Frederic Stout, pp. 93–96. Routledge, New York.

Nichols, Deborah L. and Thomas H. Charlton (editors) 1997 *The Archaeology of City-States: Cross-Cultural Approaches*. Smithsonian Institution Press, Washington, DC.

Nissen, Hans J. 1988 *The Early History of the Ancient Near East*. The University of Chicago Press, Chicago and London.

Oates, Joan, Augusta McMahon, Philip Karsgaard, Salam Al Quntar, and Jason Ur 2007 Early Mesopotamian Urbanism: A New View from the North. *Antiquity* 81:585–600.

O'Brien, Patricia J. 1989 Cahokia: The Political Capital of the "Ramey" State? *North American Archaeologist* 10:275–292.

Osborne, Robin 1996 *Greece in the Making, 1200–479 BC*. Routledge, New York and London.

Osborne, Robin and Barry W. Cunliffe 2005 *Mediterranean Urbanization, 800–600 BC*. Oxford University Press, Oxford.

Pauketat, Timothy R. 1994 *The Ascent of Chiefs*. University of Alabama Press, Tuscaloosa.

1998 Refiguring the Archaeology of Greater Cahokia. *Journal of Archaeological Research* 6:45–89.

2007 *Chiefdoms and Other Delusions*. Altamira, Lanham, MD.

Pollock, Susan 1999 *Ancient Mesopotamia*. Cambridge University Press, Cambridge.

Pred, Allan. 1984 Place as Historically Contingent Process: Structuration and the Time-Geography of Becoming Places. *Annals of the Association of American Geographers* 74(2): 279–297.

1990 *Making Histories and Constructing Human Geographies: The Local Transformation of Practice, Power Relations, and Consciousness*. Westview Press, Boulder, CO.

Preucel, Robert W. and Lynn Meskell 2004 Places. In *A Companion to Social Archaeology*, edited by Lynn Meskell and Robert W. Preucel, pp. 215–229. Blackwell, Malden, MA.

Proshansky, Harold M., Abbe K. Fabian, and Robert Kaminoff 1983 Place Identity: Physical World Socialization of the Self. *Journal of Environmental Psychology* 3: 57–83.

Pyburn, Anne K. 2008 Pomp and Circumstance before Belize: Ancient Maya Commerce and the New River Conurbation. In *The Ancient City: New Perspectives on Urbanism in the Old and New World*, edited by J. Marcus and J. A. Sabloff, pp. 247–272. School for Advanced Research Resident Scholar Book, Santa Fe, NM.

Rapoport, Amos 1988 Levels of Meaning in the Built Environment. *Cross-Cultural Perspectives in Nonverbal Communication*, edited by F. Poyatos, pp. 317–336. C. J. Hogrefe, Toronto.

1990 *The Meaning of the Built Environment*. University of Arizona Press, Tucson.

Redman, Charles L. 1978 Mesopotamian Urban Ecology: The Systematic Context of the Emergence of Urbanism. In *Social Archaeology: Beyond Subsistence and Dating*, edited by Charles Redman, Mary Jane Berman, Edward V. Curtin, William T. Longacre Jr., Nina M. Versaggi, and Jeffery C. Wanser, pp. 329–347. Academic Press, New York.

Rodman, Margaret C. 1992 Empowering Place: Multilocality and Multivocality. *American Anthropologist* 94(3):640–656.

Russell, James A. and Jacalyn Snodgrass 1987 Emotion and the Environment. In *Handbook of Environmental Psychology*, edited by David Stokols and Irwin Altman, pp. 245–280. Wiley, New York.

Sanders, William T. and David Webster 1988 The Mesoamerican Urban Tradition. *American Anthropologist* 90(3):521–546.

Scarre, Christopher and Brian M. Fagan 2008 *Ancient Civilizations*. 3rd ed. Prentice Hall, Upper Saddle River, NJ.

Shen, Chen 1994 Early Urbanization in the Early Eastern Zhou in China (770–221 BC): An Archaeological View. *Antiquity* 68:724–744.

2003 Compromises and Conflicts: Production and Commerce in the Royal Cities of Eastern Zhou, China. In *The Social Construction of Ancient Cities*, edited by Monica L. Smith, pp. 290–310. The Smithsonian Institution, Washington, DC.

Sjoberg, Gideon 1960 *The Preindustrial City, Past and Present*. Free Press, Glencoe, IL.

Smith, Adam T. 2003 *The Political Landscape: Constellations of Authority in Early Complex Societies*. University of California Press, Berkeley.

Smith, Michael E. 2007 Form and Meaning in the Earliest Cities: A New Approach to Ancient Urban Planning. *Journal of Planning History* 6(3):3–47.

2008 *Aztec City-State Capitals*. University Press of Florida, Gainesville.

2010a The Archaeological Study of Neighborhoods and Districts in Ancient Cities. *Journal of Anthropological Archaeology* 29(2):137–154.

2010b Sprawl, Squatters and Sustainable Cities: Can Archaeological Data Shed Light on Modern Urban Issues? *Cambridge Archaeological Journal* 20(2):229–253.

2011 Empirical Urban Theory for Archaeologists. *Journal of Archaeological Method and Theory* 18:167–192.

Smith, Michael E. and Frances F. Berdan 2000 The Postclassic Mesoamerican World System. *Current Anthropology* 41(2):283–286.

Smith, Monica. L. (editor) 2003a *The Social Construction of Ancient Cities*. The Smithsonian Institution, Washington, DC.

2003b Introduction: The Social Construction of Ancient Cities. In *The Social Construction of Ancient Cities*, edited by Monica L. Smith, pp. 1–36. The Smithsonian Institution, Washington, DC.

2008 Urban Empty Spaces. *Archaeological Dialogues* 15:216–231.

Soja, Edward W. 1989 *Postmodern Geographies*. Verso, London.

2000 *Postmetropolis*. Blackwell, Oxford.

Southall, Aidan William 1973 Introduction. In *Urban Anthropology: Cross-Cultural Studies of Urbanization*, edited by Aidan William Southall, pp. 3–14. Oxford University Press, New York.

Storey, Glenn R. (editor) 2006 *Urbanism in the Preindustrial World: Cross-Cultural Approaches*. The University of Alabama Press, Tuscaloosa.

Thomas, Carol G. and Craig Conant 2003 *Citadel to City-State: The Transformation of Greece, 1200–700 BC*. Indiana University Press, Bloomington.

Trigger, Bruce G. 1972 Determinants of Urban Growth in Pre-Industrial Societies. In *Man, Settlement, and Urbanism*, edited by Peter J. Ucko, R. Tringham, and G. W. Dimbleby, pp. 577–599. Duckworth, London.

  2003 *Understanding Early Civilizations*. Cambridge University Press, Cambridge.

Tringham, Ruth 1995 Archaeological Houses, Households, Housework and the Home. In *The Home: Words, Interpretations, Meanings and Environments*, edited by David N. Benjamin, David Stea, and Eje Arén, pp. 79–107. Avebury, Aldershot, Brookfield, VT.

Tuan, Yi-Fu 1977 *Space and Place: The Perspective of Experience*. University of Minnesota Press, Minneapolis.

Twigger-Ross, Clare L. and David L. Uzzell 1996 Place and Identity Processes. *Journal of Environmental Psychology* 16(3):205–220.

United Nations Department of Economic and Social Affairs, Population Division 2012 *World Urbanization Prospects, the 2011 Revision*. Final Report with Annex Tables, New York. Electronic document, http://esa.un.org/unpd/wup/Documentation/final-report.htm, accessed March 3, 2013.

Ur, Jason A. 2010 Cycles of Civilization in Northern Mesopotamia, 4400–2000 BC. *Journal of Archaeological Research* 18:387–431.

Ur, Jason A., Philip Karsgaard, and Joan Oates 2007 Urban Development in the Ancient Near East. *Science* 317:1188.

Van de Mieroop, Marc 1999 *The Ancient Mesopotamian City*. Oxford University Press, Oxford.

von Falkenhausen, Lothar 2008 Stages in the Development of "Cities" in Pre-Imperial China. In *The Ancient City: New Perspectives on Urbanism in the Old and New World*, edited by Joyce R. Marcus and Jeremy A. Sabloff, pp. 209–228. School for Advanced Research Resident Scholar Book, Santa Fe, NM.

Wolf, Eric 1990 Distinguished Lecture: Facing Power – Old Insights, New Questions. *American Anthropologist* 92:586–596.

  1999 *Envisioning Power: Ideologies of Dominance and Crisis*. University of California Press, Berkeley.

Yaeger, Jason 2003 Untangling the Ties that Bind: The City, the Countryside, and the Nature of Maya Urbanism at Xunantunich, Belize. In *The Social Construction of Ancient Cities*, edited by Monica L. Smith, pp. 121–155. The Smithsonian Institution, Washington, DC.

2

The Social Production of Space in Third-Millennium Cities of Upper Mesopotamia

Andrew T. Creekmore III

This chapter analyzes the production and construction of space in third-millennium cities of Upper Mesopotamia. I argue that space is constructed at multiple levels, including city or state government, institutions, developers, and households. Past planning episodes structure future life in the city, but are also modified to meet the needs of later residents. Within this process, I identify several characteristics of Mesopotamian city space, including a high level of nucleation, multiple centers within the city, defensible spaces such as culs-de-sac, conservative use of space, and linkage of key features into a system of armature. These features demonstrate how the social needs of residents are expressed in the fabric of the city. In these features, we see urban planning that is not strictly top-down or bottom-up, nor solely planned or organic.

In this chapter, I explore several aspects of urban space in third-millennium Upper Mesopotamian cities. These cities developed between 2700–2200 BC when a second wave of urbanism spread cities and city-states across Upper Mesopotamia (Figure 2.1) (for a fuller discussion of the city-state system, see Nishimura, Chapter 3 in this volume).[1] The size of these states is variable, but based on some of the better-known examples, they may have had core territories[2] of approximately 1,000 km² and extended political territories up to 5,000 or 10,000 km². The largest urban centers were 35–125 ha and hosted 10,000–25,000 people.[3] The primary subsistence base of these polities was dry-farmed barley supplemented by milk or meat from sheep, goats, cattle, and pigs. Production of textiles and metals, along with trade, were also important parts of the economy (Stein 2004). Urban administration consisted of palace and temple households, as well as city councils comprised of elders or other representatives of various groups within the city. The degree of power sharing among these groups is unclear and may have varied over

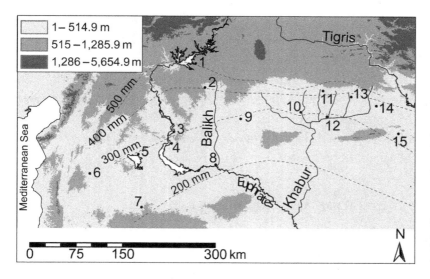

Figure 2.1 Topography, rainfall isohyets, and selected third-millennium sites in Upper Mesopotamia. 1-Titriş, 2-Kazane, 3-Banat, 4-Sweyhat, 5-Umm el-Marra, 6-Ebla, 7-Al-Rawda, 8-Bi'a, 9-Chuera, 10-Beydar, 11-Mozan, 12-Brak, 13-Leilan, 14-Hamoukar, 15-Taya. (Modified from Creekmore 2010; for a fuller list of cities, see Nishimura, Chapter 3 in this volume, Figure 3.1).

time (Cooper 2006b:63–66; Durand 1989; Fleming 2004). An analysis of urban space provides insight into how these groups negotiated the complex process of making cities.

I examine several features or factors in the generation and use of city space, including city shape, accessibility, nucleation, multiple centers, conservative development, defensible space, parceled lots, and armature, or the linkage of important monuments across a city (MacDonald 1986:5). My goal is to broaden our understanding of how these cities form and the roles of different social groups in making cities. Accordingly, I review specific cities that serve as examples of each feature or factor and infer the motivations behind the creation and use of different kinds of city space. I argue that the process of urbanization is best understood through a life-history approach that considers the social production and construction of space. As defined by Setha Low and employed by many scholars, the *social production* of space includes the processes that generate the tangible portions of city-space, such as buildings, streets and other physical features whereas the *social construction* of space is human behavior that transforms *space* into historically contingent *place* through the actions of people in their everyday lives, often over long periods of time (Anderson and Gale 1992:4; Gillespie 2000; Hodder 2007:22; Low 2000:127–128; Tringham 2003:94–95; Pred 1984:279; Rodman 1992; Verhoeven 1999:20). These concepts describe the urban process that forms the life history of a city, and acknowledge that cities are not static or fully formed, but always in motion, changing over time through dynamic human activities (Soja 2000:9). By examining the production and construction of urban space, we can identify vectors of growth and decline and the structuring impact of past spatial decisions on future residents. This approach views cities as "lived spaces" from which we can compose stories or histories (Soja 1989:14, 2000:11; de Certeau 1998:142). Over time, local planning episodes, combined with mid-level and centralized planning, create a collage of urban spaces.

URBANIZATION AND URBAN SPACE

The plans of ancient cities show how the population, institutions, and industries were distributed within them. From the spatial relationship between these and other urban features we can infer aspects of socioeconomic and political organization. The urban plan also provides clues to how urbanization took place, the role of the central authority, major institutions and "everyday" residents in this process, and how the city changed over time. In this context, "plan" refers to the physical relationship between structures, streets, and features – such as open areas – within the city. An orthogonal urban plan is generally considered the hallmark of a planned city whereas anything less than orthogonal is deemed "organic," that is, natural, emergent, irregular, and unplanned (Castagnoli 1971:124; Smith 2007:5).

In general, evidence for orthogonal planning is assumed to reflect decision making and funding at the highest level of city governance. In contrast, "organic" or unplanned urban growth is deemed to reflect the spontaneous activities of multiple households and institutions in the city. Adam Smith (2003:225) argues that this view of urban planning implies that western notions of rectilinear planning are the ideal when, in fact, "curvilinear" planning may simply reflect a different aesthetic, or a case when a king or ruler does not want to control certain aspects of the urban plan. One could add that topography structures the urban plan since uneven, variable terrain is less susceptible to rectilinear construction than flat, open land (see Fitzsimons, Chapter 7 in this volume). In practice, cities are rarely, if ever, purely planned or organic. Instead, cities contain both planned and unplanned space; even highly planned space, such as at Pompeii, may be remodeled or redeveloped by a city's inhabitants according to their specific and changing needs (Laurence 1994:19).

To close the gap between planned and organic descriptions of cities, Michael Smith draws on the work of Simon Ellis (1995) and Harold Carter (1983), among others, to devise a scheme to analyze levels of urban planning in ancient cities. Smith divides urban planning into two main components: coordination among buildings and standardization among cities. Coordination often involves formal arrangements of structures, such as around a plaza, or with respect to other features such as a temple, palace, street, or city wall (Smith 2007:9–12). Standardization occurs when we see a similar suite of features and relationships among them at several cities in a region, which suggests that they were built with a common idea about how to construct a city (Smith 2007:25–27) (see Buell, Chapter 8 in this volume, for a more complete discussion of Smith's model). Smith's analytical approach encourages scholars to look for planning principles rather than a single, unified plan and makes it possible to find evidence for planning in otherwise "organic" cities. This chapter attempts to do just that, although I do not adhere strictly to Smith's definitions of coordination or standardization.

City Size and the Cities Discussed Here

Cities discussed in this chapter range in size from 20 to more than 100 hectares. The relatively larger cities were presumably more populous, wealthier, hosted more institutions, administered more territory, and wielded greater regional power than their smaller neighbors, which may have played subservient political roles within the state. This observation does not diminish the potential political, economic, or ritual importance of even very small cities that may have been the seat of a respected family, produced a desired commodity, or hosted a revered shrine. Although the size differences among these cities can be striking, their basic structure and the spatial principles found within them are very similar. Many of these spatial principles probably predate cites and are rooted in agrarian villages in which nucleated households are the dominant features. Yet, Elizabeth Stone's remote-sensing research in Lower Mesopotamia has identified monumental architecture at the smallest of sites (less than 0.5 hectares), indicating that the built environment of small sites included more than simple houses (Stone 2007:231). Stone elaborates:

> ...just as the population of Mesopotamian cities seems to have
> been very agrarian, with well over 50 percent of the population

making their living through agriculture, so too does the rural sector look very urban. Indeed I will close with the suggestion that Mesopotamian households, and the neighborhoods or villages that they form, were the real building blocks of society, but it was the ability of the urban centers to provide both a larger political arena and an efficient resource base that led to their popularity. (Stone 2007:231)

It may be simplistic to state that Mesopotamian cities, Upper and Lower, were simply villages writ large, but it is clear that the spatial principles we see in cities are not exclusive to large urban environments. These shared principles make it possible to compare cities of vastly different sizes because their urban character does not depend solely on the size of their population or their footprint (see Yoffee, Chapter 12 in this volume for a fuller discussion of "different cities" and the problem of city size).

In my analysis, I examine the structure of several Upper Mesopotamian cities of the third millennium. Although I reference features in many cities, I give several special attention to Beydar, Chuera, Kazane, Al-Rawda, and Titriş because we know more about their built environments. Instead of identifying types of city plans, such as those defined by Heinz (1997), I prefer to identify principles of the production and construction of space in these cities, including multiple centers (in nucleated settlements), conservative notions of space, defensible space, housing parcels, and armature. Some of these features contain coordination or standardization that is relatively highly planned, according to Michael Smith's (2007) scheme, while others derive from supra-household, mid-level efforts, and others still from the smaller scale, so-called organic efforts of residents. Yet, the latter demonstrate patterned behaviors from city to city that indicate which aspects of city space appealed to residents, and point to cultural norms regarding the structure and appearance of the built environment. Accordingly, these aspects are often executed at a supra-household level. The main difficulties in examining these factors are that we usually lack the full plan of an ancient city, data from different cities are not equivalent, and it is difficult to know if the disconnected parts of the city that we uncover in our excavations are contemporary. Despite these problems, through a careful examination of several cities, we can gain a better understanding of their urban structure. At the close of my analysis, I discuss briefly the implications of the results for understanding sociopolitical organization in Upper Mesopotamia.

UPPER MESOPOTAMIAN URBAN PLANNING

According to the aforementioned notions of urban planning, Upper Mesopotamian cities are not highly planned in that they lack strict orthogonal or rectilinear layouts. Instead, these cities often form semi-orthogonal plans when adjacent structures are built with the same orientation as their neighbors, or additions to existing structures are added in orthogonal segments, often for reasons of convenience and efficiency rather than urban planning (Smith 2007:13). Yet, several sites discussed here exhibit semi-orthogonal architectural elements that clearly developed from supra-household planning. The most obvious centralized planning in these cities is found in infrastructure, including streets, city walls, sector walls, and water works. Decentralized, or mid- and low-level planning, is most evident in residential areas that were built and rebuilt according to varying codes of spatial production.

There are six major categories of urban features in Upper Mesopotamian cities:

1) infrastructure, including circuit walls and dividing walls between sectors or neighborhoods (in a few cases), city gates, streets, water and sewer systems;
2) institutional structures, including palaces, temples, and associated storage, living, and support facilities;
3) residential neighborhoods;
4) industry or craft-production facilities;
5) open areas; and
6) burial installations. This category is highly variable, including burials beneath house floors, special (sometimes mass) burials in tombs or monuments, and a variety of types of burial in intramural or extramural cemeteries.

Due to the high cost of infrastructure, features such as city walls and streets often become fixed and shape the direction and form of later development and the movement of people through the city (Herman and Ausubel 1988:13; Hillier 2008:226). Thus, urban plans may be shaped early in the developmental process with later development acting within the boundaries set by roads, city walls, and waterworks. Accordingly, realignment or rebuilding of these features requires major organization of labor and funds. Although institutional, residential and craft production facilities are subject to remodeling and rebuilding by their inhabitants, shared walls among neighboring buildings in built-up cities require supra-household organization to accomplish significant reorientation of structures. This may explain in part why, despite opportunities for flexibility in the use or definition of spaces between elements of infrastructure, these areas generally maintained their primary use or function.

Spatially, palaces tend to be located on the citadel or upper city (at Leilan [Ristvet et al. 2004; de Lillis-Forrest et al. 2007], Ebla [Matthiae 1981], Mozan [Buccellati and Kelly-Buccellati 2001], Beydar [Lebeau and Suleiman 2009], and Chuera [Meyer 2006]), although Beydar has palaces both upon its mini-acropolis and below in the upper city, and administrative buildings – including possible palaces – have been excavated in the lower and outer town at Kazane (Creekmore 2008, 2010). Magnetometry data show some larger, possibly administrative or elite buildings in the outer town at Titriş and Chuera (Meyer 2006; see also Nishimura Chapter 3, this volume). Temples are found in a variety of locations, including on citadels, in the center of the city (at Beydar [Lebeau 2006a], Chuera [Meyer 2006], Mozan [Buccellati and Kelly-Buccellati 2001], and Sweyhat [Danti and Zettler 2007]), in solitary walled compounds (at Al-Rawda [Castel and Peltenburg 2007]),[4] or as small individual structures tucked away in neighborhoods (at Chuera, possibly also Kazane[5]). Industrial activities sometimes cluster (at Banat [McClellan 1999; Porter 1995, 2002]), but in other cases are scattered throughout domestic areas (as at Sweyhat [Danti and Zettler 2007]) or located in isolated workshops (for example, in the Titriş suburbs; see Nishimura, Chapter 3 in this volume). Houses form contiguous clusters within blocks defined by wide main streets and narrow lanes. Burials occur both within tombs beneath house floors (at Kazane and Titriş) and in extramural cemeteries (at Titriş, Chuera, Sweyhat, and Al-Rawda). With the possible exception of Titriş, for which magnetometry data indicate somewhat large, open, unpaved areas toward the periphery (see Nishimura, Chapter 3 in this volume), open space is limited in these cities, and is usually paved, or grey space, as opposed to unpaved, green space consisting of gardens, parks, and the like (see Stark, Chapter 11 in this volume, for a complete discussion of types of open space). When present, open space occurs in narrow spaces between buildings, in courtyards or public plazas, in culs-de-sac, and sometimes on the periphery, just within the city wall.

CITY SHAPES

Upper Mesopotamian cities have two general shapes defined by their city walls and the location of the pre-urban settlement tell (Figure 2.2). The first shape is oblong cities – such as Sweyhat, Leilan, Titriş, and Kazane – in which the tell (mound of earlier period ruins) is located off-center and its elevated terrain, sometimes greater than twenty meters high, formed a convenient citadel for the city. In some cases, this location may have a practical purpose in providing a quick exit for officials or soldiers leaving the city to escape or confront an enemy. This location may also make it easier to transport valuable goods to the citadel. Stone (1995:243) notes that very tall temple platforms in Lower Mesopotamian cities are located outside the center of the city, perhaps setting a precedent or at least a parallel for the high versus low spatial division in Upper Mesopotamian cities between the upper city on the citadel and expansive lower towns. Although this high versus low division may serve an ideological purpose, it may just as well result from convenience or land tenure (see "Land Tenure" section later in this chapter), and the many stratigraphic layers within citadels testify to the long life history of these places (see Nishimura, Chapter 3 in this volume, for another perspective on citadel mounds, lower towns, and city shapes).

The second Upper Mesopotamian city shape is round – such as Chuera, Beydar, Bati, and Al Rawda – in which the pre-urban tell, if present, is located in the center of the site and is generally larger, forming a full-fledged upper city rather than a steep-sided citadel with limited flat space. Dubbed *Kranzhügeln* by early German archaeologists,[6] many of these cities are found in the relatively marginal (low rainfall) steppe between the Balikh and Khabur Rivers, and in the vicinity of the low mountain Jebel 'Abd al-'Aziz in northeastern Syria (Meyer 2006; Moortgat-Correns 1972). In some cases, the lower city was walled but not inhabited (as at Beydar) or does not exist (as at Al-Rawda, which has some extramural settlement, but not a striking high-low difference in elevation or a walled settlement beyond the core). Because these cities are located in a dry environment, some scholars suggest that they were built and inhabited by people with a shared culture, such as pastoral nomads who thrived through

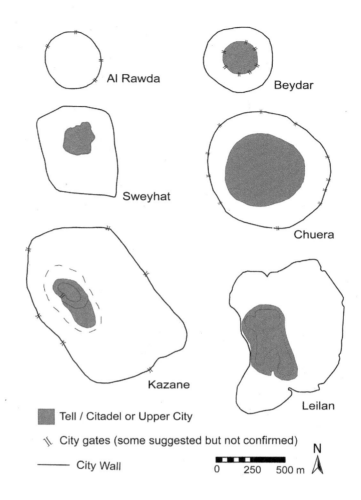

Figure 2.2 Outlines of selected cities. Scale is approximate. Al-Rawda after Gondet and Castel 2004; Beydar after Lebeau 2006a; Sweyhat after Danti and Zettler 2007; Chuera after Meyer 2006:Abb. 2; Kazane after Creekmore 2008:figure 9.3; Leilan after Weiss 1990:Abb. 1. For plan of Titriş, see Nishimura, Chapter 3 in this volume, Figure 3.2.

trade with other states in the region (Kouchoukos 1998; Lyonnet 1998; McClellan and Porter 1995:63). The excavators of Chuera and Al-Rawda claim that these cities were intentionally established in a round shape, rather than developing from the gradual expansion of a pre-existing village (Castel and Peltenburg 2007:604; Pruss 2000:1432). The variation in the life history of these cities calls into question the usefulness of the *Kranzhügeln* category; I will return to this question later in this chapter.

CITY ACCESSIBILITY

In the few cases where a significant portion of the town plan of ancient cities is exposed by magnetometry or excavations, we may begin to extend theories of architectural structuralism to entire settlements. I favor a soft structuralism in which structure is highly

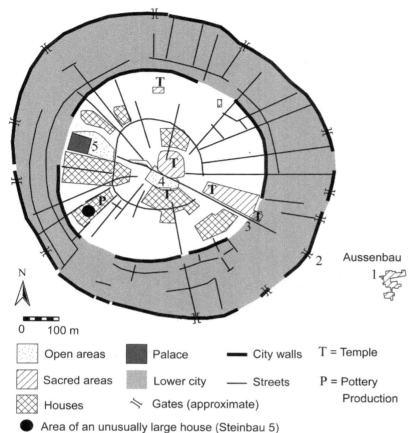

Figure 2.3 Tell Chuera, schematic plan of infrastructure and the primary use of various areas. Numbers 1–5 mark potential armature: 1) Aussenbau, 2) City gate, 3) Entry to upper city and temple complex, 4) Plaza, 5) Palace. Redrawn and modified from Meyer 2006:Abb. 2; Pruss 2000:figure 1; and Goethe Universität, Institut für Archäologische Wissenschaften 2007. Some information was also derived from Tell Chuera reports.

influential, but does not determine behavior (see Trigger 2003:654). In doing so we can construct spatial maps, such as those described by Bill Hillier and Julienne Hanson (1984:90–142), to identify similarities and differences in spatial patterning within and between cities. These spatial patterns show how people organized and moved through space in the city (see, for example, Scott Branting's [2010] computer modeling of pedestrian traffic in an Anatolian city for which the entire street network has been reconstructed with remote sensing techniques). In round cities with known street patterns, such as Tell Chuera or Al-Rawda, main streets form ring roads and spokes that define fairly regular wedge-shaped city blocks (Figures 2.3 and 2.4). This structure is more "symmetric" and "distributed," which suggests a "tendency towards the *diffusion of spatial control*" (Hillier and Hanson 1984:97 [italics in original]). Such readily discernible segments of space may make it easy to grasp the structure of a city, and provide greater access to outsiders (Lawrence

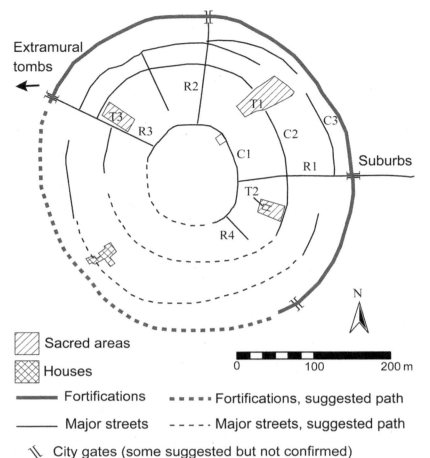

Figure 2.4 Al-Rawda, schematic plan showing city wall, temples (T1,2,3), major streets (R1,2,3; C1,2,3), excavated housing, and suburbs. Derived from Castel and Peltenburg 2007:figure 5; Castel et al. 2005:figures 2a and 3; and Gondet and Castel 2004:figure 8.

and Low 1990:471; Lynch 1964:67–70). Wheel or deformed wheel-shaped street networks funnel outsiders along certain routes, mark the boundaries of residential areas, and preserve residential privacy (Hillier 2008:10).

No matter where you go in round cities, you are never too far from a major spoke or loop road that will convey you rapidly to other parts of the city, including the very center. Gates and topography notwithstanding, lines of sight and passage on radial roads often run directly to the city center, and ring roads make it possible to reach many sectors of the city quickly while bypassing side streets or potentially congested areas. Over time, some main roads are blocked by expanding buildings, forcing pedestrians to detour through less-direct secondary streets. Without deep excavations in these spaces, it is not clear whether these obstructions are primary, marking planned defensible space (see the section on defensible space in this chapter) or secondary, marking conflicting claims to space (Low 1996:876) in which various groups block the street adjacent to their houses or workshops in order to produce defensible space. An example of the latter may be found at Al-Rawda, where streets or architecture are asymmetrical or interrupt the general pattern. The excavators of this site argue that these features result from changes to a formerly integrated master plan (Castel and Peltenburg 2007).

In contrast with the accessibility of round cities, streets in oblong cities tend to meander along a semi-straight course, as at Titriş, or at best form a semi-orthogonal structure in which cross streets create rectilinear city blocks. These streets have less-direct lines of sight than perfectly straight streets and may impede transit for visitors. We might expect irregular streets to be emergent (i.e., unplanned), but excavations at Titriş demonstrate that at least some of its streets were cut into sterile soil and built before adjacent houses, indicating that their pattern was planned and coordinated (Matney 2002:26–27), with their route influenced by topography (see Nishimura, Chapter 3 in this volume). Similar planning of streets is noted at the oblong cities of Kazane and Leilan, albeit with small exposures that do not clarify the entire path of the street (Creekmore 2008:167–168, 2010:78; Weiss 1990:201–203, abb. 3, 7–9).

NUCLEATION

Upper Mesopotamian cities were highly nucleated, built-up settlements with wall-to-wall architecture and little open space. Extramural areas contained fields, pasture, burial grounds, and small villages. Given that the growth of these cities was rarely restricted on all sides by natural features, how do we explain this nucleation? The universal presence of city walls, sometimes matched with a glacis and ditch or moat (as at Titriş, Mozan, Al-Rawda, Beydar, and Chuera) suggests that protection from theft or conflict was one motivation for nucleation. Yet, even if violence were the exception rather than the rule, nucleation makes infrastructure less expensive to build and maintain by reducing the length of city walls, streets, and drainage systems. Another impetus for nucleation is land tenure, which may have limited sprawling settlement on communal or crown land. Finally, city walls have important symbolic value, were often constructed in the earliest period of the city, and may have fostered nucleation by encouraging compaction within the walls. In the following discussion, I explore these explanations for nucleation.

Defense

The existence of substantial defensive structures at large cities, small towns, and even small villages (e.g., Cooper 2006b:70) indicates strongly that violence was a real threat. In addition, city walls are symbols of power and they project power by making it possible for a city to send its army or militia out to confront or threaten others, leaving smaller forces behind to defend the homeland (Pauketat 2007:122, 131). Violence was clearly a part of life in these societies, especially in the later third millennium (Sallaberger 2007:422–423). The Ebla texts include accounts of conflict between Mari and Ebla, a forced treaty between Ebla and Abarsal, tribute gifts sent to Ebla from threatened cities, and weapons exchanged with allies (Archi and Biga 2003; Merola 2008; Sollberger 1980). Archaeological evidence for violence at these cities is not as plentiful as lists of tribute from subject polities, but excavations reveal destruction layers at several sites, weapons in burials, and victory iconography from Mari and Ebla (Akkermans and Schwartz 2003:269). Other examples of violence or suggestive of violence include a mass burial, changes in regional settlement patterns, and local urban structure (abandoned villages and suburbs), a shift from extramural to intramural burials, and construction of new defenses at Titriş (Algaze et al. 2001:68–70), and possibly the burning of the sacred structures of *Steinbauten* I–II at Chuera (Klein and Orthmann 1995:75; Orthmann 1995a, plans 6, 13, 1995b:32; Moortgat 1962:35; Pruss 1998).

Symbolism

Aside from their role in defense, city walls also have important symbolic value that is recorded in texts, images, and their physical manifestation (Ristvet 2007:184). Upper Mesopotamian city walls defined the city, marking a clear perimeter with gates mediating entry and exit. A barrel cylinder from Mashkan-shapir, a second-millennium city in Lower Mesopotamia, celebrates the building of the city wall as a defining act in establishing the city (Steinkeller 2004:135–146). Third-millennium texts from Beydar list state workers – in this case, shepherds – under gate names, indicating that in at least some cases, gate names represented quarters or neighborhoods (Sallaberger 2004:18–19). In many examples, city walls were built early in the life of the city, as at Kazane, Mozan, Chuera, Beydar, Leilan, Al-Rawda, and others. These may be instances of conspicuous consumption and expressions of power, as described by Trigger (1990:127), although the labor and resources required to build a city wall that benefits all residents may involve more negotiation among corporate groups than the centralization of power described by Trigger (see for example the range of professions involved in building a city wall, as described in Ristvet 2007). Thus, the city wall may have first marked officially the establishment of a city, and later constricted growth and intensified nucleation as residents packed into the area behind the walls in order to be part of the city. In general, extramural settlement is rare, but it is documented at Al-Rawda and Titriş.

Land Tenure

Although defense, symbolism, or economizing construction can be considered sensible reasons to nucleate, another possible factor is land tenure. Tony Wilkinson combines archaeological survey, analysis of period textual sources, and analogy with recent historical practice in the region to argue that Bronze Age villages probably had a communal land-tenure system. In this system, use rights shifted regularly and land did not belong to a single family (Wilkinson 2010:59). This type of land tenure explains in part the ever-increasing height of tells, which were repeatedly occupied because building outside the village on communal land was discouraged. If this system was maintained during the urbanization process, then tightly packing into a nucleated city would limit the amount of former field or pasture land that would have to be taken over by the city during the development of a lower town around the tell. Although powerful city rulers may have claimed ownership over all the land in a given region (Wilkinson 2010:57), at least initially one would expect former land tenure practices to present a roadblock to the development of low-density settlement with copious open space between residential areas. A complicating factor affecting the use of land around cities is squatters, or those constructing housing, gardens, and other features in unused open space without necessarily possessing use or tenure rights. These activities may be temporary, but if tolerated, their product may become a permanent part of the city (see Neuwirth 2005 for modern examples).

Wilkinson notes that texts record villages, their land, and their inhabitants changing hands as a single entity owned by the state or private families (Wilkinson 2010:58; see also Steinkeller 1993:125–126). This practice could leave local land-use or land-tenure patterns intact, despite the knowledge that an overlord was the official owner. The case of city land ownership is more complicated. Although private home ownership within cities is attested by texts from the second millennium (Stone 1987; Van De Mieroop 1999), the division of extramural land is less clear. Highly generalized summaries of textual evidence for land exchanges across the third to second millennia throughout Mesopotamia suggest that traditional systems of communal ownership were eroded as a few landowners amassed vast holdings while the size of the average family's plot shrank (Zaccagnini 1999:339). In other cases, ruling institutions laid claim to all land and redistributed it to citizens according to their social rank (Dahl 2002). Inherited property may be absent from most texts, which chronicle sales, leaving open the possibility of larger, privately owned plots not listed in texts (Zaccagnini 1999:339). Texts from Beydar suggest that a handful of state officials controlled most of the land and male labor in its region (Sallaberger and Ur 2004:57–58; Widell 2003:723). However, this evidence is selective, and Jason Ur argues that the center controlled only part of village land (Sallaberger and Ur 2004:57, footnote 13). In any case, long-lived pathways between fields endure in some areas as "hollow ways" on the landscape, indicating continuity in the structure of fields adjacent to cities (Casana 2013; Ur 2003).

In sum, nucleation in Upper Mesopotamian cities may derive from a combined need for security and efficient infrastructure, which generated constrictive, highly symbolic walls. Nucleation is also compatible with traditional notions of land tenure that discourage dispersed housing, and building structures side-by-side along narrow streets is consistent with principles of defensible space (see defensible space section later in this chapter). It is difficult to determine with certainty which of these factors was primary. I favor an interpretation based on a pre-urban preference for close-knit living in clustered neighborhoods, combined with shared land tenure in which the defensive value, if not the symbolic value, of circuit walls varied over time with the degree of conflict.

MULTICENTRICITY

Because many Upper Mesopotamian cities developed from pre-existing villages and were highly nucleated, it is easy to assume that these settlements grew from the center or tell to the periphery in an oil-stain-like spread in which new residents joined neighborhoods that expanded around a single administrative, elite nucleus, as expressed in Sjoberg's model of preindustrial cities (1960:323). Current data are not sufficient to determine if urban growth followed major streets defining sectors in a process akin to Homer Hoyt's sector model (1939), or leap-frogged open spaces as multiple centers were established in a fashion that recalls Chauncy Harris and Edward Ullman's multiple nuclei model (1945). The fortified cluster of a palace, temples, markets, and storage at the center of Beydar comes closest to Sjoberg's model, but the social structure or status of surrounding neighborhoods is not yet clear. Recent research has uncovered multiple administrative and elite centers in several cities, and all of these cities must have had other social centers measured in terms of neighborhoods, pedestrian traffic, a convergence of major roads, or the value of land (Hoyt 1939:18).

At Kazane, elite and institutional structures form at least three administrative centers in the city. These centers include the presumed (but not excavated) administrative citadel on the tell; a probable palace or other administrative building east of the tell, marked by a massive wall; and numerous monumental structures revealed by magnetometry and excavations in the southern portion of the city. These include large storage facilities, a large house, and another possible palace or massive administrative building (Figure 2.5) (Creekmore 2010; Wattenmaker 1997). At Titriş, a small exposure of mid-third millennium remains in the outer town revealed monu- ... ture characteristic of elite housing or public build- ... nd Pournelle 2003:107; Matney 2002:25; Matney and ... . This may mark a second center, far from the citadel, ... ring the earliest period of the city. Although standard ... tures were later built over these buildings, Nishimura ... in this volume) identifies several larger buildings at ... in the outer town during the later third millennium ... k additional centers in the final period of the city.

... vda, ring and radial roads demarcate sectors containing ... it represent multiple ritual centers (Figure 2.4). On the basis of magnetometry data, two and possibly three ritual areas were

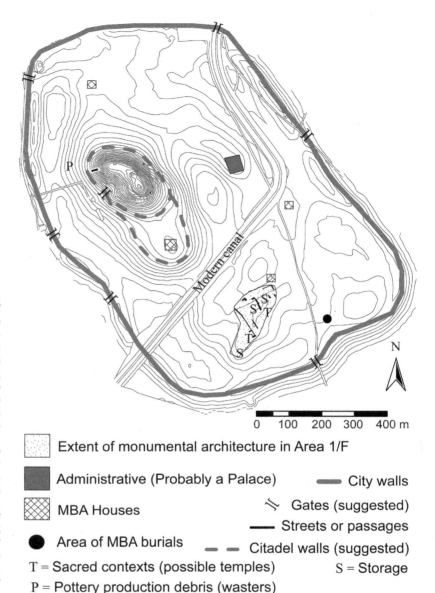

Figure 2.5 Kazane, schematic plan of Early Bronze Age infrastructure, administrative, sacred, and other areas. Middle Bronze Age housing and burials are also marked owing to possible continuity in the use of these spaces from the prior period. Note: the location of the citadel walls and city gates are suggestions, and are not based on any excavated evidence. Palace and Middle Bronze Age housing areas are shown larger than the actual exposures to enhance visibility. After Creekmore 2008:figure 9.3.

Extent of monumental architecture in Area 1/F

Administrative (Probably a Palace)

MBA Houses

Area of MBA burials

T = Sacred contexts (possible temples)
P = Pottery production debris (wasters)

City walls

Gates (suggested)

Streets or passages

Citadel walls (suggested)

S = Storage

identified in the city, one of which was confirmed by excavations. Each consists of one or two small temples surrounded by open space enclosed by a wall (Gondet and Castel 2004:104, figures 8a and 8c; Castel et al. 2005:figure 6a; Castel and Peltenburg 2007:606, figures 7 and 8). Notably, the inner sanctuary of the temples in all three areas is oriented toward the center of the site, and a single ring road, C2, intersects or passes all three compounds (Figure 2.4). The existence of multiple, spatially separated temples in a relatively small city may

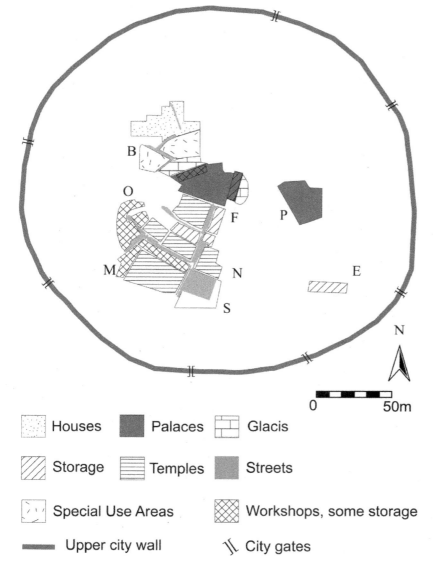

Houses   Palaces   Glacis

Storage   Temples   Streets

Special Use Areas   Workshops, some storage

Upper city wall   City gates

Figure 2.6 Beydar, upper city, schematic plan of infrastructure and the primary use of various areas, with excavation areas marked with letters. Use areas derived from Lebeau 2006a:plan 1; Lebeau and Suleiman 2008, 2009; and excavation reports. Gates placed after Bluard 1997: figure 1.

indicate the worship of multiple gods, the presence of different social or ethnic groups, and multiple nodes of religious power.

Chuera contains at least two major but separate administrative centers (Figure 2.3). These include the palace on the western edge of the upper city and the cluster of small but monumental temples and related structures on the eastern edge of the city. Small, isolated temples also exist within residential areas in the upper city. At Beydar, a second palace was recently discovered, just below but adjacent to the acropolis mound that contained a palace and multiple temples (Figure 2.6: Areas F and P) (Lebeau and Suleiman 2009).

Aside from ritual and administrative centers, multiple residential areas served as centers of social life. Street patterns, as discussed earlier, formed wedge-shaped or rectilinear blocks of housing areas subdivided by small lanes. Major intersections, culs-de-sac, and other less-visible features such as utilization of a particular neighborhood temple or shrine, could define neighborhoods or centers of social activity in the city. Thus, although a particular sector may have an elevated status owing to association with particular residents or proximity to certain features in the city, and some administrative or religious centers may have been higher in the pecking order of the city governance and devotion, these features were not relegated to a single business, religious, or housing district. Instead, they formed multiple centers of urban life.

CONSERVATIVE DEVELOPMENT

The production of space in Upper Mesopotamian cities was conservative; spatial principles established early in the life of the city were maintained over long periods of time. During the course of their life history, streets and city walls tended to be rebuilt in the same space, houses were built over houses, palaces over palaces, and temples over temples. Thus, it is rare to find examples of what Ernest Burgess (1925) called "organization" and "disorganization," in which the primary use of different parts of the city changed over time. These episodes usually occurred during major regional transitions, such as in the late third to early second millennium when many polities experienced a collapse, decline, hiatus, or reorganization of settlement (Cooper 2006a; Ur 2010). Even massive rebuilding efforts, such as after a fire that destroyed the sacred precinct at Chuera, tend to maintain the primary use or function of an area (Orthmann 1995b:32). Although this might be expected for sacred or political structures, the endurance of housing – and presumably neighborhoods, in most cities – is striking and indicates the probable importance of land ownership and inheritance within the city.[7] An exception to this pattern may be found at Titriş, where the lower town shows continuity while the outer town contains significant changes from the mid- to late third millennium, reflecting either a shift from public to private architecture, or elite to non-elite housing (Algaze and Pournelle 2003:107; Matney 2002:25; Matney and Algaze 1995:49).

Explanations for conservative production of space vary. As previously noted, for reasons of cost, infrastructure tends to remain in place and shape later development (Herman and Ausubel 1988:13). City planners note that urban space can become relatively fixed and resist change despite changes in economics or society (Herbert and Thomas 1990:126). Manuel Castells argues that the production and construction of urban space is fraught with conflict in which dominant institutions resist changes to urban structure (Castells 1983:xviii). In this view, substantial change in urban planning requires top-down decisions or major grassroots efforts (Castells 1983:303–304). Although Castells' interpretation makes sense in the context of very powerful institutions, I argue that in cases of increased power-sharing, conservative city plans may derive from a desire among residents for comfort and continuity. Although desire may be impossible to analyze with archaeological data, studies of human behavior indicate that if one's immediate surroundings are orderly or familiar, then one feels empowered whereas disorder enhances feelings of powerlessness (Geis 1998:243). A sense of order or disorder derives as much from the construction of space as the production of space, but the structuring effect of the latter may have a significant effect on maintaining social order. Thus, contra Louis Wirth's assertions – based in part on the writings of Durkheim, Weber, and Simmel – that the anonymity of cities diminishes the importance of neighborhoods (Wirth 1938:11, 21); in Mesopotamian cities, as in some modern cities, the neighborhood was very important for building and maintaining social ties (Logan and Spitze 1994; Stone 1987:129). This social importance would have contributed to conservative production of space in neighborhoods, and enhanced *place attachment*, "the symbolic relationship formed by people giving culturally shared emotional/affective meanings to a particular space or piece of land that provides the basis for the individual's and group's understanding of and relation to the environment" (Low 1992:165). This meaning may be especially strong in cases where family tombs were located within houses, as at Titriş (Laneri 2007, 2010; see also Nishimura, Chapter 3 in this volume).

DEFENSIBLE SPACE

Defensible space is a key component of Upper Mesopotamian cities. Defensible space is a conscious effort by residents and city planners to define urban space by erecting barriers or markers that indicate ownership, enhance security, and discourage or manage passage (Newman 1973:3–4). Persons walking through the city 'read' these markers and understand what kind of space they are entering or passing (de Certeau 1998:98–99; Rapoport 1990). Defensible space plays an important role in defining neighborhoods in a city (Abu-Lughod 1987). Defensible spaces in Upper Mesopotamian cities include gates along the city wall or at entrances to palaces, temples and other administrative structures, street patterns and types (wide versus narrow) that define neighborhoods, culs-de-sac within residential and administrative contexts, and houses, which are designed to interrupt the line of sight from entrances to inner rooms.

City walls and gates are found in every Upper Mesopotamian city, and gated entrances for major structures are found in most. Within the city, wide main streets demarcate sectors and probably neighborhoods as well. Narrow, branching passageways discourage entry into the heart of residential blocks, generating defensible space (Costa and Noble 1986:165; Biewers 1997:77–80; both cited in Düring 2006:47). In some cases, neighborhoods may have been bounded by long party walls (e.g., at Leilan, see Ristvet 2005:figure 3.11). Many multiroom houses exhibit defensible space in that they were entered through a small vestibule that functioned as a gate (see Nishimura, Chapter 3 in this volume, for a more detailed discussion of house form and function). This room protected the privacy of inner rooms both by limiting the view from the street and by adding layers of doorways (Rainville 2005:149; also see Nishimura, Chapter 3 in this volume, Figure 3.4). Smaller houses, such as those with just one or two rooms, did not have the luxury of a vestibule. Another form of defensible space in these cities are culs-de-sac, found in residential areas at Chuera, Beydar, Titriş, and Taya (Figure 2.7) (Pfälzner 1997:Abbildung 11; Lebeau and Suleiman 2008:9, street east of "Tablet House" and south of House 6; Algaze et al. 2001:figure 2; Rainville 2005:figure 5.7b; Reade 1973:plates LIX, LX, LXI), and in elite or administrative areas at Beydar and Kazane (Lebeau and Suleiman 2003:plan 7 [approach to palace]; Creekmore 2008:figure 4.5). Culs-de-sac are also very likely present at Al-Rawda within dense housing blocks, although published plans do not permit their identification.

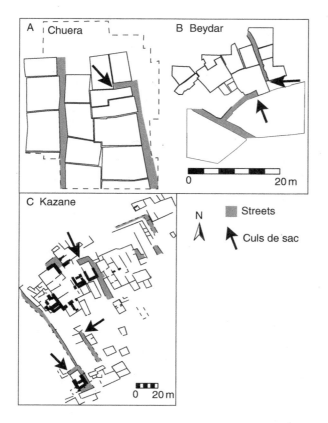

Figure 2.7 Examples of culs-de-sac in Upper Mesopotamian cities. A: Tell Chuera – Area K, excavated houses, period EJ IIIa (2600–2450 BC). Redrawn after Pfälzner 1997: Abb. 11. B: Beydar – Area B, excavated houses and special-use structures (large blocks to the south), period EJ IIIb phase 3c (2450–2300 BC). After Lebeau and Suleiman 2008:9. C: Kazane – Area 1 / F, magnetometry plan, and excavated structures (dark, thick lines), (ca. 2500–2300 BC). After Creekmore 2010:figure 4. Culs-de-sac are suggested but not confirmed by excavation.

In some cases, culs-de-sac were probably part of the original city plan; in other cases, they may represent the activities of residents creating defensible space by expanding their homes across narrow lanes, thereby blocking traffic and creating culs-de-sac. Aside from discouraging entry, culs-de-sac and alleys provide additional protected outdoor space for storage, tying up animals, and children's play. At Titriş, at least one cul-de-sac occurs at the break between terraced segments of outer-town housing, in a space possibly cut off from the street and only accessible from adjacent houses (Matney 2002:27; Nishimura, see Chapter 3 in this volume, Figure 3.3, space between Houses 3, 4, and 7). Areas with such limited access may be more likely to function as gardens, garbage dumps, or meeting places for social and even illicit activities.

PARCELED HOUSES

Because the amount of walled, protected space within a city is limited, and extending city walls, streets, and other infrastructure is expensive, it should not be surprising if central institutions – and residents themselves – attempt to control the distribution of space within the city. In the cities discussed in this chapter there is evidence for similar lot sizes in residential areas at Titriş, Chuera, and Leilan, and in the monumental buildings of Area 1 at Kazane (Matney 2002:27; Pfälzner 1997; Ristvet 2005:figure 3.11; Creekmore 2008, 2010). These similar lots are not seen in all periods, but when they appear, they demonstrate what Peter Pfälzner terms *Parzellenhäuser*, or parceled houses (Pfälzner 1997). The parceled houses identified by Pfälzner come in standard widths of 6, 7.5, 9, 12, or 15 meters, and have similar ground plans (Pfälzner 1997:figure 8). At Chuera and Bderi, these standard plots are limited to a specific time frame, 2600–2450 BC. After this period, non-parceled houses replace some parceled lots at Chuera and parceled lots disappear altogether at Bderi. Pfälzner argues that parceled lots are evidence for centralized city planning and their disappearance is owing to thinning of the city population and increasing ethnic diversity (Pfälzner 1997:251, 258).

Although the similar lot dimensions identified by Pfälzner seem to indicate an organized distribution of city land, they do not necessarily reflect top-down city planning. Instead, these lots indicate that the standard units for measuring land were agreed upon and upheld by the residents (Smith 2007:29). Rather than marking a top-down city plan, similarly sized lots are an efficient way of managing land. These lots facilitate construction of similarly sized houses and minimize space lost to leftover spaces that are too small or too large for a practical house. Regardless of lot size, residents could expand or shrink their houses by buying or selling rooms to or from adjacent structures, a practice noted in later periods in Lower Mesopotamia (Stone 2007:217; Van De Mieroop 1999:256). Thus, a homeowner could purchase two rooms from an adjacent house and incorporate them into his own house by cutting doorways into adjacent walls and blocking entrances from the new rooms to the now smaller neighboring house.

The most convincing case of house lots as evidence of formal planning comes from Titriş, where double walls bound plots of land with regular dimensions in the outer town (Matney 2002; see also Nishimura's discussion of the 2300 BC reconstruction, Chapter 3 in this volume). These plots are not equivalent to individual houses. Instead, multiple-walled plots are combined to form

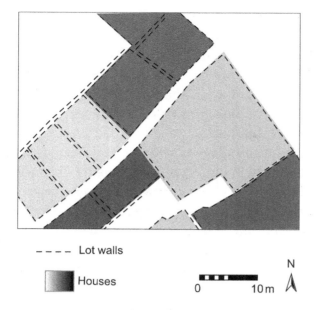

- - - - Lot walls

▨ Houses

0 ◼◻◻◼ 10 m

N
𝐀

Figure 2.8 Titriş,
building lots in the
outer town (generated
from Algaze et al.
2001:figure 2, and
Matney 2002:26). Note
doubled walls and
possible cul-de-sac. Cf.
Nishimura, Chapter 3
in this volume,
Figures 3.3–3.4.

houses of various sizes, which together are founded on regular, walled terraces (Figure 2.8). In addition, in some cases, the walls within these plots share the same orientation across multiple plots, houses, and streets (Matney 2002:27). Thus, although the internal division of space within each house differs, the plots themselves and their main walls were laid according to supra-household spatial principles, perhaps by developers (Algaze et al. 2001:69; Matney 2002:27). In sum, although parceled lots do indicate some level of land management within the city, they do not necessarily indicate a formal plan designed at the supra-household level except when combined with shared architectural principles and features.

ARMATURE

Another concept that contributes to an understanding of space in third-millennium Upper Mesopotamian cities is armature. Defined for Roman cities by William MacDonald, armature consists of "main streets, squares, and essential public buildings linked together across cities and towns from gate to gate, with junctions and entranceways prominently articulated" (MacDonald 1986:5). MacDonald argues that armature develops independently from city planning and evolves as new parts are added and old parts extended (MacDonald 1986:30–31). In most Upper Mesopotamian cities, we lack enough of the urban plan to evaluate a key part of the definition of armature – unimpeded passage across a city – but here I suggest a few possible examples of this feature.

At Mozan, a city in the Upper Khabur region, the approach to and placement of Temple BA may be an example of armature. This small temple was built in the mid-third millennium at the top of a long staircase on an isolated platform on the highest part of the upper city (Buccellati 1998; Buccellati and Kelly-Buccellati 1997, 2000, 2001). Although the temple's connection to the rest of the city is unknown, the grand staircase is suggestive of an armature system. In a similar fashion, a narrow street that climbs the mounded center of Beydar, passing temples en route to a cul-de-sac terminating at the palace, may also mark the end of an armature route (Figure 2.6) (Lebeau 2006a:120).

In contrast to the preceding partial examples, the more complete city plan available from Chuera may better illustrate a case of armature. At Chuera, a main street traverses the upper city from southeast to northwest (Figure 2.3). This street may begin (or end) outside the city to the east, in the area of a temple and extramural burials (the *Aussenbau*; "1" in Figure 2.3). From this ritual space one passes the outer city gate ("2" in Figure 2.3) and continues to the upper city. Although the upper city wall went out of use after the construction of the lower city wall (Meyer 2006:184), the beginning of an extended temple complex echoes the location of the former gate ("3" in Figure 2.3). In keeping with the armature concept, the main street next passes a temple complex marked by a stone platform, high stone terrace, and monumental gateway to this precinct. Beyond this temple area, the street continues west through a public plaza ("4" in Figure 2.3) and on to the palace and adjacent open area on the western side of the upper city ("5" in Figure 2.3). A grand entrance marks the palace, and perhaps other architectural features mark the intersections of the open areas. It is not clear if this main street continues past the palace into the lower town, but according to the armature concept, it could detour along a different axis that articulates with other public buildings or spaces before exiting the city at a major gate. One can imagine this armature developing from an initial core of the central plaza flanked by the palace and temple areas, and later expanding as the city grew to include the lower city gate and new structures in the extramural area.

Other examples of armature may include the articulation of the outer town city gate with public space at Titriş (Nishimura, Chapter 3 in this volume), the intersection of street C2 with Temples 1, 2, and 3 at Al-Rawda (Figure 2.4), and passages through or by monumental architecture in Area 1/F at Kazane (Figures 2.5 and 2.7). Although these possibilities cannot be verified without further excavations, and the static city plan provided by magnetograms (magnetometer data) fails to capture the life history of armature, it is worth considering this aspect of city space when looking for examples of coordination among buildings or linkages of seemingly disconnected aspects of city space.

THE IMPORTANCE OF LIFE HISTORIES

In this chapter, I focused on spatial and planning principles shared by many Upper Mesopotamian cities. Although I emphasized similarities, it is also important to consider differences between cities and how these cities formed and changed over time. Here I consider briefly the contrasting features and life histories of two of the archaeologically better-known round cities, Beydar and Chuera. This comparison reveals that, despite their similar shape, they have very different developmental pathways.

Chuera consists of a walled, 28 ha inner mound, and a walled, 37 ha lower town (Figure 2.3).[8] In the earliest phases at Chuera, the focal point of the city was a public plaza flanked by residences, while the palace and temple-related facilities were concentrated at the edges of the upper city along easily accessible streets. Additional small temples were situated within residential areas. In this scheme, the public plaza was the focal point that unified the households of the residents, the palace, and the temple. Yet, a few hundred years after its construction, the central plaza began to fill with garbage from adjacent residential areas. This garbage eventually rose to more than 8 meters high, along with the houses themselves, which were rebuilt again and again (Orthmann 1995a). These developments demonstrate that the original purpose and meaning of this plaza changed significantly as the city evolved. This shift may have impacted the linkage of the armature discussed earlier, or at least removed the plaza from this system. The remarkable shift from open to closed space indicates that the use and meaning of this space was changing or at least contested, and possibly created or derived from a sense of disorder among residents, as previously discussed.

Compared to Chuera, Beydar is a considerably smaller city covering 22.5 ha with 17 ha of settled area, including the top of the outer city wall and the 7 ha, 20 m high tell inside the inner city wall (Figure 6) (Lebeau 2006a:101; Ur and Wilkinson 2008:313). Between the inner and outer city walls, a moat adds further protection and a glacis accompanies the inner city wall (Lebeau 2006a, 2006b:3). In contrast to settlement at Chuera, which began in the upper city and later expanded to the lower town, at Beydar, the lower town and outer fortification were built at the very beginning of settlement but the lower town was not inhabited. In contrast to the plaza that formed the centerpiece of early settlement at Chuera, Beydar's core was dominated by a palace and five temples set upon a three-tiered terrace flanked by a glacis on two sides and accessed by a single street that narrows to provide choke or control points as it ascends toward the palace (Lebeau 2006a; Sténuit and Van der Stede 2003). Residential housing is found at the northern base of the palace glacis (Area B), while a second palace lies to the east below the central palace (Area P). From what is known of its life history, the central palace and temples remained the focal point of Beydar throughout the habitation of this city, even during the decline of its last years.

The fundamental difference in the focal point, viewshed, location, and accessibility of the palace, temples, and residences indicates very different developmental pathways for Beydar and Chuera. From its founding, Beydar looks like a small fort-city designed to protect the wealth of the palace and temple households, which probably had a close political alliance, whereas Chuera's founding plan gave prominence to residences and public space, and provided access to temples and the palace, which were spatially on a par with regular residences and located near or next to large open areas. The separation between the palace and major temple area at Chuera may indicate that these institutions were also more politically independent than at Beydar. Finally, if the second palace in Area P at Beydar proves to be surrounded by additional administrative buildings, then the space for housing at Beydar will shrink further, suggesting a lower population than we would expect from the site area alone.

IDEAL CITIES

Thus far I have argued that Upper Mesopotamian cities were planned and constructed by multiple groups in society who generated a collage of urban spaces. In most cases, the structure of the earliest phases of these cities is poorly known, lying beneath remains from later periods and making it difficult to state with certainty the extent to which later urban plans reflect an original spatial model. I noted that infrastructure shapes later development and construction of space is conservative in these cities. In two cases, Chuera and Al-Rawda, their researchers argue explicitly that significant parts, if not all of their city structure, were planned at the outset. If these cities were indeed planned on a large scale from their earliest period, then they may represent ideal cities in which the construction of space conforms to their builders' notions of a "good" city.

The excavators of Chuera argue that the site "was a town from its very beginning ... Its existence is the result of a deliberate town-planning process" (Pruss 2000:1432). This statement derives from the finding that the large plaza at the center of the site overlies mid-fourth millennium and earlier remains, but not material from the early third millennium that immediately preceded the growth of the city (Pruss 1998). Yet it does not consider that a small early third-millennium settlement could be located anywhere on the high mound, not just beneath the central plaza. Nonetheless, it does appear that the plaza, main street, and probably the basic parameters of housing and sacred areas were defined early in the life of the city. If further excavations demonstrate that the earliest foundations of each of these areas date to the same narrow period, then Chuera may indeed represent a town plan enacted by a central government, but this does not rule out participation by residents.

The excavators of Al-Rawda argue that specialists under the direction of the central authorities built the major infrastructure in the city – including the main streets, city gates, city wall, and central sector – in one single, concerted effort (Castel and Peltenburg 2007:604; Gondet and Castel 2004:108). They further argue that the plan of Al-Rawda could not have developed without a model, and they cite Tell Chuera, more than 200 kilometers to the northeast, and Tell Sheirat, 32 kilometers south of Al-Rawda, as examples of round cities that may have inspired the builders of Al-Rawda. It is possible that the architects, builders, and workers at Al-Rawda visited other round cities before or during the construction of their own settlement. In his study of the texts from Ebla, Archi notes that attached craft specialists, or those working explicitly for a government or institution, traveled between cities to work for other rulers. For example, smiths or carpenters traveled between Ebla and other nearby cities – even as far as Mari and Kish – presumably to complete special projects for which their skills were needed (Archi 1988:28). This exchange of specialists undoubtedly spread ideas about technology and style, and may have influenced city planning.

To my knowledge, no one has argued that any of the non-round (oblong) cities were built all at once according to a single master plan. The closest example to this kind of planning may be the *re*building of portions of Titriş, as described earlier. Yet, oblong cities also demonstrate ideals of city space through the repeated use of major streets to funnel traffic between major nodes, narrow lanes and culs-de-sac to restrict or inhibit access to housing, the construction of clustered structures, and the establishment of multiple centers.

DISCUSSION

This chapter identifies several important factors in the production and construction of space in Upper Mesopotamian cities. I argue that these highly nucleated settlements had multiple administrative and social centers that formed during urbanization. The production of space in these cities was conservative, often maintaining the use or function of an area even during extensive rebuilding or renovation. A key planning principle was the production of defensible space, whether by original design or subsequent modification. I suggest that the concept of armature may be applicable to these cities, and may unify otherwise scattered elements of a city's structure. Although winding streets and semi-orthogonal architecture give an appearance of an organic growth pattern, streets and, in some cases, whole neighborhoods show supra-household planning, both through designation of lot size and coordinated construction. Finally, I argue that careful attention to the life history of these cities is the best way to reveal similarities and differences in their development and the interplay between activities that structure space and the structuring effects of space.

Taken together, these observations show that the production of space in Upper Mesopotamian cities took place in multiple overlapping social spheres, including the city government that focused on infrastructure, mid-level planners or developers (Algaze et al. 2001: 69; Matney 2002) who built some residential areas in conjunction with neighborhood organizations and leaders, and residents who modified space according to their needs. Viewed in this manner, the production of space in Upper Mesopotamian cities suggests a sociopolitical order consisting of power sharing rather than top-down domination or purely disorganized, organic development. The spatial result of the sociopolitical order suggested here is a varying degree of city planning, as described by Michael Smith's scale (2007). Thus, these cities have examples of coordination among buildings in institutions, public space, and neighborhoods; supra-household planning of neighborhoods, streets, and infrastructure; and some standardization in the kinds of spaces preferred by city residents. In some cases, coordination may be expressed very loosely or in a nonlinear fashion, as in armature, requiring large horizontal exposures of sites before patterns can be identified.

Although this analysis focuses on examples from third-millennium Upper Mesopotamia, many of the spatial principles discussed here are seen in earlier, pre-urban periods and in subsequent urban periods throughout much of Upper and Lower Mesopotamia (Henrickson 1981; Keith 1999, 2003; Stone 1995, 2007; Ur 2012). The maintenance of notions of social space across the millennia throughout Mesopotamia may testify to the continuance of social structures such as tribes and lineages during the shift to cities and states (Cooper 2006b:61). The emphasis on kinship and consensual decision making in these social structures resists domination by urban authorities. The complex and often new social roles formed in cities served to integrate a diverse society, but also resisted yielding autonomy to city government (Yoffee 1979:21, 1995:289, 2005:62, 214). In this context, urban authorities may have had to work hard to build a loyal population. Stone (2007:228) argues that second-millennium Lower Mesopotamian cities competed with one another for prestige, and may have installed or refurbished infrastructure to attract residents.

Despite textual evidence for powerful rulers at different places and times, and the assertion by some that third-millennium Upper

Mesopotamian cities were oligarchies ruled coercively by the palace and a few elite households (Sallaberger and Ur 2004; Steinkeller 1993:124; Weiss et al. 2002), many scholars of these polities view the city as a bastion of heterarchy (Crumley 1995) and corporate political strategies (Blanton, Feinman, and Kowalewski 1996) in which everyday residents and individual households played a central role in urbanization and the production and governance of urban space (Creekmore 2008; Fleming 2004; Stone 2007; Ur 2004). This assertion does not deny the existence of social stratification or even possibly segregation among city residents in some cases. Instead, I argue that the making of cities is a shared, conflicting process that incorporates the needs of multiple social groups within society. In the production of space in the city, we see the give and take between Adam Smith's (2003) "regime" or John Mollenkopf's (1992) "ruling coalition," made up of the ruling families and associated factions, and the "grassroots," or "everyday" people. At the same time, a careful consideration of a city's life history reveals that cities with similar basic structure may have very different developmental pathways. Future attention to the principles of the production and construction of space discussed here, in conjunction with a life history approach and the range of theoretical angles summarized by Michael Smith (2011) may help us unpack the complexity of urbanization and recognize the agency of different sociopolitical groups in society.

ACKNOWLEDGMENTS

This work is derived from my dissertation, which was supervised by Jim Brown, Tim Earle, Cynthia Robin, Gil Stein, and Patricia Wattenmaker. Field research at Kazane and writing of portions of the text were funded by a National Science Foundation Dissertation Improvement Grant (BCS-0434788), a grant from the Center for International and Comparative Studies at Northwestern University, a Dolores Zohrab Liebmann Fellowship, a Kress Fellowship from the American Research Institute in Turkey, and a Northwestern University Summer Fellowship. Earlier drafts of this chapter benefited greatly from comments by Kevin Fisher, Britt Hartenberger, Nicola Laneri, Ellie Moseman, Rana Özbal, and Elizabeth Stone. I also thank Yoko Nishimura for providing valuable clarification of

data from Titriş, and two anonymous reviewers for catching errors
and providing thought-provoking comments.

NOTES

1 An earlier wave of urbanism is known from recent research at Tell Brak (Emberling
   2003; Emberling and McDonald 2003; Matthews 2003; Oates 2005; Oates et al. 2007;
   Ur, Karsgaard, and Oates 2007) and Hamoukar (Gibson et al. 2002) in northeastern
   Syria, and Arslantepe (Frangipane 2002) in eastern Anatolia. This work revealed
   evidence for large, urban settlements at these sites in the fourth millennium, prior
   to the appearance of Uruk colonies from Lower Mesopotamia. These finds indicate
   that urbanism developed in both Upper and Lower Mesopotamia simultaneously
   in the fourth millennium, rather than beginning in the south and spreading
   north.
2 These territory estimates are based on Jason Ur's figure for Nager/Tell Brak (Ur
   2004:273).
3 Population estimates are based on ethnographic cases and generally assume 100
   to 200 persons per ha (Adams 1981:69; Kramer 1980, 1982a, 1982b; Van Beek 1982)
   but consider Postgate (1994) for a wider range.
4 Located about 75 km east of Hama in Southern Syria, Al-Rawda is outside the
   primary region of this study, but I discuss it here because a cesium magnetometer
   survey revealed most of its plan (Castel et al. 2004, 2005; Gondet and Castel 2004).
5 Kazane's building Unit 8 may be a temple, but this is not confirmed (Creekmore
   2010).
6 *Kranzhügel* is German for "wreath mound."
7 Michael Smith (2010) is correct that the presence of neighborhoods in Upper
   Mesopotamian cities is often assumed, rather than proven, because contiguous
   housing blocks make it difficult to identify social boundaries. Yet, neighborhoods
   are not necessarily defined by housing blocks, but by shifting social connections based in part on dwelling proximity (Creekmore 2008; Keith 2003; Rainville
   2005:144; Stone 1987). Thus, even hard lines, such as the street patterns discussed
   here, may not define neighborhoods.
8 The size of Chuera is reported to be 65, 80, and 90 ha. From the published maps
   (Meyer 2006: Abb.2; Pruss 2000:figure 1), it measures closer to 65 ha, and it
   seems that the larger figures were derived from the diameter without account-
   ing for the actual shape (Meyer 2006:180; Orthmann 1997 :491; Pruss 2000:1431).
   Alternatively, the larger figures may include unreported extramural settlement
   considerably larger than the excavated area of the *Aussenbau* and *Stelenstraße* in
   area L.

REFERENCES CITED

Abu-Lughod, Janet L. 1987 The Islamic City – Historical Myth, Islamic
    Essence, and Contemporary Relevance. *International Journal of Middle
    East Studies* 19:155–176.
Adams, Robert McC. 1981 *Heartland of Cities: Surveys of Ancient Settlement
    and Land Use on the Central Floodplain of the Euphrates.* University of
    Chicago Press, Chicago.
    2005 Critique of Guillermo Algaze's "The Sumerian Takeoff." *Structure
    and Dynamics: eJournal of Anthropological and Related Sciences* 1 (1), Article

9. http://escholarship.org/uc/item/5m8043vf?query=robertadams#page-1, accessed March 2013.

Akkermans, Peter M. M. G. and Glenn M. Schwartz 2003 *The Archaeology of Syria From Complex Hunter-Gatherers to Early Urban Societies (ca. 16,000 – 300 BC)*. Cambridge University Press, Cambridge.

Algaze, Guillermo, Gulay Dinckan, Britt Hartenberger, Timothy Matney, Jennifer Pournelle, Lynn Rainville, Steven Rosen, Eric Rupley, Duncan Schlee, and Regis Vallet 2001 Research at Titriş Höyük in Southeastern Turkey: The 1999 Season. *Anatolica* 27:23–106.

Algaze, Guillermo and Jennifer Pournelle 2003 Climatic Change, Environmental Change, and Social Change at Early Bronze Age Titriş Höyük: Can Correlation and Causation be Untangled. In *From Villages to Towns. Studies Presented to Ufuk Esin*, edited by Mehmet Özdoğan, H. Hauptman, and N. Başgelen, pp. 104–128. Arkeoloji ve Sanat Publications, Istanbul.

Anderson, Kay and Fay Gale 1992 Introduction. In *Inventing Places, Studies in Cultural Geography*, edited by Kay Anderson and Fay Gale, pp. 1–12. Wiley, Halsted Press, New York.

Archi, Alfonso 1988 Prices, Workers' Wages and Maintenance at Ebla. *Altorientalische Forschungen* 15(1):24–29.

Archi, Alfonso and Maria Giovanna Biga 2003 A Victory over Mari and the Fall of Ebla. *Journal of Cuneiform Studies* 55:1–44.

Biewers, Michele 1997 *l'Habitat traditionelle à 'Aima, Enquête ethnoarchéologique dans un village Jordanien*. Archaeopress, Oxford.

Blanton, Richard E., Gary M. Feinman, Stephen A. Kowalewski, and Peter N. Peregrine 1996 A Dual-Processual Theory for the Evolution of Mesoamerican Civilization. *Current Anthropology* 37:1–14.

Bluard, Christine 1997 Recherches sur le perimeter externe (chantier H). In *Tell Beydar, Three Seasons of Excavations (1992–1994)*, edited by Marc Lebeau and Antoine Suleiman, pp. 179–191. Subartu III. Turnhout: Brepols, Belgium.

Branting, Scott 2010 Agents in Motion. In *Agency and Identity in the Ancient Near East*, edited by Sharon R. Steadman and Jennifer C. Ross, pp. 47–59. Equinox, London.

Buccellati, Giorgio 1998 Urkesh as Tell Mozan: Profiles of the Ancient City. In *Urkesh and the Hurrians*, edited by Giorgio Buccellati and Marilyn Kelly-Buccellati, pp. 11–34. Bibliotheca Mesopotamica 26. Undena Publications, Malibu, CA.

Buccellati, Giorgio and Marilyn Kelly-Buccellati 1997 Tell Mozan. In *The Oxford Encyclopedia of Archaeology in the Near East*, edited by Eric M. Meyers, pp. 60–63. Oxford University Press, New York.

2000 The Royal Palace of Urkesh. Report on the 12th Season at Tell Mozan/Urkesh: Excavations in Area AA, June–October 1999. *Mitteilungen der Deutschen Orient-Gesellschaft* 132:133–183.

2001 Überlegungen zur funktionellen und historischen Bestimmung des Königspalastes AP in Urkesch, Bericht über die 13. Kampagne in Tall Mozan.Urkesh: Ausgrabungen im Gebiet AA, Juni–August 2000. *Mitteilungen der Deutschen Orient-Gesellschaft* 133:59–96.

Burgess, Ernest W. 1925 The Growth of the City. In *The City*, edited by Robert E. Park, Ernest W. Burgess, and Roderick D. McKenzie, pp. 47–62. University of Chicago Press, Chicago.

Carter, Harold 1983 *An Introduction to Urban Historical Geography*. Edward Arnold, Baltimore, MD.

Casana, Jesse 2013 Radial Route Systems and Agro-pastoral Strategies in the Fertile Crescent: New Discoveries from western Syria and southwestern Iran. *Journal of Anthropological Archaeology* 32(2): 257–273.

Castagnoli, Ferdinando 1971 *Orthogonal Town Planning in Antiquity*. MIT Press, Cambridge, MA.

Castel, Corinne and Edgar Peltenburg 2007 Urbanism on the Margins: Third Millennium BC Al-Rawda in the Arid Zone of Syria. *Antiquity* 81:601–616.

Castel, Corinne D., O. Barge Archambault, T. Boudier, P. Courbon, A. Cuny, S. Gondet, L. Herveux, F. Isnard, L. Martin, J. Y. Monchambert, B. Moulin, N. Pousaz, and S. Sanz 2005 Rapport préliminaire sur les activités de la mission archéologique franco-syrienne dans la micro-région d'Al-Rawda (Shamiyeh): deuxième et troisième campagnes (2003 et 2004). *Akkadika* 126:51–95.

Castel, Corinne, Nazir Awad, Olivier Barge, Thomas Boudier, Alexandra Cuny, Liliane Delattre, Francis Joannès, Bertrand Moulin, and Séverine Sanz 2004 Rapport préliminaire sur les activités de la première mission archéologique franco-syrienne dans la micro-région d'Al-Rawda (Syrie intérieure): la campagnes de 2002. *Akkadika* 125:27–77.

Castells, Manuel 1983 *The City and the Grassroots: A Cross-Cultural Theory of Urban Social Movements*. University of California Press, Berkeley.

Cooper, Lisa 2006a The Demise and Regeneration of Bronze Age Urban Centers in the Euphrates Valley of Syria. In *After Collapse: The Regeneration of Complex Societies*, edited by Glenn M. Schwartz and John J. Nichols, pp. 18–37. University of Arizona Press, Tucson.

2006b *Early Urbanism on the Syrian Euphrates*. Routledge, New York.

Costa, F. J. and A. G. Noble 1986 Planning Arabic towns. *Geographical Review* 76:160–172.

Creekmore III, Andrew Theodore 2008 Kazane Höyük and Urban Life Histories in Third Millennium Upper Mesopotamia. Unpublished Ph.D. Dissertation, Department of Anthropology, Northwestern University, Evanson, IL.

2010 The Structure of Upper Mesopotamian Cities: Insight from Fluxgate Gradiometer Survey at Kazane Höyük, southeastern Turkey. *Archaeological Prospection* 17(2):73–88.

Crumley, Carole L. 1995 Heterarchy and the Analysis of Complex Societies. In *Heterarchy and the Analysis of Complex Societies*, edited by R. M. Ehrenreich, Carole L. Crumley, and J. E. Levy, pp. 1–6. Archaeological Papers, No. 6, American Anthropological Association, Washington D.C.

Dahl, Jacob 2002 Land Allotments During the Third Dynasty of Ur. *Altorientalische Forschungen* 29:330–338.

Danti, Michael D. and Richard L. Zettler 2007 The Early Bronze Age in the Syrian north-west Jezireh: The Tell es-Sweyhat Region. In *Euphrates*

River Valley Settlement: The Carchemish Sector in the Third Millennium BC, edited by Edgar Peltenburg, pp. 164–183. Levant Supplementary Series 5. Oxbow Books, Oxford.

de Certeau, Michael 1998 *The Practice of Everyday Life, Volume 2: Living and Cooking*, edited by Luce Giard, translated by Timothy J. Tomasik. University of Minnesota Press, Minneapolis.

de Lillis-Forrest, Francesca, Lucio Milano, and Lucia Mori 2007 The Akkadian Occupation in the Northwest Area of the Tell Leilan Acropolis, *KASKAL* 4:43–64.

Durand, Jean-Marie 1989 L'assemblée en Syrie à l'époque pré-amorite. In *Miscellanea Eblaitica*, edited by Pelio Fronzaroli, vol. II pp. 27–44. Quaderni di Semitistica 16. Università di Firenze, Dipartimento di Linguistica, Florence.

Düring, Bleda 2006 *Constructing Communities. Clustered Neighborhood Settlements of the Central Anatolian Neolithic ca. 8500–5500 cal. BC.* Nederlands Instituut voor het Nabije Oosten, Leiden.

Ellis, Simon P. 1995 Prologue to a Study of Roman Urban Form, in *Theoretical Roman Archaeology: Second Conference Proceedings*, edited by Peter Rush, vol. 14, Worldwide Archaeology Series, pp. 92–104. Avebury, Brookfield, Vermont.

Emberling, Geoff 2003 Urban Social Transformation and the Problem of the "First City": New Research From Mesopotamia. In *The Social Construction of Ancient Cities*, edited by Monica L. Smith, pp. 254–268. Smithsonian Institution Press, Washington D.C.

Emberling, Geoff and Helen McDonald 2003 Excavations at Tell Brak 2001–2002: Preliminary Report. *Iraq* 65:1–75.

Fleming, Daniel E. 2004 *Democracy's Ancient Ancestors: Mari and Early Collective Governance*. Cambridge University Press, Cambridge.

Frangipane, Marcella 2002 'Non-Uruk' Developments and Uruk-Linked Features on the Northern Borders of Greater Mesopotamia. In *Artefacts of Complexity. Tracking the Uruk in the Near East*, edited by J. N. Postgate, pp. 123–148. Aris and Phillips, Wiltshire, UK.

Geis, Karlyn J. 1998 A New Look at Urban Alienation: The Effect of Neighborhood Disorder on Perceived Powerlessness. *Social Psychology Quarterly* 61(3): 232–246.

Gibson, McGuire, Amr al-Azm, Clemens Reichel, Salam Quntar, Judith A. Franke, Lamya Khalidi, Carrie Hritz, Mark Altaweel, Colleen Coyle, Carlo Colantoni, Jonathan Tenney, Ghassan Abdul Aziz, and Tobin Hartnell. 2002 Hamoukar: A Summary of Three Seasons of Excavation. *Akkadika* 123:11–34.

Gillespie, Susan D. 2000 Beyond Kinship: An Introduction. In *Beyond Kinship: Social and Material Reproduction in House Societies*, edited by Rosemary A. Joyce and Susan D. Gillespie, pp. 1–21. University of Pennsylvania Press, Philadelphia.

Goethe Universität, Institut für Archäologische Wissenschaften 2007 *Tell Chuera – ein urbanes Zentrum in Nordsyrien*. Electronic document, http://web.uni-frankfurt.de/fb09/vorderasarch/tch.htm, accessed October 2007. See also "Zum Tell des 3. Jahrtausends" [*Die frühsyrische Stadt des 3. Jts. v.Chr.*], http://web.uni-frankfurt.de/fb09/vorderasarch/tch3jt.htm.

Gondet, Sébastian and Corinne Castel 2004 Prospection Géophysique à Al-Rawda et Urbanisme en Syrie au Bronze Ancien. *Paléorient* 30(2):93–110.

Harris, Chauncy D. and Edward L. Ullman 1945 The Nature of Cities. *Annals of the American Academy of Political and Social Science* 242:7–17.

Heinz, Marlies 1997 How Town Plans Reflect Society. *Archaeological Review from Cambridge* 14(2):23–44.

Henrickson, Elizabeth F. 1981 Non-Religious Residential Settlement Patterning in the Late Early Dynastic of the Diyala Region. *Mesopotamia* XVI:43–105.

Herbert, David T. and Colin J. Thomas 1990 *Cities in Space: City As Place.* Fulton Publishers, London.

Herman, Robert and Jesse H. Ausubel 1988 Cities and Infrastructure: Synthesis and Perspectives. In *Cities and Their Vital Systems: Infrastructure Past, Present and Future,* edited by Jesse H. Ausubel and Robert Herman, pp. 1–12. National Academy Press, Washington D.C.

Hillier, Bill 2008 Space and Spatiality: What the Built Environment Needs from Social Theory. *Building and Research Information* 36(3):216–230.

Hillier, Bill and Julienne Hanson 1984 *The Social Logic of Space.* Cambridge University Press, Cambridge.

Hodder, Ian 2007 Some Intriguing New Finds at Çatalhöyük. *Anatolian Archaeology* 13:20–22.

Hoyt, Homer 1939 *The Structure and Growth of Residential Neighborhoods in American Cities.* U.S. Government Printing Office, Washington D.C.

Keith, Kathryn 1999 *Cities, Neighborhoods, and Houses: Urban Spatial Organization in Old Babylonian Mesopotamia.* Unpublished Ph.D. dissertation, Department of Anthropology, University of Michigan, Ann Arbor.

2003 The Spatial Patterns of Everyday Life in Old Babylonian Neighborhoods. In *The Social Construction of Ancient Cities,* edited by Monica L. Smith, pp. 56–80. Smithsonian Books, Washington D.C.

Klein, Harald and Winfried Orthmann 1995 Grabungen im Bereich des Steinbau 2. In *Ausgrabungen in Tell Chuera in Nordost-Syrien I: Vorbericht über die Grabungskampangen 1986 bis 1992,* edited by Winfried Orthmann, pp. 73–94. Saarbrücker Druckerei und Verlag, Saarbrücken.

Kouchoukos, Nicholas. 1998 Landscape and Social Change in Late Prehistoric Mesopotamia. Unpublished Ph.D. dissertation, Department of Near Eastern Languages and Civilizations, Yale University, New Haven, CT.

Kramer, Carol 1980 Estimating Prehistoric Populations: An Ethnoarchaeological Approach. In *L'archéologie de l'Iraq du début de l'époque néolithique à 333 avant notre ère,* edited by M. T. Barrelet, pp. 315–334. Editions du CNRS, Paris.

1982a *Village Ethnoarchaeology: Rural Iran in Archaeological Perspective.* Academic Press, New York.

1982b Ethnographic Households and Archaeological Interpretation. *American Behavioral Scientist* 25 (6):663–675.

Laneri, Nicola 2007 Burial Practices at Titriş Höyük, Turkey: An Interpretation. *Journal of Near Eastern Studies* 66(4):241–266.

2010 A Family Affair: The Use of Intramural Funerary Chambers in Mesopotamia During the Late Third and Early Second Millennia BC. *Archeological Papers of the American Anthropological Association* 20(1):121–135.

Laurence, Ray 1994 *Roman Pompeii: Space and Society*. Routledge, London.

Lawrence, Denise and Setha M. Low 1990 The Built Environment and Spatial Form. *Annual Review of Anthropology* 19:453–505.

Lebeau, Marc 2006a Les Temples de Tell Beydar et leur environment immediate à l'époque Early Jezirah IIIb. In *Les espaces Syro-Mésopotamiens*, edited by Pascal Butterlin, Marc Lebeau, Jean-Yves Monchambert, Juan Luis Montero-Fenollos, and B. Muller, pp. 101–140. Subartu XVII. Brepols, Turnhout, Belgium.

2006b Nabada (Tell Beydar), an Early Bronze Age City in the Syrian Jezirah. *Lecture presented in Tübingen (October 2, 2006)*. Electronic document, http://www.beydar.com/pdf/nabada-conf-en.pdf, accessed January 2013.

Lebeau, Marc and Antoine Suleiman 2003 *Tell Beydar, The 1995–1999 Seasons of Excavations. A Preliminary Report*. Subartu X. Brepols, Turnhout, Belgium.

2008 *Report on the 15th Season of Excavations and the 6th Season of Architectural Restoration at Tell Beydar (2008)*. Electronic document, http://www.beydar.com/pdf/Beydar_2008-en.pdf, accessed November 2010.

2009 *Report on the 16th Season of Excavations at Tell Beydar (2009)*. Electronic document, http://www.beydar.com/pdf/beydar-2009.pdf, accessed November 2010.

Logan, John R. and Glenna D. Spitze 1994 Family Neighbors. *American Journal of Sociology* 100(2):453–476.

Low, Setha M. 1992 Symbolic Ties That Bind: Place Attachment in the Plaza. In *Place Attachment*, edited by Irwin Altman and Setha M. Low, pp. 165–185. Plenum Press, New York.

1996 Spatializing Culture: the Social Production and Social Construction of Public Space in Costa Rica. *American Ethnologist* 23(4):861–879.

2000 *On the Plaza*. University of Texas Press, Austin.

Lynch, Kevin 1964 *The Image of The City*. Massachusetts Institute of Technology Press, Cambridge, MA.

Lyonnet, Bertille 1998 Le peuplement de la Djéziré occidentale au début du 3e millénaire, villes circulaires et pastoralism: questions et hypotheses. In *About Subartu: Studies Devoted to Upper Mesopotamia*, edited by Marc Lebeau, pp. 179–193. Subartu IV,1. Brepols, Turnhout, Belgium.

MacDonald, William Lloyd 1986 *The Architecture of the Roman Empire, Volume II: An Urban Appraisal*. Yale University Press, New Haven, CT.

Matney, Timothy 2002 Urban Planning and the Archaeology of Society at Early Bronze Age Titriş Höyük. In *Across the Anatolian Plateau: Readings in the Archaeology of Ancient Turkey*, edited by David C. Hopkins, pp. 19–34. The Annual of the American Schools of Oriental Research 57. The American Schools of Oriental Research, Boston.

Matney, Timothy and Guillermo Algaze 1995 Urban Development at Mid-Late Early Bronze Age Titriş Höyük in Southeast Anatolia. *Bulletin of the American Schools of Oriental Research* 299–300:33–52.

Matthews, Roger 2003 (editor) *Excavations at Tell Brak Vol. 4: Exploring an Upper Mesopotamian Regional Center, 1994–1996*. British School of Archaeology in Iraq, London.

Matthiae, Paolo 1981 *Ebla: An Empire Rediscovered*. Translated by Christopher Holme. Doubleday and Company, Garden City, NY.

McClellan, Thomas L. 1999 Urbanism on the Upper Syrian Euphrates. In *Archaeology of the Upper Syrian Euphrates. The Tishrin Dam Area. Proceedings of the International Symposium Held at Barcelona, Jan. 28th–30th, 1998*, edited by Gregorio del Olmo Lete and Juan Luis Montere Fenollós, pp. 413–425. Editorial Ausa, Barcelona.

McClellan, Thomas L. and Anne Porter 1995 Jāwa and North Syria. *Studies in the History and Archaeology of Jordan* V:49–65. Department of Antiquities, Amman.

Merola, Marco 2008 Royal Goddesses of a Bronze Age State. *Archaeology* 61(1):9.

Meyer, Jan-Waalke 2006 Zur Frage der Urbanisierung von Tell Chuera. In *Les espaces syro-mésopotamiens: Dimensions de l'expérience humaine au Proche-Orient ancien: volume d'hommage offert à Jean-Claude Margueron*, edited by Butterlin, Pascal, M. Lebeau, J.-Y. Monchambert, J. L. Montero Fennolós and B. Muller, pp. 179–189. Subartu XVII. Brepols, Turnhout, Belgium.

Mollenkopf, John 1992 *A Phoenix in the Ashes: The Rise and Fall of the Koch Coalition in New York City Politics*. Princeton University Press, Princeton, NJ.

Moortgat, Anton 1962 *Tell Chuera in Nordost-Syrien. Vorläufiger Bericht über die dritte Grabungskampagne*. Westdeutscher Verlag, Köln, Germany.

Moortgat-Correns, Ursula 1972 *Die Bildwerke vom Djebelet el Beda in ihrer räumlichen und zeitlichen Umwelt*. Walter de Gruyter, Berlin.

Neuwirth, Robert 2005 *Shadow Cities*. Routledge, New York.

Newman, Oscar 1973 *Defensible Space*. Collier Books, New York.

Oates, Joan 2005 Archaeology in Mesopotamia: Digging Deeper at Tell Brak. *Proceedings of the British Academy* 131:1–40. Oxford University Press, Oxford.

Oates, Joan, Augusta McMahon, Philip Karsgaard, Salam Al Quntar, and Jason Ur 2007 Early Mesopotamian Urbanism: A New View from the North. *Antiquity* 81:585–600.

Orthmann, Winfried 1995a *Ausgrabungen in Tell Chuera in Nordost-Syrien I: Vorbericht über die Grabungskampangen 1986 bis 1992*. Saarbrücker Druckerei und Verlag, Saarbrücken, Germany.

1995b Die Grabungen am Steinbau I. In *Ausgrabungen in Tell Chuera in Nordost-Syrien I:Vorbericht über die Grabungskampangen 1986 bis 1992*, edited by Winfried Orthmann, pp. 17–72. Saarbrücker Druckerei und Verlag, Saarbrücken, Germany.

1997 Tell Chuera. In *The Oxford Encyclopedia of Archaeology in the Near East*, edited by E. M. Meyers, pp. 491–492, Oxford: Oxford University Press.

Pauketat, Timothy R. 2007 *Chiefdoms and other Archaeological Delusions*. AltaMira, New York.

Pfälzner, Peter 1997 Wandel und Kontinuität im Urbanisierungsprozess des 3. Jtsds. V. Chr. in Nordmesopotamien. In *Die Orientalische*

Stadt: Kontinuität, Wandel, Bruch, edited by G. Wilhelm, pp. 239–265. Saarbrücker Druckerei und Verlag, Saarbrücken, Germany.

Porter, Anne 1995 The Third Millennium Settlement Complex at Tell Banat: Tell Kabir. *Damaszener Mitteilungen* 8:125–163.

2002 The Dynamics of Death: Ancestors, Pastoralism, and the Origins of a Third-Millennium City in Syria. *Bulletin of the American Schools of Oriental Research* 325:1–36.

Postgate, John Nicholas 1994 How Many Sumerians per Hectare? Probing the Anatomy of an Early City. *Cambridge Archaeological Journal* 4:47–65.

Pred, Allan 1984 Place as Historically Contingent Process: Structuration and the Time-Geography of Becoming Places. *Annals of the Association of American Geographers* 74(2):279–297.

Pruss, Alexander 1998 Tell Chuera 1996: The 19th Campaign of Excavations. Electronic Document, http://www.orientarch.uni-halle.de/digs/chuera/chu96_e.htm, accessed September 2007.

2000 Recent Excavations at Tell Chuera and the Chronology of the Site. In *Proceedings of the First International Congress of the Archaeology of the Ancient Near East*, edited by Paolo Matthiae, Alessandra Enea, Luca Peyronel, and Frances Pinnock, pp. 1431–1446. Dipartimento di Scienze Storiche, Archeologiche e Antropologiche dell'Antichità, Rome.

Rainville, Lynn 2005 *Investigating Upper Mesopotamian Households using Micro-Archaeological Techniques*. British Archaeological Reports S1368, Oxford.

Rapoport, Amos 1990 *The Meaning of the Built Environment*. University of Arizona Press, Tucson.

Reade, Julian 1973 Tell Taya. *Iraq* 35:155–187.

Ristvet, Lauren 2005 Settlement, Economy, and Society in the Tell Leilan Region, Syria, 3000–1000 BC. Unpublished Ph.D. Dissertation, Department of Ancient Near Eastern Studies, University of Cambridge, Cambridge.

2007 The Third Millennium City Wall at Tell Leilan, Syria: Identity, Authority, and Urbanism. In *Power and Architecture*, edited by J. Bretschneider, J. Driessen, and K. Van Lerberghe, pp. 183–211. Orientalia Lovaniensia Analecta 156. Uitgeverij Peeters en Departement Oosterse Studies, Leuven, Belgium.

Ristvet, Lauren, Thomas Guilderson, and Harvey Weiss 2004 The Dynamics of State Development and Imperialization at Third Millennium Tell Leilan, Syria. *Orient Express* 8:68–75.

Rodman, Margaret C. 1992 Empowering Place: Multilocality and Multivocality. *American Anthropologist* 94(3):640–656.

Sallaberger, Walther 2004 A Note on the Sheep and Goat Flocks. Introduction to Texts 151–167. In *Third Millennium Cuneiform Texts from Tell Beydar (Seasons 1996–2002)*, edited by Lucio Milano, Walther Sallaberger, Philippe Talon, and Karel Van Lerberghe, pp. 13–21. Subartu XII. Brepols, Turnhout, Belgium.

2007 From Urban Culture to Nomadism: A History of Upper Mesopotamia in the Late Third Millennium. In *Sociétés humaines et changement climatique à la fin du troisième millénaire: Une Crise a-t-elle eu lieu en Haute*

Mésopotamie? Actes du Colloque de Lyon, 5–8 decembre 2005, edited by Catherine Kuzucuoğlu and Catherine Marro, pp. 417–456. Institute Francais D'Études Anatoliennes-Georges Dumezil, Paris.

Sallaberger, Walther and Jason Ur 2004 Tell Beydar / Nabada in its Regional Setting. In *Third Millennium Cuneiform Texts from Tell Beydar (Seasons 1996–2002)*, edited by Lucio Milano, Walther Sallaberger, Philippe Talon, and Karel Van Lerberghe, pp. 51–71. Subartu XII. Brepols, Turnhout, Belgium.

Sjoberg, Gideon, 1960 *The Preindustrial City: Past and Present*. The Free Press, New York.

Smith, Adam T. 2003 *The Political Landscape: Constellations of Authority in Early Complex Polities*. University of California Press, Berkeley.

Smith, Michael E. 2007 Form and Meaning in the Earliest Cities: A New Approach to Ancient Urban Planning. *Journal of Planning History* 6(3):3–47.

    2010 The Archaeological Study of Neighborhoods and Districts in ancient Cities. *Journal of Anthropological Archaeology* 29(2):137–154.

    2011 Empirical Urban Theory for Archaeologists. *Journal of Archaeological Method and Theory* 18:167–192.

Soja, Edward W. 1989 *Postmodern Geographies*. Verso, London.

    2000 *Postmetropolis*. Blackwell, Oxford.

Sollberger, Edmond 1980 The So-Called Treaty Between Ebla and "Ashur." *Studi eblaiti* 3:129–155.

Stein, Gil J. 2004 Structural Parameters and Sociocultural Factors in the Economic Organization of North Mesopotamian Organization in the Third Millennium BC. In *Archaeological Perspectives on Political Economies*, edited by Gary M. Feinman and Linda M. Nichols, pp. 61–78. University of Utah Press, Salt Lake City.

Steinkeller, Piotr 1993 Early Political Development in Mesopotamia and the Origins of the Sargonic Empire. In *Akkad: The First World Empire*, edited by Mario Liverani, pp. 107–129. Sargon, Padova, Italy.

    2004 A Building Inscription of Sin-iddinam and Other Inscribed Materials from Abu Duwari. In *The Anatomy of a Mesopotamian City: Survey and Soundings at Mashkan-shapir*, by Elizabeth C. Stone and Paul Zimansky, pp. 135–152. Eisenbrauns, Winona Lake, IN.

Sténuit, Marie-Eve, and Véronique Van der Stede 2003 *Du Palais au quartier de aisons privées*. In *Tell Beydar, The 1995–1999 Seasons of Excavations, a Preliminary Report*, edited by Marc Lebeau and Antoine Suleiman, pp. 225–241. Subartu X. Brepols, Turnhout, Belgium.

Stone, Elizabeth C. 1987 *Nippur Neighborhoods*. Oriental Institute, Chicago.

    1995 The Development of Cities in Ancient Mesopotamia. In *Civilizations of the Ancient Near East* Vol. 1, edited by J. Sasson, pp. 235–248. Simon and Schuster, New York.

    2007 The Mesopotamian Urban Experience. In *Settlement and Society*, edited by Elizabeth C. Stone, pp. 213–234. Cotsen Institute of Archaeology and the Oriental Institute, Los Angeles and Chicago.

Trigger, B. 1990. Monumental Architecture: A Thermodynamic Explanation of Symbolic Behaviour. *World Archaeology* 22(2):119–132.

    2003 *Understanding Early Civilizations*. Cambridge University Press, Cambridge.

Tringham, Ruth 2003 (Re)-Digging the Site at the End of the Twentieth Century: Large-Scale Archaeological Fieldwork in a New Millennium. In *Theory and Practice in Mediterranean Archaeology: Old World and New World Perspectives*, edited by John K. Papadopoulos and Richard M. Leventhal, pp. 89–108. Cotsen Institute of Archaeology, University of California, Los Angeles.

Ur, Jason A. 2003 CORONA Satellite Photography and Ancient Road Networks: A Northern Mesopotamian Case Study. *Antiquity* 77:102–111.

2004 Urbanism and Society in the Third Millennium Upper Khabur Basin. Unpublished Ph.D. Dissertation, Department of Near Eastern Languages and Civilizations, University of Chicago, Chicago.

2010 Cycles of Civilization in Northern Mesopotamia, 4400–2000 BC. *Journal of Archaeological Research* 18:387–431.

2012 Southern Mesopotamia. In *A Companion to the Archaeology of the Ancient Near East Vol. 1*, edited by Daniel T. Potts, pp. 533–555. Blackwell, Malden, MA and Oxford.

Ur, Jason A., P. Karsgaard, and J. Oates 2007 Urban Development in the Ancient Near East. *Science* 317:1188.

Ur, Jason A. and Tony J. Wilkinson 2008 Settlement and Economic Landscapes of Tell Beydar and its Hinterland. In *Beydar Studies 1*, edited by Marc Lebeau and Antoine Suleiman, pp. 305–327. Subartu XXI. Brepols, Turnhout, Belgium.

van Beek, G. 1982 A Population Estimate for Marib: A Contemporary Tell Village in North Yemen. *Bulletin of the American Schools of Oriental Research* 248:61–67.

Van De Mieroop, Marc 1999 Thoughts on Urban Real Estate in Ancient Mesopotamia. In *Urbanization and Land Ownership in the Ancient Near East*, edited by Michael Hudson and Baruch A. Levine, pp. 254–287. Peabody Museum of Archaeology and Ethnology, Cambridge, MA.

Verhoeven, Marc 1999 *An Archaeological Ethnography of a Neolithic Community*. Nederlands Historisch-Archaeologisch Instituut te Istanbul, Istanbul.

Wattenmaker, Patricia 1997 Kazane Höyük, 1995: Excavations at an Early City. *Kazi Sonuçları Toplantısı* 18:81–91.

Weiss, Harvey 1990 New Data for Mid-Third Millennium Urbanism and State Formation. *Mitteilungen der Deutschen Orient-Gesellschaft*, 122:193–218.

Weiss, Harvey, Francesca deLillis, Dominique deMoulins, Jesper Eidem, Thomas Guilderson, Ulla Kasten, Torben Larsen, Lucia Mori, Lauren Ristvet, Elena Rova, and Wilma Wetterstrom 2002 Revising the Contours of History at Tell Leilan. *Annales Archeologiques Arabes Syriennes*, Cinquantenaire, 45: 59–74.

Widell, Magnus 2003 Some Observations on the Administration, Agriculture, and Animal Management of Tell Beydar. *Ugarit Forschungen* 35:717–735.

Wilkinson, Tony J. 2010 The Tell: Social Archaeology and Territorial Space. In *The Development of Pre-State Communities in the Ancient Near East*, edited by Diane Bolger and Louise C. Maguire, pp. 55–62. Oxbow, Oxford.

Wirth, Louis 1938 Urbanism as a Way of Life. *American Journal of Sociology* 44(1):1–24.

Yoffee, Norman 1979 The Decline and Rise of Mesopotamian Civilization: An Ethnoarchaeological Perspective on the Evolution of Social Complexity. *American Antiquity* 44(1):5–35.

1995 Political Economy in Early Mesopotamian States. *Annual Review of Anthropology* 24:281–311.

2005 *Myths of the Archaic State: Evolution of the Earliest Cities, States and Civilizations*. Cambridge University Press, Cambridge.

Zaccagnini, Carlo 1999 Economic Aspects of Land Ownership and Land Use in Northern Mesopotamia and Syria from the Late Third Millennium to the Neo-Assyrian Period. In *Urbanization and Land Ownership in the Ancient Near East*, edited by Michael Hudson and Baruch A. Levine, pp. 331–361. Peabody Museum of Archaeology and Ethnology, Cambridge, MA.

3

North Mesopotamian Urban Neighborhoods at Titriş Höyük in the Third Millennium BC

Yoko Nishimura

While our understanding of the general layout of north Mesopotamian cities has improved in recent years, our reconstruction of socio-spatial patterns produced by the bulk of the population has not kept pace. Large-scale excavations and surveys at late-third millennium Titriş produced rich data that enable us to reconstruct the socio-spatial organization across its ancient urban residential districts. The analysis and interpretation of these data illuminate the hitherto underrepresented aspects of daily life in the city that were experienced by the majority of the residents. These aspects include relative socioeconomic homogeneity within densely occupied neighborhoods, as well as daily social interaction among neighbors and accessibility within habitation zones.

Mesopotamia has long been studied by scholars interested in the origins of the first cities, but recently this interest has shifted from the traditional emphasis on southern Mesopotamia to the recognition of the north as an important region of urban development in its own right. Early trends toward urbanism in northern Mesopotamia can now be traced back to the fourth millennium BC or even as early as 4400 BC (Emberling 2003; Gibson et al. 2002; Oates et al. 2007; Ur 2010). The growth of early cities in the northern region is explained increasingly as an indigenous development, largely independent of the influences of contemporary settlements in the southern region. The appearance of the first northern cities was followed by a second surge of urbanism in the middle centuries of the third millennium BC, resulting in the rapid and explosive growth of dozens of densely populated sites in northern Mesopotamia and its surrounding regions. The archaeologically best-understood key sites in this period include Chuēra, Beydar, Brak (ancient Nagar), Mozan (ancient Urkesh), Leilan, Hamoukar, Taya, Sweyhat, Mardikh (ancient Ebla), Titriş, and Kazane (see Creekmore, Chapter 2 in this volume)

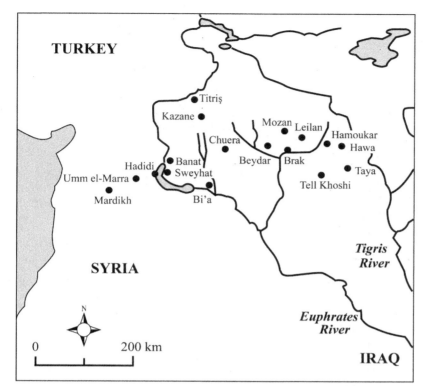

Figure 3.1 Third-millennium urban centers in north Mesopotamia and its vicinity (drawn by author; base map adapted from Oriental Institute Computer Laboratory 2010).

(Figure 3.1). The archaeological investigations at these ancient cities have greatly increased our knowledge about the developmental trajectory, spatial configuration, and decline of the mid–late third-millennium settlements in this region. However, the concentration of the excavations at the majority of these sites on and around the high mounds, where public buildings tend to be found, still limits our understanding of the extensive lower cities that surround the high mounds. When these early northern cities flourished, what did residential areas look like? How did the common city inhabitants organize their everyday environment spatially and socially? In this chapter, I present my analyses of the excavation and survey data obtained from Titriş Höyük, with the focus of attention on the vast habitation sections in the lower town. In so doing, I will illustrate the homogenous nature of the crowded urban occupation areas, as well as daily social interaction among neighbors and the accessibility both to and within the city proper at this northern Mesopotamian community. Horizontal excavations and extensive magnetometry surveys were carried out across much of the lower town at this site, making available diverse data on the bulk

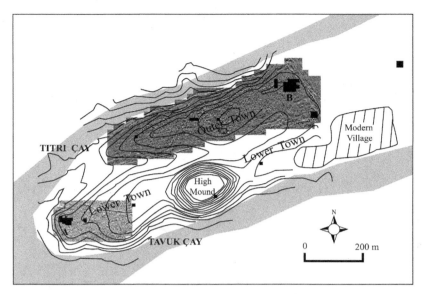

Figure 3.2 Site plan of Titriş Höyük, with areas where magnetic-field gradient surveys were conducted. The excavated areas are shown in black. "A" and "B" are two extensively excavated areas (drawn by author; base map adapted from Algaze et al. 2001:82).

of the population, as well as revealing the overall spatial configuration (Figure 3.2). In order to reconstruct the use of domestic space at Titriş, a systematic activity-area analysis was conducted based on the large quantity of household remains derived from the horizontal excavations at two opposing sectors of the settlement (Nishimura 2008, 2012). Magnetometry surveys covering almost half of the lower town allowed me to reconstruct the overall, site-wide use of space by tracing architectural plans and streets.

PREVIOUS STUDIES ON ANCIENT URBAN RESIDENTIAL NEIGHBORHOODS

As a consequence of greater interest by researchers in the analysis of both ancient cities and households, a growing number of studies have recently been conducted on socio-spatial patterning at the intermediate level (e.g., neighborhoods, districts) within ancient urban residential quarters (Arnauld et al. 2012; Cahill 2002; Chapdelaine 2009; Clayton 2011; Colantoni and Ur 2011; Creekmore 2010, Chapter 2 in this volume; Fisher, Chapter 6 in this volume; Healan 2009; Keith 2003; Kenoyer 2012; Manzanilla 2009; Nishimura 2008, 2012; Rainville 2005; M.E. Smith 2010, 2011; Spence et al. 2005; Stone 2000, 2008; York et al. 2011).

One of the focal points in the analyses of habitation sections within ancient cities has been the question of whether or not each section typically conflated different groups of people in terms of their socioeconomic classes, occupations, and/or ethnic backgrounds. For instance, Stone (2008) has presented a model linking political organization to spatial configuration at the second-millennium site of Mashkan-shapir in southern Mesopotamia and the first-millennium site of Ayanis in eastern Turkey. Stone distinguishes between state societies that were based on heterarchical/consensual (Mashkan-shapir) and hierarchical/exclusionary (Ayanis) governance, and states that these different types of political strategy developed in distinct ecological contexts. According to her socio-spatial model, cities with a more heterarchical political system would most likely exhibit housing areas that were not segregated by wealth, but rather mixed with different social classes. Such areas contained not only houses of both the rich and poor, but also loci for various manufacturing activities. In contrast, the housing areas of state societies that exercised exclusionary domination were socioeconomically more segregated, containing relatively similar domestic structures.

Whereas Stone's model connects heterogeneity and homogeneity in urban communities to the political structure of each settlement, Keith (2003) describes heterogeneous neighborhoods in ancient Mesopotamian cities as a result of everyday household and occupational activities. Following Rapoport's (1969, 1990) conceptualization of the organization of space as "systems of activities that take place in systems of settings" (Keith 2003:60), Keith defines the neighborhood as "the area within which local residents conducted most of their daily activities" (2003:58). Accordingly, Keith reconstructs residential zones within the Old Babylonian cities (e.g., Ur, Nippur, Sippar) by tracking the daily activities that the local residents performed in areas adjoining their houses. Using excavation and textual evidence, Keith identifies neighborhood facilities (e.g., shops, bakeries, mills, taverns, chapels) and examines patterns of common, everyday activities within the living areas. In her reconstruction of the Old Babylonian neighborhoods, Keith concludes that there was a mixture of various household tasks as well as occupational activities within the habitation quarters.

Michael E. Smith and his colleagues in their interdisciplinary research project on urban neighborhoods believe that residential areas in both ancient and contemporary cities are commonly socially diverse (Smith 2010, 2011; York et al. 2011). Rather than various interspersed social classes, however, these researchers maintain that urban habitation quarters often exhibit concentrations of particular groups of people who share common social identities, in terms primarily of ethnicity, socioeconomic class, religion, and occupation. Smith (2010) distinguishes and defines neighborhoods and districts as archaeological concepts. In so doing, he argues that these distinct areas in ancient cities are discernible archaeologically and offers archaeological methods that are applicable to habitation sections cross-culturally across time and space. Once these separate zones are recognized, the identified spatial patterning can be interpreted in social terms, such as social clustering of particular ethnic groups and socioeconomic classes. In order to explain the existence and development of distinct neighborhoods and frequent occurrence of social clustering, in particular ethnic and class clustering, York et al. (2011) enumerate a number of causal factors as top-down (the actions of state authorities, local regimes, and institutions) or bottom-up (the actions of individuals, households, and small groups) forces. According to these authors, ethnic and class clustering in separate habitation areas develops as a result of a complex mixture of these top-down and bottom-up processes.

The identification of such social clustering in urban residential neighborhoods is best exemplified by the studies of foreign enclaves and other discrete habitation areas at the Classic period regional center of Teotihuacán, located in the Valley of Mexico (e.g., Clayton 2011; Manzanilla 2009; Spence 1996; Spence et al. 2005). Using primarily mortuary, architectural, ceramic, and lithic data, sociocultural differences of ethnicity, occupation, wealth, and status among the inhabitants were spatially discernible at this settlement. These studies at Teotihuacán have recently been extended to include several isotope analyses on human bone and teeth to investigate places of origin, dietary changes, and marriage customs among the populations who resided within the foreign enclaves (Price et al. 2000; White et al. 2004a, 2004b).

We also have a glimpse of the presence/absence of socioeconomic differences within a residential context at the late-third millennium city of Hamoukar in northern Mesopotamia, where six housing units were excavated in a habitation quarter at the eastern edge of the site (Colantoni and Ur 2011). In the absence of evidence for administration or specialized manufacturing, these dwelling units exhibit traces of activities that were largely domestic in nature. Based on the size of House H I, the only house that was more or less completely exposed, the house size at Hamoukar is considered average in the region. Nevertheless, Colantoni and Ur suggest that this was a prosperous neighborhood, owing especially to the frequent use of baked brick in architectural features. These houses show similarities in architectural construction (e.g., house forms, courtyards with occasional baked brick pavements, and drainage), as well as in the use of domestic space (e.g., activity areas). But Colantoni and Ur (2011:59) still admit some architectural variations (e.g., house size) between the houses, and these variations are thought to reflect slight differences in socioeconomic status.

Through the reconstruction of socio-spatial patterns at the community level, the analysis of the rich excavation data and survey results obtained at Titriş will contribute to the discussion of neighborhood variability and will also bring insights into the social interaction among neighbors and accessibility within the habitation sections. In this chapter, I first outline the overall political configuration of the region in which Titriş was a flourishing urban center. The settlement layout will then be characterized, especially as related to public structures, which we can infer based on comparisons with other contemporary centers in the region. Finally, I offer an analysis of the spatial patterning within the lower town at Titriş, using both the excavation and survey data from this site.

THE ENVIRONMENT OF CITY-STATES

Contemporary written documents and settlement pattern studies indicate that the third-millennium cities in northern Mesopotamia belonged to independent city-state polities in their respective regions, embedded in turn within a larger interregional network of political, diplomatic, and economic interactions. Indirect historical references from the contemporary site of Ebla (modern Tell Mardikh) reflect the interregional political landscape to which Titriş most likely belonged. Although cuneiform tablets have also been unearthed in other contemporary, or slightly later sites such as Tell Beydar and Tell Brak, it is only the political documents of Ebla that provide significant information on the nature of the sociopolitical interactions between major cities in northern Mesopotamia and its environs around 2300 BC. The most useful Ebla documents for understanding the nature of the interstate politics in the region deal with diplomatic alliances (e.g., "Hamazi Letter"), wars (e.g., "Enna-Dagan Letter"), and treaties (e.g., "Treaty with 'Abarsal'") (Pettinato 1981:95–109). These clearly indicate that at this time, a small number of powerful and centralized kingdoms – including Ebla itself – dominated smaller, subject communities within their spheres of influence (Pettinato 1981, 1991). In this interregional city-state system, their respective capital cities were in constant contact with each other for various political and economic matters.

The picture of the international political landscape reconstructed from the Ebla texts is in accordance with Wilkinson's observations based on site survey results for mid-third millennium northern Mesopotamia. Wilkinson (2003:123, 125) characterizes this region as "landscapes of tells" in which "the system of nucleated tell-based settlement existed within a variegated and patchy landscape comprising intensive cultivation around settlements with zones of pasture beyond." During the period under consideration, the northern cities were the focal points of large population agglomeration, and the maximum occupation area of these northern sites, except for Tell Taya and possibly Tell Brak, was about 100 ha. Sustaining the growth of these urban sites were smaller, neighboring villages and their immediate rural hinterlands that provided agricultural products to their regional centers (Wilkinson 1994). After thriving for several centuries, most of these cities declined toward the end of the millennium, in some cases being abandoned altogether.[1]

NORTH MESOPOTAMIAN CITY LAYOUT

Archaeologists have noted a number of recurrent characteristics in the overall physical configuration of urban settlements across northern Mesopotamia in the mid-late third millennium. Stone (2000:243–244) describes the general patterns evident in the spatial layout of cities in this region. She states that a typical northern city of this period contains a high mound from which the lower town spreads in different directions. As the highest point of the settlement, the high mound is usually the location for the main temple, while an extensive lower town is largely given over to residential sections. The lower town tends to be circumvallated with defensive walls, at one point along which the high mound can be found. Palatial structures may also be found along the fortification wall, but such structures are probably within the lower town at some distance away from the religious precinct on the high mound.

This pattern is generally repeated among the contemporary large settlements in northern Mesopotamia and the region to the west of the Upper Euphrates, particularly Taya (Reade 1973, 1982, 1997), Leilan (Weiss et al. 1990, 1993), Hamoukar (Colantoni and Ur 2011; Gibson et al. 2002), Beydar (Lebeau 2012; Lebeau and Suleiman 2011), Chuēra (Dohmann-Pfälzner and Pfälzner 1996; Pruss 2000), Mozan (Buccellati 2005; Buccellati and Kelly-Buccellati 1998; Pfälzner 2012), Brak (Emberling and McDonald 2003; D. Oates, J. Oates, and McDonald 2001; Ur, Karsgaard, and Oates 2011), Kazane (Creekmore 2010; see also Creekmore, Chapter 2 in this volume), Sweyhat (Danti and Zettler 1998, 2002, 2006), and Mardikh (Matthiae 1981, 2010) (Figure 3.1). All of these cities, except Brak, are walled, and the settlement size ranges between approximately 30–160 ha during this time, with the average site size of ca. 80 ha.[2] Some of these cities are roughly oval and oblong (Leilan, Kazane, Mardikh, Brak, Hamoukar, and Sweyhat), while some others form a circular shape (Chuēra, Beydar, and Mozan).[3] These circular sites, known as *Kranzhügeln* ("wreath-mounds"), are also a common type, particularly seen between the Upper Khabur and Balikh regions as well as in northeast Syria (Akkermans and Schwartz 2003:256; Wilkinson 2000:239). *Kranzhügel* sites hold the citadel mound at the center, and the lower town surrounding the citadel mound is in turn circled with the outer fortification wall.

Although a single high mound is a consistent element of these northern urban centers,[4] its location can be either near the center of the mounds (Beydar, Chuēra, Kazane, Mardikh, Mozan, Sweyhat, and Taya) or at one end of their larger settlements (Brak, Hamoukar, and Leilan). The high mound was frequently fortified with an inner wall (e.g., Beydar, Chuēra, Leilan, Mozan, Sweyhat, and Taya) demarcating the high mound from the rest of the settlement during this period. The size of the high mound as a proportion of the total community size varies from one site to another. At Mardikh and Taya, the high mound occupies only 3–5 percent of the total occupied area, whereas more than half of the site is comprised of the high mound at Brak and Chuēra. The size of these high mounds ranges from 3 ha to as large as 43 ha with an average size of approximately 17 ha.[5]

The high mound was the primary location for not only main temples, but also royal and governmental residences, administrative buildings with storage facilities, and elite houses that were likely built around these public buildings. Whereas main temples tend to have been incorporated within a multiroom, 'palace-temple' complex in the southern Mesopotamian tradition, temples in northern Mesopotamia frequently stood independently. Temples excavated at these northern sites (e.g., Beydar, Brak, Chuēra, Mozan, and Taya) are located at the highest point of the settlement, on the high mound. As the main temple was recently discovered at the southeastern edge of the lower town at Mardikh, it is possible, however, that major temples also existed in other parts of the community, but have not been identified because the excavations at these large settlements have focused on the areas on or near the high mound. The elevated location must have meant that the main temple was the most prominent landmark of their landscape, for both the inhabitants and populations outside the city proper. At the same time, the availability of space on the high mound seems to have dictated the physical scale of the main temple, as well as the locations for secondary temples, if any existed. For example, the temple at Mardikh was constructed away from the small high mound (ca. 3 ha) which was already dominated by the presence of the Royal Palace G. In contrast, the large (ca. 43 ha) high mound at Chuēra provided enough space for the construction of the royal palace as well as of the main temples, allowing some distance between these massive structures.

Secular public buildings – including palaces, governors' houses, and administrative structures – are increasingly seen at these urban settlements. A mid-late third millennium palatial structure has been securely identified at four northern sites (Beydar, Chuēra, Mardikh, and Mozan), and Akkadian administrative buildings have been found at two other cities (Brak and Leilan). Many of the palatial buildings found at these sites were rectilinear with large courtyards embedded among smaller rooms. As with main temples, these structures are all located on the high mound, at its periphery (in many cases, the western periphery), rather than at the central summit, keeping some distance from the main temples.[6] It is also possible, or even likely, that more than one secular public structure existed in some cities, and that not all of these buildings would have been accommodated within the limited space of the high mound (Creekmore 2010; also see Creekmore, Chapter 2 in this volume). When secondary and tertiary secular buildings were to be constructed, there may have been a spatial limit on the high mound, which was already crowded with preexisting ceremonial and royal structures. This may be precisely the reason why, by the first half of the second millennium BC, palaces and other major public buildings are increasingly seen within the lower towns at north Mesopotamian cities (e.g., Leilan and Mardikh). At these sites, many other secular public buildings or possible public buildings with unclear functions have been excavated from third-millennium contexts. Many of these possible public structures are administrative in nature, and they appear to have been clustered also on the high mound (e.g., the "Unfinished Building" at Leilan, the "U-Shaped Complex" and "B1 Building" at Beydar, and the "Kitchen Building" at Sweyhat).[7]

All of these regional centers contained vast residential quarters. These areas tend to have been concentrated in the lower town and filled with domestic structures, streets, and side alleys. Most structures stood contiguously on both sides of streets, often sharing party walls (e.g., Beydar, Chuēra, Hamoukar, and Leilan). Even though some houses were built away from each other, leaving open spaces between them that were largely devoid of other structures (e.g., Taya), most of the examples – extensively excavated settlements, in particular – show that the densely crowded environment was the more common phenomenon. Streets were usually straight and sherd-paved, ca. 2–5 m in width. These streets provided direct access to domestic buildings (e.g., Chuēra and Taya), whereas many houses could only be accessed via side alleys (e.g., Hamoukar and Leilan). Many of the dwelling structures in these urban settlements seem to have been the central-courtyard house type with varying sizes and numbers of rooms. The average house sizes are estimated for the Chuēra houses as 63–147 m^2, and for the Taya houses as 130–178 m^2 (Pfälzner 2001:399), whereas the majority of the houses in these cities fall between 127–205 m^2 (Colantoni and Ur 2011:36). Thus, we have steadily been building the large picture of the general city layout in the north Mesopotamian sites, but our ability to reconstruct socio-spatial patterns for the bulk of the population in the extensive residential quarters is still highly limited. The analysis and interpretation of the rich data from Titriş help fill this gap and illuminate hitherto underrepresented aspects of city life.

TITRIŞ HÖYÜK

The ancient city at Titriş shows many of the common spatial characteristics discussed in the section on the general city layout of the northern cities. Similar to Tell Beydar, Titriş is smaller than most other regional centers in site area (ca. 43 ha at its maximum). Titriş flourished in a strategic location along the interregional trade route that led to one of three historically important river crossings in the Upper Euphrates (Algaze 1999:535–536). The site is an oblong shape with the high mound (ca. 3 ha) located in the south (Figure 3.2). Two lower towns flank the high mound in the east and west, and the outer town spreads to the north from the high mound. A linear fortification wall with a water-filled moat was constructed along the eastern end of the settlement. The provision of the fortification wall only at the eastern edge was probably because the northern, western, and southern sides of the mound were naturally protected by ancient rivers (Titriş Çay and Tavuk Çay) (Algaze et al. 2001:58–62). Even though the high mound at Titriş remains unexcavated, there is little doubt that this elevated land unit was the main location for public buildings for ceremonial, political, and administrative purposes.

Titriş was first occupied at the beginning of the third millennium BC and grew to become a small urban center, reaching its maximum occupied area of about 43 ha around 2500 BC. At the peak of its site history, Titriş enjoyed a role as a focal point for crafts and manufacturing activities, economic exchanges, and political and administrative affairs. After an occupational hiatus, a centrally planned construction took place around 2300 BC. The re-urbanization process apparently involved a massive reconstruction of the entire settlement that fortified the city along the unprotected eastern slopes of the mound and largely circumscribed its habitation area within the fortified mound. The reconstruction resulted in a contraction in its total occupied size from 43 ha to 35 ha, owing to the abandonment of the "suburbs" and the nucleation of the population within the limits of the city. Subsequently, in the period of urban decline in northern Mesopotamia from about 2100–1900 BC, much of the habitation area at Titriş was also abandoned, and occupation continued only within the limits of the high mound (Algaze et al. 2001).

The investigation of settlement patterns also testifies to the development of Titriş toward an urbanized capital. The survey in this region exposes a relatively undifferentiated configuration with dispersed hamlets and villages during the first centuries of the third millennium BC (Wilkinson 1990:94). This pattern then transforms to a sharply hierarchical one between about 2600–2400 BC, during which time the total settled area in the surveyed region increased greatly (Wilkinson 1990:97). A four-tier hierarchy is recognized with the site of Titriş (ca. 43 ha) at the top, four times larger than the two second-tier towns of Lidar Höyük (ca. 12 ha) and Tatar Höyük (ca. 10 ha) (Algaze et al. 2001:56–57). The markedly hierarchical pattern continues after about 2300 BC, until the population is once again dispersed into small villages and hamlets after 2100 BC, as shown by an increase in site numbers, but substantial decrease in total settled area within the surveyed region (Algaze et al. 2001:54–58; Wilkinson 1990:102–103).

ANALYSIS OF THE EXCAVATION DATA

Archaeological excavations at Titriş Höyük were carried out between 1991 and 1999 (Algaze et al. 1992, 1995, 1996, 2001; Algaze and Mısır 1993, 1994; Matney et al. 1997; Matney, Algaze, and Rosen 1999). Horizontal excavations (a total of about 2,500 m²) exposed two residential sections located at opposite ends of the site, about 900 m apart. These excavations brought to light thirteen completely or partially exposed housing units, together with their intramural family tombs, in the two habitation sections (Figure 3.3). It is thought that all the dwelling structures were built during the comprehensive rebuilding of the settlement that took place around 2300 BC (Matney 2002:24–27; Matney et al. 1997:70). This centrally planned building program is most strongly felt in the preplanned nature of street systems, as well as communal drainage and terracing systems that were constructed beneath the houses and which extended across houses and neighborhoods. City streets were long and straight, showing deliberate organization and arrangement. When the fortification wall was built, the rectilinear houses were arranged perpendicular to the wall across a street that parallels the wall.

Through the quantitative examination of the distribution of domestic material remains, the investigation of household activities and the use of space was carried out across the excavated houses (Nishimura 2008, 2012). To reflect the daily activities at this site, this investigation incorporated various architectural and spatial factors (e.g., room size, accessibility to each room), built-in features (e.g., ovens, tombs, floor types), small finds (e.g., stone tools, metal items, figurines, ceramic pots), lithic debitage, animal bones, and ceramic sherds obtained from the floor levels within the thirteen housing units (Figures 3.3–3.6).

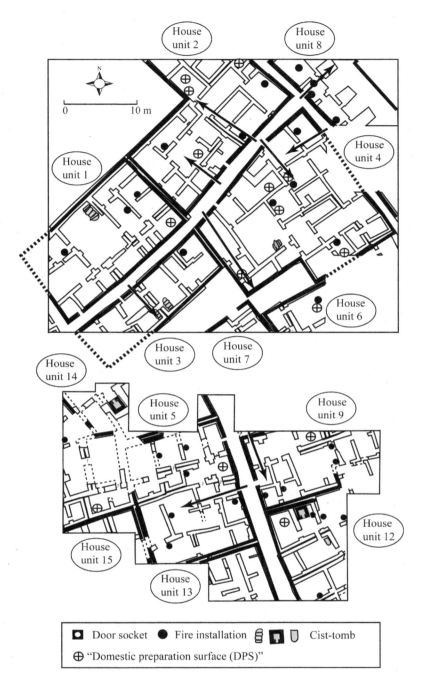

Figure 3.3 Thirteen excavated houses with features in the outer town (top) and lower town (bottom). The arrows indicate the high visibility and accessibility from the street to the internal rooms (drawn by author; base maps adapted from Algaze et al. 2001:83 and Matney, Algaze, and Pittman 1997:74).

Based on the nature and amount of the household material, it is apparent that these were nonelite private houses. Having an average house size (including the walls) of ca. 240 m², these houses are relatively large for north Mesopotamian cities.[8] As I discussed in the section on house types and sizes among the northern cities, for

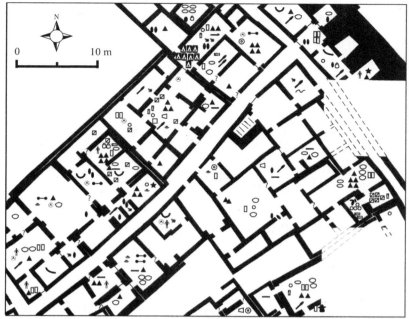

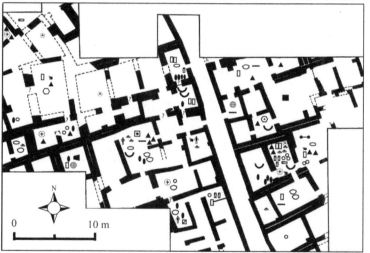

○ Scraper	◁ Axe	↔ Metal Jewelry Item
→ Pointed Piece	◀ Flint Hammer	○ Small Cup
⊚ Worked Chunk	▣ Jewelry Mold	▯ Small Jar
■ Heavy Chopper	⌒ Pounder	◮ Medium Jar
— Borer	⌣ Mortar or Pestle	◪ Small or Medium Jar
▯ Blade	◗ Grinding Stone	▱ Bowl or Plate
▲ Flake Tool	✝ Human Figurine	⊛ Terra Cotta Lid
◟ Bronze Chisel	⚘ Animal Figurine	◔ Loom Weight
▭ Stone Rubber	✦ "Aegean Stone Figurine"	⊕ Stone Spindle Whorl
∿ Metal Object	★ Seal	⁄ Bronze Needle
○ Lead Spout	◉ Model Chariot Wheel	
◎ Lead Rod	◆ Bead	

Figure 3.4 Small finds in the excavated houses indicating room functions (drawn by author; base maps adapted from Algaze et al. 2001:83; Matney, Algaze, and Pittman 1997:74).

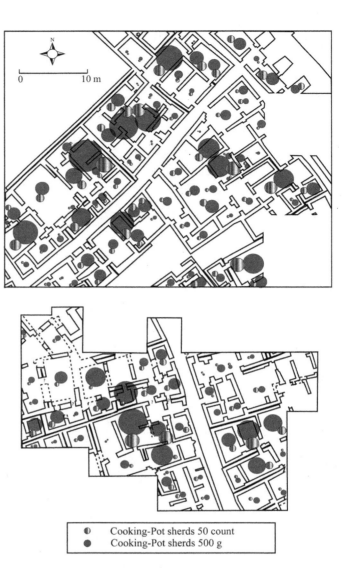

Figure 3.5 Quantitative distribution of cooking-pot sherds (drawn by author, base maps adapted from Algaze et al. 2001:83; Matney, Algaze, and Pittman 1997:74).

example, the area for the majority of the houses falls between ca. 127–205 m² at Taya and Chuēra (Colantoni and Ur 2011:36). Apart from the relatively larger size, however, there is little evidence that these structures were elite residences or public structures. The material remains and features within the houses were largely domestic in nature, including ovens, grinding stones, cooking pots, and garbage pits. Luxurious items indicative of elite status were only sporadically found as grave goods within the intramural tombs that were present beneath the floors of many of the houses. However, the inhabitants may well have taken such valuable items with them when the houses in the lower town were gradually abandoned and settlement

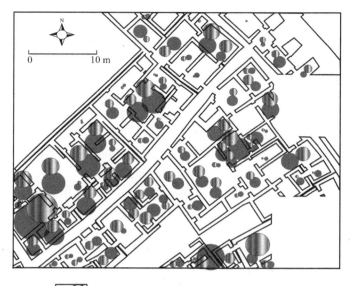

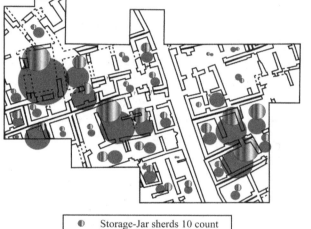

◑ Storage-Jar sherds 10 count
● Storage-Jar sherds 1000 g

Figure 3.6 Quantitative distribution of storage-jar sherds (drawn by author, base maps adapted from Algaze et al. 2001:83; Matney, Algaze, and Pittman 1997:74).

was confined to the high mound around 2100 BC. These houses lacked the architectural features often associated with public buildings, such as thick walls with decorative niches, religious altars, and podiums. The absence of evidence for specialized craft activities, as well as the minimal presence of record-keeping devices such as seals and sealings, further testifies that commercial and administrative affairs played almost no role in these areas. The two neighborhoods that contained these houses were located at opposite ends of the site, about 900 m apart, and yet these houses show considerable similarities in terms of both architectural features and artifacts recovered from them.

The two excavated sectors were packed with dwelling structures, leaving only the streets and blind alleys devoid of architectural structures. That the city dwellers used the small rectilinear rooms built within the outer wall also as domestic space emphasizes the crowded nature of the residential quarters. In such a crowded environment where side alleys and communal open space were minimized, it was a natural choice that house walls be shared between adjoining houses. Many of the inhabitants lived in relatively large, rectangular or square houses containing 15–20 rooms of different sizes. Owing probably to the lack of space to conduct household activities outside the houses in these habitation areas, these houses in general provided ample space for their occupants to conduct domestic activities within them. The availability of space within houses, in terms of a courtyard and a high number of rooms, also makes it seem less likely that the occupants would have gone to the trouble of building second floors for their houses, although the space on the roof must have been of some use.

The houses were entered directly from the city streets (Figure 3.3). There were chains of small rooms along the streets, which served as entrance rooms and storage space for many of these houses. The houses typically had more than one entrance from the main street, suggesting a distinction between private thresholds and those for guests. The entrance rooms almost always led to a reception room or courtyard. Directly entered from the streets, the doorways were often in alignment with the internal doorsteps or openings between rooms, facilitating relatively easy accessibility inside the house, as well as the high visibility of the house interior from outside (see the arrows in Figure 3.3).

The houses encompassed one or two large centrally located courtyards, which the household occupants frequently used as multipurpose workshops. Besides culinary activities, the house dwellers spent some time making and reshaping their domestic stone tools in the courtyards and also in the largest rooms of the houses. They also spun and wove textiles, butchered livestock, and processed animal hides on a regular basis. A number of houses had more than one kitchen and living room, indicating the presence of more than a single nuclear family at a time. Kitchens were usually set up in relatively large rooms and many storage jars were kept nearby, most likely to store grains and water for cooking. What is interesting is the separation of kitchens where food was actually cooked from rooms in which food was processed before cooking. Food processed in these food preparation rooms was probably for long-term use. It may have included ground grains and nuts (barley, emmer wheat, pistachio nuts, acorns, and hawthorn), dried meats, pressed olive oils, and pickled vegetables and fruits.[9] These houses also possessed a number of storage rooms, typically located in the backrooms and in the chains of small rooms along the street. The household members stored drinking cups, cooking pots, and other culinary implements and ceramic vessels in their storage rooms. Although the house occupants used some of the centrally located large rooms or courtyards extensively for everyday activities, the sacred space containing the family crypt was kept clean of everyday tools, installations, or debris. In other words, when a family cist-tomb was present beneath the floor level, other secular daily activities seem to have been deliberately restricted in the room or courtyard.

On the whole, this study of domestic activities in the excavated structures at Titriş reveals that the organization and use of space was consistent across houses. These consistent patterns are repeated in each of the two widely separated excavated areas. Very similar activities were performed in all of the dwelling structures, producing the same kinds and amounts of material remains. This consistency of patterning in spatial organization and daily activities indicates homogeneity in economic status within these residential sections. That is to say, there are no clear qualitative differences in the household activities that point to differences in wealth distribution or social class among the thirteen housing units.

This observation is supported by the analyses of faunal, floral, and skeletal remains excavated from these houses at Titriş. When investigating the rich faunal remains excavated from the late-third millennium houses at Titriş, Allentuck and Greenfield (2010) detected little evidence for differential access to animal resources by the occupants of these houses. Although a systematic comparison of the zooarchaeological data between each house has yet to be conducted, the similarity in the distribution and consumption patterns of the animal products between the two separate neighborhoods further corroborates the idea that these households were of similar economic status. Hald's (2010) comparative analysis of the paleobotanical remains between each house in the outer town also reinforces the picture of the homogeneous economic status within the habitation sections at Titriş. The archaeobotanical data found in the households show similarities in the types and the relative proportion of plants, as well as uniformity in the processing of crops. These consistent similarities led Hald to suggest that the agricultural products were preprocessed, organized, and distributed to the households by a central administration in the city. Moreover, a preliminary report of paleopathological studies of the skeletal remains recovered from the intramural tombs also revealed little difference in nutritional conditions between these households, strongly supporting the idea that there was close similarity in economic status in the habitation areas at Titriş (Honça and Algaze 1998:117).

There are noticeable variations in the size of intramural cist-tombs as well as the number of both individuals and grave goods that are buried in these family crypts at the Titriş houses. Some houses did not have tombs, whereas others contained more than one such tomb (Houses 3 and 12 had two tombs each). At least seven intramural cist-tombs were exposed within five houses across the two residential neighborhoods. Rather than differences in wealth, however, the variation in the tomb architecture and contents appears to have been related to the frequency of the use of these family crypts. For instance, House 4 had a small cist-tomb buried in a central courtyard, which contained skeletal remains of only a baby and a child, together with a simple cup and a jar as grave goods (Nishimura, forthcoming). Although House 4 was one of the largest houses excavated, this is not reflected in the scale of its tomb structures nor the quantity of funerary goods. In addition, Laneri states that, based on the kinds and amounts of grave offerings, one of the neighborhoods was wealthier than the other (2007:262). However, apart from a bronze dagger and a spearhead, a systematic comparison of the accompanying grave offerings between the two neighborhoods can readily show the close similarity in the type and quantity of these grave goods, equally represented in both habitation areas (Nishimura, forthcoming).

Thus, the excavated houses in the two widely separated habitation sections showed that these household members were most likely farmers, with little difference in economic status. These house occupants performed everyday activities that were similar in type and intensity, producing the same kinds and amounts of material remains within the houses. Compared with other contemporary city houses in the region, these urban families at Titriş lived in relatively large houses. That these house occupants could also obtain a few imported items in their everyday, as well as mortuary, material culture suggests that these families led a relatively prosperous lifestyle.

ANALYSIS OF THE MAGNETOMETRY DATA

The magnetometry data obtained at Titriş significantly enlarge the area of the site that can be studied from the perspective of spatial configuration at the settlement level. This is especially true if the excavated areas can be shown to be representative of the extensive residential quarters known only through magnetometry survey. From 1992–1994, Dr. Lewis Somers of Geoscan Research Inc. conducted magnetic field gradient surveys in both the outer and lower town at Titriş (Algaze et al. 1995:22–23, 25–26). Using a fluxgate gradiometer (FM-36), 3,200 measurements were recorded in each 20 × 20 m grid square. The surveys covered a total of 323 such grid squares (ca. 12.9 ha) in the outer town, and 89 grid squares (ca. 3.6 ha) in the lower town (Figure 3.2). Using *Geoplot* and *Illustrator*, I processed and analyzed the magnetometry data and visualized the traces of architecture and streets in magnetometry maps (Nishimura 2008).

Preliminary examination of the magnetometry data demonstrated that the reconstructed images correspond to the latest phases of occupation around 2100 BC (Algaze et al. 1995:22). During this time, the walls of the domestic structures rested on limestone foundations whose magnetic signatures are usually lower than the surrounding iron-rich, house-floor matrix. These limestone wall foundations are often preserved in the lower town, since these areas were never reoccupied after 2100 BC. House plans were reconstructed by tracing these wall lines on the magnetometry map. However, city streets that ran through the dwelling structures were paved with a number of highly magnetic materials including pot sherds (Algaze et al. 1995:23). Therefore, the magnetometry data from Titriş offered the ideal opportunity to trace the house plans and street systems where the house walls and streets created a vivid positive-negative contrast in the geomagnetic image (Figure 3.7). The accuracy of the interpretations of the positive and negative features was confirmed by twelve test soundings that were made in many parts of the surveyed areas in the outer and lower towns (Algaze et al. 1995:22).

Within the occupied areas in the outer town, architectural structures are most clearly visible in the northern and eastern parts of the surveyed areas (Figure 3.8). Structural plans and street systems

YOKO NISHIMURA

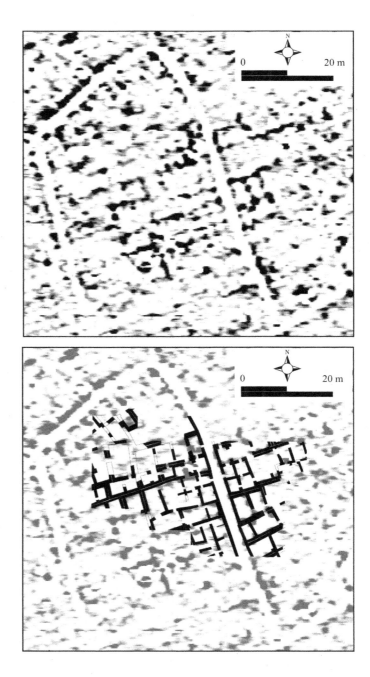

Figure 3.7 A portion of the residential neighborhood in the lower town (top). Streets are reflected in white lines, and wall foundations are revealed in black here. The excavated area superimposed over the magnetometry map (bottom).

appear less clearly, to varying degrees, in other parts of the magnetometry map of the outer town. As for the surveyed areas in the lower town, traces of architectural structures and streets are most clearly reflected in the northern and western areas. In contrast, these traces are barely visible in the southern half and in the northwestern corner of the surveyed areas. The reasons for this lack of clarity

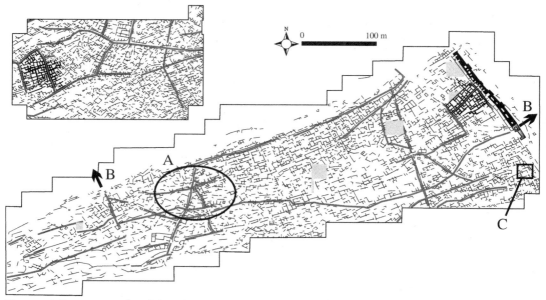

Figure 3.8 Reconstructed wall foundations and streets in the lower town (top left) and outer town (bottom). "A" is a complex intersection in the northwestern area of the outer town. Two arrows ("B") show the directions of the ancient roads that extended from the settlement (drawn by author).

can be manifold, but the accumulation of slope wash obscuring the architectural plans is probably the primary cause, particularly in the southern parts of the surveyed areas.

When the general layout of the surveyed occupied areas was reconstructed, it became apparent that there were many recurring spatial and architectural patterns throughout the lower town, owing probably to the centrally planned nature of the construction at Titriş. The most noticeable of such recurring patterns is a highly crowded environment within the habitation quarters. Apart from some peripheral areas in the lower town, the residential areas appear packed with architectural structures and streets during the final phase of the occupation period. The city inhabitants seem to have been building houses even within irregular and often narrow land units defined by intersecting main streets (Figure 3.9). The scarcity or absence of traces of architecture in the area east of the fortification wall and in the northern peripheries of the site along the ancient river indicates that the agglomeration of architectural structures within the city proper was an effect of the wall and the surrounding rivers that defined and delimited the occupation areas.

Major roadways that emerged in the magnetometry map in the lower town were not rigidly grid-like, but always followed long,

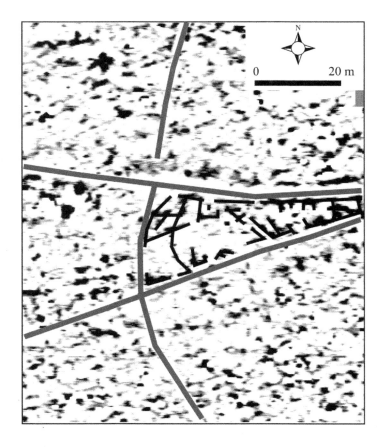

Figure 3.9 An architectural structure in the lower town built in a narrow space delimited by major roadways (drawn by author).

straight lines, extending between 40 m and 400 m within the surveyed areas (Figure 3.8). The main streets created architectural blocks of differing sizes between them, partly because many of these main roads, especially those running in a north-south direction, simply followed the topographic contours of the mound. Consequently, even though Titriş was centrally planned and constructed, the major architectural divisions created by the main streets are not uniform in size or shape. In the outer town, a very long, straight thoroughfare – stretching in an east-west direction – appeared to demarcate the northern limits of the occupation area. To the south of this northern street was another very long thoroughfare that also stretched in a roughly east-west direction. Besides the main roads, which were roughly in an east-west direction, other major roads ran in a north-south direction, clearly following the topographic contours of the mound. The lower town was also connected to the high mound by a number of straight north-south as well as east-west streets, indicating that these main streets made the central mound quite visible from the residential areas and facilitated easy access between the central mound and lower town in all directions. Another aspect of the streets that was not observed within the excavated areas was the presence of intersections of multiple streets. Intersections between two streets were not uncommon, but the surveyed areas in the outer town revealed several points where at least three main streets intersected. The most obvious was located in the northwestern area, but two other such intersections possibly existed in the further west and eastern parts of the lower town (Figure 3.8, "A").[10]

Some of these major thoroughfares radiating from the high mound clearly extended even beyond the settlement. For instance, an ancient road – appearing from the air as straight, narrow elongated depressions – was identified extending eastward from the midpoint of the eastern limit of the habitation section, apparently going through the outer wall and heading toward the third-tier site of Millisaray (Algaze et al. 2001:59–60). Another such road was discerned, which extended to the northwest from the northwestern edge of the settlement, leading most likely to the second-tier site of Lidar Höyük and an important river crossing approximately 12 km northwest of Titriş (Algaze et al. 2001:59–60). The main streets within the city proper, which connected to these ancient interregional roads, were clearly visible in the reconstructed magnetometry imagery (Figure 3.8, see the arrows "B").

Streets were flanked with walls on both sides. The walls often extended throughout the architectural blocks, and inside the walls were chains of rectangular or square rooms of small to medium size, most often oriented parallel or perpendicular to the direction of the nearby streets. As was the case with the excavated houses, sets of these rectilinear rooms apparently made up dwelling structures. Because house walls were often shared between the structures, it is difficult to determine where one structure ended and where another began. Nevertheless, it seems likely that the majority of the houses in the lower town maintained relatively standard house plans and sizes, like those of the excavated houses. For instance, this similarity is seen in a house plan detected by magnetometry, which is remarkably similar to the excavated House 5 (Figure 3.10). These structures almost always had direct access to and from the street and were almost always oriented with respect to the nearby streets. It is not clear from the magnetometry image whether the longer or the shorter walls of the rectangular structures tended to face the streets.

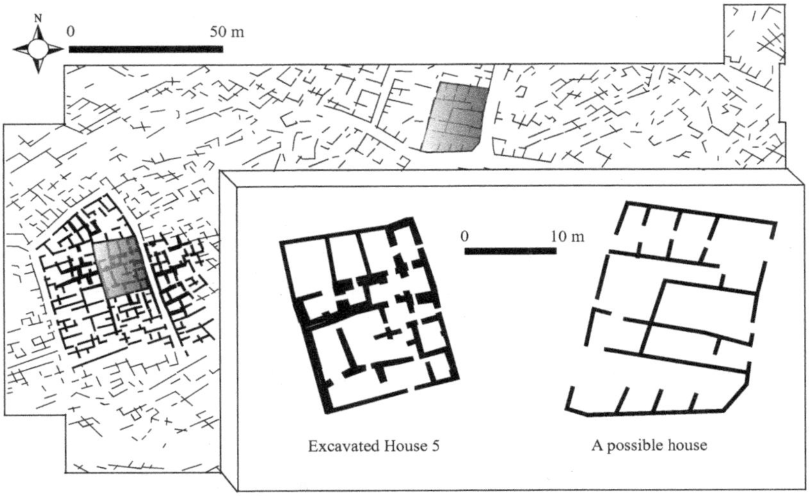

Figure 3.10 Comparison of plans of House 5 and an architectural structure in the lower town (drawn by author).

In the excavated area, rectangular rooms were typically oriented with their major axis parallel to the streets. Although open space devoid of architectural traces was rare within the residential quarters, the occupied areas were clearly demarcated by empty spaces at the peripheries of the settlement.

The magnetometry data also reveal some distinctive features, mostly connected with public spaces or buildings that the excavated areas did not expose (Figure 3.11). On the basis of the magnetometry map, for example, the excavators have previously traced and estimated the extent of the fortification wall as being at least 148 m in length (Algaze et al. 2001:33). Unless poor preservation or accumulation of slope wash obscured the rest of the city wall in the southeastern corner of the outer town, it seems evident from the magnetometry map that the wall was intentionally brought to an end there. The northern end of the wall also seems to terminate abruptly where it intersects the possible street running in a northeast-southwest direction. Excavation of parts of the defensive wall revealed a chain of small rectangular rooms built inside it, and these rooms were used as domestic space. On the magnetometry map, similar rooms are also discernible in other parts of the fortification wall.

I suspect that the southern end of the wall may have been a separate structure, such as a city gate (Figure 3.11, "B"). It was certainly a continuation of the rest of the fortification wall, but the walls of this terminal structure, about 20 m long, appear to have been much more massive, and it had a large open space in front located at the end of an east-west thoroughfare (Figure 3.11, "A"). This open space in front of

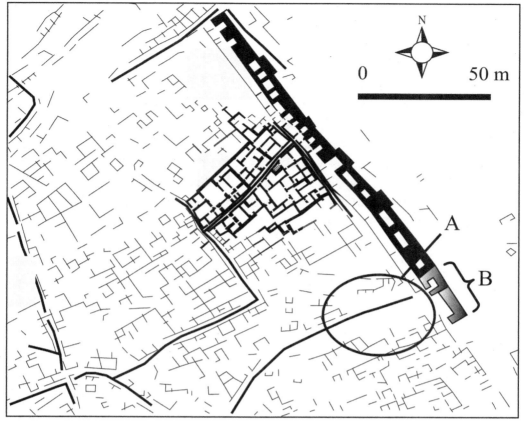

Figure 3.11 The northeastern portion of the outer town. "A" is a possible open area along the city wall at the end of a street in a southwest-northeast direction. "B" is a possible city gate (drawn by author).

the gate may well have served as a focal point of socioeconomic interactions among the inhabitants and with populations from outside the city proper. That this public field also connected this community to the outside world is supported by the presence of the path, which stretches out of the habitation section from this point. The possible location for a gateway along a fortification wall has been discussed at the other contemporary north Mesopotamian sites, including Mozan (Pfälzner 2012) and Leilan (Ristvet 2007). None of these gateway areas, however, have been adequately excavated to illuminate the architectural and spatial configuration, in particular the possible presence of a public plaza in such a peripheral zone of the site.

The excavators previously suspected the existence of possible public buildings in the area south of this city gate and the public space (Algaze et al. 1996:134) (Figure 3.8, "C"). They had opened up small trenches (ca. 100 m²), exposing massive stone foundations, 2.5 m in width. These structures appear to have been regularly aligned, and some of the rooms within these structures seem substantial in size. Although floor levels were poorly preserved, the walls in this spot, much thicker than those of excavated houses, imply that these structures were not ordinary domestic houses. Thus, it seems that this large open space in the eastern edge of the settlement was one of the communal interaction nodes where city dwellers interacted with each other as well as with visitors from outside the fortification wall. There may have been administrative buildings located nearby and managed the flow of goods and people into and out of the community. A substantial structure that probably served as a gateway was incorporated into the southern end of the fortification wall, physically and symbolically demarcating the extensive habitation sections from the area outside the city proper.

DISCUSSION

The combination of the analyses of the excavation and geophysical survey data demonstrate that the two extensively excavated areas at the opposite ends of the community contain houses that are representative in size and floor plan of the much larger, mostly homogeneous communities of which they are a part. Because of the close architectural similarities and overlaps, the spatial and architectural patterns seen within the excavated areas can safely be taken as representative of the rest of the residential quarters. By extension, I consider that the recurring patterns of domestic activities and use of space observed in the excavated houses would also have been repeated within the similar architectural structures reconstructed through the magnetometry data. The majority of the structures visible on the magnetometry map must therefore have been similar in nature to the excavated houses and were in all probability houses of ordinary city inhabitants with little socioeconomic differentiation.

The overall view of the vast habitation quarters revealed on the two separate magnetometry maps raises some intriguing questions regarding the planned nature of the settlement at Titriş. The city planning at this site did not integrate a rigid standardized land unit at the community level in either the lower or the outer town. There were a number of very long, straight streets, many leading straight to the high mound from different quarters of the community, which could not have developed without central planning. But the surveyed architectural compounds defined by the main streets do not exhibit clear regularity in shape and size. At the household level, however, many of the individual houses in the lower town seem to have maintained relatively standard house plans and sizes, like those of the excavated houses. Delougaz, Hill, and Lloyd (1967:143) observed a tendency in the living areas at the contemporary urban center of Tell Asmar in the Diyala region for poorer and smaller houses to be located toward the deeper areas of the architectural blocks without direct access from the roads. To the extent that house plans and room shapes could be reconstructed on the magnetometry map, this tendency does not seem to apply to Titriş. At Titriş, each house seems to have had direct access to the street, and when irregularly shaped structures occurred in the habitation areas, it was primarily as a result of the inhabitants' efforts to maximize use of the available land unit in an environment that was packed with dwelling structures. Matney (2002:27) suspected that two uniform plot sizes – one in a rectangular shape (12 m × 7 m) and the other in a square form (11 m × 11 m) – were used as basic land units for some of the excavated houses in the outer town. It is not clear if these basic units were used for other excavated and surveyed houses in the outer and lower towns, but this could well be the reason of why many of the individual houses show relatively standard plans and sizes at the household level.

The large-scale investigations of the use of city space at Titriş clearly show the residential areas packed with commoners' houses. The crowded environment was made more extreme by the restrictions on occupation space imposed by the fortification wall in the eastern end of the habitation section, the long street that skimmed the northern peripheries of the outer town, and ancient rivers that flowed along the northern, western, and southern sides of the mound. As a result, domestic space was created even inside the fortification wall, as well as within irregular and narrow land units between main streets, indicating that the value of land within the city proper was high. The relative economic homogeneity is consistently seen even within such irregular housing units because these house occupants also performed everyday activities that were similar in type and intensity, producing the same kinds and amounts of material remains within the houses.

Access to the urban community was probably limited to the gateways, located at the eastern edge and northwestern end of the settlement. The most obvious example of an entrance point to the community is located at the midpoint of the eastern limit of the site where the flow of people and goods was concentrated in the large open space in front of the eastern gate. As one of the major public spaces, this area most likely acted as the heart of exchange activities or more general face-to-face social interactions among the inhabitants and with populations from outside the outer wall. Because this open space was located immediately behind the gate, the out-of-the-city visitors could conduct their business and affairs without proceeding to the central areas of the settlement. Officials may have been based in the nearby administrative buildings and controlled human traffic and economic transactions in this section of the city. The use of such a large open space in a densely populated community, however, may have been constantly negotiated at various levels of authority and prone to rapid alteration (M.L. Smith 2008:220). Thus, while many of the primary public buildings probably dominated the areas within the high mound, other public structures seem to have also been built at separate strategic points within the larger lower town, such as in the immediate vicinity of the high mound, near gateways, and at other elevated points within the community (see also Creekmore 2010).

Besides the public plaza at the eastern gate, because of the general scarcity of open space within the crowded residential areas at Titriş, daily face-to-face interactions were most frequently carried out among neighbors whose houses faced mutual streets (cf. a 'face-block' in Smith 2010:139–40; also see Fisher, Chapter 6 in this volume). Other than these streets as a way to enter individual houses, there was, as a rule, no space between the houses, and these houses were adjoined by sharing walls within architectural blocks demarcated by the often orthogonal streets. Vacant land units were rare, although small open spaces serving as garbage dumps or side alleys may have been sporadically interspersed between dwelling structures, as was seen in the excavated area in the outer town. Even though the dwelling structures shared a house wall, the inhabitants of these houses did not necessarily have daily interactions, unless these houses shared a mutual street. This idea is supported by the multiple thresholds of the excavated houses, many of which faced each other between separate houses across the streets. Although these thresholds may not have been used simultaneously, this 'openness' corroborates the idea that the mutual streets were the axes of daily face-to-face interactions among residents. Moreover, because the doorway is aligned with other openings between internal rooms in a straight line, there was an easy accessibility and movement between the rooms, as well as a high visibility of the inside of the house from the street. This relative 'openness' also suggests that the spacious intramural courtyards within the ordinary houses were the loci where the occupants not only carried out household-related activities, but also conducted daily social interactions with their neighbors and relatives.

CONCLUSION

Few investigations have been conducted that enable us to generalize about the overall layout of the largely residential lower cities in mid–late third-millennium settlements in northern Mesopotamia. Titriş Höyük represents an unprecedented and ideal case study for comprehending the nature of domestic life and the socio-spatial configurations of the extensive urban living quarters as a whole. The excavated and surveyed areas in the lower town at Titriş show habitation areas indicative of residents of uniform status leading a moderately prosperous lifestyle. These houses commonly exhibit similar house plan and size, as well as standardized architectural features and household material remains. The spread of these relatively large houses created crowded neighborhoods, and such homogeneous living areas were pervasive in this ancient city. Besides public structures and elite residences most likely clustered on the high mound, functionally different areas – such as the one in front of the eastern gateway – were interspersed sporadically across the settlement. Such public or elite districts were located at specific loci, segregated from and surrounded by the more common habitation quarters. The long, straight streets not only served as communal space for daily interactions among neighbors, but also facilitated easy access between the different habitation quarters. The regular face-to-face interactions were commonly seen in the open plaza at the gate, while the flow of people and goods into and out of the city may also have been monitored in this important public area.

Residence inside the defensive wall may have been quite attractive to many because the 'suburb' populations in the immediate vicinity abandoned their houses and moved inside the fortification wall at the time of the centralized reconstruction of the settlement around 2300 BC. The ancient inhabitants may have felt it necessary to live within the limits of the city, or coercive measures may even have been applied to them by the ruling cadre. Nevertheless, the relatively comfortable standard of living guaranteed for the majority of the common residents at this northern Mesopotamian city, as well as economic opportunities in public spaces and the protection afforded by the fortification wall, all point to the general desirability of living in the urban residential neighborhoods.

ACKNOWLEDGMENTS

I would like to thank the directors of the Titriş excavations and surveys, Guillermo Algaze and Timothy Matney, for their support in my analyses of the excavation and survey data. Magnetometry survey data and faunal remains, as well as the plans and field notes, were made accessible to me by the field directors. I greatly appreciate both Andrew Creekmore and Kevin Fisher for inviting me to participate in their Society for American Archaeology (SAA) session, as well as for the enormous amount of time and work that they spent to make this edited volume successful. Although this work is a revised section of my dissertation, the writing up of this research was made possible while I was at Stone Brook University by an American Council of Learned Societies (ACLS) New Faculty Fellows award, with support of The Andrew W. Mellon Foundation.

NOTES

1 For recent studies on the settlement history of the north Mesopotamian cities at the end of the third millennium BC, see Pfälzner 2012, Ur 2010, and Weiss 2012.
2 Taya (ca. 155 ha), Leilan (ca. 90 ha), Hamoukar (ca. 98 ha), Beydar (ca. 28 ha), Chuēra (ca. 80 ha), Kazane (ca. 100 ha), Mozan (ca. 120 ha), Brak (ca. 70 ha), Mardikh (ca. 56 ha), Sweyhat (ca. 40 ha).
3 For the site plan for Tell Brak and Tell Mozan, see Ur et al. 2011 and Pfälzner 2012.
4 But see Kepinski 1990 for the double mound at Tell Khoshi.
5 The size of the high mound at Taya (ca. 5 ha), Leilan (ca. 15 ha), Hamoukar (ca. 15 ha), Beydar (ca. 9.6 ha), Chuēra (ca. 43 ha), Kazane (ca. 8–12 ha), Mozan (ca. 18 ha), Brak (ca. 43 ha), Mardikh (ca. 3 ha), Sweyhat (ca. 5–6 ha).
6 At Hamoukar, a mid–late third-millennium palace might have existed at the northeastern corner of the city (Reichel 2010–2011).
7 But a third-millennium monumental administrative structure has also been found in the lower town at Kazane (see Creekmore, Chapter 2 in this volume).

8　The average house size at Titriş was calculated with five housing units that were more or less completely excavated: House 1 = ca. 270 m², House 2 = ca. 280 m², House 3 = ca. 165 m², House 4 = ca. 205 m², and House 5 = ca. 280 m², including the walls.

9　See Hald 2010 for the assemblage of charred plant remains.

10　This intersection of three streets bears a close resemblance to an intersection excavated in the residential quarter of the early second-millennium urban settlement of Ur, located in southern Mesopotamia (Woolley and Mallowan 1976: Plate 124).

REFERENCES CITED

Akkermans, Peter and Glenn M. Schwartz 2003 *The Archaeology of Syria: From Complex Hunter-Gatherers to Early Urban Societies (ca. 16,000–300 BC)*. Cambridge University Press, Cambridge and New York.

Algaze, Guillermo 1999 Trends in the Archaeological Development of the Upper Euphrates Basin of Southeastern Anatolia during the Late Chalcolithic and Early Bronze Ages. In *Archaeology of the Upper Syrian Euphrates: The Tishrin Dam Area*, edited by G. del Olmo Lete and J. L. Montero Fenollós, pp. 5345–5572. Ausa, Barcelona.

Algaze, Guillermo and Adnan Mısır 1993 Excavations and Surveys at Titriş Höyük, A Small Mid-Late Third Millennium Urban Center in Southeastern Anatolia, 1992. *Kazı Sonuçları Toplantısı* 15:153–170.

1994 Titriş Höyük: An Early Bronze Age Urban Center in Southeastern Anatolia, 1993. *Kazı Sonuçları Toplantısı* 16:107–120.

Algaze, Guillermo, Adnan Mısır, Tony Wilkinson, Elizabeth Carter, and Ronald Gorny 1992 Şanlıurfa Museum/University of California Excavations and Surveys at Titriş Höyük, 1991: A Preliminary Report. *Anatolica* 18:33–60.

Algaze, Guillermo, Gulay Dinckan, Britt Hartenberger, Timothy Matney, Jennifer Pournelle, Lynn Rainville, Steven Rosen, Eric Rupley, Duncan Schlee, and Regis Vallet 2001 Research at Titriş Höyük in Southeastern Turkey: The 1999 Season. *Anatolica* 27:23–106.

Algaze, Guillermo, John Kelly, Tomothy [sic] Matney, and Duncan Schlee 1996 Late EBA Urban Structure at Titriş Höyük, Southeastern Turkey: The 1995 Season. *Anatolica* 22:129–143.

Algaze, Guillermo, Paul Goldberg, Deirdre Honça, Timothy Matney, Adnan Mısır, Arlene M. Rosen, Duncan Schlee, and Lewis Somers 1995 Titriş Höyük, A Small EBA Urban Center in SE Anatolia: The 1994 Season. *Anatolica* 21:13–64.

Allentuck, Adam and Haskel J. Greenfield 2010 The Organization of Animal Production in an Early Urban Center: The Zooarchaeological Evidence from Early Bronze Age Titriş Höyük, Southeast Turkey. In *Anthropological Approaches to Zooarchaeology: Complexity, Colonialism, and Animal Transformations*, edited by D. Campana, A. M. Choyke, P. Crabtree, S. D. deFrance, and J. Lev-Tov, pp. 12–29. Oxbow Books, Oxford.

Arnauld, M. Charlotte, Linda R. Manzanilla, and Michael E. Smith (editors) 2012 *The Neighborhood as a Social and Spatial Unit in Mesoamerican Cities*. The University of Arizona Press, Tucson.

Buccellati, Giorgio 2005 The Monumental Urban Complex at Urkesh: Report on the 16th Season of Excavations, July–September 2003. In *Studies on the Civilization and Culture of Nuzi and the Hurrians Vol.15, General Studies and Excavations at Nuzi 11/1*, edited by David L. Owen and Gernot Wilhelm, pp. 3–28. CDL Press, Bethesda, MD.

Buccellati, Giorgio and Marilyn Kelly-Buccellati (editors) 1998 *Urkesh and the Hurrians. A Volume in Honor of Lloyd Cotsen*. Urkesh/Mozan Studies, 3. Bibliotheca Mesopotamic 26. Undena Publications, Malibu, CA.

Cahill, Nicholas 2002 *Household and City Organization at Olynthus*. Yale University Press, New Haven, CT.

Chapdelaine, Claude 2009 Domestic Life in and around the Urban Sector of the Huacas of Moche Site, Northern Peru. In *Domestic Life in Prehispanic Capitals: A Study of Specialization, Hierarchy, and Ethnicity*, edited by Linda R. Manzanilla and Claude Chapdelaine, pp. 181–196. University of Michigan, Ann Arbor.

Clayton, Sarah C. 2011 Gender and Mortuary Ritual at Ancient Teotihuacan, Mexico: A Study of Intrasocietal Diversity. *Cambridge Archaeological Journal* 21(1):31–51.

Colantoni, Carlo and Jason Ur 2011 The Architecture and Pottery of a Late 3rd Millennium BC Residential Quarter at Tell Hamoukar, Northeastern Syria. *Iraq* 73:21–69.

Creekmore, Andrew T. 2010 The Structure of Upper Mesopotamian Cities: Insight from Fluxgate Gradiometer Survey at Kazane Höyük, Southeastern Turkey. *Archaeological Prospection* 17:73–88.

Danti, Michael and Richard L. Zettler 1998 The Evolution of the Tell es-Sweyhat (Syria) Settlement System in the Third Millennium BC. In *Espace Naturel, Espace Habité en Syrie du Nord (10e – 2e millénaires av. J-C.)*, edited by M. Fortin and O. Aurenche, pp. 209–228. Travaux de la Maison de l'Orient 28. Maison de l'Orient Méditerranéen, Lyon, France.

2002 Excavating an Enigma: The Latest Discoveries from Tell es-Sweyhat. *Expedition* 44(1):36–45.

2006 The Early Bronze Age in the Upper Euphrates River Valley and Northwest Jezireh, Syria. In *Euphrates River Valley Settlement: The Carchemish Sector in the Third Millennium BC*, edited by Edgar Peltenburg, pp. 164–183. Levant Supplementary Series 5. Oxbow, Oxford.

Delougaz, Pinhas, Harold D. Hill, and Seton Lloyd 1967 *Private Houses and Graves in the Diyala Region*. University of Chicago Press, Chicago.

Dohmann-Pfälzner, Heike and Peter Pfälzner 1996 Untersuchungen zur Urbanisierung Nordmesopotamiens im 3. Jt. v.Chr.: Wohnquartierplanung und städtische Zentrumsgestaltung in Tall Chuera. *Damazsener Mitteilungen* 9:1–13.

Emberling, Geoff 2003 Urban Social Transformations and the Problem of the "First City": New Research from Mesopotamia. In *The Social Construction of Ancient Cities*, edited by Monica L. Smith, pp. 254–268. Smithsonian Institution Press, Washington D.C.

Emberling, Geoff and Helen McDonald 2003 Excavations at Tell Brak 2001–2002: Preliminary Report. *Iraq* 65:1–75.

Gibson, McGuire, Muhammad Maktash, Judith A. Franke, Amr al-Azm, John C. Sanders, Tony Wilkinson, Clemens Reichel, Jason Ur, Peggy Sanders, Abdulillah Salameh, Carrie Hritz, Brigitte Watkins, and

Mahmoud Kattab 2002 First Season of Syrian-American Investigations at Hamoukar, Hasekeh Province. *Iraq* 64:45–68.

Hald, Mette Marie 2010 Distribution of Crops at Late Early Bronze Age Titriş Höyük, Southeast Anatolia: Towards a Model for the Identification of Consumers of Centrally Organised Food Distribution. *Vegetation History and Archaeobotany* 19:69–77.

Healan, Dan M. 2009 Household, Neighborhood, and Urban Structure in an "Adobe City": Tula, Hidalgo, Mexico. In *Domestic Life in Prehispanic Capitals: A Study of Specialization, Hierarchy, and Ethnicity*, edited by Linda R. Manzanilla and Claude Chapdelaine, pp. 67–88. Memoirs of the Museum of Anthropology, University of Michigan, Ann Arbor.

Honça, Deirdre M. and Guillermo Algaze 1998 Preliminary Report on the Human Skeletal Remains at Titriş Höyük: 1991–1996 Seasons. *Anatolica* 24:101–141.

Keith, Kathryn 2003 The Spatial Patterns of Everyday Life in Old Babylonian Neighborhoods. In *The Social Construction of Ancient Cities*, edited by Monica L. Smith, pp. 56–80. Smithsonian Institution Press, Washington D.C.

Kenoyer, J. Mark 2012 Households and Neighborhoods of the Indus Tradition: An Overview. In *New Perspectives on Household Archaeology*, edited by Bradley J. Parker and Catherine P. Foster, pp. 373–406. Eisenbrauns, Winona Lake, IN.

Kepinski, Christine 1990 Hōšī (In Archaeology in Iraq, by Khaled Nashef). *American Journal of Archaeology* 94(2):275–277.

Laneri, Nicola 2007 Burial Practices at Titriş Höyük, Turkey: An Interpretation. *Journal of Near Eastern Studies* 66(4):241–266.

Lebeau, Marc 2012 Notes sur l'architecture et l'urbanisme du Royaume de Nagar: Main Street, une "voie royale" à Tell Beydar. In *"L'Heure immobile" Entre ciel et terre. Mélanges en l'honneur d'Antoine Souleiman*, Subartu 31, edited by Phillipe Quenet and Michel al-Maqdissi, pp. 49–68. Brepols, Turnhout, Belgium.

Lebeau, Marc and Antoine Suleiman (editors) 2011 Tell Beydar: The 2004/2–2009 Seasons of Excavations, the 2004/2–2009 Seasons of Architectural Restoration: A Preliminary Report. Subartu 29. Brepols, Turnhout, Belgium.

Manzanilla, Linda R. 2009 Corporate Life in Apartment and Barrio Compounds at Teotihuacan, Central Mexico. In *Domestic Life in Prehispanic Capitals: A Study of Specialization, Hierarchy, and Ethnicity*, edited by Linda R. Manzanilla and Claude Chapdelaine, pp. 21–42. Memoirs of the Museum of Anthropology, University of Michigan, Ann Arbor.

Matney, Timothy 2002 Urban Planning and the Archaeology of Society at Early Bronze Age Titriş Höyük. In *Across the Anatolian Plateau: Readings in the Archaeology of Ancient Turkey*, edited by David C. Hopkins, pp. 19–34. American Schools of Oriental Research, Boston.

Matney, Timothy, Guillermo Algaze and Holly Pittman 1997 Excavations at Titriş Höyük in Southeastern Turkey: A Preliminary Report of the 1996 Season. *Anatolica* 23:61–84.

Matney, Timothy, Guillermo Algaze, and Steven Rosen 1999 Early Bronze Age Urban Structure at Titriş Höyük, Southeastern Turkey: The 1998 Season. *Anatolica* 25:185–201.

Matthiae, Paolo 1981 *Ebla: An Empire Rediscovered*. Doubleday, New York.

2010 Recent Excavations at Ebla 2006–2007. In *Proceedings of the 6th International Congress on the Archaeology of the Ancient Near East, 5 May–10 May 2008*, Sapienza, Università di Roma Vol. 2, edited by Paolo Matthiae, Frances Pinnock, Lorenzo Nigro, and Nicolò Marchetti, pp. 3–26. Harrassowitz Verlag, Wiesbaden, Germany.

Nishimura, Yoko 2008 North Mesopotamian Urban Space: A Reconstruction of Household Activities and City Layout at Titriş Höyük in the Third Millennium BC. Unpublished Ph.D. dissertation, University of California, Los Angeles.

2012 The Life of the Majority: A Reconstruction of Household Activities and Residential Neighborhoods at the Late–Third-Millennium Urban Settlement at Titriş Höyük in Northern Mesopotamia. In *New Perspectives on Household Archaeology*, edited by Bradley J. Parker and Catherine P. Foster, pp. 347–372. Eisenbrauns, Winona Lake, IN.

Oates, David, Joan Oates, and Helen McDonald 2001 *Excavations at Tell Brak Vol.2: Nagar in the Third Millennium BC*. McDonald Institute for Archaeological Research, Cambridge and British School of Archaeology in Iraq, London.

Oates, Joan, Augusta McMahon, Philip Karsgaard, Salam al-Quntar, and Jason Ur 2007 Early Mesopotamian Urbanism: A New View from the North. *Antiquity* 81:585–600.

Oriental Institute Computer Laboratory 2010 *Ancient Near East Site Maps – Syrian Site Map*. Electronic document, http://oi.uchicago.edu/research/lab/map/maps/syria.html, accessed June 15, 2013.

Pettinato, Giovanni 1981 *The Archives of Ebla: An Empire Inscribed in Clay*. Doubleday, New York.

1991 *Ebla: A New Look at History*. Johns Hopkins University Press, Baltimore, MD.

Pfälzner, Peter 2001 *Haus und Haushalt: Wohnformen des Dritten Jahrtausends vor Christus in Nordmesopotamien*. Damaszener Forshungen 9. Philipp von Zabern, Mainz, Germany.

2012 The Socioeconomic Dynamics of the Northern Mesopotamian and Anatolian Regions during the Late Third and Early Second Millennium BC. In *Looking North: The Socioeconomic Dynamics of Northern Mesopotamian and Anatolian Regions during the Late Third and Early Second Millennium BC*, edited by Nicola Laneri, Peter Pfälzner, and Stefano Valentini, pp. 51–80. Harrassowitz Verlag, Wiesbaden, Germany.

Price, Douglas T., Linda Manzanilla, and William D. Middleton 2000 Immigration and the Ancient City of Teotihuacan in Mexico: A Study Using Strontium Isotope Ratios in Human Bone and Teeth. *Journal of Archaeological Science* 27:903–913.

Pruss, Alexander 2000 Recent Excavations at Tell Chuera and the Chronology of the Site. In *Proceedings of the First International Congress of the Archaeology of the Ancient Near East*, edited by Paolo Matthiae, Alessandra Enea, Luca Peyronel, and Frances Pinnock, pp. 1431–1446. Dipartimento di Scienze Storiche, Archeologiche e Antropologiche dell 'Antichità, Rome.

Rainville, Lynn 2005 *Investigating Upper Mesopotamian Households Using Micro-archaeological Techniques*. Archaeopress, Oxford.

Rapoport, Amos 1969 *House Form and Culture*. Prentice-Hall, Englewood Cliffs, New Jersey.

1990 *History and Precedent in Environmental Design*. Plenum Press, New York.

Reade, Julian E. 1973 Tell Taya (1972–73): Summary Report. *Iraq* 35:155–187.

1982 Tell Taya. In *Fifty Years of Mesopotamian Discovery: the Work of the British School of Archaeology in Iraq, 1932–1982*, edited by John Curtis, pp. 72–78. British School of Archaeology in Iraq, London.

1997 Taya, Tell. In *Oxford Encyclopedia of Archaeology in the Near East*, edited by Eric M. Meyers, pp. 158–160. Oxford University Press, New York and Oxford.

Reichel, Clemens 2010–2011 Oriental Institute Annual Report, Hamoukar. Electronic document, http://oi.uchicago.edu/pdf/10_11_Hamoukar.pdf, accessed March 1, 2013.

Ristvet, Lauren 2007 The Third Millennium City Wall at Tell Leilan, Syria: Identity, Authority and Urbanism. In *Monumental Public Architecture in the Bronze Age Near East and Aegean*, edited by J. Bretschneider, J. Driessen, and K. Vanlerberghe, pp. 183–212. Peters, Leuven, Belgium.

Smith, Michael E. 2010 The Archaeological Study of Neighborhoods and Districts in Ancient Cities. *Journal of Anthropological Archaeology* 29:137–154.

2011 Classic Maya Settlement Clusters as Urban Neighborhoods: A Comparative Perspective on Low-Density Urbanism. *Journal de la Société des Américanistes* 97(1):51–73.

Smith, Monica L. 2008 Urban Empty Spaces: Contentious Places for Consensus-Building. *Archaeological Dialogues* 15(2):216–231.

Spence, Michael W. 1996 A Comparative Analysis of Ethnic Enclaves. In *Arqueología Mesoamericana: Homenaje a William T. Sanders* Vol. 1, edited by A. Mastache, J. Parsons, R. Santley, and M. C. Serra Puche, pp. 333–353. Institute Nacional de Antropología e Historia, Mexico City, Mexico.

Spence, Michael W., Christine D. White, Evelyn C. Rattray, and Fred J. Longstaffe 2005 Past Lives in Different Places: The Origins and Relationships of Teotihuacan's Foreign Residents. In *Settlement, Subsistence, and Social Complexity: Essays Honoring the Legacy of Jeffrey R. Parsons*, edited by Richard E. Blanton, pp. 155–197. Cotsen Institute of Archaeology, University of California, Los Angeles.

Stone, Elizabeth C. 2000 The Development of Cities in Ancient Mesopotamia. In *Civilizations of the Ancient Near East*, edited by Jack M. Sasson, pp. 235–248. Hendrickson, Peabody, MA.

2008 A Tale of Two Cities: Lowland Mesopotamia and Highland Anatolia. In *The Ancient City: New Perspectives on Urbanism in the Old and New World*, edited by Joyce Marcus and Jeremy A. Sabloff, pp. 141–164. School for Advanced Research Resident Scholar Book, Santa Fe, NM.

Ur, Jason A. 2010 Cycles of Civilization in Northern Mesopotamia, 4400–2000 BC. *Journal of Archaeological Research* 18:387–431.

Ur, Jason A., Philip Karsgaard, and Joan Oates 2011 The Spatial Dimensions of Early Mesopotamian Urbanism: The Tell Brak Suburban Survey, 2003–2006. *Iraq* 73:1–19.

Weiss, Harvey (editor) 2012 *Seven Generations Since the Fall of Akkad*. Studia Chaburensia 3. Harrassowitz Verlag, Wiesbaden, Germany.

Weiss, Harvey, M. A., W. Wetterstorm Courty, F. Guichard, L. Senior, R. Meadow, and A. Curnow 1993 The Genesis and Collapse of Third Millennium North Mesopotamian Civilization. *Science* 261:995–1004.

Weiss, Harvey, Peter Akkermans, Gil J. Stein, Dominique Parayre, and Robert Whiting 1990 1985 Excavations at Tell Leilan, Syria. *American Journal of Archaeology* 94:529–581.

White, Christine D., Michael W. Spence, Fred J. Langstaffe, and Kimberley R. Law 2004a Demography and Ethnic Continuity in the Tlailotlacan Enclave of Teotihuacan: The Evidence from Stable Oxygen Isotopes. *Journal of Anthropological Archaeology* 23:385–403.

White, Christine D., Rebecca Storey, Fred J. Longstaffe, and Michael W. Spence 2004b Immigration, Assimilation, and Status in the Ancient City of Teotihuacan: Stable Isotopic Evidence from Tlajinga 33. *Latin American Antiquity* 15(2):176–198.

Wilkinson, Tony J. 1990 *Town and Country in Southeastern Anatolia*. Oriental Institute of the University of Chicago Press, Chicago.

1994 The Structure and Dynamics of Dry-Farming States in Upper Mesopotamia. *Current Anthropology* 35:483–520.

2000 Regional Approaches to Mesopotamian Archaeology: The Contribution of Archaeological Surveys. *Journal of Archaeological Research* 8:219–267.

2003 *Archaeological Landscapes of the Near East*. University of Arizona Press, Tucson.

Woolley, Leonard and Max Mallowan 1976 *Ur Excavations: the Old Babylonian Period*. Vol. 7, British Museum Publications, London.

York, Abigail M., Michael E. Smith, Benjamin W. Stanley, Barbara L. Stark, Juliana Novic, Sharon L. Harlan, George L. Cowgill, and Christopher G. Boone 2011 Ethnic and Class Clustering through the Ages: A Transdisciplinary Approach to Urban Neighborhood Social Patterns. *Urban Studies* 48(11):2399–2415.

4

Swahili Urban Spaces of the Eastern African Coast

Stephanie Wynne-Jones and Jeffrey Fleisher

The study of urban space among the eighth to fifteenth-century Swahili of the eastern African coast is dominated by a social model that sees formalized town plans as crystallizations of relationships between clans and moieties over the centuries. In this paper, we develop instead a practice model, emphasizing town plans as the result of daily practice, particularly the construction and repeated alteration of stone houses, in the development of townscapes. We argue that the lifecycle of houses was likely a key element in the formation of urban space and developed the linked concepts of confined and delimited space as ways of understanding Swahili townscapes.

Dozens of coral-built towns dot the coast of eastern Africa from southern Somalia to Mozambique (Figure 4.1). The ruins of these towns – including houses, mosques, and tombs – have been the object of archaeological investigation for more than fifty years. Although once thought to be the remains of Persian colonies, these sites are now recognized as those of an African mercantile society that emerged in the mid- to late first millennium AD and reached its efflorescence between AD 1300 and 1500 (Horton and Middleton 2000; Kusimba 1999). The towns were relatively independent city-states that successfully managed long-distance trade relationships between the African continent and the Indian Ocean world, a negotiation reflected in the Islamic community and self-conscious cosmopolitanism that was part of their character since earliest times (LaViolette 2008). The foundations of most Swahili towns lay in mid-first millennium villages that engaged in trade relationships with Muslim merchants from the Persian Gulf; some of these became the coral-built towns of later centuries (Abungu 1989, 1998; Chittick 1974; Fleisher 2010; Horton 1986, 1996). The chronological development of

STEPHANIE WYNNE-
JONES AND JEFFREY
FLEISHER

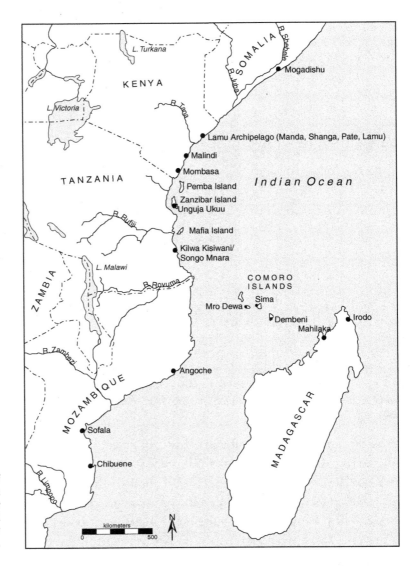

Figure 4.1 Map of
the eastern African
coast, showing major
stonetowns mentioned
in the text (drawn by
authors).

town plans is known only through a few well-excavated examples
(e.g., Horton 1996), but understood as a process in which less permanent structures of earth and thatch were slowly replaced with
those built of coral (Wright 1993). By the end of the first millennium
AD, mosques were built with cut coral foundations; by the thirteenth
century, coral rag became the preferred building material for elite
houses in many towns.

The nature of Swahili urbanism has been the subject of considerable archaeological theorizing over recent decades, resulting in an
increasingly sophisticated view of these stonetowns as regional and
international centers. Politically and economically, they seem always

to have been independent, functioning as "city-states" (Sinclair and Håkansson 2000): levying taxes, minting coins, and engaging in distinctive and varied relationships with groups in their broader hinterlands. Yet, continuity and similarity in architectural styles, comparative assemblages of locally produced and imported goods, as well as adherence to a common faith, provide a measure of the close contact maintained along the eastern African coast throughout the period in question. Archaeological approaches to Swahili urbanism have tended to move in one of two directions. First, there has been a turn toward understanding towns within their regions, exploring urban function in relation to a broader settlement pattern (Abungu and Muturo 1993; Chami 1988, 1992, 1994, 1999, 2001; Fawcett and LaViolette 1990; Fleisher 2003; Fleisher and LaViolette 1999; LaViolette et al. 1989; Schmidt et al. 1992; Wynne-Jones 2007a, 2007b). This fits into a larger-scale movement in African archaeology that seeks to characterize the unique urban formations of the continent, with an emphasis on what a city does, rather than what a city is. The series of complex interactions and material signatures that constitute urbanism have been questioned, building on models that emphasize the social aspects of urban life (M. L. Smith 2003; also Fisher and Creekmore, Chapter 1 in this volume). Second, archaeologists have focused on the institutions of the town – notably houses and mosques – and drawn upon a rich record of ethnographies and histories from recent centuries to help interpret the uses of space within the buildings (Allen 1979, 1981; Donley 1982, 1987; Donley-Reid 1990). Although the specific applicability of these models to earlier centuries might be questioned, these latter explorations demonstrate the interplay of economic, social, and ritual concerns that structured Swahili spaces and activities.

Together, the two strands of research open a space for more complex understandings of ancient Swahili urban settings. In this chapter, we suggest that an understanding of urban plans can combine the insights from these recent movements and we outline a practice-based approach to the study of town layout. By thinking through the function of city spaces, in terms of how places were used and experienced at all levels, we supplement the regional understandings of urban character with an appreciation of the spaces of the towns themselves; we simultaneously bring the insights from regional studies into the town. The important emphasis on chronology in exploring Swahili towns, which has revolutionized models of their origins

STEPHANIE WYNNE-
JONES AND JEFFREY
FLEISHER

and development, has resulted in a lack of focus on horizontal complexity and understanding towns as spaces for social interaction. Likewise, concentration on particular structures, such as houses and mosques, has rarely been expanded to encompass the spaces outside the walls. Here, we attempt to rectify this imbalance and provide a consideration of Swahili urban spaces as the settings for complex interactions and practices; building on recent approaches to urbanism, we emphasize the social aspects of ancient towns as constitutive of their materiality.

SWAHILI URBANISM

The coral-built towns of the eastern African coast figure prominently in discussions of African forms of precolonial urbanism (LaViolette and Fleisher 2005; McIntosh 1997). Earlier questions about the origins of urbanism – often invoking external inspiration – have been supplanted by recent research investigating urban function (McIntosh and McIntosh 1993). The crucial insight regarding what functions cities carry out for associated populations has helped to reinvigorate the study of African urbanism, and reveal the distinctive qualities of precolonial urban formations across the continent (Fleisher 2010; LaViolette and Fleisher 2009; McIntosh and McIntosh 1993; Pikirayi 2001; Wynne-Jones 2007c). Swahili towns have been explored with reference to their wider hinterland, seen as market centers and ritual foci, the apex of a settlement hierarchy, and home to an emergent mercantile elite (Wright 1993:670).

On the Swahili coast, this conceptual turn is based on a series of regional surveys that set the coral-built towns within their larger settlement context. In all regions subjected to such analysis, the stonetowns have emerged as just one component of a much larger landscape of occupation. Foundational research of the 1980s and 1990s, which sought the earliest earth-and-thatch iterations of the stonetowns (Abungu 1989; Horton 1996; Sinclair 1987) proceeded concurrently with a series of surveys that mapped the distribution of settlement in the coastal regions (Chami 1994; Fawcett and LaViolette 1990; LaViolette et al. 1989; Schmidt et al. 1992; Wilson 1982); the overall picture that emerged was of coral-built towns developing out of settlements of impermanent architecture, which were themselves part of a network of similar settlements across the region. The African roots of the towns were thus firmly established. More recently, regional studies have explored areas around specific towns, with the objective of examining town-country interactions during the period of urbanization (Fleisher 2003, 2010; Helm 2000; Wynne-Jones 2007c). Within the context of the broader regions, it had been assumed that the settlement pattern reflected a simple relationship of increasing hierarchy, with the developing stonetowns emerging as political and economic foci (Wright 1993:665). These studies have begun to explore the types of relationship that might be manifest between developing centers and their regions, exploring centripetal processes that go beyond the economic. Fleisher (2003, 2010), for example, has suggested that the stonetown of Chwaka functioned as a ritual center and brought the community together under the banner of Islam, with the construction of the elaborate mosque manifesting the central position of that religion for a wider community. In Chwaka's surrounding region of northern Pemba, urban development was accompanied by a dramatic decline in countryside settlement, while in southern Kenya (Helm 2000) and southern Tanzania (Wynne-Jones 2007c), urban formation had less of an effect on the surrounding populations. In the latter examples, different kinds of economic, and possibly ritual, communities have been postulated that did not lead to a focus of regional population within the emerging coral-built centers.

These approaches to urban function explore particular types of practice – whether political, economic, or religious – and gauge those forms of production in relation to surrounding populations. The focus of attention moves away from a search for definition to one of process. Despite recognizing the complexity and diversity of Swahili society, and the towns' relationships to broader populations, this turn toward urban function has somewhat neglected the study of urban planning within the stonetown settlements. Yet, the seeds of an understanding are present, through an emphasis on interaction and activity. Therefore, we see the movement toward a more functional interpretation of African urbanism as an important step toward thinking through the way human practice came to define (and be defined by) urban spaces.

In this chapter, we begin by discussing what Smith (2007), following Rapoport (1988), calls "high-level meaning," explored through ethnographic studies of the Swahili (see Fisher and Creekmore, Chapter 1 in this volume). High-level meaning relates to "cosmologies, world views and the domain of sacred" (Smith 2007:30), whereas middle-level meaning reflects the more worldly concerns of communities and elites in the manipulation of space and the "transmission of messages about identity, status and power" (Smith 2007:30). It is at this latter level that archaeologists have often explored the manipulation and use of space as a crucial resource through which power and authority were legitimized, constituting the "political landscape" of the ancient world (A. T. Smith 2003). Low-level meaning "concerns the recursive relationship between architecture and behavior" (Smith 2007:30) and is often sought in archaeologies of daily practice. Following the consideration of ethnographic data, we discuss archaeological attempts to decipher the meaning of town plans, arguing that these most commonly fall under the rubric of middle-level meaning, thus favoring the agency of elite members of society. Finally, we explore the way that previous researchers on the Swahili have emphasized the role of practice in the development of key institutions in Swahili towns, most importantly the stonehouse tradition, and argue that this practice-based understanding, which seeks low-level meaning in urban plans, has the potential to transform our understanding of Swahili urban spaces. As such, the levels of meaning give structure to our discussions. Yet, as Rapoport himself states (1988:325), levels of meaning should not be thought of as mutually exclusive categories, but as heuristic tools for subdividing a continuum of practical action. Here, we attempt to show that it is equally unhelpful to separate out different features of Swahili town planning, but that an approach that incorporates both ritual and worldly concerns, as well as the ways that people lived in and used spaces, can unite the disparate understandings already achieved through ethnography and archaeology.

"CITIES OF THE MIND"

Studies of space within the towns have tended to draw on the rich ethnographic record available for the towns of the twentieth-century coast, and particularly Lamu, on the northern coast of Kenya (el-Zein 1974; Ghaidan 1975; Middleton 1992; Prins 1971). This somewhat anachronistic approach to the exploration of ancient town plans is nonetheless valuable in delineating certain principles that may have been present over the long term. The influence of Islam on Swahili urban spaces is, for example, an interesting avenue because the period of greatest town growth in the fourteenth to fifteenth centuries was also a time of large-scale mosque construction. It is therefore necessary to look to the Islamic world for the kind of "high-level" structuring principles, or "normative urban theory" (M.E. Smith 2011:180) that would account for the overall form of a town according to cosmology or world view (cf. Kelly and Brown, Chapter 9 in this volume).

At this level, Swahili towns might be seen as part of the world of Islamic cities that have been explored in detail elsewhere. The extent to which Islam creates a distinctive pattern has been widely debated: the idealized (and orientalized) "Islamic city" based around the mosque, market, and public baths has been sought across the Islamic world (Lapidus 1969; al-Sayyad 1991). In Swahili towns – which do not contain these latter two features – the influence of Islam has instead been seen through the centrality of the mosque, the evocation of concepts of ritual purity, and on the seclusion and control of women.

The most extensive treatment of the structures of Swahili urbanism draws on Islam as an overarching cosmology that provides context and content for the specific patterns seen on the eastern African coast. El-Zein (1974) considers contemporary Lamu, and his account is based largely on the testimony of informants of the 1970s. This has important ramifications for the ways that Swahili tradition is presented in the immediate postcolonial context, with much weight given to historicity; a sense of Lamu society as timeless and enduring, as well as an emphasis on notions of pedigree, entitlement to land, and to local identity. Nevertheless, it represents an important study for the exploration of the structures of Swahili life here, based around concerns of Islam and historical memory. El-Zein's structuralist approach seeks the deep grammars of Swahili social interaction, explained through a series of conceptual oppositions traced through the oral histories related within the town. The Lamu "myths of creation" are given particular precedence (el-Zein 1974:167–220), shown to be based upon the monotheistic tradition with certain local adaptations and interpretations; through these myths, el-Zein draws a binary distinction between light and dark, white and black, angels and *jinns* (unseen spirits that were the first inhabitants of the earth), and life and death. For him, these structure every aspect of social life, including spatial prescriptions, and they are "not only a logical model but also part and parcel of the social reality shared by the people" (el-Zein 1974:172). El-Zein thus suggests that the particular ways that Islamic beliefs were structured in the town of Lamu were of fundamental importance in the shaping of the urban milieu. This sense echoes throughout architectural histories of Swahili towns, with Gensheimer's study of Swahili urban spaces concluding with the suggestion that it was the:

> acorporeal world of spirits and dead ancestors, which were used to distinguish the palaces, mosques, houses and tombs within the Swahili city. This figureless and formless construct of the city which gave meaning to the built environment and guided its construction, this city of the mind, was the essence of the Swahili city (Gensheimer 1997:359).

The notion of purity identified by el-Zein is also picked up in an architectural study of Lamu conducted at roughly the same time (Ghaidan 1975). Despite eschewing the notion of an overarching plan for the town, Ghaidan (1975:61) claims that Swahili concepts of space are based around systems of behavior that require specific "shells." He identifies these shells in three guiding principles for the architecture of the town, which could be extended to the town plan: *purity*, *involvement*, and *pedigree*. Purity refers largely to ritual purity and the avoidance of pollution. Like el-Zein, Ghaidan sees Swahili urban spaces as being structured around the concerns of maintaining this purity through the strict segregation of clean and unclean activities and persons; elsewhere, he links this explicitly to the stonehouses and associated notions of privacy (Ghaidan 1971). Again, this is linked back to Islam and to the specific rituals that accompany observance within Lamu. Involvement and pedigree are more worldly concerns, associated with the establishment of social relations through spatial proxemics (involvement) and to the main-tenance of exclusivity for elite groups (pedigree). For Ghaidan, these relations of kinship and distinction are key overarching principles of the same order as the concern with privacy, demonstrating the over-lapping nature of "high-" or "mid-level" meanings and the fact that in practice, these are not separated out. Pedigree leads, he suggests, to the establishment of certain delineated areas associated with par-ticular social classes, and is the reason for the maintenance of histor-ical tradition and the importance attached to ancestral places. Thus, the bipartite division of Lamu (Figure 4.2) into the wards of Mkomani and Langoni (see also Prins 1971) reflects an ongoing concern with social distinction between patrician and commoner, a belief about

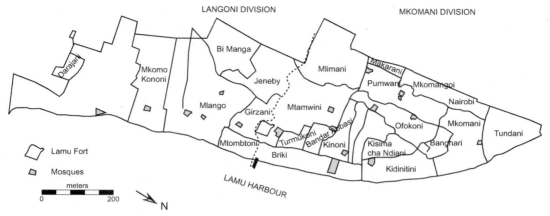

Figure 4.2 Schematic plan of twentieth-century Lamu, showing bipartite division and locations of mosques (adapted from el-Zein 1974:16).

the structure of society rendered in spatial form. Likewise, the predominance of trade-related structures (market stalls and craft workshops) in Langoni is linked to their lesser status, while the patrician ward of Mkomani is instead purely residential, and home to eleven of Lamu's nineteen mosques (Ghaidan 1975:62–64). *Pedigree* is therefore seen to be mapped fairly straightforwardly onto the town plan of contemporary Lamu, reflecting the social order in spatial form. *Involvement*, by contrast, creates the character of the Swahili town: Ghaidan argues for an extremely sociable form of urbanism (contrasting strongly with the Weberian model of alienation as intrinsic to urban life). The high involvement ratio has, for Ghaidan (1975:71), "set the scale of streets and open spaces at an intimate level … Involvement is also responsible for the absence of any expression of grandeur from Swahili architectural patterns."

Although Ghaidan and el-Zein locate the concept of purity within the realms of overarching cosmology or the "city of the mind," their development of the concept sees it played out through the more quotidian concerns of what have been termed "mid-level" meanings (Rapoport 1988; Smith 2007). These are more bound up with the social negotiation, communication, and power struggles of the inhabitants as they seek to inscribe their vision onto the urban spaces. The notions of involvement and pedigree, although elevated to the level of cosmology or worldview by Ghaidan, also clearly fall into this category. For these writers, the centrality of the mosque reflects its central position in the Islamic worldview, but is also interpreted through the social negotiations and communications of the residents of Swahili towns. Thus, for el-Zein (1974:14–15), the mosque represents the unity of the town beyond the multiplicity of ethnic and social backgrounds found in the various *mitaa* or quarters, but also, in its Mkomani position, as part of the power negotiations between the *khatib* or religious leader and the *waungwana* or mercantile elite, who are most associated with the Pwani mosque near the foreshore. The separation of worldly and religious power is seen reflected in this separation of the mosques themselves and their locations within the town. This conflation of spatial and conceptual centrality is also assumed for the earlier towns (Garlake 1966:3), as will be discussed.

Apart from the prominence of mosques, however, suggestions of how Islam might have influenced town planning focus around the ways that daily life was structured and movement constrained by the concepts of purity and the kinship relations of contemporary Lamu inhabitants. This is similar to the ways that the Islamic city has been visualized elsewhere, as analysis has moved away from the more rigid definitions of specific institutions, and toward a sense of the ways that Islam structures daily life and – through that – creates a distinctive urban form. Islamic cities are defined by Abu-Lughod (1987:172) as "processes, not products," born of an interplay between the prescriptions of religion and the ways that this is exacted in diverse environments and social settings. Wheatley (2001) has aptly demonstrated how the same fundamentals of Islamic practice led to diverse and functionally distinct urban forms in different areas – the centrality of the mosque often the only point of commonality.

The literature on high-level meaning within Swahili towns is therefore actually quite varied. Despite a claim to speak of structuring principles, and the ways that these controlled daily life in and around the town, most of the cases we examined assume that spatial differentiation will reflect social differentiation without much analysis of how this process occurs. The classic model of this is the didemic Lamu model, with the fundamental division between Mkomani and Langoni seen as reflecting a social division that is further broken down into *mitaa* or clan distinctions. Although this demonstrates the interplay between top- and mid-level meaning at all stages, it is actually at odds with the kind of process-based analysis el-Zein and Ghaidan suggest, by which activity is structured through overarching principles, and then creates a unique Islamic urban form: instead, the urban plan is seen simply to mirror the structure of society. The difference is between urban plans based on high-level meaning – pedigree, purity, Islam – and one where urban plans reflect social divisions.

COMPARING FOURTEENTH- AND FIFTEENTH-CENTURY SWAHILI TOWN PLANS

Archaeological studies of ancient Swahili urban plans have likewise tended to assume a straightforward mapping of social structure onto architecture, implicitly assuming intentionality in the creation of the townscape. It is assumed that control is present over the town plan, and patterns are correlated with particular elite concerns or social patterns; another effect of this assumption is a functional approach to urban space. Both of these features are evident in the work of Horton (1994, 1996), which constitutes the most complete consideration of an archaeological town plan, and are also seen in other approaches to ancient Swahili towns (Kusimba 2008; Pradines 2004; Wright 1993).

Horton argues that the urban plan reflects the social makeup of the Swahili town, with houses grouped according to kin patterns, and with features such as the mosque positioned centrally to reflect their importance. Excavations at the site of Shanga, on the northern Kenyan coast, have formed the basis for Horton's (1994, 1996) detailed evocation of a social model of Swahili urban space. Unparalleled detail on every phase of the town's life has offered a developmental sequence from an early phase of earth-and-thatch architecture through to the dense pattern of coral-and-lime built houses that characterized the urban landscape by the fifteenth century (Figure 4.3). In the initial stages of development, Shanga contained a central enclosure, with seven gateways, surrounded by the domestic architecture of the town. Another wall enclosed this settlement with only four gateways on the cardinal axes. Horton argues that the central area would have been the site of the market as well as of communal rituals or activities; access to this area could have been controlled by the communities that lived outside the gateways. It is also in this central area that the eighth-century congregational mosque was constructed in earth and thatch, and replaced in stone in the tenth century, offering further corroboration to this theory that the open space provided for the coming together of the urban community. Horton (1994) suggests that different areas of the town may have been functionally specialized; as such, the urban layout

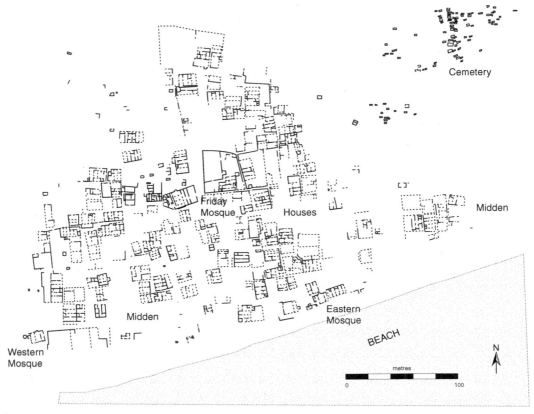

Figure 4.3 Plan of Shanga showing fourteenth- to fifteenth-century structures. Cemetery extends to the north and east (adapted from Horton 1996:figure 9).

of Shanga would have reflected both the multicultural nature of the community and the function of the town itself as a cosmopolitan and controlled setting for the coming together of these different groups for certain activities.

Horton sees this foundation of multicultural communities living in various quarters of the town in the eighth and ninth centuries as the basis for the continued division of the site into quarters or *mitaa* into the fourteenth and early fifteenth centuries. It was through these divisions that clans were able to control movement through and use of the urban space, particularly the public and communal areas. One major transformation at Shanga was the construction of stone houses in the fourteenth century, at which time the focus of control is seen to have begun to turn inward, as trade became intertwined with hospitality within the houses of the merchants. We return to this idea later, in the context of the uses of the stonehouses that became characteristic of the Swahili urban environment.

The illustration of urban development at Shanga has transformed understandings of Swahili urban spaces and makes an important step toward thinking through urban plans in terms of function and social components. The problem, however, is that the model of Shanga, with its central, focal area, and evidence for defined *mitaa*, has become an idealized model of the Swahili town. As such, the historicity of the settlement is somewhat lost; despite claims to chronological precision, the analysis is based on the very different towns of later periods. In developing his interpretation of eighth- and ninth-century Shanga, Horton draws on plans of nineteenth- and twentieth-century settlements of the near coastal hinterland, as well as historical and ethnographic evidence of quartered towns built during the sixteenth to nineteenth centuries. In a later publication, Horton and Middleton (2000:123) argue that the centralized town plan can be traced through to the settlements of the sixteenth to nineteenth centuries, with the "idea of gateways into the central enclosure moved to the outer perimeter" at sites such as Pate and Siyu, the very sites that provided conceptualization for the original model.

It is certainly the case that Swahili settlements contained foci of activity, of which the mosque was clearly the most prominent, as well as open areas and community structures such as cemeteries; to a certain extent, we can think of the towns as being focused toward these areas or as having daily activity structured through them. Yet this is not necessarily the same as an "ideal" Swahili settlement pattern, epitomized by the settlement at Shanga (conveniently also the best excavated site) and achieved to greater or lesser extent by sites elsewhere on the coast. Only at Gedi do we seem to have an echo of this arrangement in an early site (Figure 4.4), as a recent study recognizes the imprint of a former central enclosure in the shape of the town wall to the northeast surrounding the mosque (Pradines 2004).

Exploring these aspects in other Swahili towns is not without its challenges; these include problems in reconstructing chronological development and of whether the extant ruins might be seen as representative. As Horton (1996) has so ably demonstrated at Shanga, the plans of some towns developed through time, with some parts of towns extending older spatial orderings, whereas other parts of the town developed as needs emerged and populations grew. At Shanga, the central area was filled, slowly, with additional domestic structures, larger mosques, and tombs such that, by the fifteenth

STEPHANIE WYNNE-
JONES AND JEFFREY
FLEISHER

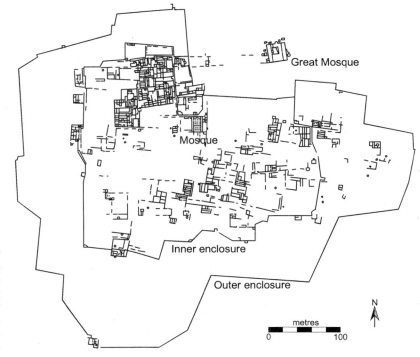

Figure 4.4 Plan of
Gedi, showing shape
of enclosure walls to
northeast, suggesting
possible earlier
enclosure (adapted from
Pradines 2004:figure 72,
p. 119).

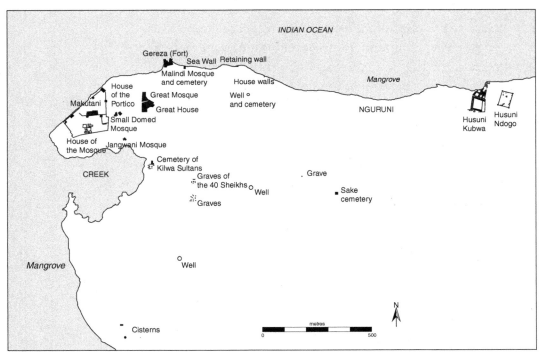

Figure 4.5 Plan of Kilwa Kisiwani, showing major monumental structures (adapted
from Chittick 1974:figure 2).

century when the site was abandoned, this "central" zone can only be recognized by the presence of the mosque. Similarly, in discussing Takwa, Wilson explores the processes through which visible town plans came to be structured, suggesting that it may be possible to read a "horizontal stratigraphy" (Wilson 1982) by charting out successive building episodes. Although it may be possible to do this for short-lived settlements like Takwa, or sites dominated by coral architecture, picking apart the "horizontal" development of Swahili towns with 700-year occupations is more of a challenge.

Another concern is the degree to which visible ruins represent a full town plan. Many of the historically significant towns are archaeologically known from a very small sample of the total area; at Kilwa, Mombasa, Malindi, and Mogadishu, only fragments can be reconstructed. In some cases, this is the result of continued occupation and subsequent destruction or overbuilding (as with Mombasa). In the case of Kilwa, however, it appears that much of the town was actually built of wood, as noted by Ibn Battuta in the early fourteenth century (Freeman-Grenville 1962:32). Despite Kilwa's coastal prominence, little of a town plan is discernible today beyond a handful of monumental structures including the Great Mosque, the palace of Husuni Kubwa, and a large and enigmatic associated structure known as Husuni Ndogo (Figure 4.5). The case of Kilwa points to another major issue of visibility: namely, the likely former predominance of earth-and-thatch architecture (Fleisher and LaViolette 1999:707; Kusimba 1996). It is now clear that some important towns were built almost exclusively of earth-and-thatch buildings, as at Chwaka on Pemba Island, with only one or two houses of coral rag, as well as mosques and tombs. Even in towns that appear to have intact plans, such as Gedi and Shanga, significant portions of the town would have been filled with earth-and-thatch houses, no longer visible, but archaeologically detectable (Fleisher and LaViolette 1999; Horton 1996; Koplin and LaViolette 2008).

Despite these problems, a number of archaeologists have attempted to interpret intra-site settlement patterns in Swahili towns. The earliest and perhaps most systematic effort was by Wilson (1979b, 1982) at Takwa. This site, dated to the sixteenth and seventeenth centuries (after which it was abandoned), provides a useful case study in that it had a relatively discrete settlement history as well as a comprehensive settlement plan (Figure 4.6). Wilson (1982:207) defined two types of space within Takwa: confined and delimited. Confined

STEPHANIE WYNNE-
JONES AND JEFFREY
FLEISHER

Figure 4.6 Plan of Takwa (adapted from Wilson 1982:figure 2, p. 204).

space is coterminous with interior, architectural spaces, whereas delimited space is "formed by the arrangement or occurrence of structures or natural features upon the settlement landscape." This distinction, we believe, captures well the important linkage between interior and exterior spaces, especially in urban contexts where much of the "open" or "empty" space is itself defined – or delimited – by architecture; we take up this distinction later in this chapter. Wilson conducted a full inventory of all structures and examined the distribution of houses with one, two, and three rooms. He found that distributions of structures in quarters of the settlement revealed few distinctions, but a higher frequency of three-room houses clustered near the central part of the site around the main congregational mosque. This pattern, he suggests, may represent the ability of wealthier families to add rooms to their houses or may reflect the longer occupational histories of more central houses. Wilson also examined the distribution of niche styles and the development of compound blocks of houses ("courtyard" and "street groups") as a means to explore possible past social units. In sum, he found that "a

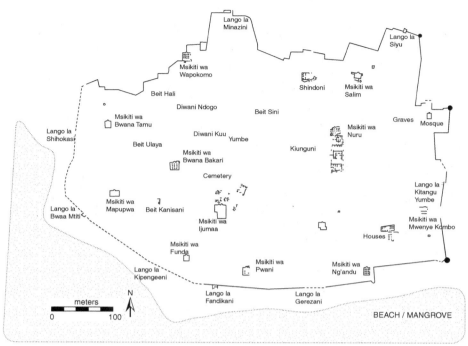

Figure 4.7 Schematic plan of Pate, showing gates (marked *lango*) and mosques (*msikiti*) (adapted from Wilson and Omar 1997:figure 1, p. 32).

distributional analysis … [shows] that community-wide patterns of settlement exist that do not reveal themselves to casual observations, and that even simple quantitative analysis can be applied to isolate such patterns" (Wilson 1982:206).

The number of published town plans that permit a more general comparison of town planning is small, and includes (from north to south) Shanga, Pate (Figure 4.7), Takwa, Gedi, Mtwapa (Figure 4.8), Jumba la Mtwana (Figure 4.9), and Songo Mnara (Figure 4.10). What unites these town plans is the dominance of the coral-built tradition, a centrally located mosque, and a town wall. Most contain a mosque positioned at or near the center of the town; in most cases, the most central mosque is the largest mosque in the town – the congregational mosque – used for the holiest of prayers on Friday. Only at Songo Mnara and Ungwana is the main mosque not centrally located, although the central area at Songo Mnara does contain a smaller mosque.

The physical centrality of monumental structures like mosques is perhaps the most important structuring feature of Swahili towns. Proximity to this mosque, as Wilson notes, is a marker of prestige in

Figure 4.8 Plan of standing buildings at Mtwapa, Kenya (courtesy of Chapurukha Kusimba).

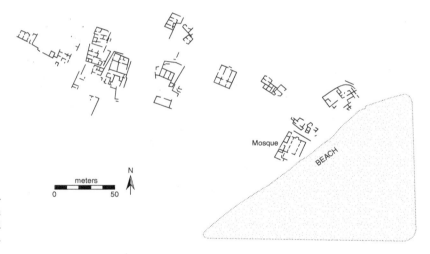

Figure 4.9 Plan of standing buildings at Jumba la Mtwana (adapted from Sassoon 1981).

both life and death. In most towns, large, sprawling palace complexes are closely associated with the central mosque, as at Gedi, Shanga, Mtwapa, and Takwa. At Songo Mnara, one of two grand domestic structures opens directly opposite the congregational mosque. Tombs and cemeteries are also directly related to these mosques, often found surrounding the northern extent of the mosque; examples include the Ijumaa cemetery at Pate, tombs clustered north of the mosque at Shanga, and walled cemeteries north of mosques at Takwa, Songo Mnara, and Chwaka (Wilson 1979a).

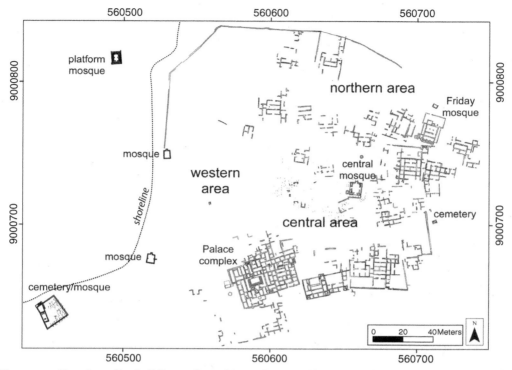

Figure 4.10 Plan of standing buildings at Songo Mnara, Tanzania (drawn by authors).

The form and distribution of domestic structures is much more highly varied. Most towns show no sign of orthogonal layout of domestic structures, although Takwa does contain a single street that bisects the settlement from north to south. Radial paths can be seen in other town plans, as at Shanga, but the quality of most town plans does not allow similar analysis. Despite a literature that suggests a normative pattern of Swahili domestic structures (Allen 1979; Donley 1982), the layout of houses is extremely variable, both within and between towns. Some towns, like Gedi, contain mostly large compound domestic structures, which were likely made up of blocks of housing units, built out over time. However, others, like Takwa, contain only one- to three-room buildings, each relatively independent. Shanga also contains mostly independent structures, yet these often have four or more rooms as well as a walled courtyard. Sites such as Mtwapa and Songo Mnara contain a combination of both individual and compound houses; Kusimba (1996:710) describes five different categories of stone houses at Mtwapa, including "single, double, triple, compound and complex houses" with compound houses containing four defined rooms, and complex with five or more rooms. These variations in house size may be one way to explore possible variations in household organization, and general changes in households through time.

LEVELS OF MEANING

The explorations of structuring principles in twentieth-century Lamu and discussions of space in more ancient Swahili settlements therefore have common themes. Both focus on the centrality of the mosque in discussing meaning in the built environment and the principles of planning that produced Swahili towns. In this, as well as in other details of the town plan, these approaches assume a relationship between social structure and physical plan. Horton has extended this to map out the social constitution of ancient Shanga through its spatial manifestation. As such, all of these studies demonstrate how high-level principles such as Islam are played out through practice and more worldly interactions. For all of the studies mentioned, these worldly interactions occur in the realm of what Rapoport (1988) has dubbed "mid-level meanings," referring to the ways that the town plan reflects the agency of elite groups within society. The category of "elite" in Swahili includes rulers of towns who were organized as ranked hierarchies (e.g., Chwaka; see LaViolette and Fleisher 2009), but also groups of wealthy merchants that formed more oligarchic town organizations. Those who shared in these more horizontally differentiated power bases were called *waung-wana* and were themselves distinct from, and hierarchically ranked over, urban newcomers and other non-freeborn members of society (LaViolette and Fleisher 2005:340). Thus, claims to historicity, grand monumental statements, and piety, might all be expressed through the built environment in different ways. Space might also be controlled and manipulated within towns, to the benefit of elite groups. Although this is not always explicitly discussed, there is an assumption that architectural and spatial control exists, giving agency to certain groups and their concerns within the Swahili towns.

These assumptions have the effect of assigning agency only to a certain portion of the population: this is actually at odds with the ethnographies that see structuring principles being played out through the agency of all inhabitants. Thus, the town layout is seen as being "planned" according to the intentions of particular, elite inhabitants. Secondly, the dominance of a particular model of Swahili urban form, linked in a circular argument with a historical model of Swahili society, means that there is little room to account for diversity. The vast majority of fourteenth- to fifteenth-century towns therefore appear "unplanned" as they do not match with this model, or elaborate arguments and chronological leaps are required to make the spaces match the supposedly universal model.

Thus, while these studies have gone a long way toward socializing our understandings of Swahili urban spaces, we suggest that it is necessary to take seriously the insights of the ethnographies with regard to structure played out through practice. As well as exploring the actions of powerful people, and the communal spaces and structures of the town, this means entwining daily practice – Rapoport's "low-level meaning" – into our explorations.

PRACTICE AND THE STONEHOUSE

The practice model has not previously been developed with regard to urban layout, although some of Wilson's (1982) ideas developed at Takwa do move in this direction. Rather, practice has been invoked during discussion of institutions within the town, most notably the Swahili stonehouse. The wholesale introduction of domestic architecture in coral and lime construction occurs with the towns of the fourteenth to fifteenth centuries, although the development of this architectural tradition is seen earlier at sites like Shanga and in the construction of mosques from the eleventh century. The stonehouse has been seen as the quintessential expression of Swahili identity (Allen 1974, 1979; Donley 1982, 1987; Donley-Reid 1990) and becomes widespread during this explosion of town building in the fourteenth century. At this time, towns also began to assume a different character as an increasing number of small community mosques supplemented the main congregational mosque, and town walls were built at some sites.

Stonehouses have therefore been studied as miniature worlds with the practices and rituals of the domestic spaces seen as key aspects of the construction of Swahili identity (Fleisher and LaViolette 2007). The importance attributed to these structures has also led to the suggestion that it was the requirements of the houses that structured the urban spaces (for a similar argument regarding Upper Mesopotamia, see Creekmore, Chapter 2 in this volume). The concomitant assumption is that the site layout had no overarching plan: Garlake (1966), who conducted the largest survey of coastal architecture to date, described the towns as having little in the way of urban planning, at least in the sense of regular streets, or an over-

STEPHANIE WYNNE-
JONES AND JEFFREY
FLEISHER

all pattern evident in the layout. He argues that this was owing to the houses:

> strong preferences for orientation [to the north or, less often, east] made the planning of towns difficult, for no house will have entrances to any street bordering its western or southern sides. Blocks of building surrounded by streets are therefore scarcely practical, and street plans are as a result irregular or, more correctly, non-existent. (Garlake 1966:89)

Yet, Garlake also laid the seeds of an important approach to the study of Swahili urban space, when he emphasized the Swahili house as the most important feature of the urban environment, defining the way that the townscape developed:

> One of the most interesting features of the town buildings is the communal approach to, and cooperation in, planning. All adjoining houses invariably share a single common party wall (there is a single exception in Songo Mnara). Moreover, in almost every case, where houses adjoin, the plans interlock rather than simply abut one another, making for compactness and economy of building. This is evidence of a far greater degree of cooperation in planning and construction than that which would be found if just one owner allowed his neighbour to build against the irregular line of his outside wall. It entailed complete cooperation and joint planning from the start, followed by simultaneous building. (Garlake 1966:89)

He (1966:90) suggests that this is most likely attributable to "a close degree of kinship, or very firm family or tribal ties," recalling Ghaidan's notion of involvement in the town plan of Lamu. This idea was developed by Allen (1979:6) who links the apparently chaotic patterning of Swahili urban spaces to the lifecycles of the houses themselves and the importance attached to spatial prescriptions over the ways the houses were used. Garlake emphasized the orientation of the houses, of which 75–80 percent face north, and cited environmental reasons, claiming that this direction favored ventilation. Allen develops instead the social aspects of the houses' design, and particularly the importance of ritual in the orientation and layout.

Allen's (1979) analysis of the Swahili stonehouse draws on a combination of ethnographic data (from Lamu) and the evidence of stonehouses in the archaeological record from the fourteenth century onward. He feels that the continuity of the stone-building tradition and similarities in form of the houses justify this extrapolation, a justification later taken up by Donley-Reid (1990). Allen's interpretation of the houses is twofold: as the settings for economic activity and as important sites for domestic ritual and self-identification. He suggests that both would have had an effect on the developing house plan, and hence the cumulative urban space. First, Allen considers the demands of finding space for family members and for the conduct of trade. Trade seems, by the fourteenth to fifteenth centuries, to have been conducted in the context of the houses and through a system of hospitality and the use of a trusted patron. Ibn Battuta's eye-witness description of fourteenth-century Mogadishu helps us understand how this might have worked:

> when a ship comes into port, it is boarded from *sanbuq*, that is to say, little boats. Each *sanbuq* carries a crowd of young men, each carrying a covered dish, containing food. Each one of them presents his dish to a merchant on board, and calls out: "This man is my guest." And his fellows do the same. Not one of the merchants disembarks except to go to the house of his host among the young men ... when a merchant has settled in his host's house, the latter sells for him what he has brought and makes his purchases for him. Buying anything from a merchant below its market price or selling him anything except in his host's presence is disapproved of by the people of Mogadishu. (Freeman-Grenville 1962:27–28)

The houses are seen to cater for this through the provision of porches for the conduct of business, and an adjoining guest room where visiting merchants might stay. At the same time, the privacy and purity of the household itself – and particularly of the women within it – would be ensured by the design of the house around an "intimacy gradient" (Ghaidan 1971), with successive rooms of increasing levels of privacy. Over time, with what appears to have been increasing proscriptions on female appearances in public life, this could have led to the development of the house blocks seen in eighteenth-century towns such as Lamu, in which women were able to move between houses without having to venture outdoors. An earlier form of this was simply the idea that family houses would exist in compound arrangements, or courtyard blocks.

Ethnographically known Swahili houses were fundamentally associated with women, who might only rarely leave the house or block in which they lived. Matrilocal marriage patterns meant that over the course of generations, houses would need to be extended and divided to cater for incoming husbands and the growing family. This fluidity of house size, and evolving architecture, necessitated against a rigid town plan and meant that inhabitants would prioritize the spaces around houses, and that house blocks or compound plans would develop organically. In addition, the interior spaces of the houses were strictly controlled by the rituals associated with marriage, birth, and death, with the family's links with, and understanding of, the spaces of the houses being renewed through these practices. In particular, this has been explored by Donley-Reid, who drew on a specific ritual in which a newborn baby is formally introduced to the interior spaces as a means of elaborating the spatiality of Swahili social structures and the ways that the house is both the medium and the expression of these.

These interpretations of the houses also rely heavily on ethnographic data from twentieth-century Lamu, and it is necessary to take into account the diversity of houses in the fourteenth to fifteenth centuries, as well as the importance of change over time that might reflect changing meanings relating to the houses (Fleisher and LaViolette 2007). Rather than simply assuming an unchanging conceptual map for the confined spaces, though, these approaches do provide an important dynamic approach to space. The emphasis on practice and ritual as linked to the lifecycle of the houses could be extended to think through the delimited exterior spaces of the urban layout on a larger scale. A focus on practice, and the lifecycle of the house through the generations of its inhabitants, offers a more flexible and useful mechanism for understanding the layout of Swahili sites, and incorporating the diversity observed among the different town plans. It also brings some of the insights of the regional studies of Swahili urbanism into the town, thinking through the ways that urbanism was created through mapping interactions, rather than simply documenting its form.

At sites such as Jumba la Mtwana on the Kenyan coast (Figure 4.9), which do not seem to conform to the centralized pattern at all, the practice-based model offers a heuristic tool that allows us an entry point into an otherwise anomalous layout. In fact, the scattered town plan of Jumba, which it has been suggested may have offered space for individual farmsteads or gardens (Sassoon 1981), could also have been a tactic within a new settlement for families building houses that they knew might need expansion over time. Such a consideration would tend to favor a dispersed site pattern. Likewise, one of the standing buildings at Jumba – the one known as the "House of the Many Doors" – offers a direct glimpse of the process of development in microcosm, as the building was adapted numerous times during its period of occupation, resulting in the many in-filled doors that give it its name. With each change, the building was further extended and subdivided – once so extensively that it seems to have been almost demolished and rebuilt at a higher level – until it ended its days as a series of "apartments," which Sassoon (1981) suggests may even have housed visiting merchants, as they appear to be small housing units.

At Songo Mnara, in Tanzania, the numerous stone houses arranged around the site without any obvious street pattern or regular plan also speak to this type of spatial structuring (Figure 4.10). The orientation of the houses is clear, and what regular patterning does exist is formed by the house blocks, which have been built up around courtyards and through houses that shared some of the partition walls. Even the town wall, which enclosed the site to the landward side, is developed in parts through the joining together of several houses: a pattern that is mirrored at other walled sites. Songo Mnara also speaks to one of the advantages of exploring Swahili urban space in this way, as the site contains a structure known as the "palace" (Garlake 1966), as well as several other huge domestic structures. Each can actually be seen as compound structures, with numerous room blocks leading onto central areas, and sharing adjoining walls. These structures are very different from the palace of Husuni Kubwa at Kilwa, which is a unique example of a planned layout associated with a particular sultan. If a correlation of space and social structure based on a single elite ruler is assumed, the "palace" at Songo Mnara must be seen as analogous, despite the presence of numerous other contenders for that title, ignoring the very real differences between it and Husuni Kubwa. Likewise, palaces have been identified at Tumbatu (Pearce 1920:402) and at Gedi (Kirkman 1963). A practice-based approach to the urban layout that instead explores these structures as built up through the functions and lifecycles of the inhabitants allows a more nuanced discussion of the differences between these sites and thus a greater understanding of the way the urban configurations would have been created.

Importantly, an approach to function, practice, and activity within the towns also allows for a consideration of the delimited spaces, built up through the positioning of the structures, but nonetheless implicated in the activities and needs of daily life. Delimited spaces within Swahili towns commonly include areas within and against town walls, courtyards, areas surrounding central congregational mosques, especially near entrances and' outside the north-facing *mihrab* or prayer niche, central open spaces delimited by domestic architecture, and less frequently by streets and alleys. Although few archaeologists have developed methodologies adequate to investigate these spaces, most support Wilson (1982:207), who argues that open spaces in Swahili towns "played an important part in the social, political and economic life of the community." Suggestions as to the use of these spaces, which are present in most Swahili towns, include: open-air meeting places (Garlake 2002:181), market areas, protected space for future town growth (Kusimba 1993:122; 1996:711), gardens and/or orchards (Garlake 2002; Kusimba 1993; see also Stark, Chapter 11 in this volume, for Mesoamerican examples); areas of impermanent architecture, and areas of industrial production (Garlake 2002; Gensheimer 1997:328–339; Kusimba 1993:122). Historic and ethnographic data support some of these hypotheses: Early sixteenth-century Portuguese accounts indicate that the sultan of Kilwa was crowned in an open space adjacent to the palace, while specially designated open spaces in Comorian cities, called *fumboni*, were contexts for social gatherings, weddings, feasts, and game playing (Gensheimer 1997:334). Archaeologists have also explored certain aspects of these spaces; on Pemba Island, Tanzania (Fleisher and LaViolette 1999; LaViolette and Fleisher 2009) and Gedi, Kenya (Koplin and LaViolette 2008), excavations have demonstrated that some "open areas" were actually dense with earth-and-thatch houses; at Shanga in Kenya, evidence of possible trade kiosks has been located in the central open space of the town (Horton 1996).

CITIES AS PROCESSES, NOT PRODUCTS

We suggest that a practice-based model is an important route to understanding Swahili urban spaces. It does not deny or replace the models derived from Shanga's plan, but instead attempts to take into account the historicity of Swahili sites, and the ways that urban spaces can be built up through daily practice and through the lifecycles of the inhabitants and their social spaces. Approaching the site plans through the buildings that make them up can also provide insights into the ways that sites can develop, even at those places where there does seem to have been some element of regularized patterning, such as Takwa (Horton and Middleton 2000; Smith 2007; Wilson 1982). As Allen (1979:8) puts it: "[A]s settlements developed in size and complexity, the need for a town plan became more pressing, and the owners of interlocking stone houses had to take this into account." Although we might question whether the "need" for a town plan develops with size, this quotation does illustrate the notion that a plan is built up from the houses, rather than imposed on them.

What is compelling about the notion of town planning through delimited space and through practices that were intertwined with architecture is that it allows us to start thinking beyond the interior spaces or monumental architecture. The delimited space of the site, which – although external – is defined through the built structures, could include those communal spaces and structures that are created through their placement. In particular, many Swahili sites seem often to have contained open areas commonly associated with the mosque area. At Mtwapa, Kusimba (1996) suggests several uses for the open areas near the mosque, assuming that elite members of society deliberately created and controlled them. He suggests that open areas were reserved for future expansion, causing less powerful residents to have to build outside the town walls. Similarly, at Takwa, Wilson explains the open spaces just inside the town wall gates as possible storage areas for market produce. Both of these explanations rely on the notion of centralized planning and elite control of open space. As Horton cogently argues, open spaces surrounding the mosque assumed important roles. However, rather than seeing such spaces as atomistic parts of an idealized Swahili town plan, a practice-based approach to open spaces might explore them as the spatial effects of house development, which may themselves have structured the patterning of buildings, and as spaces that came to have meaning through their use rather than by design (M.L. Smith 2008). Thus, for example, Horton assumed that a central open space was part of Shanga's plan from the start, a protected space with ritual structures; yet, there is little consideration that this space may have become important through the process of building a mosque, as well as other flanking domestic structures nearby. In this alternative, rather than seeking out town plans from twentieth-century Mijikenda *kayas* or Swahili towns, we might rather examine the architectural development of the town, and the changing use of delimited spaces. At Shanga, we can ask questions about why the central space, imbued with such importance, was encroached upon in later centuries, such that by the settlement's abandonment the central space ceased to exist. A narrow focus on architecture and street layout does not give us the tools to approach such questions or to view the towns as products of the activities conducted within them. We therefore feel that the approach pioneered by Allen for the Swahili house, which has already been extremely influential in the ways that we have viewed stonehouses, can be usefully extended to the entire urban environment and give us the tools to better understand Swahili urban space.

We have begun that work at the fifteenth- to sixteenth-century site of Songo Mnara, on the southern Tanzanian coast (Fleisher and Wynne-Jones 2010). There, a central open space seems to be a constant part of the town plan, albeit for a short period of occupation. However, even this open space emerges through practices that delimited it, and seems to be anchored more closely to houses in the southern part of the site rather than those in the north. Although we are only beginning to tease apart the developmental history of open spaces at Songo Mnara, the central space there provides a crucial place to examine the interplay between high/middle and low-level meanings. As yet, it is unclear whether this area was structured around the building of a small central mosque and cemetery or if it was the delimited result of domestic structures to the south, east, and north. In either case, the space itself evidently became the place of a set of practices related to burial and memorialization. These ongoing acts of commemoration were crucial to the way that the area was preserved and maintained, a striking contrast to the open space at Shanga. In the case of Songo Mnara, then, we need not envision that the town was built with a predetermined idea of a memorial, open space. Through the construction of houses, their expansion, as well as the placement of a mosque and burials associated with it, the "open space" at Songo Mnara, may have emerged through a history of only loosely interlinked practices. This does not, in any way, take away from the prominence and importance that this space assumed in the daily life of the town.

What we argue is that the acts of powerful people and places need not have been predetermined; the emergence of a town plan does not need to be the result of elites directing the construction and maintenance of town buildings and spaces. The generational power of elite people at Swahili sites relied not so much on structuring a town around the high-level meanings of Islam, purity, and pedigree, but rather their ability to imbue places and spaces with meaning that emerged through the developmental life of the town. The construction of tombs in the central open space, and the conduct of memorial practices at these sites is one example of how this might have been manifest. In this way, high-level meaning was easily located in the form and development of urban town plans, as el-Zein demonstrates. However, we need to be careful not to substitute elite ideological notions of town plans, ones that were probably part of their ongoing power and authority within towns, for an historical model of how towns actually grew into various forms. Although we cannot lose sight of high- and middle-level meanings that contributed to the structuring of Swahili towns, we would be foolish to assume that these alone were the determinants of town plans. There is no doubt that structural power was a contributing factor in the organization of Swahili towns, but as we learn from the regional study of Swahili towns and the emergence of the Swahili house, the practices of people are foundational in understanding how they emerge.

ACKNOWLEDGMENTS

This chapter was written while we were formulating our research project at Songo Mnara and we thank the editors for the opportunity to present an early version of it at the Society for American Archaeology (SAA) annual meeting in Atlanta in 2009. Wynne-Jones's participation in that meeting was funded by a British Academy Conference Grant. We are now pursuing many of the topics discussed here in our current project, the Songo Mnara Urban Landscape Project, which is funded by the National Science Foundation (USA, BCS 1123091) and the Arts and Humanities Research Council (UK, AH/J502716/1). Thank you also to Chapurukha Kusimba, Mark Horton, the National Museums of Kenya, and the British Institute in Eastern Africa for allowing us to adapt and use plans from other Swahili sites.

Abu-Lughod, Janet L. 1987 The Islamic City – Historic Myth, Islamic Essence, and Contemporary Relevance. *International Journal of Middle East Studies* 19(2):155–176.

Abungu, George H. O. 1989 Communities on the River Tana, Kenya: An Archaeological Study of Relations between the Delta and the River Basin AD 700–1890. Unpublished Ph.D. dissertation, Department of Archaeology, University of Cambridge, Cambridge.

1998 City-States of the East African Coast and their Maritime Contacts. In *Transformations in Africa: Essays on Africa's Later Past*, edited by Graham Connah, pp. 204–218. Leicester University Press, London.

Abungu, George H. O. and Henry W. Muturo 1993 Coast-Interior Settlements and Social Relations in the Kenya Hinterland. In *The Archaeology of Africa: Food, Metals and Towns*, edited by Thurstan Shaw, Paul J. J. Sinclair, Bassey Andah, and Alex Okpoko, pp. 694–704. Routledge, London.

Allen, James de Vere 1974 Swahili Architecture in the Later Middle Ages. *African Arts* 7(2):42–84.

1979 The Swahili House: Cultural and Ritual Concepts Underlying its Plan and Structure. In *Swahili Houses and Tombs of the Coast of Kenya*, edited by James de Vere Allen and Thomas H. Wilson, pp. 1–32. Art and Archaeology Research Papers, London.

1981 Swahili Culture and the Nature of East Coast Settlement. *International Journal of African Historical Studies* 14(2):306–334.

Al-Sayyad, Nezar 1991 *Cities and Caliphs: On the Genesis of Arab Muslim Urbanism*. Greenwood Press, New York.

Chami, Felix 1988 A Coastal EIA Site in Kisarawe District. *Nyame Akuma* 30:34–35.

1992 Current Archaeological Research in Bagamoyo District, Tanzania. In *Urban Origins in East Africa, Proceedings of the 1991 Workshop in Zanzibar*, edited by Paul Sinclair and Abdurahman Juma, pp. 16–34. The Swedish Central Board of National Antiquities, Stockholm.

1994 *The Tanzanian Coast in the Early First Millennium AD: An Archaeology of the Iron-Working, Farming Communities*. Studies in African Archaeology 7. Societas Archaeologica Uppsaliensis, Uppsala, Sweden.

1999 The Early Iron Age on Mafia Island and its Relationship with the Mainland. *Azania* 34:1–10.

2001 The Archaeology of the Rufiji Region since 1987 to 2000: Coastal and Interior Dynamics from AD 00–500. In *People, Contacts and the Environment in the African Past*, edited by Felix Chami, Gilbert Pwiti, and Chantal Radimilahy, pp. 7–20. Studies in the African Past. Vol. 1. Dar es Salaam University Press, Dar es Salaam, Tanzania.

Chittick, H. Neville 1974 *Kilwa: An Islamic Trading City on the East African Coast*. British Institute in Eastern Africa, Nairobi, Kenya.

Donley, Linda W. 1982 House Power: Swahili Space and Symbolic Markers. In *Symbolic and Structural Archaeology*, edited by Ian Hodder, pp. 63–73. Cambridge University Press, Cambridge.

1987 Life in the Swahili Town House Reveals the Symbolic Meaning of Spaces and Artefact Assemblages. *African Archaeological Review* 5:181–192.

Donley-Reid, Linda 1990 A Structuring Structure: The Swahili House. In *Domestic Architecture and the Use of Space*, edited by Susan Kent, pp. 114–126. Cambridge University Press, Cambridge.

el-Zein, Abdul Hamid M. 1974 *The Sacred Meadows: A Structural Analysis of Religious Symbolism in an East African Town*. Northwestern University Press, Chicago.

Fawcett, William B. and Adria LaViolette 1990 Iron Age Settlement around Mkiu, South-Eastern Tanzania. *Azania* 25:19–25.

Fleisher, Jeffrey B. 2003 Viewing Stonetowns from the Countryside: An Archaeological Approach to Swahili Regional Systems, AD 800–1500. Unpublished Ph.D. dissertation, Department of Anthropology, University of Virginia, Charlottesville.

2010 Swahili Synoecism: Rural Settlements and Town Formation on the Central East African Coast, AD 750–1500. *Journal of Field Archaeology* 35:265–282.

Fleisher, Jeffrey B. and Adria LaViolette 1999 Elusive Wattle-and-Daub: Finding the Hidden Majority in the Archaeology of the Swahili. *Azania* 34:87–108.

Fleisher, Jeffrey B. 2007 The Changing Power of Swahili Houses, Fourteenth to Nineteenth Centuries AD. In *The Durable House: House Society Models in Archaeology*, edited by Robin A. Beck, pp. 175–197. Occasional Papers, Center for Archaeological Investigations, Southern Illinois University, Carbondale.

Fleisher, Jeffrey B. and Stepahnie Wynne-Jones 2010 *Archaeological Investigations at Songo Mnara, Tanzania: Urban Space, Social Memory and Materiality on the 15th- and 16th-century Southern Swahili Coast*. Submitted to Antiquities Division, Tanzania, Dar es Salaam. Copies available at <www.songomnara.rice.edu/results.htm>.

Freeman-Grenville, Greville S. P. 1962 *The East African Coast. Select Documents from the First to the Earlier Nineteenth Centuries*. Clarendon Press, London.

Garlake, Peter S. 1966 *The Early Islamic Architecture of the East African Coast*. Oxford University Press, London.

2002 *Early Art and Architecture of Africa*. Oxford University Press, Oxford.

Gensheimer, Thomas R. 1997 At the Boundaries of the Dar-al-Islam: Cities of the East African Coast in the Late Middle Ages. Unpublished Ph.D. dissertation, Department of Architecture, University of California, Berkeley.

Ghaidan, Usam. 1971 African Heritage: The Stone Houses of Lamu. *Journal of the Architectural Association of Kenya*, May–June: 23–28.

1975 *Lamu: A Study of the Swahili Town*. East African Literature Bureau, Dar es Salaam, Tanzania.

Helm, Richard 2000 Conflicting Histories: The Archaeology of Iron-Working, Farming Communities in the Central and Southern Coast Region of Kenya. Unpublished Ph.D. dissertation, Department of Archaeology and Anthropology, University of Bristol, Bristol, UK.

Horton, Mark C. 1986 Asiatic Colonization of the East African Coast: The Manda Evidence. *Journal of the Royal Asiatic Society* 2:201–213.

1994 Swahili Architecture, Space and Social Structure. In *Architecture and Order*, edited by Michael Parker-Pearson and Colin Richards, pp. 147–169. Routledge, London.

1996 *Shanga: The Archaeology of a Muslim Trading Community on the Coast of East Africa*. British Institute in Eastern Africa, Nairobi, Kenya.

Horton, Mark C. and John Middleton 2000 *The Swahili: The Social Landscape of a Mercantile Society*. Blackwell, Oxford.

Kirkman, James S. 1963 *Gedi: The Palace*. Mouton, The Hague, The Netherlands.

Koplin, Lynn and Adria LaViolette 2008 Archaeology of Swahili Social Differentiation: Excavation of Earth-and-Thatch Neighborhoods at Gede, Kenya, 11th–16th Centuries AD. Manuscript on file, Anthropology Department, University of Virgina, Charlottesville.

Kusimba, Chapurukha M. 1993 The Archaeology and Ethnography of Iron Metallurgy on the Kenya Coast. Unpublished Ph.D. dissertation, Bryn Mawr College, Bryn Mawr, PA.

1996 Spatial Organization at Swahili Archaeological Sites in Kenya. In *Aspects of African Archaeology: Papers of the 10th Conference of the Pan African Association of Prehistory and Related Subjects*, edited by Gilbert Pwiti and Robert Soper, pp. 703–714. University of Zimbabwe, Harare.

1999 *The Rise and Fall of Swahili States*. Altamira Press, Walnut Creek, CA.

2008 Early African Cities: Their Role in the Shaping of Urban and Rural Interaction Spheres. In *The Ancient City: New Perspectives on Urbanism in the Old and New World*, edited by Joyce Marcus and Jeremy Sabloff, pp. 229–246. SAR Press, Santa Fe, NM.

Lapidus, Ira M. 1969 Muslim Cities and Islamic Societies. In *Middle Eastern Cities: A Symposium on Ancient, Islamic, and Contemporary Middle Eastern Urbanism*, edited by Ira M. Lapidus, pp. 47–79. University of California Press, Berkeley.

LaViolette, Adria 2008 Swahili Cosmopolitanism in Africa and the Indian Ocean World, AD 600–1500. *Archaeologies: Journal of the World Archaeological Congress* 1:24–49.

LaViolette, Adria and Jeffrey B. Fleisher 2005 The Archaeology of Sub-Saharan Urbanism: Cities and their Countrysides. In *African Archaeology: A Critical Introduction*, edited by Ann Stahl, pp. 327–352. Blackwell Publishing, Oxford.

2009 The Urban History of a Rural Place: Swahili Archaeology on Pemba Island, Tanzania, 700–1500 AD. *International Journal of African Historical Studies* 42(3):433–455.

LaViolette, Adria, William B. Fawcett, and Peter R. Schmidt 1989 The Coast and the Hinterland: University of Dar es Salaam Archaeological Field Schools, 1987–88. *Nyame Akuma* 32:38–46.

McIntosh, Susan K. 1997 Urbanism in Sub-Saharan Africa. In *Encyclopedia of Precolonial Africa*, edited by Joseph O. Vogel, pp. 461–465. Altamira Press, Walnut Creek, CA.

McIntosh, Susan K. and Roderick J. McIntosh 1993 Cities without Citadels: Understanding Urban Origins along the Middle Niger. In *The Archaeology of Africa: Food, Metals and Towns*, edited by Thurstan Shaw, Paul J. J.

Sinclair, Bassey Andah, and Alex Okpoko, pp. 622–641. Routledge, London.

Middleton, John, 1992. *The World of the Swahili: An African Mercantile Civilization*, Yale University Press, New Haven, CT.

Pearce, Francis B. 1920 *Zanzibar: The Island Metropolis of Eastern Africa*. Unwin, London.

Pikirayi, Innocent 2001 *The Zimbabwe Culture: Origins and Decline of Southern Zambezian States*. Altamira Press, Walnut Creek, CA.

Pradines, Stephane 2004 *Fortifications et Urbanisation en Afrique Orientale*. Cambridge Monographs in African Archaeology. British Archaeological Reports, International Series 1216, Oxford.

Prins, Adriaan H. J. 1971 *Didemic Lamu, Social Stratification and Spatial Structure in a Muslim Maritime Town*. Instituut voor Culturele Antropologie der Rijkuniversiteit, Groningen, The Netherlands.

Rapoport, Amos 1988 Levels of Meaning in the Built Environment. In *Cross-cultural Perspectives in Nonverbal Communication*, edited by F. Poyatos, pp. 317–336. C.F. Hogrefe, Toronto.

Sassoon, Hamo 1981 *Jumba la Mtwana Guide*. Kenya Museum Society and the Friends of Fort Jesus, Mombasa.

Schmidt, Peter R., N. Jonathan Karoma, Adria LaViolette, William B. Fawcett, Audax Z. Mabulla, L. N. Rutabanzibwa, and Charles M. Saanane 1992 *Archaeological Investigations in the Vicinity of Mkiu, Kisarawe District, Tanzania*. Occasional Paper 1. University Press, Dar es Salaam, Tanzania.

Sinclair, Paul 1987 *Space, Time and Social Formation: A Territorial Approach to the Archaeology and Anthropology of Zimbabwe and Mozambique c. 0–1700 AD*. Societas Archaeologica Upsaliensis, Uppsala, Sweden.

Sinclair, Paul and Thomas Håkansson 2000 The Swahili City-State Culture. In *A Comparative Study of Thirty City-State Cultures*, edited by Mogens H. Hansen, pp. 463–482. Royal Danish Academy of Sciences and Letters, Copenhagen.

Smith, Adam T. 2003 *The Political Landscape: Constellations of Authority in Early Complex Polities*. University of California Press, Berkeley, CA.

Smith, Michael E. 2007 Form and Meaning in the Earliest Cities: A New Approach to Ancient Urban Planning. *Journal of Planning History* 6(1):3–43.

2011 Empirical Urban Theory for Archaeologists. *Journal of Archaeological Method and Theory* 18: 167–192.

Smith, Monica L. (editor) 2003 *The Social Construction of Ancient Cities*. Smithsonian Institution Press, Washington, DC.

2008 Urban Empty Spaces. Contentious Places for Consensus-Building. *Archaeological Dialogues* 15(2):216–231.

Wheatley, Paul 2001 *The Places Where Men Pray Together: Cities in Islamic Lands, Seventh through Tenth Centuries*. University of Chicago Press, Chicago.

Wilson, Thomas H. 1979a Swahili Funerary Architecture of the North Kenya Coast. In *Swahili Houses and Tombs of the Coast of Kenya*, edited by James de Vere Allen and Thomas H. Wilson, pp. 33–46. Art and Archaeology Research Papers, London.

1979b Takwa: An Ancient Swahili Settlement of the Lamu Archipelago. *Kenya Past and Present* 10:6–16.

1982 Spatial Analysis and Settlement Patterns on the East African Coast. *Paideuma* 28:201–219.

Wilson, Thomas H. and Athman L. Omar 1997 Archaeological Investigations at Pate. *Azania*, 32: 31–76.

Wright, Henry T. 1993 Trade and Politics on the Eastern Littoral of Africa, AD 800–1300. In *The Archaeology of Africa: Food, Metals and Towns*, edited by Thurstan Shaw, Paul J. J. Sinclair, Bassey Andah, and Alex Okpoko, pp. 658–670. Routledge, London.

Wynne-Jones, Stephanie 2007a Creating Urban Communities at Kilwa Kisiwani, Tanzania, AD 800–1300. *Antiquity* 81:368–380.

2007b Multiple Landscapes and Layered Meanings: Scale, Interaction and Process in the Development of a Swahili Town. In *Socialising Complexity: Approaches to Power and Interaction in the Archaeological Record*, edited by Sheila E. Kohring and Stephanie Wynne-Jones, pp. 142–160. Oxbow Press, London.

2007c It's What You Do with It that Counts: Performed Identities in the East African Coastal Landscape. *Journal of Social Archaeology* 7(3):325–345.

5

The Production of Space and Identity at Classic-Period Chunchucmil, Yucatán, Mexico

Aline Magnoni, Traci Ardren, Scott R. Hutson, and Bruce Dahlin

While some researchers have questioned the degree of lowland Maya urbanism, this chapter demonstrates that Chunchucmil was a major urban center, with a population of 30,000–40,000 people and the highest settlement density of any site in the Maya lowlands. Located along a vigorous maritime trade route, it developed as a city in the late Early Classic (AD 400–650) with a complex infrastructure and market economy to accommodate its residents and the influx of rural and foreign visitors. This paper looks at the production and construction of urban spaces by Chunchucmil's residents and how lived experience helped to create a distinctive built environment.

In vain, great-hearted Kublai, shall I attempt to describe Zaira, city of high bastions. I could tell you how many steps make up the streets rising like stairways, and the degree or the arcades' curves, and what kind of zinc scales cover the roofs; but I already know this would be the same as telling you nothing. The city does not consist of this, but of relationships between the measurement of its space and the events of its past .... As this wave from memories flows in, the city soaks it up like a sponge and expands. A description of Zaira as it is today should contain all of Zaira's past. The city, however, does not tell its past, but contains it like the lines of a hand, written in the corner of streets, the gratings of windows, the banisters of the steps, the antennae of the lightning rods, the poles of the flags, every segment marked in turn with scratches, indentations, scrolls.

Italo Calvino, *Invisible Cities* (1974 [1972]:10)

In this chapter we reconstruct the experience of urbanism in ancient Chunchucmil, a large Classic Maya urban trading center in northwest

A. MAGNONI,
T. ARDREN,
S. R. HUTSON, AND
B. DAHLIN

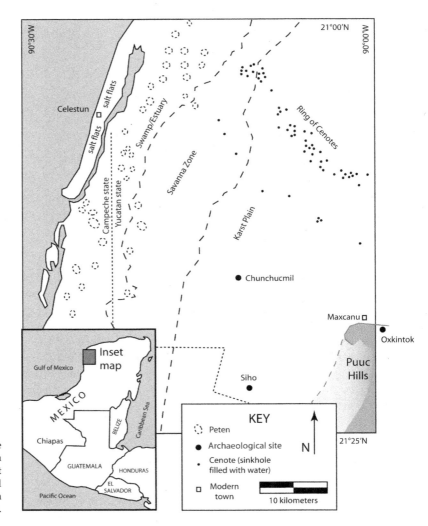

Figure 5.1 Map of the Chunchucmil region showing the different ecological areas and map of the Maya region (drawn by authors).

Yucatán (Figure 5.1). First, we define the material characteristics of urbanism at Chunchucmil and then we focus on the social experience of living in a distinctive Maya urban center. Just like the explorer Marco Polo in Italo Calvino's novel (1974 [1972]), *Invisible Cities* describes to the emperor Kublai Khan a myriad of fantastic cities with a multiplicity of forms and inhabitants – each unique and distinct in its own way and each being the result of the relations between peoples and their places; we also attempt to show that Chunchucmil is substantially different from other Classic-period cities in the Maya region. In addition, in agreement with what Marco Polo says about the city of Zaira, we understand that the description of a city's material characteristics and its spatial measurements is limited unless we recognize that peoples' actions, memories, stories, and lives have been engraved in and have shaped the materiality of the urban landscape.

There is no agreement on the criteria used in the definition of ancient or modern cities (Marcus and Sabloff 2008; Smith 2003). Even today criteria for defining modern cities, mostly based on population size, vary from country to country. For the definition of preindustrial cities, population size and density, aerial extent of the site, and presence of specialization are some of the major criteria used by most researchers (e.g., Sanders and Webster 1988). Other scholars have chosen to define cities as central places that fulfill political, economic, religious, and sociocultural functions to their hinterland, regardless of their population size (e.g., Blanton 1976, 1981; Hardoy 1999[1962]; Marcus 1983). In Mesoamerica, there has been much debate and speculation about the level of cultural complexity and the degree of urbanism reached by ancient Maya centers (Chase and Chase 1996; Ciudad Ruiz et al. 2001 Demarest 1992; Folan 1989; Fox et al. 1996; Haviland 1970; Kurjack 1999; Marcus 1983, 1993; Martin and Grube 1995; Sanders and Webster 1988; Webster 1997; Webster and Sanders 2001; and articles in Trejo 1998). Contrasts between the Central Mexican highland centers and the sites of the Eastern Mesoamerican lowlands have been emphasized, often to suggest that Maya centers were not truly urban (Sanders and Webster 1988; Webster and Sanders 2001). Maya sites have been characterized as having a dispersed settlement (Bullard 1960; Drennan 1988; Freidel 1981). This lack of compact nucleation has often been used to argue against the urban nature of these centers. Researchers agree that the dispersed settlement of Maya sites is the result of the incorporation of the rural into the urban by retaining field space that was intensively cultivated (Becker 2001; Chase and Chase 1998; Chase et al. 2001; Cobos 2001; Drennan 1988; Dunning 1992; Killion et al. 1989; cf. Stark, Chapter 11 in this volume).

Many Mayanists prefer to use a functional definition of urbanism based on the sociopolitical functions of sites rather than their demographic characteristics because population size and density of Maya sites was much smaller than that of most Old World cities or Central Mexican cities. The application of Richard Fox's (1977) typology of preindustrial cities to Mesoamerica confines all Mesoamerican centers into two major categories: regal-ritual cities or administrative cities (Sanders and Webster 1988). This is misleading because it fails to capture the diversity of urban forms, and thus reduces the variability of Mesoamerican cities (Chase et al. 1990; Cowgill 2004; Smith 1989). According to this typology, most Mesoamerican centers and all Maya sites are considered regal-ritual centers, whereas only a few administrative cities existed in the Basin of Mexico (Sanders and Webster 1988; Webster 1997; Webster and Sanders 2001). Although Fox's typology was useful in the 1980s for understanding the close ties between ritual theater and nascent urbanism within the Maya area, the strict dichotomy of two separate categories of city has not held up over time. Evidence for large-scale specialized craft production and administration has now been documented at many royal Maya cities (Moholy-Nagy 1997) while small hamlets with little architectural complexity have yielded noble burials (Hageman 2004). A new model of Maya urbanism that accounts for the multiplicity of urban forms is needed. In this chapter, we provide a detailed account of a distinctively large trading city in the Maya area. The data discussed here form a basis for further comparative examination in order to build a more complex and nuanced model of Maya urbanism.

CHUNCHUCMIL AS AN ANCIENT MAYA URBAN CENTER

Here we argue that Chunchucmil, in the northern Maya lowlands, was a demographically large urban center that functioned as a central place for the surrounding region during the middle of the Classic period ca. AD 400–600 (Ardren et al. 2003; Dahlin 2003; Hutson et al. 2008; Magnoni et al. 2012). Chunchucmil fulfills both the demographic pattern and the variety of functions performed by regional central places, characteristics required by most definitions of urbanism. According to the *Archaeological Atlas of Yucatán* compiled in the 1970s, Chunchucmil was the only Rank II, or town-sized, site in the immediate region, surrounded by forty Rank IV sites, which were hamlet size (Garza Tarazona and Kurjack 1980). In the Classic period, there were only four Rank I sites in Yucatán: Chichén Itzá, Izamal, Uxmal, and T'ho (now under the city of Merida), which were characterized by large settlements and substantial monumental architecture at their site centers. Chunchucmil was one of fourteen Rank II sites, while there were more than a thousand Rank III, IV, and V sites recorded in western Yuctán. The main reason Chunchucmil is not considered a Rank I site is the lack of large

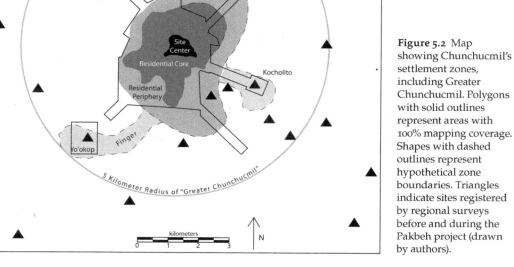

Figure 5.2 Map showing Chunchucmil's settlement zones, including Greater Chunchucmil. Polygons with solid outlines represent areas with 100% mapping coverage. Shapes with dashed outlines represent hypothetical zone boundaries. Triangles indicate sites registered by regional surveys before and during the Pakbeh project (drawn by authors).

monumental architecture at its site center; the extensive and dense settlement is otherwise comparable to Rank I sites.

From 1993–2006, the Pakbeh Regional Economy Project (PREP) mapped a contiguous area of 9.4 km² and five transects to estimate the site limits (extending the map coverage to 11.7 km²) (Figure 5.2). These transects together with aerial photographs and satellite imagery allowed us to define the limits of urban Chunchucmil to an area of 20–25 km² (Hutson et al. 2008). Regional surveys conducted by PREP members David Hixson and Daniel Mazeau to the west, north, and east of the site documented several previously unrecorded hamlet-size sites, but have confirmed that Chunchucmil was the only Rank II site in the region (Hutson et al. 2008). Because of its size, and the lack of any competing site in the surrounding region, Chunchucmil must have provided all urban functions for its hinterland. In Chunchucmil, the dense residential core (ca. 8.5 km²) has 950 structures/km² and the surrounding residential periphery (ca. 17 km²) has 350 structures/km², whereas beyond the city boundaries in the rural hinterland, structural density drops to 39–64 structures/

A. MAGNONI,
T. ARDREN,
S. R. HUTSON, AND
B. DAHLIN

Figure 5.3 Map of Chunchucmil (9.4 km²). The lines indicate the boundary walls (*albarradas*) that enclose residential groups and demarcate winding streets, whereas the solid black features are structures (drawn by authors).

km² (Hutson et al. 2008) (Figure 5.2). Hamlets within a 5 km radius showed strong economic and social ties with the city of Chunchucmil through the participation in economic exchange (visible from obsidian distribution) and the use of boundary walls to emulate the urban layout. Because such connections were absent from sites outside of the 5 km radius, we defined the 64 km² area (enclosed by the 5 km radius) as Greater Chunchucmil to emphasize the strong economic and social ties between the urban center and its hinterland (Hutson et al. 2008) (Figure 5.2).

In a separate publication, Magnoni (2007) has shown that Chunchucmil was the most densely settled Classic-period site in the Maya area with 31,000–43,000 people residing in the 20–25 km^2 urban area during the middle of the Classic period (AD 400–600) (Figures 5.2 and 5.3). At Chunchucmil, like other Maya sites, space was retained around residences to conduct a variety of domestic activities (including crafts and gardening), yet structural density was the highest known for a Classic period Maya site. Because residences are generally used to estimate past population in this region, this high structural density (8,213 residential structures in 25 km^2 or an average of 329 residential structures per km^2) implies a high population density.[1] To put these results in perspective, we can weigh them against population estimates for Tikal, considered to be the largest Maya site. If we compare Chunchucmil's population estimates to Tikal's highest population estimates (Culbert et al. 1990), we can see that the total population estimated for Tikal – 62,000 people – is considerably larger than Chunchucmil's figure of 31,000–43,000. Tikal residents, however, were spread out over an area of 120 km^2, while urban Chunchucmil covered only 20–25 km^2. More specifically, if we compare the central 9 km^2 of these sites, central Chunchucmil had three times (24,000 persons) the population of central Tikal (8,300 persons). Only the central core of Late Classic Copán had a higher density of structures and population (5,797–9,464 people/km^2) than the one estimated for Chunchucmil, but it covered a restricted area of 0.6 km^2 (Webster and Freter 1990). The whole Copán valley (500 km^2) at its peak of occupation in the Late Classic period is estimated to have been home to only 18,000–25,000 people (Webster and Freter 1990).

One of the research questions PREP tried to answer is what attracted so many people to settle in such an agriculturally marginal region. Chunchucmil is located in the northwest corner of the Yucatán peninsula, the driest portion of the entire Maya area. Besides having low rainfall, this region has shallow and sparse soils, a high evapotranspiration rate (i.e., the rate at which water evaporates before infiltrating the ground), and bedrock covers a third of the landscape (Beach 1998; Dahlin et al. 2005; Sweetwood et al. 2009; Vlcek et al. 1978) (Figure 5.1). All these characteristics severely limit the region's agricultural potential (Dahlin et al. 2005). Palaeoclimatic studies indicate that conditions were similar in the past, particularly during the middle of the Classic period (Curtis et al. 1996; Hodell et al. 1995; Leyden et al. 1996; Whitmore et al. 1996). PREP has proposed that Chunchucmil's emergence as a densely populated urban place in such an agriculturally marginal area was the result of its strategic location with respect to the exploitation of coastal and savannah resources (especially salt), redistribution of goods to the interior, and the provisioning of maritime and overland traders (Ardren et al. 2003; Dahlin 2003; Dahlin et al. 1998; Dahlin and Ardren 2002; Hutson et al. 2010). Chunchucmil was located as far west toward the Gulf of Mexico as possible on the last cultivable soils at the edge of a seasonally inundated savannah. This strategic location provided access to the rich resources of the savannah and positioned Chunchucmil to dominate coastal-inland trade as well as most urban functions for the surrounding region.

THE BUILT ENVIRONMENT OF THE CITY OF CHUNCHUCMIL

The settlement layout and architectural design of Chunchucmil suggest that it was not a typical regal-ritual city (Fox 1977; Sanders and Webster 1988), but an urban center that relied on commerce for its livelihood. Maya sites are characterized by having large acropoli and a concentration of monumental architecture in their site centers, which represent the focus of divine rulership and power. These buildings required substantial resources to construct and such resources were only available within the ruling class. In addition, at many Maya centers, carved stelae portrayed rulers and recorded their historical actions, such as accession to the throne, victory or defeat in battles, and capture of prisoners from an enemy site. Chunchucmil lacks such a concentration of elaborate monumental architecture and no carved monuments have been discovered to date. Instead, Chunchucmil has several architectural complexes of similar size and shape dispersed over the central 1 km² (Figure 5.4). These architectural complexes – quadrangles – consist of a relatively large, quadrangular patio with low-range structures on three sides, a monumental pyramid on the fourth side, and a low freestanding platform in the center of the patio. With the exception of a handful of isolated examples found in sites a few dozen km to the east of Chunchucmil, other Maya centers lack quadrangles. We have mapped fifteen of these quadrangles, eleven of which are in

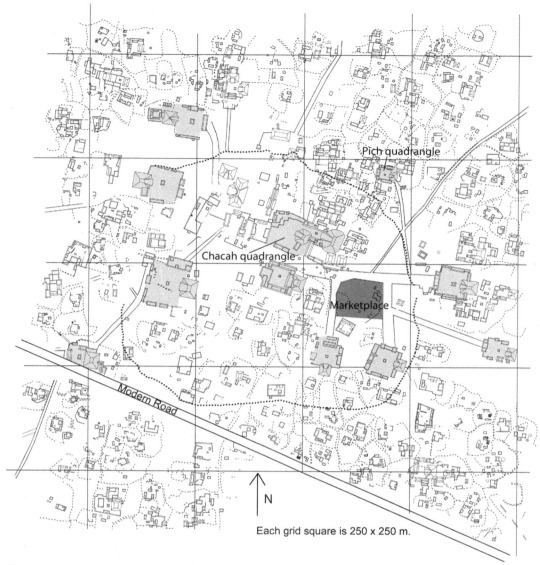

Each grid square is 250 x 250 m.

Figure 5.4 Map of central Chunchucmil showing eleven quadrangles (marked in gray) and connecting *sacbes* (drawn by authors).

the site center and mostly connected by *sacbes* – raised processional avenues – whereas four quadrangles are located at varying distances of 800 m to 2 km from the site center.

Given the absence of other ritual or elite residential architecture, each quadrangle may have been the ceremonial and administrative focus of a certain segment of the population. Because of the limited size of the patio (640–7,700 m^2 of enclosed area, with an average area of 2,760 m^2) of each quadrangle, only portions of the Chunchucmil population and of visiting traders could have participated in the ceremonies and rituals conducted within these architectural complexes (Magnoni et al. 2008). The groups with larger patio areas (1,765–7,000 m²), which also had a higher volume of architecture, were concentrated in the site center, while those at a distance from the site center had smaller patios (640–1,700 m²) and a smaller volume of architecture. These differences in scale, in addition to the lack of more traditional forms of Maya royal architecture, suggest to us that the quadrangles were the key locations of political and economic power at Chunchucmil. Long range structures surrounding a central patio with restricted access and an adjacent pyramid temple could have provided a relatively private environment for the trade and exchange of goods that fueled the economy of Chunchucmil.

Excavations at the smallest of these central quadrangles, the Pich Quadrangle, carried out by Traci Ardren, revealed that the flanking structures faced into the patio of the quadrangle: a pyramid framed the east side of the patio and flanking staircases were identified on the range structures of at least two other sides of the patio (Figure 5.5). This architectural configuration, while limiting access to the interior patio area, put emphasis on this patio as a performative space for ceremonies and rituals. The small central platform facing the pyramid could have been an important staging area. The internal patio, thus, could have been an area for the resident elite to receive tribute payments, as suggested by Ringle and Bey (2001) based on ethnohistoric literature, or as a place from which to conduct trading negotiations and bestow exotic gifts. In addition to the structures arranged along the sides of the patio, in a few cases, clusters of elite domestic structures were also attached to the side of the central patio of some quadrangles. These attached residential structures seem to have served as elite living areas, based on the scale of living space, quality of stonework including vaulted architecture, and their proximity to the Pich group pyramidal structure. This cluster may have replaced the more typical palace compound found at other Maya sites. We believe this architectural difference indicates a conceptual difference as well, and that the many quadrangles of Chunchucmil represent multiple elite house societies, or social groups, which each held significant economic, political, and social power at the site.

One of the quadrangles, the centrally located Chacah quadrangle, has several distinctive features that set it apart from the others (Figure 5.4). Although its main pyramid is only slightly taller (17.5

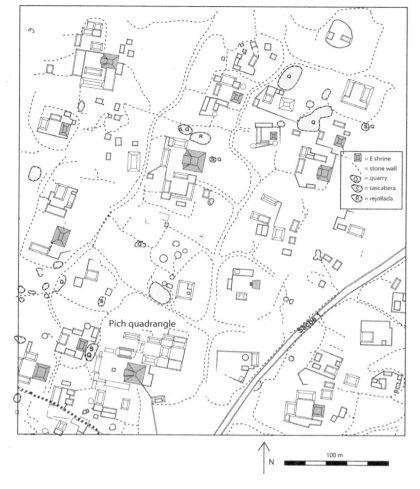

= E shrine
= stone wall
= quarry
= sascabera
= rejollada

Pich quadrangle

Sacbe 1

100 m

N

Figure 5.5 Map of Chunchucmil showing Pich quadrangle (the smallest of the centrally located quadrangles) and the dense residential areas with house lots demarcated by boundary walls. Also note the presence of streets between residential groups and how these streets intersect with the narrow *sacbe* leading northwest (drawn by authors).

m) than other quadrangle pyramids, the volume of its main and secondary pyramids and its attached architecture are significantly larger than that of other quadrangles. In addition, the only ball court at the site is associated with the Chacah quadrangle. These features, together with the central location at the junction of the two main *sacbes*, suggest that this architectural complex may have functioned as the primary locus for administrative functions at Chunchucmil. Keeping in mind that the lack of extensive excavations at this group or other quadrangles limits our interpretations, we argue that if consolidation of power in the hands of one governing faction took place at the Chacah quadrangle, political power had to be shared to a certain degree among strong competing factions at Chunchucmil. The presence of fifteen quadrangles throughout the site, and especially the concentration of ten large quadrangles around Chacah in

A. MAGNONI,
T. ARDREN,
S. R. HUTSON, AND
B. DAHLIN

the central portion of the site, indicate that strong competing power holders would have hindered a hierarchical monopoly of power in the hands of one ruling lineage (Dahlin 2003; Magnoni et al. 2008). This may be indicative of a more heterarchical system, perhaps one based on a market-and-trading economy that provided multiple sources of economic and political power to competing factions as well as to a more widespread portion of the Chunchucmil population (Dahlin 2003; Hutson et al. 2010), similar to the corporate power strategy described by Blanton et al. (1996) or the heterarchical/consensual political organization described by Stone (2008) (see Nishimura, Chapter 3 in this volume, for a discussion of a heterarchical/consensual polity in northern Mesopotamia).

In addition to the distinctive character of the central part of the site, with its lack of concentrated monumental architecture so common at other Maya sites, the residential areas of Chunchucmil were also markedly distinct (Figures 5.3, 5.4, and 5.5). Residential quarters were characterized by the presence of stone boundary walls that enclosed groups of structures and adjacent open areas. These boundary walls were rare at other Classic period sites – with the exception of Cobá, where, however, they did not always completely enclose residential groups and did not form streets as in Chunchucmil (Folan et al. 1983). Stone boundary walls enclosing small residential areas, empty lots (possibly gardens), and in some cases, streets became more common at some Postclassic sites, like Mayapán (Bullard 1952, 1954; Smith 1962) and those of the eastern Caribbean Coast (e.g., Benavides Castillo 1981; Sierra Sosa 1994; Vargas et al. 1985). In addition to stone boundary walls to demarcate residential groups, narrow, raised, winding causeways – *chichbes* – were also used. *Chichbes* (less than 1 m high and 0.5–3 m wide) were less common than the stone boundary walls, but the two could have been used interchangeably to demarcate the same house lot. *Chichbes* may have been used as planting surfaces for cacti such as nopal, or other plants, to provide a tall boundary delimitation as well as to create raised and well-drained planting surfaces for economically viable species (Magnoni et al. 2012).

At Chunchucmil, the arrangement of domestic groups is similar to the typical patio layout (Ashmore 1981) present throughout the Maya area, but the use of boundary walls and *chichbes* to completely demarcate household groups is original (Magnoni et al. 2012). Because of the high density of structures, most of Chunchucmil's residential groups shared these stone boundary walls and in some cases, space was left between parallel running walls to create narrow streets that allowed the flow of foot traffic. These streets, which in some cases intersected *sacbes*, directed traffic in the crowded urban landscape. They also provided important venues for communication between local residents as well as between locals and outsiders, such as merchants and visitors. Only in the residential periphery, where structure density diminishes, were open spaces left between distinct residential groups and streets no longer appeared.

The erection of boundary walls and *chichbes* at Chunchucmil points to the intention of demarcating household land by creating physical barriers between adjacent house lots to protect the household space not only from neighbors, but also from the numerous visitors, traders, and passersby who would have entered the city. These stone walls – in some cases, only a course high – and the *chichbes* that may have been planted with vegetation served as symbolic, yet tangible, boundary markers that helped forge a household identity, in terms of a claim to and identification with a designated space in the city. By delineating the space belonging to individual households, the mate-riality of the stone boundary walls defined the spatial arena for daily practices. Because households were the primary production and consumption units, the definition of the private realm would have been necessary to demarcate the place for household cooperation and everyday practices. These activities that related people, places, and objects in a daily entanglement would have been essential in the creation of a shared household identity (Hutson 2010; Hutson et al. 2004; Magnoni et al. 2012) and "sense of place" (Feld and Basso 1996, Lynch 1981). A sense of place refers to the recognition and attach-ment to the distinctive and particular qualities and characteristics that set a place – household, neighborhood, city – apart from other places (Lynch 1981:131). The symbolic importance of stone boundary walls is underscored by their presence in the residential periphery of Chunchucmil, where the structural density was lower and there-fore, physical boundary markers would not have been necessary to delineate individual households.

Some of the hamlet-size sites within Greater Chunchucmil also have boundary walls around residential groups, suggesting that the use of stone walls in these low-density hinterland sites would have been for the purpose of social affiliation with the urban center, to be part of the "imagined community" (Anderson 1991; see Hutson et al. 2008:33–34 for a longer description). The concept of imagined community was developed by Anderson (1991) to describe the recent phenomenon of nationalism, where a nation is a socially produced community made of people who imagine themselves as part of that group, but who are not necessarily engaged in everyday face-to-face interactions. This concept, however, has been successfully employed in archaeological contexts to define communities that are not necessarily spatially contiguous, but which share material symbols, cultural practices of affiliation, or elements of an identity discourse (e.g., Isbell 2000; Joyce and Hendon 2000; Knapp 2003; Preucel 2000; Yaeger 2000). In our interpretation, we view the use of stone boundary walls around domestic groups by rural residents as a strategic practice of cultural affiliation and ideological connection toward the urban center to create "a continuity of place across discontinuous space" (Hutson et al. 2008:34).

The boundary walls and *chichbes* at Chunchucmil enclosed both the household's structures and the non-built space adjacent to the structures. In the tropics, many activities take place outside and ethnographic studies of domestic yards (*solares*) in Mesoamerica indicate that outdoor spaces were essential for conducting a variety of domestic activities, such as food preparation, washing clothes, tending animals, processing agricultural products, and craft activities (e.g., pottery and basketry) (Anderson 1996; Arnold 1990; Caballero 1992; Hayden and Cannon 1983, 1984; Herrera Castro 1993, 1994; Isendahl 2002; Killion 1990; Ortega et al. 1993; Rico-Gray et al. 1990; see Stark this volume for an extensive discussion of the importance of urban open spaces in Mesoamerica). In addition, two separate areas for growing plants can be found in these ethnographic *solares*: an area of intensive or horticultural management close to the living quarters, where economically useful species are grown, and an extensively managed portion of the garden containing trees, which often mimic the forest composition, and other useful economic species (Anderson 1996; Caballero 1992; Herrera Castro 1993, 1994; Ortega et al. 1993; Rico-Gray et al. 1990; cf. Stark, Chapter 11 in this volume). Our detailed excavations at several of these Early Classic residential groups have shown that *solares* were used for similar activities in the past (Hutson 2010; Hutson et al. 2007; Magnoni 2008).

In the crowded urban landscape, the retention of *solar* space would be an important economic asset. The empty area around the structures and enclosed by the boundary walls at Chunchucmil varied in size from 442–15,206 m² with an average space consisting of 3,595 m² and a standard deviation of 2,351 m^2 (Magnoni et al. 2012). A strong correlation was found between the size of *solar* and the area covered by architecture, as well as the volume of architecture. Of these last two variables, volume of architecture can be a good indicator of the amount of power a household can exercise in controlling labor and resources, and thus, can be a proxy for group prosperity and wealth (Abrams 1994). It is important to note that prosperous households with higher volumes of architecture and larger *solares* were dispersed throughout urban Chunchucmil and not concentrated in the site center (Hutson et al. 2006; Magnoni et al. 2012:figures 9 and 10). In Maya sites, we tend to see concentrations of larger and wealthier residential groups in site centers with smaller habitational complexes in the surrounding areas (e.g., Fletcher and Kintz 1983; Folan et al. 2009; Folan et al. 1982; Kurjack 1974). At Chunchucmil, instead, prosperous residences with a large volume of architecture and extensive garden areas were located next to smaller and less-affluent households throughout the site, often sharing boundary walls and streets (Figures 5.3 and 5.5). Although we may not fully understand the forces that brought people of different socioeconomic status to reside close together, we can certainly envision the impact of such arrangements, as we will explain in more detail. As a result of living in a settlement with closely spaced neighbors of different socioeconomic backgrounds, Chunchucmil residents would have engaged in extra-household interactions, regardless of social distinctions.

SOCIAL PRODUCTION OF PLACE AND IDENTITY AT CHUNCHUCMIL

Cultivating a Sense of Place

Physical features alone, like large settlement size and high population density, cannot fully define the urban nature of a city. As Marco Polo tells the Chinese emperor, "The city does not consist of this [spatial materiality], but of relationships between the measurement of its space and the events of its past" (Calvino 1974:10) and those past events are inscribed in every material aspect of the city. Early definitions of urbanism (Childe 1950; Simmel 2002 [1903]; Weber 1958; Wirth 1938) stressed the social experience of living in a city. Recent considerations of urbanism continue to place importance on how human action and human relations play integral roles in

A. MAGNONI,
T. ARDREN,
S. R. HUTSON, AND
B. DAHLIN

constituting cities. For example, in discussing the "spatial specific-ity of urbanism," Soja (2000:5) considers not just the configuration of the built environment, but also the social relations and the human activities that take place within it. The proximity caused by dense settlement creates an increase in social interactions between urban dwellers. As a result, interdependencies among social groups and individuals are formed, which in turn affect the spatialization of social life (Bourdieu 1977; Joyce 2001; Joyce and Hendon 2000). Thus, the materiality of the built environment is simultaneously the means, medium, and outcome of social reproduction (Soja 1989). The inter-dependencies about which Soja writes make cities the center of large social networks. Experience of and involvement in these networks can cause residents, as well as the hinterland inhabitants, to identify with cities (e.g., Yaeger 2003). Cities are "places – that is, specific loca-tions in space that provide an anchor and a meaning to who we are" (Orum and Chen 2003:1). This sense of placeness and identity is real-ized through everyday interactions of people with the materiality of the urban setting (Bourdieu 1977; Joyce and Hendon 2000; Yaeger and Canuto 2000; see also Fisher, Chapter 6 in this volume).

In sum, cities are not just buildings and demography, but also a set of shared experiences that cultivate a sense of place with which people come to identify. In this section of the paper, we claim that a unique sense of place did indeed develop at Chunchucmil, dif-ferentiating it from other Maya cities. People did things differently at Chunchucmil and, to be expected of anthropologists, we attempt to pinpoint the factors that made Chunchucmil different. The basic notion that people come to identify with cities appears in widely cir-culated readers about urban anthropology (e.g., Rotenberg 2002). Yet even a whiff of the word "identity" may occasion discontent among those with materialist leanings. Without doubt, the concept of iden-tity, like all broad concepts, is imprecise. For example, Brubaker and Cooper (2000) argue that identity has come to mean too many things – philosophical notions of permanence, psychoanalytic notions of the self, sociological notions of roles, subaltern notions of race, class, gender, and more. At the same time, Brubaker and Cooper recog-nize that even if the term identity has become too ambiguous and encumbered, the work it has been tasked with – charting how peo-ple's histories, predicaments, commonalities, and self-understand-ings inform the claims they make and the way they live – remains important and valid. The florescence of archaeology books on the subject of identity (e.g., Casella and Fowler 2005; Díaz-Andreu et al. 2005; Insoll 2007) suggest that the relevance of identity will not soon abate. In the interests of semantic hygiene, we limit our use of the word identity to refer to the shared bonds that result from the process of establishing similarities and differences (Jenkins 2004:5).

Experiencing the Materiality of the Built Environment

Two aspects of Chunchucmil's built environment make it quite different from other Maya centers: houselot boundary walls and quadrangles. We have already discussed both of these at length and will only add short comments about them before attempting to explain how these features came to be shared. With regard to stone boundary walls, whatever practical function they served (for example, clarifying claims to space in a dense context where space was at a premium) cannot fully explain why so many people chose to build them. This is because the people of Chunchucmil built these walls not just where occupation was dense and space was scarce, but also at the edge of the site where space was abundant and walls would no longer be needed for communicating claims to space or creating privacy. Quadrangles and domestic groups at Chunchucmil share the same basic layout. Quadrangles, which have a tall pyramid on the east side and range structures facing the patio on the other three sides, repeat on a larger scale the layout of domestic groups: residential structures arranged around a patio with a domestic shrine on the east side. Although this plan is a common architectural arrangement for small domestic groups at other Maya sites, it is very rare as a template for monumental architecture at other Maya sites. It is unusual to find that nearly all of Chunchucmil's large architectural compounds take a form so rarely found in monumental compounds beyond Chunchucmil. Also, in large residential groups at Chunchucmil with tall eastern shrines, a small central platform (similar to that found in quadrangles) is often present, indicating a continuity of architectural form and meaning (Figure 5.5). The elite architectural complexes at Chunchucmil seem to have grown from the bottom-up emulation of the common disposition of Maya domestic architecture arranged around a patio and with a shrine on the eastern side, albeit at a larger scale (Ardren et al. 2003; Magnoni 2008).

What can explain these two distinguishing features of Chunchucmil's built environment? In other words, why did nearly all households use boundary walls and why did nearly all massive building projects take the form of quadrangles? Unlike other sites that have massive plazas for ceremonies that may have integrated their populaces, Chunchucmil lacked any spaces large enough to accommodate more than a fraction of the people living at the site (see Inomata 2006). In fact, Chunchucmil is better known for ceremonial spaces in domestic contexts. Of particular relevance here are the domestic shrines located on the east side of the domestic patios, where residents would have participated in common rituals and ceremonies (Figure 5.5). At least 34 percent and possibly as many as two-thirds of residential groups at Chunchucmil showed an eastern domestic shrine (Magnoni et al. 2012). Eastern domestic shrines were commonly found at other Maya sites (Becker 1991, 1999, 2003; Leventhal 1983; Tourtellot 1983), but they were not present in such abundance at all sites. For instance, at Tikal where the eastern shrines have been extensively studied, only 14 percent of residential groups had a domestic shrine (Becker 1999). The large quantity of eastern shrines at Chunchucmil is particularly significant given the absence of large public religious buildings and plazas for the practice of worship at an urban level. Instead, worship took place within the walls of the residential groups or in the quadrangles, the largest of which could not hold even a tenth of the site's maximum estimated population.

These rituals would have helped reinforce social bonds among residential groups or larger groups that shared an affiliation with a particular quadrangle, but they would not have created a city-wide identity. Each of the four excavated domestic shrines had unique architectural aspects that set them apart from their neighbors and reinforced a distinctive household identity (Ardren and Lowry 2011; Hutson et al. 2004, Magnoni et al. 2012). These domestic shrines with continuous architectural remodeling and the presence of ancestor burials and dedicatory offerings with inalienable goods would have been places for negotiating household power relations and expressing social coherence and identity (see Nishimura, Chapter 3 in this volume, for a discussion of household tombs underneath house floors in northern Mesopotamia). These shrines would have also been important in creating and maintaining the household's social memory by permanently inscribing these sacred places in the domestic landscape (Connerton 1989). Detailed excavations in these shrines have revealed the reaccession of the sealed deposits, indicating that the knowledge of the location of such deposits – together with their histories and memories – were passed down from generation to generation and formed part of the social memory of the household (Hutson 2010; Magnoni 2008).

Participating in Long-Distance Trade and Commerce

Thus, the shared bonds implied by similarities found across Chunchucmil – boundary walls and quadrangles – could not have been created by site-wide ceremonies because Chunchucmil lacked a venue for such large ceremonies. If participation in ceremonies did create a sense of unity at Chunchucmil, such unity was fostered at much smaller scales in residences and quadrangles. We argue that understanding how people at Chunchucmil came to share bonds requires looking at other practices and the relations engendered by those practices. A critical practice at Chunchucmil was participation in long-distance trade and market exchange. Participation in long-distance trade and the presence of a marketplace where local residents and visiting traders could have exchanged their goods is corroborated by the widespread distribution of obsidian in households at Chunchucmil. The large majority (97 percent) of the obsidian at Chunchucmil comes from El Chayal, located 670 km away in highland Guatemala. Our excavations in 162 locations across the site representing each type of architectural and residential group has shown an abundant and equal distribution of obsidian prismatic blades across all households independent of size and socioeconomic status (Hutson and Dahlin 2008; Hutson et al. 2010). Such an egalitarian distribution of obsidian blades would not have been possible under economies based on redistribution or reciprocity; only market exchange could have distributed so widely an exotic material like obsidian (Hirth 1998; Masson and Freidel 2012). Configurational data support the presence of a marketplace at Chunchucmil. Dahlin (2003; Dahlin et al. 2007) interpreted a flat, leveled 1 ha area bounded by the three major *sacbes* in the site center as a marketplace (Figure 5.4). Excavations exposed several short rock alignments – the remains of makeshift market stalls – accompanied by unusually high phosphate values, which accumulated as the result of intense wastage and spillage of organic items. Moreover, the battered condition of small sherds and tiny fragments of obsidian, which were recovered close to the market stalls, would be consistent with continuous trampling and sweeping.

A. MAGNONI,
T. ARDREN,
S. R. HUTSON, AND
B. DAHLIN

The presence of similar amounts of obsidian at large quad-rangles and small residential groups indicated that everybody in Chunchucmil, independent of their social status, had access to this long-distance traded material through market exchange. The abundance of obsidian prismatic blades across large and small households alike shows that socioeconomic hierarchical relations may have been mitigated by heterarchical ones (Hutson and Magnoni 2011). In fact, Hutson et al. (2010) suggested that supra-household collectives based in the quadrangles, but in collaboration with other households, may have managed the obsidian trade and redistribution because the scale of the undertaking would have been too significant for individual households. This level of supra-household cooperation, which would have crossed social hierarchies, would have reinforced a common identity built around the experiences of long-distance trade and market exchange. In addition, it would have been in the best interest of the collectives to reduce competition and increase cooperation in order to foster optimal conditions for long-distance trade and a flourishing market economy (Hutson et al. 2010).

As discussed in greater length in Hutson et al. 2008, hamlets in the rural hinterland belonging to Greater Chunchucmil showed six times the amount of obsidian found in settlements outside of the 5-km radius of Greater Chunchucmil. Even though the amount of obsidian present at the rural hamlets within Greater Chunchucmil was only a third of the amount present in urban Chunchucmil, it indicated participation in the Chunchucmil economy. Given that inhabitants of the rural hinterland of Greater Chunchucmil participated in Chunchucmil's obsidian market, it may come as no surprise that these rural inhabitants also used stone boundary walls to demarcate their residential groups. In this hinterland portion of Chunchucmil, consisting of hamlets with low-settlement density, boundary walls would not have been needed for practical purposes of defining space or maintaining privacy. Rural inhabitants chose to mark their connection with the city in an effort to emulate the urban life and be part of Chunchucmil's "imagined community" (Anderson 1991; see also Isbell 2000; Knapp 2003; Yaeger 2000). Were these rural house lots with boundary walls the product of urban household fissioning as households in the city grew in size through time? If so, these would have been urban dwellers moving to the hinterland and taking with them their own internalized way of experiencing and recreating the material settings. Or were these rural inhabitants newcomers to the area trying to create a sense of place and identity by emulating the urban lifeways? Unfortunately, our data cannot provide us answers with respect to the origins of these rural dwellers, but it is clear that in Greater Chunchucmil, the production of a spatial materiality at the residential level that attempted to replicate the urban form was a statement of affiliation and participation in the urban identity (Hutson et al. 2008).

Reinforcing Social Bonds

Another component that reinforced the social bonds that resulted in shared ways of doing things at Chunchucmil was the lack of spatial segregation between residential groups of different sizes and economic levels. No neighborhoods with a concentration of large and wealthy households (measured in terms of volume of architecture and yard size) were found at Chunchucmil; instead, small domestic units were often placed next to large ones, whereby they shared a common wall or a street (Figures 5.3 and 5.5). In addition, our detailed mapping and testpitting program at 162 locations across the site and detailed excavations at six groups have failed to identify neighborhoods inhabited by different ethnic groups, or specific craftsmen. Even though we cannot detect archaeologically distinctive neighborhoods at Chunchucmil, we suspect that intermediate social units of interaction between the household and the city would have been present at the level of the neighborhood, particularly in a city as dense as Chunchucmil. Although we cannot identify a spatial concentration of archaeological markers of ethnic groups or the clustering of specific occupations or crafts at Chunchucmil, we suspect that spatial segments of the city bounded by streets may have been neighborhoods – localized spatial units created from the bottom-up where residents would have had face-to-face social interactions and shared use of space (Feinman and Nicholas 2012; Smith and Novic 2012). The low boundary walls (never higher than 1–1.5 m); the low, winding *chichbes* (which may have supported tall plants); and the narrow streets, on average 2 m wide, provided frequent opportunities for neighbors of different socioeconomic levels to interact with each other and form extra-household relations. Whether walking down the narrow streets or being able to see and relate to neighbors over the low boundary walls in the crowded urban landscape,

A. MAGNONI,
T. ARDREN,
S. R. HUTSON, AND
B. DAHLIN

Chunchucmil citizens were never isolated from their neighbors and passersby walking down the streets. The spatial materiality of the urban environment – the lack of segregation of domestic units based on wealth in conjunction with the shared fences and narrow alleyways interspersed in the dense settlement – favored continued social interactions among households, which would have contributed enormously to the strengthening of social bonds (Hutson and Magnoni 2011; Magnoni et al. 2012). In turn, the built environment that Chunchucmil residents left for us to study was the outcome of social negotiations and collaborations among neighbors. Levels of supra-household coordination and cooperation, at least at the neighborhood level, are visible in the irregular, yet functional, layout of boundary walls and streets allowing traffic across the city, which would not have required a centralized planning effort (Dahlin and Ardren 2002; Hutson et al. 2008). This adaptive strategy of self-organization at the neighborhood level – "the introversion of the intermediate units" (Blanton and Fargher 2012:42) – is the result of multiple self-governing neighborhoods providing public goods when these are not offered by the state. These stone boundary walls were erected around living spaces by individual households, but in coordination with neighbors, to place boundaries in the appropriate places and leave enough space for narrow streets (see Creekmore, Chapter 2 in this volume, for examples of supra-household, but decentralized planning, in Upper Mesopotamian cities of the third millennium).

The layout of the central portion of the city – the lack of impressive focal monumental architecture and the arrangement of quadrangles interspersed with residential groups within the central portion of the site – suggests a lack of centralized planning. We believe that this architectural configuration is indicative of the lack of hierarchical and centralized ruling authority that would have supervised civic administration of the city. Only six quadrangles and the four main connecting *sacbes* in the site center seem to have been spatially organized following a "coordinated arrangement of buildings and space" (Smith 2007:8) (Figure 5.4). In addition, the spontaneous and organic growth of tightly bound residential groups and winding streets, generated by individual household practices, also indicates a lack of centralized civic planning of residential areas. Another important distinction in Chunchucmil's settlement pattern is the use of *sacbes*. At sites throughout the Maya region, these straight and broad processional avenues are considered the product of organized labor from a centralized authority, as they connected large monumental groups symbolizing the alliances and relations between elite groups (Kurjack and Andrews 1976; Shaw 2001). Chunchucmil's central *sacbes* (15–25 m-wide processional causeways that extended for 130–300 m) were no different as they connected several of the central quadrangles, but ten additional *sacbes*, which were narrower (maximum width of 6 m), radiated out of the site center (up to 800 m away) and intersected with the street network (Figures 5.4 and 5.5). Whereas a centralized authority may have created these narrow and, in some cases, curving *sacbes* to allow easy access to the central part of the site, city dwellers built boundary walls against these *sacbes* to protect the privacy of their residential groups and created intersections of the streets with the *sacbes* to facilitate traffic (Figure 5.5). In this process, Chunchucmil residents were appropriating the urban features, possibly imposed by a centralized authority, and producing a different urban landscape that would fit their needs (cf. Fisher, Chapter 6 in this volume, for a discussion of similar processes in Cyprus). Thus, even though the central *sacbes* may have been used for public, ceremonial processions and events as in other Maya sites, the long and narrow *sacbes* leading away from the site center and intersecting with the connective tissues of the urban layout – streets and boundary walls – may have carried more mundane traffic of local residents, as well as traders and visitors coming and going on a day-to-day basis.

By dwelling at Chunchucmil, its citizens were no longer simply part of kin-based social networks, but participated in extra-household social networks such as cooperative associations based on commerce and neighborhood maintenance. This increase in the network of contacts through participation in groups outside the households in turn created a high level of economic and social interdependence between a variety of groups from the city, its hinterland, and the trading partners (Ardren et al. 2003; Feinman and Nicholas 2012; Smith 2003). In this recursive process of spatialization and social production, we have to acknowledge the practices of individual social actors, even though it can be hard to isolate specific people in the archaeological record (e.g., Cowgill 2004; Smith 2003).

Cities are loci for socially generative practices: partaking in political or civic performances and administrative occurrences, or simply daily trading activities, would have provided the opportunity for interactions with a wide range of urban dwellers, as well as visiting

A. MAGNONI,
T. ARDREN,
S. R. HUTSON, AND
B. DAHLIN

traders. In these circumstances, social relations were built across the resident and visiting population spectrum regardless of social distinctions. This continuous interaction would have facilitated the creation of a shared identity that united them as the residents of this city, beyond the level of the household identity (Hutson et al. 2008, Magnoni et al. 2012). This mutual understanding of similarities was shaped by their common experiences of sharing an urban landscape charged with the architectural identifiers of hierarchy, such as the quadrangles and *sacbes*, and densely populated by similar social units based in the bounded house lots with which they interacted in supra-household groups (Magnoni 2008). This shared urban identity generated by supra-household interactions may have, on some occasions, stood in contrast to – and on other occasions, complemented – the specific social identities created at the household level, which have been extensively documented by our intensive research in specific residential groups (Hutson 2010; Hutson et al. 2004; Magnoni 2008; Magnoni et al. 2012).

Urban Imaginary

To better understand the notion of urban identity, we now turn to the concept of the "urban imaginary" (Ardren, et al. 2003; LiPuma and Koelble 2005). The urban imaginary can be conceptualized as a "culturally imaginary space" that is created and continuously transformed on one side by the overlapping circulations of people, goods, ideas, and ways of life, and on the other side by the stabilizing practices of the city's administrative powers and its infrastructure (LiPuma and Koelble 2005:154). The urban imaginary is constructed and transformed by the social experience of dwelling in the city and even its hinterland, in part by the constant interactions with the materiality of the city (the crowded residential groups, the narrow streets, the tall pyramids of the quadrangles) and in part by the continuous intersections of individual and collective ways of being and experiencing the city (the circulation of stories, shared experiences, and social identities at the household or supra-household level). Chunchucmil residents, like those inhabiting other cities, may have perceived their social existence through the "urban imaginary," or the "enabling socio-semiotic matrix within which those that inhabit the city imagine and act as urban-making collective agents" (LiPuma and Koelble 2005:155). The daily circulations of local and exotic goods, residents and foreigners, stories, experiences, and ideas through Chunchucmil's built environment led to specific understandings and production of the identity of "being from there." We acknowledge that despite the presence of many factors favoring the creation of a shared urban identity, multifarious ways of internalizing, experiencing, and expressing this urban identity must have been present at Chunchucmil and its hinterland as the result of individual idiosyncrasies and histories.

CONCLUSION

In this chapter, we have attempted to reconstruct the experience of urbanism at ancient Chunchucmil. First we looked at a variety of data that reflect the built environment in order to define the notion of urbanism at this unique city. We argued that the large extent of settlement – with a dense core of 8.5 km² and a greater metropolitan zone of 64 km², coupled with the highest population density of any known Classic-period Maya city – qualifies Chunchucmil as a central place of truly urban proportions. The use of boundary walls around modest domestic groups and internal roads that directed foot traffic in and out of the center likewise contributed to a highly interactive and dynamic city in which diverse groups of people lived in close association. The presence of trade goods at all socioeconomic levels and across the metropolitan area suggests a notion of the city as an unbounded arena for exchange and social interaction.

Our second goal was to explore the social experience of living at Chunchucmil, in part because it is a distinctive urban center when compared to other Classic Maya cities and faces particular environmental challenges. Lacking a central acropolis, the urban core is instead characterized by a series of eleven quadrangles that vary in dimension, but conform to the same design. We suggest that these monumental architectural spaces were the loci of political and economic powers; perhaps the materializations of competing house societies or economic networks. With these spaces as a framework for trade and negotiation, the walled house groups and narrow winding streets all suggest that claims to privacy and use rights were valued. These architectural forms indicate an urban imaginary that promoted the simultaneous economic activities of multiple groups of people who in turn must have helped maintain such an imaginary

A. MAGNONI,
T. ARDREN,
S. R. HUTSON, AND
B. DAHLIN

by constructing, living, and performing their shared identity within these spaces.

The draw to become a Chunchucmil resident must have been strong because, despite poor agricultural soils and dense urban crowding, people were willing to move to the city in large numbers in the middle of the Classic period. The prospect for increased wealth through commerce, the access to a variety of goods and opportunities that were not available in rural settings, and, more importantly, the participation in social experiences larger than the individual and the household – or simply the expectations of all these factors – must have been powerful attractions for hinterland and rural people to consider moving to Chunchucmil. The process of urban growth was likely a rapid one, according to our ceramic chronology. Chunchucmil grew from a small Preclassic settlement to a large city in a relatively brief period, but the dense urban settlement did not last for long. By AD 650–700, the site was mostly depopulated and in the Late-Terminal Classic period (AD 700–1100), only 300–700 people were living on twenty platforms dispersed among the ruins of the site. The urban grandeur and its imaginary were forever gone, although new memories of the ancient urban center may have developed among later inhabitants and possibly created new identities around the ruined city (Magnoni et al. 2008).

ACKNOWLEDGMENTS

First of all, we want to acknowledge the passing of Bruce Dahlin during the preparation of this manuscript. Bruce started investigations at Chunchucmil in 1993 and directed the Pakbeh Regional Economy Project until 2006. His initial insight into the unique nature of the city of Chunchucmil in conjunction with his enthusiasm and commitment to unraveling the distinctive characteristics of the political economy of Chunchucmil have made it possible to obtain a comprehensive understanding of this important city in the Maya region. Bruce always fostered a collaborative, interdisciplinary, and supportive research environment and for that we are deeply indebted to him. We also thank all the other PREP members and the people from the villages of Chunchucmil, Kochol, San Mateo, Cohauila, and Halacho, without whose help this research could not have been carried out. Special gratitude goes to Instituto Nacional de Antropología e Historia and the Consejo de Arqueología for giving us the permission to work at Chunchucmil. Support for the research discussed in this paper has come from the National Geographic Society and the National Science Foundation. We are deeply grateful to Andrew Creekmore and Kevin Fisher for the patience and support they showed during the preparation of this manuscript. We also want to thank Michael Smith and an anonymous reviewer for their comments; any inaccuracies are the sole responsibility of the authors.

NOTES

1 It is important to note that estimates for structural density at Chunchucmil only include residential structures, which are used for calculating population estimates. Ancillary structures, temples, shrines, and large nonresidential architecture have been removed from this figure. Thus, the figures reported for Chunchucmil with only residential structures are different from the commonly cited figures at other Maya sites, which report total numbers of structures including nonresidential ones. The full details for these calculations are explained in Magnoni 2007, but a few points are important to mention here. First, the presence of boundary walls and streets indicate that this settlement functioned as a contemporaneous site. In addition, 115 of these residential groups have been tested with off-mound test pits, while four have undergone extensive excavations, confirming that these groups were contemporaneous domestic units in the middle of the Classic period. Finally, a correction factor to account for abandoned structures and structures not in use for a specific period of time was used in the calculation. We should still be mindful, however, that the figures proposed here are estimates and without census figures, we cannot accurately calculate the number of residences and inhabitants at prehistoric sites.

REFERENCES CITED

Abrams, Elliot M. 1994 *How the Maya Built Their World: Energetics and Ancient Architecture.* University of Texas Press, Austin.

Anderson, Benedict 1991 *Imagined Communities: Reflections on the Origin and Spread of Nationalism.* Revised Edition. Verso, London and New York.

Anderson, E. N. 1996 Gardens of Chunhuhub. In *Los Mayas de Quintana Roo: Investigaciones Antropologicas Recientes,* edited by Ueli Hostetter, pp. 63–75. Institut fur Ethnologie, Universitat Bern, Bern, Germany.

Ardren, Traci, Aline Magnoni, and David Hixson 2003 The Nature of Urbanism at Ancient Chunchucmil. Paper presented at the Second Annual Tulane Maya Symposium, New Orleans, LA.

Ardren, Traci and Justin Lowry 2011 Long Distance Trade and Identity Maintenance at Early Classic Chunchucmil. Paper presented at the Tercero Congreso Internacional de Cultura Maya, Merida, Yucatán, Mexico.

Arnold, Philip J. III 1990 The Organization of Refuse Disposal and Ceramic Production with Contemporary Mexican Houselots. *American Anthropologist* 92:915–932.

A. MAGNONI,
T. ARDREN,
S. R. HUTSON, AND
B. DAHLIN

Ashmore, Wendy 1981 *Some Issues of Method and Theory in Lowland Maya Settlement Archaeology.* In *Lowland Maya Settlement Patterns*, edited by Wendy Ashmore, pp. 37–69. University of New Mexico Press, Albuquerque.

Beach, Timothy 1998 Soil Constraints in Northwest Yucatán, Mexico: Pedoarchaeology and Maya Subsistence at Chunchucmil. *Geoarchaeology* 13:759–791.

Becker, Marshall J. 1991 Plaza Plans at Tikal, Guatemala, and at Other Lowland Maya Sites: Evidence for Patterns of Culture Change. *Cuadernos de Arquitectura Mesoamericana* 14:11–26.

1999 *Excavations in Residential Areas of Tikal: Groups with Shrines.* Tikal Report 21, University Museum Monographs 104. University of Pennsylvania, Philadelphia.

2001 Houselots at Tikal Guatemala: It's What's Out Back that Counts. In *Reconstruyendo la Ciudad Maya: El Urbanismo en las Sociedades Antiguas*, edited by Andrés Ciudad Ruiz, Maria Josefa Iglesias Ponce de León, and Maria del Carmen Martínez Martínez, pp. 427–460. Sociedad Española de Estudios Mayas, Madrid.

2003 Plaza Plans at Tikal: A Research Strategy for Inferring Social Organization and Processes of Culture Change at Lowland Maya Sites. In *Tikal: Dynasties, Foreigners, and Affairs of State*, edited by Jeremy Sabloff, pp. 253–280. School of American Research, Santa Fe, NM.

Benavides Castillo, Antonio 1981 Coba y Tulum: Adaptación al Medio Ambiente y Contról del Medio Social. *Estudios de Cultura Maya* XIII:205–222.

Blanton, Richard 1976 Anthropological Studies of Cities. *Annual Review of Anthropology* 5: 249–264.

1981 The Rise of Cities. In *Archaeology*, edited by Jeremy A. Sabloff, pp. 392–400. Handbook of Middle American Indians, Supplement I, Victoria Reifler Bricker, general editor. University of Texas Press, Austin.

Blanton, Richard E. and Fargher Lane F. 2012 Neighborhoods and the Civic Constitution of Premodern Cities as Seen from the Perspective of the Collective Action. In *The Neighborhood as a Social and Spatial Unit in Mesoamerican Cities*, edited by M. Charlotte Arnould, Linda R. Manzanilla, and Michael E. Smith, pp.27–52. The University of Arizona Press, Tucson.

Blanton, Richard, Gary Feinman, Stephen Kowalewski, and Peter Peregrine 1996 A Dual-Processual Theory for the Evolution of Mesoamerican Civilization. *Current Anthropology* 37(1):1–14.

Bourdieu, Pierre 1977 *Outline of a Theory of Practice.* Cambridge University Press, Cambridge.

Brubaker, Rogers and Frederick Cooper 2000 Beyond "Identity." *Theory and Society* 29(1):1–47.

Bullard, William 1952 Residential Property Walls at Mayapan. *Carnegie Institution of Washington, Current Reports* 3:36–41.

1954 Boundary Walls and House Lots at Mayapan. *Carnegie Institution of Washington, Current Reports* 13:234–253.

1960 Maya Settlement Pattern in Northeastern Petén, Guatemala. *American Antiquity* 25(3):355–372.

Caballero, J. 1992 Maya Homegardens: Past, Present, and Future. *Etnoecologica* 1:35–53.

Calvino, Italo 1974 [1972] *Invisible Cities*. Translated from the Italian by William Weaver. Harcourt Brace Jovanovich, New York.

Casella, Eleanor C. and Chris Fowler (editors) 2005 *The Archaeology of Plural and Changing Identities*. Kluwer, New York.

Chase, Arlen F. and Diane Z. Chase 1996 More than Kin and King. Centralized Political Organization among the Late Classic Maya. *Current Anthropology* 37(5):803–810.

    1998 Scale and Intensity in Classic Period Maya Agriculture: Terracing and Settlement at the "Garden City" of Caracol, Belize. *Culture and Agriculture* 20:60–70.

Chase, Arlen F., Diane Z. Chase, and Christine D. White 2001 El Paisaje Urbano Maya: La Integración de los Espacios Construidos y la Estructura Social en Caracol, Belice. In *Reconstruyendo la Ciudad Maya: El Urbanismo en Las Sociedades Antiguas*, edited by Andrés Ciudad Ruiz, Maria Josefa Iglesias Ponce de León and Maria del Carmen Martínez Martínez, pp. 95–122. Sociedad Española de Estudios Mayas, Madrid.

Chase, Diane Z., Arlen F. Chase, and Wiliam Haviland 1990 The Classic Maya City: Reconsidering the "Mesoamerican Urban Tradition." *American Anthropologist* 92(2):499–506.

Childe, V. Gordon 1950 The Urban Revolution. *The Town Planning Review* 21:3–17.

Cobos Palma, Rafael 2001 El Centro de Yucatán: de Área Periférica a la Integración de la Comunidad Urbana en Chichen Itzá. In *Reconstruyendo la Ciudad Maya: El Urbanismo en Las Sociedades Antiguas*, edited by Andrés Ciudad Ruiz, Maria Josefa Iglesias Ponce de León, and Maria del Carmen Martínez Martínez. Sociedad Española de Estudios Mayas, Madrid.

Connerton, Paul 1989 *How Societies Remember*. Cambridge University Press, Cambridge.

Cowgill, George 2004 Origins and Development of Urbanism: Archaeological Perspectives. *Annual Review of Anthropology* 33: 525–549.

Culbert, T. Patrick, Laura J. Kosakowsky, Robert E. Fry, and William A. Haviland 1990 The Population of Tikal, Guatemala. In *Precolumbian Population History in the Maya Lowlands*, edited by T. Patrick Culbert and Don S. Rice, pp. 103–121. University of New Mexico Press, Albuquerque.

Curtis, Jason H., David A. Hodell, and Mark Brenner 1996 Climate Variability on the Yucatán Peninsula (Mexico) during the Last 3500 Years and Implications for Maya Cultural Evolution. *Quaternary Research* 46:37–47.

Dahlin, Bruce H. 2003 Chunchucmil: A Complex Economy in NW Yucatán. *Mexicon* 25:129–138.

Dahlin, Bruce H. and Traci Ardren 2002 Modes of Exchange and their Effects on Regional and Urban Patterns at Chunchucmil, Yucatán, Mexico. In *Ancient Maya Political Economies*, edited by M. A. Masson and D. A. Freidel, pp. 249–284. Altamira Press, Walnut Creek, CA.

Dahlin, Bruce H., Anthony P. Andrews, Timothy Beach, Clara I. Bezanilla, Patrice Farrell, Sheryl Luzzadder-Beach, and Valerie McCormick 1998 Punta Canbalam in Context: A Peripatetic Coastal Site in Northwest Campeche, Mexico. *Ancient Mesoamerica* 9(1):1–16.

Dahlin, Bruce H., Christopher T. Jensen, Richard E. Terry, David R. Wright, and Timothy Beach 2007 In Search of an Ancient Maya Market. *Latin American Antiquity* 18(4):363–384.

Dahlin, Bruce H., Timothy Beach, Sheryl Luzzadder-Beach, David Hixson, Scott Hutson, Aline Magnoni, Eugenia Mansell, and Daniel Mazeau 2005 Reconstructing Agricultural Self-Sufficiency at Chunchucmil, Yucatán, Mexico. *Ancient Mesoamerica* 16(2):1–19.

Demarest, Arthur A. 1992 Ideology in Ancient Maya Cultural Evolution: The Dynamics of Galactic Polities. In *Ideology and Pre-Columbian Civilizations*, edited by A. A. Demarest and G. W. Conrad, pp. 135–157. School of American Research Press, Santa Fe, NM.

Díaz-Andreu, Margarita, Sam Lucy, Staša Babić, and David N. Edwards 2005 *The Archaeology of Identity: Approaches to Gender, Age, Status, Ethnicity and Religion*. Routledge, London.

Drennan, Robert D. 1988 Household Location and Compact versus Dispersed Settlement in Prehispanic Mesoamerica. In *Household and Community in the Mesoamerican Past*, edited by R. Wilk and Wendy Ashmore, pp. 273–293. University of New Mexico Press, Albuquerque.

Dunning, Nicholas P. 1992 *Lords of the Hills: Ancient Maya Settlement in the Puuc Region, Yucatán, Mexico*. Prehistory Press, Madison, WI.

Feinman, Gary M. and Linda M. Nicholas 2012 Compact versus Dispersed Settlement in Pre-Hispanic Mesoamerica: The Role of Neighborhood Organization and Collective Action. In *The Neighborhood as a Social and Spatial Unit in Mesoamerican Cities*, edited by M. Charlotte Arnould, Linda R. Manzanilla, and Michael E. Smith, pp. 132–155. The University of Arizona Press, Tucson.

Feld, Steven and Keith Basso 1996 *Senses of Place*. School of American Research Press, Santa Fe, NM.

Fletcher, Laraine A. and Ellen R. Kintz 1983 Solares, Kitchen Gardens, and Social Status at Coba. In *Cobá: A Classic Maya Metropolis*, edited by W. J. Folan, E. R. Kintz, and L. A. Fletcher, pp. 103–119. Academic Press, New York.

Folan, William J. 1989 Questions and Hypothesis: Coba, Quintana Roo, Mexico, Revisited. *Mexicon* 11(1):7–12.

Folan, William J., Armando Anaya Hernandez, Ellen R. Kintz, Laraine A. Fletcher, Raymundo Gonzalez Heredia, Jacinto May Hau, and Nicolas Caamal Canche 2009 Coba, Quintana Roo, Mexico: A Recent Analysis of the Social, Economic, and Political Organization of a Major Maya Urban Center. *Ancient Mesoamerica* 20:59–70.

Folan, William J., Ellen R. Kintz, and Laraine A. Fletcher (editors) 1983 *Coba: A Classic Maya Metropolis*. Academic Press, New York.

Folan, William J., Ellen R. Kintz, Laraine A. Fletcher, and Burma H. Hyde 1982 An Examination of Settlement Patterns at Coba, Quintana Roo, Mexico, and Tikal, Guatemala: A Reply to Arnold and Ford. *American Antiquity* 47(2):430–436.

Fox, John W., Garret W. Cook, Arlen F. Chase, and Diane Z. Chase 1996 Questions of Political and Economic Integration. Segmentary versus Centralized States among the Ancient Maya. *Current Anthropology* 37(5):795–801.

Fox, Richard G. 1977 *Urban Anthropology: Cities in their Cultural Settings*. Prentice-Hall, Englewood Cliffs, NJ.

Freidel, David 1981 The Political Economies of Residential Dispersion among the Lowland Maya. In *Lowland Maya Settlement Patterns*, edited by Wendy Ashmore, pp. 371–382. University of New Mexico Press, Albuquerque.

Garza Tarazona de Gonzalez, Silvia and Edward B. Kurjack 1980 *Atlas Arqueológico del Estado de Yucatán*. 2 Vols. Instituto Nacional de Antropología e Historia, Centro Regional del Sureste, Mexico City.

Hageman, Jon B. 2004 The Lineage Model and Archaeological Data in Late Classic Northwestern Belize. *Ancient Mesoamerica* 15:63–74.

Hardoy, Jorge 1999[1962] *Ciudades Precolombinas*. Ediciones Infinito, Buenos Aires.

Haviland, William A. 1970 Tikal, Guatemala, and Mesoamerican Urbanism. *World Archaeology* 2:186–198.

Hayden, Brian D. and Aubrey Cannon 1983 Where the Garbage Goes: Refuse Disposal in the Maya Highlands. *Journal of Anthropological Archaeology* 2:117–163.

1984 *The Structure of Material Systems: Ethnoarchaeology in the Maya Highlands*. Society for American Archaeology Papers, No. 3, Washington, DC.

Herrera Castro, Natividad D. 1993 Los Huertos Familiares Mayas en X-uilub, Yucatán, México. Aspectos Generales y Estudio Comparativo entre la Flora de los Huertos Familiares y la Selva. *Biotica* 1:19–36.

1994 *Los Huertos Familiares Mayas en el Oriente de Yucatán*. Etnoflora Yucatánense Fascículo 9. Universidad Autónoma de Yucatán, Mérida, Mexico.

Hirth, Kenneth G. 1998 The Distributional Approach: A New Way to Identify Marketplace Exchange in the Archaeological Record. *Current Anthropology* 39:451–476.

Hodell, David A., Jason H. Curtis, and Mark Brenner 1995 Possible Role of Climate in the Collapse of Classic Maya Civilization. *Nature* 375:391–394.

Hutson, Scott R. 2010 *Dwelling, Identity and the Maya: Relational Archaeology at Chunchucmil*. Altamira, Lanham, MD.

Hutson, Scott R. and Aline Magnoni 2011 Identidad Social en el Mosáico Urbano de Chunchucmil, Yucatán, México. In *Identidad Social: Localidad y Globalidad en el Mundo Maya Prehispánico e Indígena Contemporáneo. Estudios de Espacio y Género*, edited by Miriam Judith Gallegos Gómora, pp. 65–78. Instituto Nacional de Antropologia e Historia, Mexico City.

Hutson, Scott R., Aline Magnoni, and Travis W. Stanton 2004 House Rules? The Practice of Social Organization in Classic-Period Chunchucmil, Yucatán, Mexico. *Ancient Mesoamerica* 15:73–90.

Hutson, Scott R., Aline Magnoni, Daniel Mazeau, and Travis Stanton 2006 The Archaeology of Urban Houselots at Chunchucmil, Yucatán, Mexico. In *Lifeways in the Northern Lowlands: New Approaches to Maya Archaeology*, edited by J. P. Mathews and B. A. Morrison, pp. 77–92. University of Arizona Press, Tucson.

Hutson, Scott R. and Bruce H. Dahlin 2008 Desenredando Una Paradoja: Asentamiento y Economía en Chunchucmil, Yucatán. *Los Investigadores de la Cultura Maya* 16:75–89.

Hutson, Scott R., Bruce H. Dahlin, and Daniel Mazeau 2010 Commerce and Cooperation among the Classic Maya: The Chunchucmil Case. In *Cooperation in Social and Economic Life*, edited by R. Marshall, pp. 81–103. Altamira Press, Lanham, MD.

Hutson, Scott R., David Hixson, Aline Magnoni, Daniel Mazeau, and Bruce H. Dahlin 2008 Site and Community at Chunchucmil and Ancient Maya Urban Centers. *Journal of Field Archaeology* 33(1):19–40.

Hutson, Scott R., Travis W. Stanton, Aline Magnoni, Richard Terry, and Jason Craner 2007 Beyond the Buildings: Formation Processes of Ancient Maya Houselots and Methods for the Study of Non-Architectural Space. *Journal of Anthropological Archaeology* 26:442–473.

Inomata, Takeshi 2006 Plazas, Performers and Spectators: Political Theaters of the Classic Maya. *Current Anthropology* 47:805–842.

Insoll, T. 2007 *The Archaeology of Identities*. Routledge, London.

Isbell, William H. 2000 What We Should Be Studying: The "Imagined Community and the Natural Community." In *The Archaeology of Communities. A New World Perspective*, edited by Marcello Canuto and Jason Yaeger, pp. 243–266. Routledge, London and New York.

Isendahl, Christian 2002 *Common Knowledge: Lowland Maya Urban Farming at Xuch*. Studies in Global Archaeology I. Department of Archaeology and Ancient History, Uppsala University and Universidad Autónoma de Campeche, Uppsala, Sweden.

Jenkins, Richard 2004 *Social Identity*. 2nd ed. Routledge, London.

Joyce, Rosemary A. 2001 Planificación Urbana y Escala Social: Reflexiones sobre Datos de Comunidades Clásicas en Honduras. In *Reconstruyendo la Ciudad Maya: El Urbanismo en las Sociedades Antiguas*, edited by Andrés Ciudad Ruiz, Maria Josefa Iglesias Ponce de León, and Maria del Carmen Martínez Martínez, pp. 12–136. Sociedad Española de Estudios Mayas, Madrid.

Joyce, Rosemary A. and Julia A. Hendon 2000 Heterarchy, History, and Material Reality: Communities in Late Classic Honduras. In *The Archaeology of Communities. A New World Perspective*, edited by Marcello Canuto and Jason Yaeger, pp. 143–160. Routledge, London and New York.

Killion, Thomas W. 1990 Cultivation Intensity and Residential Site Structure: An Ethnoarchaeological Examination of Peasant Agriculture in the Sierra de los Tuxtlas, Veracruz, Mexico. *Latin American Antiquity* 1:191–215.

Killion, Thomas W., Jeremy A. Sabloff, Gair Tourtellot, and Nicholas P. Dunning 1989 Intensive Surface Collection of Residential Clusters at Terminal Classic Sayil, Yucatán, Mexico. *Journal of Field Archaeology* 16:273–294.

Knapp, A. Bernard 2003 The Archaeology of Community on Bronze Age Cyprus: Politiko Phorades in Context. *American Journal of Archaeology* 107:559–580.

Kurjack, Edward B. 1974 *Prehistoric Lowland Maya Community Social Organization: A Case Study at Dzibilchaltun, Yucatán, Mexico*. Middle American Research Institute, Publication 38. Tulane University, New Orleans, LA.

1999 Was Dzibilchaltun a Preindustrial City? In *The Land of the Turkey and the Deer: Recent Research in Yucatán*, edited by Ruth Gubler, pp. 119–128. Labyrinthos, Lancaster, CA.

Kurjack, Edward B. and E. Wyllys Andrews V 1976 Early Boundary Maintenance in Northwest Yucatán, Mexico. *American Antiquity* 41:318–325.

Leventhal, Richard M. 1983 Household Groups and Classic Maya Religion. In *Prehistoric Settlement Patterns: Essays in Honor of Gordon Willey*, edited by Richard M. Leventhal and Alan L. Kolata, pp. 55–76. University of New Mexico Press, Albuquerque, and Peabody Museum of Archaeology and Ethnology, Harvard, Cambridge.

Leyden, B., M. Brenner, J. Curtis, D. Piperno, T. Whitmore, and B. H. Dahlin 1996 A Record of Long- and Short-Term Climatic Variation from Northwest Yucatán: Cenote. San Jose Chulchaca. In *The Managed Mosaic: Ancient Maya Agriculture and Resource Use*, edited by S. Fedick, pp. 30–52. University of Utah Press, Salt Lake City.

LiPuma, Edward and Thomas Koelble 2005 Cultures of Circulation and the Urban Imaginary: Miami as Example and Examplar. *Public Culture*: 17(1):153–179.

Lynch, Kevin 1981 *A Theory of Good City Form*. The Massachusetts Institute of Technology, Cambridge, MA.

Magnoni, Aline 2007 Population Estimates at the Ancient Maya City of Chunchucmil, Yucatán, Mexico. In *Digital Discovery: Exploring New Frontiers in Human Heritage. CAA 2006. Computer Applications and Quantitative Methods in Archaeology. Proceedings of the 34th Conference, Fargo, United States, April 2006*, edited by Jeffrey Clark and Emily Hagemeister, pp. 175–182. Archaeolingua, Budapest.

2008 *From City to Village: Landscape and Household Transformations at Classic Period Chunchucmil, Yucatán, Mexico*. Unpublished Ph.D. dissertation, Department of Anthropology, Tulane University, New Orleans, LA.

Magnoni, Aline, Scott Hutson, and Bruce Dahlin 2012 Living in the City: Settlement Patterns and the Urban Experience at Classic Period Chunchucmil, Yucatán, Mexico. *Ancient Mesoamerica* 23:313–343.

Magnoni, Aline, Scott R. Hutson, and Travis W. Stanton 2008 Landscape Transformations and Changing Perceptions at Chunchucmil, Yucatán. In *Ruins of the Past: Use and Perception of Abandoned Structures in the Maya Lowlands*, edited by Travis Stanton and Aline Magnoni, pp. 193–222. University of Colorado Press, Boulder.

Marcus, Joyce 1983 On the Nature of Mesoamerican City. In *Prehistoric Settlement Patterns: Essays in Honor of Gordon Willey*, edited by E. Z. Vogt and R. M. Leventhal, pp. 195–242. University of New Mexico Press, Albuquerque.

1993 Ancient Maya Political Organization. In *Lowland Maya Civilization in the Eighth Century A.D.*, edited by J. A. Sabloff and J. S. Henderson, pp. 111–183. Dumbarton Oaks Research Library and Collection, Washington, DC.

Marcus, Joyce and Jeremy A. Sabloff 2008 Introduction. In *The Ancient City: New Perspectives on Urbanism in the Old and New World*, edited by Joyce

Marcus and Jeremy A. Sabloff, pp. 3–26. School for Advanced Research Press, Santa Fe, NM.

Martin, Simon and Nikolai Grube 1995 Maya Superstates. *Archaeology* 48(6):41–46.

2001 Post-Classic and Terminal Classic Courts of the Northern Maya Lowlands. In *Royal Courts of the Ancient Maya, Vol. 2*, edited by Takeshi Inomata and Stephen D. Houston, pp. 266–307. Westview Press, Boulder, CO.

Martínez 2001 *Reconstruyendo la Ciudad Maya: El Urbanismo en las Sociedades Antiguas*. Sociedad Española de Estudios Mayas, Madrid.

Masson, Marilyn A. and David A. Freidel 2012 An Argument for Classic Era Maya Market Exchange. *Journal or Anthropological Archaeology* 31:455–484.

Moholy-Nagy, Hattula 1997 Middens, Construction Fill, and Offerings: Evidence for the Organization of Classic Period Craft Production at Tikal, Guatemala. *Journal of Field Archaeology* 24(3):293–313.

Ortega, Luz María, Sergio Avendaño, Arturo Gómez-Pompa, and Edilberto Ucán Ek 1993 Los Solares de Chunchucmil, Yucatán, Mexico. *Biotica* 1:37–51.

Orum, Anthony M. and Xiangming Chen 2003 *The World of Cities: Places in Comparative and Historical Perspective*. Blackwell, Madden, MA.

Preucel, Robert 2000 Making Pueblo Communities: Architectural Discourse at Kotyiti, New Mexico. In *The Archaeology of Communities. A New World Perspective*, edited by Marcello Canuto and Jason Yaeger, pp. 58–77. Routledge, London and New York.

Rico-Gray, Victor, José G. García Franco, Alexandra Chemas, Armando Puch, and Paulino Sima 1990 Species Composition, Similarity, and Structure of Maya Homegardens in Tixpehual and Tixcacaltuyub, Yucatan, Mexico. *Economic Botany* 44(4):470–487.

Ringle, W. M. and G. J. Bey 2001 Post-Classic and Terminal Classic Courts of the Northern Maya Lowlands. In *Royal Courts of the Ancient Maya, Vol. 2*, edited by T. Inomata and S. D. Houston, pp. 266–307. Westview Press, Boulder, CO.

Rotenberg, Robert 2002 The Metropolis and Everyday Life. In *Urban Life: Readings in the Anthropology of the City*, 4th edition, edited by G. Gmelch and W. P. Zenner, pp. 93–105. Waveland Press, Prospect Heights, IL.

Sanders, W. T. and D. Webster 1988 The Mesoamerican Urban Tradition. *American Anthropologist* 90:521–546.

Shaw, Justine M. 2001 Maya Sacbeob: Form and Function. *Ancient Mesoamerica* 12:261–272.

Sierra Sosa, Thelma 1994 *Contribución al Estudio de los Asentamientos de San Gervasio, Isla de Cozumel*. Instituto Nacional de Antropología e Historia, Mexico City, Mexico.

Simmel, Georg 2002 [1903] The Metropolis and Mental Life. In *The Blackwell City Reader*, edited by Gary Bridge and April A. Watson, pp. 11–19. Blackwell, Malden MA.

Smith, A. L. 1962 *Mayapan, Yucatán. Mexico, Part 3: Residential and Associated Structures at Mayapan*. Carnegie Institution of Washington, Washington, DC.

Smith, Michael E. 1989 Cities, Towns, and Urbanism: Comment on Sanders and Webster. *American Anthropologist* 91(2):454–460.

2007 Form and Meaning in the Earliest Cities: A New Approach to Ancient Urban Planning. *Journal of Planning History* 6(3):3–47.

2012 Introduction: Neighborhoods and Districts in Ancient Mesoamerica. In *The Neighborhood as a Social and Spatial Unit in Mesoamerican Cities*, edited by M. Charlotte Arnould, Linda R. Manzanilla, and Michael E. Smith, pp.1–26. The University of Arizona Press, Tucson.

Smith, Monica L. 2003 Introduction: The Social Construction of Ancient Cities. In *The Social Construction of Ancient Cities*, edited by Monica L. Smith, pp. 1–36. Smithsonian Books, Washington, DC.

Soja, Edward W. 1989 *Postmodern Geographies: The Reassertion of Space in Critical Social Theory*. Verso Press: New York.

2000 *Postmetropolis: Critical Studies of Cities and Regions*. Blackwell, Malden, MA.

Stone, Elizabeth C. 2008 A Tale of Two Cities: Lowland Mesopotamia and Highland Anatolia. In *The Ancient City: New Perspectives on Urbanism in the Old and New World*, edited by Joyce Marcus and Jeremy A. Sabloff, pp.141–164. School for Advanced Research Resident Scholar Book, Santa Fe, NM.

Sweetwood, Ryan, Timothy Beach, Bruce H. Dahlin, and Richard Terry 2009 Maya Footprint: Soil Resources of Chunchucmil, Yucatán, Mexico. *Soil Science Society of America Journal* 73:1209–1220.

Tourtellot, Gair III 1983 An Assessment of Classic Maya Household Composition. In *Prehistoric Settlements Patterns: Essays in Honor of Gordon Willey*, edited by E. Z. Vogt and R. M. Leventhal, pp. 35–54. University of New Mexico Press, Albuquerque.

Trejo, Silvia (editor) 1998 *Modelos de Entidades Políticas Mayas*. Conaculta, Instituto de Antropología e Historia, Mexico.

Vargas, Ernesto, Patricia S. Santillan, and Marta Vilalta 1985 Apuntes para el Análisis del Patrón de Asentamiento de Tulum. *Estudios de Cultura Maya* 16:55–83.

Vlcek, David T., Sylvia Garza Tarazona de Gonzalez, and Edward B. Kurjack 1978 Contemporary Farming and Ancient Maya Settlements: Some Disconcerting Evidence. In *Prehispanic Maya Agriculture*, edited by Peter. D. Harrison and B. L. Turner II, pp. 211–233. University of New Mexico Press, Albuquerque.

Weber, Max 1958 *The City*. Translated and edited by D. Martindale and G. Neuwirth. The Free Press, Glencoe, IL.

Webster, David L. 1997 City-States of the Maya. In *The Archaeology of City-States Cross Cultural Approaches*, edited by D. L. Nichols and T. H. Charlton, pp. 135–154. Smithsonian Institution Press, Washington, DC and London.

Webster, David and AnnCorrine Freter 1990 The Demography of Late Classic Copan. In *Precolumbian Population History in the Maya Lowlands*, edited by T. Patrick Culbert and Don S. Rice, pp. 37–61. University of New Mexico Press, Albuquerque.

Webster, David and William T. Sanders 2001 La Antigua Ciudad Meso-americana: Teoría y Concepto. In *Reconstruyendo la Ciudad Maya: El Urbanismo en Las Sociedades Antiguas, Vol. 6*, edited by Andrés Ciudad Ruiz,

Maria Josefa Iglesias Ponce, de León and Maria del Carmen Martínez, pp. 34–64. Sociedad Española de Estudios Mayas, Madrid.

Whitmore, Thomas J., Mark Brenner, Jason H. Curtis, Bruce H. Dahlin, and Barbara W. Leyden 1996 Holocene Climate and Human Influences on Lakes of the Yucatán Peninsula, Mexico: An Interdisciplinary, Palaeolimnological Approach. *The Holocene* 6(3):273–287.

Wirth, Louis 1938 Urbanism as a Way of Life. *The American Journal of Sociology* 44(1):1–24.

Yaeger, Jason 2000 The Social Construction of Communities in the Classic Maya Countryside. In *The Archaeology of Communities. A New World Perspective*, edited by Marcello Canuto and Jason Yaeger, pp. 123–142. Routledge, London and New York.

2003 Untangling the Ties that Bind: Urbanism at Xunantunich, Belize. In *The Social Construction of Ancient Cities*, edited by M. L. Smith, pp. 121–155. Smithsonian Institution, Washington, DC.

Yaeger, Jason and Marcello Canuto 2000 Introducing an Archaeology of Communities. In *The Archaeology of Communities. A New World Perspective*, edited by Marcello Canuto and Jason Yaeger, pp. 1–15. Routledge, London and New York.

6

Making the First Cities on Cyprus: Urbanism and Social Change in the Late Bronze Age

Kevin D. Fisher

Compared with its eastern Mediterranean neighbors, the island of Cyprus is remarkable for the rapid and rather late appearance of urban centers during the Late Bronze Age. Using an approach that focuses on the role of built environments as contexts for social interaction, I argue instead that the first cities were the result of place-making by the various groups and individuals that made up an increasingly complex Late Bronze Age society. This took place at multiple spatial scales from the top-down planning of ruling elites that gave shape to the urban landscape, through the formation of neighborhoods, to the bottom-up actions of individual households and their members. As such, the new urban centers were both product and producers of social life and catalysts for the far-reaching social transformations that characterized the Late Bronze Age on Cyprus.

Even before V. Gordon Childe first coined the phrase "urban revolution," the eastern Mediterranean and Near East had long been recognized as one of the so-called cradles of urbanism (Childe 1936). Cities first appear in Mesopotamia by the mid-fourth millennium BC and by the early third millennium, we see the emergence of fortified urban centers, generally thought to represent city-states, in the Levant and Anatolia. In the Aegean, urban centers with vast palace complexes were built on Crete by the beginning of the second millennium BC, if not earlier. Amid these developments, the island of Cyprus is somewhat of an anomaly, with urban centers not appearing until the Late Bronze Age (LBA; ca. 1650–1100 BC) and scholars have frequently noted its late arrival on the urban scene (e.g., Held 1993:29; Keswani 1996:217–218; Wright 1992:84–85). Explanations for the eventual appearance of cities on Cyprus have tended to see the process as an almost natural outcome of demographic growth and politico-economic development through secondary state formation.

The aim of this paper is to rethink the emergence of urbanism on Cyprus by placing it at the center of the profound social changes that took place during the Late Bronze Age. I see the new cities as intentional creations resulting from a process of place-making by which space was appropriated, defined, and turned into meaningful contexts for social interaction. By the fully urban period of the fourteenth through twelfth centuries BC, this process manifested itself at a number of levels from the top-down planning of the streets and fortifications of urban centers by ruling elites, to the design and construction of neighborhoods, individual buildings, and their constituent spaces, which involved decisions by various stakeholders, including the grassroots actions of various individuals and urban communities. This was truly an urban revolution in that it utterly changed the way many Cypriotes lived their lives. The new built environments became the primary arenas in which the social dynamics of the LBA were enacted, forging new relationships and identities in the process.

To examine these developments, I will begin by briefly discussing previous considerations of LBA Cypriot urbanism, before introducing an approach that investigates the mutually constituting relationship between people and places through a focus on social interaction. I then outline what we know about the rapid rise of urbanism during the LBA and address the social production of space in the first Cypriot cities by examining place-making at various scales, from the top-down planning of ruling elites, through the formation of neighborhoods, to the bottom-up actions of individual households.

WAYS OF LOOKING AT LATE CYPRIOT CITIES

In spite of excavations at a number of LBA (or Late Cypriot [LC], as it is called locally) urban sites, there has been a notable absence of research into the social aspects of their architectural remains. Until recently, most studies of ancient Cypriot built environments, informed by traditional art-historical and culture-historical paradigms, have been descriptive rather than explanatory, focusing on issues such as stylistic classification and change, chronology, or the technical aspects of construction. In probably the most comprehensive work on ancient Cypriot architecture, Wright (1992), while recognizing the significance of the emergence of "urban society" in the Bronze Age, offers no explanation as to its cause or profound social effects. Recognizing the limitations of such approaches, some scholars in the 1990s tried to explain the rise of urbanism in terms of the emergence and development of sociopolitical complexity (e.g., Keswani 1993; Knapp 1993; Knapp et al. 1994). Influenced by the processual paradigm in archaeology, the appearance of cities on Late Bronze Age Cyprus was viewed as the result of processes of demographic growth and nucleation and politico-economic development, usually characterized as "state formation." Such an approach emphasized the function of the new settlements within systems of production and exchange, classifying them according to their place within a politico-economic hierarchy (Keswani 1993, Knapp 1997:ch. 5; Negbi 2005; Peltenburg 1996).

Although these approaches are important in highlighting the function and articulation of settlement systems in a general sense, they ultimately fail to shed light on the far more significant social role that cities played in revolutionizing the lives of the people that lived in and around them. Even recent agent-based approaches that recognize the vital role of the built environment in social reproduction (e.g., Bolger 2003; Knapp 2008) have not adequately addressed the transformative nature of the new cities. Archaeologists working in Cyprus have often been reluctant to call the new urban settlements "cities," preferring instead to use the terms "centers" or, more often, "towns" (e.g., Knapp 2008; Negbi 2005; South 1995; Wright 1992). This reluctance likely stems in part from the relatively small size attributed to most LC urban sites, with two of the best known, Enkomi and Kalavasos-*Ayios Dhimitrios*, having sizes of 14 and 11.5 ha, respectively.[1] As Iacovou (2007) rightly points out, however, such estimates as published in various tables and charts (e.g., Knapp 1997:figure 5 and table 2) have taken on the weight of fact, in spite of being based on sources that use very little hard data or that amalgamate data from several phases of occupation. In any case, I have no difficulty defining the urban centers discussed here as cities.

Trying to define *city* is a complicated matter and there is no consensus among archaeologists, or even among scholars of contemporary urbanism. Factors such as large size, a dense aggregation of people, socioeconomic heterogeneity, and the performance of specialized functions in relation to their hinterlands are commonly cited as characteristics of cities (Kostof 1991:37; Trigger 2003:120; Wirth 1938:8). Yet, I would agree with Cowgill's (2004:526) argument that a "somewhat fuzzy core concept" is more appropriate than definitions based on specific sizes or population levels – neither of which is easily determined in archaeological contexts (also Trigger 2003:120). We might define a city, therefore, as "a permanent settlement within the larger territory occupied by a society, considered home to a significant number of residents whose activities, roles, practices, experiences, identities, and attitudes differ significantly from those of other members of the society who identify most closely with 'rural' lands outside such settlements" (Cowgill 2004:526). An important distinction between *urban* (referring to "city-ness" [Cowgill 2004:527]) and nonurban, then, is one of identities. Monica Smith (2003:8) refers to it as an urban "ethos."

To see a city as being about its effects on people's lives and the formation of their identities is to see it as a *place*: the dynamic, socially constructed and meaningful context of human action and experience (Feld and Basso 1996; Low and Lawrence-Zúñiga 2003; Preucel and Meskell 2004; Rodman 1992; Tuan 1977). In trying to understand the relationship between people and their built environments, I take an approach that acknowledges the agency of both. It is informed on a theoretical level by the work of Giddens (1979, 1984) and others (e.g., Bourdieu 1973, 1977; Lefebvre 1991) who argue for a mutually constituting relationship between human action and social reproduction. More than mere settings for these actions, built environments play an active role in the structuring and routinizing of embodied practice through which the structural properties of social systems are produced, reproduced, and transformed. In this way cities are both producer and product of social life. Their creation and transformation are acts of place-making carried out by a range of individuals and groups at various spatial scales (M. L. Smith 2003; Soja 2000).

To investigate how this social dynamic played out in the LC built environment, I have developed an integrative approach (see Lawrence and Low 1990:482–491) that allows one to examine how built form provides contexts for various social interactions, including public-inclusive and private-exclusive social occasions, through which social boundaries and identities are negotiated and materialized (Fisher 2007, 2009a; see also Goffman 1963). The approach examines how built environments influence movement and interaction potential through their configuration and by encoding and nonverbally communicating meanings that are perceived by their occupants and visitors, potentially influencing their behavior (see Hillier and Hanson 1984; Rapoport 1990). The aim of the integrative approach, therefore, is to repopulate the contexts in which past social interactions took place. I have applied this approach to the analysis of LC monumental buildings (Fisher 2007, 2009b) and, more recently, used it to examine the changing nature of house and household in the LC period and their articulation with urban communities (Fisher 2014). These are what Isbell (2000; after Anderson 1991) refers to as "imagined communities," which are dynamic, fluid, and changing social institutions, formed as actors select among available alternatives while striving to create new ones in order to achieve their goals. They are historically contingent and "ever-emergent" communities that generate and are generated by supra-household interactions that are structured and synchronized by a set of places within a particular span of time (Yaeger and Canuto 2000:5–6; also Knapp 2003).

Building on this work, I will discuss how acts of place-making were materialized in LC urban landscapes at a range of spatial scales, from various levels of urban community such as the city itself and its neighborhoods, to individual buildings and their constituent spaces. First, however, I will briefly outline some of the key developments that accompanied the rise of the first cities on Cyprus.

THE RISE OF URBANISM ON CYPRUS

It is important to bear in mind that, up until the mid-third millennium BC, Cypriotes continued to live in small villages of circular, stone and mudbrick single-room dwellings, a settlement form dating back at least to the Late Aceramic Neolithic (ca. 7000/6500–5500 BC). The transition to the Early Bronze Age (locally, Early Cypriot) ca. 2500 BC brought important cultural changes, spurred in part by the exploitation of Cyprus's rich copper resources by local emerging elites and the adoption and adaption of cultural innovations brought by immigrants from Anatolia (Knapp 2008:ch.3; Manning 1993; Steel 2004:ch.5). Emerging social inequalities were manifested most clearly in the elaboration of burial practices and deposition of wealth seen in some cemeteries (notably at Lapithos-*Vrysi tou Barba* and Bellapais-*Vounous*) in the northwestern part of the island (see Keswani 2004:42–46; Figure 6.1). Although these cemeteries are exceptional, it is clear that the funerary realm became the primary arena for display and supra-household social interaction at this time (Keswani 2005). The growing social complexity seen in the northern cemeteries is not, however, borne out in other elements of the built

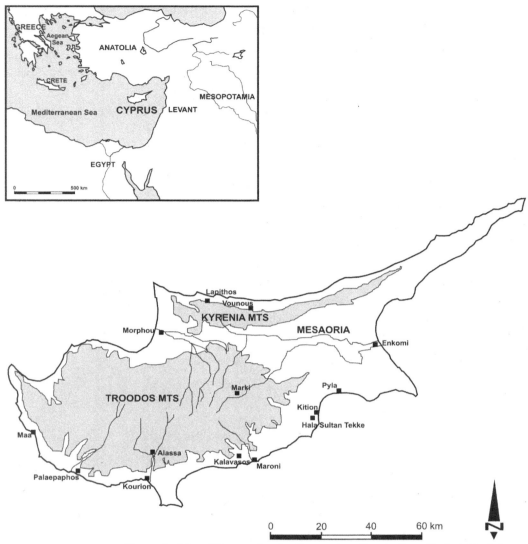

Figure 6.1 Map of Cyprus showing Bronze Age sites mentioned in text. Shaded area is land greater than 300 m asl (drawn by author).

environment. In spite of the appearance at this time of rectilinear, multiroom, agglomerative domestic architecture, there is currently no evidence for urban settlements, settlement hierarchies, or monumental architecture of any sort until the seventeenth century BC (Keswani 1996). If the evidence from Marki-*Alonia*, which spans most of the Early and Middle Bronze Age, is any indication, the typical house consisted of two or three covered rooms at the back of a larger courtyard, an "idealized concept" that remained in place throughout the life of the settlement (Frankel and Webb 2006:299).

The long-standing adherence to traditional "rural" architectural types can perhaps be tied to what Peltenburg (1993; 1996:27) has described as an "egalitarian ethos" and segmentary social organization that characterized pre-Bronze Age Cypriot society and largely persisted outside of the northern part of the island until the near end of the Middle Bronze Age (locally, the Middle Cypriot).

Cyprus then entered a period of rapid and profound change, culminating in what some scholars see as the emergence of state-level sociopolitical organization. Whether the island was ruled as a unified political entity or as a series of independent, regional "peer" polities (or possibly vacillated between these two forms of organization) is a matter of debate (see Knapp 2008:144–159, 324–341 for a detailed discussion of these issues; cf. Peltenburg 2012). In any case, it is clear that emerging inequalities gave way to social hierarchies as elites institutionalized their power through intensified control over increasingly specialized systems of production and exchange, legitimized through ideological means (see Knapp 1986; 2008:159–172). The basis for this control extended beyond the island's boundaries as Cyprus became ever more integrated into the wider politico-economic relations of the eastern Mediterranean and Near East. At the same time, society became increasingly heterarchical as various collectivities emerged in the context of new social, political, and economic networks and opportunities (Keswani 1996; 2004:154–157). These changes took place within the context of further agricultural intensification that supported demographic growth and nucleation, seen in an increase in settlement numbers and, more importantly, size and density (Knapp 1997:47–48). At the same time, we see far-reaching changes to the island's built environment, including the rise of the island's first urban centers and the appearance of monumental buildings and new types of domestic and mortuary architecture. As I noted in the introduction, I would see the new built environments as a driving force behind the profound sociopolitical changes of the LBA, rather than as their side effect. Cities were both product and producer of these transformations through the creation and use of meaningful contexts for social interactions.

The Proto-Urban Period

The earliest urban centers on the island were founded during what I have termed a "Proto-urban" period covering roughly the Middle

Cypriot (MC) III through Late Cypriot (LC) IIB; ca. 1750–1340/15 BC. Admittedly, my use of this term speaks more to the lack of data about the formative period of Cypriot cities than any certainty about the nature of these first urban settlements. We are greatly hampered by the relatively limited exposures of nearly all sites. Generally less than 5 percent of any site has been excavated and even those exposures tend to be fragmented into discontinuous areas. It is also likely that the earliest foundations of the cities have been obscured by the more substantial remains of their fully urban successors. Even though it appears that Enkomi, Morphou-*Toumba tou Skourou*, Hala Sultan Tekke, and Maroni are among the first of these Proto-urban settlements, only Enkomi provides any significant insight into its formative levels.

Excavations have revealed two important features from Proto-urban Enkomi: the so-called Fortress – one of the island's first monumental buildings – and a large domestic complex. Located at the northern end of the site, the Fortress is a large rectangular building, roughly 30 x 10 m in size, that contained evidence for large-scale copper working (Dikaios 1969–1971:plates 245–248; Figure 6.2). This is but one of a series of so-called forts, some twenty-one in all, which appear in the northern and eastern parts of the island during the transition from the Middle to Late Bronze Age (Fortin 1981; Peltenburg 1996). These were by far the largest structures built on the island to this point, representing an unprecedented investment in material and human resources. Peltenburg (1996) has argued that these forts were part of a strategy to secure the routes from new coastal settlements, like Enkomi, to the copper sources in the Troodos Mountains. Control of this copper production was undoubtedly one of the primary economic underpinnings of the power of emerging elites. I have argued that Enkomi's Fortress materialized both the large-scale appropriation and enclosure of space, as well as efforts to control physical and visual access to the vital copper-working facilities and their associated technologies in its west wing (Fisher 2007:199–204, figure 7.4).

If excavations in the later city center are any indication, the initial settlement that was constructed to the south of Enkomi's Fortress was fundamentally different from the agglomerative, village-based domestic architecture of the Early through Middle Bronze Age periods. It was characterized, at least in part, by large domestic complexes (see Dikaios 1969–1971:plates 267–271). The earliest complex

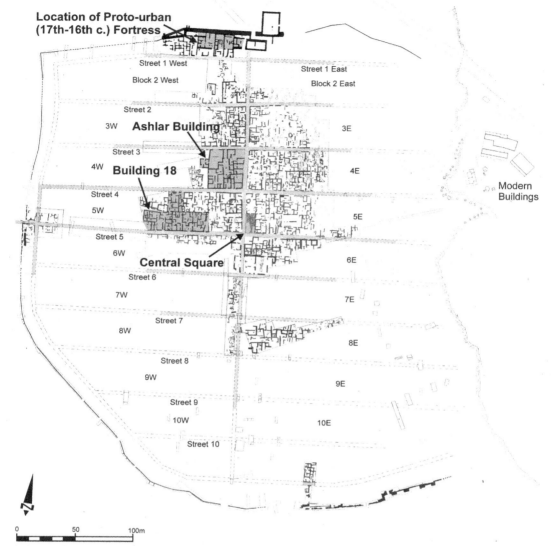

Figure 6.2 Schematic plan of Enkomi, c. 1200 BC (adapted by author from Courtois et al. 1986:figure 1 and Schaeffer 1971:plan IV).

recovered beneath the Ashlar Building occupies an area of about 30 x 22 m and has wings of rooms arranged around a central court, open on one end. It is important to note that this structure is freestanding, separated from other possible adjacent structures by open spaces. And, in a distinct break from thousands of years of burial in extramural cemeteries, we see that these open spaces are used for burials in subterranean chamber tombs. These tombs were a vital part of the Proto-urban built environments. Their location in the open space between individual buildings (rather than collective placement in extramural cemeteries) and their continued reuse throughout the Proto-urban period indicates that they were the primary means of status display (Keswani 2004) and were used in the negotiation and demarcation of both physical and social boundaries between rival groups. These tombs provided a direct link to ancestors as well as a statement of territoriality, legitimizing these groups' claims to spatial control. They were undoubtedly meant to be encountered in the course of daily practice, as seen in the two tombs built directly in front of the Fortress's main entrance.

Keswani's (2004) important study of Cypriot mortuary practices reveals that this dynamic would change significantly over the course of the LBA. She notes a decreasing elaboration of ritual treatment accompanied by a decline in investment in mortuary architecture and the value of deposited grave goods. These trends point to a decline in the importance of funerary ritual. I agree with Keswani's (2004:143–144,159–160) suggestion that increasingly complex political and economic opportunities became available as the LBA progressed, creating new contexts for the accumulation of wealth and the establishment of social status. This supported the emergence of political and religious institutions with officials, dependents, and functionaries whose social status and identity were increasingly independent of their associations with the earlier (Proto-urban) kin groups. It is no coincidence that the island's first urban centers were built at this same time.

PLACE-MAKING IN LATE CYPRIOT URBAN LANDSCAPES

The Proto-urban phase was followed by a phase from the mid-fourteenth century BC through to the end of the Bronze Age in ca. 1100 BC (LC IIC–IIIA periods) that witnessed the (re)construction, urbanization, and monumentalization of a number of settlements. Although we can bring evidence to bear from a larger number of sites to discuss this, it is important to emphasize that the following account is still based on limited and discontinuous exposures. Enkomi is the exception with nearly 20 percent of the known area of the site from this phase excavated (Figure 6.2), but there are various unresolved issues regarding the site's stratigraphic sequence that limit its use in understanding some aspects of LC urbanism (see Fisher 2007:120–122 for a summary). In any case, if excavations at sites such as Enkomi and Kalavasos-*Ayios Dhimitrios* are any indication (and to this we can add glimpses from Alassa, Hala Sultan Tekke, Kition, Episkopi (Kourion)-*Bamboula*, and Pyla-*Kokkinokremos*), the construction of many of the new cities involved the architectural definition and enclosure of the majority of space within the urban areas through the contiguous placement of building walls and streets (Åström 1996; Courtois et al. 1986:5–8, figure 1; Hadjisavvas 1986; Karageorghis and Demas 1984, 1985; Weinberg 1983; Wright 1992:115). We can begin by examining this at the spatial scale of the city as a whole – the urban landscape – and attempts by ruling elites to impose order on it.

The Planned City: Elite Place-Making Writ Large

One of the most striking features of many LC cities is the extensive use of urban planning, often characterized by particular street arrangements, which determined the position and alignment of most of their constituent buildings. This is seen most clearly at Enkomi, which, after a major destruction ca. 1200 BC, was rebuilt in an impressive manner exhibiting a number of the hallmarks of centralized planning recently discussed by Michael Smith (2007). These include formality and a coordinated arrangement of buildings and spaces combined through the use of a modular orthogonal plan (Figure 6.2). The grid, oriented to about 7 degrees west of north, consists of a single, central north-south artery dissected by nine evenly spaced, east–west running streets, forming twenty blocks. The fact that the outer walls of the Ashlar Building follow the boundaries of an underlying building from the previous phase might suggest that at least some elements of this layout were already in place before the city's reconstruction (see Dikaios 1969–1971:plates 292–293; Wright 1992). This was demarcated by a "cyclopean" fortification wall (i.e., made with a base of massive roughly shaped boulders) with towers that enclosed an area of about 14 ha (Courtois et al. 1986:5–8, figure 1). A ring road appears to have run around the inside of the fortifications. The plan also exhibits monumentality in the construction of a number of monumental buildings built partially or wholly of ashlar masonry, some of the most impressive of which (Building 18 [which is actually a series of elite residential units] and the Ashlar Building) are found along the city's central axes. The existence or nature of any settlement outside the walls is unknown (Iacovou 2007:10).

The failure of the published plans from the French excavations (e.g., Schaeffer 1971:plan IV) to distinguish among walls of various phases makes it difficult to ascertain the precise boundaries and internal structure of many of Enkomi's individual buildings. The centrally located Ashlar Building (Dikaios 1969–1971:171–190; Fisher 2007:ch. 6) is substantially larger than any other structure, but it appears to have been an elite residence and lacks compelling evidence for administrative activities. The lack of a single obvious administrative center and the generally widespread distribution of the highest status goods among elite graves throughout the city has led Keswani (1996; 2004:115) to suggest that there was no single focus of administrative power at Enkomi and that the site was therefore characterized by a heterarchical sociopolitical organization with power dispersed among multiple nodes (also Manning 1998:53; see Magnoni et al., Chapter 5 of this volume for a similar situation at the Classic Maya site of Chunchucmil).

The city of Kalavasos-*Ayios Dhimitrios*, dating mainly to the LC IIC period (ca. 1340/15–1200 BC), represents a somewhat different spatial configuration. Excavations in several areas of this site reveal various buildings and roads that are generally oriented to 25 degrees west of north, indicating that the city was laid out on a preconceived plan (South 1980, 1995; Figure 6.3). No fortification wall has yet been found, but the distribution-of-surface finds and architectural remains suggest that the site was about 11.5 ha in size. The plan consists of at least one major "north-south" street and one or more transverse "east-west" streets (Wright 1992:115).[2] The main north-south street, roughly 3.8 m wide, appears to extend at least 150 m through three separate excavation areas. Not enough of the urban fabric has been recovered to determine whether the plan is a modular orthogonal grid such as at Enkomi, or a simpler integrated orthogonal plan in which the buildings are aligned to one or more large-scale features (see Smith 2007:12–21). Some form of zoning may have been imposed in which the monumental administrative buildings were in the northeast, whereas higher-status residences, some of which also contained industrial facilities, were found in the eastern and central parts of the city, and smaller, and nonelite dwellings were on the western outskirts (Wright 1992:115). The latter are on a slightly different alignment (closer to north) than the rest of the city's buildings and infrastructure. Elsewhere, the plan exhibits symmetry and conformity, seen in the alignment of buildings on opposite sides of the street and the possible existence of "lots" demarcated by long stretches of wall (South 1995:192).

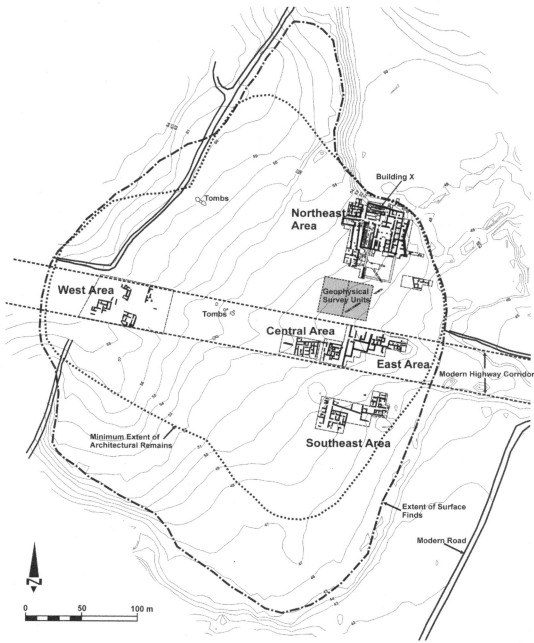

Figure 6.3 Schematic plan of Kalavasos-*Ayios Dhimitrios* (drawn by author based on topographic data provided by Alison South).

South (1988:223) has argued that a large wall excavated along the north and east side of the Northeast Area may have enclosed this part of the site, which contained monumental structures, including Building X – the largest and most architecturally elaborate building

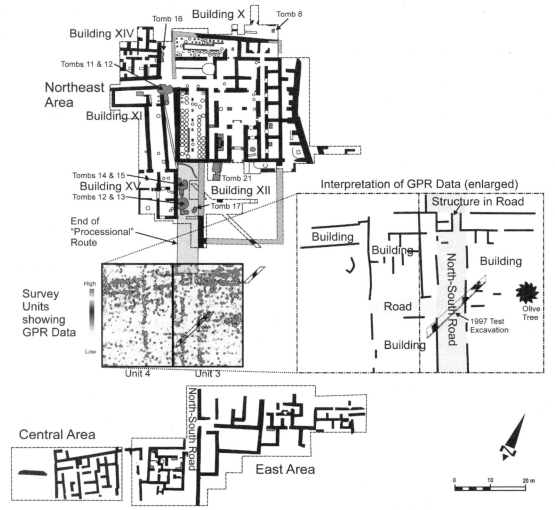

Figure 6.4 Detail of Northeast, Central and East excavation areas at Kalavasos-*Ayios Dhimitrios*, including results of ground-penetrating radar (GPR) survey (see Fisher et al. 2011–2012 for details; adapted by author from plan provided by Alison South).

yet found at the site and likely its administrative focus. A recent survey by the Kalavasos and Maroni Built Environments (KAMBE) Project using archaeological geophysics appears to support this contention, suggesting an arrangement of structures delineating the southern limit of the Northeast Area (Fisher et al. 2011–2012; Figure 6.4). Where these features intersect with the main north-south road, there appears to be a structure that narrowed the roadway, possibly indicating an attempt to control physical and visual access to this area of the city, yet another hallmark of centralized planning (Smith 2007:23–25). The presence of this single and separate administrative area implies a hierarchical organization of power at Kalavasos-*Ayios Dhimitrios*, with a paramount ruling individual or group (Keswani 1996).

The urban centers of Maroni and Alassa likewise had monumental zones that appear to have been the primary focus of elite power at each site, although it is unclear how they articulated with nearby settlement areas. A survey in the Maroni Valley suggests a fairly continuous 15–25 ha area of LC occupation down to the shoreline, although it is presently unclear whether remains of buildings and tombs found at *Vournes*, *Aspres*, *Kapsaloudhia* and *Tsaroukkas* represent continuous or dispersed urban development (Fisher et al. 2011–2012; Manning 1998:42; Manning et al. 1994; Manning and Conwell 1992; Manning and De Mita 1997; cf. Iacovou 2007:7; Figure 6.5). Excavations of an elevated zone at Maroni-*Vournes* revealed a monumental building complex dating to Late Cypriot IIC that included the Ashlar Building, a 30.5 x 21 m structure built in part with ashlar masonry and separated from an adjacent storage building by a 4.5 m wide street (Cadogan 1984, 1992). A few small sterile trenches to the east of *Vournes* led Cadogan (1984:2) to conclude that it was physically separated from contemporaneous utilitarian buildings and tombs found at the coastal site of Maroni-*Tsaroukkas*, nearly 500 m to the southeast. These buildings are on a different alignment (ca. 25 degrees west of north) than those at *Vournes* (ca. 45 degrees west of north). Ongoing geophysical survey and test excavations by the KAMBE Project at Maroni between *Vournes* and *Tsaroukkas* (Fisher et al. 2010–2011) have revealed the remains of contemporary LBA structures interspersed with open spaces, suggesting a lower-density or less-integrated form of urbanism than seen at sites such as Kalavasos or Enkomi.

Like Maroni, Alassa-*Paliotaverna* is characterized by the presence of monumental structures dating to the LC IIC-IIIA, including Building II, a massive court-centered building (37.7 m per side) built almost entirely of elaborate ashlar masonry (see Hadjisavvas 1986; 1996). To the south, across a 4.3 m wide street, was a large, pillared hall, also built of ashlar masonry (Building I). *Paliotaverna* appears to have been separated from an area of nonelite domestic architecture found downslope at Alassa-*Pano Mandilaris*, nearly 200 m to the east and built on a different alignment (Figure 6.6).

The coordinated arrangement of buildings and spaces seen within the monumental areas of both Maroni and Alassa is indicative

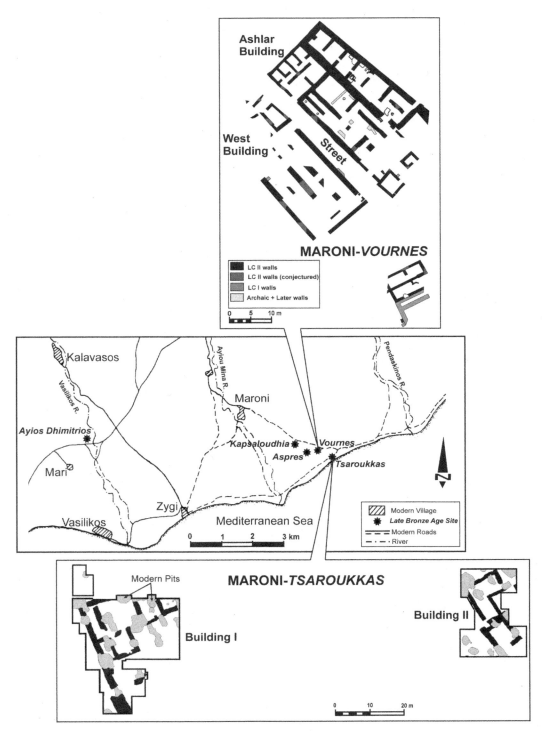

Figure 6.5 Map of the Maroni region with schematic plans of excavation areas at *Vournes* and *Tsaroukkas* (adapted by author from Manning 1998:figure 2; Fisher 2007:figure 7.24; Fisher et al. 2011–2012:figure 9).

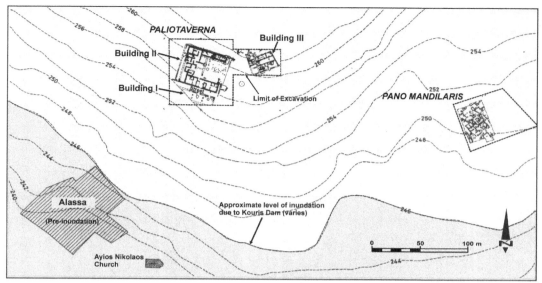

Figure 6.6 Map of the site of Alassa, showing the *Paliotaverna* and *Pano Mandilaris* localities (adapted by author from map by A. Kattos in Hadjisavvas 2003:figure 2).

of centralized planning, even if these areas were not tied to nearby domestic areas through an orthogonal grid. Similarly, one could perhaps see areas of domestic architecture at both Hala Sultan Tekke and Pyla-*Kokkinokremos*, in which several adjoined houses were aligned on the same orientation, as the result of higher-level planning (Åström 1989; Karageorghis and Demas 1984; Figures 6.7 and 6.8). As Smith (2007:14–16) points out, however, this sort of pattern could potentially arise from the actions of individual builders who made additions or new structures next to existing ones based on factors of practicality, efficiency, or, in the case of Pyla, the presence of the plateau edge. Åström (1996:10) claims that Hala Sultan Tekke had an orthogonal town plan with streets at right angles (he uses the term "Hippodamic"), but it is difficult to substantiate this on the basis of the published plans (e.g., Åström 1989:figure 2; Figure 6.7).

Based on the available evidence, it appears that there was no ideal plan for a Late Bronze Age city on Cyprus and that each was a product of individual site histories and trajectories of urban development (Iacovou 2007). The urban landscape of Maroni, and perhaps the still poorly understood LBA occupation of Palaepaphos (Iacovou 2007:3–6), may represent lower-density forms of urbanism than those materialized in the more integrated or nucleated plans of cities such as Enkomi and Kalavasos. In many cases, these cities share spatial configurations in which physical and social boundaries

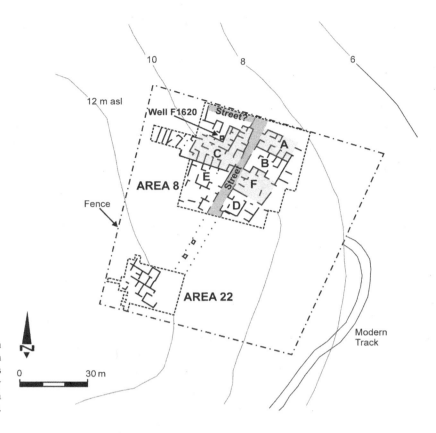

Figure 6.7 Hala Sultan Tekke, schematic plan of excavation Areas 8 and 22 (adapted by author from Åström 1989:figure 2).

were increasingly defined through the construction of buildings and street systems. For the most part, open spaces – the control of which had likely been negotiated among competing groups through the placement of tombs in the Proto-urban phase (again, based mainly on limited exposures from Enkomi) – were now incorporated within the structure of contiguously placed buildings on well-defined streets. This is quite clear in Area I at Enkomi, where a succession of Proto-urban buildings centered around multiple courtyards that were open on one side was replaced by the fully enclosed LC IIIA Ashlar Building (Dikaios 1969–1971:153–190). Here, the function of the tombs as territorial markers was preserved in the LC IIIA street pattern on the north and south of the new Ashlar Building. In some cases, earlier elite tombs continued to be used in the new urban environments, marking an attempt to demonstrate real or fictive continuity of ownership and power (e.g., Tomb 13 and its newly built subsidiary Tomb 12 in the street west of Building X at Kalavasos-*Ayios Dhimitrios*; South 1995:72). In other cases, as at Maroni-*Vournes* (Manning 1998), new elites marked their ascendancy over the

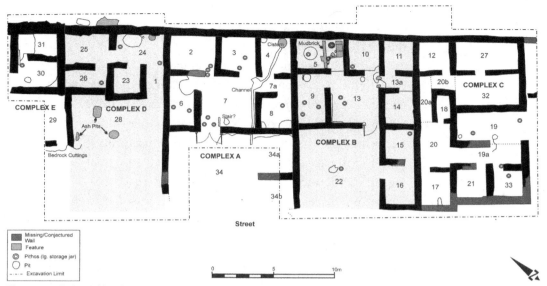

Figure 6.8 Pyla-*Kokkinokremos*, schematic plan of Complexes A–E (adapted by author from Karageorghis and Demas 1984:plan 1).

previous sociopolitical order by constructing their new buildings directly on top of the earlier tombs.

I would argue that the overall plans (streets, fortifications, and monumental buildings) of the new cities were products of top-down decision making by ruling elites, whether they exercised political power locally or at some wider regional or island-wide level. As Kostof (1991:33) argues in *The City Shaped*, "[c]ities, even those attributed to spontaneous processes inherent in a region, are never entirely processual events: at some level, city making always entails an act of will on the part of a leader or collectivity." Indeed, the general form of the new urban environments was a product of elite place-making writ large, symbolized at some sites by the use of the grid, which has been recognized as a tool of dominance and oppression in societies engaged in centralizing authority (e.g., Grant 2001; Love 1999). A close association exists between the constitution of authority of political regimes and the form and aesthetic of urban political landscapes (A. Smith 2003). In a similar vein, Foucault (1977) has demonstrated how the configuration of space contributes to the maintenance of power of one group over another through the control and surveillance of the movement of bodies through space.

In addition, other than the streets, there is a notable lack of large, open, publically accessible spaces that could be used for spontaneous gatherings or planned public-inclusive social occasions among a city's inhabitants and visitors. This could be seen as an attempt by those who planned the city's infrastructure to limit the occurrence of large-scale, uncontrolled social gatherings. A number of studies have found that open public spaces stimulate political action, civic engagement, and democratic practices (Shin 2009:426). Monica Smith (2008) argues that open spaces provide flexible venues for planned and unplanned performances and the opportunity for consensus building in dense populations. The central square at Enkomi (see Figure 6.2), located at the city's main crossroads (the North-South Artery and Street 5), was one of few such spaces and likely an important venue for both informal gatherings and public-inclusive social occasions. Given its capacity (as many as 380 standing persons based on modern architectural conventions [see Fisher 2009a:444], not including the adjoining road space), such a place had the potential to serve as a prime context for interactions aimed at resisting or undermining the social order represented by the nearby monumental buildings and the overall urban plan.

Other large, open spaces tended to be more carefully controlled. For example, I previously noted that the main north-south road at Kalavasos-*Ayios Dhimitrios* may have reached some form of intervening structure as it approached the Northeast Area (see Figure 6.4). Beyond this point, the road widens to 6 m, creating a large space more than 30 m long that may have functioned as the terminus of a processional or ceremonial way or similar performative space. Here, earlier elite tombs (Tombs 12, 13, 14, and 15) would have been visible in the street, their entrances marked with vertically placed stones and possibly posts (South 1997:170). The street was bounded on the east by the poorly preserved ashlar façade of Building XII, and ended at the southwest corner of Building X. This was Building X's most impressive façade, made with a plinth of monumental ashlar blocks with drafted margins and lifting bosses, topped by an orthostat of large blocks, also with drafted margins. The space defined by these façades undoubtedly provided an imposing context for social occasions that took place here, including the arrival or departure of Building X's elite inhabitants, as well as the arrival of visitors who were permitted access to this part of the city, perhaps as participants in the feasting events that occasionally took place within Buildings X and XII (see Fisher 2009b; South 2008).

The cities of the fully urban phase of the LBA were the ultimate expressions of the desire to control movement and interaction, first seen in the Proto-urban forts. Their extant remains indicate the large-scale appropriation of space and its incorporation into planned, imageable built environments. Kevin Lynch (1960:9) sees *imageability* as "that quality in a physical object which gives it a high probability of evoking a strong image in any given observer. It is that shape, color, or arrangement which facilitates the making of vividly identified, powerfully structured, highly useful mental images of the environment." The enclosure of some urban environments (e.g., Enkomi and Kition) by massive cyclopean fortifications undoubtedly contributed to this imageability, while providing ruling elites additional means to control movement and participation in particular social interactions. In addition to their military and defensive functions, these walls vividly materialized the boundaries of the city proper and those who lived within them may have increasingly identified themselves in terms of a built-up, complex, ordered, and perhaps cosmopolitan cityscape that stood in contrast to the rural lands beyond – regardless of the failure of such an ideal to reflect the socioeconomic reality of city-hinterland interdependence.

The highly imageable urban center was likely one the more clearly defined places with which many Late Cypriot people identified. Indeed, Cowgill's definition of a city outlined earlier emphasizes the formation of a distinct urban identity through daily practice. Environmental psychologists have long noted the important role of place attachment at various scales in the formation of self- and group identities (Fisher and Creekmore, Chapter 1 of this volume; Proshansky 1978; Proshansky et al. 1983; Twigger-Ross and Uzzell 1996). Proshansky (1978:161) argues that an urban identity arises from the physical characteristics and requirements of life in urban contexts that socialize individuals to move, think, feel, play social roles, and solve problems in ways that are uniquely urban. Therefore, the experience of living in urban environments (i.e., an urban lifestyle) or, in some cases, attachment to particular cities, can form the basis of urban identities (Feldman 1990; Graumann 2002:109–110; Lalli 1992; Magnoni et al., Chapter 5 of this volume; Proshansky et al. 1983:78). This sort of place identity also developed through more localized forms of place-making that resulted in the production of (and attachment to) neighborhoods and households.

Between City and Household: Late Cypriot Neighborhoods

Urban communities that were intermediate between the city and the household undoubtedly existed in LC cities, although defining their social and material boundaries is no simple matter. Michael Smith (2010) recently argued that the division of cities into neighborhoods and districts was a universal of urban life for all time periods. He defines a *neighborhood* as a residential zone that exhibits a great deal of face-to-face interaction and is distinctive on the basis of physical and/or social characteristics, while a *district* is a larger administrative unit within a city (Smith 2010:139–140). Distinct districts are difficult to substantiate in LC urban centers, given their relatively small size and limited exposures, but we are perhaps better able to identify neighborhoods. In modern urban settings, neighborhoods have long been acknowledged as an important level of social organization (recently, Garrioch and Peel 2006). They become political and social communities, providing a frame of reference for the individual and a venue for the exchange of skills, emergency assistance, and mutual protection (Hallman 1984:11; M. L. Smith 2003:20–21). Neighborhoods have also been noted as being particularly important in the formation of individual and group identities and place attachment (often referred to as "neighborhood attachment") among their residents (Brown et al. 2003; Comstock et al. 2010). Although mostly absent from discussions of LC cities (cf. Weinberg 1983), neighborhoods have been recognized in other ancient contexts, including Mesoamerica (e.g., Arnauld et al. 2012) and Mesopotamia (e.g., Creekmore 2008, Chapter 2 of this volume; Nishimura, Chapter 3 of this volume; Stone 1996; cf. van de Mieroop 1992). Textual sources from Mesopotamian cities of the Old Babylonian period indicate that neighborhood associations actively mediated between households and the city-level bureaucracy (Keith 2003). In Mesoamarica, Cowgill (1992) has suggested the existence of neighborhoods based on ethnic groups at Teotihuacan.

An early form of neighborhood on Cyprus might be traced back to the founding of Proto-urban Enkomi and Morphou-*Toumba tou Skourou* in the seventeenth century BC. Keswani (1996) argues that these sites were initially formed by residents of other communities and even other regions, who gathered in localities well suited to exploiting foreign trade. The dispersed arrangement of compounds at early Enkomi and the residential and industrial zones associated with multiple mounds attested at *Toumba tou Skourou* (Vermeule and Wolsky 1990) might reflect the existence of nascent neighborhoods rooted in these heterogeneous origins. This contrasts with fully urban Enkomi during the LC IIIA (ca. 1200 BC), which was arranged in clearly defined blocks by the street system previously discussed (see Figure 6.2). Although the internal arrangements of most of these blocks are unclear owing to the conflation of various architectural phases in published plans (e.g., Courtois et al. 1986:figure 1), it appears that each consisted of a number of contiguously placed buildings of various shapes and sizes. Several blocks (especially blocks 4E, 5E, 5W, and 6E) exhibit a fairly regular wall line bisecting them along their east-west axes, perhaps further evidence of higher-level planning through the use of regular lot depths. While it is possible that these blocks might have constituted some form of neighborhood, residents would likely have had greater occasion to interact with those who lived in units across the main streets. This socio-spatial arrangement is referred to as a "face-block" neighborhood, defined as two sides of one street between intersecting streets (Suttles 1972; American Planning Association 2006:409). Distinctive features, such as the ashlar façade pierced with unique windows that ran along the north side of Street 5 West (i.e., the south wall of Building 18), gave some of these face-blocks high imageability.

Karageorghis and Demas (1988:58) appear to be referring to a neighborhood when they suggest that Buildings II and IV at Maa-*Palaeokastro* combined with Areas 96 and 99 and Rooms 73, 76, and 77 to form an "architectural grouping" that might have represented a level of integration between individual households and the wider settlement (Figure 6.9). In other cities, there were areas defined by the concentration of particular building types that might also be seen as neighborhoods. The administrative areas of Kalavasos (the Northeast Area), Maroni (the *Vournes* locality), and Alassa (the *Paliotaverna* locality) discussed earlier, with their monumental ashlar buildings and evidence for production and storage, or Area II at Kition where five temples connected by courtyards and workshops were recovered (Karageorghis and Demas 1985; cf. J. Smith 2009), were all distinct in this way. But, these areas were not primarily residential and many social interactions would have been limited to particular times of day or other activity cycles.

At Kalavasos-*Ayios Dhimitrios*, the area of what Wright (1992:115) describes as "poorer" dwellings in the western-most part of the site

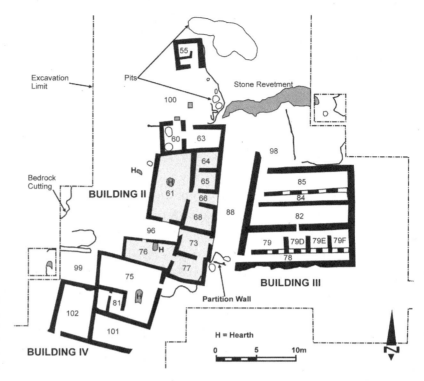

Figure 6.9 Schematic plan of Maa-*Palaeokastro*, Area III (adapted by author from Karageorghis and Demas 1988:figure 15).

might be an example of a neighborhood based on socioeconomic status (see Figure 6.3). As noted previously, the buildings (likely houses) in this part of the site are on a slightly different alignment (closer to north) than the rest of the site's architecture and appear to have significant spaces between the buildings, in contrast to the contiguous and more ordered construction seen along the main north-south road. It is important to bear in mind that this part of the site was incompletely excavated and that any conclusions regarding the status of its inhabitants are based mainly on the generally smaller size of these buildings and the lower quality of their extant masonry compared with houses recovered to the east (South 1980:42). A similar dynamic may have existed at Episkopi-*Bamboula*, where Area E has generally larger houses, which were arranged in orderly blocks delimited by streets, in contrast with the smaller and more organically arranged dwellings of Area A (Weinberg 1983:52–57, figures 18–20). This could represent a form of zoning as part of the overall urban plan. Such practices have sociopolitical implications as authority (legally based or otherwise) is employed to control social relations through the segregation or exclusion of certain groups (Madanipour 1998; Shin 2009:431). In modern cities, spatial and residential segregation is

known to create social enclaves and categorical relationships by limiting social interaction within racially, socioeconomically, and culturally homogeneous social groups, raising the potential for conflict
and tension among segregated groups (Shin 2009:434).

The use of shared facilities could have been an additional basis
for the kind of face-to-face interactions that defined particular neighborhoods (Keith 2003). For example, in spite of Bolger's (2003:49) contention that the water supply became increasingly privatized in LBA
Cyprus, dwellings from a number of sites have no evidence for their
own permanent water extraction or collection facilities, such as wells
or cisterns. This suggests that many, if not most, households would
have used communal water facilities, such as the large, well-built
well found in Area B at Episkopi-*Bamboula*. This feature was 1.8 m
square, aligned to the cardinal points, and does not appear to have
been enclosed by any architecture (Weinberg 1983:32, plate 8). At
Hala Sultan Tekke, even though Buildings A, C, and D had their own
wells, the well (F 1620) located in Room 59 was located at the end of
what Åström (1998:54–8) describes as a raised, communal passage-
way accessed by a street that ran along the northern edge of Building
C (Figure 6.7). In addition, Karageorghis and Demas (1988:61) suggest
that Buildings II and IV at Maa- *Palaeokastro* may have shared communal food preparation facilities in Area 96, Room 76, and possibly
Area 99 (Figure 6.9).

Urban Households: Place-Making from the Bottom-up

It is clear that there were likely several overlapping bases around
which neighborhoods might have formed, but each would have consisted of a number of individual households. Like neighborhood,
household is a concept with interwoven material-spatial and social
components. It is traditionally seen as a minimal social unit that meets
certain basic needs of its members (economic, social, and biological)
and is generally distinguished from family by co-residence, or at least
locality, rather than kinship (Bender 1967; Rogers 1995; Santley and
Hirth 1993; Yanagisako 1979). Current approaches instead emphasize
the social interactions within and between households, seeing them
not as functional units, but rather as a set of social relations enacted
through practice (Hendon 2004; Meskell 1998). As Wilk and Rathje
(1982:618) famously stated, archaeologists do not dig up households,
but must infer them from the material record of houses and their

associated artifacts. The house can act as a medium through which the wider community can exercise a measure of control over what goes on within, yet it also provides a means of separating the actions of household members from that wider community (Allison 1999:1; Ardener 1993:11; also Altman and Gauvain 1981:287). The design of domestic space interacts with human action and meaning to create places "in which the house becomes integral to the construction of social identities through a process of … movements, views and spatial arrangements" (Hendon 2004:276).

Individual houses have been identified in all of the major LC urban centers. Unfortunately, individual urban buildings have often been distinguished in binary terms of "private" domestic architecture and "public" monumental architecture, in spite of the fact that both building types contained spaces that were, to varying degrees, public and private (domestic). Whatever administrative, economic, and ideological functions they may have had (and in spite of their size and architectural elaboration), most monumental buildings were, in fact, dwellings for elite households, likely including a number of retainers. I have presented detailed arguments elsewhere regarding the vital roles that the monumental buildings and new types of nonelite housing both played in LC sociopolitical dynamics (Fisher 2007, 2009b, 2014). These new types of urban buildings and their constituent spaces provided the contexts for much of daily practice as well as occasional social interactions (such as feasts) that brought various individuals and groups together as social identities, roles, and statuses were negotiated, established, and displayed. Here I will briefly consider how these individual buildings and the households who lived in them were woven into the wider urban fabric.

In spite of the perception of LC settlement plans consisting of independent freestanding structures (e.g., Bolger 2003:49), most of the buildings from the fully urban period show, rather, an agglomerative (albeit ordered) arrangement in which they were constructed side by side and often shared outer walls. It was necessary for residents of such built environments, where nearly all space was architecturally defined, to demarcate and maintain the boundaries of the area under their direct control as unambiguously as possible. These boundaries defined what Altman (1975:111–120) refers to as household members' *primary territory* – spaces used by them on a relatively permanent basis and central to their day-to-day lives. Such spaces tend to have markers more closely reflective of the personal qualities and central values of the occupants (Brown 1987). They also reflect an increased concern for privacy during the LBA and Bolger's (2003:49) contention that this period witnessed greater privatization of domestic activities is borne out in the limited physical and visual accessibility of LBA houses from the outside (Fisher 2014). Given the relationship between power and knowledge through surveillance (Foucault 1977), this might be seen on one level as an act of resistance against the power structures that came to intervene in various aspects of LBA life.

The importance of boundary maintenance is also apparent in the number of LC houses that show evidence of rebuilding on the same or nearly identical plan. For example, at LC IIIA Episkopi-*Bamboula*, the houses of Area A were destroyed at the end of Stratum D (Weinberg 1983:9–26). Houses A.V and A.VI were rebuilt in Stratum E using the same layout by leveling the debris, raising the floors and thresholds, and constructing new walls directly on top of the old foundations (Figure 6.10). Such continuity is not merely a demonstration of enduring property ownership, but indicates a constancy of dwelling that materialized a household's attachment to a particular place through the accumulation of meanings and the formation of individual and collective memories (Ingold 2000:175; Zerubavel 2003:41). Attempts to demonstrate such continuity of spatial use and control were an essential part of place-making throughout the urban social hierarchy.

In spite of such efforts at boundary demarcation and maintenance, LC urban landscapes were also places of negotiation, fluidity, and change. House A.VIII at Episkopi was built *de novo* in Stratum E and extended beyond the remains of House A.VIa, which it replaced, whereas House A.IV went out of use (see Figure 6.10), demonstrating that urban development was a dynamic process as some households in a given neighborhood grew or contracted; owners vacated, transferred, or subdivided their properties – processes that were materialized in the unique biographies of individual houses (see Tringham 1995; Düring 2005). The transformation of the Fortress at Enkomi from a freestanding monumental building and center of power at the beginning of the LC period, to a series of non-monumental domestic units that formed part of an urban block in LC II–III also attests to this dynamic (Fisher 2007:199–217; Pickles and Peltenburg 1998).

A notable example of the ambiguity of some boundaries can be seen in the design of the large external courtyards that fronted Complexes A, B, and D at Pyla-*Kokkinokremos* (see Karageorghis and

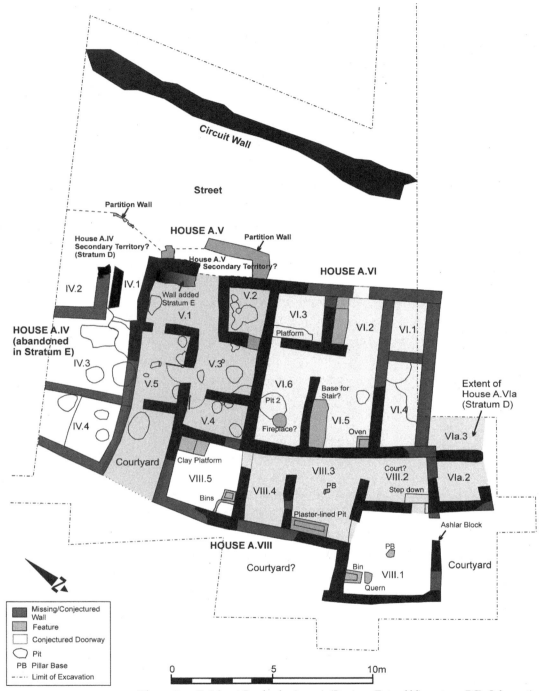

Figure 6.10 Episkopi-*Bamboula*, Area A (Stratum E, twelfth century BC). Schematic plan showing houses A.IV, A.V, A.VI (now abandoned) and the newly built A.VIII. Shaded area in House A.VIII shows extent of earlier House A.VIa (from Stratum D). Note appropriation of street space by House A.IV (Stratum D) and House A.V (Strata D and E) (adapted by author from Weinberg 1983:figures 7, 23, and 24).

Demas 1984:6–32; Figure 6.8). The fact that these courtyards appear to have been completely open to the space in front of the houses – presumably a street – indicates that they were intended to be both readily accessible and completely visible from the street. The function of these courts is unclear. The one in Complex A (Room 34) was not entirely excavated, while three ashy deposits that may have been hearths were found in the court in Complex D (Room 28). The court in Complex B (Room 22) contained a bronze "foundry hoard" hidden in a pit, as well as a fragmentary pithos and another pit containing copper slag, but with no associated ash (thus, likely ruling out metallurgical activity). The courts otherwise contained no built features. Although it is possible that their boundaries with the street were regulated through implicit norms or conventions (e.g., Lawrence 1990:77), the lack of a material border is rather unusual given the tendency to define spaces architecturally in LC IIC–IIIA urban environments, and introduces opportunities for negotiation and contestation. I would argue that these spaces were likely what Altman (1975) refers to as *secondary territories*, which are accessible to a wider range of users, although regular occupants often exert some degree of control over who can enter a space and their behavior. Because secondary territories combine public or semipublic access with control by regular occupants, there is potential for uncertainty and social conflict as boundaries are established, tested, and violated (Altman 1975:114; see also Lawrence's [1990] discussion of "collective" spaces).

In addition to the negotiation invited by the ambiguous boundaries of these transitional spaces, there is evidence suggesting that the efforts of ruling elites to impose order through top-down urban planning were sometimes undermined by bottom-up actions of individual households. In some cities, there are instances of households laying some claim to sections of what would appear to be public streets. At Maa-*Palaeokastro*, a screen made of wooden posts and other perishable materials was erected, running perpendicular to the east wall of Room 73, blocking off part of the open space (likely a street) between Buildings II and III (Karageorghis and Demas 1988; see Figure 6.9). Elsewhere, the owners of Houses A.V and A.IV at Episkopi-*Bamboula* (Stratum D) constructed partition walls in front of their houses using wooden posts or shallow trenches and field stones, thereby appropriating part of the street that ran inside the circuit wall (Figure 6.10). The relative permanence of this arrangement is seen by the fact that the wall in front of House A.V was rebuilt along with the rest of the house in Stratum E. The placement of new tombs in the streets and open areas in Area E at Episkopi-*Bamboula* (Benson 1972; Weinberg 1983:figure 25) and at Alassa-*Pano Mandilaris* (Hadjisavvas 1986) was one of the most potent symbols of the contesting, if not appropriation, of public space and indicates that at least some streets were deemed by adjacent households as a secondary territory or collective space. These acts of place-making suggest that even established, well-marked boundaries could be ignored, challenged, or at least open to negotiation. The success or permanence of such actions likely depended on the existence and degree of enforcement of norms or laws regarding the use of space established at the neighborhood and city levels, as well as the changing sociopolitical and economic fortunes of the people involved.

CONCLUSIONS

The new cities of the LC period fundamentally altered the island's physical and social landscape. They were created in the interplay of decisions made at various levels by multiple stakeholders, taking into account factors such as available material and human resources, topography, and whether or not there was preexisting architecture that had to be incorporated or removed (Fisher 2009b:189; Locock 1994:5; Markus 1993:23). On one hand, people made these decisions influenced by shared cultural ideas of what constitutes proper built form, giving rise to standardized building types or methods of construction and embellishment. We can see this in terms of the structural properties of social systems that, according to Giddens (1984:17), make it possible for similar social practices to exist across various spans of space and time and that give systemic form to these practices. This is manifested in the culturally contingent "limited palette of elements" and "display rules," which people combine to create their built environments (Rapoport 1990:figure 17). On the other hand, Rapoport (1990:15–16, 21) argues that many of the meanings that make a building a place are those encoded by its occupants and users through the process of *personalization* as they take possession of, complete, and change their built environment. This can be seen as a form of marking one's primary territory by encoding messages regarding self- or household identity (Brown 1987:519–521). The numerous idiosyncrasies in configuration and design even between the so-called twin Complexes A and B at Pyla-*Kokkinokremos*

(Karageorghis and Demas 1984: 9; see Figure 6.8) are testament to this process (Fisher 2014).

I have argued that the overall form of LC cities was largely the result of top-down decision making by ruling elites who rose to power in the LBA. As Knapp (2008:159) recently claimed, these elites "sought to integrate society more closely than in the past, to resolve ambiguities … and to restructure social relationships in a manner that clarified their identity beyond doubt." The large-scale appropriation and control of space through urban planning was a vital component of these efforts, materialized in the gridded streets and fortifications of cities like Enkomi. Yet, this place-making could be met with resistance or subject to negotiation as individual households sought to create places of their own. Shared socioeconomic status or prior community affiliations among these households and the use of common facilities helped to generate the social interactions and built forms that characterized particular neighborhoods. These processes made LC cities places of contestation and fluidity, despite efforts to define social boundaries unambiguously through architectural design and other forms of nonverbal communication. The unique urban landscapes that resulted were at once creator and materialization of the increasingly complex and heterogeneous society that characterized LBA Cyprus. The new cities became an important element in the identities of these individuals and groups, drawn together in the "evocative potency" (A. Smith 2003:27) and "social drama" (Mumford 1937[2003]:94) of the urban experience.

ACKNOWLEDGMENTS

Research presented in this chapter was funded or otherwise supported by a number of agencies and institutions, including the National Science Foundation (Awards # BCS-0917732 and 0917734), the Social Sciences and Humanities Research Council of Canada, the Archaeological Institute of America, the Cyprus American Archaeological Research Institute, the University of Toronto, Wilfrid Laurier University, the Department of Classics at Cornell University, and the Joukowsky Institute for Archaeology and the Ancient World at Brown University. I thank the Department of Antiquities of Cyprus for their permission to conduct this work and my codirectors and crew of the Kalavasos and Maroni Built Environments (KAMBE) Project for all their hard work. Alison South has kindly provided ongoing moral and logistical support of our investigations at Kalavasos-*Ayios Dhimitrios*. Earlier drafts of this chapter benefited from the comments and criticisms of Andrew Creekmore, Sturt Manning, Michael Smith, and an anonymous reviewer. I am grateful for their efforts; any errors or omissions are my own. I would especially like to acknowledge the tireless work of my coeditor, Andrew Creekmore – this volume would have been impossible without his efforts.

NOTES

1 The name of a Cypriot archaeological site typically consists of both a first name referring to the municipality in which it is found, followed by an italicized toponym that refers to the specific locality. Some sites, such as Enkomi-*Ayios Iakovos* are more typically known only by their first name.

2 Unless otherwise noted, architectural descriptions at Kalavasos-*Ayios Dhimitrios* are given as though the roads and buildings were aligned to the cardinal points (rather than 25° west of north, etc.).

REFERENCES CITED

Allison, Penelope M. (editor) 1999 *The Archaeology of Household Activities*. Routledge, London, New York.

Altman, Irwin 1975 *The Environment and Social Behavior: Privacy, Personal Space, Territory, Crowding*. Brooks/Cole Publishing, Monterey, CA.

Altman, Irwin and Mary Gauvain 1981 A Cross-cultural and Dialectic Analysis of Homes. In *Spatial Representation and Behavior Across the Life Span: Theory and Application*, edited by Lynn S. Liben, Arthur H. Patterson, and Nora Newcombe, pp. 283–320. Academic Press, New York.

American Planning Association 2006 *Planning and Urban Design Standards*. John Wiley and Sons, Hoboken, NJ.

Anderson, Benedict 1991 *Imagined Communities: Reflections on the Origins and Spread of Nationalism*. 2nd edition. Verso, London.

Ardener, Shirley (editor) 1993 *Women and Space: Ground Rules and Social Maps*. Berg, Oxford, UK and Providence, RI.

Arnauld, M. Charlotte, Linda R. Manzanilla, and Michael E. Smith (editors) 2012 *The Neighbourhood as Social and Spatial Unit in Mesoamerican Cities*. University of Arizona Press, Tucson.

Åström, Paul 1989 *Hala Sultan Tekke. Vol. 9, Trenches 1972–1987, with an Index for Volumes 1–9*. P. Åströms Förlag, Göteborg, Sweden.

— 1996 Hala Sultan Tekke – a Late Cypriot Harbour Town. In *Late Bronze Age Settlement in Cyprus: Function and Relationship*, edited by Paul Åström and Ellen Herscher, pp. 9–14. P. Åströms Förlag, Jonsered, Sweden.

— 1998 *Hala Sultan Tekke. 10, The Wells*. P. Åströms Förlag, Jonsered, Sweden.

Bender, Donald R. 1967 A Refinement of the Concept of Household: Families, Co-Residence, and Domestic Functions. *American Anthropologist* 69(5):493–504.

Benson, Jack L. 1972 *Bamboula at Kourion: the Necropolis and the Finds Excavated by J. F. Daniel.* University of Pennsylvania Press, Philadelphia.

Bolger, Diane R. 2003 *Gender in Ancient Cyprus: Narratives of Social Change on a Mediterranean Island.* AltaMira Press, Walnut Creek, CA.

Bourdieu, Pierre 1973 The Kabyle House. In *Rules and Meanings; the Anthropology of Everyday Knowledge,* edited by Mary Douglas, pp. 98–110. Penguin Education, Harmondsworth, UK.

1977 *Outline of a Theory of Practice.* Vol. 16, Cambridge University Press, Cambridge, New York.

Brown, Barbara, Douglas D. Perkins, and Graham Brown 2003 Place Attachment in a Revitalizing Neighborhood: Individual and Block Levels of Analysis. *Journal of Environmental Psychology* 23(3):259–271.

Brown, B. B. 1987 Territoriality. In *Handbook of Environmental Psychology,* edited by Daniel Stokols and Irwin Altman, pp. 505–531. Wiley, New York.

Cadogan, Gerald 1984 Maroni and the Late Bronze Age of Cyprus. In *Cyprus at the Close of the Late Bronze Age,* edited by Vassos Karageorghis and James D. Muhly, pp. 1–10. A.G. Leventis Foundation, Nicosia, Cyprus.

1992 Maroni VI. *Report of the Department of Antiquities, Cyprus:*51–58.

Childe, V. Gordon 1936 *Man Makes Himself.* Watts and Co., London.

Comstock, Nicole L. Miriam Dickinson, Julie A. Marshall, Mah-J Soobader, Mark S. Turbin, Michael Buchenau, and Jill S. Litt 2010 Neighborhood Attachment and its Correlates: Exploring Neighborhood Conditions, Collective Efficacy, and Gardening. *Journal of Environmental Psychology* 30(4):435–442.

Courtois, Jacques-Claude, Jacques Lagarce, and Elisabeth Lagarce 1986 *Enkomi et le Bronze Récent à Chypre.* Zavallis, Nicosia, Cyprus.

Cowgill, George L. 1992 Social differentiation at Teotihuacan. In *Mesoamerican Elites: An Archaeological Assessment,* edited by Arlen F. Chase and Diane E. Z. Chase, pp. 206–220. University of Oklahoma Press, Norman, London.

2004 Origins and Development of Urbanism: Archaeological Perspectives. *Annual Review of Anthropology* 33:525–549.

Creekmore, Andrew T. 2008 Kazane Höyük and Urban Life Histories in Third Millennium Upper Mesopotamia. Unpublished Ph.D. dissertation, Department of Anthropology, Northwestern University, Evanston, IL.

Dikaios, Porphyrios 1969–1971 *Enkomi: Excavations 1948–1958.* Philipp von Zabern, Mainz, Germany.

Düring, Bleda S. 2005 Building continuity in the Central Anatolian Neolithic: Exploring the Meaning of Buildings at Aşıklı Höyük and Çatalhöyük. *Journal of Mediterranean Archaeology* 18(1):3–29.

Feld, Steven and Keith H. Basso (editors) 1996 *Senses of Place.* 1st edition. School of American Research Press, Santa Fe, NM.

Feldman, Roberta M. 1990 Settlement-Identity: Psychological Bonds with Home Places in a Mobile Society. *Environment and Behavior* 22(2):183–229.

Fisher, Kevin D. 2007 Building Power: Monumental Architecture, Place and Social Interaction in Late Bronze Age Cyprus. Unpublished Ph.D. dissertation, Department of Anthropology, University of Toronto, Toronto.

2009a Placing Social Interaction: An Integrative Approach to Analyzing Past Built Environments. *Journal of Anthropological Archaeology* 28(4):439–457.

2009b Elite place-making and Social Interaction in the Late Cypriot Bronze Age. *Journal of Mediterranean Archaeology* 22(2):183–209.

2014 Rethinking the Late Cypriot Built Environment: Households and Communities as Places of Social Transformation. In *Cambridge Prehistory of the Bronze and Iron Age Mediterranean World*, edited by A. B. Knapp and P. van Dommelen. Cambridge University Press, Cambridge, in press.

Fisher, Kevin D., Jeffrey F. Leon, Sturt W. Manning, Michael Rogers, and David A. Sewell 2011–2012 Kalavasos and Maroni Built Environments Project: Introduction and Preliminary Report on the 2008 and 2010 Field Seasons. *Report of the Department of Antiquities, Cyprus*, in press.

Fortin, Michel 1981 *Military Architecture in Cyprus during the Second Millennium B.C.* Unpublished Ph.D. dissertation, University of London, London.

Foucault, Michel 1977 *Discipline and Punish: the Birth of the Prison.* Pantheon Books, New York.

Frankel, David and Jennifer M. Webb 2006 Neighbours: Negotiating Space in a Prehistoric Village. *Antiquity* 80:287–302.

Garrioch, David and Mark Peel 2006 Introduction: the Social History of Urban Neighborhoods. *Journal of Urban History* 32(5):663–676.

Giddens, Anthony 1979 *Central Problems In Social Theory: Action, Structure And Contradiction In Social Analysis.* University of California Press, Berkeley.

1984 *The Constitution of Society: Introduction of the Theory of Structuration.* University of California Press, Berkeley.

Goffman, Erving 1963 *Behavior in Public Places: Notes on the Social Organization of Gatherings.* Free Press of Glencoe, New York.

Grant, Jill 2001 The Dark Side of the Grid: Power and Urban Design. *Planning Perspectives* 16(3):219–241.

Graumann, Carl F. 2002 The Phenomenological Approach to People-Environment Relations. In *The Handbook of Environmental Psychology*, edited by R. B. Bechtel and A. Churchman, pp. 95–113. John Wiley and Sons, New York.

Hadjisavvas, Sophocles 1986 Alassa. A new Late Cypriote site. *Report of the Department of Antiquities, Cyprus*:62–67.

1996 Alassa: A Regional Centre of Alasia? In *Late Bronze Age Settlement in Cyprus: Function and Relationship*, edited by Paul Åström and Ellen Herscher, pp. 23–38. P. Åströms Förlag, Jonsered, Sweden.

2003 Dating Alassa. In *The Synchronisation of Civilisations in the Eastern Mediterranean in the Second Millennium BC II. Proceedings of the SCIEM 2000 EuroConference*, edited by M. Bietak, pp. 431–436. Verlag der Österreichischen Akademie der Wissenschaften, Wien, Austria.

Hallman, Howard W. 1984 *Neighborhoods: Their Place in Urban Life.* Sage Publications, Beverly Hills, CA.

Held, Steve O. 1993 Insularity as a Modifier of Culture Change: The Case of Prehistoric Cyprus. *Bulletin of the American Schools of Oriental Research* 292:25–33.

Hendon, Julia A. 2004 Living and Working at Home: the Social Archaeology of Household Production and Social Relations. In *A Companion to Social Archaeology*, edited by Lynn Meskell and Robert W. Preucel, pp. 272–286. Blackwell Publishing, Malden, MA.

Hillier, Bill and Julienne Hanson 1984 *The Social Logic of Space*. Cambridge University Press, Cambridge.

Iacovou, Maria 2007 Site Size Estimates and the Diversity Factor in Late Cypriot Settlement Histories. *Bulletin of the American Schools of Oriental Research* 348:1–23.

Ingold, Tim 2000 *The Perception of the Environment: Essays on Livelihood, Dwelling and Skill*. Routledge, London and New York.

Isbell, William H. 2000 What We Should be Studying: The "Imagined Community" and the "National Community." In *The Archaeology of Communities: a New World Perspective*, edited by Jason Yaeger and Marcello A. Canuto, pp. 243–266. Routledge, London and New York.

Karageorghis, Vassos and M. Demas 1984 *Pyla-Kokkinokremos: a Late 13th-Century BC Fortified Settlement in Cyprus*. Department of Antiquities, Nicosia, Cyprus.

1985 *Excavations at Kition V, The Pre-Phoenician Levels*. Department of Antiquities, Nicosia, Cyprus.

1988 *Excavations at Maa-Palaeokastro 1979–1986*. Department of Antiquities, Nicosia, Cyprus.

Keith, Kathryn 2003 The Spatial Patterns of Everyday Life in Old Babylonian Neighborhoods. In *The Social Construction of Ancient Cities*, edited by Monica L. Smith, pp. 56–80. Smithsonian Books, Washington, DC.

Keswani, Pricilla 1993 Models of Local Exchange in Late Bronze Age Cyprus. *Bulletin of the American Schools of Oriental Research* 292:73–83.

1996 Hierarchies, Heterarchies, and Urbanization Processes: the view from Bronze Age Cyprus. *Journal of Mediterranean Archaeology* 9(2):211–250.

2004 *Mortuary Ritual and Society in Bronze Age Cyprus*. Equinox Publishing, London and Oakville, CT.

2005 Death, prestige, and copper in Bronze Age Cyprus. *American Journal of Archaeology* 109(3):341–401.

Knapp, A. Bernard 1986 *Copper Production and Divine Protection: Archaeology, Ideology and Social Complexity on Bronze Age Cyprus*. Studies in Mediterranean Archaeology and Literature Pocket-book 42. P. Åströms Förlag, Göteborg, Sweden.

1993 Social Complexity: Incipience, Emergence, and Development on Prehistoric Cyprus. *Bulletin of the American Schools of Oriental Research* 292:85–106.

1997 *The Archaeology of Late Bronze Age Cypriot Society: the Study of Settlement, Survey and Landscape*. University of Glasgow, Glasgow, Scotland.

2003 The Archaeology of Community on Bronze Age Cyprus: Politiko Phorades in Context. *American Journal of Archaeology* 107(4):559–580.

2008 *Prehistoric and Protohistoric Cyprus: Identity, Insularity, and Connectivity*. Oxford University Press, Oxford and New York.

Knapp, A. Bernard, Steve O. Held, and Sturt W. Manning 1994 The Prehistory of Cyprus: Problems and Prospects. *Journal of World Prehistory* 8(4):377–453.

Kostof, Spiro 1991 *The City Shaped: Urban Patterns and Meanings through History*. Thames and Hudson, London.

Lalli, Marco 1992 Urban-related Identity: Theory, Measurement and Empirical Findings. *Journal of Environmental Psychology* 12:285–303.

Lawrence, Denise L. and Setha M. Low 1990 The Built Environment and Spatial Form. *Annual Review of Anthropology* 19:453–505.

Lawrence, Roderick J. 1990 Public, Collective and Private Space: A Study of Urban Housing in Switzerland. In *Domestic Architecture and the Use of Space: an Interdisciplinary Cross-cultural Study*, edited by Susan Kent, pp. 73–91. Cambridge University Press, Cambridge UK and New York.

Lefebvre, Henri 1991 *The Production of Space*. Blackwell, Oxford, UK and Cambridge, MA.

Locock, Martin 1994 Meaningful Architecture. In *Meaningful Architecture: Social Interpretations of Buildings*, Vol. 9, edited by Martin Locock, pp. 1–13. Avebury/Ashgate Publishing, Aldershot, Hampshire, UK.

Love, Michael 1999 Ideology, Material Culture, and Daily Practice in Pre-classic Mesoamerica: a Pacific Coast Perspective. In *Social Patterns in Pre-Classic Mesoamerica : a Symposium at Dumbarton Oaks, 9 and 10 October 1993*, edited by David C. Grove and Rosemary A. Joyce, pp. 127–153. Dumbarton Oaks Research Library and Collection, Washington, DC.

Low, Setha M. and Denise Lawrence-Zúñiga (editors) 2003 *The Anthropology of Space and Place: Locating Culture*. Blackwell, Malden, MA.

Lynch, Kevin 1960 *The Image of the City*. MIT Press, Cambridge, MA.

Madanipour, Ali 1998 Social Exclusion and Space. In *Social Exclusion in European Cities : Processes, Experiences, and Responses*, edited by Ali Madanipour, Goran Cars and Judith Allen, pp. 75–94. Jessica Kingsley; Regional Studies Association, London; Philadelphia; London.

Manning, Sturt W. 1993 Prestige, Distinction, and Competition: The Anatomy of Socioeconomic Complexity in Fourth to Second Millennium BCE. *Bulletin of the American Schools of Oriental Research* 292:35–58.

1998 Changing Pasts and Socio-political Cognition in Late Bronze Age Cyprus. *World Archaeology* 30(1):39–58.

Manning, Sturt W. and D. H. Conwell 1992 Maroni Valley Archaeological Survey Project: Preliminary Report on the 1990–1991 Seasons. *Report of the Department of Antiquities, Cyprus*:271–283.

Manning, Sturt W., Diane R. Bolger, M. J. Ponting, Louise Steele, and A. Swinton 1994 Maroni Valley Archaeological Survey Project: Preliminary Report on the 1992–1993 seasons. *Report of the Department of Antiquities, Cyprus*:345–367.

Manning, Sturt W. and Frank A. De Mita 1997 Cyprus, the Aegean, and Maroni-*Tsaroukkas*. In *Proceedings of the International Archaeological Conference: Cyprus and the Aegean in Antiquity: from the prehistoric period to the 7th century AD: Nicosia 8–10 December 1995*, edited by Kypros Tmēma Archaiotēton, pp. 102–142. Department of Antiquities, Nicosia, Cyprus.

Markus, Thomas A. 1993 *Buildings and Power: Freedom and Control in the Origin of Modern Building Types*. Routledge, London and New York.

Meskell, Lynn 1998 An Archaeology of Social Relations in an Egyptian Village. *Journal of Archaeological Method and Theory* 5(3):209–243.

Mumford, Lewis 1937 [2003] What is a City? In *The City Reader*, edited by Richard T. LeGates and Frederic Stout, pp. 92–96. Routledge, New York and London.

Negbi, Ora 2005 Urbanism on Late Bronze Age Cyprus: LC II in Retrospect. *Bulletin of the American Schools of Oriental Research* 337:1–45.

Peltenburg, Edgar J. 1993 Settlement Discontinuity and Resistance to Complexity in Cyprus, ca. 4500–2500 B.C.E. *Bulletin of the American Schools of Oriental Research* 292:9–23.

1996 From Isolation to State Formation in Cyprus, c. 3500–1500 B.C. In *The Development of the Cypriot Economy: From the Prehistoric Period to the Present Day*, edited by Vassos Karageorghis and Dēmētrēs Michaēlidēs, pp. 17–44. University of Cyprus and Bank of Cyprus, Nicosia.

2012 Text meets Material Culture in Late Bronze Age Cyprus. In *Cyprus: An Island Culture. Society and Social Relations from the Bronze Age to the Venetian Period*, edited by A. Georgiou, pp. 1–23. Oxbow Books, Oxford.

Pickles, Sydney and Edgar J. Peltenburg 1998 Metallurgy, Society and the Bronze/Iron Transition in the east Mediterranean and the Near East. *Report of the Department of Antiquities, Cyprus*:67–100.

Preucel, Robert W. and Lynn Meskell 2004 Places. In *A Companion to Social Archaeology*, edited by Lynn Meskell and Robert W. Preucel, pp. 215–229. Blackwell, Malden, MA.

Proshansky, Harold M. 1978 The City and Self-identity. *Environment and Behavior* 10(2):147–169.

Proshansky, Harold M., Abbe K. Fabian, and Robert Kaminoff 1983 Place Identity: Physical World Socialisation of the Self. *Journal of Environmental Psychology* 3:57–83.

Rapoport, Amos 1990 *The Meaning of the Built Environment: a Nonverbal Communication Approach*. University of Arizona Press, Tucson.

Rodman, Margaret C. 1992 Empowering Place: Multilocality and Multivocality. *American Anthropologist* 94(3):640–656.

Rogers, J. Daniel 1995 Introduction. In *Mississippian Communities and Households*, edited by J. Daniel Rogers and Bruce D. Smith, pp. 1–6. University of Alabama Press, Tuscaloosa.

Santley, Robert S. and Kenneth G. Hirth (editors) 1993 *Prehispanic Domestic Units in Western Mesoamerica: Studies of the Household, Compound, and Residence*. CRC Press, Boca Raton, FL.

Schaeffer, Claude F. A. 1971 *Alasia, Première série*. Mission Archéologique d'Alasia: Klincksieck. E. J. Brill, Paris and Leiden, Netherlands.

Shin, Yong J. 2009 Understanding Spatial Differentiation of Social Interaction: Suggesting a Conceptual Framework for Spatial Mediation. *Communication Theory* 19(4):423–444.

Smith, Adam T. 2003 *The Political Landscape: Constellations of Authority in Early Complex Polities*. University of California Press, Berkeley.

Smith, Joanna S. 2009 *Art and society in Cyprus from the Bronze Age into the Iron Age*. Cambridge University Press, Cambridge, UK and New York.

Smith, Michael E. 2007 Form and Meaning in the Earliest Cities: A New Approach to Ancient Urban Planning. *Journal of Planning History* 6(1):3–47.

2010 The Archaeological Study of Neighborhoods and Districts in Ancient Cities. *Journal of Anthropological Archaeology* 29(2):137–154.

Smith, Monica L. 2003 Introduction: The Social Construction of Ancient Cities. In *The Social Construction of Ancient Cities*, edited by Monica L. Smith, pp. 1–36. Smithsonian Books, Washington, DC.

2008 Urban Empty Spaces. Contentious Places for Consensus-Building. *Archaeological Dialogues* 15(2):216–231.

Soja, Edward W. 2000 *Postmetropolis: Critical Studies of Cities and Regions*. Blackwell, Malden, MA.

South, Alison K. 1980 Kalavasos-Ayios Dhimitrios 1979: a summary report. *Report of the Department of Antiquities, Cyprus*:60–68.

1988 Kalavasos-Ayios Dhimitrios 1987: an important ceramic group from Building X. *Report of the Department of Antiquities, Cyprus*:223–228.

1995 Urbanism and trade in the Vasilikos Valley in the Late Bronze Age. In *Trade, Contact, and the Movement of Peoples in the Eastern Mediterranean: Studies in Honour of J. Basil Hennessy*, edited by Stephen Bourke and Jean-Paul Descœudres, pp. 187–197. Meditarch, Sydney.

1997 Kalavasos-Ayios Dhimitrios 1992–1996. *Report of the Department of Antiquities, Cyprus*:151–175.

2008 Feasting in Cyprus: a view from Kalavasos. In *Dais: the Aegean Feast. Proceedings of the 12th International Aegean Conference, University of Melbourne, Centre for Classics and Archaeology, 25–29 March 2008*, edited by Louise Hitchcock, Robert Laffineur, and Janice Crowley, pp. 309–15. Université de Liège, Liège, Belgium.

Steel, Louise 2004 *Cyprus Before History: From the Earliest Settlers to the End of the Bronze Age*. Duckworth, London.

Stone, Elizabeth C. 1996 Houses, households and neighborhoods in the Old Babylonian Period: the role of extended families. In *Houses and Households in Ancient Mesopotamia: Papers Read at the 40e Rencontre Assyriologique Internationale, Leiden, July 5–8, 1993*, edited by Rencontre Assyriologique Internationale, Klaas R. Veenhof and Nederlands Historisch-Archaeologisch Instituut te Istanbul., pp. 229–235. Nederlands Historisch-Archaeologisch Instituut te Istanbul, Istanbul.

Suttles, Gerald D. 1972 *The social construction of communities*. University of Chicago Press, Chicago.

Trigger, Bruce G. 2003 *Understanding Early Civilizations: A Comparative Study*. Cambridge University Press, Cambridge and New York.

Tringham, Ruth 1995 Archaeological Houses, Households, Housework and the Home. In *The Home: Words, Interpretations, Meanings and Environments*, edited by David N. Benjamin, pp. 79–107. Avebury, Aldershot, UK and Brookfield, VT.

Tuan, Yi-fu 1977 *Space and Place: the Perspective of Experience*. University of Minnesota Press, Minneapolis.

Twigger-Ross, Clare L. and David L. Uzzell 1996 Place and Identity Processes. *Journal of Environmental Psychology* 16(3):205–220.

Van de Mieroop, Marc 1992 Old Babylonian Ur: portrait of an ancient Mesopotamian city. *The Journal of the Ancient Near Eastern Society* 21:119–130.

Vermeule, Emily and Florence Z. Wolsky 1990 *Toumba tou Skourou: a Bronze Age Potters' Quarter on Morphou Bay in Cyprus*. Harvard University-

Museum of Fine Arts, Boston Cyprus Expedition; Distributed by Harvard University Press, [Boston, MA]; Cambridge, MA.

Weinberg, Saul S. 1983 *Bamboula at Kourion: the Architecture*. Vol. 42, University of Pennsylvania, Philadelphia.

Wilk, Richard R. and William L. Rathje 1982 Household Archaeology. *American Behavioral Scientist* 25(6):617–639.

Wirth, Louis 1938 Urbanism as a Way of Life. *American Journal of Sociology* 44(1):1–24.

Wright, G. R. H. 1992 *Ancient Building in Cyprus*. E.J. Brill, Leiden, Netherlands and New York.

Yaeger, Jason and Marcello A. Canuto 2000 Introducing an Archaeology of Communities. In *The Archaeology of Communities: a New World Perspective*, edited by Marcello A. Canuto and Jason Yaeger, pp. 1–15. Routledge, London and New York.

Yanagisako, Sylvia J. 1979 Family and Household: The Analysis of Domestic Groups. *Annual Review of Anthropology* 8:161–205.

Zerubavel, Eviatar 2003 *Time maps: Collective Memory and the Social Shape of the Past*. University of Chicago Press, Chicago.

7

Urbanization and the Emergence of the Greek *Polis*: The Case of Azoria, Crete

Rodney D. Fitzsimons

Perhaps the most striking development accompanying the emergence of the Greek city-state (ca. 1200–480 BC) was the appearance of new urban centers whose form, contents, and construction provided the most visible and effective means of creating, reinforcing, and symbolizing the social, political, and economic relationships that characterized the new polis *system. Excavations at the site of Azoria (East Crete) have brought to light an unparalleled collection of architectural data, largely unobscured by later activities, that provides one of the best opportunities to study the architectural correlates of urbanization in the Greek world. This paper explores three levels of the built environment at Azoria – the domestic, the civic, and the urban – and demonstrates that the architectural landscape of the nascent city-state not only served to reflect the dramatic social and political developments that accompanied the emergence of the* polis, *but in effect, also functioned as an active agent in their creation.*

Current models of state formation in the Greek world envision a radical shift in sociopolitical structure from either pastoral or mixed village-farming communities operating within a chiefdom-based or big-man society to more elaborate sociopolitical and economic systems characterized by drastically rearranged social organizations, complex inter- and intraregional trade networks, and more extensive integration between rural landscapes and their new urban centers (Donlan 1985, 1997; Foxhall 1995; Morris 1997a; Nowicki 1999, 2002; Osborne 1996; Small 2010; Tandy 1997; Wallace 2001, 2003a, 2006). This process of transformation, which unfolded at different paces in different regions of the Aegean world from the end of the Late Bronze Age (ca. 1200–1050 BC), through the Early Iron Age (ca. 1050–600 BC) to the end of the Archaic Period (ca. 600–480 BC), culminated in the appearance of that characteristic Greek political institution, the city-state or *polis* (e.g., Hansen 2006; Hansen and Nielsen

2005; Morris 1997b; Mitchell and Rhodes 1997; Perlman 2004; Small 2010; Snodgrass 2006; Wallace 2010). One important, yet understudied, aspect of the emergence of the Greek *polis* involves the process of urbanization, a phenomenon that resulted in the appearance of cities throughout much of the Aegean Basin over the course of the eighth through sixth centuries BC (Andersen et al. 1997; Andreev 1989; Kotsonas 2002:50–57; Lang 2002, 2007; Osborne 2005). Indeed, even though the precise definition of the term urbanization varies from culture to culture (Cowgill 2004:526–528; Vink 1997:111–118), studies of numerous preindustrial societies throughout the Old and New Worlds have demonstrated the intimate connection between the creation of urban space and state formation (Adams 1966; Blanton 1976; Cowgill 2004; Fox 1977; Marcus 1983; A. Smith 2003; M. Smith 2003; Hansen 2000, 2002; Nichols and Charlton 1997; Sanders and Santley 1983; Storey 2006). As these studies have shown, the construction of these new urban landscapes provides perhaps the most visible and effective means of creating, reinforcing, and symbolizing the new social, political, and economic relationships in these developing polities (Abrams 1989:48; Abrams and Bolland 1999:263–264; Cowgill 2004:528; A. Smith 2003; see Miller 1995 for Athens).

Despite the integral relationship between urbanization and *polis* formation, however, previous examinations of the role played by the built environment have been hampered by the general paucity of structural remains dating to the seventh and sixth centuries BC (Kotsonas 2002:48–50; Nowicki 2002:150, 170). Whereas studies of larger, "successful" city-states such as Corinth and Athens have yielded abundant historical and archaeological evidence for this field of study, the majority of the architectural data dating to the relevant periods from non-sanctuary contexts remain buried or otherwise obscured by centuries, even millennia, of later construction activities and, as a result, the overall form of these early urban centers beyond their primary cult centers is fragmentary at best (e.g., Harris-Cline 1999; Hurwit 1999:85–137; Papadopoulos 2003:280–297; Pfaff 2003; Rhodes 2003; Robertson 1998; Schmalz 2006; Shear 1994; Weir 1995). Similarly, although the eighth-century BC architectural remains at smaller sites such as Emporio on Chios (Boardman 1967), Koukounaries on Paros (Schilardi 1983), Vroulia on Rhodes (Kinch 1914; Melander 1988), and Zagora on Andros (Cambitoglou et al. 1971, 1988; Green 1990; Vink 1997) are clearly visible in the archaeological record, their potential contribution to this discussion is limited by the fact that they were abandoned at a relatively early phase in their development.

The dearth of evidence for these initial stages of urbanization is even more pronounced on the island of Crete, where there is a remarkable decline in the quantity not only of settlement remains, but also funerary and ritual activity in the sixth century BC. This situation has led many scholars to suggest that the island witnessed a dramatic drop in population during this period (e.g., Coldstream and Huxley 1999; Kotsonas 2002; Prent 1996–1997; Van der Vliet 1996–1997; Vink 1996–1997). Such a population decline is particularly surprising considering that the preceding three centuries were characterized by intense and dynamic cultural interaction between the inhabitants of Crete, the Aegean islands, the Greek mainland, and the Near East. Moreover, it was precisely during this period that the state entities that dominated the political landscape of the island during the second half of the first millennium BC seem to have had their formative years. New studies being conducted at such sites as Afrati and Kato Syme (Erickson 2002), Eleutherna (Erickson 2004; Stampolidis 1990, 2002), Itanos (Apostolakou et al. 2004–2005; Duplouy 2009; Greco et al. 2003), Kommos (Shaw 2000), Praisos (Whitley 2006; Whitley et al. 1995; Whitley et al. 1999), and Vrokastro (Hayden 2004a, 2004b), however, have begun to shed some much-needed light on this so-called Dark Age and, as a result, challenge more traditional views of stagnation on the island. Of particular importance in this regard is the site of Azoria, where recent excavations have produced a wealth of evidence suggesting that the seventh and sixth centuries BC was a period of active sociopolitical development.

Azoria is located atop a double-peaked hill in eastern Crete, roughly 1 km southeast of the modern village of Kavousi and 3 km from the Aegean Sea (Figure 7.1). The site commands an excellent view of the coastal plain of Tholos to the north, and is strategically located at the western end of the system of mountain valleys that leads to the eastern end of the island, and at the northern end of the Ierapetra Isthmus, a narrow neck of land roughly 15 km in length. This isthmus served as a primary route of land-based communication linking the Aegean Sea to the Mediterranean Sea throughout the history of the island. Azoria was first explored by Harriet Boyd in 1900 (Boyd 1901), but it was not until 2002, when a five-year campaign of excavation under the direction of Donald C. Haggis and Margaret S. Mook was initiated, that systematic investigations of the

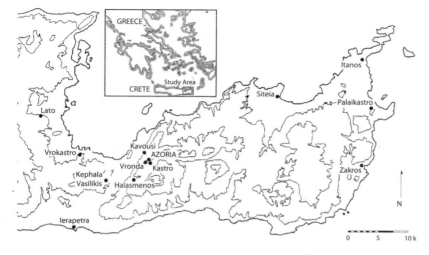

Figure 7.1 Map of
eastern Crete, showing
the location of sites
mentioned in the
text (redrawn by
author from Coulson
and Tsipopoulou
1994:figure 1; inset
redrawn from Azoria
I:figure 1).

site began (Azoria I–VI). Although these excavations have yielded
abundant artifactual and scattered architectural evidence for occupation as early as the Final Neolithic Period (Azoria I:390; Azoria
II:276; Azoria III:668–696, 706–707), the primary phase of occupation
appears to date to the seventh through early fifth centuries BC, the
very period of the so-called Cretan "Dark Age." Moreover, unlike
the majority of other relevant sites in the Aegean, Azoria was abandoned in the first quarter of the fifth century BC, and reoccupied on
a very limited scale for only a brief period in the late third and early
second centuries BC (Azoria I:372, 379; Azoria II:266–269, 294–295,
305; Azoria IV:1–4). This exceptional occupational history has thus
preserved the urban landscape of the seventh and sixth centuries BC
in a relatively intact fashion, and provides a unique opportunity to
study the process of urbanization as it unfolded in this region of the
Greek world (Figure 7.2). This paper explores three functional and
ideological levels of the built environment at Azoria (dubbed here,
landscapes) – the domestic, the civic, and the urban – and demonstrates that the architectural landscape of the nascent city-state not
only served to reflect the dramatic social and political developments
that accompanied the emergence of the *polis*, but in effect also functioned as an active agent in their creation.

THE DOMESTIC LANDSCAPE

Excavations along the eastern and western slopes of the North
Acropolis and the northern, western, and southern slopes of the

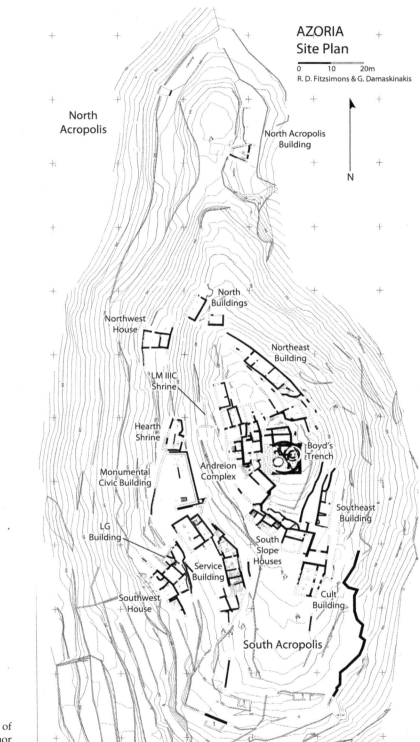

Figure 7.2 Site plan of Azoria (drawn by author and G. Damaskanakis).

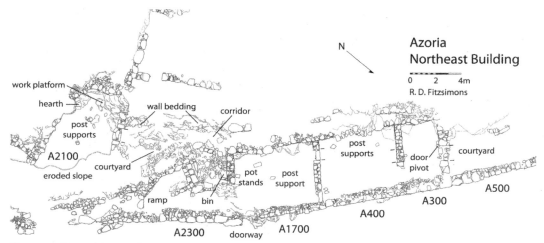

Figure 7.3 Plan of the Northeast Building at Azoria, late seventh/early sixth century BC (drawn by author).

South Acropolis have brought to light the remains of up to a dozen houses, the best preserved and most illustrative example of which is the Northeast Building (Figure 7.3; Azoria I:364–367; Azoria II:246–252; Azoria V:434–437). This structure was composed of a suite of three rectangular rooms (A300, A400, A1700) and one irregularly shaped room (A2300) arranged in axial fashion (northwest-southeast) along a single, broad terrace (ca. 5.30 m wide). The narrow, northwest façade of the building faced onto a small courtyard (A500) that sat at the end of a street leading from the north and was pierced by a well-built doorway framed by megalithic masonry set in the center of the wall. This door opened onto a shallow room (A300), perhaps an entry vestibule, which in turn opened onto a deep, rectangular chamber (A400) that yielded a large collection of drinking, dining, and storage vessels and that has been identified as the main hall of the house. A well-built doorway set into the western part of the rear wall of this room granted access to another large chamber (A1700) found littered with smashed pithoi (storage jars), pot stands, and the remains of cereal grains and olive pits, attesting to its function as the primary storage facility of the house. Additional storage and work space was provided by the stone-lined bin and work platform set into the triangular alcove southwest of the corridor (A2300) that ran southeast from the south corner of A1700. This passage ended at the bottom of a sloped ramp cut into the bedrock at the bottom of a short staircase that opened onto the street running northwest-southeast along the terrace immediately southwest of and above the Northeast

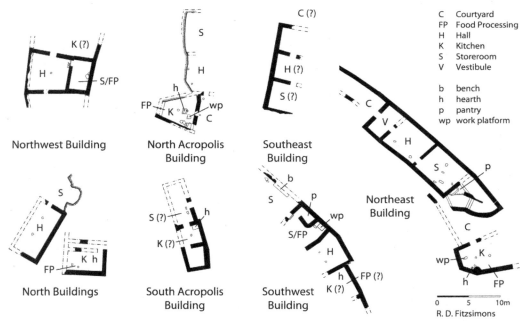

Figure 7.4 Plan of the Archaic houses at Azoria, showing the distribution of room functions, late seventh/early sixth century BC (drawn by author).

Building. The southeast end of this street was marked by a triangular-shaped courtyard (A1800) set before a large, irregularly shaped room (A2100) with a side hearth and work platform that appears to have functioned as the kitchen for the Northeast Building.

Although only partially preserved or awaiting further excavation, the scattered fragments of house remains unearthed elsewhere on the South Acropolis appear to conform to the same basic blueprint of formal and functional arrangement evident in the Northeast Building (Figure 7.4; Azoria I:370–372; Azoria II:265–269; Azoria V).[1] Moreover, the presence of a similarly designed domestic structure on the North Acropolis, the North Acropolis Building (Azoria V:463–477), suggests that this blueprint was not restricted to a specific subsection of the settlement (i.e., the South Acropolis or its summit), but rather extended across the entire site (Figures 7.1 and 7.4). Thus, even though it is true that no two houses were identical in terms of plan, elaboration, or scale, the repeated pattern of archaeological features evident in the extant remains suggests that their builders subscribed to a single, common approach to the conception, design, and utilization of domestic space. This approach was characterized by an emphasis on the front of the house through the construction of an elaborate façade and/or the presence of an exterior court; the separation of spaces devoted to the storage, processing, and consumption of foodstuffs (i.e., storeroom, kitchen, main hall), with the kitchen often set in isolation from the rest of the house and the storeroom juxtaposed with the main hall; the use of the main hall for multiple domestic, industrial, and social activities, most notably the performance of dining and drinking rituals; and the preference for arranging these functional spaces in axial fashion along a single terrace.

The axial approach to house planning was not unique to Azoria, but appears to have been standard practice on Crete well into the fourth century BC, when the court-centered house common elsewhere in the Greek world made its first appearance on the island (Westgate 2007a).[2] In fact, the axial house plan can be traced as far back as the end of the Late Bronze Age on Crete, when the collapse of the Mycenaean palatial administration that had dominated the Aegean for the preceding two or three centuries necessitated a radical restructuring of the sociopolitical landscape. Three Early Iron Age sites in the immediate vicinity of Azoria preserve substantial remains of houses that seem to conform to this pattern (Figure 7.1). Although two of them, Kastro (Coulson 1997, 1998; Haggis et al. 1997; Mook 1998, 2004) and Halasmenos (Coulson and Tsipopoulou 1994; Paschalides 2006; Rupp 2007; Tsipopoulou 2004), await detailed publication before a thorough analysis of their domestic landscape can be undertaken, the third, Vronda, provides clear evidence for the prevalence of the axial house plan and its role in both shaping and reflecting the sociopolitical landscape prior to the emergence of the *polis*.

Excavations at Vronda have brought to light the remains of twelve to fifteen houses dating to the twelfth and early eleventh centuries BC (Figure 7.5; Day et al. 1986; Day et al. 2009; Gesell et al. 1995:68–92, 116–117). These houses were organized into several large clusters scattered over the hilltop (Buildings A-B, C-D, E, G, I-O-N, J-K, and L-M), the best preserved of which is Building I-O-N, an agglomeration of at least twelve partially interconnected rooms located along the southwest edge of the settlement (Figure 7.6). Detailed analysis of the structural remains associated with this complex has revealed that its final form resulted from the addition and expansion of several new suites of rooms, collectively dubbed Buildings O and N, to an initial three-room complex, Building I, over the course of several generations (Glowacki 2002:39–42, 2004:127–131, 2007:132). Similar

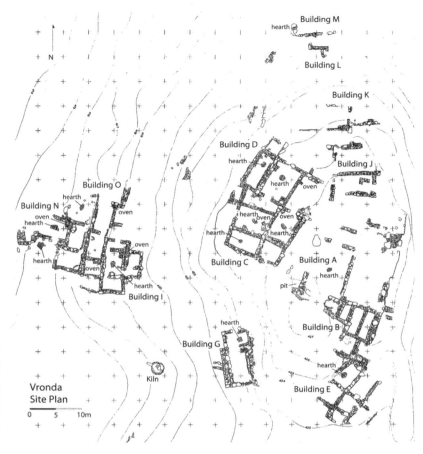

Figure 7.5 Site plan of Vronda, showing the location of house clusters, twelfth and eleventh centuries BC (after Glowacki 2007:figure 14:1).

analysis of four additional building clusters on the site (Buildings C-D, E, J-K, and L-M), despite their more fragmentary state of preservation, suggests a conformance to the same basic arrangement evident in Building I-O-N,[3] with each cluster being composed of two or more suites of rooms (Glowacki 2002:38, 42, 2004:134, 2007:134–135, 136–137).

Even though great strides have been made in the study and reconstruction of domestic groupings on the basis of archaeological and ethnographic evidence in other parts of the world in recent decades (e.g., Allison 1999; Johnston and Gonlin 1998; Samson 1990; Yanagisako 1979), the definition and identification of such basic features as "family," "house," and "household" are much less developed for Early Iron Age Crete, in large part because of the paucity of relevant remains from across the island. Nevertheless, despite the small sample size, the extant evidence from across the island (e.g., Coulson 1998; Haggis et al. 1997; Hayden 1983; Mook 1998; Nowicki

Figure 7.6 Plan of Building I-O-N at Vronda, showing phases of construction, twelfth and eleventh centuries BC (after Glowacki 2007:figure 14:4).

2002:156–158, 161; Yasur-Landau 2003–2004, 2006) supports current scholarly opinion that the basic building block of Cretan society throughout the first half of the first millennium BC was the *oikos* unit (e.g., Day and Snyder 2004:78; Donlan 1985:299–300; Glowacki 2004:134; Small 1998:289; Nowicki 1999:147), a somewhat fluid entity comprised of an extended nuclear family (i.e., three generations) and its varied cadre of non-kin retainers.

Although the evidence is admittedly fragmentary, the remains at both Vronda and Azoria seem to confirm this pattern. At the former, the best example is provided by Building I-O-N, where the recurrence of repetitive suites of artifact types and the duplication of fixed installations such as hearths and ovens throughout its various component parts has led Glowacki to argue that each suite of rooms was occupied by a single, nuclear family – in other words, an *oikos* unit (Glowacki 2002:46, 2004:129, 2007:133–134). Similarly, at Azoria, the repetition of formal and functional areas in each of the excavated domestic structures across the settlement has led the excavators to suggest that each axial unit served to house an individual *oikos* unit (Azoria V:484–485). On one level, then, the evidence from Vronda and Azoria reveals that the individual family, embodied in the basic axial unit, continued to play a dominant role in the social, political, and physical fabric of Cretan settlements throughout the first half of the first millennium BC.

At the same time, however, the widespread building program undertaken on the hilltops at Azoria toward the end of the seventh century BC ushered in several significant structural changes that both reflected, and perhaps served as a catalyst for, corresponding changes in the position of the family within the new urban environment. Most obvious, perhaps, is the increase in the size of the basic axial unit: the footprint of the largest house at Vronda (N2-N3-N5) measures roughly 82.9 m² (Glowacki 2007:135, 2012:134–135, 2013 personal communication), while that of the Northeast Building (A300, A400, A1700, A2300) covers an area of approximately 144 m². Moreover, if the area covered by the two courtyards, A500 and A1800, and the associated kitchen, A2100, were included in this measurement (totaling approximately 260 m²), the size of the Northeast Building would even exceed that calculated for the so-called Big Man's house, Building A/B, at Vronda (approximately 198 m²; Day et al. 2009:26–27; Glowacki 2007:135, 2013 personal communication). Associated with this increase in the size of the houses at Azoria is a corresponding escalation in the absolute wealth of at least some of its inhabitants, a phenomenon marked not only by the extensive provisions for the storage and production of agricultural goods, but also the expansion of household property and membership reflected in the addition of non-adjacent structures (e.g., A2100) and intervening spaces to the basic axial unit. Just as, if not more, significant, however, was the resulting physical and symbolic change in the distribution of houses across the settlement. At Vronda, Glowacki has reasonably concluded that the larger clusters of room suites across the settlement (i.e., Buildings A-B, C-D, E, G, I-O-N, J-K, and L-M) were occupied by extended family groups (i.e., groups of related families), with each appended suite of rooms representing the appearance of a newly spawned *oikos* unit. The resulting agglomerations likely reflect the underlying importance of kinship-based associations in the definition of social and political identity in the early Iron Age (Glowacki 2002:38, 42, 2004:134, 2007:134–135, 136–137). At Azoria, on the other hand, the distribution of axial (i.e., family) units in more disparate and isolated fashion across the hilltops and the absence of any evidence for their subsequent expansion over the course of five or six generations of occupation at the site suggests a weakening of these more traditional affiliations and the emergence of the individual family as a more independent entity within the community. What appears to have emerged with the urbanization of the landscape in the seventh and sixth centuries BC was less a change in the internal nature of the individual family, but rather a transformation in the manner in which it advertised its position within the sociopolitical fabric of the new urban environment. Although kinship relations continued to play an important role in negotiating power relationships within the community, and indeed while the house continued to serve as a significant vehicle for the advertisement of wealth and status,[4] it was now the position of the family within the larger *polis* landscape, rather than its juxtaposition to previous or contemporary generations, that afforded the highest levels of rank and prestige (cf. Westgate 2007b).

THE CIVIC LANDSCAPE

Coinciding with and serving as a prime catalyst for this redefinition of the sociopolitical position of the individual household unit within the larger urban community was a dramatic change in settlement pattern that took place at the end of the seventh century BC in the Kavousi region (Haggis 1993, 1996, 2001, 2005). Intensive survey in the area has demonstrated that whereas the Early Iron Age landscape was dotted by a series of small, agricultural villages organized into regional clusters reflecting larger kinship groupings, by the beginning of the Archaic Period, the majority of these rural settlements had been partially or entirely abandoned as their inhabitants flooded into the new urban center at Azoria. This nucleation of disparate population groups, a phenomenon that has also been noted for other areas of the island during this period (Wallace 2003b:256–262), necessitated a dramatic reorganization of the sociopolitical and economic relationships within the nascent community. In the process, the traditional kinship groups of the preceding era coalesced into a single, political entity.

Throughout Greek history, one of the primary means of negotiating social and political status between and among the various competing factions within a community was through the performance of ritualized dining and drinking activities (e.g., Murray 1983, 1990; Lissarrague 1991; Lynch 2007; Topper 2009; Wright 2004). Such rituals provide opportunities not only to forge and negotiate inter- and intragroup relationships through the sharing of food and drink and the exchange of information in institutionalized settings, but also to establish and reinforce social and political inequalities through the display, exchange, and consumption of superior resources (Arnold 1999; Dietler 1990, 1996, 1999; Dietler and Hayden 2001; Joffee 1998). The emphasis on the main hall, the proximity of the storeroom with its richly decorated pithoi, and the prevalence of vessels intended for the production and consumption of foodstuffs in the Archaic houses at Azoria illustrate the importance of such activities operating at the household level in the new urban environment of the seventh and sixth centuries BC. A similar focus on the hearth, the oven, and the processing of foodstuffs at Vronda indicates a corresponding emphasis on household dining and drinking activities during the twelfth and eleventh centuries BC.

There is also evidence for the performance of more complex rituals involving participants drawn from beyond the individual household or kinship group at Vronda. Building A/B (Figure 7.4; Day et al. 2009:48–63; Day and Snyder 2004; Glowacki 2002:38–39, 2007:135–136), situated on the eastern slope of the hill at its highest point, assumed the form of a large, rectangular room with a central hearth (Building A) flanked to the north by a narrower room, perhaps a storeroom, and to the south by an open court. A second suite of four small, doorless rooms bordering the court to the east (Building B) and containing numerous pithoi, cooking vessels, and drinking cups, has been interpreted as storage magazines. Externally, a long, megalithic terrace wall provided a monumental façade to viewers from the east. The size and elaboration of the architecture of Building A/B, together with the quantity and quality of its contents, led Day and Snyder to identify it as the house of the local ruler, who may have sponsored communal dining and drinking activities at his own expense in order to forge and reinforce social and political ties among the various members of the community (Day and Snyder 2004:73, 78).

At Azoria, too, there is clear evidence for the performance of similarly elaborate rituals attended by a wider cross-section of the

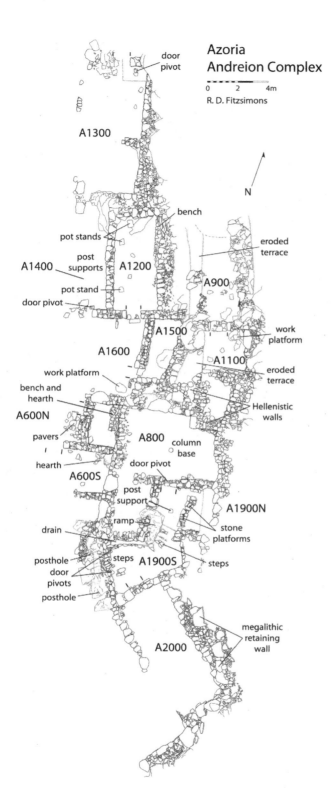

Azoria
Andreion Complex

0   2   4m
R. D. Fitzsimons

door pivot

A1300

N

bench

pot stands

eroded terrace

post supports   A1200

A1400

pot stand

A900

door pivot

work platform

A1500

A1600

A1100

eroded terrace

work platform

bench and hearth

Hellenistic walls

A600N

pavers

A800   column base

hearth

A600S   door pivot

post support

A1900N

ramp

drain

stone platforms

posthole   steps   A1900S   steps

door pivots

posthole

megalithic retaining wall

A2000

Figure 7.7 Plan of the Communal Dining Building at Azoria, late seventh/early sixth century BC (drawn by author).

community, although here the buildings in which they were enacted assumed a distinctly civic character. One such building (Figure 7.7), dubbed the Communal Dining Building, is a sprawling complex of at least ten rooms divided into two functional sections distributed across the upper two terraces of the West Acropolis, immediately below the summit (Azoria I:367–370, 373–390; Azoria II:253–265; Azoria IV:4–16). The rooms to the north were devoted to cooking (A600, A1600), the processing of wine (A1300), and the storage of foodstuffs (A1200, A1500, and perhaps A1400) and cooking and drinking vessels (A1500), whereas those to the south and east appear to have housed activities associated with dining and drinking (A800, A2000) and the display of prestige artifacts (A1900), including martial paraphernalia.

A second public facility (Figure 7.8) devoted, at least partially, to communal feasting was unearthed a short distance to the south and has been dubbed the Monumental Civic Building (Azoria II:295–301; Azoria IV:16–28, 39–41). This structure, which assumed the form of a huge trapezoidal chamber (D500) measuring 10 m in width and 20.5 m and 22.5 m long along its eastern and western sides respectively, was lined with two tiers of benches composed of hammer-dressed stones arranged along its southern, eastern, and northern walls. Substantial quantities of roofing material preserved along the eastern wall and two well-dressed post supports, as well as numerous outcroppings of roughly worked bedrock that would have functioned in a similar capacity, and traces of burnt beam impressions, indicate that the entire space, despite its immense size (ca. 200 m^2) was roofed (Azoria II:298; Azoria IV:21–22). The main entrance to the building appears to have been located at the southern end of its western wall. Here, a handful of risers and a large schist slab bearing a massive pivot hole mark the position of a short staircase leading up to a double door. Although few complete vessels were recovered, copious amounts of food debris found atop the floor of the building suggest at least one of its functions was to house feasting and sacrificial activities. A second, smaller entrance cut through the north wall of this room granted access to a short corridor running along the top of a set of theatral-like seats (D1400) that lined the street below, which in turn opened onto an irregularly shaped kitchen (D1000) and a small, rectangular room (D900). This small room (D900) contained a central hearth abutting the north face of a stone altar that was found littered with ritual implements (Azoria IV:28–38). Also associated with

Azoria
Monumental Civic Complex

0   2   4m
R. D. Fitzsimons

hearth

D1000

Hearth
Shrine

N

theatral
steps

hearth

D1400

altar

D900

stepped
doorway

column
base

trench
line

Monumental
Civic
Building

D500

column
base

erosion
line

bedrock
foundations

socket

later
paved
platform

risers

Early Iron
Age wall

stepped
entrance

Figure 7.8 Plan of the
Monumental Civic
Building and the
Archaic Hearth Shrine
at Azoria, late seventh/
early sixth century BC
(drawn by author).

this complex was a suite of interconnecting rooms and open courts located a short distance to the south, which the excavators have identified as a Service Building (Azoria II:274–295; Azoria IV:43–62). Two large kitchens (B1500, B2200/2300) ran along the east side of an as yet unexcavated street connecting two open spaces (B1700, B3100) in which various activities, including food processing and perhaps textile manufacture (Azoria II:286, 288–289, 301; Azoria IV:43), took place. Both kitchens contained a rectangular hearth and multiple work platforms as well as numerous vessels for storage, dining, and drinking, whereas an adjoining room (B700) was devoted to the storage of foodstuffs and serving and processing equipment. An isolated room to the south of the south court (B3300) housed additional food processing activities, whereas two large rooms at the northern end of the complex were devoted to the production and storage of olive oil (D300).

The absence of both inscriptional evidence from Azoria and architectural comparanda from elsewhere on the island makes it impossible to determine the specific nomenclature applied to these complexes by the ancient inhabitants of the site. The evidence for the large-scale processing, storage, and consumption of food and the display of aristocratic artifacts in the first building (Figure 7.7) has led the excavators to suggest a possible identification as an Andreion Complex (Azoria I:380–382, 387–390, 391–393; Azoria II:253, 263–265; Azoria IV:4–16). This building type is known from literary and epigraphic sources to have housed such activities and to have acted as a forum for the competition for status by elite males (Azoria I:387–390; Azoria IV:4–6; Koehl 1997). Similar activities have also been ascribed to the Monumental Civic Building, where the presence of theatral-like seating designed for accommodating large-scale public gatherings and the intimate connection with the cult activities housed in the neighboring shrine building both find parallels in the formal and functional arrangement of the later city centers at Lato (Demargne 1903:216–221; Ducrey and Picard 1971, 1972; Miller 1978:78–86) and Dreros (Demargne and van Effenterre 1937:10–16; Marinatos 1936:254; Xanthoudides 1918).[5] These features also recall the descriptions of the so-called Prytaneion, known from later historical and epigraphic sources (Miller 1978). Whether or not the inhabitants of the site referred to these structures as an Andreion and a Prytaneion, however, is less relevant than the fact that they housed the sorts of activities that would come to be ascribed to such complexes by later authors (Azoria IV:4–6, 39–41). Indeed, the scale on which both of these structures were designed and constructed, the multiplicity of facilities devoted to the production, consumption, and storage of foodstuffs they housed, and the sheer volume of material unearthed within them makes it clear that they operated well above the level of the individual household, and instead belonged to the purview of the nascent civic authority.

Despite the functional similarities between these two complexes and the fact that they were both designed to accommodate public, or perhaps rather communal (Sjögren 2007:149–150), activities, they nevertheless appear to have been designed for somewhat different purposes and audiences. The relatively small size of the dining facilities in A2000, the measures taken to limit visual and physical access to its inner rooms through the creation of multiple doorways and circuitous routes of passage, and the emphasis on the display of elite artifacts in A1900 and A800 suggest that the gatherings housed in the Communal Dining Building were of a more restricted, intimate nature and it is tempting to associate them with commensal meetings attended and/or hosted by the traditional leaders and senior members of individual kinship associations. By contrast, the strikingly open design of the Monumental Civic Building, the extensive provisions for seating or standing arranged along its perimeter, and the expansive arrangement of associated facilities – that is, the Civic Shrine to the north and the Service Building to the south – arranged in a very unrestricted fashion along a major thoroughfare, indicate that this complex was designed to accommodate much larger gatherings of people in a much more public setting, and it is tempting to identify it as a sort of public assembly hall where citizens of the new *polis* would convene to discuss and deliberate social, political, and economic matters affecting the city-state as a whole.

THE URBAN LANDSCAPE

The emergence of new social and political bodies operating at the civic level also finds its expression in the overall plan of the settlement that, although lacking the symmetry of the so-called Hippodamian arrangement so characteristic of many contemporary colonies in Magna Graecia and later cities throughout the Aegean, nevertheless displays a marked degree of overall organization. Here, the cohesive element is not the orthogonal street plan, but rather the network of

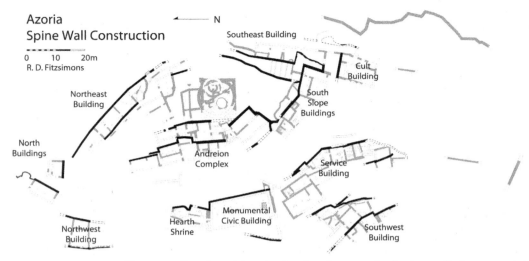

Figure 7.9 Site plan of Azoria, showing the network of spine walls, late seventh/ early sixth century BC (drawn by author).

megalithic spine walls erected in roughly concentric fashion along the natural contours of both Acropolis hills (Figure 7.9; Azoria I:349– 352; Azoria IV:2; Azoria V:432–434; for spine walls, see Fagerström 1988:113–114). These structures, characterized by the frequent use of massive, cyclopean boulders reaching upwards of 1 m in length along their maximum dimensions, served to retain the terraces on which the refashioned settlement was constructed, and thus acted as the armature around which the new urban landscape was fashioned (Figure 7.10).

Although no detailed energetics approaches comparable to the studies conducted by Abrams on the Maya have yet been applied to Early Iron Age Greece (Abrams 1989, 1994; Abrams and Bolland 1999), it seems unlikely that the volume of human and animal labor required for the successful completion of this undertaking could have been supplied by members of a single or limited number of kinship groups. Instead, it seems more reasonable to hypothesize that the creation of this new urban landscape could only have been achieved through the participation and cooperation of gangs of workmen drawn from the expanded population base of the newly coalesced community. Indeed, the ambitious nature of this building program and the extensive scale on which it was executed, as well as the absence of any substantial later modifications to it (Azoria IV:2; Azoria V:439, 477), would seem to provide clear indication of the existence of a communal authority operating far above the level

Figure 7.10. Photograph of Wall A602 from the south, showing typical spine wall construction, late seventh/early sixth century BC (photograph by author).

of the earlier family or extended kinship groups that would appear to have been responsible for the organization and execution of construction projects undertaken in the Early Iron Age. If this deduction is correct, it therefore follows that the widespread renovations undertaken to the hilltops at Azoria themselves indicate the corresponding emergence of some sort of civic administration capable of mobilizing, organizing, and directing quantities of human, capital, and symbolic resources on a scale not evident since the Mycenaean Age, one perhaps able to provide its own forms of compensation to its citizens (see Perlman 2004 for epigraphic evidence for various forms of state and non-state compensation in Archaic Crete).

More than acting as a mere passive reflection of the new sociopolitical order, however, the very creation of this urban landscape also played an active role in the restructuring of social and political networks within the community. It is likely that the construction of most private dwellings would still have been undertaken by individuals from the immediate family unit for whom they were originally erected, aided by various members of that particular family's extended kinship and social network (for ethnographic parallels, see Cameron 1999). In the process, some familial groups with access to superior resources may have assumed (a larger) responsibility for the creation of certain civic monuments or parts thereof as a means of reinforcing or enhancing their social and political status. On the other hand, the majority of the public building projects that

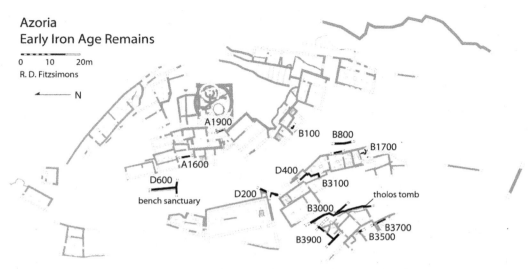

Azoria
Early Iron Age Remains

0   10   20m
R. D. Fitzsimons

← N

A1900
B100   B800
B1700
A1600
D400
D600   B3100
bench sanctuary   D200   tholos tomb
B3000
B3700
B3900   B3500

Figure 7.11 Plan of Azoria, showing the location of Early Iron Age architectural remains (drawn by author).

comprised the new urban landscape must have been the products of enterprises that assumed a much more communal character. Thus, for example, decisions regarding the course and layout of the spine wall system and the network of terraces it framed; the location and design of major civic structures such as the Cult Building (Azoria II:269–273, 301–302; Small 2010:201), the Communal Dining Building, and the Monumental Civic Building and its Service Building; and the allotment of land to private families for house construction, farming, and other economic activities must have arisen, at least in part, through the consensus and collaboration of community leaders. The collective nature of these building activities, with individuals from different kinship groups working side-by-side across the settlement for extended periods of time, would have served as one more cohesive mechanism that reinforced the notions of group membership and civic identity fostered by the new city-state by obscuring the more traditional kinship ties that had characterized the first few centuries of the first millennium BC. In this context, it is perhaps worth noting that large-scale public building projects often serve as effective vehicles for promoting group solidarity during times of social and political stress (Abrams 1989:62; Trigger 1990:127–128), a description that seems highly applicable to an era that witnessed both the widespread movement of population groups resulting in the nucleation of settlement at the site, the dissolution of long-standing social and political affiliations, and the institution of new forms of kinship and civic relationships that would characterize the nascent *polis*.

Interestingly, this rearrangement of the traditional sociopolitical network and the creation of a new, more inclusive civic identity may have been further reinforced through the transformation of the physical landscape itself. Scattered traces of architecture dating to the Early Iron Age have been revealed in numerous places along the western slope of the South Acropolis (Figure 7.11; Azoria III:696–705; Azoria IV:45; Azoria V:432, 456–457, 461; Azoria VI), notably in the areas west of the northern rooms of the Communal Dining Building (Trench D600, the bench sanctuary), north (Trenches B3100, D200, and D400), east (Trench B800), and south (Trench B1700) of the Service Building, and north of, east of, and beneath the Southwest Building (Trenches B3000, B3500, B3700, and B3900). Even though these remains are preserved in too fragmentary a form to allow for a reliable reconstruction of their overall appearance, they nevertheless provide tantalizing evidence that the architectural landscape of the Early Iron Age settlement may have been intentionally obscured during the seventh and sixth century renovations undertaken at the site (Azoria III:701).

The clearest evidence for such activity can be seen in the area of the northern room of the Service Building (Figures 7.12–7.13; Trenches B2200/2300, 3100, and D400), where the course and position of the preexisting structural remains were not only ignored by the builders of the Archaic complex, but also obscured, perhaps deliberately, by the deposition of massive amounts of cobble fill that preceded the construction of the later complex. Similar deposits of cobble fill have been found in connection with a large number of structures, both private and public, erected across the settlement in the Archaic Period, including the Northeast Building (Azoria I:364), the Communal Dining Building (Azoria I:366, 370, 375; Azoria II:253, 265; Azoria IV:10), and the area south of the Monumental Civic Building (Azoria III:701). Although it is possible that these fills were laid for purely practical reasons – namely, to provide stable foundations and drainage for the new constructions – the ubiquitous nature of the cobbles, the massive amounts of labor required for their laying, and the fact that none of the preexisting walls were reused, raises the distinct possibility, if not likelihood, that the resulting disappearance of the Early Iron Age landscape was entirely intentional.

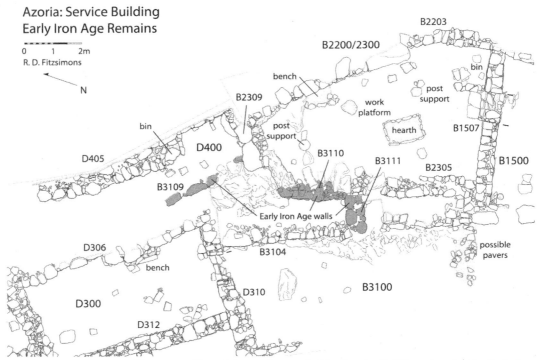

Azoria: Service Building
Early Iron Age Remains

0   1   2m
R. D. Fitzsimons

N

Figure 7.12 Plan of the northern end of the Service Building, showing the Early Iron Age and Archaic structural remains (drawn by author).

Figure 7.13 Photograph of the northern end of the Service Building, showing the Early Iron Age and Archaic structural remains (photograph by author).

Interestingly, this obfuscation of the preexisting architectural landscape differs markedly from the treatment afforded to the material possessions of its occupants. Indeed, the presence, for example, of the Late Minoan (LM) IIIC (twelfth century BC) pithos in the storeroom (B300) of the so-called East Corridor House (Azoria I:354), the Daedalic plaque in the kitchen of the North Acropolis Building (Azoria V:468), the Early Iron Age figurine from the south kitchen of the Service Complex (Azoria III:700–701), the Protogeometric krater in the north room of the Civic Shrine (Azoria IV: 36), and the handful of early figurines from its altar (Azoria IV:31–35), suggest an interest on the part of (at least) some individual families in preserving some of the material elements from earlier generations. Although some of these objects may well have been kept for purely practical purposes, in some cases at least (notably the ritual artifacts from the Hearth Shrine and its attendant storeroom), the likelihood is that they were intentionally preserved and displayed as heirlooms in an effort to maintain physical, symbolic, and emotional ties to the social environment of the immediate and more distant past (Azoria II:304; Azoria III:699, 708; Azoria IV:37; Lillios 1999).

If the residents of Azoria were in fact keeping heirlooms, it would appear that the dramatic sociopolitical changes that accompanied the process of urbanization at this site did not necessitate the total eradication of the entire social network that had operated in the region in the first few centuries of the first millennium BC, but rather, resulted in its removal (in architectural form) from the physical and visible realm of public spectacle. Interestingly, this situation appears to contrast with evidence elsewhere on the island, where the deliberate reuse of and reference to earlier settlement, cultic, and mortuary sites as a means of legitimizing and strengthening kinship structures and regional identities has been stressed (Azoria III:707–708; Prent 2003; Wallace 2003b). The setting of Early Iron Age shrines within, or in close proximity to, clearly visible Bronze Age remains at Ayia Triada and Kommos is a manifestation of this phenomenon (see Wallace 2003b:263–264 for references). The ambitious building program undertaken by the leaders of the new *polis* community at Azoria, which resulted in the deletion of the preexisting settlement plan, might therefore be understood as a deliberate initiative intended to eliminate the social and political relationships embodied in the preexisting built environment from the new corporate consciousness (Abrams 1989:62). In effect, then, the new urban landscape created in the final decades of the seventh century BC operated not only as a physical expression of the nascent *polis*, but also as a social and ideological symbol of the sociopolitical transformations that had accompanied its appearance.

CONCLUSIONS

The factors that led to the abandonment of the hilltops at Azoria in the first quarter of the fifth century BC and prevented the immediate return of its inhabitants remain unidentified. Nevertheless, the fiery destruction that swept across the settlement shortly after their departure served to preserve in reasonably intact condition the structural and material environment that existed at the time of their exodus. Moreover, although there are clear indications that minor alterations were made to some of the buildings on the site prior to its final desertion, it is nevertheless the case that the original physical framework that was established during the dramatic reshuffling of population that transpired around the transition from the seventh to the sixth century BC survived relatively unchanged until the final demise of the settlement. As a result, the recent excavations at Azoria have yielded unparalleled insight into the archaeological correlates of state formation and urbanization as it unfolded on Crete at the beginning of the Archaic Period.

Analysis of the results from these excavations demonstrates that the urbanization of the landscape at Azoria was a complex, active process stemming from, and in turn encouraging, a series of deliberate and conscious decisions undertaken by, and ultimately affecting, a wide variety of different social and political levels throughout the community (Cowgill 2004:528). The effects of these decisions were not restricted to the tangible components of settlement, but rather encompassed a wide range of intangible elements as well, signaling the redefinition of preexisting sociopolitical and economic relationships between and within the various vertical and horizontal factions of the community, necessitating the creation and implementation of new mechanisms for negotiating standing and identity for and between citizens, and marking the emergence of the "civic" rather than the "kin" as the primary measure of status and prestige within the new urban environment. In effect, then, this transformational process resulted not only in the creation of a new physical and ideological landscape, but also – intimately connected with its appearance – the destruction and obliteration of the preexisting settlement topography and the traditional social, political, and economic associations it had once embodied.

ACKNOWLEDGMENTS

I would like to thank Andy Creekmore and Kevin Fisher for inviting me to contribute to this volume, Donald C. Haggis and Margaret S. Mook for granting me permission to study the architectural material from their excavations at Azoria, and the Social Sciences and Humanities Research Council of Canada and Trent University for providing partial funding for my research. Many thanks to the above-mentioned individuals, as well as David Small and the two anonymous reviewers, for the helpful and insightful comments and criticisms they provided on early drafts of this paper; any lapses in judgment and interpretation remain the author's responsibility.

NOTES

1 Two structures excavated on the southern slope of the South Acropolis, the so-called East and West Corridor Houses (Azoria I:352–363), were first identified as having belonged to a different type of house plan, one characterized by the presence of a corridor/storeroom running alongside a main hall (Azoria I:360–361; Haggis and Mook 2011). Recent reanalysis of the architectural, ceramic, and stratigraphic evidence from these buildings, however, suggests that this original interpretation may not be entirely accurate, although whether they conform to the same pattern of design exemplified by the Northeast Building is yet to be ascertained.

2 It is true that, to some extent, the form of the axial house is dictated by the fact that artificial terraces are required for construction because of the topography of many Cretan settlements. However, there are, as of yet, no indications that these axial units were constructed on adjacent terraces at Azoria, nor that any attempt was made to provide direct communication between terraces from within the houses – as was the case, for example, in the houses erected on the west slope of Lato (Demargne 1903:207–210).

3 Two complexes on the site, Buildings A-B and G, do not conform to the general pattern of house design discussed here. The former has been interpreted as the leader's house, and will be discussed in the context of the civic landscape below. The latter (Day 1997:400–403; Eliopoulos 2004; Klein 2004; Glowacki 2007:135, 137–138) belongs to a class of structure known as a bench sanctuary (Eliopoulos 2004; Klein and Glowacki 2009; Prent 2005:188–200, 616–617), an integral element in the architectural landscape of Early Iron Age Crete known from several sites in the immediate vicinity of Vronda, including Azoria, Halasmenos (Tsipopoulou 2001), Kephala Vasilikis (Eliopoulos 1998, 2004), and Pakhlitzani Agriadha (Alexiou 1965).

4 Of particular interest in this regard was the discovery of two pairs of agrimi (a wild or feral domestic goat on Crete, also known as the kri-kri) horn cores in rooms

A400 and A1700 of the Northeast Building, which the excavators have interpreted as symbolic expressions of power (Azoria II:248). A collection of agrimi horns and cattle skulls in Building B at Vronda has been similarly interpreted as representations of elite male power (Day and Snyder 2004:69–71; Prent 2005453).

5 Despite attempts to identify the complex of rooms south of the Geometric Temple at Dreros as a Prytaneion (Demargne and van Effenterre 1937:16–26; Miller 1978:93–98), two more likely candidates for such a structure at this site are provided by the so-called Agora (Demargne and van Effenterre 1937:10–16) and the building excavated by Xanthoudides (1918) on the Western Acropolis. Both of these structures are the subject of new excavations currently being conducted by Alexandre Farnoux of the French School of Archaeology in Athens.

REFERENCES CITED

Abrams, Elliot M. 1989 Architecture and Energy: An Evolutionary Perspective. *Journal of Archaeological Method and Theory* 1:47–87.

1994 *How the Maya Built Their World: Energetics and Ancient Architecture.* University of Texas Press, Austin.

Abrams, Elliot M. and Thomas W. Bolland 1999 Architectural Energetics, Ancient Monuments, and Operations Management. *Journal of Archaeological Method and Theory* 6:263–291.

Adams, Robert M. 1966 *The Evolution of Urban Society: Early Mesopotamia and Prehispanic Mexico.* Aldine Publishing, Chicago, IL.

Alexiou, Stelios 1965 Ιερόν παρά το Καβούσι Ιεραπέτρας (A Shrine near Kavousi, Ierapetra). *Κρήτικα Χρόνικα* 10:7–19.

Allison, Penelope M. (editor) 1999 *The Archaeology of Household Activities.* Routledge, London.

Andersen, Helle Damgaard, Helle W. Horsnæs, Sanne Houby-Nielsen, and Annette Rathje (editors) 1997 *Urbanization in the Mediterranean in the 9th to 6th Centuries BC. Acta Hyperborea 7.* Museum Tusculanum Press, Copenhagen.

Andreev, Y. V. 1989 Urbanization as a Phenomenon of Social History. *Oxford Journal of Archaeology* 8:167–177.

Apostolakou, Stavroula, Emanuele Greco, T. Kalpaxis, Alain Schnapp, and Didier Viviers 2004–2005 Travaux menés en collaboration avec l'École française en 2003 et 2004: Itanos (Crète orientale). *Bulletin de correspondance hellénique* 128–129:988–1005.

Arnold, Bettina 1999 'Drinking the Feast': Alcohol and the Legitimation of Power in Celtic Europe. *Cambridge Archaeological Journal* 9:71–93.

Azoria I = Haggis, Donald C., Margaret S. Mook, C. Margaret Scarry, Lynn M. Snyder, and William C. West, III 2004 Excavations at Azoria, 2002. *Hesperia* 73:339–400.

Azoria II = Haggis, Donald C., Margaret S. Mook, Rodney D. Fitzsimons, C. Margaret Scarry, and Lynn M. Snyder 2007 Excavations at Azoria in 2003 and 2004, Part 1: The Archaic Civic Complex. *Hesperia* 76:243–321.

Azoria III = Haggis, Donald C., Margaret S. Mook, Tristan Carter, and Lynn M. Snyder 2007 Excavations at Azoria in 2003 and 2004, Part 2: The Final Neolithic, Late Prepalatial, and Early Iron Age Occupation. *Hesperia* 76:665–716.

Azoria IV = Haggis, Donald C., Margaret S. Mook, Rodney D. Fitzsimons, C. Margaret Scarry, Lynn M. Snyder, and William C. West, III 2011 Excavations in the Archaic Civic Buildings at Azoria in 2005–2006. *Hesperia* 80:1–70.

Azoria V = Haggis, Donald C., Margaret S. Mook, Rodney D. Fitzsimons, C. Margaret Scarry, and Lynn M. Snyder 2011 The Excavation of Archaic Houses at Azoria in 2005–2006. *Hesperia* 80:431–489.

Azoria VI = Haggis, Donald D., Margaret S. Mook, Rodney D. Fitzsimons, Melissa Eaby, Maria Liston, C. Margaret Scarry, Lynn M. Snyder, and Roger Doonan 2012 The Excavation of Early Iron Age and Orientalizing Levels at Azoria in 2005–2006. *Hesperia*, forthcoming.

Blanton, Richard E. 1976 Anthropological Studies of Cities. *Annual Review of Anthropology* 5:249–264.

Boardman, John 1967 *Greek Emporio: Excavations in Chios 1952–1955*. British School at Athens Supplement 6. Thames and Hudson, London.

Boyd, Harriet 1901 Excavations at Kavousi, Crete, in 1900. *American Journal of Archaeology* 5:125–157.

Cambitoglou, Alexander, J. J. Coulton, Ann Birchall, and J. R. Green 1988 *Zagora 2: Excavation of a Geometric Settlement on the Island of Andros, Greece. Excavation Season 1969, Study Season 1969–70*. Sydney University Press, Sydney.

Cambitoglou, Alexander, J. J. Coulton, Judy Birmingham, and J. R. Green 1971 *Zagora 1: Excavation of a Geometric Settlement on the Island of Andros, Greece. Excavation Season 1967, Study Season 1968–69*. Sydney University Press, Sydney.

Cameron, Catherine M. 1999 Room Size, Organization of Construction, and Archaeological Interpretation in the Puebloan Southwest. *Journal of Anthropological Archaeology* 18:201–239.

Coldstream, J. Nicolas, and G. L. Huxley 1999 Knossos: The Archaic Gap. *Annual of the British School at Athens* 94:289–307.

Coulson, William D. E. 1997 The Late Minoan IIIC Period on the Kastro at Kavousi. In *La Crète mycénienne. Actes de la Table Ronde Internationale organisée par l'École française d'Athènes, 26–28 mars 1991*, edited by Jan M. Driessen and Alexandre Farnoux, pp. 59–72. *Bulletin de correspondance hellénique* Supplement 30. De Boccard, Paris.

1998 The Early Iron Age on the Kastro at Kavousi in East Crete. In *Post-Minoan Crete. Proceedings of the First Colloquium on Post-Minoan Crete held by the British School at Athens and the Institute of Archaeology, University College, London, 10–11 November 1995*, edited by William G. Cavanagh and Michael Curtis, pp. 40–44. British School at Athens Studies 2. The British School at Athens, London.

Coulson, William D. E. and Metaxia Tsipopoulou 1994 Preliminary Investigations at Halasmenos, Crete, 1992–1993. *Aegean Archaeology* 1:65–97.

Cowgill, George L. 2004 Origins and Development of Urbanism: Archaeological Perspectives. *Annual Review of Anthropology* 33:525–549.

Day, Leslie Preston 1997 The Late Minoan IIIC Period at Vronda, Kavousi. In *La Crète mycénienne. Actes de la Table Ronde Internationale organisée par l'École française d'Athènes, 26–28 mars 1991*, edited by Jan M. Driessen and Alexandre Farnoux, pp. 391–406. *Bulletin de correspondance hellé-nique* Supplement 30. De Boccard, Paris.

Day, Leslie Preston and Lynn M. Snyder 2004 The "Big House" at Vronda and the "Great House" at Karphi: Evidence for Social Structure in LM IIIC Crete. In *Crete beyond the Palaces: Proceedings of the Crete 2000 Conference*, edited by Leslie Preston Day, Margaret S. Mook, and James D. Muhly, pp. 63–79. Institute for Aegean Prehistory Academic Press, Philadelphia.

Day, Leslie Preston, Nancy L. Klein, and Lee Ann Turner 2009 *Kavousi IIA: The Late Minoan IIIC Settlement at Vronda. The Buildings on the Summit*. Prehistory Monographs 26. Institute for Aegean Prehistory Academic Press, Philadelphia.

Day, Leslie Preston, William D. E. Coulson, and Geraldine C. Gesell 1986 Kavousi, 1983–1984: The Settlement at Vronda. *Hesperia* 55:355–387.

Demargne, J. 1903 Fouilles à Lato en Crète 1899–1900. *Bulletin de correspondance hellénique* 27:206–232.

Demargne, Pierre and Henri van Effenterre 1937 Recherches à Dreros. *Bulletin de correspondance hellénique* 61:5–32.

Dietler, Michael 1990 Driven by Drink: The Role of Drinking in the Political Economy and the Case of Early Iron Age France. *Journal of Anthropological Archaeology* 9:352–406.

——— 1996 Feasts and Commensal Politics in the Political Economy: Food, Power, and Status in Prehistoric Europe. In *Food and the Status Quest: An Interdisciplinary Perspective*, edited by Polly Weissner and Wulf Schiefenhovel, pp. 87–125. Berghahn Books, Oxford.

——— 1999 Rituals of Commensality and the Politics of State Formation in the "Princely" Societies of Early Iron Age Europe. In *Les princes de la proto-histoire et l'émergence de l'état. Actes de la table ronde internationale organisée par le Centre Jean Bérard et l'École française de Rome, Naples, 27–29 octobre 1994*, edited by Pascal Ruby, pp. 135–152. L'École Française de Rome, Naples, Italy.

Dietler, Michael and Brian Hayden (editors) 2001 *Feasts: Archaeological and Ethnographic Perspectives on Food, Politics, and Power*. Smithsonian Institution Press, Washington, DC.

Donlan, Walter 1985 The Social Groups of Dark Age Greece. *Classical Philology* 80:293–308.

——— 1997 The Homeric Economy. In *A New Companion to Homer*, edited by Ian Morris and Barry B. Powell, pp. 649–667. E. J. Brill, Leiden, The Netherlands.

Ducrey, Pierre and Olivier Picard 1971 Recherches à Latô IV. Le théâtre. *Bulletin de correspondance hellénique* 95:515–531.

——— 1972 Recherches à Latô V. Le prytanée. *Bulletin de correspondance hellénique* 96:567–592.

Duplouy, Alain, Alain Schnapp, Annie Schnapp-Gourbeillon, C. Tsigonaki, and Didier Viviers 2009 Recherches archéologiques à Itanos (Crète orientale). *Revue archéologique*:103–122.

Eliopoulos, Theodore 1998 A Preliminary Report on the Discovery of a Temple Complex of the Dark Ages at Kephala Vasilikis. In *Eastern Mediterranean: Cyprus – Dodecanese – Crete 16th-6th Cent. BC Proceedings of the International Symposium held at Rethymnon – Crete in May 1997*, edited by Vassos Karageorghis and Nikolas Stampolidis, pp. 301–313. A. G. Leventis Foundation, Athens.

2004 Gournia, Vronda Kavousi, Kephala Vasilikis: A Triad of Interrelated Shrines of the Expiring Minoan Age on the Isthmus of Ierapetra. In *Crete beyond the Palaces: Proceedings of the Crete 2000 Conference*, edited by Leslie Preston Day, Margaret S. Mook, and James D. Muhly, pp. 81–90. Institute for Aegean Prehistory Academic Press, Philadelphia.

Erickson, Brice L. 2002 Aphrati and Kato Syme: Pottery, Continuity, and Cult in Late Archaic and Classical Crete. *Hesperia* 71:41–90.

2004 Eleutherna and the Greek World, ca. 600–400 B.C. In *Crete beyond the Palaces: Proceedings of the Crete 2000 Conference*, edited by Leslie Preston Day, Margaret S. Mook, and James D. Muhly, pp. 199–212. Institute for Aegean Prehistory Academic Press, Philadelphia.

Fagerström, Kåre 1988 *Greek Iron Age Architecture: Developments through Changing Times*. Studies in Mediterranean Archaeology 81. Paul Åströms Förlag, Göteborg, Sweden.

Fox, Richard G. 1977 *Urban Anthropology: Cities in Their Cultural Settings*. Prentice-Hall, Englewood Cliffs, NJ.

Foxhall, Lin 1995 Bronze to Iron: Agricultural Systems and Political Structures in Late Bronze Age and Early Iron Age Greece. *Annual of the British School at Athens* 90:239–250.

Gesell, Geraldine C., Leslie Preston Day, and William D. E. Coulson 1995 Excavations at Kavousi, Crete, 1989 and 1990. *Hesperia* 64:67–120.

Glowacki, Kevin T. 2002 Digging Houses at LM IIIC Vronda (Kavousi) Crete. *Pallas* 58:33–47.

2004 Household Analysis in Dark Age Crete. In *Crete beyond the Palaces: Proceedings of the Crete 2000 Conference*, edited by Leslie Preston Day, Margaret S. Mook, and James D. Muhly, pp. 125–136. Institute for Aegean Prehistory Academic Press, Philadelphia.

2007 House, Household and Community at LM IIIC Vronda, Kavousi. In *Building Communities: House, Settlement and Society in the Aegean and Beyond. Proceedings of a Conference Held at Cardiff University 17–21 April 2001*, edited by Ruth Westgate, Nick Fisher, and James Whitley, pp. 129–139. British School at Athens Studies 15. British School at Athens, London.

2012 Building Complex I-O-N. In *Kavousi IIB: The Late Minoan IIIC Settlement at Vronda. The Buildings on the Periphery*, edited by Leslie Preston Day and Kevin T. Glowacki, pp. 57–141. Prehistory Monographs 39. Institute for Aegean Prehistory Academic Press, Philadelphia.

Greco, Emanuele, T. Kalpaxis, Alain Schnapp, and Didier Viviers 2003 Travaux menés en collaboration avec l'École française en 2002: Itanos (Crète orientale). *Bulletin de correspondance hellénique* 127:546–553.

Green, J. R. 1990 Zagora – Population Increase and Society in the Later Eighth Century BC. In *Eumousia: Ceramic and Iconographic Studies in Honour of Alexander Cambitoglou*, edited by Jean-Paul Descœudres, pp. 41–47. Mediterranean Archaeology Supplement 1. Mediterranean Archaeology, Sydney.

Haggis, Donald C. 1993 Intensive Survey, Traditional Settlement Patterns and Dark Age Crete: The Case of Early Iron Age Kavousi. *Journal of Mediterranean Archaeology* 6:131–174.

1996 Archaeological Survey at Kavousi, East Crete: Preliminary Report. *Hesperia* 65:373–432.

2001 A Dark Age Settlement System in East Crete, and a Reassessment of the Definition of Refuge Settlements. In *Defensive Settlements of the Aegean and the Eastern Mediterranean Area after c. 1200 BC. Proceedings of an International Workshop Held at Trinity College, Dublin, 7th-9th May, 1999*, edited by Vassos Karageorghis and Christine Morris, pp. 41–57. Trinity College, Dublin and the Anastasios G. Leventis Foundation, Nicosia, Cyprus.

2005 *The Archaeological Survey of the Kavousi Region, Kavousi I. The Results of the Excavations at Kavousi in Eastern Crete*. Prehistory Monographs 16. Institute for Aegean Prehistory Academic Press, Philadelphia.

Haggis, Donald C. and Margaret S. Mook 2011. The Archaic Houses at Azoria. In *STEGA: The Archaeology of Houses and Households in Ancient Crete from the Neolithic Period through the Roman Era*, edited by Kevin T. Glowacki and Natalia Vogeikoff-Brogan, pp. 367–380. Hesperia Supplement 44. American School of Classical Studies at Athens, Princeton, NJ.

Haggis, Donald C., Margaret S. Mook, William D. E. Coulson, and Jennifer L. Tobin 1997 Excavations on the Kastro at Kavousi: An Architectural Overview. *Hesperia* 66:315–390.

Hansen, Mogens H. (editor) 2000 *A Comparative Study of Thirty City-State Cultures*. Historisk-Filosofiske Skrifter 21. The Royal Danish Academy of Science and Letters, Copenhagen.

(editor) 2002 *A Comparative Study of Six City-State Cultures*. Historisk-Filosofiske Skrifter 27. The Royal Danish Academy of Science and Letters, Copenhagen.

2006 *Polis: An Introduction to the Ancient Greek City-State*. Oxford University Press, Oxford.

Hansen, Mogens H. and Thomas H. Nielsen (editors) 2005 *An Inventory of Archaic and Classical Poleis: An Investigation Conducted by the Copenhagen Polis Centre for the Danish National Research Foundation*. Oxford University Press, Oxford.

Harris-Cline, Diane 1999 Archaic Athens and the Topography of the Kylon Affair. *Annual of the British School at Athens* 94:309–320.

Hayden, Barbara J. 1983 New Plans of the Early Iron Age Settlement of Vrokastro. *Hesperia* 52:367–387.

2004a *Reports on the Vrokastro Area, Eastern Crete, Volume 2: The Settlement History of the Vrokastro Area and Related Studies*. University Museum Monograph 119. University of Pennsylvania Press, Philadelphia.

2004b Vrokastro and the Settlement Pattern of the LM IIIA-Geometric Periods. In *Crete beyond the Palaces: Proceedings of the Crete 2000 Conference*, edited by Leslie Preston Day, Margaret S. Mook, and James D. Muhly, pp. 233–245. Institute for Aegean Prehistory Academic Press, Philadelphia.

Hurwit, Jeffrey M. 1999 *The Athenian Acropolis: History, Mythology, and Archaeology from the Neolithic to Present*. Cambridge University Press, Cambridge.

Joffee, Alexander H. 1998 Alcohol and Social Complexity in Ancient Western Asia. *Current Anthropology* 39(3):297–322.

Johnston, Kevin J. and Nancy Gonlin 1998 What Do Houses Mean? Approaches to the Analysis of Classic Maya Commoner Residences. In *Function and Meaning in Classic Maya Architecture*, edited by Stephen D. Houston, 141–185. Dumbarton Oaks Research Library and Collection, Washington, DC.

Kinch, Karl F. 1914 *Vroulia*. G. Reimer, Berlin.

Klein, Nancy L. 2004 The Architecture of the Late Minoan IIIC Shrine (Building G) at Vronda, Kavousi. In *Crete beyond the Palaces: Proceedings of the Crete 2000 Conference*, edited by Leslie Preston Day, Margaret S. Mook, and James D. Muhly, pp. 91–101. Institute for Aegean Prehistory Academic Press, Philadelphia.

Klein, Nancy and Kevin T. Glowacki 2009 From Vronda to Dreros: Architecture and Display in Cretan Cult Buildings 1200–700 B.C. In *Archaeologies of Cult: Essays on Ritual and Cult in Crete*, edited by Anna Lucia D'Agata, Aleydis van der Moortel, and Molly B. Richardson, pp. 153–167. *Hesperia* Supplements 42. The American School of Classical Studies at Athens, Princeton.

Koehl, Robert B. 1997 The Villas at Ayia Triada and Nirou Chani and the Origin of the Cretan Andreion. In *The Function of the Minoan Villa. Proceedings of the Eighth International Symposium at the Swedish Institute at Athens, 6–8 June 1992*, edited by Robin Hägg, pp. 137–149. Skrifter utgivna av Svenska Institutet i Athen, 4°, XLVI. Paul Åströms Förlag, Stockholm.

Kotsonas, Antonios 2002 The Rise of the Polis in Central Crete. ΕΥΛΙΜΕΝΗ 3:37–74.

Lang, Franziska 2002 Housing and Settlement in Archaic Greece. *Pallas* 58:13–32.

　2007 House – Community – Settlement: The New Concept of Living in Archaic Greece. In *Building Communities: House, Settlement and Society in the Aegean and Beyond. Proceedings of a Conference Held at Cardiff University 17–21 April 2001*, edited by Ruth Westgate, Nick Fisher, and James Whitley, pp. 183–193. British School at Athens Studies 15. British School at Athens, London.

Lillios, Katina T. 1999 Objects of Memory: The Ethnography and Archaeology of Heirlooms. *Journal of Archaeological Method and Theory* 6:235–262.

Lissarrague, François 1991 *The Aesthetics of the Greek Banquet: Images of Wine and Ritual*. Translated by Andrew Szegedy-Maszak. Princeton University Press, Princeton, NJ.

Lynch, Kathleen M. 2007 More Thoughts on the Space of the Symposium. In *Building Communities: House, Settlement and Society in the Aegean and Beyond. Proceedings of a Conference Held at Cardiff University 17–21 April 2001*, edited by Ruth Westgate, Nick Fisher, and James Whitley, pp. 243–249. British School at Athens Studies 15. British School at Athens, London.

Marcus, Joyce 1983 On the nature of the Mesoamerican City. In *Prehistoric Settlement Patterns: Essays in Honor of Gordon R. Willey*, edited by Evon Z. Vogt and Richard M. Leventhal, pp. 195–242. University of New Mexico Press, Albuquerque.

Marinatos, Spyridon 1936 Le temple geométrique à Dreros. *Bulletin de correspondance hellénique* 60:214–285.

RODNEY D.
FITZSIMONS

Melander, Torben 1988 Vroulia: Town Plan and Gate. In *Archaeology in the Dodecanese*, edited by Søren Dietz and Ioannis Papachristodoulou, pp. 83–87. National Museum of Denmark, Copenhagen.

Miller, Stephen G. 1978 *The Prytaneion: Its Function and Architectural Form*. University of California Press, Berkeley.

 1995 Architecture as Evidence for the Identity of the Early *Polis*. In *Sources for the Ancient Greek City-State. Symposium August, 24–27 1994*, edited by Mogens G. Hansen, pp. 201–242. Acts of the Copenhagen Polis Centre 2. The Royal Danish Academy of Sciences and Letters, Copenhagen.

Mitchell, Lynette G. and P. J. Rhodes (editors) 1997 *The Development of the Polis in Archaic Greece*. Routledge, London.

Mook, Margaret S. 1998 Early Iron Age Domestic Architecture: The Northwest Building on the Kastro at Kavousi. In *Post-Minoan Crete. Proceedings of the First Colloquium on Post-Minoan Crete held by the British School at Athens and the Institute of Archaeology, University College, London, 10–11 November 1995*, edited by William G. Cavanagh and Michael Curtis, pp. 45–57. British School at Athens Studies 2. The British School at Athens, London.

 2004 From Foundation to Abandonment: New Ceramic Phasing for the Late Bronze Age and Early Iron Age on the Kastro at Kavousi. In *Crete beyond the Palaces: Proceedings of the Crete 2000 Conference*, edited by Leslie P. Day, Margaret S. Mook, and James D. Muhly, pp. 163–179. Institute for Aegean Prehistory Academic Press, Philadelphia.

Morris, Ian 1997a Homer and the Iron Age. In *A New Companion to Homer*, edited by Ian Morris and Barry B. Powell, pp. 535–559. E. J. Brill, Leiden, The Netherlands.

 1997b An Archaeology of Equalities? The Greek City-States. In *A New Companion to Homer*, edited by Ian Morris and Barry B. Powell, pp. 91–105. E. J. Brill, Leiden, The Netherlands.

 1998 Archaeology and Archaic Greek History. In *Archaic Greece: New Approaches and New Evidence*, edited by Nick Fisher and Hans van Wees, pp. 1–92. Duckworth, London.

Murray, Oswyn 1983 The Symposion as Social Organisation. In *The Greek Renaissance of the Eighth Century BC: Tradition and Innovation. Proceedings of the Second International Symposium at the Swedish Institute in Athens, 1–5 June, 1981*, edited by Robin Hägg, pp. 195–200. Skrifter utgivna av Svenska Institutet i Athen, 4°, XXX. Paul Åströms Förlag, Stockholm.

 (editor) 1990 *Sympotica: A Symposium on the Symposion*. Clarendon Press, Oxford.

Nichols, Deborah L. and Thomas H. Charlton (editors) 1997 *The Archaeology of City-States: Cross-Cultural Approaches*. Smithsonian Institution Press, Washington, DC.

Nowicki, Krzysztof 1999 Economy of Refugees: Life in the Cretan Mountains at the Turn of the Bronze and Iron Ages. In *From Minoan Farmers to Roman Traders: Sidelights on the Economy of Ancient Crete*, edited by Angelos Chaniotis, pp. 145–172. Franz Steiner Verlag, Stuttgart, Germany.

 2002 From Late Minoan IIIC Refuge Settlements to Geometric Acropoleis: Architecture and Social Organization of Dark Age Villages and Towns in Crete. *Pallas* 58:149–174.

Osborne, Robin 1996 *Greece in the Making 1200–479 B.C.* Routledge, London.

2005 *Mediterranean Urbanization 800–600 B.C.* Oxford University Press, Oxford.

Papadopoulos, John K. 2003 *Ceramic Redivivus: The Early Iron Age Potter's Field in the Area of the Classical Athenian Agora.* Hesperia Supplement 31. American School of Classical Studies at Athens, Princeton, NJ.

Paschalides, Konstantinos P. 2006 Στοιχεία Μυκηναϊκού Χαρακτήρα στην Ανατολική Κρήτη κατά το Τέλος της Εποχής του Χαλκού. Νέα Μέγαρα στο Χαλασμένο Ιεράπετρας (Elements of Mycenaean Character in East Crete at the End of the Bronze Age. New Megara at Halasmenos, Ierapetra). In Πεπραγμένα Θ' Διεθνούς Κρητολογικού Συνεδρίου (Proceedings of the 9th International Cretological Congress, Elounda, 1–6 October 2001), Ελούντα, 1–6 Οκτωβρίου 2001, Α1, pp. 219–232. Etairia Kritikon Istorikon Meleton, Herakleion, Greece.

Perlman, Paula 2004 Tinker, Tailor, Soldier, Sailor: The Economies of Archaic Eleutherna, Crete. *Classical Antiquity* 23:95–136.

Pfaff, Christopher A. 2003 Archaic Corinthian Architecture, ca. 600 to 480 BC. In *Corinth: The Centenary 1896–1996*, edited by Charles K. Williams and Nancy Bookidis, pp. 95–140. The American School of Classical Studies at Athens, Princeton, NJ.

Prent, Mieke 1996–1997 The Sixth Century BC in Crete: The Best Candidate for a Dark Age? In *Debating Dark Ages*, edited by Marianne Maaskant-Kleibrink and Marja Vink, pp. 35–46. *Caeculus* 3. Archaeological Institute, Groningen University, Groningen, The Netherlands.

2003 Glories of the Past in the Past: Ritual Activities at Palatial Ruins in Early Iron Age Crete. In *Archaeologies of Memory*, edited by Ruth M. Van Dyke and Susan E. Alcock, pp. 81–103. Blackwell Publishing, Oxford.

2005 *Cretan Sanctuaries and Cults: Continuity and Change from Late Minoan IIIC to the Archaic Period.* E. J. Brill, Leiden, The Netherlands.

Rhodes, Robin F. 2003 The Earliest Greek Architecture in Corinth and the 7th Century Temple on Temple Hill. In *Corinth: The Centenary 1896–1996*, edited by Charles K. Williams and Nancy Bookidis, pp. 85–94. The American School of Classical Studies at Athens, Princeton, NJ.

Robertson, Noel 1998 The City Center of Archaic Athens. *Hesperia* 67:283–302.

Rupp, David W. 2007 Building Megara for Dummies: The Conception and Construction of Architectural Forms at Late Minoan IIIC Halasmenos (Monasteraki, Ierapetra, Crete). In Κρίνοι και Λιμένες: *Studies in Honor of Joseph and Maria Shaw*, edited by Philip P. Betancourt, Michael C. Nelson, and Hector Williams, pp. 61–66. Prehistory Monographs 22. Institute for Aegean Prehistory Academic Press, Philadelphia.

Samson, Ross (editor) 1990 *The Social Archaeology of Houses.* Edinburgh University Press, Edinburgh, Scotland.

Sanders, William T. and Robert S. Santley 1983 A Tale of Three Cities: Energetics and Urbanization in Pre-Hispanic Central Mexico. In *Prehistoric Settlement Patterns: Essays in Honor of Gordon R. Willey*, edited by Evon Z. Vogt and Richard M. Leventhal, pp. 243–291. University of New Mexico Press, Albuquerque.

Schilardi, Demetrius U. 1983 The Decline of the Geometric Settlement of Koukounaries at Paros. In *The Greek Renaissance of the Eighth Century BC:*

Tradition and Innovation. Proceedings of the Second International Symposium at the Swedish Institute in Athens, 1–5 June, 1981, edited by Robin Hägg, pp. 173–183. Skrifter utgivna av Svenska Institutet i Athen, 4°, XXX. Paul Åströms Förlag, Stockholm.

Schmalz, Geoffrey C. R. 2006 The Athenian Prytaneion Discovered? *Hesperia* 75:33–81.

Shaw, Joseph W. 2000 Ritual and Development in the Greek Sanctuary. In *Kommos IV: The Greek Sanctuary*, edited by Joseph W. Shaw and Maria C. Shaw, pp. 669–732. Princeton University Press, Princeton, NJ.

Shear, T. Leslie, Jr. 1994 Ισονόμους τ'Αθήνας εποιησάτην: The Agora and the Democracy. In *The Archaeology of Athens and Attica under the Democracy*, edited by W. D. E. Coulson, O. Palagia, T. L. Shear, Jr., H. A. Shapiro, and F. J. Frost, pp. 225–248. Oxbow Monograph 37. Oxbow, Oxford.

Sjögren, Lena 2007 Interpreting Cretan Private and Communal Spaces (800–500 BC). In *Building Communities: House, Settlement and Society in the Aegean and Beyond. Proceedings of a Conference Held at Cardiff University 17–21 April 2001*, edited by Ruth Westgate, Nick Fisher, and James Whitley, pp. 149–155. British School at Athens Studies 15. British School at Athens, London.

Small, David B. 1998 Surviving the Collapse: The Oikos and Structural Continuity between Late Bronze Age and Later Greece. In *Mediterranean Peoples in Transition: Thirteenth to Early Tenth Centuries BCE In Honor of Professor Trude Dothan*, edited by Seymour Gitin, Amihai Mazar, and Ephraim Stern, pp. 283–291. Israel Exploration Society, Jerusalem.

2010 The Archaic *Polis* of Azoria: A Window into Cretan 'Political' Social Structure. *Journal of Mediterranean Archaeology* 23:197–217.

Smith, Adam T. 2003 *The Political Landscape: Constellations of Authority in Early Complex Polities*. University of California Press, Berkeley.

Smith, Monica L. (editor) 2003 *The Social Construction of Ancient Cities*. Smithsonian Institution Press, Washington, DC.

Snodgrass, Anthony M. 2006 *Archaeology and the Emergence of Greece*. Cornell University Press, Ithaca, NY.

Stampolidis, Nikolas 1990 Eleutherna on Crete: An Interim Report on the Geometric-Archaic Cemetery. *Annual of the British School at Athens* 85:375–403.

2002 From the Geometric and Archaic Necropolis at Eleutherna. In *Excavating Classical Culture: Recent Archaeological Discoveries in Greece*, edited by Maria Stamatopoulou and Marina Yeroulanou, pp. 327–332. The Beazley Archive and Archaeopress, Oxford.

Storey, Glenn R. (editor) 2006 *Urbanism in the Preindustrial World: Cross-Cultural Approaches*. University of Alabama Press, Tuscaloosa.

Tandy, David W. 1997 *Warriors into Traders: The Power of the Market in Early Greece*. University of California Press, Berkeley.

Topper, Kathryn 2009 Primitive Life and the Construction of the Sympotic Past in Athenian Vase Painting. *American Journal of Archaeology* 113:3–26.

Trigger, Bruce G. 1990 Monumental Architecture: A Thermodynamic Explanation of Symbolic Behaviour. *World Archaeology* 22:119–132.

Tsipopoulou, Metaxia 2001 A New Late Minoan IIIC Shrine at Halasmenos, East Crete. In *POTNIA: Deities and Religion in the Aegean Bronze Age*, edited by Robert Laffineur and Robin Hägg, pp. 99–101. *Aegaeum* 22. Université de Liège, Liège, Belgium.

2004 Halasmenos, Destroyed but not Invisible: New Insights on the LM IIIC Period in the Isthmus of Ierapetra. First Presentation of the Pottery from the 1992–1997 Campaigns. In *Crete beyond the Palaces: Proceedings of the Crete 2000 Conference*, edited by Leslie Preston Day, Margaret S. Mook, and James D. Muhly, pp. 103–123. Institute for Aegean Prehistory Academic Press, Philadelphia.

Van der Vliet, Edward Ch. L. 1996–1997 The Seventh Century BC as a Dark Age: A Historian's Perspective. In *Debating Dark Ages*, edited by Marianne Maaskant-Kleibrink and Marja Vink, pp. 25–33. *Caeculus* 3. Archaeological Institute, Groningen University, Groningen, The Netherlands.

Vink, Marja C. 1996–1997 The Archaic Period in Greece: Another Dark Age? In *Debating Dark Ages*, edited by Marianne Maaskant-Kleibrink and Marja Vink, pp. 1–18. *Caeculus* 3. Archaeological Institute, Groningen University, Groningen, The Netherlands.

1997 Urbanization in Late and Sub-Geometric Greece: Abstract Considerations and Concrete Case Studies of Eretria and Zagora c. 700 BC. In *Urbanization in the Mediterranean in the 9th to 6th Centuries BC*, edited by Helle Damgaard Andersen, Helle W. Horsnæs, Sanne Houby-Nielsen, and Annette Rathje, pp. 111–141. Acta Hyperborea 7. Museum Tusculanum Press, Copenhagen.

Wallace, Saro 2001 Case Studies of Settlement Change in Early Iron Age Crete (*c.* 1200–700 BC): Economic Interpretations of Cause and Effect Assessed in a Long-Term Historical Perspective. *Aegean Archaeology* 4:61–99.

2003a The Changing Role of Herding in the Early Iron Age of Crete: Some Implications of Settlement Shift for Economy. *American Journal of Archaeology* 107:601–628.

2003b The Perpetuated Past: Re-Use or Continuity in Material Culture and the Structuring of Identity in Early Iron Age Crete. *Annual of the British School at Athens* 98:251–277.

2006 The Gilded Cage? Settlement and Socioeconomic Change after 1200 BC: A Comparison of Crete and Other Aegean Regions. In *Ancient Greece: From the Mycenaean Palaces to the Age of Homer*, edited by Sigrid Deger-Jalkotzy and Irene S. Lemos, pp. 619–664. Edinburgh Leventis Studies 3. Edinburgh University Press, Edinburgh, Scotland.

2010 *Ancient Crete: From Successful Collapse to Democracy`s Alternatives, Twelfth to Fifth Centuries BC*. Cambridge University Press, Cambridge.

Weir, Robert G. A. 1995 The Late Archaic Wall around Athens. *Phoenix* 49:247–258.

Westgate, Ruth 2007a House and Society in Classical and Hellenistic Crete: A Case Study in Regional Variation. *American Journal of Archaeology* 111:423–457.

2007b The Greek House and the Ideology of Citizenship. *World Archaeology* 39(2):229–245.

Whitley, James 2006 Praisos: Political Evolution and Ethnic Identity in Eastern Crete c. 1400–300 BC. In *Ancient Greece: From the Mycenaean Palaces to the Age of Homer*, edited by Sigrid Deger-Jalkotzy and Irene S. Lemos, pp. 597–617. Edinburgh Leventis Studies 3. Edinburgh University Press, Edinburgh, Scotland.

Whitley, James, Kieran O'Conor, and Howard Mason 1995 Praisos III: A Report on the Architectural Survey Undertaken in 1992. *Annual of the British School at Athens* 90:405–428.

Whitley, James, Mieke Prent, and Stuart Thorne 1999 Praisos IV: A Preliminary Report on the 1993 and 1994 Survey Seasons. *Annual of the British School at Athens* 94:215–264.

Wright, James C. (editor) 2004 *The Mycenaean Feast*. The American School of Classical Studies at Athens, Princeton, NJ.

Xanthoudides, Stephanos A. 1918 Παράρτημα του Αρχαιλογικού Δελτίου 1918 – Δρήρος (Supplement to the 1918 Αρχαιολογικόν Δελτίον). *Αρχαιολογικόν Δελτίον* 4:23–30.

Yanagisako, Sylvia Junko 1979 Family and Household: The Analysis of Domestic Groups. *Annual Review of Anthropology* 8:161–205.

Yasur-Landau, Assaf 2003–2004 (2006) The Last *Glendi* in Halasmenos: Social Aspects of Cooking in a Dark Age Cretan Village. *Aegean Archaeology* 7:49–66.

2006 *Halasmeno Fagito*: Burnt Dishes and Scorched Pots. Some Preliminary Observations on LM IIIC Cooking Ware. In Πεπραγμένα Θ' Διεθνούς Κρητολογικού Συνεδρίου, Ελούντα, 1–6 Οκτωβρίου 2001 (Proceedings of the 9th International Cretological Congress, Elounda, 1–6 October 2001), A1, pp. 233–51. Etairia Kritikon Istorikon Meleton, Herakleion, Crete.

8

The Rise of a Minoan City and the (Re)Structuring of Its Hinterlands: A View from Galatas

D. Matthew Buell

Data from both recent excavation and survey work at the Minoan city of Galatas, which is located in the Pediada in central Crete, allow one to situate an early Neopalatial (ca. 1700–1600 BC) palace in both its urban and rural contexts. Through the employment of Michael Smith's novel approach to analyzing city planning, and consideration of the associated meanings that may be attached to it, it becomes clear that certain elements of the city of Galatas were constructed with a view toward promoting group cohesion, while at the same time emphasizing, maintaining, and enforcing social differentiation. The fact that these were real concerns for those who constructed the city is highlighted by the various changes to the region's sociopolitical and economic framework. The impetus for the construction of the city of Galatas remains little understood, but it is tentatively posited that it was owing to the expansion of Knossos in the early part of the Neopalatial period.

To date, there have been relatively few discussions concerning the nature of Minoan urbanism, especially as it pertains to city planning. Scholars have suggested that Minoan society was not very urban (e.g., Renfrew 1972:242–244), and that if it was, there was little formal organization or planning involved (e.g., Branigan 2001:45; Hutchinson 1950). Those who argue for planning within Minoan cities do so through models emphasizing the presence of street grids (e.g., Cunningham 2001:78–81), or the use of modular planning (e.g., Palyvou 2002; Preziosi 1983), and metrological systems (e.g., Graham 1960, 1987) in the construction of one element of the urban environment, the palace. Perhaps the fact that very few have attempted to assess the urban environment in its totality is not so surprising, given that there has been an almost exclusive focus on excavation of the palaces. This myopic viewpoint has led to a general reluctance among scholars to describe such settlements as cities. I argue that Minoan settlements with palatial complexes were in fact cities because they were highly differentiated from their rural hinterlands, yet functionally interconnected to them as they served as the locations for a number of specialized activities ranging from the political to the ideological; many scholars consider these to be defining characteristics of cities (cf. Cowgill 2004:527; Grove 1972:560; Redman 1978:215–216; Smith 2007:4; Southall 1973:6; Trigger 1972). On this basis, I contend that settlements with palatial complexes were cities and that significant parts of these cities were planned by rulers with a view toward promoting specific messages about identity and social status.

Rapoport (1990:10) argues that parts of the built environment are actively created in order to reflect social expressions of culture, including groups, family structures, institutions, social networks, and status relations. For Rapoport (1988, 1990) there are three levels of meanings embedded within the built environment, including high-level meanings (cosmological and supernatural), mid-level meanings (identity, status, and power), and low-level meanings (behavior and movement). According to Smith (2007:30), these three levels provide an appropriate framework for examining both the intentions of rulers and builders, and the effects of city planning on urban visitors and inhabitants. These different levels of meaning are neither independent, nor are they mutually exclusive as two or three levels are often conveyed in cities and their individual buildings (cf. Fisher and Creekmore, Chapter 1 of this volume; Fitzsimons, Chapter 7 of this volume). I will examine only mid-level and low-level meanings, for high-level ones are difficult to substantiate in the present case study and more generally (Smith 2007:34–35).

Because parts of the built environment convey messages associated with identity and power relationships, it should be understood that certain aspects of a cultural group's ideology are infused within it. The creation, control, and proliferation of ideology serve as important instruments of social stability and change (Miller and Tilley 1984:8; Mumford 2003; Preucel and Meskell 2003; Whitley 1998:17). Through the strategic employment of ideology, here in its materialized sense, elites may use it as a powerful tool to both reproduce and transform their own social roles within society (DeMarrais et al. 1996; Knapp 1988:139). Because specific parts of the built environment are the products of deliberate, strategic planning by certain individuals, personal agency is implied (cf. Dobres and Robb 2000:8–9). Thus, there is a link between the elites, agency, and power, which is manifested in certain parts of the built environment.

Minoan cities were planned with a view toward promoting both mid- and low-level meanings, for buildings and spaces were organized with specific reference (i.e., simple coordination) to one another, a number of buildings were both formally arranged and monumental in scope, and they were often designed with a view toward controlling and restricting both access and visibility. Taken as a group (i.e., simple coordination, formality, and monumentality) these elements of planning may be referred to as coordination among buildings and spaces (Carter 1983; Smith 2007:8). When cities across Crete are compared to each other, a remarkable number of similarities in design, form, orientation, building materials, and, perhaps, even the use of a common metrological system can be noted. In other words, Minoan cities shared a number of standardized features (cf. Ellis 1995; Smith 2007:8). At its most basic level, the presence of a coordination of buildings, along with some degree of standardization, suggests that there was an active program of central planning that was shared among Minoan cities.

In light of the foregoing discussion, I argue that Minoan cities were distinct and differentiated from their hinterlands, and that significant parts of them were planned by specific individuals in order to promote mid-level and low-level meanings, specifically those that are concerned with group identity and hierarchical institutions. I assess the relative degree of planning using Smith's (2007, 2008) model for ancient city planning. The constituent parts of this model include: simple coordination, formality, and monumentality; access and visibility; and standardization amongst a number of other cities within a cultural *koine*. These units of analysis can then be linked to meaning. The clearest mid-level meanings of ancient cities, for example, are derived from expressions of monumentality and formality, whereas low-level meanings – those that are concerned with the recursive relationship between architecture and behavior – may be analyzed through a study of visibility and accessibility (Smith 2007:35–37). As is the case for certain elements of Minoan cities, I believe that the hinterlands of cities were often reorganized to meet certain demands imposed by the rulers living within cities.

In order to illustrate the claims presented here, I apply Smith's (2007) model for urban planning to the Minoan city of Galatas, which is located in central Crete in the region of the Pediada (Figure 8.1). Galatas, which has been continuously excavated by G. Rethemiotakis since 1992, presents an excellent case study for

Table 8.1 *Minoan chronology (after Warren and Hankey 1989:137–169)*

Ceramic Phase		Date
Early Minoan I (EM I)		3650/3500–3000/2900 BC
Early Minoan II (EM II)		2900–2300/2026 BC
Early Minoan III (EM III)		2300/2150–2160/2025 BC
Middle Minoan IA (MM IA)	Prepalatial	2160/1979–20th century BC
Middle Minoan IB (MM IB)		19th century BC
Middle Minoan II (MM II)	Protopalatial	19th century–1700/1650 BC
Middle Minoan IIIA (MM IIIA)		1700/1650–1640/1630 BC
Middle Minoan IIIB (MM IIIB)		1640/1630–1600 BC
Late Minoan IA (LM IA)		1600/1580–1480 BC
Late Minoan IB (LM IB)	Neopalatial	1480–1425 BC
Late Minoan II (LM II)		1425–1390 BC
Late Minoan IIIA1	Postpalatial	1390–1370/1360 BC

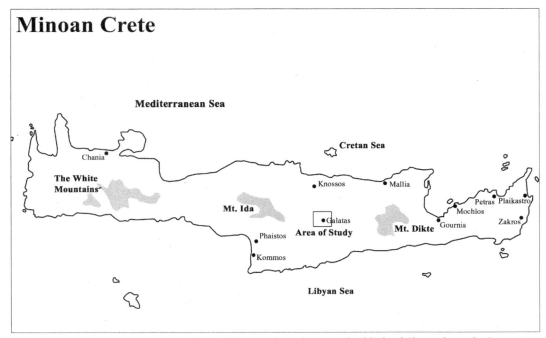

Figure 8.1 Plan of Crete with study region highlighted (drawn by author).

investigations of Minoan urbanism, especially those pertaining to city planning, because it was built anew in Middle Minoan IIIA following a period of abandonment in Middle Minoan II (see Table 8.1 for Minoan chronology). As a result of its clear building history, one can fully assess the level of planning and the sociopolitical messages that it conveyed. In addition, the recent survey of Galatas's territory conducted by the State University of New York at Buffalo allows us to expand the scope of analysis to examine how the newly imposed city changed traditional rural lifestyles (Watrous et al. 2014). The survey data suggest that the ruler(s) of Galatas's concern for promoting messages connected to social rank, power, and group identity was very real and that these messages significantly affected the day-to-day lives of people living within Galatas's hinterlands. The integrated excavation and survey data also offer some tantalizing clues as to the identity of those who built the city on the Galatas Kephala (i.e., hilltop). It seems as though the construction of this new city in the Pediada may have been part of a political strategy employed by Knossos as it expanded the scope of its regional state.

THE CITY

Excavation and surface survey indicate that the Galatas Kephala was first occupied in Early Minoan I (Buell 2014a; Rethemiotakis and Christakis 2011: 195), whereas the first recorded architectural remains at the settlement belong to Middle Minoan IA. Following Middle Minoan IB, the Kephala was abandoned until Middle Minoan IIIA when an extensive building program, which included a palatial complex, was initiated (Figure 8.2). Besides the palace, Middle Minoan IIIA witnessed the construction of several new, elite residential buildings on the Kephala, including Buildings 1, 6, and 7. Building 3, which was initially constructed in Middle Minoan IA-IB, was also rebuilt in this period (Rethemiotakis 2007–2008:105, 2008–2009:95–97). Following a destruction event at the end of Middle Minoan IIIA – probably the result of an earthquake – all buildings, including the palatial compound, were immediately rebuilt and occupied in Middle Minoan IIIB. As was the case for other Neopalatial palaces on Crete (i.e., Knossos, Phaistos, Malia, and Zakros) the complex at Galatas consisted of four wings organized around a central courtyard. Occupying an area of nearly 1 ha, the palace possessed spaces

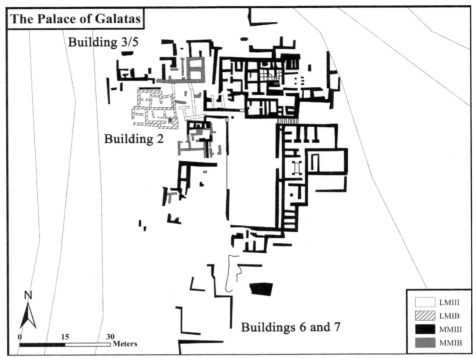

Figure 8.2 Plan of the palace of Galatas (redrawn from Rethemiotakis and Christakis 2011:figure 2).

for storage, ceremonial activities, and industry. Galatas ultimately lost its palatial character in the early Late Minoan IA as only a small part of the palace remained in use (Rethemiotakis 2002:63). The settlement continued to be occupied until the end of Late Minoan IB when it was destroyed by fire. Besides the buildings that have been excavated, the University at Buffalo survey has identified the remains of a number of other Neopalatial structures spread throughout the settlement (Buell 2014b; Figure 8.3). Although a precise date cannot be assigned to these buildings, it is assumed, based on the dates of their associated surface pottery, that they are contemporary with the Middle Minoan IIIA-B palace.

Coordination of Buildings and Spaces

According to Smith (2007:8), simple coordination refers to cases in which buildings and spaces are arranged with *specific* reference to one another. At Galatas, all features of the urban environment shared a common reference to the palace in that they all possessed a general north-south orientation (Figure 8.3). Because all buildings of

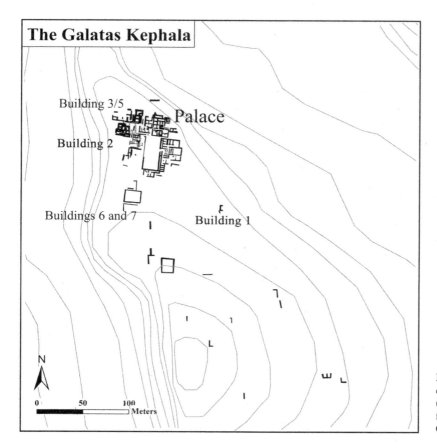

The Galatas Kephala

Building 3/5

Palace

Building 2

Buildings 6 and 7

Building 1

N

0   50   100
Meters

Figure 8.3 Site plan
of the city of Galatas
(redrawn and adapted
from Rethemiotakis and
Christakis 2011:figure 1).

the palace complex were oriented with respect to the central courtyard, this space should be seen as the principal organizing feature of
the city. What makes this more acute is that buildings situated in different topographical locations, including Building 1 and two other
buildings identified by the University at Buffalo survey, adhered to
this common orientation (Buell 2014b; Figure 8.3). Topography, therefore, did not seem to be a key factor in the orientation of buildings
on the Kephala.

Buildings and spaces at Galatas were also constructed with reference to streets. Roads, streets, and paths serve as key elements in
the armature of urban environments because they provide coherence for different structures and they unite these same buildings
(MacDonald 1986:256; see also Creekmore, Chapter 2 in this volume).
These features also help social actors in their negotiations within
a particular environment because they may be used to direct individuals to spaces important in structuring and enforcing social
relationships (Lynch 1960:49–62). Evidence for the construction of

roads and streets at Galatas is unfortunately quite limited.[1] There does, however, seem to have been a main north-south artery (i.e., a main city street) on the Kephala, which ran from the bottom of the hill through the settlement and then up to the palace. Large urban blocks, with narrow alleyways providing access to individual buildings within these blocks, were laid out along it (Rethemiotakis 2008–2009:94–95). Once the street reached the southern courtyard of the palace, it split into two branches with each one running along opposite sides of the palace's exterior before joining together at the northern-most part of the palace, creating a ring road. Because the main street led up to and terminated at the palace, it can be said that it possessed a specific directional quality that situated the palace as the most prominent feature in the urban environment. This was reinforced by the fact that as one traveled toward the palace, one was constantly moving upward in elevation. The effect of this is that the palace would have been seen to loom above the individual, creating a visual effect wherein it was made more imposing (cf. Moore 1996:92–120). According to Rapoport (1990:107), the use of higher elevation is a nearly universal nonverbal cue indicating higher status. The belief that this was indeed planned is suggested by the fact that there was an open courtyard on the palace's southern side (the direction of its major approach), which provided travelers with an unobstructed view of the palace and its monumental southern façade (cf. Letesson and Vansteenhuyse 2006:93–94). This concern for providing clear views of the palace's monumental facades was repeated on its northern and eastern sides, as neither topographical features nor architecture restricted the views of these elements. In fact, because the palace occupied the most prominent part of the settlement on the northern tip of the ridge, it was visible in some areas to the north and east for distances of nearly 6 km as verified by geographic information system (GIS) viewshed analysis (Buell 2014b). Given its placement on the Kephala, the power and prestige of the palace would have been communicated to both local inhabitants and visitors to the city.

The street system also linked three courtyards (i.e., the southern, northwestern, and northern courtyards), which were themselves built with specific reference to the palace as they were positioned on its periphery. Because these three courtyards interrupted the linear flow of the primary street system, they would have served as junctions or nodes within the armature of the city of Galatas. Given the ceremonial functions of these courtyards, as will be discussed, and their architectural elaborations, which included the ashlar facades of the palace walls that faced them, the streets that connected them would have possessed prominence in the minds of travelers (cf. Lynch 1960:50–51). In addition to directing individuals to places of social interaction, the palace's abilities to command both material and human labor would have been reflected in the construction of the street system. Thus, apart from having served as a unifying or structuring element, one that helped in the simple coordination of buildings and spaces, Galatas's street system served as a material-ized form of ideology as it helped to highlight the social position of those responsible for its construction.

One final element that highlights the notion of simple coordina-tion is that there may have been districts of similarly designed build-ings within the city of Galatas. Unfortunately, given the current focus of excavation on the monumental core, we are, at present, unable to discuss the presence and composition of specific neighborhoods. In contrast, districts, which often possess multiple neighborhoods, are discernible in Galatas's archaeological record, for these areas are usually separated from each other through the use of homogenous architecture (Smith 2010:140). The distinct architectural forms and the social activities conducted within districts provide them with specific social identities, which, in turn, allow observers to mentally visualize them (Lynch 1960:66; Smith 2010:140). At Galatas, two or perhaps three distinct districts are apparent within its architectural remains.

Galatas's monumental core served as an administrative dis-trict, for it acted as the political, economic, and ideological center for the city and the region. This urban core was surrounded by a number of large, freestanding structures (i.e., Buildings 1, 3, 5, 6, and 7), all of which possessed a number of architectural elabora-tions including the use of ashlar masonry, wall paintings, or spe-cialized rooms like the Minoan Hall complex.[2] Given the size and elaboration of some of these residences, it may be that these build-ings comprised an elite district at Galatas. A nonelite district may have existed at the fringes of the settlement as a number of walls belonging to distinct, small structures constructed from fieldstones were identified by the University at Buffalo survey (Buell 2014b). Because these houses were constructed in a common architectural style, seem to have been about the same size, and were all located within the same general area, it may be that they formed a discrete district of residential units on the fringes of the settlement at Galatas. Within such a scenario, one where successive districts radiated out from a central point, Galatas's monumental core served as the city's epicenter or nucleus (cf. Park et al. 1925).

Formality and Monumentality

When buildings, spaces, and their layouts are constructed in clearly articulated and directed space, they can be said to be formally arranged (Lynch 1960:105–108; Steinhardt 1990:5–12; Smith 2007:12). At Galatas, formality is recognized in the construction of the courtyards associated with the palace (i.e., the central, southern, northwestern, and northern courtyards) as each one was constructed in a clearly delineated space and each one possessed a clearly recognizable and simplistic (i.e., easily understood) architectural form, consisting of a large open space facing at least one of the palace's monumental facades (cf. Lynch 1960:105–108). Because the courtyards served as junctions or breaks in the transportation network of the settlement, they would have forced travelers to make decisions, and, as a consequence, attention would have been heightened and nearby elements perceived with more than normal clarity (Lynch 1960:72–73). One particular element that would have been noticed was the change in architectural form from rubble and mudbrick house exteriors to the ashlar facades of the palace that framed the activities conducted within these spaces. Because of the expense of the ashlar facades, individuals would have been constantly reminded of the power and wealth of those who commissioned their construction while using the courtyards or simply passing through them.

The relative levels of accessibility and visibility among Galatas's courtyards suggests that there was a hierarchy of courtyards and that each one was designed to be used by a specific group of people. The central courtyard, which occupied the central position of the palatial complex, was quite restricted in terms of both accessibility and visibility. The narrowness of the corridors that provided access into the central courtyard, for example, produced a funneling effect as one moved from the street into it, limiting the number of people that could enter concurrently. Two of the three corridors also possessed flights of steps, which, given the uneven ground levels, limited visibility into the central courtyard and the activities conducted within it. The restricted nature of both the accessibility and visibility into the central courtyard suggests that it was only used by select groups of individuals, perhaps the elite (cf. Gesell 1987:125).

The open space of the central courtyard was framed by an elaborate architectural setting utilizing ashlar masonry, which created a boundary for the ceremonial activities conducted within it. Deposits containing many drinking, pouring, and serving vessels – along with faunal refuse (Rethemiotakis 1999a, 1999b, 2002:56–57) and architectural spaces including areas for cooking, storage, and dining (e.g., Rooms 17 and 22) – were found within close proximity to the central courtyard, suggesting that feasting and associated ritual activities took place in this area (cf. Borgna 2004; Dietler and Hayden 2001; Gero 1992). Unequal social relationships between local elites (those who were able to participate in the activities in the central courtyard) and other segments of society (those who were not), may have been stressed and reaffirmed through the process of exclusion. Likewise, the act of inclusion served the purpose of creating a sense of group identity among those permitted into this space through the communal act of sharing food and drink (cf. Hayden 2001:28; Potter 2000:471; Wright 2004:134). And finally, the relative scale of the feast demonstrated the palace's abilities, and thus its position within society, to command substantial amounts of foodstuffs collected through tribute assessments within the territory.

The rest of the community may have used the northern, northwestern, and southern courtyards, for these were each easily accessed via streets that led into and through them, and they were highly visible. As with the central courtyards, the open public courtyards almost certainly served as venues for ceremonial activities, as suggested by the presence of exedras, raised causeways, or tripartite facades (Rethemiotakis 2002–2003:78–80). The latter are often connected to ceremonial activities because of their appearance in conjunction with cultic activity in Minoan iconography (e.g., the relief *rhyton* from Kato Zakros, the "Grand Stand" fresco from Knossos, etc.) (Goodison 2004; Shaw 1978:443–445, figures 17 and 18). Additional evidence for ceremonial activity can be seen in the southern courtyard where a *baetyl* was located. Like the tripartite facades, these objects often appear in Minoan glyptic art in association with ritual or ceremonial activity (Warren 1990:193). The material remains recovered in these areas also support their association with ritual or ceremonial activities as a number of objects related to these activities – including pedestalled chalices, animal figurines, and a stone libation table – were found within close proximity to the northern and southern courtyards (Rethemiotakis and Christakis 2013). The close proximity of the palace suggests its sponsorship of the activities conducted within these courtyards. It may be that ceremonial activities were conducted in all courtyards at the same time in an effort to unite groups of people together in a social setting (cf. Fitzsimons, Chapter 7 in this volume, for a similar case of building civic identity through ceremonial activities).

The promotion of messages connected to wealth, power, and status was also reflected in the monumentality of buildings and spaces within the city of Galatas. For Trigger (1990:119), the principle-defining feature of monumental architecture is that both its scale and elaboration exceed the requirements of utilitarian or practical functions that a particular building is intended to perform. Through the conspicuous consumption of both materials and human labor, power relations are displayed and reinforced (Trigger 1990:124–125, 128). Thus, monumental buildings play an active role in both the constitution and the reproduction of asymmetrical relations of power and authority (Fisher 2009:184). Monumental architecture should be considered to be a form of indexical communication because it is concerned with claims of advancement in wealth and status (cf. Blanton 1993). In fact, it serves as a relatively efficient means of indexical communication because these types of buildings, given their size, were visible to large populations and their seemingly permanent nature guarantees that they would have been seen by many people over a long period of time (Blanton 1989:413; DeMarrais et al. 1996:18). As Dovey (1999:15–16) argues, monumental edifices can provide illusions of stability and/or change, and they help to promote and differentiate group identity. These types of buildings are often constructed when group solidarity is needed most, such as during periods of sociopolitical or economic stress (Abrams 1989:62). In a specifically Minoan context, Driessen (1995), for instance, argues that there was a period of monumental building following the Santorini eruption at the end of Late Minoan IA in an effort to help stabilize society. Surely, this could also be said for the *formation* of a polity, especially one such as Galatas, which, as will be discussed later, may have been built by Knossos as it expanded its state system.

Measuring the monumentality of a building (i.e., a quantitative analysis) is a difficult task, especially given the poor state of preservation of Galatas's architectural remains (cf. Abrams 1989, 1994; Abrams and Bolland 1999). Instead, a number of qualitative aspects may be used to verify a particular building's monumentality. These aspects may include the use of specialized masonry styles, the presence of certain decorative elements, and the complexity of design and layout. Further qualitative variables may include the relative permanence of a construction, its location within a settlement, its degree of visibility, and its ubiquity (cf. Moore 1996:139–140).[3] It is these qualitative elements that make monumental buildings both imageable and legible (Lynch 1960), ensuring that their meanings are quite clear and easily understood by observers.

The cost of building, both in terms of materials and human labor, is reflected in all stages of the palace at Galatas's creation. Prior to its construction, suitable building space for the palace had to be prepared. This included the leveling of ground and the construction of a number of retaining walls and terraces to help support the building against the edge of the ridge, especially in the areas of the northern and eastern wings of the palace. Because the preparatory work was quite complex and time consuming, there was considerable expenditure in terms of both materials and human labor (cf. Fotou 1990). The high cost of building is also reflected in the ordinary utilitarian walls of the palace, for these walls, which were constructed of rubble foundations with plastered mudbrick superstructures, could be quite long (upward of ca. 30 m) and many were required in the construction of the building, which approached nearly 1 ha in total area (cf. Devolder 2012).

Important areas of the palace, including the walls of the central court, the Minoan Hall in the northern wing, the Pillar and Columnar Halls in the eastern wing, and the external walls of the palatial complex, were fitted with extensive facades of limestone ashlar blocks, several of which bore mason's marks similar to those found at Knossos. The limestone itself was quarried from the area of Alagni, a distance of 4 km from Galatas (Rethemiotakis 2002:60). Other specialized materials and building techniques, including the use of special stones for pillars and column bases and the construction of elaborately paved floors, were used to decorate select areas of the palace complex, including the Minoan Hall and the Pillar and Columnar Halls (Rethemiotakis 2000–2001:127, 2002:60, 2002–2003:79). Gypsum, which was quarried from an outcrop 13 km away, was used as a building material for the door jambs and two pillar bases of the Minoan Hall (Chlouveraki 2005:294–305). The excavators also uncovered a fragment of a miniature pictorial fresco in the Pillar Hall (Rethemiotakis 1999b, 2002:57, plate XVIa). This fragment may have formed part of a landscape scene complete with a red wavy terrain line, stylized rocks, and a floral arrangement. Based on stylistic affinities with frescoes from Knossos, Rethemiotakis (2002:57) argues that those at Galatas may have been the work of painters trained at Knossos. The Knossian mason's marks and Knossian-style frescoes found at Galatas suggest that there was a special relationship between the two cities. The presence of these architectural elements may serve as an indication of the deployment of skilled stone masons and artists from Knossos to the Galatas Kephala (Bevan 2010:42–43; Chlouveraki 2002; Warren 2004:160). Whatever the case may be, these particular elements document the arrival of a new sociopolitical order, one with specific elements of Knossian design, in an area that possessed no previous comparable architectural tradition.

The areas that employed specialized materials and techniques in their construction were all highly conspicuous spaces where visitors may have participated in a number of special activities. Although the evidence is far from complete, the Pillar Hall and, perhaps, the Columnar Hall, may have served as the locations for commensal activities, judging from their semi-fixed features (i.e., hearths and benches) and close connection to the East Magazines, and areas associated with food preparation (i.e., Rooms 11 and 12) (Christakis 2008:50–15, figure 15; Rethemiotakis 1999a, 1999b, 2002). Because of the restricted access and visibility of these interior spaces, it is hypothesized that they were used only by elites. In this way then, architectural elaboration served as a material agent at Galatas, one that complemented a number of specialized activities that drew separate audiences together (e.g., the general populace in the courtyards outside of the palace and groups of elites within the interior rooms of the palace).

Each stage in the construction of the palace and, indeed, as Abrams (1989:54) reminds us, its continued maintenance, required much in terms of organization or central planning, along with the ability and authority to command both materials and human labor. In the case of Minoan Crete, this may have been derived from both specialized craftsmen, either itinerant or attached to the palace, and corvée labor. It is even possible that through participation in monumental building projects, such as that of the palace of Galatas, these individuals developed a sense of identity with their city and ruler as they took pride in their endeavors, as was the case in a number of historically documented examples (e.g., Smith 2000; Pauketat 2000).

Standardization

Smith (2007:25) argues that the presence of similar buildings and layouts within a series of related cities suggests some adherence to a common plan or idea of city planning. Standardization can be discussed in terms of common architectural inventories, spatial patterns, orientation, and metrology (Smith 2007:25). Although there may have been earlier monumental buildings, which served as predecessors to the palaces, the earliest unambiguous evidence for the development of the first (i.e., Protopalatial) palaces belongs to the Middle IB-II periods (Schoep 2004; Shaw 2009:161; Warren 1987:47). The palace at Galatas seems to be one of the earliest constructed in the Neopalatial period, for those at Malia, Phaistos, and Zakros were seemingly built in either Late Minoan IA or IB (Carinci 1989; La Rosa 2002; MacDonald 2002; Platon 2004; van Effenterre 1980:336–337). Although it is poorly understood because of intensive rebuilding throughout its life history, it seems as though a new palace was also constructed in Middle Minoan III at Knossos (MacDonald 2002).

Despite their relative periods of construction, all of the palaces employed similar concepts in planning, design, and function, although they often differed in scale and configuration. For example, although each palace's central courtyard shares proportions of roughly 1:2 and all, with the exception of that at Zakros, follow a general north-south orientation, their relative areas differ dramatically.[4] Additionally, although other spaces such as storage, those devoted to ritual and ceremony, and "residential suites" were present and often possessed similar architectural forms, they were often positioned in different places within the palaces (McEnroe 2010:87). It can thus be stated that on the one hand, each palace possessed similar types of areas dedicated to specific functions, while on the other hand, these areas were often of dissimilar sizes and situated in different locations.

Turning to orientation, four of the five palaces shared a similar north-south orientation, falling within about 15 degrees of one another (Shaw 1973:47). Zakros is the only palace that does not share the general north-south orientation. Many buildings, within each of these cities, regardless of their topographic situation, shared a similar orientation to their respective palaces. Malia, for example, provides a good example of this because of its flat topography. Here, where builders were not limited by topography, buildings were constructed following a similar orientation to the palace (McEnroe 1979:342; Shaw 1973:52). Such an orientation, which according to Shaw (1973) and later Goodison (2004) was a long-standing principal of design going back to at least the Protopalatial period, may have been the product of a cosmological desire to orient the buildings in the western wings of the palaces to the rising sun, which was itself an important iconographical element present in depictions of ritual activity in glyptic art (e.g., Goodison 2001:plates XVIIIa-XVIIIe).

As noted in the introduction to this paper, both metrology and modularity have been utilized in discussions of Minoan architectural planning. Graham (1960, 1987), Preziosi (1983:489–493), and Cherry (1986), for instance, have proposed that the Minoans used a common metrological system in their buildings. As the issue stands today, however, there is no scholarly agreement on this subject as each scholar proposes a different standard of measurement. Generally speaking, as Smith (2007:29) notes, although the metrology of ancient cities has been examined, the results, as is the case for Minoan Crete, are often not widely accepted and remain controversial. Preziosi (1983) and later Palyvou (2002:170–171, plate LVI) suggest that the palaces may have been laid out according to the principles of a grid-based design, following the 1:2 proportions of the central courts, which represented one half of an original square module. McEnroe (1984:601), however, points out several shortcomings to this approach, including the extreme flexibility of this application and the fact that building histories (e.g., construction, reconstruction, rebuilding, and destruction) are seldom taken into account. Given the inherent problems with these two approaches, neither metrology nor modular planning can at present be used as reliable evidence for urban planning in Minoan cities.

The Planned City of Galatas

On the basis of the evidence previously detailed, certain key aspects of the Minoan city of Galatas were centrally planned as they possessed some degree of simple coordination, formality, and monumentality. Architectural elements following these principles of design were constructed with the very specific intention of conveying messages concerned with the promotion of status differentiations and social cohesion, those which are associated with Rapoport's mid- and low-level meanings. Relative levels of accessibility and visibility within and between spaces were used as a means of further reinforcing these very specific sociopolitical messages. Further, this planning followed a somewhat standardized formula; one which was, perhaps, developed in the preceding Protopalatial period, and can be seen in cities geographically removed from each other. This suggests the existence of some preconceived ideas concerning the planning of Minoan cities. Given the specific messages conveyed by Galatas's built environment, it is posited that the city, or at least specific parts of it such as the urban core, was built at the behest of a central authority – perhaps, given certain architectural affinities, one originating from Knossos. It is of interest that the city of Galatas was built in an area that, as we shall see, was sparsely populated and where no prior city existed. The rapid construction of the city corresponded to a complete restructuring of the local political and socioeconomic situation. Through this restructuring, the inhabitants of Galatas's hinterlands became intimately bound to the new city and, as a consequence, its rulers.

THE REGION

On the basis of surface surveys, there was a substantial rise of 60.5 percent in the number of sites between the Protopalatial period and the Neopalatial period in the Upper Pediada (cf. Figures 8.4 and 8.5).[5] Not only did the number of sites increase, but several (i.e., 44, 82, and 139) also became quite large in the Neopalatial period. The expansion of the city of Galatas following a period of abandonment in Middle Minoan II was the most significant, as it expanded to an area of around 25 ha in Middle Minoan III. The dramatic increase in the number of new sites and the substantial growth of others suggests that the local population increased dramatically at the beginning of the Neopalatial period, far beyond what could be accounted for by normal growth.[6] For the most part, the Protopalatial settlement pattern was much like that of earlier periods (e.g., Neolithic and Early Minoan) in that sites remained fairly small (less than 1 ha) and were situationally dispersed from one another on hilltops, perhaps reflecting a concern for defense (Figure 8.4). The situation

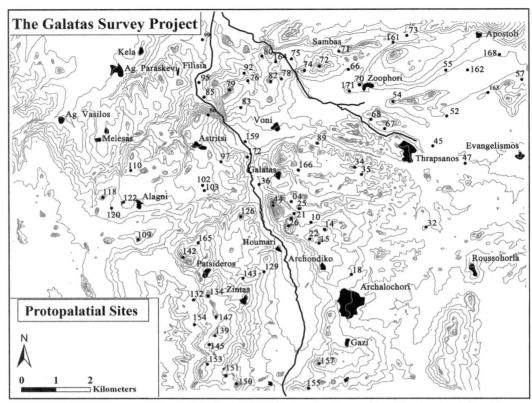

The Galatas Survey Project

Protopalatial Sites

N

0   1   2
Kilometers

Figure 8.4 Plan detailing all Protopalatial sites identified by the Galatas Survey Project (drawn by author).

in the Neopalatial period, however, was quite different as a number of larger sites (greater than 3 ha) – including 44 (Galatas), 82, and 139 – came to be spread out evenly across the landscape at distances of approximately 4 km away from their next-nearest neighbor (Figure 8.5). Such a settlement situation suggests that these larger settlements possessed agricultural catchments of about 2 km in radius (Figure 8.6). This distance of 2 km may perhaps be explained as the distance in which urban-based farmers began to experience diminished returns on their agricultural production owing to excessive travel times between home and field (cf. Marchetti 1994; Blanton 2004:212). A number of smaller sites – which probably represent small numbers of households or, perhaps, agricultural villages – were spread throughout every class of land within each one of these agricultural catchments. These smaller sites may be understood as the agricultural producers for the larger sites within each catchment.

Several sites with seemingly specialized functions also appeared in the Neopalatial period (Buell 2014b). Site 17, which is located on

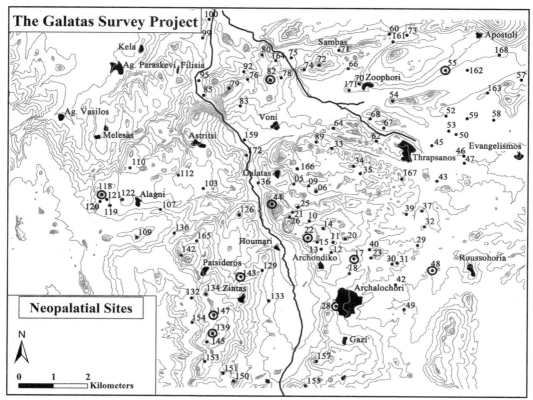

Figure 8.5 Plan detailing all Neopalatial sites identified by the Galatas Survey Project (drawn by author). Sites mentioned in text are circled.

the periphery of Galatas's local catchment, is particularly important because a large, monumental multiroomed structure was found there. A mason's mark in the shape of a cross (+) was found on one of the building's ashlar blocks. Similar marks also appear on the monumental buildings at both Knossos and Galatas. The building's monumental size and its fine building materials, along with the presence of the mason's mark, suggest that it served some special purpose and that it was constructed at the behest of a central authority, presumably one at Galatas. Because the building's material assemblage consisted primarily of large storage vessels, its purpose may have been connected to storage. Taken at face value, this new Neopalatial situation – one that sees a number of smaller agricultural sites situated on all types of land and a number of seemingly special-purpose sites such as Site 17 – is indicative of a process of increased sociospatial stratification of the landscape.

In order to feed the new, predominantly urban population and, perhaps, to meet the demands for tribute imposed by the new

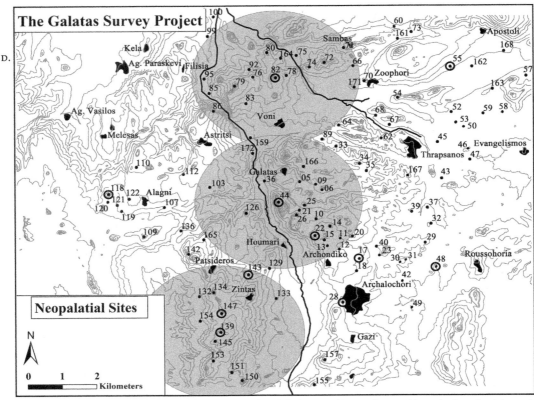

Figure 8.6 Plan of Neopalatial Galatas and its territory with agricultural catchments indicated (drawn by author). Sites mentioned in text are circled.

political regime centered at Galatas, agricultural practices became more intensive in the Neopalatial period. As mentioned previously, Neopalatial sites in the survey zone were located in more diverse topographic positions (i.e., all classes of land) and, often, away from water, suggesting a desire to exploit all potential land. Furthermore, the land within close proximity to most Neopalatial sites was intensively utilized, for these sites possessed distinctive "haloes" of material remains; perhaps representing the residual artifacts that were spread on fields and gardens along with manure (cf. Bintliff and Howard 1999; Bintliff and Snodgrass 1988; Wilkinson 1982, 1988, 1989). The fact that the Minoans used manuring in their fields and gardens is known from the site of Pseira where fecal biomarkers mixed with sherds were found in the excavation of a Neopalatial terrace (Bull et al. 1999, 2001). The use of manuring is indicative of a highly organized agricultural strategy, one that was aimed at achieving the maximum potential output from fields and gardens because the use of manure encourages general productivity; it renews nutrients, improves root penetration, and it helps to both aerate the soil and keep it moist. One final correlate to this evidence for agricultural intensification is that the number of groundstone tools associated with agricultural production (e.g., rubbers, pounders, and querns) increased dramatically as more than 50 percent of all Neopalatial sites produced at least one of these objects.

Other than cereals, olive and grapevine cultivation became important in the Upper Pediada during the Neopalatial period as many sites were situated in more marginal locations on the thin soils of hills; sites that were suitable for these types of agricultural endeavors (Foxhall 2007:112). The expansion of olive and vine cultivation is further confirmed by the substantial increase in the number of sites that produced storage vessels in the Neopalatial period (i.e., 75 percent of Neopalatial sites compared with only 19 percent of Protopalatial sites). Ethnographic work testifies to the significant proportion (greater than 60 percent) of storage pithoi being dedicated to olive oil and wine (Christakis 1999:6). The tending of vines and, perhaps to a lesser extent, olive trees, is a time-consuming and expensive endeavor, which requires some degree of specialized knowledge for successful harvests (cf. Hamilakis 1999; Stallsmith 2004:41). Because these practices may have been more suitable for people who had the ability to take risks and experiment, the palace itself may have sponsored certain individuals involved in these operations. The fact that wine, in particular, was a commodity that the palatial elite desired is confirmed by the later Linear B documents from Knossos, which do not record wine as having been a ration for lower-level personnel, but rather as a commodity used in banqueting and feasting within the palaces and some associated sanctuaries (Palmer 1989).

The intensified agricultural regime may be related to one part of Galatas's more general political economy. In short, these new practices may have been a product of the newly founded palace's demand for tribute. Movement of local products upward as tribute involved the functioning of three distinct types of storage: central, regional, and household (Smyth 1989). The end point in this mobilization, central storage, is represented by the storage magazines within the palace at Galatas (Christakis 1999:6). The presence of these architecturally recognized storage areas points to a formalized economic system of storage (Adams 2006:21). Regional storage may have been required because of the palace's limited storage capacity and the long distances in which bulky agricultural goods would have to travel before reaching it. Regional storage may have been conducted at Site 17, which, as described earlier, was positioned on the edge of Galatas's agricultural catchment and possessed suitable evidence for an official character and storage function. If Site 17 served as a storage facility, it would have expanded Galatas's local catchment significantly.

Once collected, surpluses – whether stored at central or regional locations – may have been used to support palace dependents (e.g., bureaucrats, priests, craftsmen, architects, laborers, etc.) and to fund various state enterprises, one of which was almost certainly feasting as evidenced by the deposits indicative of this activity found at Galatas (cf. Earle 1978:184–185; Brumfiel and Earle 1987; Dietler and Hayden 2001:13; Hayden 2001:29–30). The direct control of storage equates to some control of the economy and, as a result, the livelihoods of individuals within this area (cf. D'Altroy and Earle 1985:192). There is thus an implicit ideological aspect in both centralized and regional storage because direction of the surplus and the mechanism of this control guaranteed the independence and viability of the palace itself.

The presence of household storage in the Upper Pediada is reflected in the rise in the absolute number of storage vessels found on all sites. It may be that household storage was increased in order to meet the demands for tribute imposed on the household by the newly developed polity. These developments, which include increased agricultural production and more complex storage strategies, may be related to the development of a system of staple finance, wherein obligatory payments (i.e., tribute) are sent to the state in the form of basic goods (cf. D'Altroy and Earle 1985:188; Earle 1997; Earle and D'Altroy 1982:266).

It is noteworthy that amphibolite-stone drill guides, which are usually associated with the production of stone vases, were found at five sites: 22, 44 (Galatas Kephala), 48, 55, and 118 (cf. Bevan 2007:58, figure 4.13; Carter 2004:71–72, plate 21, nos. IC.389–393). As suggested by the close spatial proximity between stone vessel workshops and the palace itself, the stone-vase industry at both Site 44 (Galatas) and Site 22, which is located on a hilltop immediately to the south of Galatas, may have operated under direct palatial control, whereas the other three sites (e.g., 48, 55, and 118) seem to have been outside of its control – these were located far from the city of Galatas at distances upward of 6 km. Because stone vases were prestige objects, given the labor and specialized knowledge involved in their production, they, like monumental architecture, served as a form of materialized ideology, which helped to structure and enforce unequal social relationships (Bevan 2007:188–192).[7] Given the ideological value attached to these products, and the fact that some stone-vase workshops on Crete tended to be associated with elite buildings, it is reasonable to suggest that the other three centers of production in our survey area were attached to and working for local elites.[8] If this is the case, then stone vessels may have circulated within a system of prestige exchange between the elites centered on the palace and those living in other areas of the survey zone.

Stone vessels may therefore have formed part of a wealth-finance system in operation within the Upper Pediada (D'Altroy and Earle 1985). This is a system wherein a central polity employs high-value goods to fund state operations (Nakassis 2010:128). Craft specialists – those who did not have the opportunity or time to produce their own subsistence products because they worked at the palace or within its immediate locale (i.e., Site 22) – may have been supported by the staple goods that were collected through tribute and later stored within the palace (cf. Brumfiel and Earle 1987). As such, some staple products, because they were used to fund dependent craft workers, were converted directly into wealth by the palace (cf. D'Altroy and Earle 1985:188; Halstead 1999, 2000). By directing the flow of these objects, the palace could use specialized products as a form of political currency because high-value goods may have been given to local elites in exchange for various obligations (Earle 1994:445). In other words, they may have been used to create reciprocal debt and to foster loyalty to the palace. These objects would have, in turn, been used by local elites as a means of displaying their connection to the palace, and thus legitimizing their own local social status (cf. Knapp 1997:49).

One activity that seems to have operated outside of palatial involvement is ceramic production, which was identified by the presence of kiln fragments and wasters at a number of sites (i.e., 28, 82, 143, and 147) within the survey zone. The Neopalatial sites possessing evidence for this activity were long-lived and all were situated on natural trade routes along the Karteros River, which connected the northern and southern coasts. Furthermore, the local potting tradition is long-standing, stretching from the Neolithic period to the present (e.g., Voyatzoglou 1984). With this stated, it is important to note that there was an abrupt change in local production in the Neopalatial period as local potters began to make vessels imitative of those made at Knossos (cf. Rethemiotakis 2002:57). Because these vessels were found at both urban and rural sites, it may be that they formed some part of the local tribute system.

DISCUSSION

The factors that led to the rapid construction of the city of Galatas – including its monumental urban core – remain undetermined, but it is important to note that the construction of this city corresponds to a period of reconstruction at the city of Knossos in Middle Minoan IIIA through IIIB (cf. McDonald 2002). Indeed, the city of Knossos appears to have grown to such a size in the Neopalatial period that the land needed to sustain its population encroached upon Galatas's territory (e.g., Christakis 2008:134; Hood 1958; Hood and Smyth 1981:10; Panagiotakis 2004; Warren 2004; Whitelaw 2004:figure10.6). At the same time, a new architectural form (i.e., palatial architecture), one that employed specific elements of Knossian design and materials (e.g., gypsum) from the area of Knossos, appeared rather suddenly on the Galatas Kephala in an area with little previous evidence for the sort of political organization that would have been required to build a city *ex nihilo* (cf. Bevan 2010). These data should be viewed comparatively with those from the survey of Galatas and its hinterlands. One of the most important of these is the evidence for the growth and development of the city of Galatas and the corresponding increase in population within its local environs. There is an undeniable correlation between this massive rise in population and the adaptation of specific aspects of Knossian material culture as represented by the change in local potting traditions. Given such evidence, slight as it is, it may be proposed that Galatas and its territory came to be populated by individuals from the area of Knossos in the early part of the Neopalatial period. If this is the case, it may be that Knossos built the city of Galatas and populated it as a means of drawing the resource-rich Upper Pediada into its state system (cf. Warren 2004; Wiener 2007). This falls in line with several studies suggesting that the process of urbanization may, in some cases, be connected to the development and growth of state systems (Blanton 1976; Cowgill 2004; Marcus 1983; A. Smith 2003). If we accept this, then the city of Galatas could be viewed as a second-tier site in a much larger regional-settlement system, one that was centered on Knossos.

Although this is somewhat speculative, we are, given the arguments presented in this paper, still left with two strong conclusions. First, I have argued that the city of Galatas was well planned, presumably by some central authority, perhaps at the initiative of Knossos itself. This is revealed through the employment of Smith's (2007) approach to analyzing urban planning, which highlights the concepts of a coordination of space between buildings, formality, and monumentality, and standardization between cities. Such planning is particularly noted in the city's monumental urban core, an area that was charged with symbolic meaning. Through consideration of these planning schemes, it can be seen that the builders of the city were specifically concerned with creating, enforcing, and legitimizing unequal social relationships. At the same time, these rulers were also concerned with promoting messages associated with the establishment of group identity, probably for the purposes of creating social cohesion. Given the fact that the city was rapidly constructed in an area that did not possess an earlier urban center, this strategy would have been essential for maintaining political and economic control of the territory around the city. In this way, the city itself became an active player in the daily lives of its inhabitants and those living in its hinterlands. Secondly, I discussed how the landscape outside of the confines of the city also changed dramatically with the founding of the city. It is my belief that Galatas's rural hinterlands were restructured in order to meet the demands imposed by the new political order situated on the Galatas Kephala. As such, the city became functionally interconnected with the hinterland. Its reorganization, therefore, serves as evidence for top-down planning initiated by elites at Galatas (possibly at the behest of Knossos), resulting in the formation of a new urban landscape in the Neopalatial period.

ACKNOWLEDGMENTS

I owe a particular debt of gratitude to both Andrew Creekmore and Kevin Fisher who invited me to contribute to this volume. I express further thanks to these two individuals for their patience and helpful suggestions during the editing process. On this same note, I thank Kapua Iao who also helped in the editing process, providing useful feedback and commentary. Without the steady and excellent publications of Giorgos Rethemiotakis and Kostis Christakis, this work could not have been completed. Additional thanks go to all members of the Galatas Survey Project, especially its director L. Vance Watrous, who has provided me with innumerable opportunities, excellent guidance, and sincere friendship over the years. I wrote this paper while at the American School for Classical Studies in Athens holding the Doreen Canaday Spitzer Fellowship.

NOTES

1 "Street" is used here in reference to a built track within an urban environment, whereas "road" refers to a track that connects further distances (i.e., town to town).

2 The Minoan Hall was a standardized suite of rooms consisting of a large main room, which was divided by a pier-and-door partition, with at least one side opening onto a portico, and a light well and forehall.

3 Although Moore (1996:139–140) applies these variables to buildings and spaces with ritual associations, I believe that they may broadly be applied to all types of monumental buildings.

4 Knossos's central courtyard, for example, possessed an area of 1484 m², whereas that at Galatas was 525 m².

5 The University at Buffalo survey project was an intensive and diachronic pedestrian survey. One of its principal aims was to situate the city of Galatas within its regional framework (Watrous et al. 2014). Because the survey monograph is still in preparation, all data and interpretations made in this section remain preliminary in nature.

6 Using the formula $PR = \dfrac{(V present - V past)}{V past} \times 100$ with the University at Buffalo survey's estimate for populations in the Protopalatial period (1,870–2,580) and Neopalatial period (10,840–13,480) and then dividing the number by N (the total number of years, which amounts to 200 between the two periods), provides a yearly growth rate of between 2.11 and 2.38 percent (Buell 2014a). Annual growth rates in prehistory were normally on the order of about 0.1 percent, whereas a growth rate of more than 1 percent per annum was as unlikely as it was unsustainable (Cowgill 1975; Hassan 1981:253).

7 It is noted that, as Bevan (2007, 2010) argues, different types of vessels probably possessed different values. At present, because no unfinished or broken stone vessels were found at any of the sites identified by the survey project, we do not know what kind kinds of vessels were being manufactured.

8 For later, Late Minoan IB examples of stone-vase workshops in close association to elite buildings, see Building BS/BV and, perhaps, AE at Pseira and the Artisans' Quarters and Chalinomouri at Mochlos.

REFERENCES CITED

Abrams, Elliot M. 1989 Architecture and Energy: An Evolutionary Perspective. *Archaeological Method and Theory* 1:47–87.

    1994 *How the Maya Built their World: Energetics and Ancient Architecture.* University of Texas Press, Austin.

Abrams, Elliot M. and Thomas W. Bolland 1999 Architectural Energetics, Ancient Monuments, and Operations Management. *Journal of Archaeological Method and Theory* 6(4):263–291.

Adams, Ellen 2006 Social Strategies and Spatial Dynamics in Neopalatial Crete: An Analysis of the North-Central Area. *American Journal of Archaeology* 110:1–36.

Bevan, Andrew 2007 *Stone Vessels and Values in the Bronze Age Mediterranean.* Cambridge University Press, Cambridge.

    2010 Political Geography and Palatial Crete. *Journal of Mediterranean Archaeology* 23(1):27–54.

Bintliff, John L. and Anthony Snodgrass 1988 Off-Site Pottery Distribution: A Regional and Interregional Perspective. *Current Anthropology* 29:506–513.

Bintliff, John L. and Phil Howard 1999 Studying Needles in Haystacks: Surface Survey and the Rural Landscape of Central Greece in Roman Times. *Pharos* 7:51–91.

Blanton, Richard E. 1976 Anthropological Studies of Cities. *Annual Review of Anthropology* 5:249–264.

    1989 Continuity and Change in Public Architecture: Periods I through V of the Valley of Oaxaca, Mexico. In *Monte Alban's Hinterland Part II: Settlement Patterns in Tlacolula, Etla, and Ocatlan, Valley of Oaxaca, Mexico, vol. I.,* edited by S. Kowalewski, G. Feinman, R. Blanton, L. Finsten, and L. Nichols. University of Michigan, Ann Arbor.

    1993 *Houses and Households: A Comparative Study.* Springer-Verlag, New York.

    2004 A Comparative Perspective on Settlement Pattern and Population Change in Mesoamerican and Mediterranean Civilizations. In *Side by Side Survey: Comparative Regional Studies in the Mediterranean World,* edited by Susan E. Alcock and John F. Cherry, pp. 206–240., Oxbow, Oxford.

Borgna, Elisabetta 2004 Aegean Feasting: A Minoan Perspective. *Hesperia* 73:247–279.

Branigan, Keith 2001 Aspects of Minoan Urbanism. In *Urbanism in the Aegean Bronze Age,* edited by Keith Branigan, pp. 38–50. Sheffield Academic Press, London.

Brumfiel, Elizabeth M. and Timothy K. Earle 1987 Specialization, Exchange, and Complex Societies: An Introduction. In *Specialization, Exchange, and Complex Societies,* edited by Elizabeth M. Brumfiel and Timothy K. Earle, pp. 1–9. Cambridge University Press, Cambridge.

Buell, D. Matthew 2014a. The Early Minoan Period. In *The Galatas Survey: A History of the Upper Pediada Region of Crete During the Neolithic-Ottoman Periods,* edited by L. V. Watrous. The Institute for Aegean Prehistory Academic Press, Philadelphia, PA, in preparation.

2014b. The Neopalatial Period. In *The Galatas Survey: A History of the Upper Pediada Region of Crete during the Neolithic-Ottoman Periods*, edited by L. V. Watrous. The Institute for Aegean Prehistory Academic Press, Philadelphia, PA, in preparation.

Bull, Ian D., Phillip P. Betancourt, and Richard P. Evershed 1999 Chemical Evidence for a Structured Agricultural Manuring Regime on the Island of Pseira, Crete, During the Minoan Period. In *Meletemata: Studies in Aegean Archaeology Presented to Malcolm H. Wiener as He Enters His 65th Year*, Vol. 1, edited by Phillip P. Betancourt, Vassos Karageorghis, Robert Laffineur, and Wolf-Dietrich Niemeier, pp. 69–73. Universite de Liège, Liège, Belgium.

Bull, Ian D., 2001 An Organic Geochemical Investigation of the Practice of Manuring at a Minoan Site on Pseira Island, Crete. *Geoarchaeology* 16:223–243.

Carinci, F. 1989. The "III fase protopalaziale" at Phaestos: Some Observations. In *Transition.Le monde égéen du Bronze moyen au Bronze récent. Actes de la deuxième Rencontre égéenne internationale de l'Université de Liège, 18–20 avril 1988*, edited by R. Laffineur, pp. 73–80. Universitè de l'Etat à Liège, Liège, Belgium.

Carter, Harold 1983 *An Introduction to Urban Historical Geography*. Edward Arnold, Baltimore, MD.

Carter, Tristan 2004 The Stone Implements. In *Mochlos IC: Period III. Neopalatial Settlement on the Coast: The Artisans' Quarter and the Farmhouse at Chalinomouri. The Small Finds*, edited by Jeffery Soles and Costis Davaras, pp. 61–108. Prehistory Monographs 9. The Institute for Aegean Prehistory Academic Press, Philadelphia, PA.

Cherry, John 1986 Polities and Palace: Some Problems in Minoan State Formation. In *Peer Polity Interaction and Socio-Political Change*, edited by A. Colin Renfrew and John F. Cherry, pp. 19–45. Cambridge University Press, Cambridge.

Chlouveraki, Stephania 2002 Exploitation of Gypsum in Minoan Crete. In *Interdisciplinary Studies on Ancient Stone. ASMOSIA VI: Proceedings of the Sixth International Conference (Venice, June 15–18, 2000)*, edited by L. Lazzarini, pp. 25–34. Bottega D'Erasmo, Padua, Italy.

2005 Gypsum in Minoan Architecture: Exploitation, Utilisation and Weathering of Prestige Stone. Unpublished Ph.D. Dissertation, University College London, London.

Christakis, Kostis S. 1999 Pithoi and Food Storage in Neopalatial Crete: A Domestic Perspective. *World Archaeology* 31(1):1–20.

2008 *The Politics of Storage: Storage and Sociopolitical Complexity in Neopalatial Crete*. Institute for Aegean Prehistory, Philadelphia, PA.

Cowgill, George L. 1975 On Causes of Ancient and Modern Population Changes. *American Anthropologist* 77(3):505–525.

2004 Origins and Development of Urbanism: Archaeological Perspectives. *Annual Review of Anthropology* 33:525–549.

Cunningham, Timothy 2001 Variations on a Theme: Divergence in Settlement Patterns and Spatial Organization in the Far East of Crete during the Proto- and Neopalatial Periods. In *Urbanism in the Aegean Bronze Age*, edited by Keith Branigan, pp. 72–86. Sheffield Academic Press, London.

D'Altroy, Terrence N. and Timothy K. Earle 1985 Staple Finance, Wealth Finance, and Storage in the Inka Political Economy. *Current Anthropology* 26(2):187–206.

DeMarrais Elizabeth, Luis J. Castillo, and Timothy K. Earle 1996 Ideology, Materialization, and Power Strategies. *Current Anthropology* 37(1):15–31.

Devolder, Maud 2012 Labour Costs and Neopalatial Architecture: A Study of the Buildings at Klimataria-Manares and Achladia and the Palace at Gournia. In *Minoan Realities, Approaches to Images, Architecture, and Society in the Aegean Bronze Age*, Aegis 5, edited by D. Panagiotopoulos and U. Gükel-Maschek, pp. 165–179. Presses Universitaires de Louvain, Louvain-la-Neuve, Belgium.

Dietler, Michael and Brian Hayden 2001 *Feast*. Smithsonian Institution Press, Washington, DC.

Dobres, Marcia-Anne and John E. Robb 2000 *Agency in Archaeology*. Routledge, London.

Dovey, Kim 1999 *Framing Places: Mediating Power in Built Form*. Routledge, London.

Driessen, Jan 1995 Crisis Architecture? Some Observations on Architectural Adaptations as Immediate Responses to Changing Socio-Cultural Conditions. *Topoi Orient-Occident* 5:63–88.

Earle, Timothy K. 1978 *Economic and Social Organization of a Complex Chiefdom: The Halelea Distric, Kaua'I, Hawaii*. Anthropological Papers of the Museum of Anthropology 63. University of Michigan, Ann Arbor.

1994 Wealth Finance in the Inka Empire: Evidence from the Calchaqui Valley, Argentina. *American Antiquity* 59:443–460.

1997 *Cahokia and the Archaeology of Power*. University of Alabama Press, Tuscaloosa.

Earle, Timothy K. and Terrence N. D'Altroy 1982 Storage Facilities and State Finance in the Upper Mantaro Valley, Peru. In *Contexts for Prehistoric Exchange*, edited by Jonathon E. Ericson and Timothy K. Earle, pp. 265–290. Academic Press, New York.

Ellis, Simon P. 1995 Prologue to a Study of Roman Urban Form. In *Theoretical Roman Archaeology: Second Conference Proceedings*, edited by Peter Rush, pp. 92–104. Worldwide Archaeology Series Vol. 14. Avebury, Brookfield, VT.

Fisher, Kevin D. 2009 Elite Place-Making and Social Interaction in the Late Cypriot Bronze Age. *Journal of Mediterranean Archaeology* 22(2):183–209.

Fotou, Vasso 1990 L'implantation des batiments en Crete a l'epoque Neopalatiale: amenagement du terrain et mode. In *L'Habitat égéen préhistorique: actes de la Table Ronde internationale, Athènes, 23–25 juin, 1987, organisés par le Centre National de la echerche Scientifique, l'Université de Paris et l'École française d'Athènes (Athènes, 23–25 juin 1987)*, edited by R. Pascal and R. Treuil, pp. 45–73. École française d'Athènes, Athens, Greece.

Foxhall, Lynne 2007 *Olive Cultivation in Ancient Greece: Seeking the Ancient Economy*. Oxford University Press, Oxford.

Gero, Joan 1992 Feasts and Females: Gender Ideology and Political Meals in the Andes. *Norwegian Archaeological Review* 25:1–16.

Gesell, Geraldine C. 1987 The Minoan Palace and Public Cult. In *The Function of the Minoan Palaces: Proceedings of the fourth international symposium at the*

Swedish Institute in Athens, 10–16 June, 1984, edited by Robin Hägg and Nanno Marinatos, pp. 123–127. Studies In Mediterranean Archaeology 34, Paul Åströms Förlag, Göteborg, Sweden.

Goodison, Lucy 2001 From Tholos Tomb to Throne Room: Perceptions of the Sun in Minoan Ritual. In *Potnia: Deities and Religion in the Aegean Bronze Age*, edited by Robert Laffineur and Robin Hägg, pp. 77–88. Aegaeum 22. Université de Liège, Liège, Belgium.

2004 From Tholos Tomb to Throne Room: Some Considerations of Dawn Light and Directionality in Minoan Buildings. In *Knossos: Palace, City, State. Proceedings of the Conference in Herakleion Organized by the British School at Athens and the 23rd Ephoreia of Prehistoric and Classical Antiquities of Herakleion, in November 2000, for the Centenary of Sir Arthur Evans's Excavations at Knossos*, edited by Gerald Cadogan, Eleni Hatzaki, and Andonis Vasilakis, pp. 339–350. British School at Athens Studies 12. The British School at Athens, London.

Graham, J. Walter 1960 The Minoan Unit of Length and Minoan Palace Planning. *American Journal of Archaeology.* 64:335–341.

1987 *The Palaces of Crete.* 2nd revised edition. Princeton University Press, Princeton, NJ.

Grove, David 1972 The Function and Future of Urban Centres. In *Man, Settlement and Urbanism*, edited by Peter J. Ucko, Ruth Tringham, and G. W. Dimbleby, pp. 559–567. Duckworth, Gloucester, UK.

Halstead, Paul 1999 Surplus and Share-croppers: The Grain Production Strategies of Mycenaean Palaces. In *Meletemata: Studies in Aegean Archaeology Presented to Malcom H. Wiener as he Enters his 65th Year. Vol. II*, edited by Philip. P. Betancourt, Vassos Karageorghis, Robert Laffineur, and Wolf-Dietrich Niemeier, pp. 319–326, Université de Liège, Liège, Belgium.

2000 Land Use in Postglacial Greece: Cultural Causes and Environmental Effects. In *Landscape and Land Use in Postglacial Greece*, edited by Paul Halstead and Charles Fredrick, pp. 110–128, Sheffield Studies in Aegean Archaeology. Sheffield Academic Press, Sheffield, UK.

Hamilakis, Yannis 1999 Food Technologies/Technologies of the Body: The Social Context of Wine and Oil Production and Consumption in Bronze Age Crete. *World Archaeology* 31:38–54.

Hassan. Fekri A. 1981. *Demographic Anthropology.* Academic Press, New York.

Hayden, Brian 2001 Fabulous Feasts: A Prolegomenon to the Importance of Feasting. In *Feasts: Archaeological and Ethnographic Perspectives on Food, Politics and Power*, edited by Michael Dietler and Brian Hayden, pp. 23–54, Smithsonian Books, Washington, DC.

Hood, M. F. Sinclair 1958 *Archaeological Survey of the Knossos Area.* British School at Athens, London.

Hood, M. Sinclair F. and David Smyth 1981 *Archaeological Survey of the Knossos Area*, BSA Supplement 14. British School at Athens, London.

Hutchinson, R. W. 1950 Prehistoric Town Planning in Crete. *The Town Planning Review* 41(1):5–21.

Knapp, A. Bernard 1988 Ideology, Archaeology and Polity. *Man* 23(1):133–163.

1997 *The Archaeology of Late Bronze Age Cypriot Society: The Study of Settlement, Survey and Landscape*. University of Glasgow Department of Archaeology, Glasgow, UK.

La Rosa, Vincenzo 2002 Pour une révision préliminaire du second palais de Phaistos In *Monuments of Minos: Rethinking the Minoan Palaces: Proceedings of the International Workshop "Crete of the Hundred Palaces?" Held at the Université Catholique de Louvain, Louvain-la-Neuve, 14–15 December 2001*, edited by Jan Driessen, Ilse Schoep, and Robert Laffineur, pp. 71–97, Aegaeum 23, Université de Liège, Liège, Belgium.

Letesson, Quentin and Klaas Vansteenhuyse 2006 Towards an Archaeology of Perception: "Looking" at the Minoan Palaces. *Journal of Mediterranean Archaeology* 19(1):91–119.

Lynch, Kevin A. 1960 *The Image of the City*. Massachusetts Institute of Technology Press, Cambridge, MA.

MacDonald, Colin F. 2002 The Neopalatial Palaces of Knossos. In *Monuments of Minos: Rethinking the Minoan Palaces: Proceedings of the International Workshop "Crete of the Hundred Palaces?" Held at the Université Catholique de Louvain, Louvain-la-Neuve, 14–15 December 2001*, edited by Jan Driessen, Ilse Schoep, and Robert Laffineur, pp. 35–55, Aegaeum 23, Université de Liège, Liège, Belgium.

MacDonald, William L. 1986 *The Architecture of the Roman Empire II: An Urban Appraisal*. Yale University Press, New Haven, CT.

Marchetti, Cesare 1994 Anthropological Invariants in Travel Behaviour. *Technological Forecasting and Social Change* 47:75–88.

Marcus, Joyce 1983. On the nature of the Mesoamerican City. In *Prehistoric Settlement Patterns: Essays in Honor of Gordon R. Willey*, edited by Evon Z. Vogt and Richard M. Leventhal, pp. 195–242. University of New Mexico Press, Albuquerque.

McEnroe, John C. 1979 *Minoan House and Town Arrangement*. Unpublished Ph.D. Dissertation, University of Toronto, Toronto.

1984 Review of Preziosi. *American Journal of Archaeology* 88(4):600–601.

2010 *Architecture of Minoan Crete: Constructing Identity in the Aegean Bronze Age*, University of Texas Press, Austin.

Miller, Daniel and Christopher Tilley 1984 Ideology, Power and Prehistory: An introduction. In *Ideology, Power and Prehistory*, edited by Daniel Miller and Christopher Tilley, pp. 1–17. Cambridge University Press, Cambridge.

Moore, Jerry 1996 *Architecture and Power in the Ancient Andes: the Archaeology of Public Buildings*. Cambridge University Press, Cambridge.

Mumford, Lewis 2003 What is a City? In *The City Reader*, edited by Richard T. Legates and Frederic Stout, pp. 93–96, Routledge, New York.

Nakassis, Dimitri 2010 Reevaluating Staple and Wealth Finance at Mycenaean Pylos. In *Political Economies of the Aegean Bronze Age: Papers from the Langford Conference, Florida State University, Tallahassee, 22–24, February 2007*, edited by D. J. Pullen, pp. 127–148. Oxbow, Oxford.

Palmer, Ruth 1989 *Wine in the Mycenaean Palace Economy*. Unpublished Ph.D. Dissertation University of Cincinnati, Cincinnati, OH.

Panagiotakis, Nikos 2003 L'évolution archéologique de la Pédiada (Crète centrale): premier bilan. *Bulletin de Correspondance Hellénique* 127(2):327–430.

2004 Contacts between Knossos and the Pediada Region in Central Crete. In *Knossos: Palace, City, State. Proceedings of the Conference in Herakleion Organized by the British School at Athens and the 23rd Ephoreia of Prehistoric and Classical Antiquities of Herakleion, in November 2000, for the Centenary of Sir Arthur Evans's Excavations at Knossos*, edited by Gerald Cadogan, Eleni Hatzaki, and Andonis Vasilakis, pp. 177–186. British School at Athens Studies 12. The British School at Athens, London.

Park, Robert, Ezra W. Burgess, and Roderick D. McKenzie 1925 *The City*. University of Chicago Press, Chicago.

Pauketat, Timothy R. 2000 The Tragedy of the Commoners. In *Agency in Archaeology*, edited by M. Dobres and J. E. Robb, pp. 113–129. Routledge, London.

Paylvou, Clary 2002 Central Courts: The Supremacy of the Void. In *Monuments of Minos: Rethinking the Minoan Palaces: Proceedings of the International Workshop "Crete of the Hundred Palaces?" Held at the Université Catholique de Louvain, Louvain-la-Neuve, 14–15 December 2001*, edited by Jan Driessen, Ilse Schoep, and Robert Laffineur, pp. 167–172, Aegaeum 23. Université de Liège, Liège, Belgium.

Platon, Lefteris 2004 To Ysterominoiko I anaktoro tis Zakrou: mia 'Knosos' exo apo tin Knoso. In *Knossos: Palace, City, State. Proceedings of the Conference in Herakleion Organized by the British School at Athens and the 23rd Ephoreia of Prehistoric and Classical Antiquities of Herakleion, in November 2000, for the Centenary of Sir Arthur Evans's Excavations at Knossos*, edited by Gerald Cadogan, Eleni Hatzaki, and Andonis Vasilakis, pp. 381–392. British School at Athens Studies 12. The British School at Athens, London.

Potter, James M. 2000 Pots, Parties, and Politics: Communal Feasting in the American Southwest. *American Antiquity* 65(3):471–492.

Preucel, Robert W. and Lynn Meskell 2003 Places. In *A Companion to Social Archaeology*, edited by Lynn Meskell and Robert W. Preucel, pp. 315–329. Blackwell, Malden, MA.

Preziosi, Donald 1983 *Minoan Architectural Design: Formation and Signification*. Approaches to Semiotics 63. Mouton, Berlin

Rapoport, Amos 1988 Levels of Meaning in the Built Environment. In *Cross-Cultural Perspectives in Non Verbal Communication*, edited by F. Pyatos, pp. 317–336. C. J. Hogrefe, Toronto.

1990 *The Meaning of the Built Environment: A Nonverbal Communication Approach*, revised edition. University of Arizona Press, Tucson.

Redman, Charles L. 1978 *The Rise of Civilization: from early farmers to urban society in the ancient Near East*. W. H. Freeman, San Francisco, CA.

Renfrew, A. Colin 1972 *The Emergence of Civilisation: The Cyclades and the Aegean in the Third Millennium BC*. Methuen and Company, London.

Rethemiotakis, Giorgos 1999a The Hearths of the Minoan Palace at Galatas. In *Meletemata: Studies in Aegean Archaeology Presented to Malcolm H. Wiener as He Enters His 65th Year*, edited by Philip P. Betancourt, Vassos Karageorghis, Robert Laffineur, and Wolf-Dietrich Niemeier, pp. 721–727. Université de Liège, Liège, Belgium.

1999b Social Rank and Political Power. The Evidence from the Minoan Palace at Galatas In *Eliten in der Bronzezeit: Ergebnisse zweier Colloquien in Mainz und Athen*, edited by I. Kilian-Dirlmeier and M. Egg, pp. 19–26.

Verlag des Römisch-Germanischen Zentralmuseums, in Kommission bei Dr. Rudolf Habelt, Mainz, Germany.

2000–2001 Galatas. *Archaeology in Greece*. 47:127–128.

2002 Evidence on Social and Economic Changes at Galatas and Pediada in the New-Palace Period. In *Monuments of Minos: Rethinking the Minoan Palaces*. Aegaeum 23, edited by Jan Driessen, Ilse Schoep, and Robert Laffineur, pp 55–70. Université de Liège, Liège, Belgium.

2002–2003 Galatas. *Archaeology in Greece*. 49:78–79.

2007–2008 Galatas. *Archaeology in Greece*. 54:101–102.

2008–2009 Galatas. *Archaeology in Greece*. 55:95–97.

Rethemiotakis, Giorgos and Kostis Christakis 2011 LM I Pottery Groups from the Palace and the Town of Galatas, Pediada. In *LM IB Pottery: Relative Chronology and Regional Differences. Acts of a Workshop Held at the Danish Institute at Athens in Collaboration with the INSTAP Study Center for East Crete, 27–28 June 2007*, edited by T. M. Brogan and E. Hallager, pp. 205–228. Dutch Institute at Athens, Athens, Greece.

Rethemiotakis, Giorgos 2013 Middle Minoan III Period at Galatas: Pottery and Historical Implications. In *Intermezzo: Intermediacy and Regeneration in Middle Minoan III Palatial Crete*, edited by C. F. Macdonald and C. Knappett, pp. 93–106. British School at Athens, London.

Schoep, Ilse 2004 Assessing the Role of Architecture in Conspicuous Consumption in the Middle Minoan I–II Periods. *Oxford Journal of Archaeology* 23:243–269.

Shaw, Joseph W. 1973 The Orientation of the Minoan Palaces. *Antichità Cretesi: Studi in onore di Doro Levi 1. Chronache di Archeologia*. 12:47–59.

1978 Evidence for the Minoan Tripartite Shrine. *American Journal of Archaeology* 82(4): 429–448.

2009 *Minoan Architecture: Materials and Techniques*. Studi Di Archaeologia Cretese VII. Bottega D'Erasmo, Padova, Italy.

Smith, Adam T. 2000 Rendering the Political Aesthetic: Political Legitimacy in Urartian Representations of the Built Environment. *Journal of Anthropological Archaeology* 19:131–163.

2003 *The Political Landscape: Constellations of Authority in Early Complex Polities*. University of California Press, Berkeley.

Smith, Michael E. 2007 Form and Meaning in the Earliest Cities: A New Approach to Ancient Urban Planning. *Journal of Planning History* 6(1):3–47.

2008 *Aztec City-State Capitals*. University of Florida Press, Gainesville.

2010 The Archaeological Study of Neighborhoods and Districts in Ancient Cities. *Journal of Anthropological Archaeology* 29:137–154.

Smyth, Michael P. 1989 Domestic Storage Behaviour in Mesoamerica: An Ethnoarchaeological Approach. *Archaeological Method and Theory* 1:89–138.

Southall, Aiden W. 1973 Introduction. In *Urban Anthropology: Cross-cultural Studies of Urbanization*, edited by Aiden W. Southall, pp. 3–14. Oxford University Press, New York.

Stallsmith, Allaire B. 2004 The Agriculture Year in the Vrokastro Survey Area. In *Reports on the Vrokastro Area, Eastern Crete. Volume 2: The Settlement History of the Vrokastro Area and Related Studies*, edited by

Barbara J. Hayden, Appendix 4. University of Pennsylvania Museum Publications, Philadelphia.

Steinhardt, Nancy S. 1990 *Chinese Imperial City Planning*. University of Hawaii Press, Honolulu.

Trigger, Bruce G. 1972 Determinants of Urban Growth in Pre-industrial Societies. In *Man, Settlement, and Urbanism*, edited by Peter J. Ucko, Ruth Tringham, and G. W. Dimbleby, pp. 577–599. Duckworth, London.

1990 Monumental architecture: a thermodynamic explanation of symbolic behaviour. *World Archaeology* 22(2):119–132.

van Effenterre, Henri 1980 *Le palais de Malia et la cite minoenne*. Incunabula Graeca 76. Edizioni dell'Ateneo, Rome.

Voyatzoglou, M. 1984 Thrapsano, Village of Jar Makers. In *East Cretan White-on-Dark Ware: Studies on a Handmade Pottery of the Early to Middle Minoan Periods*, edited by P. P. Betancourt, pp. 130–142. Philadelphia University Museum, Philadelphia.

Warren, Peter 1987 The genesis of the Minoan palace. In *The Function of the Minoan Palaces: Proceedings of the Fourth International Symposium at the Swedish Institute in Athens, 10–16 June, 1984*, SIMA 34, edited by Robin Hägg and Nanno Marinatos, pp. 47–56. Paul Åströms Förlag, Göteborg, Sweden.

1990 Of Baetyls. *Opuscula Atheniensia* 18:193–206.

2002 Political Structure in Neopalatial Crete. In *Monuments of Minos: Rethinking the Minoan Palaces*, Aegeum 23, edited by Jan Driessen, Ilse Schoep, and Robert Laffineur, pp. 201–205. Université de Liège, Liège, Belgium.

2004 Terra Cognita? The Territory and Boundaries of the Early Neopalatial Knossian State. In *Knossos: Palace, City, State. Proceedings of the Conference in Herakleion Organized by the British School at Athens and the 23rd Ephoreia of Prehistoric and Classical Antiquities of Herakleion, in November 2000, for the Centenary of Sir Arthur Evans's Excavations at Knossos*, edited by Gerald Cadogan, Eleni Hatzaki, and Andonis Vasilakis, pp. 159–168. British School at Athens Studies 12. The British School at Athens, London.

Warren, Peter and Vronwy Hankey 1989. *Aegean Bronze Age Chronology*. Bristol: Bristol Classical Press.

Watrous, L. Vance, D. Matthew Buell, Lee Ann Turner, Scott Gallimore, Kapua Iao, and Mark Hammond 2014. *The Galatas Survey: A History of the Upper Pediada Region of Crete During the Neolithic-Ottoman Periods*. The Institute for Aegean Prehistory Academic Press, Philadelphia, PA.

Whitelaw, Todd 2004 Estimating the Population of Neopalatial Knossos. In *Knossos: Palace, City, State. Proceedings of the Conference in Herakleion Organized by the British School at Athens and the 23rd Ephoreia of Prehistoric and Classical Antiquities of Herakleion, in November 2000, for the Centenary of Sir Arthur Evans's Excavations at Knossos*, edited by Gerald Cadogan, Eleni Hatzaki, and Andonis Vasilakis, pp. 147–158. British School at Athens Studies 12. The British School at Athens, London.

Whitley, David S. 1998 New Approaches to Old Problems: Archaeology in Search of an Ever Elusive Past. In *Reader in Archaeological Theory: Post-Processual and Cognitive Approaches*, edited by David S. Whitley, pp. 1–28. Routledge, London.

Wiener, Malcolm 2007 Neopalatial Knossos: Rule and Role. In *Krinoi kai Limenes. Studies in Honor of Joseph and Maria Shaw*, edited by P. P. Betancourt, M. C. Nelson, and H. Williams, pp. 231–242. The Institute for Aegean Prehistory, Philadelphia, PA.

Wilkinson, Tony J. 1982 The Definition of Ancient Manured Zones by Extensive Sherd-Sampling Techniques. *Journal of Field Archaeology* 9:323–333.

1988 The Archaeological Component of Agricultural Soils in the Middle East: The Effects of Manuring in Antiquity. In *Man-Made Soils*, edited by W. Groenman-van Waateringe and M. Robinson, pp. 93–114. BAR International Series 410. British Archaeological Reports, Oxford.

1989 Extensive Sherd Scatters and Land-Use Intensity: Some Recent Results. *Jorunal of Field Archaeology* 16:31–46.

Wright, James C. 2004 A Survey of Evidence for Feasting in Mycenaean Society. *Hesperia* 73.2:133–178.

9

Cahokia: The Processes and Principles of the Creation of an Early Mississippian City

John E. Kelly and James A. Brown

As North America's only pre-Columbian city, Cahokia represents a unique configuration characterized some fifty years after its outset by four quadrilateral plazas centered on Monks Mound. This ritualized core of large earthen platform mounds, large constructed plazas, and massive wooden architecture comprises a landscape encompassing more than 100 ha. This built environment is at the heart of a ritual city covering nearly 15 km² and has its roots in the site's late-Emergent Mississippian community. This chapter focuses on the processes leading to the creation of this urban space and the American Indian cosmological principles that underlie them.

Only in the last few decades has the definition of urbanism been broadened to accommodate large and socially diversified Amerindian settlements that lack the political apparatus of the state or the stimulus of market-driven economies. At the same time, the finding has been generally accepted that cities emerged independently in a number of areas of the world. In many cases of pristine development, urbanism was sustained – often for millennia (Marcus and Sabloff 2008; Smith 2003). But what of those that faltered early and fell short of sustained growth? For any understanding of the processes of urbanism, it is precisely these areas that offer crucial information about the inception of the process. Cahokia (Figure 9.1) is a place that offers just such a window and one that comes from eastern North America, an area that has yet to contribute to a comprehensive picture on the origins of urbanism. In the following discussion, we focus on the processes leading to the creation of Cahokia and the American Indian cosmological principles that structure its space.

Recent comparative studies (Cowgill 2004; Smith 2002, 2007) have effectively disengaged the city from its timeworn role as a marker

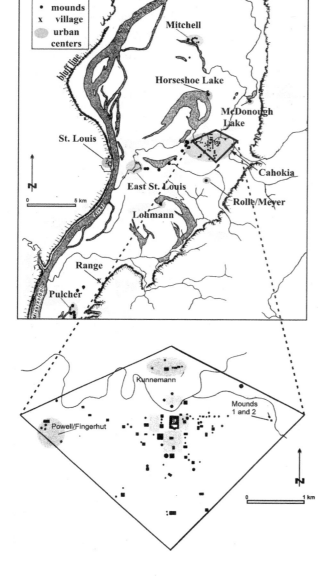

Figure 9.1 (a) Map of the American Bottom (base map adapted from Bushnell 1922); (b) plan of central Cahokia (base map adapted from Mink 1999:27).

of the state and a market economy. As a result, the number of places now defined as ancient cities has blossomed. As part of this rethinking, Fletcher (2009) has pointed to the presence of "low density, agrarian urbanism" in different parts of the globe. In discussing the early stages of urbanism in the Middle Niger in West Africa and the Late Neolithic along the Yellow River of northeast China, McIntosh (1991, 2005) has proposed the concept of "urban cluster" to describe large settlements in which monumental architecture is not present. Heckenberger and his colleagues (2008) have argued that the large (ca. 30–50 ha) pre-Columbian communities of the Amazon Basin are urban and part of a "galactic" settlement system. Michael Smith (2002, 2007) has pinpointed internal site planning and the relationship a site has to its hinterland as especially critical to what defines a city.

By removing the city as a defining element of the state, research in the ancient Americas has moved away from traditional models of cities and has instead focused on the role of religion, ritual, cosmology, and ideology as important elements in the creation and configuration of the city (Ashmore 1991), as well as how these cities articulate with smaller communities within the region. We argue here that with respect to site plan, scale, monumentality, and a socially differentiated hinterland, Cahokia merits serious consideration as being a city. We believe it is important to lay out the basis for defining Cahokia's urban character with attention to its historical antecedents and Amerindian cosmological principles (Kelly 1996a). In what follows, we first review the context of the debate over Cahokia's status as a city and then describe in detail its physical structure. Finally, we interpret Cahokia's structure and meaning in light of ethnohistoric and ethnographic data. Key features of Cahokia that we consider in our analysis include the horizontal organization of plazas and mounds, the vertical differentiation between sunken plazas and elevated platforms and mounds, the pairing of mounds, the removal of soil, and the use of specific kinds of soils in the construction of the site's monuments. In these features, we see the hands of different corporate groups in Cahokian society (Saitta 1994; Trubitt 2000) whose actions cemented sociopolitical relationships and emphasized group identity even as they competed to make their mark on urban space. Our application of indigenous beliefs and meaning to Cahokia from ethnographic sources cannot be fully corroborated by archaeological data, but we believe that our interpretations are well-grounded possibilities that enrich an understanding of the city.

CAHOKIA AS A CITY: PAST PERSPECTIVES

The 'City of the Sun' is the theme of the Interpretive Center at Cahokia, a World Heritage site located just east of St. Louis, Missouri. Although the site's sociopolitical complexity and degree of centralization have

received substantial discussion (Holt 2009; Pauketat 2004, 2007)
remarkably little has been devoted to Cahokia as a city. O'Brien
(1972), using Childe's (1950) criteria, was perhaps the first to argue
that Cahokia was a city. She also followed Childe's link between
urbanism and state-level society, consistently arguing for Cahokia
being a state (O'Brien 1989, 1992; see also Gibbon 1974 and, for a more
recent novel perspective, Holt 2009). The early writings of Fowler
(1974, 1975, 1976) and a more recent volume (Young and Fowler 2000)
often allude to Cahokia as a city, with particular emphasis on the
alignments and axes that undergird the site's spatial arrangement
(Morgan 1980; Rolingson 1996; Sherrod and Rolingson 1987).

O'Brien's perspective received renewed emphasis from Kehoe
(1998:169), who not only advocated the site as the center of a state, but
who has also consistently argued that both Chaco and Cahokia were
basically derived from the Toltec Empire of central Mexico during
its apogee between 900–1200 AD. Although there is little significant
interaction between the southwest and Cahokia, there is even less
between Cahokia and Mexico (Brown 2004; Brown and Kelly 2012;
Hall 1989). There is no question that ideological parallels exist in the
latter case and that some form of interaction was being maintained
(Brown and Kelly 2012; Hall 2006), yet Cahokia remains an indigenous development together with the rest of Mississippian culture.

Several historians – including Roger Kennedy, Francis Jennings,
and William Swagerty – have also provided perspectives on Cahokia
as a city, "metropolis," or "empire" (Jennings 1993:64–65; Kennedy
1994; Swagerty 2000), whereas other recent volumes on Cahokia discuss its complexity to varying degrees (Chappell 2002; Dalan 1993;
Dalan et al. 2003). Pauketat (2004, 2007, 2009) has followed in the
earlier footsteps of O'Brien and Kehoe in pushing the level of the
site's sociopolitical complexity to a point beyond what can be supported by extant data, especially when it is asserted mainly because
Cahokia is large. Iseminger (2010), following Smith's recent work on
degrees of urban planning and the key features of cities (Smith 2002,
2007) treats Cahokia as "America's First City," echoing Pfeiffer's
(1973, 1974) use of this label decades earlier.

Large, complex sites in North America are generally considered
incapable of contributing to the study of ancient cities. In the Eastern
Woodlands, the emergence of urbanism is commonly denied or
basically ignored (Welch 2004) although the region is known for its
long tradition of earthen monumental architecture. Southeastern

archaeologists, in fact, go out of their way not to describe Cahokia as a city, but instead as a "mega-center" or Great Town (Holley 1999). Although Cahokia, the largest site in eastern North America, is sometimes thought of as urban, it is just as often dismissed as a standard temple-town settlement writ large. The general lack of discussion about Cahokia as a city is indicative of the discomfort that many archaeologists have with the idea. We advocate examining the problem in an unaccustomed way. Instead of judging the merits of the urban label with definitive criteria in a checklist or trait list, it is more worthwhile, generally speaking, to think of urbanism as a process in which no definitive line exists to separate non-cities from cities. Consequently, many of the distinguishing traits of cities are ones that emerge or develop in more differentiated ways during the expansion of large, internally diversified central places through the social production of space.

For Amerindians of the mid-continent, it is not until the eleventh century AD that the process of urbanization becomes clearly identifiable near St. Louis in the central Mississippi Valley. The nature of these changes in community aggregation and nucleation over a period of 500 years ultimately is the foundation of Cahokia (Kelly 1992). The creation of Cahokia and its configuration as a city may have been the inspiration for urban centers that developed elsewhere in the Midwest and Southeast (cf. Pauketat 2004, 2007), such as Moundville (Knight and Steponaitis 1998), where parallel but slightly later developmental processes appear to have been well underway. Beginning in the twelfth century, smaller nucleated settlements, traditionally referred to by indigenous Muskogean peoples as *talwas* or towns, emerged at the core of most southeastern polities (Ethridge 2003:96).

In many respects, the Mississippian world can be visualized as an example of *incipient* urbanism, and arguably a pristine case of development within the Eastern Woodlands of North America. Certainly, Mississippian towns are more than large villages with mounds; they are planned residential communities with large central plazas and monumental architecture such as mounds, public buildings, and in many instances, wooden fortification walls (see Lewis and Stout 1998). What makes this important to understanding developments on a global scale is the short-lived nature of the Mississippian tradition (i.e., five centuries) and thus the lack of a long, drawn-out history of urbanization compared with many other parts of the world. It is extremely difficult at this time to investigate the onset of urbanism in these other areas through plans of excavated cities, but Cahokia's relatively short chronology provides a unique opportunity to analyze this process.

We choose to address the process of urbanism at Cahokia from the inhabitants' points of view by interpreting the built environment through the lens of ethnographic records from the region. Although we cannot capture the expectations, motivations, and adjustment strategies of living in large communities, we can make use of aspects of the material record, both major and minor, that reflect the agency of those that inhabit any major aggregation. What impresses us most is the strength of multigenerational trends that measure a group's material response to the challenge of continued close living. The cultural structures "inhabited" by groups at all social and political levels have moments of conscious creation – "events" in Sewell's terms – in which structural transformation is achieved through the addition of a new structural element (Sewell 2005).

Throughout its nearly four centuries of history, Cahokia reveals a dynamic interplay between its size and the production of differentiated space. This makes Cahokia particularly appropriate for the theme of how space in cities is configured and socially produced. Our primary focus in this chapter is the epicenter that dominates the heart of this Amerindian community (Figure 9.2). Covering nearly 150 ha, this is an area much larger than most ancient cities elsewhere in the world. The principles that underlie the creation of Cahokia's heart are those embedded in Amerindian communities historically and are intricately linked to their cosmology.

CAHOKIA: THE CITYSCAPE

Cahokia is situated within the widest expanse of the Mississippi floodplain 180 km north of the Mississippi river embayment where the floodplain expands dramatically outward (Figure 9.1a). As a 13 km^2 place on the landscape with more than 100 earthen mounds of varying sizes and shapes (Figure 9.1b), Cahokia is a product of human activity that has appropriated and transformed both space and nature (cf. Pred 1984:279). Cahokia was established amid a complex mosaic of abandoned Mississippi River meanders, Spring Lake and Edelhardt, which created topographically differentiated environments that accentuated aquatic resources (Delcourt and Delcourt

JOHN E. KELLY AND
JAMES A. BROWN

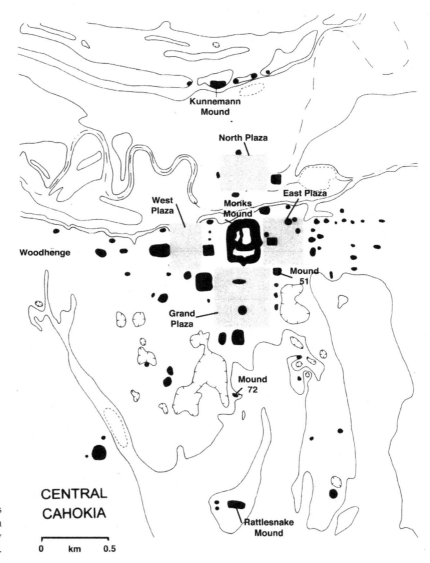

Figure 9.2 Cahokia's
Early Mississippian
Epicenter (drawn by
author).

2004; Milner 2006). Based on the earlier soil work of Woods (1987, 2004) it is probably no accident that Cahokia is situated on the western margins of the largest area of tillable soils in the region (Dalan et al. 2003:85).

The area that encompasses the immediate environs of Cahokia provided most of the subsistence resources and building materials for domestic structures and storage facilities. However, the lithic raw materials employed in the production of the basic tools used in the construction of buildings, houses, mounds, and in clearing fields for agricultural use needed to be procured at distances beyond 15 km. The Ozarks, more than 30 km to the southwest, are an important part of the larger landscape (Diaz-Granados and Duncan 2000; Kelly 1980, 1984, 2011; Koldehoff and Brennan 2011). It is here that additional lithic raw materials, such as galena and hematite, were procured along with trees such as red cedar – all of which were imbued with sacred qualities by historic Native American groups such as the Osage (e.g., Bailey 1995). This lithic landscape also included unique places such as caves and rock shelters that ethnographic studies indicate were used as important spiritual portals between different worlds for Native American communities (see Diaz-Granados 2004). Thus, the materials and places on the landscape may have formed an integral part of the Cahokian's cosmos.

The surrounding social landscape was the most dynamic aspect of Cahokia with the settlement system being highly differentiated and in a constant state of flux. In spite of its dynamic nature, Cahokia endured for nearly four centuries and thus gave people a sense of sacred place. Over the last three decades, a number of researchers have provided descriptions and interpretations of the regional settlement systems in Cahokia's immediate hinterland (Emerson 1997; Mehrer 1995; Mehrer and Collins 1995; Milner 2006; and Vermilion 2005). Other towns were established lasting about a century or less (Kelly 2008b). Researchers remain divided on the political significance of these nearby towns and debate the degree to which Cahokia dominated and effectively controlled its hinterland (Beck 2006).

The overall extent of Cahokia seems to be without firm boundaries. In size, it approaches Teotihuacán, but without the tenfold greater density of occupation of the latter (cf. Fowler 1976). Archaeologists traditionally define Cahokia's margins by four large marker mounds set at the cardinal directions (Fowler 1974). At the center lies Monks Mound, which is also at the center of four large plazas. When we examine Cahokia's landscape beyond this epicenter, the surrounding settlement scatter, particularly along the natural levee stretching to the west, resembles contemporary urban sprawl. Recent efforts to delineate the distribution of non-mound occupation (Hall et al. 1995; Holley 1990, 1995; Keller et al. 1994; Kelly and Koldehoff 1996; Kelly et al. 2001) provide a more accurate definition of the community over time. For example, Mounds 1 and 2 (Figure 9.1b), which date to the late thirteenth century and define the eastern margin of the site, are separated from the site core by nearly 1 km, and there is little evidence of occupation in the intervening area. Likewise, the western Powell group and nearby Fingerhut Tract may together represent a relatively early suburb or town dating to the site's apogee. The actual area of the Powell/Fingerhut complex stretches to the west beyond the current site boundary.

Pre-Mississippian Configuration

Over time, the structure of Cahokia as a community changed in the following ways. First, aggregated Late Woodland and early Emergent Mississippian villages of the seventh through ninth centuries AD, typically with populations of less than 100 people, were dispersed across the landscape of the American Bottom and adjacent uplands (Kelly 1990a, 1990b, 2000, 2002). These villages were scattered within the area of Cahokia; however, there is no indication of continuity until the end of the tenth and beginning of the eleventh centuries. These earlier settlements exhibit distinct plans centered on an open public space or community square with three types of symbolically charged central elements (Figure 9.3). By the middle of the tenth century, small, village populations were nucleated into larger villages with more than 200 people (Kelly 1992). The new plans integrate the central symbolic elements of the earlier communities into large (400–900 sq. m), centrally located, quadrilateral plazas and attendant courtyards (Figure 9.4). As a well-established feature of late Emergent Mississippian villages (Kelly 1990a; Kelly et al. 2007c), the largest rectangular residences fronted on these plazas, with another large (36 m²) building at the end of the earliest plaza. However, mounds were absent from village plans with very few exceptions. One exception – the Morrison site located immediately northwest of Cahokia – has two low (less than 1 m) mounds with an intervening plaza (Pauketat et al. 1998) some 70 m in length. A similar arrangement is evident at the Washausen site some 30 km south of Cahokia (Bailey 2007; Chapman 2005). Both date to the initial decades of the eleventh century.

The late Emergent Mississippian settlement at Cahokia extends at least 1.7 km along the natural levee of an abandoned meander (Figure 9.5). The population for this 17–34 ha area could have been 3,400–6,800 people if settlement was continuous and the density

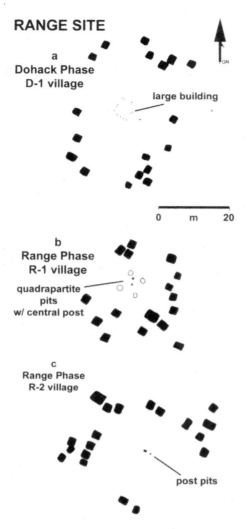

RANGE SITE

a
Dohack Phase
D-1 village

large building

0   m   20

b
Range Phase
R-1 village

quadrapartite
pits
w/ central post

c
Range Phase
R-2 village

post pits

Figure 9.3 Emergent
Mississippian 1 com-
munity plans (base map
adapted from Kelly
1996a:figure 8.6b).

corresponds to the 1 ha George Reeves-phase village at the Range site (Kelly 1990a; Kelly et al. 2007c), which had a population of approximately 200 people. Pauketat (2009) suggests a rather small population of 1,000 for pre-"Big Bang" Cahokia (i.e., the Emergent Mississippian period just before the site's rapid expansion and transformation around 1050 AD), albeit without providing supporting documentation in terms of settlement area and density. Dalan et al. (2003:figure 20) suggest an extensive (greater than 4 km²) Emergent Mississippian occupation from the eastern margins of the site to its western end, concentrated along the natural levee containing the Canteen and Cahokia Creek confluence to the north. Present

JOHN E. KELLY AND
JAMES A. BROWN

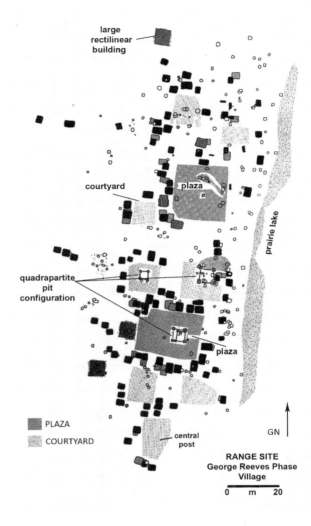

large
rectilinear
building

courtyard

plaza

quadrapartite
pit
configuration

plaza

PLAZA
COURTYARD

central
post

GN

RANGE SITE
George Reeves Phase
Village

0   m   20

Prairie lake

Figure 9.4 Nucleated
Late Emergent Missis-
sippian village at the
Range site (base map
adapted from Kelly
1990a:figure 40).

evidence for this foundational settlement, however, lacks monumental architecture and a clearly defined epicenter and may conform to
the "Urban Cluster" configuration described by McIntosh (1991) for
West Africa and the Neolithic of northeast China.

We argue that the community squares or plazas seen in the earlier Emergent Mississippian community plans were the focus of
community life and the symbolic embodiment of community cohesion that can be seen in the subsequent Mississippian communities.
Because they were essential to community integration, we believe
that these plans are the foundation for Cahokia's quadripartite
design. The community squares and plazas are symbolically the
heart and soul of these communities.

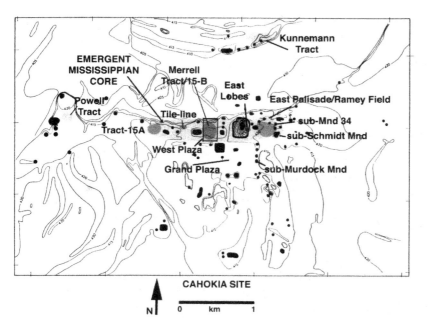

Figure 9.5 Central Cahokia's Late Emergent Mississippian occupation (drawn by author).

Early Mississippian Configuration

By the mid-eleventh century, Cahokia saw a series of rapid changes in community organization and size. These changes involve population increase (Milner 1986, 2006; Pauketat and Lopinot 1997) and subsistence intensification with the conspicuous rise in the importance of maize (Fritz and Lopinot 2007). Intensely occupied residential enclaves such as the Interpretative Center Tract southeast of the Grand Plaza exhibit a population density between 100 and 200 people per ha. More than demographic growth was involved, however. Cahokia's ritual epicenter was initially designed to accommodate large numbers of people from the region that were in excess of local demographic growth. As proposed by Pauketat (2003), migration from more distant locales must have been involved as well. Cahokia's sudden growth incorporated a number of local traditions. The ceramic record, as Vogel (1975:70) and Hall (1975) noted more than forty years ago, indicates a pluralistic amalgamation of different populations from both within and outside the region into Cahokia and, in some instances, the creation of new settlements. Significant to this review is the advocacy by Beck (2003 and 2006) of Cahokia as a magnet for ritual observance by being an active attractor of religious supplicants.

Migration is not new to the archaeological literature of the Eastern Woodlands. Gordon Willey (1953, see Waring 1968) drew

JOHN E. KELLY AND
JAMES A. BROWN

upon the origin myths of Muskhogeans to explain the appearance of the Early Mississippian center of Macon Plateau in central Georgia. The impact of immigrants on the established population is conditioned by the consideration of the relative increase in populations. As with the differences in population estimates, the issue becomes one of identifying the actual evidence of migration, the number of immigrants, and the impact of migration as a process. The importance of new faces appearing in cities relates to the pluralistic nature of the community. Researchers have long recognized the potential role of new ideas entering the American Bottom (Vogel 1975, Hall 1975). In many respects, certain Cahokians were very gifted in their ability to take new technologies and ideas and recast them into something uniquely different – a Middle Mississippian culture. As stressed by Hall (2006), adoption was one of the ways in which outsiders could be readily incorporated into Cahokian society together with their craft skills. Historically, ritual was the vehicle for this process.

At the onset of the Mississippian settlement pattern at Cahokia in the mid-eleventh century, the landscape was abruptly altered by creating a broad north-south occupational and ritual space of urban dimensions to accommodate the planned core or epicenter of the site. After Cahokia was reconfigured, the preexisting Emergent Mississippian village plan was easily quadrupled. Four monumentally sized plazas were laid out as arms of a giant cruciform (Kelly 1996a), although the precise timing of their emplacement has yet to be pinned down archaeologically. However, as Holley and his colleagues have noted (Holley et al. 1993), the creation of the Grand Plaza and possibly the West Plaza (Kelly 1996a) were already underway before the Big-Bang at 1050 AD, the conventional date for Cahokia's rapid transformation. The four-sided plaza is a well-rooted feature of public architecture. The form in which the four duplicate plazas were united expresses their subordination to a center occupied by Monks Mound. In eastern North American cosmology, the center stands for the center of the world – a concept recapitulated by the Omaha camp circle with its attendant connections to less-complex cultural organization (Brown 2011). The cross accentuates the four cardinal directions and the incorporation of a well-rooted feature of public architecture in the form of a central plaza and its internal architecture. These features expanded on past Emergent Mississippian planning principles by including an emerging vision of a larger corporate society enshrined in a cruciform of quadrilateral plazas

(Kelly 1996a). The very center, where Monks Mound now rests, may have been emptied of residential occupation at the time, although the relevant 6 ha surface is deeply buried by the colossal mound.

In the past, the initial construction of Monks Mound has been placed in the tenth century based on radiometric dates from cores (Fowler 1997). A recent reexamination of these data in conjunction with new data from cores and excavations has prompted Schilling (2010) to suggest that a rapid buildup of this earthen edifice occurred in the mid-twelfth century after Cahokia had become an urban center. This may make more sense if Monks Mound serves to connect with and commemorate what lies beneath it, similar to constructions in some of the Mesoamerican centers (cf. Heyden 1975). An important feature may lie beneath the mound. In his study of previous coring investigations beneath the northwest part of Monks Mound, Schilling (2010) identified a depression that does not appear to be a borrow pit (that is, an area where earth was removed to construct mounds) because of earlier Late Woodland deposits that are in place at the bottom of the depression. There is no clear geomorphic explanation for this feature because this area is part of the natural levee of the Edelhardt meander.

THE EPICENTER

For Cahokia, two important urban components shared with many ancient cities stand out. The first is the site's monumental epicenter. Central Cahokia is restricted to a 7.5 km² area (Figure 9.2). The 150 ha epicenter, measuring 1.5 km north-south by 1.25 km east-west, is characterized by four, large plazas centered on Monks Mound (Kelly 1996a). Fowler's work (1969, 1974), reveals the significance of its importance. The rectangular shape of each plaza creates inflexibility in the order of place setting along the perimeter (Hillier and Hanson 1984; Hunter-Anderson 1977). Corners are created that have unequal value, hence special significance. A relevant parallel is the effect that corners in quadrangular dwellings have on flexibility in rearranging furniture. The epicenter was the heart of Cahokia for more than a century. Surrounding the epicenter are additional mounds and smaller plazas with substantial residential areas (Collins 1990; O'Brien 1972; Pauketat 1998). The second urban component is the site's immediate hinterland (Smith 2007), which is very dynamic in terms of the ongoing settlement changes. A diversity of settlement types of differing orders of scale, as described by Fowler (1974) and refined by Emerson (1997) and others, included mound centers and towns of varying sizes, along with villages, numerous farmsteads, and small, specialized nodal sites that comprised the larger urban polity.

Spatially, plazas vary in size (6–21 ha) and in the number of mounds (four to nine) that ultimately defined the enclosed spaces. The largest arena, the Grand Plaza (Figure 9.6a), was originally a natural landscape of ridges and swales before it was leveled (Dalan 1993; Holley et al. 1993). More recent investigations in the Grand Plaza have proposed that the plaza was being filled in (Alt et al. 2010), although this may be related to the erosion of Monks Mound. Mapping over the last decade indicates that the plaza is actually sunken or at least accentuated by low, earthen platforms constructed on three of its four sides (Holley et al. 1990; Trubitt 2003). The north side facing Monks Mound is also elevated, naturally. The pairing of mounds around the remaining three sides of the Grand Plaza is of importance, particularly the twin mortuary mounds along the south side.

Harriet Smith's (1973) salvage work at the Murdock mound located at the south end of the east row of mounds in the Grand Plaza provided the earliest insights on the architecture of the plaza edge. Her work documented the unique nature of pre-mound build-ings (Figure 9.6b) and mound construction. The earliest building is a cross-shaped structure placed within a circular basin. This is followed by a large circular building or sweat lodge located just north of a rectangular structure. These were constructed in the area beneath the mound's northeast corner. Presumably, other structures were part of this pre-mound landscape.

In addition to this architecture, two large mounds were placed within the Grand Plaza. The Jesse Ramey mound, possibly terraced (Dalan 1993; Dalan et al. 1993; Dalan et al. 2003), was oriented north-south and located just to the southeast of the plaza's geometric center (Figure 9.6a). Testing of the east-west oriented Mound 49 by Pauketat and Rees (1996; Pauketat et al. 2010), has provided additional insights into mound construction. It is positioned just west of the plaza's north-south axis and centrally located along the east-west axis of the plaza's northwest quadrant.

The West Plaza is bounded by paired mounds on three of its sides (Figure 9.7). The west and south consist of a pair each, whereas the east side consists of two pairs. The north side is open on the

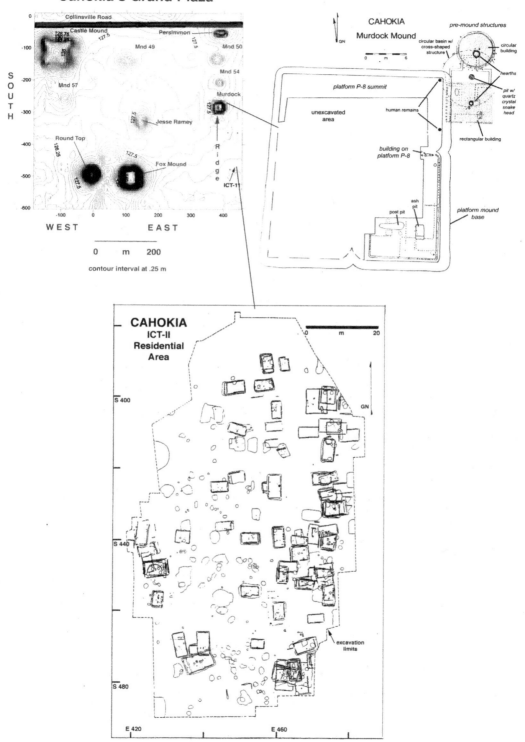

Figure 9.6 Plan of central Cahokia showing (a) Grand Plaza; (b) with Murdock mound inset (adapted from Smith 1973:figures 29, 33, 34, and 37); (c) ICT-II Residential Area inset (adapted from Collins 1990:figure 1.9).

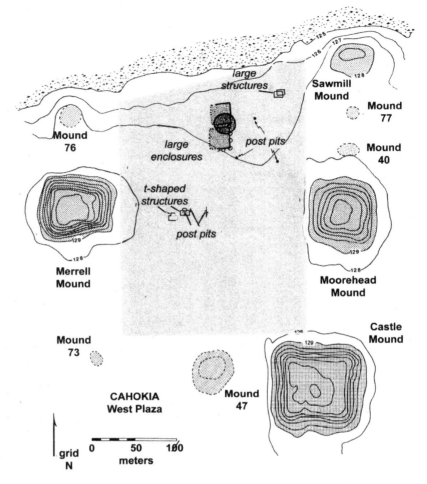

Figure 9.7 Cahokia,
plan of West Plaza area
(base map adapted from
Kelly 1996c).

Edelhardt meander and Cahokia Creek. The 1950 University of
Michigan test excavations into the low-lying Mound 76 on the plaza's northwest corner indicate that fill was added to the face of the
natural levee to accommodate an extension of the mound (Kelly and
Brown 2001). This suggests that mound placement was carefully
calculated. The floor beneath the mound was covered with a thin
veneer of sand, generally indicative of ritual purification (Adair 1930;
Hawkins 1848).

Evidence of interior plaza architecture is best expressed in the
West Plaza (Figures 9.8 and 9.9) initially defined by Wittry and
Vogel (1962) in the early 1960s salvage work at Cahokia (Valese 2012).
The sequence of unusually large enclosures (25–30 m in extent)
that occupy the north-central end of this area provides important
insights into the nature of the ritual activities taking place. There

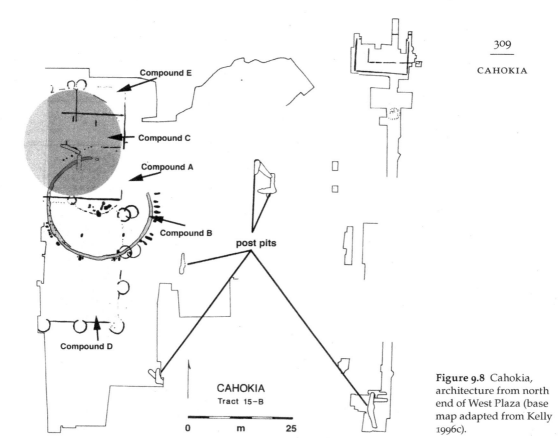

Figure 9.8 Cahokia, architecture from north end of West Plaza (base map adapted from Kelly 1996c).

is an architectural, stylistic, and presumed symbolic shift from an initial series of large (30 m in diameter) circular structures to large rectilinear enclosures with circular bastions. The latter can be stylistically linked to the initial palisade bastions from the end of the twelfth century. Subsequent excavations have identified a series of large post pits that may mark the center of the plaza. A series of other post pits to the west appear to be earlier and were placed along an east-west axis across the center of this area. Also present are two large T-shaped buildings (Kelly 1996b).

The four sides of the North Plaza are identified by four separate mounds (Figure 9.10), each of which establishes a dichotomy that accentuates size, distance, and directionality. The largest mound (Mound 5) – placed at the eastern end – is spatially distant from those on the other sides. The southernmost mound is also not oriented to the cardinal directions, but 40 degrees west of north. The whole tableau of the North Plaza has been purposely placed into the Edelhardt meander at a lower elevation than the other plazas, although this

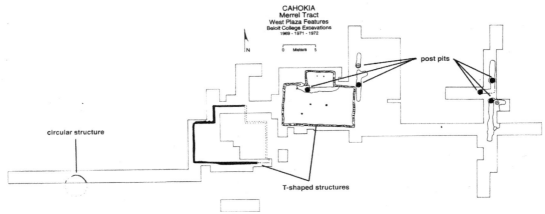

Figure 9.9 Cahokia, architecture from center of West Plaza (base map adapted from Kelly 1996c).

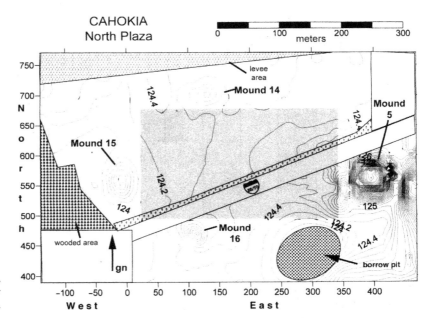

Figure 9.10 Cahokia, North Plaza (drawn by author).

landscape is slightly elevated with recent coring, thereby suggesting fill had been added to create it (Kelly et al. 2007b; Kelly 2012).

The East Plaza is the most difficult to define because, unlike the other plazas, mounds do not clearly demarcate this space (Figure 9.11). Definition of this plaza is based largely on negative evidence; that is, the lack of any early Mississippian residential occupation in the excavated palisade transect (Iseminger et al. 1990). The distribution of materials from controlled surface collections

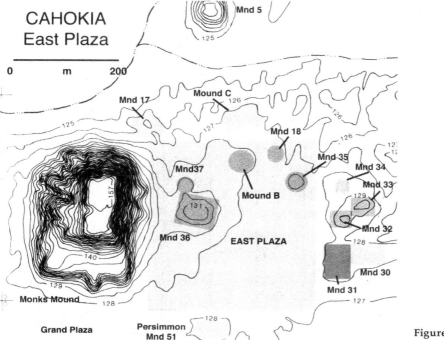

Figure 9.11 Cahokia, East Plaza (drawn by author).

exhibits a virtual lack of material in the area to the south of Mound 36 (Benchley 1981; Vander Leest 1980), an absence that appears to extend below the surface according to a recent geophysical survey (Hargrave 2011). In addition to the five mounds present within this area, two platforms are also present; one to the northeast of Mound 36 is broad and low and is cut by the palisade (Mound B). Another artificially constructed area (Mound C) is immediately north of the aforementioned platform and is also superimposed by the palisade (Kelly 2012). If this is indeed an architectural component on the northeast corner of this plaza, then it compliments Mound 76 on the northwest corner of the West Plaza. Mound 17 appears on the northwest corner of the plaza just below the northeast corner of Monks Mound. The area on the north is otherwise open on the low-lying Edelhardt meander landscape. The plaza's southern edge is delimited by Mound 51, located on the northeast corner of the Grand Plaza. Although this plaza landscape is perhaps the most difficult to understand in terms of its architectural elements, it is possible that we have a different configuration in which a large mound, Mound 36, is at its "center," although offset to the west.

312

JOHN E. KELLY AND
JAMES A. BROWN

Surrounding the epicenter lies a sprawling occupation of domestic dwellings and smaller, peripheral plazas and courtyards as evident in the case of the Interpretive Center Tract -II (ICT-II) (Collins 1990, 1997); Tract 15-A (Pauketat 1998) (see Figure 9.3 and 9.6c); and the Kunnemann Tract (Holley 1990, 1995). Residences are dispersed around courtyards and oriented along the epicenter axes, especially in the early part of the sequence. Except for its slightly larger size, domestic architecture in the city was the same as outside the site (Collins 1990). The early residential structures (i.e., late Lohmann phase), such as those on the ICT-II just southeast of the Grand Plaza, are initially oriented with the site grid, whereas the houses in the subsequent Stirling phase (1100–1200 AD) have axial orientations that are off-grid and are organized around a small plaza with mounds. This may reflect the ability of various kin groups within the site to control the organization of their subcommunities, thereby focusing inward on their community rather than outward toward the larger urban community.

As a planned city, Cahokia stood on the preceding Emergent Mississippian period site that comfortably occupied the natural levee (Dalan et al. 2003:70). However, its core expanded significantly to the north and south of this natural landscape and into areas not normally amenable to occupation. All of the plazas and most mounds rest to varying degrees on a modified landscape. An important key to this new plan was the Grand Plaza (Figure 9.6a), which was created through the physical process of infilling the natural depressions or swales that were separated from the adjacent high ground of natural ridges that were part of this point-bar landform (Holley et al. 1993). A portion of this ground on the northeast corner, at its junction with the southern margins of the East Plaza, was removed, creating a large borrow pit of unknown size that was some 3 m in depth (Chmurny 1973). Shortly thereafter, it was rapidly backfilled with midden, ritual objects, and feasting debris (Pauketat et al. 2002). Known as the sub-Mound 51 borrow pit, most of the debris was associated with feasting activity, especially during its preparation (L. Kelly 2000, 2001). As a unique episode of landscape modification, the activities provide insights into the social mechanisms employed in the mobilization of labor to create this landscape.

Late Mississippian Configuration

Toward the end of the twelfth century, a major change took place within the overall configuration of the epicenter (Figure 9.12a) involving the construction of a large palisade wall around Monks Mound, the Grand Plaza, and possibly the West Plaza (Anderson 1969; Iseminger et al. 1990; Trubitt 2003). As an example of monumental architecture, the palisade is perhaps one of the largest construction projects at the site, second only to Monks Mound itself (Milner 2006). As a 3 km long wooden wall, rebuilt three times, it encompassed nearly 200 ha and remained in use for at least another century. Immediately east of the palisade, the second largest plaza with its attendant mounds and borrow areas was created, covering nearly 50 ha. The Ramey borrow pit north of the mound and plaza complex resulted in the removal and destruction of a large (up to 10 ha) residential area (Kelly and Brown 2012). The scale of Cahokia became reduced in size, and the site appears to be made up of small, widely dispersed occupational loci such as the residential zone in the Woodhenge area (Hall 1975; Pauketat 1998); the Fingerhut Tract and an intrusive cemetery into the Powell No. 2 mound on the western margins (Keller et al. 1994; Kelly and Koldehoff 1996; Hall et al. 1995); and Mounds 1 and 2 on the east (Kelly et al. 2001).

These changes took place roughly in concert with a transformation in the way that food was served. Before about 1200 AD the presentation of food was dominated by small (ca. 1 liter in volume) serving vessels, whereas after that date, larger (ca. 3 liters in volume) openmouthed bowls, known as plates, with broad flat rims were incorporated into a ceramic assemblage in which the frequency of serving vessels doubled (Hamlin 2004; Kelly 2001). Another significant change was the transfer of a common repertoire of cosmic symbolism from the shoulders of open-mouthed (Ramey Incised) jars to the outflaring rims surrounding the centers of large open (Wells Incised) plates. Concordant with this change was a shift in the placement of concentrations of exotic materials, particularly Gulf Coast marine shell, found in house basins. Trubitt (2000) has demonstrated that between 1200–1275 AD these exotics were correlated with house size in that large houses had more exotics and small houses had fewer, whereas prior to 1200 AD, no relationship existed between the size of the residential unit and exotic accumulation. From these lines

JOHN E. KELLY AND
JAMES A. BROWN

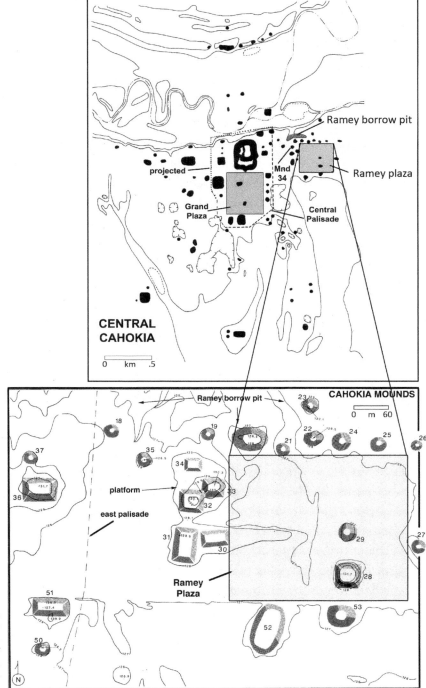

Figure 9.12 (a) Central Cahokia, Late Mississippian configuration; (b) detail of Ramey Plaza (base map adapted from Kelly 1996a:figure 8.4).

of evidence, it becomes clear that the household economics and community feasting ritual at Cahokia had shifted in a direction away from preexisting cultural norms. In general, houses increased in size during the thirteenth century (Milner et al. 1984; Vogel 1975), and household orientation at the beginning of the thirteenth century followed the site grid. Of particular importance was increased distance between households, perhaps suggestive of nearby gardens (see also Stark, Chapter 11 in this volume, and Magnoni et al., Chapter 5 in this volume, for a discussion of open spaces and household delineation in Mesoamerican cities) or an effort to minimize the ability of fires to spread if the settlement were attacked.

Outside the palisade to the east, the Ramey Plaza was created (Kelly et al. 2007a). This sunken plaza is second in size to the Grand Plaza at 10 ha. It was excavated to a depth of 1 m below the surrounding landscape. Low foundational platforms similar to those in the Grand Plaza are evident on the north and west sides. The Ramey Plaza dates to the thirteenth century and contains materials related to the pan-southeastern expression of high art on high-value materials commonly known as the Southeastern Ceremonial Complex (Brown and Kelly 2000; King 2007a, 2007b). Although there are significant changes at the end of the twelfth century, Cahokia continued to function as an incipient urban center. The density of settlements in the hinterland was reduced while the epicenter remained intact. Many of the mounds had been capped (Pauketat 1993; Trubitt 2000), including Monks Mound (Fischer 1972; Reed 2009), thereby memorializing these edifices in an act of burial. Changes continued to occur, with the urban character of the settlement no longer intact by the end of the thirteenth century. The settlement that existed was spread around Monks Mound on the west and the south among the earthen monuments. There was little evidence of any additional monumental construction.

SETTLEMENT HISTORY, EVOLUTION, AND COSMOLOGY

On the basis of the previous observations, it is possible to describe a historical process that charts shifts in social interaction that prefigure some of the forms recognizable in an established urban setting. The development of a new gustatory etiquette, together with changes to the engine of vested economic power, testifies to the strength of the effects of the urban setting on human action and vice versa. These reasons alone are sufficient to justify a consideration of Cahokia as a site that evolved toward fully urban life. The text for this process is encoded in the cosmology as expressed in the rituals undertaken by the corporate groups that lived in this urban landscape. Such an emblematically conceived "fresh start" of a macro-community construction fulfills an important criterion for cities – that is, they are more than simply villages or towns writ large. After 1050 AD, Cahokia was designed to accommodate the integration of the major corporate groups by assigning each a role in the implementation of its cosmic charter.

Although we cannot directly access the minds of the Cahokians, we can gain insight into the purpose and meaning of their settlement plan by interpreting the site's structure and features through the cosmology of related Native American groups, such as the Osage and Omaha, Dhegihan-Siouan speaking groups with origins in the Ohio River Valley, or the Chickasaw of the southeast (Bailey 1995, 2010; Burns 2004, 2005; Knight 1998; O'Shea and Ludwickson 1992; Welsch 1981). The knowledge of the cosmos that resided historically among groups such as the Osage was carefully partitioned among the religious specialists or priests of each kin group (Bailey 1995). Each clan was responsible for the knowledge that resided in their portion of the cosmos. In order for a specific ritual to work, it was necessary for the religious agents of each clan to come together with what they knew and create what was necessary. Although this rendition of Dhegiha Siouan cosmology belongs to the late nineteenth century AD, there is reason to think that this convention extended back to places such as Cahokia that have been connected with early Dhegihan society (Brown 2011; Kelly 2006). It is important to remember that Cahokia probably represents the ancestral roots of the descendant Dhegihan-speaking societies. Although the specifics have changed over the centuries, the principles remain intact and are critical in the production of public space that is at the city's core.

The principles that underlie urban planning of Cahokia are embedded in its epicenter. Paraphrasing the Osage, Garrick Bailey (1995) states that the cosmos was encoded in their community and society. The principles of reciprocity represented by dualism reflect the various elements within society and the cosmos that were in a constant state of opposition; in the end, these principles resulted in an effort to attain a balance or harmony of the whole and were thus in a constant state of negotiation. Large mounds are paired with small mounds. The dichotomy created by these pairings of unequal size reflects an important indigenous principle that focuses on maintaining a balance in the cosmos; night versus day; male versus female; large versus small; and so forth. A similar pairing is evident on the West Plaza. The square platform is placed opposite a circular conical mound, one on the east, the other to the west, respectively; or, in other instances, the former to the south and the latter to the north. Like a mountain, Monks Mound rises above the surrounding four plazas – flat expanses of space that created an arena in which people came together to negotiate with their past and to ensure societal continuity for the future.

The four mounds that demarcate the North Plaza (Figure 9.10) accentuate spatially the size, distance, and directionality of this landscape. Given their position within the Edelhardt meander at a lower elevation than the other plazas, they can be seen as being tethered to the underworld and to the origins of the earth in the selection of sediments of different colors and sources that appear to have been dictated by mythological associations. The earth diver, a mythical creature common in Native American origin stories, is one such connection (Köngäs 1960). In this case, the earth diver assists in the creation of the earth by diving beneath the primordial waters to retrieve muck from the aquatic floor (Hall 1997). Black mucky soils are occasionally inter-layered with light-colored soils in Monks Mound. It is believed that much of the earth was removed in this area to construct Monks Mound (Kelly et al. 2007b).

The four plazas with their attendant mounds reflect the principle of quadrilateralism. In ethnographic texts, four is a sacred number that points in the direction of the universe with the rising and setting of the sun each day in the east and west, respectively (Bailey 1995). The North Plaza is placed within the watery matrix of the Edelhardt meander. In the earth-diver origin stories discussed earlier, it is from this watery world that mud is collected to establish life. It is from this area that we suspect that mud was taken to create Monks Mound. To the south is death, as represented in the twin mounds at the south end of the Grand Plaza and beyond this is an earlier mortuary display of death in Mound 72 with four headless and handless males marking the center (Fowler et al. 1999). Beyond this is the largest mortuary structure, the Harding, or Rattlesnake Mound (Fowler 1997; Moorehead 1929; Pauketat and Barker 2000) placed within and rising out of a watery matrix where life begins. Mound 72 is not wholly about sacrifices, but as Brown (2003, 2006) has noted, a performance that reenacts the origins of the cosmos in the initial mound. Indigenous groups saw death as part of an intergenerational cycle. It is this geometric form – the circle – that encapsulates the continuum of life and death.

A hallmark of urban settlement complexity is the partitioning of space into places for dedicated purposes. At Cahokia, plazas, courtyards, residential areas, mounds, and other specialized architecture – such as the woodhenge – had their predetermined locations. Some of these locations, and perhaps all, were determined by cosmological order, in the vein of the Omaha summer-camp circle that will be described (Ridington and Hastings 1997). For our purposes, the plaza is the most important space to be discussed. Each of the four plazas at the heart of Cahokia are defined by large, open spaces bounded by mounds placed at the edges. In general, plazas are an integral part of the architectural space of Mississippian mound centers or towns and have a long history in the Eastern Woodlands going back into the Archaic period. Plazas continued into the historic period and are an integral part of traditional ceremonies of Indian communities today, as seen in southeastern Indian towns of the past. Although these communities, called *talwa* in the Creek Indian language, exist as a dispersed settlement pattern, they maintain a ritual/public center consisting of a town square or square ground. Thus, among Southeastern tribes, space for community activities occupies a conspicuous location and sacred sanctions are usually invoked in public rituals. Consequently, the places where such rituals are performed has to be ritually purified and declared off-limits to women and outsiders (Swanton 1931). These rituals create town-wide cohesion through appeal to the sacred. The plazas of Cahokia may have hosted similar rituals for both local inhabitants and the larger regional community.

Certain studies of urbanism have used selected spatial relationships as their guide to understanding this process of urbanization. Examples include viewsheds, visual orientation, metrification, and geometric relationships (e.g., Dalan et al. 2003). At Cahokia, objects of orientation – or the key architectural building units – are Monks Mound at the center, platform mounds generally, ridge-top mounds, conical mounds, large posts, and plazas. At a larger scale, the geometric arrangement of the epicenter and its celestial orientation become important. Surrounding the epicenter lies a sprawling, yet structured and organized occupation of domestic dwellings and smaller, peripheral plazas and courtyards, as evident in the Interpretive Center Tract-II (Collins 1990, 1997) and Tract 15-A (Pauketat 1998) (see Figures 9.3 and 9.6c). Residences are dispersed around courtyards and orientated along the epicenter axes, especially in the early part of the sequence.

Cosmology, Feasting, and the "Big Bang"

The major event of about 1050 AD, the so-called Big Bang, appears to mark the time when a sudden influx of people entered Cahokia from the surrounding region and, to a limited extent, from other nearby regions. It is possible that astronomical events provided some impetus for this cultural change (Beck et al. 2007) among people whose descendants, in ethnographic texts, were keen observers of celestial events, which they viewed as omens. Kelly (1996a) speculated on the possibility that the appearance of Haley's comet around the time of the spring equinox at 1066 coincided with the Big-Bang. Pauketat (2009; Pauketat and Loren 2005:17) suggests a link between the Big Bang and a 1054 supernova first noted by Diaz-Granados and Duncan (2000) in the rock art of eastern Missouri. It is also important to note that the largest supernova to be recorded historically appeared in the spring of 1006 AD and continued to be present intermittently for the next three years (Stephenson 2002). We have no clear material correlates of the 1006 event, but the appearance of these asterisms ties in with the elite-centered imagery of Morning Star depicted in rock art from Picture Cave in east-central Missouri (Diaz-Granados and Duncan 2000; Diaz-Granados et al. 2001) and Gottschall rock shelter in southwestern Wisconsin (Salzer and Rajnovich 2001), both of which date to around 1000 AD.

Regardless of the possible role of astronomical events in sparking the Big Bang, this influx of people may be related in part to the scheduling of annual community-wide feasts at a central location (Kelly 2008a, 2008c). The ability of leaders to host such large-scale events for the region and beyond at Cahokia may have stemmed in part from the high productivity of nearby soils (Schroeder 1999, 2004). The fields represented the most important resource that certain kin groups at Cahokia and adjacent communities may have controlled. Thus, food represents one commodity that could be used to draw others beyond the immediate sphere to participate not only in its consumption and the attendant rituals, but what others bring to the so-called table – that is Cahokia – in the way of raw materials and finished products. In sum, the local abundance of food becomes an important factor in attracting to Cahokia a population living well beyond the immediate vicinity. As a consequence, the feasts would not only reinforce the political power of the hosts, but they would mark Cahokia as the font of the largess and, by extension, the place where the spiritual power to produce food can be accessed (Byers 2006). This system, with its roots in the late Emergent Mississippian period, involved social groups from the family level up to the level of the community as a whole, with an initial invitation that extended in all four sacred directions beyond the region.

Cosmic Foundations

Interpreted on the basis of the ethnographic principles described here, Cahokian society incorporated multiple corporate groups through community ritual enacted within a purpose-built environment. These groups not only created this space, but also negotiated how that space was configured and employed to represent their vision of the larger cosmos. As we will demonstrate, this process, well rooted in local traditions, represented a rapid and dynamic implementation of a corporate vision involving the creation of a four-fold multiplication of the quadrilateral plaza configuration (Figure 9.2) that recreated the cosmos by tying them to a common center (Beck et al. 2007; Kelly 1996a) (see Howard 1968; Lankford 2007). There is not only a horizontal dimension to the production of space, formalizing the relationships between individuals and the groups they are part of, but also a distinct vertical dimension that is in concordance with the multilayered cosmos (Lankford 2007). This verticality is not necessarily translated into social standing. The horizontal dimensions of the world they live in are connected through an axial center (*axis mundi*) from the lower worlds beneath the earth's surface to the empyrean or upper world, above the sky. The creation of these different levels serves to place people with respect to the major spiritual forces represented, for example, by the sun on the one hand and the deities of the sky on the other hand (Brown 2011).

Historically, each clan of Mississippian native groups was symbolically represented within the village structure. The camp circle of the Omaha tribe represents one material version of this representation (Fletcher and LaFlesche 1911). The religious edifice known as the "House of Mystery" orders clans on a smaller scale among the Osage (Bailey 1995). As large public places, Cahokia's plazas honor the four sacred directions and are unified by a program of monumentality. Investigations by a number of different researchers provide insights into them as part of the cityscape with different architectural elements that comprise each plaza. The plazas are more than diagrammatic inscriptions on the landscape. Knight (1998) argued that the spatial organization of Moundville resembled the square ground of the Chickasaw Indians. We build on this insight to argue that plazas, particularly sunken plazas, articulate with mounds to form a vertical dimension to the surface arrangement of plazas and mounds. At Cahokia, two central plazas were sunken (the Grand Plaza and Ramey Plaza) to provide what can be regarded as an architectural way of displaying a tiered universe – this world of the cruciform plan, the beneath world of the sunken plazas, and the upper world of the summit of Monks Mound. Other levels could also be represented. The Osage believed that there were an additional four worlds placed between this world and the empyrean (Duncan 2011; Reilly 2004).

CORPORATE GROUPS AND CITY SPACE

In this cosmically ordered city, the very large core of mounds stands at the center, with plazas radiating from the center that are, in at least the southern Grand Plaza, sunken beneath the site surface. Framing the plazas are earthen mounds on broad, low platforms, the vertical dimensions of which were accentuated with the construction of wooden architecture. This arrangement, while conceptually in the builders' cosmic vision, did not come about all at once. Although the central (Monks) mound was raised within a brief span of time, the mounds around and within each plaza were added over a longer span of time, some more actively than others. Like the cosmos, a distinct verticality is evident with multiple layers of monumental construction.

Following Knight's (1998) application of the Chickasaw camp circle to the diagrammatic plan of Moundville, each mound or paired mounds along the plaza margins at Cahokia hypothetically represented a particular corporate entity. Four clans would have been represented in the North Plaza; three would be present around the West Plaza; four would have been present around the Grand Plaza; and it is unclear, given the lack of pairing, how many were associated with the East Plaza, perhaps three. In effect, at least four separate "multi-corporate communities" would have had cosmically ordained positions within the ritual epicenter. The mounds, we believe, represent the placement of specific buildings that served to personify the religious component of each respective corporate group. This is evident later at Mound 34 where an underlying complex of structures, including a copper-working house, may have been capped by an extensive 0.70 m high earthen platform that supported other structures, including what became Mounds 34, 33, and 32 along the west side of the Ramey Plaza (Figure 9.12). Harriet Smith (1973) identified a suite of unique buildings beneath the Murdock mound, along the Grand Plaza's east side, that were eventually capped by a series of thin earthen blankets. In light of ethnographic cases, each of the mound layers reflects the repetitious death of the initial pre-mound building(s) and their subsequent rebirth. The final cap, in effect a memorial, personifies an ancestral corporate group.

In some respects, we have presented an oversimplification of a complex socio-religious landscape that shows abundant evidence of shifting land use over time. We are only beginning to understand how Cahokia's citizenry were arranged within its cosmologically defined layout. The plazas laid out in cosmologically important directions created the format within which shrines were situated. Each had its designated place around the edge of each plaza. Not all construction obeyed the implicit format; several mounds invaded the central place. Judging by the size and span of time involved in mound construction and mound use, some of the clans and/or sodalities appear wealthier than others – perhaps embracing more members. With these caveats in mind, we have found it very useful to think within the framework of Dhegihan social order as represented by the Omaha and Osage systems (Bailey 1995; Brown 2011; Duncan 2011; Hall 2004, 2005; Ridington and Hastings 1997). In these systems, each individual component social group, usually a clan, was responsible for a unique component of sacred knowledge. Performance of the entirety of this knowledge in the annual ritual cycle unified these tribes by creating ritual obligations for each social segment, no matter how minor, toward the maintenance of harmonious balance in the universe.

Tapping into the persuasive politics thesis of Rob Beck (2006), we could propose that as outside social groups were attracted to Cahokia, they were allotted space according to some cosmically ordained calculus. One of the unintended effects may have been to promote alternate urban agglomerations, such as the East St. Louis town that may have attempted to undercut the political designs of the Cahokian elite (Kelly 2008b). Located some 10 km to the southwest of Cahokia, this urban complex was undoubtedly second in size to Cahokia within the larger Mississippian world. It appears that this urban complex consists of a ritual core of mounds and a central plaza with the residential area separated by a wide, low-lying slough 1 km to the north. It may be significant that East St. Louis may have had a cruciform plaza of its own. At Cahokia, one plaza – the predominant Grand Plaza with the largest number of mounds – may even have prospered at the expense of the other plazas, especially when it continued along with Monks Mound as the surviving ritualized core late into the city's existence (Figure 9.6a).

CONCLUSIONS: CAHOKIA AS A CITY REVISITED

Despite the reluctance of Eastern Woodlands archaeologists to adopt the position that Cahokia is a city, we join with students of the general topic in seeing essential aspects of urbanism at Cahokia. Beginning with a crossed-shaped plan of four plazas, the site was clearly, by the end, partitioned internally with a walled precinct, craft specialization took place in both secular and sacred contexts, an art style was refined, and a hinterland was drawn to its service. Although the limits of this settlement seem messy, recent reviews of low-density agrarian settlements make clear that compact cities are something of an exception (Fletcher 2009). It is the structural and functional differentiation of the community and its relationship to the extra-settlement catchment that make the city.

Viewing Cahokia as a city has the benefit of addressing the internal social and economic structure of the site and its hinterland along useful lines. The central Monks Mound was created to define the city architecturally and to unite each of the plazas within an ideologically potent plan. It allows us to examine the creative role of the plaza organization, which fixed the place of constituent groups within an ideologically sanctioned overarching scheme. The mound architecture associated with these groups would stand as a visible materialization of each lineage's ability to muster resources and to declare its potency to succeeding generations. If historic uses of the cult of the Sacred Hawk among the Osage are any guide to past beliefs, it would appear that its Birdman-centered corollary dealt directly with the propagation of one's lineage. Once extinct, the lineage's monuments would testify to their former relative importance in a permanent way. The strength of this city organization is testified by the appearance midway in its history of regularity in household size and economic potency. After 1200 AD, larger households came to dominate the acquisition and deposition of exotics so that the amount of exotics is more closely related to the size of the associated building. A weakness in the organizational structure lay in the inability of the collective format to survive the emergence of an overt hierarchy in an unconstrained environment. Any challenge to the collectivity would promote breakup along factional lines.

Although our interpretations of the meaning of Cahokia's structure rely heavily on ethnographic data, cultural continuity during the 400 years between the time of Cahokia's demise and the earliest ethnohistoric texts and the more recent ethnographies of the late nineteenth and early twentieth centuries makes it possible to provide reasonable explanations for the planning principles evident at Cahokia. Archaeological evidence for feasting, mortuary practices, household change over time, regional settlement restructuring, and monuments that were carefully built and maintained, dovetail with ethnographic accounts of the cosmic order in the ancient American Indian settlements of the Cahokian region. In light of the scale and complexity of this planning, along with the socioeconomic and religious factors described here, we argue that in Cahokia, we see the expression of Native North American urbanism – a process that was not taken up at the same scale as Cahokia in subsequent periods, leaving the (false) impression that North America lacks ancient cities. We further argue that this is an incipient and pristine example of the emergence of urbanism in the Eastern Woodlands of North America.

ACKNOWLEDGMENTS

The authors would like to thank the following institutions and individuals for their assistance in preparing this paper. First, Andy

Creekmore and Kevin Fisher, who not only included our paper in the 2009 SAA symposium and this volume, but were also instrumental in helping with various aspects of organizing our chapter to reflect the cosmological underpinnings of Cahokia's spatial organization as an ancient city. Second, the current investigations at Cahokia over the last two decades have been conducted through the support of Washington University and Northwestern University, and with funding from the Cahokia Mounds Museum Society, the Earthwatch Institute, and the National Geographic Society. Third, we would like to acknowledge the support of Cahokia colleagues, students, and volunteers who have participated in our endeavors. Finally, an especial note of thanks to Lucretia Kelly for help with the various drafts and the formatting at the end. The authors assume sole responsibility for the data, its interpretation, and any errors or omissions that are part of an ongoing effort to better understand this ancient city.

REFERENCES CITED

Adair, James 1930 *Adair's History of the American Indians*. Edited by Samuel Cole Williams. Promotory Press, New York.

Alt, Susan, Jeffrey Kruchten, and Timothy Pauketat 2010 The Construction and Use of Cahokia's Grand Plaza. *Journal of Field Archaeology* 35(2):131–146.

Anderson, James P. 1969 A Cahokia Palisade Sequence. In *Explorations into Cahokia Archaeology*, edited by M. L. Fowler, pp. 89–99. Illinois Archaeological Survey, Inc., Bulletin No. 7, University of Illinois, Urbana.

Ashmore, Wendy 1991 Site Planning Principles and Concepts of Directionality among the Ancient Maya. *Latin American Antiquity* 2:199–226.

Bailey, Garrick A. (editor) 1995 *The Osage and the Invisible World: From the Works of Francis La Flesche*. University of Oklahoma Press, Norman.
2010 *Traditions of the Osage: Stories Collected and Translated by Francis la Flesche*. University of New Mexico Press, Albuquerque.

Bailey, Katri Susanna 2007 Washausen Mound Center (11MO305) Ceramic Assemblage: Broken Pots from the Plaza. Unpublished Master's thesis, Department of Anthropology, Washington University, St. Louis, MO.

Beck, Robin A., Jr. 2003 Consolidation and Hierarchy: Chiefdom Variability in the Mississippian Southeast. *American Antiquity* 68:641–664.
2006 Persuasive Politics and Domination at Cahokia and Moundville. In *Leadership and Polity in Mississippian Society*, edited by Brian M. Butler and Paul D. Welch, pp. 19–42. Center for Archaeological Investigations Occasional Paper No. 33. Southern Illinois University, Carbondale.

Beck, Robin A., Douglas J. Bolender, James A. Brown, and Timothy K. Earle 2007 Eventful Archaeology: The Place of Space in Structural Transformation. *Current Anthropology* 48: 833–860.

Benchley, Elizabeth D. 1981 *Summary Report on Controlled Surface Collections of the Ramey Field, Cahokia Mounds Historic Site, Madison County Illinois.* Reports of Investigations No. 51. Archaeological Research Laboratory, University of Wisconsin, Milwaukee.

Brown, James A. 2003 The Cahokia Mound 72-Sub 1 Burials as Collective Representation. In *A Deep-Time Perspective: Studies in Symbols, Meaning, and the Archaeological Record, Papers in Honor of Robert L. Hall,* edited by John D. Richards and Melvin L. Fowler. *The Wisconsin Archeologist* 84: 81–97.

2004 Exchange and Interaction to AD 1500. *Handbook for North American Indians, Volume 14 – Southeast,* edited by Raymond D. Fogelson, pp. 677–685. Smithsonian Institution, Washington, DC.

2006 Where's the Power in Mound Building? An Eastern Woodland Perspective. In *Leadership and Polity in Mississippian Society,* edited by Brian M. Butler and Paul D. Welch, pp. 197–213. Center for Archaeological Investigations Occasional Paper No. 33. Southern Illinois University, Carbondale.

2011 The Regional Culture Signature of the Braden Art Style. In *Visualizing the Sacred: Cosmic Visions, Regionalism, and the Art of the Mississippian World,* edited by George E. Lankford, F. Kent Reilly, III and James F. Garber, pp. 37–63. University of Texas Press, Austin.

Brown, James A. and John E. Kelly 2000 Cahokia and the Southeastern Ceremonial Complex. In *Mounds, Modoc, and Mesoamerica: Papers in Honor of Melvin L. Fowler,* edited by Steven R. Ahler, pp. 469–510. Illinois State Museum Scientific Papers, Springfield.

2012 The Importance of Being Specific: Theme and Trajectory in Mississippian Iconography. In *Enduring Motives: Religious Traditions of the Americas,* edited by Linea Sundstrom and Warren DeBoer, pp. 210–234. University of Alabama Press, Tuscaloosa.

Burns, Louis F. 2004 *A History of the Osage People.* University of Alabama Press, Tuscaloosa.

2005 *Osage Indian Customs and Myths.* University of Alabama Press, Tuscaloosa.

Bushnell, David I., Jr. 1922 Archaeological Reconnaissance of the Cahokia and Related Mound Groups. Explorations and Field Work of the Smithsonian Institution in 1921. *Smithsonian Miscellaneous Collections* 72(15):92–105.

Byers, A. Martin 2006 *Cahokia: A World Renewal Cult Heterarchy.* University Press of Florida, Gainsville.

Chapman, Ellen 2005 Analysis of the Washausen Mississippian Mound Site (11MO305) Using Distribution Maps. Unpublished Senior Thesis, Department of Anthropology, Washington University, St. Louis, MO.

Chappell, Sally A. Kitt 2002 *Cahokia: Mirror of the Cosmos.* University of Chicago Press, Chicago.

Childe, V. Gordon 1950 The Urban Revolution. *Town Planning Review* 21:3–17.

Chmurny, William W. 1973 The Ecology of the Middle Mississippian Occupation of the American Bottom. Unpublished Ph.D. Dissertation, Department of Anthropology, University of Illinois, Urbana.

Collins, James M. 1990 *The Archaeology of the Cahokia Mounds ICT-II: Site Structure.* Illinois Cultural Resources Study No. 10. Illinois Historic Preservation Agency, Springfield.

1997 Cahokia Settlement and Social Structure as Viewed from the ICT-II. In *Cahokia: Domination and ideology in the Mississippian world*, edited by T. R. Pauketat and T. E. Emerson, 124–140. University of Nebraska Press, Lincoln.

Cowgill, George L. 2004 Origins and Development of Urbanism: Archaeological Perspectives. *Annual Review of Anthropology* 33: 525–549.

Dalan, Rinita A. 1993 Landscape Modification at the Cahokia Mounds Site: Geophysical Evidence of Cultural Change. Unpublished Ph.D. Dissertation, Department of Anthropology, University of Minnesota, Minneapolis.

Dalan, Rinita A., George R. Holley, and Harold W. Watters, Jr. 1993 *An Assessment of Moorehead's Investigations at Mound 56, Cahokia Mounds State Historic Site*. Submitted to the Illinois Historic Preservation Agency. Copies available from the Illinois Historic Preservation Agency, Springfield.

Dalan, Rinita A., George R. Holley, William I. Woods, Harold W. Watters, Jr. and John A. Koepke 2003 *Envisioning Cahokia: A landscape perspective*. Northern Illinois University, DeKalb.

Delcourt, Paul A. and Hazel R. Delcourt 2004 *Prehistoric Native Americans and Ecological Change: Human Ecosystems in Eastern North America since the Pleistocene*. Cambridge University Press, Cambridge.

Diaz-Granados, Carol 2004 Marking Stone, Land, Body, and Spirit: Rock Art and Mississippian Iconography. In *The Hero, Hawk, and the Open Hand: American Indian Art of the Ancient Midwest and South*, edited by Richard Townsend and Robert V. Sharp, pp. 139–149. Art Institute of Chicago, Chicago.

Diaz-Granados, Carol and James Duncan R. 2000 *The Petroglyphs and Pictographs of Missouri*. University of Alabama Press, Tuscaloosa.

Diaz-Granados, Carol, M. W. Rowe, M. Hyman, James Duncan R., and J. R. Southon 2001 AMS Radiocarbon Dates for Charcoal from Three Missouri Pictographs and their Associated Iconography. *American Antiquity* 66(3):481–492.

Duncan, James R. 2011 The Cosmology of the Osage: The Star People and their Universe. In *Visualizing the Sacred: Cosmic Visions, Regionalism, and the Art of the Mississippian World*, edited by George E. Lankford, F. Kent Reilly, III and James F. Garber, pp. 18–33. University of Texas Press, Austin.

Emerson, Thomas E. 1997 *Cahokia and the Archaeology of Power*. University of Alabama Press, Tuscaloosa.

Ethridge, Robbie F. 2003 *Creek Country: The Creek Indians and their World*. University of North Carolina Press, Chapel Hill.

Fischer, Fred W. 1972 Recent Archaeological Investigations on the 4th Elevation of Monks Mound, Madison County, Illinois. Manuscript on file, Department of Anthropology, Washington University, St. Louis, MO.

Fletcher, Alice and Franics LaFlesche 1911 *Twenty-seventh Annual Report of the Bureau of American Ethnology*. Smithsonian Institution, Washington, DC.

Fletcher, Roland 2009 Low-Density, Agrarian-Based Urbanism: A Comparative View. Institute of Advanced Study E-Journal *Insights* 2(4): 2–19. http://www.isisonline.org.uk/resources/ias/insights/Fletcher16Jan.pdf, accessed April 1, 2013.

Fowler, Melvin L. 1969 The Cahokia Site. In *Explorations into Cahokia Archaeology*, edited by M. L. Fowler, pp. 1–30. Illinois Archaeological Survey, Inc., Bulletin No. 7, University of Illinois, Urbana.

1974 *Cahokia: Ancient Capital of the Midwest*. Addison-Wesley Module in Anthropology 48. Addison-Wesley Publishing, Reading, PA.

1975 A Pre-Columbian Urban Center on the Mississippi. *Scientific American* 233:92–101.

1976 Prehistoric Urban Revolution in North America. In *Indiana Historical Society Lectures, 1973–1974: Human and Cultural Development*, edited by J. T. Robinson, Melvin L. Fowler, and Brian M. Fagan, pp. 22–41. Indiana Historical Society, Indianapolis.

1997 *The Cahokia Atlas: A Historical Atlas of Cahokia Archaeology*, rev. edition, chapters 1–3. University of Illinois Urbana-Champaign, Studies in Archaeology No. 2.

Fowler, Melvin L., Jerome Rose, Barbara Vander Leest, and Steven R. Ahler 1999 *The Mound 72 Area: Dedicated and Sacred Space in Early Cahokia*. Illinois State Museum Report of Investigations, No. 54. Illinois State Museum, Springfield.

Fritz, Gayle J. and Neal H. Lopinot 2007 Native Crops at Early Cahokia: Comparing Domestic and Ceremonial Contexts. *Illinois Archaeology* 15/16:90–111.

Gibbon, Guy 1974 A Model of Mississippian Development and Its Implications for the Red Wing Area. In *Aspects of Upper Great Lakes Anthropology*, edited by Elden Johnson, pp. 129–137. Minnesota Prehistoric Archaeology Series No. 11. Minnesota Historical Society, Saint Paul.

Hall, Abigail, John E. Kelly, and Brad Koldehoff 1995 The Nature and Context of the Mississippian Occupation on the Southern Periphery of the Powell Mound Group. Paper presented at the 40th Annual Meeting of the Midwest Archaeological Conference, Beloit, Wisconsin.

Hall, Robert L. 1975 Chronology and Phases at Cahokia. *Illinois Archaeological Survey Bulletin* 10: 15–31.

1989 The Cultural Background of Mississippian Symbolism. In *The Southeastern Ceremonial Complex: Artifacts and Analysis*, edited by Patricia K. Galloway, pp. 239–278. University of Nebraska Press, Lincoln.

1997 *An Archaeology of the Soul: North American Indian Belief and Ritual*. University of Illinois Press, Urbana.

2004 The Cahokia Site and Its People. In *The Hero, Hawk, and the Open Hand: American Indian Art of the Ancient Midwest and South*, edited by Richard Townsend and Robert V. Sharp, pp. 92–103. Art Institute of Chicago, Chicago.

2005 Contradictions as a Source of Historical Perspective: Examples from the Symbolism of Camp Circle and Sacred Poles. In *Native Symbolic Expression around the Great Lakes and Beyond*, edited by William A. Fox and Robert J. Pearce. *Ontario Archaeology* 79/80: 115–126.

2006 Exploring the Big Bang at Cahokia. In *A Precolumbian World*, edited by Jeffrey Quilter and Mary Miller, pp. 187–229. Harvard University Press, Cambridge, MA.

Hamlin, Jenna 2004 Sociopolitical Significance of the Moorehead Phase Ceramic Dataset Variation in the Cahokia Area. Unpublished Ph.D.

Dissertation, Department of Anthropology, Washington University, St. Louis, MO.

Hargrave, Michael L. 2011 Geophysical Survey of Complex Deposits at Ramey Field, Cahokia. *Southeastern Archaeology* 30(1):1–19.

Hawkins, Benjamin 1848 *A Sketch of the Creek Country in 1798 and 1799*. Collections of the Georgia Historical Society 3(1). Georgia Historical Society, Savannah.

Heckenberger, Michael J., J. Christian Russell, Carlos Fausto, Joshua R. Toney, Moran J. Schmidt, Edithe Pereira, Bruna Franchetto, and Afukaka Kuikuro 2008 Pre-Columbian Urbanism, Anthropogenic Landscapes, and the Future of the Amazon. *Science* 321:1214–1217.

Heyden, Doris 1975 An Interpretation of the Cave under the Pyramid of the Sun in Teotihuacan, Mexico. *American Antiquity* 40(2):131–147.

Hillier, Bill and Julienne Hanson 1984 *The Social Logic of Space*. Cambridge University Press, Cambridge and New York.

Holley, George R. 1990 *Investigations at the Kunnemann Tract, Cahokia Mounds Historic Site, Madison County, Illinois*. Submitted to the Illinois Historic Preservation Agency, Springfield. Copies available from the Illinois Historic Preservation Agency.

   1995 Microliths and the Kunnemann Tract: An Assessment of Craft Production at the Cahokia Site. *Illinois Archaeology* 7(1–2):1–68.

   1999 Late Prehistoric Towns in the Southeast. In *Great Towns and Regional Polities in the Prehistoric American Southwest and Southeast*, edited by Jill E. Neitzel, pp.23–43. University of New Mexico Press, Albuquerque.

Holley, George R., Neal H. Lopinot, Rinita A. Dalan, and William I. Woods 1990 *The Archaeology of the Cahokia Palisade: South Palisade Investigations*. Illinois Cultural Resources Study No. 14, Illinois Historic Preservation Agency, Springfield.

Holley, George R., Rinita A. Dalan, and Philip A. Smith 1993 Investigations in the Cahokia Site Grand Plaza. *American Antiquity* 58:306–319.

Holt, Julie Zimmerman 2009 Rethinking the Ramey State: Was Cahokia the Center of a Theater State? *American Antiquity* 74(2):231–254.

Howard, James H. 1968 The Southern Ceremonial Complex and Its Interpretations. *Missouri Archaeological Society Memoir No.6*. Columbia, MO.

Hunter-Anderson, Rosalind L. 1977 A Theoretical Approach to the Study of House Form. In *For Theory-Building in Archaeology* edited by Lewis R. Binford, pp. 287–316. Academic Press, New York.

Iseminger, William R. 2010 *Cahokia Mounds: America's First City*. History Press, London and Charleston, SC.

Iseminger, William R., Timothy R. Pauketat, Brad Koldehoff, Lucretia S. Kelly, and Leonard Blake 1990 *The Archaeology of the Cahokia Palisade: East Palisade Investigations*. Illinois Cultural Resources Study No. 14, Illinois Historic Preservation Agency, Springfield.

Jennings, Francis 1993 *The Founders of America*. W. W. Norton, New York and London.

Kehoe, Alice Beck 1998 *Land of Prehistory: A Critical History of American Archaeology*. Routledge, New York and London.

Keller, Kenneth, John E. Kelly, and Charles Witty 1994 Cahokia's Western Periphery: Recent Investigations on the Fingerhut Tract. Paper presented at the joint Southeastern Archaeological and Midwest Archaeological Conferences, Lexington, KY.

Kelly, John E. 1980 Formative Developments at Cahokia and the Adjacent American Bottom: A Merrell Tract Perspective. Unpublished Ph.D. Dissertation, Department of Anthropology, University of Wisconsin, Madison.

1984 Late Bluff Chert Utilization on the Merrell Tract, Cahokia. In *Prehistoric Chert Exploitation: Studies from the Midcontinent*, edited by Brian Butler and Ernest E. May, pp. 23–44. Occasional Papers 2, Center for Archaeological Investigations, Southern Illinois University, Carbondale.

1990a The Range Site Community Patterns and the Mississippian Emergence. In *The Mississippian Emergence*, edited by Bruce Smith, pp. 67–112. Smithsonian Institution Press, Washington, DC.

1990b The Emergence of Mississippian Culture in the American Bottom Region. In *The Mississippian Emergence*, edited by Bruce Smith, pp. 113–152. Smithsonian Institution Press, Washington, DC.

1992 The Impact of Maize on the Development of Nucleated Settlements: An American Bottom Example. In *Late Prehistoric Agriculture: Observations from the Midwest*, edited by William I. Woods, pp. 167–197. Studies in Illinois Archaeology No. 8, Illinois Historic Preservation Agency, Springfield.

1996a Redefining Cahokia: Principles and elements of community Organization. *Wisconsin Archeologist* 6:97–119.

1996b "The Realm of Public Architecture at Cahokia: The Context of the Merrell Tract 'Monuments.'" Paper presented at the 41st Annual Meeting of the Midwest Archaeological Conference, Beloit, Wisconsin.

1996c The Public Architecture on the Merrell Tract, Cahokia. Report submitted to the Cahokia Mounds Museum Society, Collinsville, IL. Central Mississippi Valley Archaeological Research Institute, Columbia, IL.

2000 The nature and context of emergent Mississippian cultural dynamics in the greater American Bottom. In *Late Woodland Societies: Tradition and Transformation across the Midcontinent*, edited by T. E. Emerson, D. L. McElrath, and A. C. Fortier, pp. 163–175. University of Nebraska Press, Lincoln.

2001 The Historical and Distributional Significance of Wells Incised Plates. Paper presented in the Symposium, The Moorehead Phase Revisited: The Historical Context of Cahokia's Second Climax, organized by John E. Kelly, James A. Brown, and Mary Beth Trubitt at the 58th Annual Meeting of the Southeastern Archaeological Conference, Chattanooga, TN.

2002 Woodland Archaeology in the American Bottom. In *The Woodland Southeast*, edited by David G. Anderson and Robert C. Mainfort, Jr., pp. 134–161. University of Alabama Press, Tuscaloosa.

2006 The Ritualization of Cahokia: The Structure and Organization of Early Cahokia Crafts. In *Leadership and Polity in Mississippian Society* edited by B. M. Butler and P. D. Welch, pp. 236–263. Center for Archaeological Investigations Occasional Paper No. 33. Southern Illinois University, Carbondale.

2008a An Historical Perspective on the Big-bang: Who Lit the Fuse. Paper presented at the 54th Annual Meeting of the Midwest Archaeological Conference, Milwaukee, WI.

2008b Contemplating Cahokia's Collapse. In *Global Perspectives on the Collapse of Complex Systems*, edited by Jim A. Railey and Richard Martin Reycraft, pp. 147–169. Anthropological Papers No. 8, Maxwell Museum of Anthropology, Albuquerque, NM.

2008c Negotiating Place and Space: The Founding of Cahokia. Paper presented at the 2008 Cahokia Conference, Cahokia Mounds State Historic Site, Collinsville, IL.

2011 The Geological and Cultural Contexts of Basalt from Late Emergent Mississippian and Early Mississippian Sites in the St. Louis Region. *Missouri Archaeologist* 71:199–216.

2012 Contextualizing Cahokia's East Plaza: the 2012 Fieldwork. Paper presented at the 58th Annual Meeting of the Midwest Archaeological Conference, East Lansing, Michigan.

Kelly, John E. and Brad Koldehoff 1996 The Nature and Context of the Mississippian Occupation on Cahokia's Western Periphery: The Fingerhut and Powell Tracts. Paper presented at the 17th Annual Midsouth Archaeological Conference, Memphis, TN.

Kelly, John E., Gayle Fritz, Bonnie Gums, and William Gartner 2001 The 1991 Test Excavations at Mound 1, Cahokia, 11-Ms-2/9. Report submitted to the Illinois Historic Preservation Agency, March 15, 2001. Copies available from the Illinois Historic Preservation [Agency], Springfield.

Kelly, John E. and James A. Brown 2001 The University of Michigan Investigations in the American Bottom and Cahokia. Paper presented in the symposium, An American Bottom Odyssey at the 47th Annual Meeting of the Midwest Archaeological Conference, La Crosse, WI.

2012 Assessing the Impact of the Ramey Plaza and Its Creation on the Cahokian Landscape. Paper presented at the Society for American Archaeology 77th Annual Meeting, Memphis, TN.

Kelly, John E., James A. Brown, Jenna M. Hamlin, Lucretia S. Kelly, Laura Kozuch, Kathryn Parker, and Juliann VanNest 2007a Mound 34: The Context for the Early Evidence of the Southeastern Ceremonial Complex. In *Southeastern Ceremonial Complex: Chronology, Iconography, and Meaning*, edited by Adam King, pp. 57–87. University of Alabama Press, Tuscaloosa.

Kelly, John E., Steven J. Ozuk, and Joyce A. Williams 2007c *The Range Site: The Emergent Mississippian, George Reeves and Lindeman Phase Components*. Illinois Transportation Archaeological Research Program, Transportation Archaeological Research Reports 18. University of Illinois, Urbana-Champaign.

Kelly, John E, TR Kidder, and Timothy Schilling 2007b Preliminary Results of the 2007 Investigations at Monks Mound, Cahokia. Paper presented at the Annual Meeting of the Illinois Archaeological Survey, Carbondale.

Kelly, Lucretia S. 2000 Social Implications of Faunal Provisioning of the Cahokia Site: Initial Mississippian, Lohmann Phase. Unpublished Ph.D. Dissertation, Department of Anthropology, Washington University, St. Louis, MO.

2001 A Case of Ritual Feasting at the Cahokia Site. In *Feasts: Archaeological and Ethnographic Perspectives on Food, Politics, and Power*, edited by Michael Dietler and Brian Hayden, pp. 334–367. Smithsonian Institution Press, Washington, DC.

Kennedy, Roger G. 1994 *Hidden Cities: The Discovery and Loss of Ancient North American Civilization*. The Free Press, New York.

King, Adam 2007a The Southeastern Ceremonial Complex: From Cult to Complex. In *Southeastern Ceremonial Complex: Chronology, Iconography, and Meaning*, edited by Adam King, pp. 1–14. University of Alabama Press, Tuscaloosa.

2007b Whether SECC? In *Southeastern Ceremonial Complex: Chronology, Iconography, and Meaning*, edited by Adam King, pp. 251–258. University of Alabama Press, Tuscaloosa.

Knight, Vernon J. 1998 Moundville as a Diagrammatic Ceremonial Center. In *Archaeology of the Moundville Chiefdom*, edited by Vernon James Knight and Vincas Steponaitis, pp. 44–62. Smithsonian Institution Press, Washington, DC.

Knight, Vernon J. and Vincas Steponaitis (editors) 1998 *Archaeology of the Moundville Chiefdom*. Smithsonian Institution Press, Washington, DC.

Koldehoff, Brad and Tamira Brennan 2011 Exploring Mississippian Polity Interaction and Craft Specialization with Ozarks Chipped-Stone Resources. *Missouri Archaeologist* 71:131–164.

Köngäs, Elli Kaija 1960 The Earth-Diver (Th. A 812). *Ethnohistory* 7(2):151–180.

Lankford, George E. 2007 Some Cosmological Motifs in the Southeastern Ceremonial Complex. In *Ancient Objects and Sacred Realms: Interpretations of Mississippian Iconography*, edited by F. Kent Reilly III and James F. Garber, pp. 8–38. University of Texas Press, Austin.

Lewis, R. Barry, Charles Stout, and Cameron B. Wesson 1998 The Design of Mississippian Towns. *Mississippian Towns and Sacred Spaces: Searching for An Architectural Grammar*, edited by R. Barry Lewis and Charles Stout, pp. 1–21. University of Alabama Press, Tuscaloosa.

Marcus, J. and J. A. Sabloff (editors) 2008 *The Ancient City: New Perspectives on Urbanism in the Old and New World*. School for Advanced Research Resident Scholar Book, Santa Fe, NM.

McIntosh, Roderick J. 1991 Early Urban Clusters in China and Africa: the Arbitration of Social Ambiguity. *Journal of Field Archaeology* 18:199–212.

2005 *Ancient Middle Niger: Urbanism and the Self-Organizing Landscape*. Cambridge University Press, Cambridge.

Mehrer, Mark W. 1995 *Cahokia's Countryside: Household Archaeology, Settlement Patterns, and Social Power*. Northern Illinois University Press, DeKalb.

Mehrer, Mark W. and James M. Collins 1995 Household Archaeology at Cahokia and Its Hinterlands. In *Mississippian Communities and Households*, edited by J. Daniel Rogers and Bruce D. Smith, pp. 32–57. University of Alabama Press, Tuscaloosa.

Milner, George R. 1986 Mississippian period population density in a segment of the central Mississippi River valley. *American Antiquity* 51:227–238.

2006 *The Cahokia Chiefdom: The Archaeology of a Mississippian Society*. University of Alabama Press, Tuscaloosa.

Milner, George R., Thomas E. Emerson, Mark W. Mehrer, Joyce A. Williams, and Duane Esarey 1984 Mississippian and Oneota Period. In *American*

Bottom Archaeology, edited by Charles J. Bareis and James W. Porter, pp. 158–186. University of Illinois Press, Urbana.

Mink, Claudia Gellman 1999 *Cahokia: City of the Sun*. Cahokia Mounds Museum Society, Collinsville, IL.

Moorehead, Warren K. 1929 The Cahokia Mounds: Part I; Explorations of 1922, 1923, 1924, and 1927 in the Cahokia Mounds. *University of Illinois Bulletin* 26(4):7–106.

Morgan, William N. 1980 *Prehistoric Architecture in the Eastern United States*. Massachusetts Institute of Technology Press, Cambridge, MA.

O'Brien, Patricia J. 1972 Urbanism, Cahokia, and Middle Mississippian. *Archaeology* 25:189–197.

1989 Cahokia: The Political Capital of the "Ramey" State? *North American Archaeologist* 10(4):188–197.

1992 "World-System" of Cahokia within the Middle Mississippian Tradition. *Review (Fernand Braudel Center for the Study of Economies, Historical Systems, and Civilizations)* 15(3):389–417.

O'Shea, John M, and John Ludwickson 1992 *Archaeology and ethnohistory of the Omaha Indians: the Big Village site*. University of Nebraska Press, Lincoln.

Pauketat, Timothy R. 1993 *Temples for Cahokian Lords: Preston Holder's 1955–1956 Excavations of Kunnemann Mound*. Memoir 26. Museum of Anthropology, University of Michigan, Ann Arbor.

1998 *The Archaeology of Downtown Cahokia: The Tract 15A and Dunham Tract Excavations*. Studies in Archaeology I. Illinois Transportation Archaeological Research Program, Urbana.

2003 Resettled Farmers and the Making of a Mississippian Polity. *American Antiquity* 68(1):39–66.

2004 *Ancient Cahokia and the Mississippians*. Cambridge University Press, Cambridge.

2007 *Chiefdoms and Other Archaeological Delusions*. AltaMira Press, Lanham, MD.

2009 *Cahokia: Ancient America's Great City on the Mississippi*. Viking, New York.

Pauketat, Timothy R. and Alex W. Barker 2000 Mounds 65 and 66 at Cahokia: Additional Details of the 1927 Excavations. In *Mounds, Modoc and Mesoamerica, Papers in Honor of Melvin L. Fowler*, edited by Steven R. Ahler, pp. 125–140. Illinois State Museum Scientific Papers, Vol. XXVIII, Illinois State Museum, Springfield.

Pauketat, Timothy R. and Diana DiPaola Loren 2005 Alternative Histories and North American Archaeology. In *North American Archaeology*, edited by Timothy R. Pauketat and Diana DiPaola Loren, pp. 1–29. Blackwell, Malden, MA.

Pauketat, Timothy R. and Neil H. Lopinot 1997 Cahokian Population Dynamics. In *Cahokia: Domination and Ideology in the Mississippian World*, edited by Timothy R. Pauketat and Thomas E. Emerson, pp. 103–123. University of Nebraska Press, Lincoln.

Pauketat, Timothy R., Lucretia S. Kelly, Gayle J. Fritz, Neal H. Lopinot, Scott Elias, and Eve Hargarve 2002 Ritual Refuse from Cahokia. *American Antiquity*, 67(2):257–279.

Pauketat, Timothy R. and Mark A. Rees 1996 *Early Cahokia Project: 1994 Excavations at Mound 49, Cahokia (11-S-34–2)*. Report Submitted to the

Illinois Historic Preservation Agency. Copies available from the Illinois Historic Preservation Agency, Springfield.

Pauketat, Timothy R., Mark A. Rees, Amber M. Vanderwarker, and Kathryn E. Parker 2010 Excavations into Cahokia's Mound 49. *Illinois Archaeology* 22 (2):397–436.

Pauketat, Timothy R., Mark A. Rees, and Stephanie L. Pauketat 1998 An Archaeological Survey of the Horseshoe Lake State Park, Madison County, Illinois. *Illinois State Museum, Reports of Investigations, No. 55.* Illinois State Museum, Springfield.

Pfeiffer, John 1973 Indian City on the Mississippi. *1974 Nature/Science Annual,* Time-Life Books, New York.

1974 America's First City. *Horizon* 16(2):58–63.

Pred, Allan 1984 Place as Historically Contingent Process: Structuration and the Time-Geography of Becoming Places. *Annals of the Association of American Geographers* 74(2):279–297.

Reed, Nelson A. 2009 Excavations on the Third Terrace and Front Ramp of Monks Mound, Cahokia: A Personal Narrative. *Illinois Archaeology* 21:1–89.

Reilly, R. Kent 2004 People of Earth, People of Sky: Visualizing the Sacred in Native American Art of the Mississippian Period. In *The Hero, Hawk, and the Open Hand: American Indian Art of the Ancient Midwest and South,* edited by Richard Townsend and Robert V. Sharp, pp. 104–123. Art Institute of Chicago, Chicago.

Ridington, Robin and Dennis Hastings (In'aska) 1997 *Blessing for a Long Time: The Sacred Pole of the Omaha Tribe.* University of Nebraska Press, Lincoln.

Rolingson, Martha A. 1996 Elements of Community Design at Cahokia. In *The Ancient Skies and Sky Watchers of Cahokia: Woodhenges, Eclipses, and Cahokian Cosmology,* edited by Melvin Fowler. *The Wisconsin Archeologist* 77(3/4):84–96.

Saitta, Dean 1994 Agency, Class, and Archaeological Interpretation. *Journal of Anthropological Archaeology* 13:201–227.

Salzer, Robert J. and Grace Rajnovich 2001 *The Gottschall Rockshelter: An Archaeological Mystery.* Prairie Smoke, St. Paul, MN.

Schilling, Timothy 2010 An Archaeological Model of the Construction of Monks Mound and Implications for the Development of Cahokian Society. Unpublished Ph.D. Dissertation, Department of Anthropology, Washington University, St. Louis.

Schroeder, Sissel 1999 Maize Productivity in the Eastern Woodlands and Great Plains of North America. *American Antiquity* 64:499–516.

2004 Power and Place: Agency, Ecology, and History in the American Bottom, Illinois. *Antiquity* 78: 812–827.

Sewell, William H., Jr. 2005 *Logics of History: Social Theory and Social Transformation.* University of Chicago Press, Chicago.

Sherrod, P. Clay and Martha A. Rolingson 1987 *Surveyors of the Ancient Mississippi Valley: Modules and Alignments in Prehistoric Mound Sites.* Research Series, no. 28. Arkansas Archeological Survey, Fayetteville.

Smith, Harriet 1973 The Murdock Mound, Cahokia Site. In *Explorations into Cahokia Archaeology,* edited by M. L. Fowler, pp. 49–99. Bulletin 7, Illinois Archaeological Survey, University of Illinois, Urbana.

Smith, Michael E. 2002 The Earliest Cities. In *Urban Life: Readings in the Anthropology of the City*, edited by George Gmelch and Walter P. Zenner, pp. 3–19. Waveland Press, Prospect Heights, IL.

2007 Form and Meaning in the Earliest Cities: A New Approach to Ancient Urban Planning. *Journal of Planning History* 6:3–47.

Smith, Monica L. (editor) 2003 *The Social Construction of Ancient Cities*. Smithsonian Books, Washington, DC.

Stephenson, F Richard 2002 *Historical supernovae and their remnants*. Oxford University Press, Oxford.

Swagerty, William R. 2000 Urban Indians before Columbus. *Journal of Urban History* 26:493–507.

Swanton, John R. 1931 Modern Square Grounds of the Creek Indians. *Smithsonian Miscellaneous Collections* 85(8): 1–46.

Trubitt, Mary Beth D. 2000 Mound Building and Prestige Goods Exchange: Changing Strategies in the Cahokian Chiefdom. *American Antiquity* 65:669–690.

2003 Mississippian Period Warfare and Palisade Construction at Cahokia. In *Theory, Method, and Practice in Modern Archaeology*, edited by Robert J. Jeske and Douglas K. Charles, pp. 149–162. Praeger, London and Westport, CT.

Valese, Immacolata 2012 Settlement Dynamics and Use of Space in the Mississippian World, an Analysis of Cahokia's Tract 15B and West Plaza (Illinois, USA), MA Thesis, Department of Archaeology, University of Bologna, Italy.

Vander Leest, Barbara J. 1980 The Ramey Field, Cahokia Surface Collection: A Functional Analysis of Spatial Structure. Unpublished Ph.D. Dissertation, Department of Anthropology, University of Wisconsin, Milwaukee.

Vermilion, Mary R. 2005 The Loyd Site (11 MS 74): A Prehistoric Moorehead Phase Nodal Site (Illinois). Unpublished Ph.D. Dissertation, Department of Anthropology, University of Illinois, Chicago.

Vogel, Joseph O. 1975 Trends in Cahokia Ceramics: Preliminary Study of the Collections from Tracts 15A and 15B. *Illinois Archaeological Survey Bulletin* 10:32–125.

Waring, Antonio J. 1968 The Southern Cult and Muskhogean Ceremonial. In *The Waring Papers, The Collected Works of Antonio J. Waring, Jr.*, edited by Stephen Williams, pp. 30–69. Papers of the Peabody Museum of Archaeology and Ethnology, Harvard University, Vol. 58, Cambridge, MA.

Welch, Paul D. 2004 How Early Were Cities in the Eastern United States? *Journal of Urban History* 30:594–604.

Welsch, Roger L. 1981 *Omaha tribal myths and trickster tales*. Sage Books, Chicago.

Willey, Gordon R. 1953 A Pattern of Diffusion-Acculturation. *Southwest Journal of Anthropology* 9:369–384.

Wittry, Warren L. and Joseph O. Vogel 1962 Illinois State Museum Projects: October 1961 to June 1962. In *First Annual Report: American Bottoms Archaeology, July 1, 1961–June 30, 1962*, edited by M. L. Fowler, pp. 15–30. Illinois Archaeological Survey, University of Illinois, Urbana.

Woods, William I. 1987 Maize and the late prehistoric: A characterization of settlement location strategies. In *Emergent Horticultural Economies of the Eastern Woodlands*, edited by W. F. Keegan, pp. 273–292. Occasional Paper No. 7. Center for Archaeological Investigations, Southern Illinois University, Carbondale.

2004 Population Nucleation, Intensive Agriculture, and Environmental Degradation: The Cahokia Example. *Agriculture and Human Values* 21(2/3):255–261.

Young, Biloine Whiting and Melvin Fowler 2000 *Cahokia, the Great Native American Metropolis*. University of Illinois, Champaign.

10

Comparing East and West: Aspects of Urban Manufacture and Retail in the Capitals of the Roman and Han Empires

Anna Razeto

This chapter explores the archaeological and literary evidence for marketplaces and urban forms connected to the manufacturing of bricks and metalworking in the capital cities of the contemporary empires of Rome and Han China (ca. 200 BC–200 AD). A comparative analysis of the physical aspects of these urban structures informs a discussion of the impact of the political, practical, ideological, and economic circumstances of the two empires on the distribution and features of the architecture and industries presented. This highlights the extent to which the urban architecture of the capitals was involved in the social and political processes that characterized the production of space in these cities.

This chapter presents a comparison of urban structures connected to the economy of the Roman and Han empires within their capital cities during the first two centuries BC and AD. During this period, Rome and China became the world's largest agrarian empires, and their capital cities were shaped for the first time by the urban elites to be symbols of the power of their relatively newly formed political systems. In 210 BC, the Western Han Dynasty took control of the Chinese territories conquered by the Qin Dynasty and created an empire that lasted until the advent of the Republic in AD 1911. In the Han period, the Chinese created a new and stable urban form representative of not only a state, but of an entire universe: the imperial capital. Simultaneously, the Han imperial ideology came to focus on the notion of the emperor as the center of the world and the link between heaven, earth, and humans. By that time in the West, the city of Rome had become the capital of a powerful Republic engaged in active territorial expansion, and its urban features had undergone the modifications necessary to transform it into the new imperial capital. Thus, it was during the same broad period, and particularly in the first centuries BC and AD, that the two capitals of Rome and Chang'an acted as theaters for the transformation of imperial ideologies and religious beliefs, which were tightly connected to the alteration of their political institutions. These changes were expressed in the material forms of the capitals, the design of city buildings, and in the location of structures within the urban landscape.

Control is a critical element that must be considered when discussing different levels of spatial production in ancient cities. In this context, control references both the ownership of land on which architecture is built and control of activities within the property. The Han Empire had a strong autonomous and absolutist character, with a strictly stratified society that showed continuous interweaving of political and administrative urban hierarchies, as well as a lack of distinct religious elites (Eisenstadt and Shachar 1987:126). Social classes were mainly determined by literary-political criteria of status definition, where the class of scholars was considered superior to those of farmers, artisans, and merchants (Ch'ü 1972:64–66, 84–88).

Considering this simplified characterization of the sociopolitical structure of the Han period, it is possible to infer that the ruling elites – composed of emperor, literati, and officials – were firmly in control of the utilization of urban land, regardless of whether or not they personally owned the property. The social and political structure of the Roman Empire was also characterized by hierarchical criteria such as social ranking classified by wealth (with senatorial and equestrian ranks at the top of the scale [Suetonius 1914a:15]), ancestry (or the division between patricians and the rest of the population – the plebeians [Livy 1919:1.8]), and the degree of citizenship possessed (Nicolet 1980). The social classification of Rome allowed room for social mobility, mainly through loss or gain of wealth and through career progression, resulting in a ruling class that was relatively fluid in its composition. It follows that, in contrast to the Han situation, the sociopolitical scene of Rome was characterized by a plurality of actors, which could influence the control over the land and the production of space, according to a combination of their own interests and those of the *res publica*.

The distinctiveness of the political and administrative systems of the two empires was ultimately reflected in the construction of their cities, and of their capitals in particular. The center of Rome, as well as of minor Roman cities, had always contained the forum, which initially served as a democratic symbol of the interests of the citizens, the locus of economic activities as well as social and political meetings, and the site of the main religious and civic buildings. In contrast, the urban space of the Chinese capital was arranged around a walled enclosure within which could be found the palace, administration, and court of the emperor (who was, by the Han period, considered ruler of the world and keystone of the universe), or at least his provincial representative. Within the city, political and economic activities appear to have been physically separated (Lewis 2006:151–152). Because common people in ancient China received no civil rights and did not take part in public religious or political affairs, a city had no need for an open center for social, political, and economic activity like the Roman forum. It follows that the production of space in Rome appears to have been driven by a combination of top-down and mid-level dynamics, in which the impact of the middle levels of society was comparatively low, but still discernible, whereas the evidence for Chang'an shows a mostly top-down process. During the transition from Republic to Principate, the production of space in the Roman capital shifted from operating at multiple levels (reflecting the plurality of sponsors constituting the top part of the Republican society) toward a concentration in the interests of the emperor. Such differences in the social drive for the production of space seem to reinforce the impression of an indissoluble link between imperialism, society, and the urban landscape that can also be observed in relation to the urban structures connected to the economy of the capitals, on which this study mainly focuses.

SOURCES

This chapter presents data from literary and archaeological sources relating to Rome and Chang'an, all of which need to be taken into account in a critical manner to provide a broader perspective on urban life in the ancient world. In highly bureaucratized empires like Han China and Rome, texts were deeply connected to the political and ideological activities of the central authorities. Chinese traditional historiography, in particular, has been explicitly and continuously produced for millennia by officials employed by the governments of successive dynasties, who created historical records combining primary and secondary sources with the aim of consolidating the legality of the status of a dynasty through the creation of moralizing accounts of past events (Mittag 2008:143; von Falkenhausen

1993:839; Wang 2000:17; Wilkinson 2000:483, 490–491). Although archaeological evidence provides a different perspective on past social, cultural, and economic conditions, it is now widely acknowledged that the remains of the past are not value-free either, as their interpretation can significantly rely on the modern social, political, and economic context within which archaeologists necessarily operate (Shanks and Tilley 1987a, 1987b; Watson 1990). Textual evidence relating to the economic structures of Rome selected for this study derives mainly from epigraphic inscriptions and from the works of Roman scholars, poets, and jurists, who sometimes referred to the existence of particular economic establishments in the capital.

The main written sources discussing economic and social conditions under the Han dynasties are official dynastic histories such as *Shi Ji (Records of the Grand Historian)*, *Han Shu (Book of Han)*, and *Hou Han Shu (Book of Later Han)*. Information on state monopolies also derives from *Yan Tie Lun (The Discourses on Salt and Iron)*, a compilation addressing themes from a political debate on state economic policies concerning the salt and iron industries, which took place in 81 BC.[1] These texts mainly offer information of general economic character, with rare references to the urban structures of the capitals. Archaeological excavations of workshops in Chang'an carried out in the 1990s, and in Rome, have also been of critical importance in the analysis of the distribution of productive and redistributive urban structures presented in this chapter.

METHODOLOGY

Significant similarities noted during the period under examination have singled out the Han and Roman Empires and their capitals as ideal cases for an intensive comparative analysis characterized by a high level of contextualization. In addition, the Han and Roman Empires displayed sufficient diversity in their cultural and sociopolitical contexts to allow for a more vibrant investigation of the connections between their specific circumstances and the material structures of the selected cities.

The scale of comparison considered in this study comprises three levels: two empires represent the broad units of the analysis, two cities constitute the medium-scale elements, and several specific urban features make up its small-scale components. At the broadest scale, the study is carried out in a more general and abstract manner in the context of the ideological, sociopolitical, and cultural specifics of the two empires, whereas at the smallest scale of investigation, the individual structures of the capitals are analyzed in a detailed and concrete manner. At the medium level of the capitals of Rome and Chang'an, the analysis is supported by a combination of less-abstract theories tailored to the study of urbanism that Smith calls "empirical urban theories" (2011), which will principally make use of a combination of theoretical approaches consisting of urban morphology (or morphogenesis), normative urban theory, and architectural communication. On one hand, the combination of urban morphology and normative urban theory provides a structure for investigating the general characteristics of a city as seen in its entirety, in relation to the form of its ground plan and its historical transformations, its internal layout, as well as its visual aspects and functions. On the other hand, architectural communication theories help to understand how certain features of the individual urban elements chosen for the comparison – namely, their scale, design, and location in relation to the existing urban environment – can be read as a projection of ideological and propagandistic messages (Favro 1993). The materialization of ideologies in the urban environment can be achieved through different mechanisms, such as topographical associations triggered through physical proximity to other structures, or through the more-or-less explicit symbolic character of design elements, which depend on the cultural traditions and context of the societies to which they pertain (Rapoport 1990). Through these different but complementary levels of analysis, the present comparative research will not only uncover similarities and differences in the economic structures of the Roman and Han capital cities, but it will also reveal unique aspects of the relationship between imperialism and urban form that would be difficult to detect when considering each context in isolation.

On the basis of the methodological framework thus presented, this chapter explores some retail and production structures in Rome and Chang'an, basing the analysis on the assumption that the economies of both empires showed high levels of commercialization, with abundant circulation of coin (Scheidel 2009), competitive markets, and precocious means of mass production (Barbieri-Low 2007). Trading in the capitals was undertaken at varying scales of activity and in different types of structures: private and state controlled or owned. Manufacturing was also carried out as private and state-controlled production. The extent to which each of these levels of activity was represented inside the confines of a city, and in what ways the location and morphology of their structures could be seen as a reflection of the social, political, and economic organization of their empires, is not yet clear. In view of this, data relating to the permanent architecture of marketplaces and to establishments connected to brickwork and metal production, which constituted important and profitable sectors of the specifically urban aspects of the economies of Rome and Han China, have been selected for analysis. Textual and archaeological data are discussed in relation to the morphology and scale of the buildings and their location in the urban environment in order to determine how different levels of state and private involvement are reflected in the architectural features and in the spatial relationship the markets and workshops had with the urban fabric. The selected elements and their dimensions of analysis will help bring into focus different levels of urban production in the ancient world, particularly private and state managed, as well as the degree of state control exercised not just over the city structures dedicated to manufacturing and retailing, but also over the distribution of finished products.

GENERAL LAYOUT, DISTRIBUTION, AND SCALE OF RETAIL AND MANUFACTURE STRUCTURES

An analysis of the morphology, location, and scale of the surviving evidence for markets and production establishments in Rome and Chang'an can be indicative of the extent to which different kinds of structures were present in the urban contexts of the two imperial capitals. Moreover, these categories can also show the influence that state policies, ideologies, and different traditions of urbanism had on the various forms of architecture dedicated to retail. Although permanent marketplaces and shops were not the only structures dedicated to commerce in the two empires, the archaeological and literary evidence for other types of architecture – such as Roman basilicas, porticoes, areas dedicated to auctions, and temporary markets – is not of comparable quality and quantity for both empires, making it impossible to analyze those features here in a convincing manner.

Markets

Permanent marketplaces were among the most important structures for the exchange and redistribution of goods in preindustrial societies and as such, they were often imposing government-built structures subjected to a high level of state control (cf. Magnoni et al., Chapter 5 in this volume). This is especially true for the markets of Chang'an. Literary sources indicate that Chang'an had nine major markets (Ban Gu, *Liang Du Fu [Rhapsody on The Two Capitals]*; Zhang Heng, *Xi Du Fu [Rhapsody on The Western Capital]*), although in Chinese tradition, the word nine might have simply been used as a general number meaning numerous markets. Some of these markets may have been situated to the northwest of the capital because several satellite towns were located in that direction, but others could have been found near key buildings (Barbieri-Low 2007:124; Sahara 1985; Zhou 2001:172–190). Inside Chang'an, there were three markets: the East Market, the West Market, and the Xiaoli Market. The location and identification of the remains of the markets of Chang'an, among other issues related to the layout of the Western Han capital, have been long debated by Yang Kuan and Liu Qingzhu (see Liu [1992:632, 640, 2000:152–176] and Yang [1984, 1989, 1993a, 1993b] for a full discussion). Liu identified the East and West Markets with the archaeological remains found inside the inner walls whereas Yang, basing his theory mainly on historical records, indicated their location as being outside the city walls. Liu's identification of the East and West Markets with the structures found inside Chang'an is the most widely accepted theory to date, although the location of the Xiaoli Market is still unclear.

The East Market was the commercial center of the capital, established by the founder of the Western Han Dynasty in 201 BC before the city walls were built, at a time when it was known as *Da Shi*, the Great Market (Sima Qian 1993, *Yearly Table of Statesmen, Generals and Officials since the Han Dynasty's Founding*, Table 10, Volume 22). The markets of the capital were probably larger than those in other cities, and surveys have shown that the East Market was much larger than the western one, occupying an extraordinary area of more than 500,000 m² (Liu 1987:264, 1996, 2003:161; Zhou 2001:174). The West Market, founded in 189 BC after the completion of the city walls, was the manufacturing center and contained workshops and factories of all sizes, the products of which could then be sold in the East Market (Liu 2000:152–161). The West Market occupied an area of more than 250,000 m² (Liu 1987:264). Both markets were located behind the imperial palaces inside the city walls, approximately north and northwest respectively of Bei and Gui Palaces (Figure 10.1).

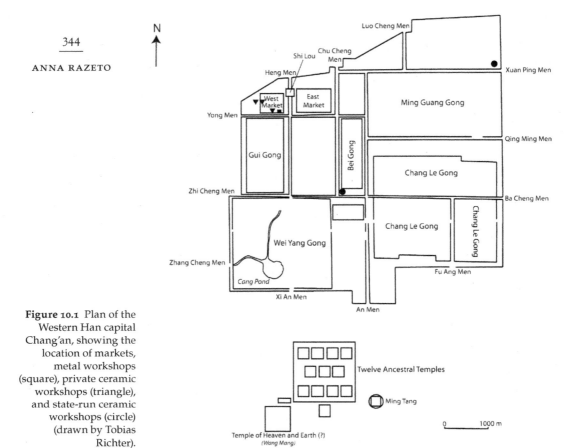

Figure 10.1 Plan of the Western Han capital Chang'an, showing the location of markets, metal workshops (square), private ceramic workshops (triangle), and state-run ceramic workshops (circle) (drawn by Tobias Richter).

These positions seem to have respected the detailed prescriptions for the layout of an ideal city contained in the *Jiang Ren Ying Guo (On Building a Capital City)* section of the *Kao Gong Ji (Record of Trades or Artificers' Record)*, a late Warring States period text substituted in the first century BC for a lost part of the *Zhou Li (Rites of Zhou)*, which is considered to be one of the Chinese historical sources most relevant to the planning of ancient cities.

It is known from archaeological surveys that the East and West Markets of Chang'an had two gates on each side and were crossed by four roads intersecting at right angles, dividing each market into nine sectors, further subdivided into rows of stalls (Liu 2003:161). In every corner of the walls were storage structures, which were among the only buildings in the markets apart from the gates and the *shi lou*, the multistoried administrative building for local government-appointed officers in charge of controlling the trade and levying taxes (Zhou 2001:172–176). Investigations in Chang'an have

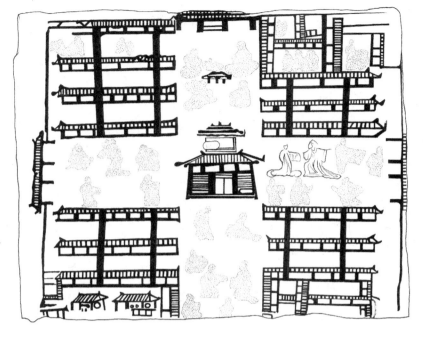

Figure 10.2 Drawing
of impressed brick
found near Chengdu in
Sichuan Province and
representing a market-
place with the central
government building, *shi
lou*, in evidence (drawn
by Guenevere Bjerre
Thaarup).

also recovered the remains of a huge structure between the East and
West Markets, which Liu suggested to be the *shi lou* (Liu 1987:942,
2003:161).

An impressed tomb brick excavated in Sichuan, probably representing the Blue Ram Market of Chengdu (one of the metropo-
lises of the Han period), seems to confirm the information on the
markets of Chang'an derived from texts and archaeological excavations (Figure 10.2). The market depicted on the brick shows walls
surrounding the compound, with gates piercing the walls and two
intersecting roads with three lanes each. In the middle of the crossroads there stands a tower building, the *shi lou*. Evidence from the
Eastern Han capital Luoyang does not further the understanding of
markets of the Han period, as none of its three main commercial
areas have so far been clearly identified or excavated. The problematic situation posed by the markets of Luoyang is somewhat mirrored by the evidence for the marketplaces of Rome.

Literary sources mention that from the sixth century BC onward,
markets in Rome were held on the banks of the Tiber, southwest of
the Roman Forum. There stood the cattle market (*forum boarium*)
and the vegetable market (*forum holitorium*), whereas the main markets for fish and meat (*fora piscarium et cuppedinis*) were held in the
Forum (Ovid 1989:6.295). Gradually, other businesses were located

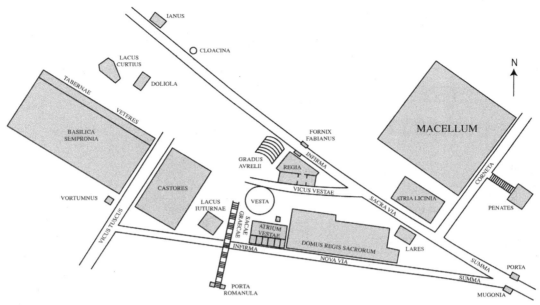

Figure 10.3. Location of the *macellum* in the Roman Forum during the Republican Period (redrawn from Coarelli 1983:33).

nearer the river, and in the Classical period, only money changers, goldsmiths, and jewelers remained in the area of the Forum (Cicero 1988:2.266; Livy 1936: 39.44.7, 1943:26.11, 26.27.2, 1963:9.40.16, 1989a:3.48.5, 1989b:44.16.10). During the third century BC, as the Forum became more monumental and thus less suitable for ordinary domestic shopping, all the commercial activities were concentrated north of it, in an area that seems to have absorbed the initially separated installations of the meat and fish markets, as well as other specialist markets (Figure 10.3).

It is known from Livy that the *forum piscarium* was one of the buildings devastated by a fire that spread in the center of Rome in 210 BC (Livy 1943:26.27.1–3, 1978: 6.17.2). Its reconstruction began in 209 BC, but this time the author, referring to the market structure, mentions a *macellum*, not a *forum* (Livy 1943:27.11.16). A statement from Varro strongly suggests that the new *macellum* integrated the various specialized markets into a centralized provision market, and perhaps the term *macellum* denoted a building, more than just a commercial function (Varro 1958:5.146–147). We can probably assume that the construction of a major, general-provision market building was part of the process of monumentalization of the Forum and its clearer division between civic and commercial roles, which had begun earlier in the Republican period.

Figure 10.4 Schematic map of Rome showing the location of permanent marketplaces (small squares), brick-making workshops (circles), and metal workshops (big squares) (drawn by Alexis Pantos).

It appears that during mid- to late Republican times, only one monumental market building existed in Rome, situated to the north of the Forum, possibly near the Argiletum (Varro 1958:5.145, 152) (Figures 10.3 and 10.4), although it is not clear if this was the same building supposed to replace the one that burned in 210 BC. During the early Principate, a growth in demand for goods distribution led to the construction of two new *macella* in Rome, of which very little remains. The *Macellum Liviae*, situated just outside the Esquiline Gate (Figure 10.4), consisted of a vast rectangle with remains of a fountain and drainage system in the center; the structure was surrounded by arcades behind which shops opened on at least three sides. These remains were discovered in the late nineteenth century and there is no real evidence to suggest when or under whose orders

348

ANNA RAZETO

Figure 10.5 Replica of
dupondius with depiction
of *Macellum Augusti*,
minted under Nero
(photo by Anna Razeto).

2 cm

the building was constructed (although its name might indicate that it was a state construction [Richardson 1992:241]).

The *Macellum Augusti*, or *Macellum Magnum*, was located on the Caelian Hill and dedicated by Nero in AD 59 (Cassius Dio 1927:62.18.3; Robinson 1992:131) (Figure 10.4). Its layout might be connected to a fragment of the *Forma Urbis Romae*, a marble map carved between AD 203 and 211, which depicted the plan of every architectural feature in the ancient city. The *Macellum* consisted of a rectangular area surrounded by arcades; the internal court was enclosed by two rows of shops and the remains of a curved colonnade point to the existence of a *tholos* element, as can be seen from epigraphic and numismatic evidence (*Corpus Inscriptionum Latinarum* 1876-2001: VI:1648, 9183; Fuchs 1969:46, figures 133–136; Mattingly 1923:1, nos. 191–197, 335–337, plate 43, nos. 5, 6, 7; Rainbird, Sear and Simpson 1971:40–46) (Figure 10.5).

At the end of the first century and beginning of the second century AD, the complex now called the Markets of Trajan was built (Amici 1982; Pensabene et al. 1989). Its creation furthered the process of removing from the Roman Forum and its surrounding area the business activity considered inappropriate to its new dignity as the official center of the empire. The markets formed an integral part of the new Forum of Trajan, apparently occupying its back end (Meneghini 2010; Packer 1997), and served multiple needs, from storage and distribution of commodities to retail business and administration (Bianchini 1991, 1992; Meneghini 1990, 2003, 2010) (Figure 10.6). In terms of layout, the markets were arranged on three floors, designed to conceal the scar left by cutting away the hillside (Sear 1982:160–164). Remains of the big hemicycle of shops echoing the eastern exedra of the forum consist of eleven commercial spaces carved out of the hillside; on the second floor, a barrel-vaulted corridor gives access to ten additional shops

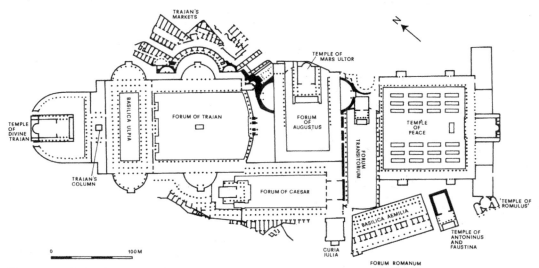

Figure 10.6 General site plan of the Imperial Fora with the Markets of Trajan highlighted (from Patterson 1992:208, figure 4).

(Coarelli 2008:121–125). The top floor was most probably a promenade gallery; shops on this level do not open on the forum, but on the Via Biberatica behind. Another building opposite the hemicycle shows groups of rooms of different sizes, probably used for the administration of the complex or as warehouses. Although their architectural arrangement was impressive, the markets were not significantly different from the shop facilities built onto the sides of the earlier fora.

Marketplaces in Rome and Chang'an seem to have represented a focal point for the urban population to mingle and socialize, as well as shop. These structures often united within their boundaries many smaller commercial premises, creating the impression of spaces more similar to modern, planned shopping centers than to any of the many ancient traditional-market structures. Although they do not appear to have been very similar in terms of aspect, mainly owing to very different architectural traditions, marketplaces in the two capitals represented the physical embodiment of the involvement of the state in their economic lives. This was evident on a visual and physical level through the use of imposing architectural forms symbolic of control over trade, but also on a legal level through the regulation of prices, measurements, and schedules. Roman and Chinese marketplaces appear to have also housed productive activities in their numerous shops and workshops. However, these permanent structures were not the only areas where commercial and manufacturing units could be found in the capitals (and other cities) of the two empires.

Production Establishments

The shops and workshops of a Roman town, also known as *tabernae*, were ubiquitous features, unavoidable by all but the richest inhabitants (Varro 1958:5.160; Laurence 1994), as attested by their frequency on the fragmentary evidence for the capital provided by the *Forma Urbis Romae* (MacDonald 1986:122; McKay 1975:77; Packer 1967:81; Purcell 1994:661). In Han towns, the situation depicted by literary sources appears to have been considerably different. As already discussed, according to the prescriptions of the *Kao Gong Ji*, markets in the ideal city were to be located at the back of the palace, within the outer walls. Most scholars suggest that, owing to the high level of state control over trade and production, from the Warring States period (circa 475–221 BC) until the Song Dynasty (AD 960–1279) all shops and the vast majority of workshops were placed inside the market wards (Sadao 1986:575–576). This view is challenged by more recent excavations in Chang'an, where certain types of private, as well as state-run workshops, have been found in other areas of the city, as in the case of brick-making facilities (Han City Archaeological Team 1996). On a morphological level, the basic form of the workshop/shop structure in Chinese and Roman cities was very comparable; a versatile walled space of various dimensions with an opening on a road from which to attract customers, provide ventilation, and facilitate transportation of goods (Barbieri-Low 2007:68, 276; Frasca 1994:246; Livy 1919:1.35.10; Luoyang Museum 1975:116–124, 134). Whether the road it opened onto was situated inside a market ward or in the open center of town seems to constitute the main difference. Workshops relying on more specialized productive techniques, like ceramic or metal working, necessitated the presence of specific instruments and installations such as kilns and furnaces. Because of this, the remains of such production establishments can be more readily identified, as I will now discuss in more detail.

BRICK MANUFACTURE

According to Chinese traditional beliefs, wood was the appropriate element for the edification of all buildings intended for the use of the living, but their foundations were made of tamped earth and tiles were used to cover the roofs (Needham 1962:61, 65). Apart from wood, bricks and tiles were the basic construction materials in China during the early dynasties. Although the creation of the new capital city of Chang'an by the first Han emperor, Gaozu, accelerated the development of the brick- and tile-making industry, masonry and brickwork in Han architecture were still confined to those elements that did not come into contact with the space inhabited or utilized by the living (Needham 1962:61, 65). Tombs, walls, defensive features, and terraces were therefore the only structures for which stones and ceramic building material were utilized. During the Han period, large molded, hollow, terracotta slabs depicting scenes of daily life or abstract patterns were also produced alongside ordinary fired bricks. They were mainly used as decoration in tombs. In the Warring States period, bricks were mostly made out of sun-dried mud, but under Han rule, the fired variety became more common. During the construction of Chang'an, many of the city's structures used brickwork, especially the numerous walls separating the individual palace wards and many quarters of the town.

Remains of kilns for bricks and tiles were located and excavated in the northwest, in the center, and in the northeast of Chang'an. The ceramic workshops found in the northwest of Chang'an were relatively small facilities, mostly located in the western and southern parts of the West Market (Han City Archaeological Team 1991:18–22, 1994: 986–995) (Figure 10.1). These types of kilns were usually privately run and did not appear to have been strictly regulated. They produced a wide variety of average quality items for the daily needs of the inhabitants of Chang'an, which were probably sold in the markets of the city (Han City Archaeological Team 1991, 1992, 1994; Liu 2003:171, 174). The eleven kilns found in the center of Chang'an, by contrast, were more likely state-run structures producing mainly tiles, such as those used for the roofing of imperial buildings; they have been dated to the early Western Han period (Liu 2003:172–174). Most of these state facilities were arranged systematically south of the Bei Palace and north of Zhi Cheng Men Street (Han City Archaeological Team 1996). State-run furnaces were also located in the northeast of the city, where twenty-one kilns have been excavated to date (Han City Archaeological Team 1994). These facilities have been identified with the official kilns of the *Shao Fu*, the major administrative center of the Han manufacturing industry (Han City Archaeological Team 1994:99–129; Liu 2003:175–180).

Several of the issues connected to the production of building material in Chang'an have also emerged from the evidence in Rome, a city characterized by frequent construction projects sponsored by the state and by private individuals. Because the Roman people had no compunction about building with permanent materials, many structures were made of bricks. Fired bricks came into general use during the Augustan period because of their higher durability and resistance to fire and pressure, thus supplanting the production of the sun-dried type, which had been popular in previous periods (DeLaine 2000; Helen 1975:16–20). Although literary sources illustrating brickwork production in Rome, or in any other city of the empire, are rare (Vitruvius 1935:2.3), there is sufficient archaeological data relating to brick manufacturing facilities in the capital to allow for an analysis of the local production.

Many of the brickyards supplying Rome seem to have been located in the suburban area as close as possible to either natural clay pits or transport routes, such as rivers or consular roads. The areas of the Esquiline, Caelian, and the beginning of the Via Appia were specifically known for their clays and clay-derived products (Petracca and Vigna 1985). The Tiber Valley was a center of brick production, thanks to the abundance of clay, fuel, and ease of transportation offered by the river. Even so, several furnaces were also discovered in the urban environment of the capital, where the availability of raw material allowed for the establishment of a ceramic industry. A passage from Varro points to the presence of specific facilities for the production of ceramic implements (*figlinae*) in the vicinity of the Esquiline Hill (1958:5.50). Excavations have confirmed this; two kilns were discovered in this area (Figure 10.4). The first furnace, dated to the Republican period, was located on the Esquiline Hill, on the corner between Via dello Statuto and Via Merulana. The second kiln was a small structure on the southwest corner of Via Isonzo and Via Tevere, accompanied by two tubs for the manipulation of clay (Cozzo 1928:133; Gatti 1925:282–288; Platner and Ashby 1929:209; Steinby 1978:1507). Remains of ceramic production were also identified on the Janiculum Hill (Moccheggiani-Carpano 1982:25–35), whereas Juvenal pointed to the existence of potters' workshops on the Vatican Hill (Juvenal 2004:6) (Figure 10.4). Furthermore, toponyms attested for the city of Rome indicate the presence of brick production in the urban area (Frutaz 1962: II, plate 103; III, plates 412, 550, 552, 570, 588, 591, 615, 620). Even so, most of Rome's brickfields were located in the suburban areas, as indicated by three furnaces discovered in the areas surrounding the Via Cassia (Messineo, Petracca, and Vigna 1984:250; Petracca and Vigna 1985:132, 134–136), and two facilities along the Via Flaminia (Petracca and Vigna 1985:134, 136), among others (Figure 10.4). These productive structures were all roughly datable to the beginning of the Principate, apart from the kiln on the Esquiline Hill near Via Merulana, which was dated by Cozzo to the Republican period (1928:133). The furnaces seem to have been typical structures for firing bricks (especially if the chamber was large), or vases and tiles (if the smaller chamber was round [Cuomo di Caprio 1971–1972:436–437]).

The high occurrence of construction projects taking place in the capitals of the Han and Roman Empires certainly relied on the intensive production of bricks, regardless of whether entire structures were made of brickwork, or whether they were used only for the surrounding walls so often mentioned for the Chinese capitals. Remains of kilns for firing bricks discovered in the central areas of Rome and Chang'an show that their production took place in the urban areas of both cities. The different location of structures for the manufacture of bricks in the two cities can probably be attributed to the difference between a city of new construction with much open space within its boundaries, as with Chang'an, and a large and already built capital with limited urban areas suitable for the bulky production of bricks. Apart from a few particular cases found in the center of the city, Roman brickfields were mostly located in the suburban area, in close proximity to the agricultural estates of the urban elites to whom they often belonged, and within easy reach of both the necessary clay pits and main roads or rivers leading to the capital. Although it is true that many of the excavated Chinese kilns for firing bricks were located near the construction sites within the city, it is not clear whether the clay was transported to the construction sites and successively manipulated, dried, and fired on site, or whether only the firing stage of production was carried out on the locations where the furnaces were found. Perhaps the position of several kilns in the northeast and northwest of Chang'an indicated a concentration of production of the finished bricks in the area. This could be further explained by the proximity of the area to the markets, the river, and the gates closest to it, which could have facilitated the transportation of large quantities of clay to be worked in these workshops.

The kilns situated closer to the construction sites of Chang'an and identified as the official sites producing bricks and roofing material for the palaces were either completely or at least heavily controlled by the state. Nevertheless, there seems to have been a certain number of structures producing items for private construction projects or for retail in the urban markets. The industry does not appear to have been entirely in the hands of the Han state, and the same observation can be made for the Roman manufacturing of bricks. Given the detailed information on Roman brick stamps, it is possible to reconstruct a fuller picture of the industry and its organization inside the capital and its suburban areas. Many stamps convey the name of the owner of the estate(s) that supplied the raw material, as well as the date of production and names of responsible managers and workers (Helen 1975). These stamps show that many of the rich landowners engaged in an industry that, because of its close ties to agriculture, did not carry the social stigma attached to commerce and small workshop production (Cicero 1923:89–90 1976:18.9–10; Kehoe 2007:561–562; Livy 1963:8.20.4; Pliny the Elder 1952: 3.49). It was also extremely profitable. A lack of any social stigma is also suggested by the high frequency of female names on the brick stamps (Helen 1975:112–113) as well as male names, showing how an association with this respectable industry did not represent a point of dishonor for the more vulnerable members of the higher social classes. These women could have been owners of the estates or tenants of the brickfields, although they almost never figured as workers (*Corpus Inscriptionum Latinarum* 1887:XV:587, 646–651; Helen 1975:113). After the accession of Antoninus Pius (AD 138–161) and Marcus Aurelius (AD 161–180), the factories owned by the emperors as private citizens became part of the estate of the imperial family, which resulted in their ownership of a large share of the brickfields of Rome and its *suburbium* (Loane 1938:102–103). Although the imperial control over brick production increased in later times, it does not appear to have ever become an official state monopoly. During the Flavian period and in later imperial years, brick stamps still show the existence of many privately owned brickyards (*Corpus Inscriptionum Latinarum* 1887:XV), proving the coexistence of state and privately owned structures in the capital, in a similar way to the contemporary situation of the Han period.

METALWORK

Aside from brick making, metalworking was another industry that benefitted from the manipulation and firing of natural materials, and whose workshops were attested in both urban and rural environments in the Han and Roman Empires. Besides the metal objects recovered from tombs of the Han period, most of the data for metalworking under the Han Dynasties are related to the organization and monopoly of iron production. Evidence derives principally from the official historical sources and from the *Yan Tie Lun*, (Ban et al. 1950: *Biography of Usurers*, Volume 91; for a deeper analysis of the contents of the text, see Wagner [2001]). From Han Wu Di's period, in 117 or 119 BC (Ban Gu et al. 1950: *Treatise on Food and Money*, Volume 24; Sima Qian 1993: *Treatise on The Balanced Standard*, Treatise 8, Volume 30), iron production from the smelting of the metal to the sale of the final products was entirely controlled by the government (Liu 2003:181–182; Pirazzoli-T'Serstevens 1982:71–72; Wagner 2001). Iron manufacture had been a long-practiced industry even before the reign of Wu Di. By monopolizing it, the Han government incorporated its vast profits, which had until then benefited private entrepreneurs. These actions caused criticism of the state and resulted in a series of government reforms throughout the Han Dynasties aimed at reorganizing the production. The state monopoly of salt and iron was abolished in 44 BC, but reinstated again in 41 BC (Ban Gu et al. 1950: *Treatise on Food and Money*, Volume 24). During the Eastern Han Dynasty, the Salt and Iron Offices were transferred from the central administration to the offices of local commanderies and prefectures, signifying a loss of power for the central Han government (Fan Ye 1958: *Treatise on The Hundred State Offices* Volumes 114 and 116). From this period onward, salt and iron were no longer a state monopoly, although their large-scale manufacture still happened under direct supervision of the government (Wagner 2001:17). Urban metal manufacture was also affected by governmental policies, particularly with respect to the location of industrial structures. Before the introduction of the iron monopoly, manufacture was carried out under private management in both large- and small-scale workshops. More often than not, these structures were located as close as possible to fuel sources necessary to operate the furnaces (Ban Gu et al. 1950: *Treatise on Food and Money*, Volume 24; Huan Kan 1967: Chapter 6). Because of the difficulty of dealing with fires, smoke, and slag residues from smelting in an urban environment, large blast furnaces processing iron from ore were situated outside the city walls. Foundries producing cast metal from material smelted elsewhere, on the other hand, could also be found inside the urban production areas (see Wagner 2001:table 2). After the institution of the iron monopoly, bureaucratic control brought many large smelting workshops within much closer range of the urban administrative centers, making their discovery somewhat easier for archaeologists investigating urban sites (Wagner 2001:38). In a way, the closer the ties of the central administration became to the metal production, the closer the physical position of the industrial workshops became to the administrative centers.

The only archaeological evidence available for metalworking in the urban area of Chang'an comes from the remains of a smelting and metal casting area in the south-central part of the West Market, where utensils like belt hooks and carriage fittings were discovered (Han City Archaeological Team 1995:792–798, 1997:581–588) (Figure 10.1). The layout of such structures was very similar to that used for ceramic production. The features excavated consisted of a series of kilns and the base of a cupola furnace (or shaft furnace, see Wagner [2001:75–76] for more detailed description of the casting process of such furnaces). Given the high degree of state control over the entire iron manufacturing cycle, it is possible that metal implements were sold only inside the market wards, where transactions could be monitored by officials.

As in Chang'an, the evidence for metalworking in Rome is also principally derived from literary and epigraphic sources, although it relates mainly to the production of precious metals, not iron. Mining of metal ore was a very profitable industry both during the Republic and the Principate. Over time, as new territories were conquered, the Roman government increased the acquisition of mines, and strengthened its control over the smelting processes associated with them, often leasing out its exploitation to private companies (Kehoe 2007:566–568; Lo Cascio 2007:643). It does not appear that Roman elites had a strong involvement in the mining industry, as this was one of the sectors of the Roman economy that saw the state taking control of the raw resources (Kehoe 2007:568).

The majority of inscriptions mentioning goldsmiths in Italy come from the capital, which suggests that Rome was a center for precious-metal production during the first century of the Principate (Gummerus 1918:262). This was probably owing to a combination of factors, including the availability of imported raw materials, the demand of the rich urban population, and the presence of skilled artisans (Loane 1938:87). Goldsmiths' *tabernae* appear to have been small structures located throughout the city; for example, some are attested along the Via Sacra (*Corpus Inscriptionum Latinarum* 1876–2001: VI:9207), Vico Longo (*Corpus Inscriptionum Latinarum* 1876–2001: VI:37469), Lacus Gallinae (*Corpus Inscriptionum Latinarum* 1876–2001: VI:33835), and outside the Porta Flumentana (*Corpus Inscriptionum Latinarum* 1876–2001: VI:9208; Loane 1938:88) (Figure 10.4). Silversmithing was highly specialized, with labor divided into the different steps of production; different titles of expert artisans responsible for various stages of manufacture are attested in the epigraphic evidence (*Corpus Inscriptionum Latinarum* 1876–2001: VI:9222, 9432, 3928, 9950, 8839, 9418). Locations of workshops indicate an analogous situation to that of the goldsmiths' *tabernae* because they were scattered throughout the city; some on the Via Sacra (*Corpus Inscriptionum Latinarum* 1876–2001: VI:9221) (Figure 10.4), others on the Via Sigillaria (Suetonius 1914b:16). Copper and bronze were also traded and worked in small shops across the city (Juvenal 2004: 7, 223). Whether larger structures existed for the production of bronze and copper items in urban contexts is not certain, as no data has so far been found in the capital. There is also evidence of inscriptions mentioning the existence of ironsmiths in Rome making small implements for everyday use, such as keys and locks (*Corpus Inscriptionum Latinarum* 1876–2001:VI:9259, 9260), although they do not seem as abundant as those relating to goldsmiths.

Evidence for metal industries in the Han and Roman capitals has yielded different kinds of information. Chinese sources provide better data on the organization of iron production, with evidence for smaller-scale workshops located inside the city. The Roman data for the capital point specifically to precious metalworking, especially gold and silver, but also copper, bronze, and iron. In view of the fragmentary evidence collected so far, it is not possible to reconstruct anything more than a very partial picture of the metal industry in the Roman and Han capitals. It appears that in Chang'an, workshops dealing with the production and retail of metal objects were located within the confines of the official markets, under the strict control of officials. In Rome, these facilities were instead found in many areas of the town, often situated in proximity to major roads, possibly to attract clientele, but also to facilitate the delivery of the rough metal that had been smelted from ore on, or near, the extraction location (Kehoe 2007:566–568). Finished products were sold in the shops/workshops that produced them, but could also be sold inside purpose-built market structures. The Chinese and Roman evidence does not point to a heavy presence of large-scale workshops for the processing of metal in urban contexts, probably owing, at least in part, to hazards associated with fire, smoke, and the large quantities of refuse. Both the workshop found in Chang'an and the ones in Rome appear to have been small-scale structures for local production and retailing of common-use metal implements. In the majority of cases documented so far, the manufacture of metal objects and bricks appears to have been confined to specific small-scale, purpose-built workshops or to assigned areas located inside or outside the urban conglomerate.

DISCUSSION

The presentation of the areas of urban manufacturing and retailing discussed in this chapter is organized according to several main dimensions that were common to both Roman and Chinese urban economic structures. These dimensions are the layout, location, and distribution of workshops and markets in the capitals, the scale and ownership of premises, and the degree of state involvement in the selected businesses. I will now consider these dimensions of analysis together, addressing how the production of space operated in Rome and Chang'an and focusing particularly on the role of the state in such processes. Both governments influenced not only the cycle of manufacture and sale of the products under study, but also the physical forms and locations of the urban structures connected to it, playing an important role in the production of space in the capitals. The extent of their impact can be estimated through a broader reading of the morphology and location of the markets and workshops of the capitals.

Retail Space, Morphology, and Location

The first and most immediate visual sign of the influence of the state on the economic structures is to be found in the design of the official market buildings. Fixed marketplaces in both Rome and Chang'an were state-built monumental constructions located in relatively central areas of the urban landscape. While in Chang'an it does not appear that the two main East and West Markets changed their form, size, or position of close proximity to the main imperial citadel in the course of their lifespans, markets in Rome underwent several changes. Such transformations, which mainly concerned their location and layout, showed a parallel evolution in the production of space and of the role of the city and its institutions, from powerful urban center to capital of an empire. The additional construction of market buildings during the Principate further reflects the increased economic necessities of a city that had become a real metropolis.

The Han marketplaces were also subjected to a higher level of governmental control than can be observed for their Roman counterparts. This can be evinced from the existence of walls surrounding the East and West Markets in Chang'an, gates regulating access to the areas, and from the presence of an administrative office in the form of a tower building situated between the two compounds. Although the markets of the Han period can be considered as the only public foci of socialization and commercial exchange in the capitals, the very segregation and monumentality of their architecture must have represented a constant reminder to the emperor's subjects of their ruler's authority and justice, especially considering that the markets of Chang'an were the customary stages for public executions and punishment. On the contrary, like other public areas, Roman marketplaces did not appear to have been intended, or at least interpreted by the urban masses, as deterrents to their free use. In the Roman world, public areas were frequently appropriated by the population and adapted to their uses, and even to their entertainment, as indicated by evidence of game boards carved onto structures of the fora of provincial centers (Trifiló 2011:312–331). There have also been recent studies that hinted at the possibility that the Basilica Aemilia in the Roman Forum could have doubled up from its commercial role to nothing less than a casino (Ertel and Freyburger 2007). This flexibility in the use of urban spaces in Rome contrasts with the strict control the Han exercised over the production of space and use of urban structures.

Manufacture Space, Distribution, and Scale

Aside from the state-constructed market buildings, a broad look at the distribution and scale of the facilities for the manufacture and sale of bricks and metal objects can offer pointers to understanding their connections to the central government. In general terms, the majority of workshops manufacturing bricks and metal implements investigated so far in Chang'an were located in the northern part of the city and within the market wards. This was because of a combination of practical and administrative reasons, such as ease of access to the routes of transportation of the raw material, and need for state control. Roman workshops were instead located throughout the capital, wherever demand arose for their services, with a predominance of units in the center of the city and along the main roads, presumably to promote their visibility and transport raw materials and final products more easily. In terms of scale of the facilities, the structures found in the urban environment were not large enough to support the idea of private or state-run large-scale production for export or wholesale. Workshops were mainly smaller units catering to the potentially high demands of the urban rulers, elites, and the common people.

The analysis of the evidence for shops and workshops in Rome shows that although the government was in command of several aspects of the state economy – such as the provisioning of grain, salt, and the extraction of metals – private entrepreneurs existed in Rome in ample number, and they belonged to all social classes, from emperor to slaves, depending on whether they were owners, employees (salaried or not), or independent workers. The existence of many private brick-making industries attested for the reign of Antoninus Pius, when a vast percentage of the brickyards of Rome and its *suburbium* were concentrated into the estates of the imperial family, makes it clear that although the *princeps* was an extremely influential player in the Roman economy, he was nonetheless a player and not solely responsible for its state (Lo Cascio 2006:225). Regardless of the more strict state control on commercial activities in the Han capitals, private workshops appear to have been present also in China, as indicated by the interpretation of several brick-making workshops in Chang'an. This situation signifies that although the level of involvement of the government in trade and production was conspicuous, such conditions did not stifle private activities. While the government policies adopted by the Han Empire in the economic sector emphasized the control of the authoritarian state, the Roman regulations were based on, and fostered, the existence of private property and the patron-client relationships typical of their society, with the influence of state administration showing mostly on structures located on public property.

Capital cities in general, and the Roman and Han ones in particular, have often been characterized by scholars as loci of concentrated consumption, veritable "consumer cities." The "consumer city" construct is built on the basis of the interpretation of the nature of the ancient economy as defined by the degree of economic reciprocity between town and hinterland. It was originally theorized by Weber and later revisited by Finley (Finley 1973; Weber 1978 [1922]:1215–1217), and is still (often begrudgingly) considered the best heuristic device available to examine the mechanisms of the ancient economic cycle of production and consumption. Keeping in mind the somewhat limited evidence for production and consumption processes in the capitals of the Han and Roman Empires presented in this chapter, it is possible to infer that although Rome and Chang'an showed strong signs of widespread commercial and productive activities, such findings do not indicate that competitive markets drove the economy and were the main form of redistribution. The Roman and Han urban societies still gained most of their livelihood from the surrounding territories, thus making the capitals of their respective empires essentially consumer cities. In view of this, the Roman and Han urban economies appear to find a more fitting element of comparison in each other than in the modern economy.

Production of Space in the Roman and Han Imperial Capitals

The analysis undertaken in this chapter indicates that the production of space dedicated to economic activities in the Han capital was driven to a very large extent by its government, a situation that is especially evident in the enforced concentration of retail businesses and many production establishments within the enclosed wards of the marketplaces. These circumstances contrast deeply with the evidence relating to the Roman capital. The foregoing analysis of the location of production and commercial activities and the degree of state control exercised over them has, in fact, indicated the existence of a plurality of actors and social dynamics influencing the production of Rome's economic space. Despite the more scattered distribution of manufacturing establishments in Rome, certain areas of the capital appear to have attracted groups of similar trades, as attested by toponyms known from modern areas or from the classical sources.

There were *Scalae Anularie*, where jewelers sold rings and other trinkets; a *Clivius Vitrarius* for glass dealers; a *Vicus Argentarius* where money lenders could be found, and many areas of Rome still carry the traces in their names of the presence of clay and the facilities connected to its use (Frutaz 1962:II, plate 103, III, plates 412, 550, 552, 570, 588, 591, 615, 620). This seems to indicate that in the Roman case, although many aspects of the ancient urban economy – especially concerning trade and permanent retail architecture – were controlled by the government, some elements such as the naming of districts of the cities could have been influenced by the daily economic activities of their inhabitants. By contrast, known names for palaces, streets, and gates in Chang'an do not appear to have reflected the existence of a tight relationship between production activities and urban space. Names of urban features and locations in the Han capital were mainly reminiscent of less prosaic and more poetic ideas, like the Cassia, Brilliant, and Everlasting Palaces (*Gui, Ming Guang* and *Wei Yang* palaces), or the Gate of Peace (*An Men*). It was the plurality of social actors existing in Rome (not solely belonging to the highest social classes) that shaped the urban space of the capital. To put it in James Anderson's words:

> The businesses and artisans gave their names, their character and ultimately their very identities to the most heavily used streets and spaces in the city, the shopping and market districts and the streets that allowed access to and from them (Anderson 1997:334).

CONCLUSION

The physical features of the capitals of the Roman and Han Empires clearly reflect the different interests driving the development of the two societies and the production of urban space, as seen in the difference in distribution of production areas and how space was used. Although the material forms of Rome and Chang'an were produced by societies with different interests, it is important to remember that these capitals were not simply passive materializations of the interests of the forces at play. Rather, they were "living cities" – highly responsive and catalyzing foci of large-scale sociopolitical processes, and their structures were both medium and outcome of such processes.

The responsiveness of the built environment to sociohistorical events observed in the course of the analysis of a selection of production and retail structures found in the Han and Roman capitals highlights the close connection existing between political structures, society, and the urban landscape. This connection has been brought out even more clearly through the comparative analysis of the urban structures of politically charged urban centers like these imperial capitals. The ways in which the daily activities of the inhabitants, as well as the great sociohistorical processes that took place in the capitals, shaped the urban space and remolded its identity, reveal the existence of multiple levels of spatial production and meaning that characterize the cities under examination not only in this chapter, but throughout this volume.

ACKNOWLEDGMENTS

I am grateful to Andrew Creekmore and Kevin Fisher, who organized the "Production of Space in Ancient Cities" session of the 2009 Society for American Archaeology (SAA) Symposium in Atlanta and edited the present volume, for their enthusiasm and support throughout the process. I would also like to thank Tobias Richter, Alexis Pantos, and Guenevere Bjerre Thaarup who helped prepare the figures for this chapter, and the reviewers of the volume, whose comments allowed me to improve my contribution. My gratitude also goes to the Graduate School of the University College of London, for funding my participation in the 2009 SAA Symposium.

NOTES

1 Ancient Chinese and Latin texts have been cited in this contribution according to the following guidelines: Chinese works have been cited with the *pinyin* transliteration of their title and the indication in English of the chapter or section discussed. Latin texts have been cited indicating the name of the author and title in Latin, and a numeral indication of the book and section of it under examination. Translations into English or French of classical texts have been referenced in the bibliography; when these were not available, modern Chinese language editions of Chinese sources have been referenced instead.
Chinese sources cited with attributed authors and dates:
Han Shu (Ban Gu, Ban Biao, Ban Zhao) (Ban Gu 32–92 AD) [covering 209 BC–25 AD]
Hou Han Shu (Fan Ye) (398–445 AD) [covering 25–220 AD]
Liang Du Fu (Ban Gu) (32–92 AD)
Shi Ji (Sima Qian) (145–86? BC) [covering earliest times to 99 BC]

Xi Du Fu (Zhang Heng) (78–139 AD)

Yan Tie Lun (Huan Kuan) [covering debate in 81 BC and previous Westen Han policies]

Zhou Li (Jiang Ren Ying Guo, Kao Gong Ji) (Liu Xin, ed.) (ca. 50 BC–AD 23) [covering ca. 476–221 BC]

REFERENCES CITED

Amici, Carla Maria 1982 *Foro di Traiano: Basilica Ulpia e Biblioteche.* Commissione Archeologica Comunale in Roma, Spoleto, Italy.

Anderson, James C. Jr. 1997 *Roman Architecture and Society.* Johns Hopkins University Press, Baltimore, MD.

Ban, Gu, Ban, Biao, and Ban, Zhao 1950 (trans.) *Han Shu.* Translated and annotated by Nancy Lee Swann in *Food & Money in Ancient China: The Earliest Economic History of China to A.D. 25: Han Shu 24, with Related Texts, Han Shu 91 and Shih-Chi 129.* Princeton University Press, Princeton, NJ.

Ban, Gu 1960 (trans.) *Liang Du Fu.* Translated by Ernest R. Hughes in *Two Chinese Poets: Vignettes of Han Life and Thought.* Princeton University Press, Princeton, NJ.

Barbieri-Low, Anthony J. 2007 *Artisans in Early Imperial China.* University of Washington Press, Seattle and London.

Bianchini, Marco 1991 I Mercati di Traiano. *Bollettino di Archeologia* 8:102–121.
    1992 Mercati Traianei. La Destinazione d'Uso. *Bollettino di Archeologia* 16–18:145–163.

Cassius Dio 1927 (trans.) *Historia Romana, Libri 61–70.* Translated by E. Cary, and H. B. Foster. Harvard University Press, Cambridge, MA.

Ch'ü, T'ung-tsu 1972 *Han Social Structure.* University of Washington Press, Seattle and London.

Cicero 1923 (trans.) *De Domo Sua.* Translated by N. H. Watts. Harvard University Press, Cambridge, MA.
    1988 (trans.) *De Oratore.* Translated by E. W. Sutton, and H. Rackham. Harvard University Press, Cambridge, MA.
    1976 (trans.) *Pro Flacco.* Translated by C. MacDonald. Harvard University Press, Cambridge, MA.

Coarelli, Filippo 1983 *Il Foro Romano, I, Periodo Arcaico.* Quasar, Rome.
    2008 *Rome and Environs; An Archaeological Guide.* University of California Press, Berkeley.

Corpus Inscriptionum Latinarum (C.I.L.) 1876–2001 *Volume VI. Inscriptiones Urbis Romae Latinae.* Edited by G. Henzen, I. B. De Rossi, E. Bormann, C. Huelsen, and M. Bang. Walter de Gruyter, Berlin.
    1887 *Volume XV. Inscriptiones Latii Veteris Latinae.* Edited by H. Dessau. Walter de Gruyter, Berlin.

Cozzo, Giuseppe 1928 *Ingegneria Romana.* Libreria Editrice Mantegazza di P. Cremonese, Rome.

Cuomo Di Caprio, Ninina 1971–1972 Proposta di Classificazione delle Fornaci per Ceramica e Laterizi nell'Area Italiana. *Sibrium* 11:436–437.

DeLaine, Janet 2000 Bricks and Mortar: Exploring the Economics of Building Techniques at Rome and Ostia. In *Economies Beyond Agriculture in* the *Classical World*, edited by David J. Mattingly and John Salmon, pp. 271–296. Routledge, London.

Eisenstadt, Shmuel Noah and Arie Shachar 1987 *Society, Culture and Urbanization*. Sage Publications, Newbury Hills, CA.

Ertel, Christine and Klaus Stefan Freyburger 2007 Nuove Indagini sulla Basilica Aemilia nel Foro Romano. *Archeologia Classica* 58:109–142.

Fan, Ye 1968 *Hou Han Shu Ji Jie* (後漢書集解). Edited by Wang Xianqian. Commercial Press, Taipei.

Favro, Diane 1993 Reading the Augustan City. In *Narrative and Event in Ancient Art*, edited by Peter J. Holliday, pp. 230–257. Cambridge University Press, Cambridge.

Finley, Moses I. 1973 *The Ancient Economy*. University of California Press, Berkeley.

Frasca, Rossella 1994 *Mestieri e Professioni a Roma. Una Storia dell'Educazione*. La Nuova Italia Editrice, Scandicci (Florence).

Frutaz, Amato P. 1962 *Le Piante di Roma*, Vols. II, III. Istituto di Studi Romani, Rome.

Fuchs, Gunter 1969 *Architekturdarstellungen auf römischen Münzen der Republik und der frühen Kaiserzeit*. Walter de Gruyter, Berlin.

Gatti, Giuseppe 1925 Notizie di Recenti Ritrovamenti di Antichitá in Roma e nel Suburbio. *Bullettino della Commissione Archeologica di Roma* 53:271–304.

Gummerus, Herman G. 1918 Die Römische Industrie. *Klio* 15:256–302.

Han City Archaeological Team, Institute of Archaeology, Chinese Academy of Social Sciences 1991 Han Chang'an Cheng 1 Hao Jiu Zhi Fa Jue Jian Bao (a Preliminary Excavation Report of Kiln Site 1 at the Han Period Chang'an City). *Kao Gu* 1:18–22.

1992 Han Chang'an Cheng 2–8 Qu Yao Ju Yi Je Chu Bu Bao Gao (a Preliminary Report on the Excavation of Kiln Sites 2–8 of Han Chang'an). *Kao Gu* 2:138.

1994 Han Chang'an Cheng Jiu Zhi Fa Jue Bao Gao (Excavation Report of the Kiln Sites of Han Period Chang'an). *Kao Gu Xue Bao* 1:99–129.

1995 Nian Han Chang'an Cheng Ye Zhu Yi Zhi Fa Jue Jian Bao (a Preliminary Report on the Excavation of a Smelting and Casting Site in Chang'an City of the Han Period in 1992). *Kao Gu* 9:792–798, 807; Plates 6–8.

1996 Han Chang'an Cheng Bei Gong De Kan Tan Ji Qi Nan Mian Zhuan Wa Yao De Fa Jue (Prospecting for the Beigong Palace of the City of Chang'an of Han Period and Excavation of Brick Kilns South of It). *Kao Gu* 10:887–896.

1997 1996 Nian Han Chang'an Cheng Ye Zhu Yi Zhi Fa Jue Jian Bao (Excavation of an Iron Foundry Site at the Han City of Chang'an in 1996). *Kao Gu* 7:581–588; Plates 1–3.

Helen, Tapio 1975 *Organization of Roman Brick Production in the First and Second Centuries AD: An Interpretation of Roman Brick Stamps*. Suomalainen Tiedeakatemia. Annales Academiae Scientiarum Fennicae, Helsinki.

Huan, Kuan 1967 [1931] (trans.) *Yan Tie Lun*. Translated by Esson McDowell Gale in *Discourses on Salt and Iron: a Debate on State Control of Commerce and Industry in Ancient China, Chapter I-XXVIII (Sinica Leidensia Edidit*

Institutum Sinologicum Lugduno-Batavum, vol. II). Cheng Wen Publishing Company, Taipei.

Juvenal 2004 (trans.) *Satires*. Translated by S. M. Braund. Harvard University Press, Cambridge, MA.

Kehoe, Dennis P. 2007 The Early Roman Empire: Production. In *The Cambridge Economic History of the Greco-Roman World*, edited by Walter Scheidel, Ian Morris, and Richard Saller, pp. 543–569. Cambridge University Press, Cambridge.

Laurence, Ray 1994 *Roman Pompeii: Space and Society*. Routledge, London.

Lewis, Mark E. 2006 *The Construction of Space in Ancient China*. State University of New York, Albany.

Liu, Qingzhu 1987 Xi'an Shi Han Chang'an Cheng Dong Shi He Xi Shi Yi Zhi (Remains of the East and West Markets of the Han City of Chang'an in Xi'an). *Zhongguo Kaoguxue Nianjian*:264.

    1992 Zai Tan Han Chang'an Cheng Bu Ju Jie Gou Ji Qi Xiang Guan Wen Ti. Da Yang Kuan Xian Sheng (Again on the Layout of Han Chang'an and the Problems Concerned. Answer to Prof. Yang Kuan). *Kao Gu* 7:632–639.

    1996 Han Chang'an Cheng De Kao Gu Fa Xian Ji Xiang Guan Wen Ti Yang Jiu (Archaeological Discoveries and Research on the Chang'an City Site of the Han Period). *Kao Gu* 10:1–14.

    2000 *Gu Dai Du Cheng Xie Di Ling Kao Gu Xue Yan Jiu, (Archaeological Studies of Capitals and Imperial Mausoleums in Ancient China)*. Kexue Chu Ban She, Beijing.

    2003 *Han Chang'an Cheng (the Han City of Chang'an)*. Wenwu Chu Ban She, Beijing.

Liu, Xin (ed.) 1851 (trans.) *Zhou Li*. Translated by Edouard Biot in *Le Tcheou-Li ou Rites des Tcheou, Tome II*. Edited by S. Julien and J. B. Biot. L'Imprimerie Nationale, Paris.

Livy 1919 (trans.) *Ab Urbe Condita Libri 1–2*. Translated by B. O. Foster. Harvard University Press, Cambridge, MA.

    1936 (trans.) *Ab Urbe Condita Libri 38–39*. Translated by E. T. Sage. Harvard University Press, Cambridge, MA.

    1943 (trans.) *Ab Urbe Condita Libri 26–27*. Translated by F. Gardner Moore. Harvard University Press, Cambridge, MA.

    1963 (trans.) *Ab Urbe Condita Libri 8–10*. Translated by B. O. Foster. Harvard University Press, Cambridge, MA.

    1978 (trans.) *Ab Urbe Condita Libri 5–7*. Translated by B. O. Foster. Harvard University Press, Cambridge, MA.

    1989a (trans.) *Ab Urbe Condita Libri 3–4*. Translated by B. O. Foster. Harvard University Press, Cambridge, MA.

    1989b (trans.) *Ab Urbe Condita Libri 43–45*. Translated by A. C. Schlesinger. Harvard University Press, Cambridge, MA.

Loane, Helen J. 1938 *Industry and Commerce of the City of Rome (50 BC–200 AD)*. The Johns Hopkins Press, Baltimore, MD.

Lo Cascio, Elio 2006 The Role of the State in the Roman Economy: Making Use of the New Institutional Economics. In *Ancient Economies, Modern Methodologies, Archaeology, Comparative History, Models and Institutions*, edited by Peter F. Bang, Mamoru Ikeguchi, and Hartmut G. Ziche, pp. 215–234. Edipuglia, Bari, Italy.

2007 The Early Roman Empire: the State and the Economy. In *The Cambridge Economic History of the Greco-Roman World*, edited by Walter Scheidel, Ian Morris, and Richard Saller, pp. 619–647. Cambridge University Press, Cambridge.

Luoyang Museum 1975 Luoyang Jian Xi Qi Li He Dong Han Mu Fa Jue Jian Bao (Preliminary Excavation Report of the Eastern Han Tomb at Qilihe, Jianxi). *Kao Gu* 2:116–24, 134.

MacDonald, William L. 1986 *The Architecture of the Roman Empire, Vol II, an Urban Appraisal*. Yale University Press, New Haven, CT and London.

Mattingly, Harold 1923 *Coins of the Roman Empire in the British Museum*, Vol I. British Museum Publications, London.

McKay, Alexander G. 1975 *Houses, Villas and Palaces in the Roman World*. Johns Hopkins University Press, Baltimore, MD.

Meneghini, Roberto 1990 Roma. Mercati di Traiano: Ricerche nell'Area della Torre delle Milizie. Rapporto Preliminare. *Archeologia Medievale* 17:419–433.

2003 Indagini Archeologiche Lungo l'Area Perimetrale dei Mercati di Traiano: Settori Settentrionale e Orientale (Scavi 1989–1997). *Bullettino della Commissione Archeologica Comunale di Roma* 104:219–234.

2010 *I Fori Imperiali e i Mercati di Traiano. Storia e Descrizione dei Monumenti alla Luce degli Studi e degli Scavi*. Istituto Poligrafico dello Stato, Rome.

Messineo, Gaetano, Lucia Petracca, and L. M. Vigna 1984 Suburbio di Roma. Notiziario Archeologico. Via Barberano Romano; Resti di una Villa Rustica Romana. *Bullettino della Commissione Archeologica Comunale di Roma* 88:248–253.

Mittag, Achim 2008 Empire and Historiography in Han China. In *Conceiving the Empire, China and Rome Compared*, edited by Fritz-Heiner Mutschler and Achim Mittag, pp. 143–165. Oxford University Press, Oxford.

Moccheggiani-Carpano, Claudio 1982 *L'Area del Santuario Siriaco del Gianicolo*. Edizioni Quasar, Rome.

Needham, Joseph 1962 *Science and Civilization in China*, Vol. 4, III. Cambridge University Press, Cambridge.

Nicolet, Claude 1980 *The World of the Citizen in Republican Rome*. Batsford, London.

Ovid 1989 (trans.) *Fasti*. Translated by J. G. Fraser. Harvard University Press, Cambridge, MA.

Packer, James E. 1967 Housing and Population in Imperial Rome and Ostia. *Journal of Roman Studies* 57:80–95.

1997 *The Forum of Trajan in Rome. A Study of the Monuments*. 3 vols. University of California Press, Berkeley.

Patterson, John R. 1992 The City of Rome: From Republic to Empire, *Journal of Roman Studies* 82:186–215.

Pensabene, Patrizio, Marina Milella, Bianca Maria Tummarello, Gioia Piazzesi, Luigi Messa, Lucrezia Ungaro, Sandro Stucchi, and Antonio Insalaco 1989 Foro Traiano. Contributi per una ricostruzione storica e architettonica. *Archeologia Classica* 41:27–327.

Petracca, Lucia and L. M. Vigna 1985 Le Fornaci di Roma e Suburbio. In *Misurare la Terra: Centuriazioni e Coloni nel Mondo Romano. Città, Agricoltura, Commercio: Materiali da Roma e dal Suburbio*, edited by

Rolando Bussi and Vittorio Vandelli, pp.131–137. Panini, Modena, Italy.

Pirazzoli-T'Serstevens, Michele 1982 *The Han Civilization of China*. Phaidon, Oxford.

Platner, Samuel B. and Thomas Ashby 1929 *A Topographical Dictionary of Ancient Rome*. Oxford University Press, London.

Pliny the Elder 1952 (trans.) *Historia Naturalis Libri 33–35*. Translated by H. Rackham. Harvard University Press, Cambridge, MA.

Purcell, Nicholas 1994 The City of Rome and the Plebs Urbanas in the Later Republic. In *The Last Age of the Roman Republic, 146–43 BC*, edited by J. A. Crook, Andrew Lintott, and Elizabeth Rawson, pp. 644–688. Cambridge University Press, Cambridge.

Rainbird, J. S., Frank B. Sear, and Jean Simpson 1971 A Possible Description of the Macellum Magnum of Nero. *Papers of the British School at Rome* 39:40–46.

Rapoport, Amos 1990 *The Meaning of the Built Environment: a Non-verbal Communication Approach*. University of Arizona Press, Tucson.

Richardson, Lawrence 1992 *A New Topographical Dictionary of Ancient Rome*. The Johns Hopkins University Press, Baltimore, MD.

Robinson, O. F. 1992 *Ancient Rome; City Planning and Administration*. Routledge, London.

Sadao, Nishijima 1986 The Economic and Social History of Former Han. In *Cambridge History of China: Volume I: the Ch'in and Han Empires, 221 BC–AD 220*, edited by Denis Twitchett and Michael Loewe, pp. 545–607. Cambridge University Press, Cambridge.

Sahara, Yasuo 1985 Han Period Markets. *Shirin* 68(5):33–71.

Scheidel, Walter 2009 The Monetary Systems of the Han and Roman Empires. In *Rome and China: Comparative Perspectives on Ancient World Empires*, edited by Walter Scheidel, pp. 137–208. Oxford University Press, Oxford.

Sear, Frank 1982 *Roman Architecture*. Batsford, London.

Sima, Qian 1993 (trans.) *Shi Ji*. Translated by Burton Watson in *Records of the Grand Historian of China: Han Dynasty II*, revised edition. The Research Centre for Translation, The Chinese University of Hong Kong, Hong Kong and Columbia University Press, NY.

Shanks, Michael and Christopher Tilley 1987a *Re-Constructing Archaeology. Theory and Practice*. Cambridge University Press, Cambridge.

Shanks, Michael 1987b *Social Theory and Archaeology*. Polity Press, Oxford.

Smith, Michael E. 2011. Empirical Urban Theory for Archaeologists. *Journal of Archaeological Method and Theory* 18:167–192.

Steinby, Eva Margareta 1978 Ziegelstempel von Rom und Umgebung. In *Paulys Realencyclopädie der Classischen Altertumswissenschaft*, edited by August Pauly and Georg Wissowa, Supplement XV, Columns 1489–1531. J.B. Metzler, Stuttgart.

Suetonius 1914a (trans.) *Divus Augustus*. Translated by J. C. Rolfe. Harvard University Press, Cambridge, MA.

1914b (trans.) *Divus Claudius*. Translated by J. C. Rolfe. Harvard University Press, Cambridge, MA.

Trifiló, Francesco 2011 Gaming in the forum and the use of space. In *Rome, Ostia, Pompeii, Movement and Space*, edited by David J. Newsome and Ray Laurence, pp. 312–331. Oxford University Press, Oxford.

Varro 1958 (trans.) *De Lingua Latina Libri XXV, Libri 5–7*. Translated by R. G. Kent. Harvard University Press, Cambridge, MA.

Vitruvius 1935 (trans.) *De Architectura*. Translated by F. Granger. Harvard University Press, Cambridge, MA.

von Falkenhausen, Lothar 1993 On the Historiographical Orientation of Chinese Archaeology. *Antiquity* 67:839–849.

Wagner, Donald B. 2001 *The State and the Iron Industry in Han China*. Nordic Institute of Asian Studies, Copenhagen.

Wang, Edward Q. 2000 *Inventing China through History: the May-Fourth Approach*. State University of New York, Albany.

Watson, Richard A. 1990 Ozymandias, King of Kings: Postprocessual Radical Archaeology as Critique. *American Antiquity* 55(4):673–689.

Weber, Max 1978 [1922] The City (Non-Legitimate Domination). In *Economy and Society: An Outline of Interpretive Sociology*, edited by G. Roth and C. Wittich, II:1212–1372. Translated from German by E. Fischoff, H. Gerth, A. M. Henderson, F. Kolegar, C. W. Mills, T. Parsons, M. Rheinstein, G. Roth, E. Shils, and C. Wittich. University of California Press, Berkeley.

Wilkinson, Endymion 2000 *Chinese History. A Manual*. Harvard University Press, Cambridge, MA and London.

Yang, Kuan 1984 Xi Han Chang'an Bu Ju jie Gou De Tan Tao (Study of the Layout Structure of Chang'an in the West Han Dynasty). *Wen Bo* 1:19–24.

1989 Xi Han Chang'an Bu Ju Jie Gou de Zai Tan Tao (Second Study of the Layout Structure of Chang'an in the West Han Dynasty). *Kao Gu* 4:348–356.

1993a *Zhong Guo Gu Dai Du Cheng Zhi Du Shi Yan Jiu (Research into the History of Chinese Ancient Urban Institutions)*. Shanghai Gu Ji Chu Ban She, Shanghai.

1993b San Lun Xi Han Chang'an de Bu Ju Jie Gou Wen Ti (Third Study of the Layout Structure of Chang'an in the West Han Dynasty). In *Zhong Guo Gu Dai Du Cheng Zhi Du Shi Yan Jiu (Research into the History of Chinese Ancient Urban Institutions)*, edited by Yang Kuan, pp. 593ff. Shanghai Gu Ji Chu Ban She, Shanghai.

Zhang, Heng 1982 (trans.) *Xi Du Fu*. Translated by David R. Knechtges in *Wen Xuan, or Selections of Refined Literature*, 1. Princeton University Press, Princeton, NJ.

Zhou, Changshan 2001 *Han Dai Cheng Shi Yan Jiu (Research on Cities of the Han Dynasty)*. Renmin Chu Ban She, Beijing.

11

Ancient Open Space, Gardens, and Parks: A Comparative Discussion of Mesoamerican Urbanism

Barbara L. Stark

Gardens and parks are part of urban open space, with elite gardens often constituting substantial investments. Proportions of open space assist evaluation of settlement nucleation. Three Mesoamerican cities demonstrate sufficient open space near elaborate residences to have had associated gardens. Cerro de las Mesas, Veracruz, Mexico, exhibits peripheral reserve spaces, which, in combination with comparative data, suggests an urban model that combines aspects of Burgess's (1925) concentric zones and Sjoberg's (1960) model of the preindustrial city. Archaeological practices for definition of settlement boundaries obscure the potential for a mosaic periphery that includes important green space as part of elite or other gardens and parks.

Issues concerning Mesoamerican urban open space, especially gardens and parks, have received scant archaeological attention despite crucial implications for interpretations of ancient urbanism as well as for archaeological practices. To address a selection of these issues, the paper is organized in four parts. First, I discuss the concepts of gardens and parks as part of urban open space. Ancient gardens and parks range in elaborateness well beyond ordinary household gardens (also termed kitchen or home gardens); similarly, the range of functions includes food production, but extends far beyond. Elite and royal gardens are substantial investments in most ancient states and empires, and they serve a variety of symbolic and social functions in addition to producing "practical items" (e.g., comestibles, wood, or medicines). Social ostentation is a frequent aspect of elaborate gardens and parks (for the Aztecs, see Evans 2000).

Second, I note the utility of open-space measurement for settlement density comparisons. Third, I examine Mesoamerican research concerning dispersed or low-density cities in the lowlands, where spaces among residences and other structures provided ample opportunities for gardens at both palatial and ordinary household scales. I focus on elaborate gardens, a neglected subject in comparison to home gardens. Possible palatial gardens are not solely an issue for low-density urbanism, however. I demonstrate that space was available for palatial gardens in Mesoamerican capitals through examples in both lowland Veracruz and highland Oaxaca. Fourth, I examine the implications of peripheral gardens and parks for archaeological decisions about settlement boundaries, arguing that settlement definitions require consideration of possible peripheral green space.

CONCEPTS ABOUT URBAN OPEN SPACE: GARDENS AND PARKS

In an urban context, gardens and parks form part of settlement open space along with streets, plazas, and other installations, such as ball courts in Mesoamerica. Open space differs from roofed architecture and other structures (e.g., pyramidal platforms) in many uses, but the two may interdigitate in planned arrangements, such as porticos, which are open-air but roofed. Modern, historic, and archaeological approaches to urban open spaces have developed in different disciplines, leading to somewhat disparate conceptual frameworks and emphases. From the point of view of urban planning, Al-Hagla (2008:164–165) subdivides modern open space into green or gray space, according to whether plantings versus paving or other hard landscaping prevail (including dirt surfaces). Among the categories of green space, elaborate gardens and parks are my focus. Green and gray spaces form a punctuated continuum because many open spaces are designed with a mixture of features in varying proportions, as in the case of house lots (Killion 1990, 1992). An elaborate park or garden may include paved terraces or walkways (even a modern parking lot may have meager marginal vegetation required by city codes). Nevertheless, there are a number of open areas for which green or gray space is a hallmark, such as plazas versus gardens; the two concepts are useful to highlight quite contrastive design and function.

I define gardens as well-delimited cultivated open spaces with a strongly designed live organic content, normally smaller in area than parks and usually more diverse in plant inventory than fields (polyculture gardens for food production are usually distinguished terminologically from fields, which at a given time have monoculture or a few inter-planted crops). Parks intergrade with gardens in the degree and kinds of manipulation (e.g., MacDougall 1972:41–44), sharing with them the characteristic of a delimited space, but accommodating less intensive efforts in a more extensive terrain – even if parts are intensively modified (see Creighton 2009 concerning English hunting parks, which may contain palaces and gardens within them). In ancient complex societies, both gardens and parks often have a residential association (although it may be part time). Gardens and parks vary in the proportions of food, raw material, condiment, and medicinal production versus aesthetic and symbolic content. Across the broad range from home gardens to elaborate, palatial gardens and parks, neither comestibles nor symbols and aesthetics are an exclusive focus.

Home gardens are intensively cultivated areas near dwellings, usually geared to a mix of foods, condiments, ornamentals, medicines, or raw materials; these contents are more prominent than those linked to social ostentation (Turner and Sanders 1992:265–266). Elaborate gardens may be attached to elite palaces, and some constitute royal pleasure grounds that mix state and social functions. Much of the organic content may be selected for symbolic or aesthetic reasons. In Mesoamerican archaeological research, home gardens have received the greatest amount of discussion and intergrade in a continuum with infield and outfield cultivation (e.g., Ball and Kelsay 1992; Dunning 1992; Hughbanks 1998; Isendahl 2002; Killion 1992; Killion et al. 1989; Smyth et al. 1995; see also Magnoni et al., Chapter 5 in this volume). The residential space may include both home gardens and outside cleared work areas (gray space [Killion 1990:202–203]). Among elaborate, ostentatious gardens and parks, Aztec royal installations are the only Mesoamerican examples that have been analyzed, primarily through documents (Alva Ixtlilxóchitl 1985[1868]:115–116; Evans 2000, 2004; Medina 1997; Mendizabál 1925; Moreno and Torres 2002; Musset 1986; Nuttall 1923; Solis Olguín 2002).

Groves may be the primary constituents in gardens or parks (Bonnechere 2007; Chandrashekara and Sankar 1998; Evans 2000:209–211; Falade 1984; Sheridan 2008; Uchiyamada 1998:181) or form an element of an internally differentiated garden or park. Groves are concentrations of trees largely cleared of any understory wood (Phibbs 1991:181). In many African societies, a solitary tree of particular species may come to represent functions of a grove and have monumental or memorial roles (Ross 1995:223–231, 2002:58–62, 2008). In Mesoamerica, species of symbolic importance included the ceiba (*Ceiba pentandra*, lowland tropics) and *ahuehuete* (*Taxodium mucronatum* Tenor, highland Mexico) (Granziera 2001). These trees or others may have appeared in green spaces, either solitary or in groves, including sacred groves (Gómez-Pompa et al. 1990). Also, cacao (*Theobroma cacao* L.), for its special economic and social value, may have been a component of gardens and parks where environmental conditions permitted. I include groves in the scope of gardens and parks.

Architecture, rather than open space, has predominated in anthropological and archaeological studies of urbanism; in Lawrence and Low's (1990:455) review of urban studies, for example, green space is scarcely mentioned. Among open spaces, plazas (spaces framed by buildings) have attracted ethnographic research (e.g., Low 2000) and archaeological studies (e.g., Inomata 2006; Moore 1996). Beyond anthropology in modern contexts, urban open spaces usually are part of planning public space (e.g., Carmona et al. 2008), with open space and public space sometimes treated interchangeably; however, authors often are more concerned with democratic ideals of the public sphere than with the physical qualities of open space. In New Urbanist planning, open space is often evaluated in terms of framing buildings and their uses (Duany et al. 2010:10.1; see also Jacobs 1993[1961]:123, 125), partly analogous to the "delimited open space" concept employed by Wynne-Jones and Fleisher (see Chapter 4 in this volume). In the New Urbanism, although access to "nature" is described as a basic right, types of green space and their social functions are given little attention (Duany et al. 2010:4.10, 6.4).

In Mesoamerican archaeology, public gray space has received more attention than green space, especially plazas because of their intimate association with buildings, accommodation of assemblies, and frequent use for display of sculpture or low platforms for rituals. Like plazas, open-air ball courts had importance early in Mesoamerica, ca. 1600 BC (Hill and Clark 2001). Even earlier in preceramic times, Gheo-Shih yielded a cleared area 20 by 7 m, lined by cobbles; it has been interpreted as a dance ground (Marcus and Flannery 1996:59), but may have been a ball court in view of its morphological resemblance to courts with flanking cobbles in Chihuahua and Sonora (Whalen and Minnis 1996:735–736).

In archaeology, we often are confronted by mapped cities or towns for which architectural and topographic features are recorded, but for which open spaces cannot be characterized as green or gray without excavation. Were we able to characterize open spaces more accurately within these two categories, we would have an improved basis for comparing urban forms. Such information would be particularly useful for gauging (1) the extent to which food production may have been conducted within the urban environment; (2) the extent of social ostentation in gardens and parks; (3) the opportunities for highly flexible social interactions and communications in certain kinds of open spaces, such as streets and plazas that could facilitate "bottom-up" social initiatives (see Wynne-Jones and Fleisher, Chapter 4 in this volume, for Swahili cities and Creekmore, Chapter 2 in this volume, for Upper Mesopotamia); and (4) the nature of urban boundaries. As addressed in this chapter, measurement of urban open space itself offers some analytical advantages for settlement comparisons.

OPEN SPACE AND SETTLEMENT COMPARISONS

Even without subdivision of predominantly green versus gray open spaces, calculations of open space provide a basis to compare settlements. The degree of nucleation of settlement has implications for a variety of urban issues, such as quality of life, sanitation and health, and urban food production. For the most part, archaeologists have compared population densities of ancient cities to analyze the degree of nucleation, rather than the proportions of open space. Whereas population figures for modern cities are readily available, such information is hard-won for ancient cities. Population calculations make a number of assumptions about household size or numbers of people in relation to architectural remains, such as residences or sleeping space (e.g., Rice and Culbert 1990), or to artifact densities (e.g., Sanders et al. 1979:34–40). Population density is valuable for comparing urban settlements, but the proportion of open space versus architectural space involves fewer assumptions. Of course, not all ancient settlements allow assessment of open spaces because surface architecture is not reliably visible.

Where we have information, the proportion of urban open space versus roofed architecture or structures covers a wide spectrum. For modern cities, Huang et al. (2007) used satellite imagery to determine the percent of open space in 47 cities in developing countries, which had a standard deviation range of 13.56–39.6 percent open space. For 30 cities in developed countries, one standard deviation encompassed 9.23–24.88 percent open space. Combined, the 77 modern cities span approximately 9–40 percent open space across one standard deviation. Occasionally, ancient cities have been evaluated for open space. Jashemski (2008:15) characterized Roman Pompeii as just over one-third open space approximately equally divided between green and gray space. Jim and Liu (2001:359, citing Zeng 1991) state that around AD 300, gardens covered half of Guangzhou, China, somewhat higher than the modern range. Not well represented in the Huang et al. (2007:185) modern sample were tropical and mountain areas where cloud cover was an impediment to imagery; thus, low-density tropical urbanism (Evans et al. 2007) is not adequately represented. At the tropical Mesoamerican capital of Cerro de las Mesas in Veracruz, where dispersed occupation is characteristic, conservatively 90 percent or more of the city is open space (mapped in my fieldwork). Clearly, marked variation characterizes open spaces among cities, with low-density tropical cities at one extreme, possibly as part of a continuum. Both Creekmore (Chapter 2 in this volume) and Fisher (Chapter 6 in this volume) remark on the paucity of open space for cities in third-millennium Upper Mesopotamia and Late Bronze Age Cyprus respectively, perhaps exhibiting extremes at the other end of the spectrum.

In the next section, I address one aspect of Mesoamerican urban open space – the archaeological potential for palatial gardens. Such gardens were recorded ethnohistorically for the Aztecs. Although other open spaces are important as well, the investments in royal and elite gardens deserve attention because of their potential labor investment and cultural and social roles. Instead, attention has focused to a considerable extent on the important subject of palaces, usually without consideration of associated open space (e.g., Christie 2003; Christie and Sarro 2006; Evans and Pillsbury 2004; Inomata and Houston 2000, 2001).

PALATIAL GARDENS: MESOAMERICAN PROSPECTS

Palatial gardens are important green space for ancient states and empires because of the considerable investment in plantings, layouts, embellishments, and upkeep. For Mesoamerica, the existence of palatial gardens before the Aztecs is an open question that must be addressed archaeologically because of the scant portrayal of gardens in imagery. Parks, because of their greater size, normally will be located beyond an ancient settlement or on its outskirts, so I focus more on gardens. Note that in modern U.S. usage, *park* is applied broadly to gardens, parks, forests, shores, and other phenomena with various sizes and functions and a broad range of locations, such as inside cities, on their edges, and far from them. Many former royal gardens in a variety of nations have been converted into public parks or gardens (local terms vary). In the garden and landscape literature, the term *garden* is applied to more intensively managed green spaces of varying sizes, usually associated with residences or public buildings, and usually with well-delimited borders (see Doolittle 2004:398; Hunt 2000:14–29).

To address urban palatial gardens in Mesoamerica, several criteria are relevant. First, I use examples of well-mapped urban settlements in order to identify candidate garden spaces. Certainly, many Aztec royal gardens described in ethnohistoric accounts were outside the Aztec Triple Alliance capitals; many gardens and parks were situated in environmentally symbolic and commanding positions or at locations suited to particular purposes, such as hunting, or a lower altitude with a milder climate to accommodate a broader range of species. Nevertheless, some gardens were established as part of elite or royal residences within cities. Elaborate gardens and parks are almost always accompanied by residential accommodations suited to the elevated status of the patron. Therefore, we can begin by examining the availability of space adjacent to palaces, with palaces defined here as elaborate residences of powerful elites or royals, not solely royals (Webster's [1963:605] second definition of "a large stately house," rather than the first definition: "the official residence of a sovereign"). Although at times archaeologists focus on rulers' residences, a broader range of elaborate residences is of interest for my purposes, and, in any case, royals may maintain multiple palaces. Certainly other institutional buildings, such as temples, may have been accompanied by elaborate gardens – as was the case in ancient Egypt and Rome, for instance – but ethnohistoric data from Mesoamerica mainly address royal gardens and parks attached to palaces.

Identification of adequate open space is a first step in my investigation of urban gardens. Regrettably, comparative literature does not always present scaled drawings of palaces and their grounds to guide us concerning how much open space to expect – and garden space surely varied. We might expect that gardens within densely built-up central districts often will be more cramped and might not be readily recognizable from surface indications. For my purposes, assessment will concentrate on evidence for sizable gardens, that is, garden space at least one or two times the area of the palace architecture; often the space will be far greater. Assessment focuses on spaces adjacent to palaces (or reached through bridges across water features) because of the characteristic integration of gardens with palatial architecture. Cross-culturally, palatial gardens were used for a variety of social entertainments, sports, strolls, contemplation, rituals, and social competition, making spatial contiguity with palaces a priority. This proximity does not preclude additional gardens and parks, also with palatial accommodations. Elites and royals often enjoyed multiple residences. Recognition of appropriate space is less straightforward than it might first appear. Palatial grounds often include kiosks, pavilions, shrines, and other structures. From a map of an abandoned city, such architectural remnants could mask the extent or presence of sufficient garden space because such structures may appear similar to surface traces of residences. A further concern is the contemporaneity of different structures. Garden space for noble families may be abandoned and reoccupied later by other city dwellers. Despite these caveats, it is of interest to know if adequate open space existed adjacent to Mesoamerican palaces.

A second consideration is waterworks or water-control devices. Waterworks (e.g., fountains, pools, streams, cascades) are one of the most common components of elaborate gardens comparatively. However, waterworks may vary enormously in scope, and only certain kinds are likely to be visible in surface mapping. In arid or semiarid environments, waterworks may have been part of the effort to sustain garden plants. Nevertheless, substantial labor for tending the garden may have been available to supply water as needed in different seasons, or parts of the garden may have been "hardscaped" with paths or other surfacing, reducing the need for water. In some cases, such as Monte Albán in Oaxaca, water supplies are not indicated with obvious canals. How would gardens have been watered? Egyptian art shows servants performing hand watering of gardens (Wilkinson 1998:20–31), pointing to the possibility at Monte Albán of a combination of rainfall, labor investment in hand watering, and use of plants reasonably well adapted to the rainfall regime. Just as in the case of monumental architecture, gardens can be examples of conspicuous use of labor. Paralleling Trigger's (1990:119) definition of monumental architecture as exceeding in scale and elaborateness what is functionally necessary, ostentatious gardens may present sizable installations and demand constant labor to water and tend plants. Thus, although water is an issue to be considered, arid or semiarid environments may rely on social solutions to the water (and nutrient) demands of plants through command of labor.

Delimitation of garden space is an additional criterion to consider, as walls may have surrounded gardens. Many gardens in ancient states are enclosed because they are associated with "private" residences, not public buildings. Without garden protection, plant delicacies might be subject to depredations by people and animals, such as deer. However, walls can be constructed in various ways; puddled mud or mud bricks may, like houses, undergo decay and erosion, leaving only a slightly elevated residue to represent the wall, or perhaps nothing visible. A more significant archaeological problem is the use of living fences that formed a blockade of trees, cactuses, or thorny plants to effectively screen off the space (Gutiérrez 2005). Thus, lack of remnant enclosing walls visible on the surface is not a secure basis to dismiss the possibility of palatial gardens. In the examples considered, walls are not evident – although caution is appropriate because faint features could be overlooked by archaeologists when not expected.

For Mesoamerica, Aztec royal gardens and parks are reported ethnohistorically (and documented archaeologically at Tetzcotzinco [Medina 1997; Parsons 1971:94–95, 122–125]). Through historical analogy and the abundant comparative cases of elaborate gardens in ancient states, we might suspect their presence earlier than the Aztecs. However, other expectations can be advanced. Perhaps sufficient space for palatial gardens will be detected in the tropical lowlands where low-density urbanism prevails, but not in compact highland cities where space is less abundant. Or, perhaps the abundance of open green space in low-density urbanism renders special gardens overly redundant and less likely to be important for elite distinction (yet content may distinguish them) (see Magnoni et al., Chapter 5 in this volume). Thus, perhaps neither highland nor lowland circumstances favor elaborate gardens. Ultimately, the issue of adequate space is an empirical question. Maps allow assessment as long as we bear in mind that urban places are remodeled with some frequency, which may obscure or blur past open spaces.

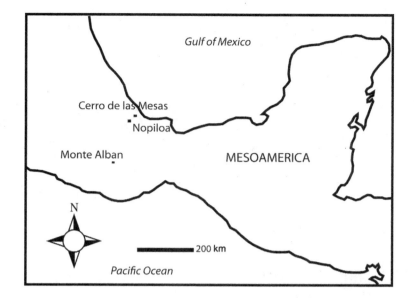

Figure 11.1 Locations
in Mexico of Cerro de
las Mesas and Nopiloa,
Veracruz, and Monte
Albán, Oaxaca (drawn
by author).

As examples, I consider Cerro de las Mesas and Nopiloa, two
successive capitals in south-central Veracruz, and Monte Albán, in
highland Oaxaca (Figure 11.1). The former two represent low-density
urbanism and the latter represents a compact capital on a series of
terraced hills. At Monte Albán, the natural constriction of the upper
hills might be thought to prohibit sufficient space for palatial gardens. As I demonstrate for all three cases, however, there is space for
gardens adjacent to palaces. For each case, I assess open space (not
occupied by architecture) in immediate proximity to palaces that is
of sufficient size to have accommodated an elaborate garden (at least
equal to the footprint of the palace or larger). The issue of water supply for plants and boundary marking is discussed for each situation.
In the designation of possible palatial garden space on figures, I arbitrarily draw rectangles to indicate open space; in some instances,
even more space might be marked, but the point of the exercise is
simply to indicate the presence of adequate space, not all potential
space nor its exact shape. Archaeological excavations are required to
assess space, in any case.

Cerro de las Mesas

This settlement is located within my Veracruz survey, which comprises several blocks along the Blanco and Guerengo Rivers in
south-central Veracruz. Cerro de las Mesas is an Early Classic (AD

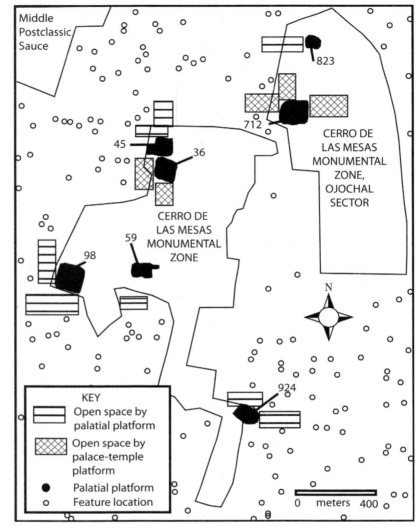

Figure 11.2 Cerro de las Mesas, possible palatial garden spaces. Contour-mapped areas of monumental construction are surrounded by a line; features outside that area were recorded during pedestrian survey (open circles). Monumental palatial platforms are 98, 59, 45, and 823; monumental palatial platforms with temple mounds atop are 712, 35, and 924 (drawn by author).

KEY
Open space by palatial platform
Open space by palace-temple platform
● Palatial platform
○ Feature location

300–600) capital in the Blanco Delta, with an earlier founding during the Late Preclassic period (600–300 BC) (Figure 11.2). It was the largest ancient center in the region, unusual in its agglomerative construction with repetition of monumental plaza groups in the core (Drucker 1943; Stark 1999, 2003; Stark and Ossa 2007; Stirling 1943). Cerro de las Mesas and other Classic-period centers in the region had waterworks – artificial ponds – integrated into the design of the centers in various ways (Daneels 2002; Stark 1999; Stark and Ossa 2007). The central pond at Cerro de las Mesas lies amid the concentration of temple mounds, but not proximate to palaces. These ponds took advantage of the proximity of the water table, and their excavation undoubtedly contributed fill to the predominantly earthen monumental architecture. The ponds appear to be part of the civic layout and only in a few cases incidentally close to palaces. Any palatial gardens could count on hand-dug wells down to the water table for "pot irrigation" of plants, that is, drawing water up by hand from a level likely only 6–8 m below (a practice employed today with gasoline pumps).

Massive rectangular platforms are the most obvious candidates for palatial residences (Stark 1999). Such functions for similar structures are confirmed by excavations at La Joya in the next drainage west (Daneels 2010). At Cerro de las Mesas, similar platforms sometimes have conical mounds added on top of the platform. Possibly these represent a conversion of a palace platform to support a funerary or commemorative temple when a royal or other prominent individual died. A commemorative temple atop the massive East Platform is reported from La Joya (Daneels, Guerrero, and Liberotti 2013), and funerary temples are known from the Maya lowlands (Coe 1956). Thus, for Cerro de las Mesas, both kinds of massive platforms can be examined, but the ones with temple superstructures are less certain to have had a palatial function without excavations. Other elite residences are likely present at the center, involving mounds with attached lower aprons (terraces), but their functions are not yet studied through excavation, and they are not analyzed here.

All five massive palatial platforms at the core of Cerro de las Mesas have adjacent space(s) sufficient for a garden, as do the two comparable platforms with a pyramid on top (Figure 11.2). None of the open spaces marked as possible gardens has obvious delimitation by a wall or other construction, but perishable or living fences may have been employed. Living fences are used in the region today around houses, and wooden posts cut from certain local species take root in the fence line around fields and form living fences.

Nopiloa

When paramount power waned at Cerro de las Mesas, several centers succeeded it, carving up the previously unified territory during the Late Classic period (AD 600–900). Nopiloa was one of the successors, located to the south along the Guerengo River (Medellín 1987; Stark 1999, 2003) (Figure 11.3). The monumental core nestles in a bend of the Guerengo River, with some peripheral artificial ponds further

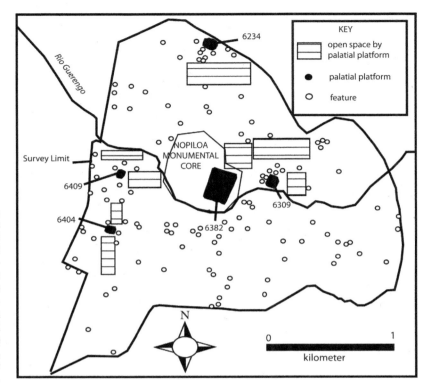

Figure 11.3 Nopiloa, possible palatial garden spaces. Contour-mapped areas of monumental construction are surrounded by a line; features outside that area were recorded during pedestrian survey (open circles). Monumental palatial platforms are 6234, 6409, 6404, 6382, and 6309 (drawn by author).

restricting the central space. The artificial ponds associated with the core are not located adjacent to the central palace platform, and thus, as with Cerro de las Mesas, they seem to have been designed as part of the civic layout, not the private purview of palaces.

At Nopiloa, the earlier tradition of massive rectangular palatial platforms continued. During the Late Classic period here (and at other capitals), some palatial platforms occurred at varying distances from the monumental core. The largest palatial platform in the region is at the south end of the main plaza at Nopiloa (feature 6382 in Figure 11.3), but possibly it is underlain by a natural hill. The river wraps around the eastern end of the monumental core where palatial platform 6382 is located. Today, a low, flooded area northeast of the large platform is partly a function of modern irrigation that drains from northern pastures to the Guerengo River. With less induced flooding, this area may have provided space for a garden, as marked on Figure 11.3. Four other palatial platforms are scattered around the monumental core, within a distance of approximately 1 km. Each has possible garden space adjacent. One platform (6309) has an artificial pond adjacent, the sole instance of a waterwork that may have been integrated into garden space. As with Cerro de las Mesas, none of the possible garden spaces is delimited with walls or other structures recognizable from the surface.

Monte Albán

Monte Albán was the capital of the Valley of Oaxaca for hundreds of years (Blanton 1978). Founded around 500 BC, it gained control of the Valley in subsequent centuries and maintained its paramount position until approximately AD 700, with some later occupation and use of the site. Monte Albán was founded on a hill located at the juncture of two branches of the Valley of Oaxaca, along the Atoyac River. Occupation eventually spread to adjacent hilltops. The settlement was mapped, and surface collections were used to date gridded segments of the site. Blanton defined fifteen districts of the settlement according to a combination of hilltops and the distribution of civic-ceremonial and elite-residential buildings away from the Main Plaza, where the preponderance of monumental and governmental structures is located. Residential occupation is located on terraces built on the hilltops and their upper sides. Blanton defined elaborate residences on the basis of mound groups (i.e., not just a terrace, but also mound structures) arranged enclosing a shared plaza or patio; outlying civic-ceremonial buildings consist of a single mound in an open area or a double-mound group. The elaborate residences are considered palaces for my analyses.

Based on Blanton's (1978) survey, Figure 11.4 locates elaborate residential mounds and instances where open space (not a terrace) was located in immediate proximity.[1] Of the thirty-five palatial residences, twenty (57 percent) have possible garden open space adjacent. More examples are found farther from the congested Main Plaza vicinity, as might be expected.

One unresolved issue concerns whether some terraces themselves may have supported elite gardens. Six additional elite residences have an adjacent terrace that is unusually long or the residence itself sits on an unusually large terrace that may have allowed garden space (elite groups 1461, 165, 174, 1306, 278, 1453 in Blanton's numbering system). In general, terraces were considered residential by the survey crews, but the possibility that some might, instead, have been devoted to ostentatious gardens should be kept in mind. Were these six to have had garden functions, 74 percent of elite residences

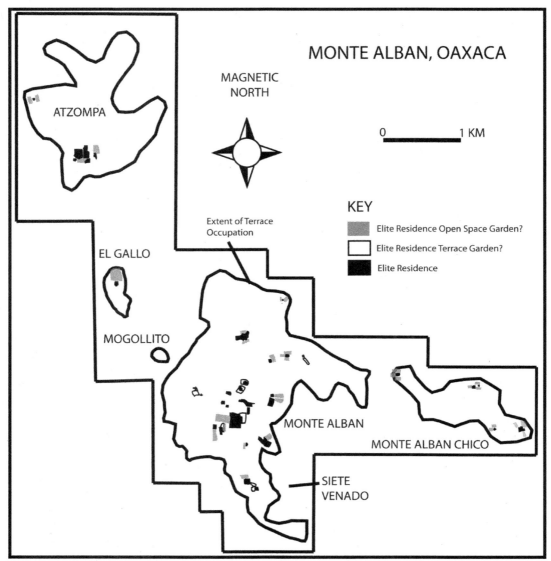

Figure 11.4 Monte Albán, possible elite garden spaces (adapted from figure 1.3 in Blanton 1978:4). Possible elite terrace gardens are unusually large terraces associated with elite residences. Possible open space gardens are not terraces, but open ground.

had adjacent open space for a garden. Aside from the six cases with adjacent terraces, which have physical delimitations, the other open space appears to have no surrounding wall.

The Valley of Oaxaca is semiarid, with a pattern of seasonal summer rains. Permanent surface water is not available on the hilltops, but the river and irrigation canals for farming provide water near the base of the main hill (Blanton 1978:54–55). Water features were noted only at Atzompa, El Gallo, and at the edge of Monte Albán proper (to the northwest). Only at Atzompa and El Gallo are

In the figure, the map is labeled:

MONTE ALBAN, OAXACA

MAGNETIC NORTH

ATZOMPA

0 ___ 1 KM

Extent of Terrace Occupation

KEY

Elite Residence Open Space Garden?
Elite Residence Terrace Garden?
Elite Residence

EL GALLO

MOGOLLITO

MONTE ALBAN

MONTE ALBAN CHICO

SIETE VENADO

water impoundments part of the possible garden spaces marked on Figure 11.4. Thus, if species intolerant of local conditions were planted, extra labor by servants or slaves or through labor tax would be required to haul water and decant it to plants.

Settlement growth seems to have played a role in the possibility for adjacent open space for elite residents (Blanton 1978: figures 2.1, 3.1, 3.2, 4.1, 4.2). Palatial residences on outlying knolls are located in parts of the city (Atzompa, El Gallo, and Monte Albán Chico) that generally have little or no pottery from the Early I period (500–200 BC) and little from the Monte Albán II period (200 BC–AD 200). By Monte Albán III–IV (AD 200–950) these areas have moderate or marked amounts of diagnostic pottery, suggesting outward growth of the settlement and a possibility that outlying elaborate residences were constructed after much of the central space was too congested to permit additional extensive gardens.

Discussion

The important conclusion of this exercise concerning open space adjacent to palatial residences is that such space *is* available for many of the elite residences at Monte Albán as well as those in the two Veracruz capitals. Therefore, the potential for elaborate gardens is not restricted to the two low-density urban capitals. Monte Albán displays a congestion of residential terraces on and around the tops of the set of hills, yet elite residences typically have space adjacent that could have accommodated gardens.

As Monica Smith (2008) notes, archaeologists have not been preoccupied with open space in settlements, an observation applicable to palatial gardens (see Wynne-Jones and Fleisher, Chapter 4 in this volume, who include attention to open space). Unless we flag and investigate possible elaborate garden spaces, we will be immensely limited in assessing investments in open spaces. As indicated by the tendency of elaborate residences to locate in newer, outer areas of Monte Albán where more open space existed, green space in settlement peripheries may be more characteristic than in the central core, which can affect our determination of settlement boundaries, as discussed next.

GREEN SPACE, URBAN BOUNDARIES, AND URBAN MODELS

Settlement limits pose more complex issues than commonly assumed, a point well illustrated by Goodman's (2007) study of Roman urban peripheries. In cases she examines, city walls and orthogonal grids suggest urban limits, yet peri-urban facilities are common. Settlement limits are particularly elusive for dispersed occupation at lowland Mesoamerican centers, where the amount of green space is magnified (cf. Magnoni et al., Chapter 5 in this volume), but dispersed occupation occurs more widely. In Mesoamerica, Graham (1999) contrasts lowland "green cities" to "stone cities." In the lowlands, occupational remains may decrease in density with greater distance from a center, continuing into the countryside. Consequently, the peripheries of a settlement have even more open space than the central settlement, and settlement limits become problematic. Much of the inter-residential space within low-density lowland settlements is assumed to have been cultivated in some fashion (Stark and Ossa 2007).

The extent to which Mesoamerican lowland settlements can be characterized as low-density urbanism has been challenged (Smith 2005:412). Smith (2005:412) shows that the degree of contrast between the Mesoamerican lowlands and highlands is exaggerated for the Postclassic period. Smith (2005:412) expressed doubt about the reality of greater residential dispersal in lowland Mesoamerica, based on his calculations for population densities in Postclassic Mesoamerican cities because three lowland settlements (Santa Rita, Mayapan, and Naco) fell within the ranges of highland low-density settlements.

The three Postclassic lowland settlements do not afford data consonant with earlier periods, however. Calculations for Classic-period lowland settlements show instances of a considerably lower density than Smith encountered in his late sample, and they also show that densities can vary considerably between the denser core of settlements and the outlying sectors (Table 11.1) (Culbert and Rice 1990). As noted earlier, calculations of open space versus architectural space could provide a more reliable physical comparison of settlement densities than interjection of demographic calculations, but population densities are the data available.

Table 11.1 shows declines in population density away from settlement cores that illustrate the challenge of defining settlement limits. In several Maya cases, settlements seem to "fade" into the countryside, which provides a backdrop of scattered rural hamlets or farmsteads. Dzibilichaltún is an example (Stuart et al. 1979), as well as Nohmul (Hammond et al. 1988; Pyburn 1990). Even with a denser concentration of residential remains within an enclosing wall, such as at Mayapan, new work showed residences scattered beyond the

Table 11.1 *Settlement population densities at lowland Mesoamerican sites*

Site	Phase or Period	Area in ha	Area km²	Pop. Estimate	Density per ha	Density per km²	Source
Santa Rita Corozal, Belize	Postclassic period	500	5.00	7,000	14	1400	Smith (2005:412) using data from Chase (1990) and Chase and Chase (1988)
Mayapan, Yucatan	Postclassic period	420	4.20	21,000	50	5,000	Smith (2005:412) using data from Pollock et al. (1962)
Naco, Honduras	Postclassic period	160	1.60	10,000	62.5	6250	Smith (2005:412) using data from Wonderly (1985, 1986)
Sayil, Campeche, Mexico	Terminal Classic period	345	3.45				Tourtellot et al. (1990:219, 245, 248, 256)
– minimum				7,159	20.8	2075	
– maximum				10,858	31.5	3147	
Seibal, Peten, Guatemala	Late/Terminal Classic period	1525	15.25	4,366	2.86	286	Tourtellot (1990:102)
Copan, Honduras	Late Classic period	1200	1.2[a]				Webster and Freter (1990:40, 46–47, 51–52, 60)
– urban core minimum				5,797	48.7	4871	
– urban core maximum				9,214	77.43	7743	
– surrounding Copan pocket minimum				9,360	4.07	407	

(continued)

Table 11.1 (*continued*)

Site	Phase or Period	Area in ha	Area km²	Pop. Estimate	Density per ha	Density per km²	Source
– surrounding Copan pocket maximum		2220		11,239	5.06	506	
Tikal, Peten, Guatemala	Imix Phase, Late Classic period	12,000	22.2[a]	62,000	5.17	517	Culbert et al. (1990:115–117, 119–120)
– central 9 km²					9.2	922	
– next 7 sq km²					7.1	711	
– remaining 104 km²					4.4	440	
– rural area 194 km²					1.5	153	
Peten Lakes area transects (non-center), Guatemala	Late Classic period	1650[b]	16.5[b]	4752[a]	2.8	288	Rice and Rice (1990:140, 143)
Quirigua, Guatemala	Late Classic period	3000	3.00	1,221	4.07	407	Ashmore (1990:71, 80)
Nohmul, Belize	Late Classic period	2200	22[c]	3,310	1.5	150	Pyburn (1990:193)
Cerro de las Mesas, Veracruz	Early Classic period	4940	49.4[c]				Stark (2003:401)
– low estimate				4,000	0.81	81	
– high estimate				10,000	2.02	202	
Komchen, Yucatan, Mexico	Late Nabanche Phase, Late Preclassic period		2.00	3000	15	1500	Ringle and Andrews (1990:223, 229)

[a] interpolated data
[b] inhabitable
[c] mapped

wall (Russell 2008) (likely not uncommon, see also Rome ca. AD 1 [Morley (1996:33)].

Tikal combines residential dispersal with delimitation of the settlement by earthworks and ditches (Puleston 1983; Puleston and Callender 1967). The more extensively documented northern earthwork and ditch were first interpreted as a defensive boundary extending between the wetlands located to the east and west. These findings proved problematic with restudy (Webster et al. 2004, 2007). A proposed southern earthwork and ditch was not found; the southeastern earthwork was accompanied by a parallel formation slightly farther in toward the center – a double-ditch alignment; the northern feature proved to be mainly a ditch; a western ditch was detected. Inconsistencies in the depth of the ditches and the height of the earthwork (often absent) cast considerable doubt on the original defensive interpretation, particularly as attacking forces would meet no obstacle to the south. Nevertheless, the constructions are "something" and suggest an emic delimitation, perhaps unfinished. From these Maya examples, we see instances in which no obvious boundary was detected (Dzibilchaltún), a clear surrounding wall did not encompass all the residences associated with the center (Mayapan) (see also Becan [Thomas 1981]), and population densities varied according to a delimiting feature (Tikal).

The Early Classic capital of Cerro de las Mesas in Veracruz offers yet another situation. There, areas without residential traces – "reserve spaces" (presumably green in that environment) –are scattered around the monumental core at a distance of 2 to 3 km (Figure 11.5). Although these spaces require future evaluations, for the moment they are considered a transitional or delimiting feature, somewhat akin to the ditches around Tikal. Residences occur beyond the reserve spaces, but the pattern of spaces seems to represent an effect of planning, as they remained unoccupied by domestic mounds during the Classic period. The reserve spaces in Figure 11.5 are marked arbitrarily because we do not know the allocation of exterior space around domestic mounds in the vicinity, nor whether subsequent occupations may have encroached on the reserve space. In addition, the survey did not locate occupation north of the Viejo River, which may also contribute to the peripheral space delimiting Cerro de las Mesas. Comparative data, discussed next, provide a broader context for understanding peripheral–urban green space.

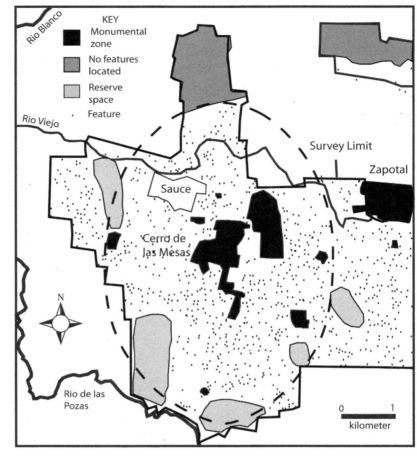

Figure 11.5 Reserve space around the monumental core of Early Classic Cerro de las Mesas. Dashed line shows transition zone of possible settlement limits. Zapotal is predominantly Late Classic, and Sauce is a Middle Postclassic town (drawn by author).

Comparative Examples of Urban Peripheral Gardens

Peripheral palatial or other institutional gardens are relatively common in ancient states and are understandable in part through a historical view of land use, city growth, and land values (Table 11.2). They are only one of a variety of open spaces and associated activities near urban peripheries; for example, Kostof (1992:130–132) notes markets, sports, and other functions (see also Goodman 2007 for the western Roman Empire). A concern with city peripheries has a counterpart in modern contexts. Today, urban planners and other scholars use the notion of a peri-urban transition area, or urban fringe, to examine multiple effects of urban centers: demand for nearby resources that may lead to agricultural, watershed, or soil changes; disposal of by-products and waste; the expansion of cities with growing populations, especially through in-migration; changes in nearby smaller (rural) settlements; and counter-urbanization as wealthy individuals

Table 11.2 *Examples of city margins with peripheral gardens and parks*

Algeria, Fes, 19th–20th centuries
Great houses and gardens predominantly on the periphery (Revault et al. 1992:363).

Assyria, Assur, Nineveh, 704–681 BC
Temple and garden built outside wall of Assur; four extramural royal gardens or "plantations" at Nineveh (Dalley 1993:6; Foster 2004:215).

Austria, Vienna, AD 1683–1720, Beidermeir AD 1812–1848
Nobles had to have a permanent residence in Vienna, and palaces were built outside the walls of the city. During this period, bourgeois building construction remained restricted to the outlying areas of the suburbs (Rotenberg 2008:118).

Aztec empire, Late Postclassic period, Tenochtitlan, Texcoco, AD 1350–1519
Royal gardens and hunting parks, most within 5–12 km of the capital (Evans 2000:209–211).

Byzantine, Thessalonike, Constantinople, AD 1204–1453
Monastery gardens inside and outside the city; suburban Constantinople villas along the sea and outside the city walls; area between two city walls included gardens, tombs, and monasteries (Constantinides 2002:87–89; Talbot 2002:61; Mango 1985:47, 49).

China, Song, and Yuan Dynasties, AD 960–1126, AD 1279–1368
Loyang, gardens on the outskirts (Lifang and Yu 1986:16).
Kaifeng, Northern Song Dynasty, 20 gardens in the city outskirts, with flower, recreational, and residential qualities (Chen and Yu 1986:16; Hammond 2008:45); environs of Kaifeng replete with gardens and orchards, with suburban villas, feasting halls, monasteries, and nunneries (West 2005:297, 298).

China, Suzhou, Jiangnan, Loyang, Ming Dynasty, AD 1450–1650
One of four gardens in gazetteer was within the walls, another on the outskirts, and the other two inside and outside the walls of Kunshan, a smaller subordinate city (Clunas 1996:16); one owner had a garden inside and another smaller one just outside the Loyang city walls; elders built gardens inside walls on vacant land, but some were outside (Hammond 2008:46, 47); survey by Ch'I of Loyang counted 191 in the county, 74 in the city and the rest outside the city (Smith 1992:67).

Dutch, AD 1650–1702
Banlieue became a transitional territory between town and country, near town walls, where kitchen gardens and orchards were rented or purchased by the economically less viable (de Jong 1990:29).

England, Birmingham, also Vienna, Austria, and Paris, France, 20th century
Fringe belts with extensive land use at the edge of an urban area, formed when the city was not growing, with recreational areas, public utilities, allotment gardens, sports clubs, and other institutions (Whitehand and Morton 2006:2048).

England, Medieval
Deer parks on the urban fringe formed, in effect, suburban green belts, in some cases arresting city growth (Creighton 2009:158).

Genoa, Republic of, 16th century
Lavish villas outside city walls, daily commute to city dwellings (Magnani 2008:55).

Greece, Classical
Delos gardens outside city, but elsewhere at Tegea, scattered among houses; Athens gardens associated with town periphery, men of property (Osborne 1992:377–379, 381); Athenian educational gymnasia outside of city in garden and grove areas (Carroll 2003:29, 50–52).

India, Mughal Empire, AD 17th and 18th centuries
Suburban gardens and residences for early ruler at Agra, not in citadels (Wescoat 1992:336); Shahjahanabad had extensive suburbs outside the city wall with gardens, important tombs, markets, and inns (Blake 1991:57–66).

Iran, Isfahan, 17th–18th centuries
Royal palace of Farahabad built in suburb ca. 10 km from the city center by last Safavid Shah, with two earlier rulers also building their own suburban palaces at Isfahan (Brignoli 2007:144); Ettinghausen (1976:7) notes some elaborate gardens in the Islamic tradition were in suburbs or the countryside.

(continued)

Table 11.2 (continued)

Italy, Rome, Renaissance
Rome included area within the walls and adjacent suburban land outside the walls; surrounding land included villas with gardens of people whose activities centered in Rome; elite villas mostly within about 35 km of Rome, but up to 70 km (Coffin 1979 especially vii).

Northeastern United States, 19th century
Use of rural cemeteries by public as parks, also informal open spaces just outside the developed area of cities (Low et al. 2005:20, 21).

Ottoman, Istanbul, 18th century
New lavish palatial gardens along suburban banks of the Bosphorus and Golden Horn, with return of court of Sultan in 1703; old suburban imperial gardens declined as foci of court life, with various outcomes, disuse, renovations, but some made into gardens for the wider public (Hamadeh 2008:91).

Roman Empire, Rome, 1st century BC–AD 1st century, Pompeii, AD 79
Many wealthy, influential Romans built private villas just outside Rome (Carroll 2003:58); at Pompeii, elite gardens were concentrated toward the southwest edge of the city (Ciarallo 2001:39).

Seljuk Alanya, Turkey, AD 1221–1250
Winter retreat and later de facto capital at Alanya, with seven or more outlying gardens and palaces (also tent pavilions), some royal, some occupied by emirs. Gardens range from 1.9 to 5.9 km from the citadel, mounted travel used. The court, with most emirs in attendance, was seasonally mobile in warfare (Redford et al. 2000:24, 27, 31–32, 40, 42, 54–55, 69).

Sri Lanka, Kandy Kingdom, 18th century
Religious buildings, including temples, built on outskirts of Kandy, also royal garden in suburb 5 miles southwest of capital (Duncan 1990:76).

Yoruba, Ile-Ife, 1388 AD–
Land between the two town walls of Ile-Ife was used for gardens, hunting, wood lots; beyond the outer wall, sacred groves merged into the town farms. Sacred groves occurred within the first wall, the second wall, and outside the second wall, but mainly at the city edge, in part owing to constraints on land (Falade 1984:29, 31, 32, 36).

use modern transport to reside outside the urban area even if they work there (Simon 2008).

Peripheral elite gardens attached to elaborate residences as well as other peripheral green spaces are documented in several historic cases, even though urban garden location is seldom the main focus of the landscape and gardening literature (Table 11.2). At Pompeii, for example, elite gardens were concentrated toward the southwest edge of the city (Ciarallo 2001:39). Royal gardens were part of a settlement boundary at Bianliang (Kaifeng) in Song Dynasty China (West 2005); elite gardens also were on the outskirts of Loyang (Lifang and Yu 1986:16). In Renaissance Rome, several elite villas were located outside the city walls, indicating that aristocratic estates may be removed from the denser, more obvious settlement, yet are a functional part of the city, with owners moving between or among residences (Coffin 1979).

Because of land values and land tenure, space for palatial grounds is more readily available at the edges of cities. As Revault

et al. (1992:363) state for Fez, Morocco, in the nineteenth and twentieth centuries, new palatial residences and grounds frequently were
located marginally because of the densely built central city and the
difficulty of acquiring appropriate land for a lavish and extensive
property. Brignoli (2007:147) remarks on similar factors in respect
to the location of a Safavid royal palace. Certainly some demoli-
tion and redesign of central space can occur, especially if initiated
by powerful rulers or governments, but this process of conversion
does not afford the only solution because peripheral locations can
be selected.

Palatial garden estates are only one of the space-hungry facilities
that may have gravitated to a peripheral location. Constantinides
(2002:87–89) notes the movement of Late Byzantine monasteries from
the countryside to cities for security reasons, often to city margins to
accommodate their orchards and gardens (see also Talbot 2002:61).
Hunting parks may be maintained outside cities in locations where
environmental conditions are suited to game (Constantinides
2002:96; Tabbaa 1992:305; Williamson 1992:74–75). In Aztec times,
royal or palatial gardens were found within the capital near the center, but also outside at considerable distances to take advantage of
particularly striking or symbolic natural locations or different climate zones (Evans 2000:209–211). Other provocations to establish
outlying estates include respite from city life (unconvincing for low-
density urbanism) and refuge from city plagues (for Constantinople,
Auzépy 1995:360; for Renaissance Rome, Coffin 1979:9, 84). Thus,
extensive gardens or parks can occur scattered into the countryside
and present a mosaic of distances despite the fact that the owners
who utilize them are city residents.

Some peripheral gardens have a food-production emphasis
rather than social ostentation, a function incorporated in land-use
models. Variation in land use with distances from a town motivates
von Thünen's (1966 [1875]) isolated state model in which transport
costs, market values of products, and cultivation frequency vary in
"rings" around a settlement (see summary and discussion of modern contexts at different scales in Bradford and Kent [1977:28–41]). In
von Thünen's model, more-distant land costs less to obtain and can
be profitable with lower economic yields, but transport costs may
negate this extra income, depending on the crop. Intensity of cultivation is adjusted to the distance and transport costs, usually with less-
intensive regimes at a greater distance, but modified according to

the weight of the crop. On the outskirts of Greek city-states (Osborne 1992:381), intensive irrigation gardening of foods reflected von Thünen-like principles of land use. As Renaissance Dutch merchant families sought country estates, individuals of lesser means rented or bought gardens or orchards on the edges of towns (de Jong 1990: 29).

A more recent expression of the phenomenon of peripheral green space, land costs, and access involves urban fringe belts. The fringe belt concept dates from 1936 in a study of Berlin by H. Louis and was then emphasized in the work by geographer Conzen (Whitehand 2001:105). Whitehand and Morton (2006:2047) point out that urban fringe belts derive from peripheral installations with associated open space (e.g., sports, health, or educational facilities) that are engulfed by leapfrog urban growth. They note that fringe belts typically have an intermittent or mosaic spatial form, which provides one morphological model for urban peripheries. Once established, despite urban growth, the peripheral uses can be difficult to replace with higher density uses, so the fringe belt remains.

Thus, peripheral open space responds to a complex set of factors. Land costs, claims on land, governmental regulation, and the history of building in the urban settlement, as well as other factors, can conspire to provide incentives for a variety of more spatially extensive land uses at the city margin. Some of these uses may finger out into the countryside, creating an indistinct or mosaic city margin. This possibility has been scarcely considered in archaeological practice. Sufficient spatial separation of architectural groups from the core of an urban settlement has normally been grounds for defining a different site. As noted, comparative data concerning peripheral gardens and parks call into question archaeological site-definition procedures.

With an urban green-space perspective, we can be alert to urban boundaries not as hard lines, nor entirely as a gradient, but also as a peripheral mosaic. Faced with the question of where to "draw the line" for a settlement boundary, an arbitrary density limit for artifacts is usually established. At Teotihuacán, a criterion of 300 m without structures or other significant materials was applied (Millon 1973:8). At Xochicalco, an interval of 100 m was used (Hirth 2000:54). Hirth (2000:54) separates the concept of settlement definition from community definition in discussing Xochicalco. Because he refers to outlying settlements linked to Xochicalco by roads and situated 1–3 km away as communities, he presumably does not consider them part of Xochicalco (the boundaries of the Xochicalco community are not stated). Such settlements would be possible candidates for accommodating peripheral palace, garden, or estate facilities. Maya settlements such as Caracol and Cobá, with stone roads to outlying architectural groups, warrant attention in regard to peripheral facilities as well.

Other archaeological reasoning also can be rethought. In the case of Monte Albán, terraces descending the hill slope had traces of residential walls and domestic artifacts, but eventually, lower terraces did not yield these traces; thus, they were excluded from the city limits (Blanton 1978:8), but such locations would be subject to greater erosional deposition that might mask occupation traces. Commonly, urban studies neglect the possibility of gardens and villas or other installations slightly removed from the built-up portion of the settlement as well as their roles as part of the urban settlement.

One example of outlying installations concerns Tikal, for which "minor ceremonial centers" were identified that fall within the area eventually discovered to be delimited by the ditch and embankment segments (Puleston 1983). In a study of Roman villas during the Renaissance, Coffin (1979:vii) developed a concept of city limits, which includes "all the land surrounding the city which is owned by persons whose political, religious, commercial, or social activities are centered within it." As a result, he accommodates villas used by Roman elites in the vicinity of the more compact portion of that capital; in his view, Rome is not the area within the city walls, but approximately the modern region of Latium or Lazio. The villas range up to 70 km distant from Rome, but most fall within half that distance, approximating ancient Rome's peri-urban extent in Goodman's (2007:20) analysis. Such distances reflect advantages of animal and wheeled transport different from Mesoamerican technologies, as well as construction of roads leading to Rome. Ethnohistoric documents mention a range of distances for royal Aztec parks and gardens (Evans 2000:209–211); most were in the Basin of Mexico within 5–12 km of the capitals.

In sum, royal or elite residences and gardens may be located at some distance from what archaeologists usually take as a settlement boundary, yet the periodic visits or seasonal uses of these diverse properties show a city with a mosaic extent (although still within an accessible area). In a behavioral sense, the city can be seen as the array of close places in regular annual use for continuing residential and social interactions connected with city life. From this perspective, the fuzzy limits of low-density tropical settlements are more understandable and constitute a more widespread phenomenon than recognized by any mechanical process of site delimitation in archaeological survey and mapping. Especially elites with peripheral estates may participate in urban affairs on a periodic basis (e.g., Coffin 1979; Tourtellot 1993).

Peripheral gardens and parks have implications for urban models. Some modern cities support Burgess's (1925) idea of higher income or status groups located toward the periphery, but Sjoberg (1960) described an inverted model for preindustrial cities, with the most powerful elements of society clustered near the urban center (see review in Abbott 1974). Here I call attention to the urban periphery and its potential as a location for social institutions or residences with elevated status that command extensive space. In some respects, peripheral elite gardens are more in keeping with Burgess's original ideas, yet peripheral palaces and grounds coexist with others near the urban core as Sjoberg (1960) contended, supporting a dual model. In some cases, such as the extension of suburban villas from Constantinople (and Istanbul) along the waterfront (Constantinides 2002:87–89; Mango 1985:47, 49; Talbot 2002:6), the pattern is more in keeping with Hoyt's (1939) radial-sector model than a concentric model.

Peripheral gardens and parks suggest that archaeological settlement definitions for major urban centers should exercise caution about peripheries and that urban studies in archaeology will benefit from more attention to open space generally. Investigators should examine what might otherwise be thought of as outlying settlements in the immediate vicinity to see whether some may reflect a mosaic urban extent. A mosaic extent in some cases may resemble modern fringe belts. At stake with palatial grounds is evidence concerning class differentiation and the allocation of labor and resources in Mesoamerican urban societies.

CONCLUSION

On several counts, greater archaeological attention to urban open space is warranted, especially gardens and parks. Computation of the percent of open space can provide a basis to compare degrees of settlement nucleation. My search for open space adjacent to elite residences produced positive results in both low- and high-density urban examples in Mesoamerica. Peripheral reserve spaces around Cerro de las Mesas suggest that green space helped delimit the settlement. Palatial and other garden or green space at settlement peripheries is not uncommon in comparative literature despite scant attention focused on the phenomenon. Despite the archaeological fascination with architecture, urban life includes many open-space activities at facilities, such as processional roadways, plazas, ballgame courts, and market areas. Elite gardens may have played a role in establishing and maintaining class differences, social interactions, and aesthetic and symbolic experiences, and they may have involved substantial investments. Our grasp of the spatial framework of ancient complex societies remains incomplete without more consideration of open spaces. Fieldwork protocols for investigating open spaces are only beginning to be elaborated to assess our prospects for investigating these parts of the urban environment, and appropriate research designs constitute an agenda for future work.

ACKNOWLEDGMENTS

I thank Andrew Creekmore and Kevin Fisher for their invitation to participate in the symposium at the 74th annual meeting of the Society for American Archaeology, Atlanta, Georgia. My comparative research was conducted with a Pre-Columbian Studies Fellowship at Dumbarton Oaks, 2010, and I am grateful to colleagues there who provided me many leads about sources. Several people provided helpful comments that benefitted this chapter, but are not responsible for the content: Richard Blanton, Grey Gundaker, Reiko Ishihara, Verónica Pérez Rodríguez, Michael Smith, Monica Smith, Ben Stanley, and Sarah Striker.

NOTES

1 More recent work at Atzompa (Robles García and Andrade Cuautle 2011) updates the information from Blanton (1978) on the basis of excavation and more detailed mapping. One elite residence is added, but another is not included, and the number of elite residences at the center of Atzompa is reduced to two. The small, published scale of the new maps does not permit incorporation of the new information in this chapter.

REFERENCES CITED

Abbott, Walter F. 1974 Moscow in 1897 as a Preindustrial City: A Test of the Inverse Burgess Zonal Hypothesis. *American Sociological Review* 39:4:542–550.

Al-Hagla, Kalid 2008 Towards a Sustainable Neighborhood: The Role of Open Spaces. *International Journal of Architectural Research* (Archnet-IJAR) 2:2:162–177.

Alva Ixtlilxóchitl, Fernando de 1985[1868] *Obras históricas : incluyen el texto completo de las las llamadas relaciones e historia de la nación chichimeca en una nueva versión establecida con el cotejo de los manuscritos más antiguos que se conocen.* Vol. 2. Instituto de Investigaciones Históricas, Universidad Nacional Autónoma de México, Mexico City.

Ashmore, Wendy 1990 Ode to a Dragline: Demographic Reconstructions at Classic Quirigua. In *Precolumbian Population History in the Maya Lowlands,* ed. by T. Patrick Culbert and Don S. Rice, pp. 63–82. University of New Mexico Press, Albuquerque.

Auzépy, Marie-France 1995 Les déplacements de l'empereur dans la ville et ses environs (VIIIe-Xe siecles). In *Constantinople and Its Hinterland,* edited by Cyril A. Mango, Gilbert Dagron, and Geoffrey Greatrex, pp. 357–366. Aldershot, Hampshire, UK.

Ball, Joseph W. and Richalene G. Kelsay 1992 Prehistoric Intrasettlement Land Use and Residual Soil Phosphate Levels in the Upper Belize Valley, Central America. In *Gardens of Prehistory: The Archaeology of Settlement Agriculture in Greater Mesoamerica,* edited by Thomas W. Killion, pp. 234–262. The University of Alabama Press, Tuscaloosa.

Blake, Stephen P. 1991 *Shahjahanabad: The Sovereign City in Mughal India, 1639–1739.* Cambridge University Press, Cambridge.

Blanton, Richard E. 1978 *Monte Albán: Settlement Patterns at the Ancient Zapotec Capital.* Academic Press, New York.

Bonnechere, Pierre 2007 The Place of the Sacred Grove (*Alsos*) in the Mantic Rituals of Greece: The Example of the *Alsos* of Trophonios at Lebadeia (Boeotia). In *Sacred Gardens and Landscapes: Ritual and Agency,* edited by Michel Conan, pp. 17–54. Dumbarton Oaks Research Library and Collection, Washington, DC.

Bradford, M. G. and William A. Kent 1977 *Human Geography: Theories and Their Applications.* Oxford University Press, Oxford.

Brignoli, Jean-Do 2007 The Royal Gardens of Farahabad and the Fall of Shah Sultan Husayn Revisited. In *Middle East Garden Traditions: Unity and Diversity: Questions, Methods and Resources in a Multicultural Perspective,* edited by Michel Conan, pp. 141–157. Dumbarton Oaks Research Library and Collection, Washington, DC.

Burgess, Edward W. 1925 The Growth of the City: An Introduction to a Research Project. In *The City,* edited by Edward W. Burgess and R. D. McKenzie, pp 47–62. University of Chicago Press, Chicago.

Carmona, Matthew, Claudio de Magalhães, and Leo Hammond 2008 *Public Space: The Management Dimension.* Routledge, London.

Carroll, Maureen 2003 *Earthly Paradises: Ancient Gardens in History and Archaeology.* J. Paul Getty Museum, Los Angeles.

Chandrashekara, U. M. and S. Sankar 1998 Ecology and Management of Sacred Groves in Kerala, India. *Forest Ecology and Management* 112(1–2):165–177.

Chase, Diane Z. 1990 The Invisible Maya: Population History and Archaeology at Santa Rita Corozal. In *Precolumbian Population History in the Maya Lowlands,* edited by T. Patrick Culbert and Don S. Rice, pp. 199–214. University of New Mexico Press, Albuquerque.

Chase, Diane Z. and Arlen F. Chase 1988 *A Postclassic Perspective: Excavations at the Maya Site of Santa Rita Corozal, Belize*. Precolumbian Art Research Institute, Monograph 4. San Francisco.

Chen, Lifang and Yu Sianglin 1986 *The Garden Art of China = [Chung-kuo tsao yüan i shu]*. Timber Press, Portland, OR.

Christie, Jessica Joyce, editor 2003 *Maya Palaces and Elite Residences: An Interdisciplinary Approach*. University of Texas Press, Austin.

Christie, Jessica Joyce and Patricia Joan Sarro, editors 2006 *Palaces and Power in the Americas: From Peru to the Northwest Coast*. University of Texas Press, Austin.

Ciarallo, Anna Maria 2001 *Gardens of Pompeii*. The J. Paul Getty Museum, Los Angeles.

Clunas, Craig 1996 *Fruitful Sites: Garden Culture in Ming Dynasty China*. Reaktion Books, London.

Coe, Michael D. 1956 The Funerary Temple among the Classic Maya. *Southwestern Journal of Anthropology* 12:387–394.

Coffin, David R. 1979 *The Villa in the Life of Renaissance Rome*. Princeton University Press, Princeton, NJ.

Constantinides, Costas N. 2002 Byzantine Gardens and Horticulture in the Late Byzantine Period, 1204–1453: The Secular Sources. In *Byzantine Garden Culture*, edited by Antony Littlewood, Henry Maguire, and Joachim Wolschke-Bulmahn, pp. 87–103. Dumbarton Oaks Research Library and Collection, Washington, DC.

Creighton, Oliver H. 2009 *Designs upon the Land: Elite Landscapes of the Middle Ages*. Boydell Press, Woodbridge, UK.

Culbert, T. Patrick and Don S. Rice, editors 1990 *Precolumbian Population History in the Maya Lowlands*. University of New Mexico Press, Albuquerque.

Culbert, T. Patrick, Laura J. Kosakowsky, Robert E. Fry, and William A. Haviland 1990 The Population of Tikal, Guatemala. In *Precolumbian Population History in the Maya Lowlands*, edited by T. Patrick Culbert and Don S. Rice, pp. 103–121. University of New Mexico Press, Albuquerque.

Dalley, Stephanie 1993 Ancient Mesopotamian Gardens and the Identification of the Hanging Gardens of Babylon Resolved. *Garden History* 21(1):1–13.

Daneels, Annick 2002 El patrón de asentamiento del período clásico en la cuenca baja del Río Cotaxtla, centro de Veracruz: Un estudio de caso de desarrollo de sociedades complejas en tierras bajas tropicales. Unpublished Tesis de Doctor en Antropología, Instituto de Investigaciones Antropológicas, Universidad Nacional Autónoma de México, Mexico City.

2010 Earthen Architecture in Classic Period Central Veracruz, Mexico: Development and Function. In *Monumental Questions, Prehistoric Megaliths, Mounds, and Enclosures*, edited by David Calado, Maximiliam Baldia, and Matthew Boulanger, pp. 223–230. Proceedings of the XV Congress of the Union of Pre-and Protohistoric Science. British Archaeological Reports, International Series 2123, Archaeopress, Oxford.

Daneels, Annick, Luis Guerrero, and Giovanna Liberotti 2013 Monumental Earthen Architecture in the Humid Tropics of Mexico: Archaeological

Evidence of a Millenary Tradition. Structural Studies, Repairs and Maintenance of Heritage Architecture XIII, edited by C. A. Brebia, pp. 457–468. WIT Press, Southampton, UK.

de Jong, Erik 1990 For Profit and Ornament: The Function and Meaning of Dutch Garden Art in the Period of William and Mary, 1650–1702. In *The Dutch Garden in the Seventeenth Century*, edited by John Dixon Hunt, pp 13–48. Dumbarton Oaks Research Library and Collection, Washington, DC.

Doolittle, William E. 2004 Gardens Are Us, We Are Nature: Transcending Antiquity and Modernity. *Geographical Review* 94:391–404.

Drucker, Philip 1943 *Ceramic Stratigraphy at Cerro de las Mesas, Veracruz, Mexico*. Smithsonian Institution, Bureau of American Ethnology Bulletin 141. U.S. Government Printing Office, Washington, DC.

Duany, Andres, Jeff Speck, and Mike Lydon 2010 *The Smart Growth Manual*. McGraw-Hill, New York.

Duncan, James S. 1990 *The City as Text: The Politics of Landscape Interpretation in the Kandyan Kingdom*. Cambridge University Press, New York.

Dunning, Nicholas P. 1992 *Lords of the Hills: Ancient Maya Settlement in the Puuc Region, Yucatán, Mexico*. Monographs in World Archaeology 15. Prehistory Press, Madison, WI.

Ettinghausen, Richard 1976 Introduction. In *The Islamic Garden*, edited by Elisabeth B. MacDougall and Richard Ettinghausen, pp. 2–10. Dumbarton Oaks, Washington, DC.

Evans, Damian, Christophe Pottier, Roland Fletcher, Scott Hensley, Ian Tapley, Anthony Milne, and Michael Barbetti 2007 A Comprehensive Archaeological Map of the World's Largest Preindustrial Settlement Complex at Angkor, Cambodia. *Proceedings of the National Academy of Sciences* 104:14277–14282.

Evans, Susan Toby 2000 Aztec Royal Pleasure Parks: Conspicuous Consumption and Elite Status Rivalry. *Studies in the History of Gardens and Designed Landscapes* 20:206–228.

    2004 Aztec Palaces and Other Elite Residential Architecture. In *Palaces of the Ancient New World*, edited by Susan T. Evans and Joanne Pillsbury, pp. 7–58. Dumbarton Oaks Research Library and Collection, Washington, DC.

Evans, Susan Toby and Joanne Pillsbury, editors 2004 *Palaces of the Ancient New World: A Symposium at Dumbarton Oaks, 10th and 11th October 1998*. Dumbarton Oaks Research Library and Collection, Washington, DC.

Falade, Johnson Bade 1984 Yoruba Sacred Groves and Squares: A Case Study of Ile-Ife. *Edinburgh Architectural Research* 11:21–49.

Foster, Karen Polinger 2004 The Hanging Gardens of Nineveh. *Iraq* 66:207–220.

Gómez-Pompa, Arturo, José Salvador Flores, and Mario Aliphat Fernández 1990 The Sacred Cacao Groves of the Maya. *Latin American Antiquity* 1:247–257.

Goodman, Penelope J. 2007 *The Roman City and its Periphery: from Rome to Gaul*. Routledge, London.

Graham, Elizabeth 1999 Stone Cities, Green Cities. In *Complex Polities in the Ancient Tropical World*, edited by Elisabeth A. Bacus and Lisa J. Lucero, pp. 185–194. Archaeological Papers of the American Anthropological Association 9. Arlington, VA.

Granziera, Patrizia 2001 Concept of the Garden in Pre-Hispanic Mexico. *Garden History* 29(2):185–213.

Gutiérrez, Gerardo 2005 Jardines Defensivos: Un Acercamiento Histórico al Uso de la Vegetación en la Guerra Antigua. *Anales de Antropología* 39(1):51–77.

Hamadeh, Shirine 2008 Garden Sociability in Eighteenth-century Ottoman Istanbul. In *Gardens, City Life and Culture: A World Tour*, edited by Michel Conan and Chen Wangheng, pp. 88–108. Dumbarton Oaks Research Library and Collection, Washington, DC.

Hammond, Kenneth J. 2008 Urban Gardens in Ming Jiangnan: Insights from the Essays of Wang Shizhen. In *Gardens, City Life and Culture: A World Tour*, edited by Michel Conan and Chen Wangheng pp. 41–52. Dumbarton Oaks Research Library and Collection, Washington, DC.

Hammond, Norman, K. Anne Pyburn, John Rose, J. C. Staneko, and Deborah Muyskens 1988 Excavation and Survey at Nohmul, Belize, 1986. *Journal of Field Archaeology* 15:1–15.

Hill, Warren D. and John E. Clark 2001 Sports, Gambling, and Government: America's First Social Compact? *American Anthropologist* 103:331–345.

Hirth, Kenneth 2000 *Archaeological Research at Xochicalco. v. 1. Ancient Urbanism at Xochicalco: The Evolution and Organization of a Pre-Hispanic Society*. University of Utah Press, Salt Lake City.

Hoyt, Homer 1939 *The Structure and Growth of Residential Neighborhoods in American Cities*. U.S. Federal Housing Administration, Washington, DC.

Huang, Jingnan, X. X. Lu, and Jefferey M. Sellers 2007 A Global Comparative Analysis of Urban Form: Applying Spatial Metrics and Remote Sensing. *Landscape and Urban Planning* 82:184–197.

Hughbanks, Paul J. 1998 Settlement and Land Use at Guijarral, Northwest Belize. *Culture and Agriculture* 20:107–120.

Hunt, John Dixon 2000 *Greater Perfections: The Practice of Garden Theory*. University of Pennsylvania Press, Philadelphia.

Inomata, Takeshi 2006 Plazas, Performers, and Spectators: Political Theaters of the Classic Maya. *Current Anthropology* 47(5):805–842.

Inomata, Takeshi and Stephen D. Houston, editors 2000 *Royal Courts of the Ancient Maya*, vol. 1. Westview Press, Boulder, CO.

  2001 *Royal Courts of the Ancient Maya*, vol. 2. Westview Press, Boulder, CO.

Isendahl, Christian 2002 *Common Knowledge: Lowland Maya Urban Farming at Xuch*. Department of Archaeology and Ancient History, Uppsala University and Universidad Autónoma de Campeche, Uppsala, Sweden.

Jacobs, Jane 1993[1961] *The Death and Life of Great American Cities*. Modern Library, New York.

Jashemski, Wilhelmina 2008 Gardens and Garden Life in Pompeii in the First Century AD. In *Gardens, City Life and Culture: A World Tour*, edited by Michel Conan and Chen Wangheng pp. 15–28. Dumbarton Oaks Research Library and Collection, Washington, DC.

Jim, C. Y. and Liu, H. T. 2001 Patterns and Dynamics of Urban Forests in Relation to Land Use and Development History in Guangzhou City, China. *The Geographical Journal* 167(4):358–375.

Killion, Thomas W. 1990 Cultivation Intensity and Residential Site Structure: An Ethnoarchaeological Examination of Peasant Agriculture in the Sierra de los Tuxtlas, Veracruz, Mexico. *Latin American Antiquity* 1(3):191–215.

1992 Residential Ethnoarchaeology and Ancient Site Structure: Contemporary Farming and Prehistoric Settlement Agriculture at Matacapan, Veracruz, Mexico. In *Gardens in Prehistory: The Archaeology of Settlement Agriculture in Greater Mesoamerica*, edited by Thomas W. Killion, pp. 119–149. The University of Alabama Press, Tuscaloosa.

Killion, Thomas W., Jeremy A. Sabloff, Gair Tourtellot, and Nicholas Dunning
1989 Intensive Surface Collection of Residential Clusters at Terminal Classic Sayil, Yucatan, Mexico. *Journal of Field Archaeology* 16:273–294.

Kostof, Spiro 1992 *The City Assembled: The Elements of Urban Form through History*. Thames and Hudson, London.

Lawrence, Denise L. and Setha M. Low 1990 The Built Environment and Spatial Form. In *Annual Review of Anthropology* 19, edited by Bernard J. Siegel, Alan R. Beals, and Stephen A. Tyler, pp. 453–505. Palo Alto, CA.

Lifang, Chen and Sianglin Yu 1986 *The Garden Art of China*. Timber Press, Portland, OR.

Low, Setha M. 2000 *On the Plaza: The Politics of Public Space and Culture*. University of Texas Press, Austin.

Low, Setha, Dana Taplin, and Suzanne Scheld 2005 *Rethinking Urban Parks: Public Space and Cultural Diversity*. University of Texas Press, Austin.

MacDougall, Elizabeth 1972 *Ars Hortulorum*: Sixteenth Century Garden Iconography and Literary Theory in Italy. In *The Italian Garden*, edited by David R. Coffin, pp. 37–59. Dumbarton Oaks, Trustees for Harvard University, Washington, DC.

Magnani, Lauro 2008 Genoese Gardens: Between Pleasure and Politics. In *Gardens, City Life and Culture: A World Tour*, edited by Michel Conan and Chen Wangheng, pp. 55–71. Dumbarton Oaks Research Library and Collection, Washington, DC.

Mango, Cyril A. 1985 *Le Développement Urbain de Constantinople, IVe-VIIe siècles*. Volume 2. Diffusion de Boccard, Paris.

Marcus, Joyce and Kent V. Flannery 1996 *Zapotec Civilization: How Urban Society Evolved in Mexico's Oaxaca Valley*. Thames and Hudson, New York.

Medellín Zenil, Alfonso 1987 *Nopiloa: exploraciones arqueológicas*. Universidad Veracruzana, Xalapa, Mexico.

Medina, Miguel A. 1997 *Arte y estética de El Tetzcotzinco : arquitectura de paisaje en la época de Netzahualcóyotl*. Colección de arte 50. Universidad Nacional Autónoma de México, Coordinación de Humanidades, Mexico City.

Mendizabál, Miguel O. de 1925 El Jardin de Netzahualcoyotl en el Cerro de Tetzcotzinco. *Ethnos: Revista Dedicada al Estudio y Mejoramiento de la Población Indígena de México* época 3, tomo 1:86–95.

Millon, René 1973 *Urbanization at Teotihuacán, Mexico*, v. 1. *Part One, Text*. University of Texas Press, Austin.

Moore, Jerry D. 1996 The Archaeology of Plazas and the Proxemics of Ritual: Three Andean Traditions. *American Anthropologist* 98(4):789–802.

Moreno, María de la Luz and Manuel Alberto Torres 2002 El Origen del Jardín Mexica de Chapultepec. *Arqueología* 10(57):41.

Morley, Neville 1996 *Metropolis and Hinterland: The City of Rome and the Italian Economy, 200 BC–AD 200*. Cambridge University Press, Cambridge.

Musset, Alain 1986 Les Jardins Préhispaniques. *Trace: Travaux et Recherches dans les Ameriques du Centre* 10:59–73.

Nuttall, Zelia 1923 The Gardens of Ancient Mexico. In *Annual Report of the Smithsonian Institution*, pp. 453–464. Smithsonian Institution, Washington, DC.

Osborne, Robin 1992 Classical Greek Gardens: Between Form and Paradise. In *Garden History: Issues, Approaches, Methods*, edited by John Dixon Hunt, pp. 373–391. Dumbarton Oaks Research Library and Collection, Washington, DC.

Parsons, Jeffrey R. 1971 Prehistoric Settlement Patterns in the Texcoco Region, Mexico. *Memoirs of the Museum of Anthropology, University of Michigan*, no. 3. Ann Arbor.

Phibbs, John 1991 Groves and Belts. *Garden History* 19(2):175–186.

Pollack, Harry E. D., Ralph L. Roys, Tatiana Proskouriakoff, and A. Ledyard Smith 1962 *Mayapan, Yucatan, Mexico*. Publication 619. Carnegie Institution of Washington, Washington, DC.

Puleston, Dennis E. 1983 *The Settlement Survey of Tikal*. Tikal Report No. 13, University Museum Monograph 48. The University Museum, University of Pennsylvania, Philadelphia.

Puleston, Dennis E. and Donald W. Callender, Jr. 1967 Defensive Earthworks at Tikal. *Expedition* 9(30):40–48.

Pyburn, Anne K. 1990 Settlement Patterns at Nohmul: Preliminary Results of Four Excavation Seasons. In *Precolumbian Population History in the Maya Lowlands*, edited by T. Patrick Culbert and Don S. Rice, pp 183–197. University of New Mexico Press, Albuquerque.

Redford, Scott, Timothy Paul Beach, and Sheryl Luzzadder-Beach 2000 *Landscape and the State in Medieval Anatolia : Seljuk Gardens and Pavilions of Alanya, Turkey*. British Archaeological Reports, International Series 893. Archaeopress, Oxford.

Revault, Jacques, Lucien Golvin, and Ali Amahan 1992 *Palais et Demeures de Fès, III, Epoque Alawite (XIVe-XXe siecles): Bilan des Recherches sur l'Architecture Domestique à Fès*. Edition du Centre Nacional de la Recherche Scientifique, Paris.

Rice, Don S. and T. Patrick Culbert 1990 Historical Contexts for Population Reconstruction in the Maya Lowlands. In *Precolumbian Population History in the Maya Lowlands*, edited by T. Patrick Culbert and Don S. Rice, pp. 1–31. University of New Mexico Press, Albuquerque.

Rice, Don S. and Prudence M. Rice 1990 Population Size and Population Change in the Central Peten Lakes Region, Guatemala. In *Precolumbian Population History in the Maya Lowlands*, edited by T. Patrick Culbert and Don S. Rice, pp. 123–148. University of New Mexico Press, Albuquerque.

Ringle, William M. and E. Wyllys Andrews, V 1990 The Demography of Komchen, An Early Maya town in Northern Yucatan. In *Precolumbian Population History in the Maya Lowlands*, edited by T. Patrick Culbert and Don S. Rice, pp. 215–243. .University of New Mexico Press, Albuquerque.

Robles García, Nelly Margarita, and Augustín E. Andrade Cuautle 2011 El Proyecto Arqueológico del Conjunto Monumental de Atzompa. In *Monte Albán en la encrucijada regional y disciplinaria. Memoria de la Quinta Mesa Redonda de Monte Albán*, edited by Nelly Margarita Robles García and Ángel Iván Rivera Guzmán, pp. 285–313. Instituto Nacional de Antropologia e Historia, Mexico City.

Ross, Eric S. 1995 Touba: A Spiritual Metropolis in the Modern World. *Canadian Journal of African Studies / Revue Canadienne des Études Africaines* 29(2):222–259.

2002 Marabout Republics Then and Now: Configuring Muslim Towns in Senegal. *Islam et Sociètès au Sud du Sahara* 16:35–65.

2008 Palaver Trees Reconsidered in the Senegalese Landscape: Arboreal Monuments & Memorials. In *African Sacred Groves: Ecological Dynamics & Social Change*, edited by Michael J. Sheridan and Celia Nyamweru, pp. 133–148. James Currey, Oxford, UK.

Rotenberg, Robert 2008 Biedermeier Gardens in Vienna and the Self-fashioning of Middle-class Identities. In *Gardens, City Life and Culture*, edited by Michel Conan and Chen Whangheng, pp. 111–121. Dumbarton Oaks Research Library and Collection, Washington, DC.

Russell, Bradley W. 2008 Postclassic Maya Settlement on the Rural-Urban Fringe of Mayapan, Yucatan, Mexico. Unpublished Ph.D. Dissertation, Department of Anthropology, State University of New York, Albány.

Sanders, William T., Jeffrey R. Parsons, and Robert S. Santley 1979 *The Basin of Mexico: Ecological Processes in the Evolution of a Civilization*. Academic Press, New York.

Sheridan, Michael J. 2008 The Dynamics of African Sacred Groves: Ecological, Social & Symbolic Processes. In *African Sacred Groves: Ecological Dynamics & Social Change*, edited by Michael J. Sheridan and Celia Nyamweru, pp. 9–41. James Currey, Oxford, UK.

Simon, David 2008 Urban Environments: Issues on the Peri-Urban Fringe. *Annual Review of Environment and Resources* 33:167–185.

Sjoberg, Gideon 1960 *The Preindustrial City, Past and Present*. Free Press, New York.

Smith, Joanna F. Handlin 1992 Gardens in Ch'i Piao-chia's Social World: Wealth and Values in Late-Ming Kiangnan. *The Journal of Asian Studies* 51:55–81.

Smith, Michael E. 2005 City Size in Late Postclassic Mesoamerica. *Journal of Urban History* 31:403–434.

Smith, Monica L. 2008 Urban Empty Spaces. Contentious Places for Consensus-Building. *Archaeological Dialogues* 15:216–231.

Smyth, Michael P., Christopher D. Dore, and Nicholas P. Dunning 1995 Interpreting Prehistoric Settlement Patterns: Lessons from the Maya Center of Sayil, Yucatan. *Journal of Field Archaeology* 22:321–358.

Solis Olguín, Felipe 2002 Chapultepec, Espacio Ritual y Secular de los Tlatoani Aztecas. *Arqueología* 10(57):36–40.

Stark, Barbara L. 1999 Formal Architectural Complexes in South-central Veracruz; Mexico: A Capital Zone? *Journal of Field Archaeology* 26:197–225.

2003 Cerro de las Mesas: Social and Economic Perspectives on a Gulf Center. In *El Urbanismo en Mesoamérica: Urbanism in Mesoamerica*, vol. 1, edited by William T. Sanders, Alba Guadalupe Mastache, and Robert Cobean, pp. 391–426. Instituto Nacional de Antropologia e Historia, Mexico City and The Pennsylvania State University, University Park.

Stark, Barbara L. and Alanna Ossa 2007 Ancient Settlement, Urban Gardening, and Environment in the Gulf Lowlands of Mexico. *Latin American Antiquity* 18:385–406.

Stirling, Matthew W. 1943 *Stone Monuments of Southern Mexico*. Bureau of American Ethnology Bulletin 138. Smithsonian Institution, Washington, DC.

Stuart, George E., John C. Scheffler, Edward B. Kurjack, and John W. Cottier 1979 *Map of the Ruins of Dzibilchaltún, Yucatan, Mexico*. Publication 47, Middle American Research Institute, Tulane University, New Orleans, LA.

Tabbaa, Yasser 1992 The Medieval Islamic Garden: Typology and Hydraulics. In *Garden History: Issues, Approaches, Methods*, edited by John Dixon Hunt, pp. 303–329. Dumbarton Oaks Research Library and Collection, Washington, DC.

Talbot, Alice-Mary 2002 Byzantine Monastic Horticulture: The Textual Evidence. In *Byzantine Garden Culture*, edited by Antony Littlewood, Henry Maguire, and Joachim Wolschke-Bulmahn, pp. 37–67. Dumbarton Oaks Research Library and Collection, Washington, DC.

Thomas, Jr., Prentice M. 1981 *Prehistoric Maya Settlement Patterns at Becan, Campeche, Mexico*. Publication 45, Middle American Research Institute, Tulane University, New Orleans, LA.

Tourtellot, Gair 1990 Population Estimates for Preclassic and Classic Seibal, Peten. In *Precolumbian Population History in the Maya Lowlands*, edited by T. Patrick Culbert and Don S. Rice, pp. 83–102. University of New Mexico Press, Albuquerque.

   1993 A View of Ancient Maya Settlements in the Eighth Century. In *Lowland Maya Civilization in the Eighth Century AD*, edited by Jeremy A. Sabloff and John S. Henderson, pp. 219–241. Dumbarton Oaks Research Library and Collection, Washington DC.

Tourtellot, Gair, Jeremy A. Sabloff, and Michael P. Smyth 1990 Room Counts and Population Estimation for Terminal Classic Sayil in the Puuc Region, Yucatan, Mexico. In *Precolumbian Population History in the Maya Lowlands*, edited by T. Patrick Culbert and Don S. Rice, pp. 245–261. University of New Mexico Press, Albuquerque.

Trigger, Bruce G. 1990 Monumental Architecture: A Thermodynamic Explanation of Symbolic Behaviour. *World Archaeology* 22(2):119–132.

Turner II, Billie Lee and William L. Sanders 1992 Summary and Critique. In *Gardens in Prehistory: The Archaeology of Settlement Agriculture in Greater Mesoamerica*, edited by Thomas W. Killion, pp. 263–284. The University of Alabama Press, Tuscaloosa.

Uchiyamada, Yasushi 1998 "The Grove is Our Temple." Contested Representations of *Kaavu* in Kerala, South India. In *The Social Life of Trees: Anthropological Perspectives on Tree Symbolism*, edited by Laura M. Rival, pp. 177–196. Berg, Oxford.

von Thünen, Johann Heinrich 1966 [1875] Von Thunen's "Isolated State": An English Edition, edited with an Introduction by Peter Hall. Carla M. Wartenberg, transl. Pergamon, Oxford.

Webster, David and AnnCorrine Freter 1990 The Demography of Late Classic Copan. In *Precolumbian Population History in the Maya Lowlands*, edited by T. Patrick Culbert and Don S. Rice, pp. 37–61. University of New Mexico Press, Albuquerque.

Webster, David, Timothy Murtha, Dirk D. Straight, Jay Silverstein, Horacio Martinez, Richard E. Terry, and Richard Burnett 2007 The Great Tikal Earthwork Revisited. *Journal of Field Archaeology* 32:41–64.

Webster, David, Jay Silverstein, Timothy Murtha, Horacio Martínez, and Kirk Straight 2004 *The Tikal Earthworks Revisited*. Occasional Papers in Anthropology No. 28. Department of Anthropology, Pennsylvania State University, University Park.

Webster's Seventh New Collegiate Dictionary 1963 *Webster's Seventh New Collegiate Dictionary, Based on Webster's Third New International Dictionary*. G. and C. Merriam Company, Springfield, MA.

Wescoat Jr., James L. 1992 Gardens versus Citadels: The Territorial Context of Early Mughal Gardens. In *Garden History: Issues, Approaches, Methods*, edited by John Dixon Hunt, pp. 331–358. Dumbarton Oaks Research Library and Collection, Washington, DC.

West, Stephen H. 2005 Spectacle, Ritual, and Social Relations: the Son of Heaven, Citizens, and Created Space in Imperial Gardens in the Northern Song. In *Baroque Gardens, Emulation, Sublimation, Subversion*, edited by Michel Conan, pp. 291–321. Dumbarton Oaks Research Library and Collection, Washington, DC.

Whalen, Michael E. and Paul E. Minnis 1996 Ball Courts and Political Centralization in the Casas Grandes Region. *American Antiquity* 61:732–746.

Whitehand, J. W. R. 2001 British Urban Morphology: The Conzenian Tradition. *Urban Morphology* 5(2):103–109.

Whitehand, J. W. R. and N. J. Morton 2006 The Fringe-belt Phenomenon and Socioeconomic Change. *Urban Studies* 43:2047–2066.

Wilkinson, Alix 1998 *The Garden in Ancient Egypt*. Rubicon Press, London.

Williamson, Tom 1992 Garden History and Systematic Survey. In *Garden History: Issues, Approaches, Method*, edited by John Dixon Hunt, pp. 59–78. Dumbarton Oaks Research Library and Collection, Washington, DC.

Wonderly, Anthony 1985 The Land of Ulua: Postclassic Research in the Naco and Sula Valleys, Honduras. In *The Lowland Maya Postclassic*, edited by Arlen F. Chase and Prudence M. Rice, pp. 254–269. University of Texas Press, Austin.

1986 Naco, Honduras: Some Aspects of a Late Precolumbian Community on the Eastern Maya Frontier. In *The Southeast Maya Periphery*, edited by Patricia A. Urban and Edward M. Schortman, pp. 313–332. University of Texas Press, Austin.

Zeng, Z. X. 1991 Historical Geography of Guangzhou. People's Press of Guangdong, Guangzhou. (In Chinese).

12

Different Cities

Norman Yoffee

I live in "The City Different," Santa Fe, New Mexico. It is "different," first, because of its look. Although Santa Fe was founded in 1608 and has accumulated a variety of architectural styles over the centuries, in 1908, city wallahs decreed that all constructions in the central Plaza and in adjacent historic neighborhoods be in the "Pueblo Revival" style, that is, resemble ancient Pueblos, and especially Taos Pueblo about an hour-and-a-half's drive to the north. Garrison Keillor now describes Santa Fe as an "adobe theme-park."

Santa Fe is a city since it has a relatively large population (around 75,000), it is reasonably large (around 100 km²), and – in accordance with followers of central place theory – it serves a hinterland. Some of these services are retail establishments; there are TV stores and computer stores that don't exist in second- or third-order settlements like Española (although it now has a Walmart) or Chimayó.

Santa Fe is a tourist attraction, and its hinterland is national and international in scope. Visitors are attracted to the city's art market, and there are (according to the chamber of commerce) more art galleries in Santa Fe than in any other city in the USA, excepting New York and Los Angeles. In the summer, there is the Santa Fe Opera, an open-air theater that is one of the major venues for opera during this time of year. There is also concurrently a chamber music festival, various choral festivals, ballets, and jazz festivals. To cater to visitors, there are hundreds of restaurants, many quite fancy, many more featuring New Mexican food, which is food with spicy chile sauce. Whereas many states have a state bird, a state tree, or (in Utah and Arizona) a state gun, in New Mexico there is a state question:

red or green? (meaning the color of chile you prefer over your flat, blue-corn enchiladas).

Santa Fe is also a market and ritual center. In the summer, there is Spanish Market, then Indian Market, where artists who are judged as appropriate sell their art in dozens of stalls set up in and near the Plaza. (The word "market" is pronounced by locals "mark-up"). Thousands of visitors from all over the globe come to these markets (and other events) and to ponder the state question. Following these markets is the Fiesta de Santa Fe, commemorating the reconquest of the city and region following the Pueblo Revolt in 1680 that expelled the Spanish immigrants for about twenty years. The highlight of the fiesta (at least for tourists and many Santa Feans) is the burning of a 15 m high paper-maché marionette called "Zozobra," the invention of a Santa Fe booster in 1924. The burning (which takes place in a park) is preceded by a performance of costumed dancers and much consumption of adult beverages by the onlookers (some of whom sit on hillsides above the park where they can barely make out the appearance of Zozobra).

Santa Fe also fits urbanologists' criteria of cities because it is extremely heterogeneous. About 50 percent of the inhabitants are Hispanics (many claiming descent directly from Spain and so do not consider themselves Mexican-Americans, and many speak Spanish as their first language), around 45 percent gringos, several percent Native Americans, and others. Native American Pueblos ring Santa Fe and are not least one of the qualities of life that differentiates Santa Fe from other cities. Santa Fe is a city in that it provides an overarching identity of sorts for its various inhabitants, a critical variable for urbanological gurus (from Weber onward) who labor to define city-ness.

Santa Fe is also legendary for its tolerance of many social, sexual, and cultural orientations. There is a substantial number of Tibetan refugees in Santa Fe, and they fit Santa Fe well since there are many converts to Buddhism in the city, and cocktail conversation is often centered around the best places to meditate. Santa Fe is also home to New Age folk. The answer to the riddle, "Why did the Santa Fean cross the road?" is "she was channeling a chicken."

THE CITY DIFFERENT AND DIFFERENT CITIES IN THIS BOOK

Santa Fe is clearly different from Albuquerque, the Gotham City of New Mexico, with about a half-million inhabitants. Some of them

Table 12.1 *Area and population figures for selected sites from this volume*

City	Size	Population	Time period
Titriş	44 ha	3,750/13,936	2700–2200 BC
Kalavasos	11.5 ha	2,000	1400–1200 BC
Azoria	9–15 ha	1,000+	7th–5th c. BC
Galatas	6–25 ha	5,000	1700–1425 BC
most Swahili sites	10–12 ha	1,000, 5–10,000	AD 600–1500
Rome	35 km²	a million	200 BC–AD 200
Chang'an	36 km²	250,000+	200 BC–AD 200
Cahokia	15 km²	20,000	AD 1000–1300
Chunchucmil	11.7 km²	30,000	AD 400–600
Cerro de las Mesas	15 km²+	4,000–10,000	AD 300–600

come to Santa Fe for its "services," that is, the art galleries, festivals, and restaurants, whereas few Santa Feans descend (2,000-feet down and 100 km to the south) to the Duke City (The Duke of Albuquerque was a conquistador in the Spanish conquest of the region). Santa Fe, as a city, is also different from New York City in ways that are obvious. Is there a great utility, then, in declaring that Santa Fe is a city and so is New York City? This is not an idle question in discussing cities in this volume. Some "cities" that are the subjects of our chapters are approximately 10 ha in area and are estimated to have a few hundred or a few thousand people; others are tens of square kilometers (or more) and have a million or more people.

I present a table (Table 12.1) of approximate areal sizes (rounded-up and usually of largest size/period) and population estimates for some cities in this volume. I draw these figures from the chapters, correspondence with the editors and authors, and published information. My purpose is only to delineate some apples and oranges in the comparisons below. Dates are those given in the chapters, with some rounding.

FULL DISCLOSURE

The editors asked me to discuss chapters in this volume since they had read my review of recent books on ancient cities (Yoffee 2009) and assumed, rightly, that I'd be interested in new studies and new perspectives on studying ancient urbanism. I also am engaged in a project to edit a volume in a new *Cambridge History of the World* in which volume three is on early cities. There has been a conference of chapter authors of that volume at the Institute for the Study of the

Ancient World in New York City, and I must write the introduction and conclusion of that volume. My edited volume will differ from other volumes on early cities, including this one, in that it does not consist solely of essays on cities. Rather, the cities are grouped in topical sections: early cities and the performance of power; early cities, writing, and administrative technologies; early cities and their landscapes; early cities and the distribution of power; cities as creations; imperial cities. The three or four authors of chapters in these sections will also write a conclusion to their section in which controlled comparisons of the cities in their section will be essayed.

When I received the table of contents of the present volume, I was intrigued with the choice of cities. Upper Mesopotamian sites, such as Titriş and Kazane, are discussed whereas the large Mesopotamian cities of the south, such as Uruk or Ur or Lagash or Babylon, are not. Are these northern Mesopotamian sites comparable to the great Mesopotamian cities to their south? For the Aegean world, cities like Athens or Corinth are not represented, but sites on Cyprus, not considered a heartland of cities, and on Crete, also not usually thought of as urban places, are. In Africa there is a chapter on Swahili sites, not Jenne-Jeno or Aksum or Great Zimbabwe or early cities in Egypt. For Mesoamerica the great Maya sites like Tikal are not discussed, nor is there much mention of the urban metropolis of Teotihuacán. Although I was pleased to see new sites being discussed, new research reported, and new perspectives on these sites advanced, one does wonder why these important sites were not represented in a volume on early cities. I was pleased to see the inclusion of Cahokia as an early city, as it is in my own forthcoming edited volume.

My discussion is, of course, not a review of the chapters in the volume; that will be someone else's task. Mine is to ascertain the qualities of "city-ness" in the presented chapters and to ask what if any qualities of "city-ness" hold the volume together.

CITY DIFFERENCES

Chunchucmil, a Maya city in Yucatán, isn't like most other Maya cities. Specifically, there is no monumental architecture as the central focus of the city, and it cannot be claimed that it's a "regal-ritual" city. Its population is quite dense, organized into quadrangles, but these segments of the population are not ethnic groups or wealth groups, according to Aline Magnoni et al. Furthermore, if there was central planning of the *sacbe*-routes through the site, the stone boundary walls of the neighborhoods were presumably constructed by the neighborhoods themselves. Does it matter that Chunchucmil was a Maya city far from the great Classic Maya cities in the Petén to the south? Why was there less of an "investment in charismatic authority," as Colin Renfrew (1978) once put it, in this Maya city? In any case, Chunchucmil collapsed, ca. AD 650–700, sharing the fate of mostly later collapses of the Petén cities.

In the other chapter on Mesoamerican cities, Barbara Stark raises the possibility that there was a great deal of open space, for example, in Cerro de las Mesas and Nopiloa, which she has studied over many years, and in Monte Albán, the famous Oaxacan site. For a comparative case, one might cite the verses from the Mesopotamian poem of Gilgamesh, who describes his city of Uruk: "One square mile is city, one square mile is orchards, one square mile is clay pits, as well as the open ground of Ishtar's temple. Three square miles and the open ground comprise Uruk" (Dalley 1989:50; archaeologists reckon Uruk at the ostensible time of Gilgamesh as 3.5 km^2 and with a population of over 30,000). Shannon Dawdy has recently also written on vacant land in modern and historical cities as ruins, negative space, and the magico-realism of cities (Dawdy 2010). Such are new perspectives on cities that deserve the attention of urban archaeologists.

Cahokia was a city in John Kelly's and James Brown's depiction, sharing the view of Tim Pauketat, whose latest book is titled *Ancient America's Great City on the Mississippi* (Pauketat 2009). In this they rehabilitate, partly, the opinion of Patricia O'Brien, whose views on the complexity of Cahokia had been generally disregarded. However, O'Brien wrote of Cahokia as a state, and Kelly and Brown write of Cahokia as a city, but not a state. Indeed, in Table 12.1, it can clearly be seen that Cahokia's size and population are certainly in the range of sites everyone calls cities and much larger than the sites that several authors in this volume call cities. If Cahokia is a city, and I do not dispute Kelly and Brown in this, what kind of city was it? Apparently, following the authors, Cahokia did not have a king or central government with specialized bureaucratic managers, but did have leaders who owed their power to their place in a kinship and/ or ceremonial system. But, could a city the size and heterogeneity of Cahokia be managed by this kind of leadership? It is a commonplace in urban studies that cities effect changes in their political, social, and demographic structure (see, for an egregious example of this kind of thought, Glaeser's *Triumph of the City* ([2011]). Cahokia, however, collapsed in the fourteenth century, around 300 years after the "Big Bang" that created it. One is tempted to infer that precisely because Cahokia did not develop state-like institutions, it was profoundly unstable, and that attempts at integration in fact led to its collapse. Moreover, if this inference from an outsider to Mississippian studies is worth considering, one might conclude that determining that Cahokia (or any other site) was a "city" can actually deflect more important questions such as what kind of leadership did it have and what sort of division of power and authority existed in the site and ultimately, why was the "city" unstable?

Anna Razeto attempts a comparison between the roughly contemporary cities of Rome and Chang'an, capitals of states and/or empires. She focuses on the nature of manufacture in workshops and the degree of control of overarching state institutions as opposed to private/non-state initiatives. Max Weber, whose influence on urban studies has been great, termed ancient cities "consumer cities;" that is, cities in which wealth was created by control of the countryside and rents paid to urban landlords and the state. Some ancient cities, certainly, were not consumer cities; in this volume, those studying Chunchucmil discuss the important role of trade and commerce, and the importance of long distance is well known from Mesopotamian cities in which the traders were entrepreneurs.

Finally, the authors of chapters on Northern Mesopotamian cities (Andrew Creekmore and Yoko Nishimura), on Cyprus (Kevin Fisher), on Azoria (Rodney Fitzsimmons) and Galatas on Crete (Matt Buell), and on Swahili cities (Stephanie Wynne-Jones and Jeffrey Fleisher) present cases for the urban character of relatively small sites (see Table 12.1), which I review next.

TO BE OR NOT TO BE: CITIES

As can be seen in Table 12.1 of some cities, the first group of five cities that are discussed in the volume are several orders of magnitude removed from the second group of cities. Fisher's and Creekmore's approach "avoids restrictive definitions of 'city' or 'urban' based solely on population size or density." Thus, Fisher declares for sites of 14 and 11.5 ha – little more than some large early villages of the early Neolithic period in Western Asia and that also provided services to and reshaped a countryside: "I have no difficulty defining the urban centers discussed here as cities." Be that as it may, cities that are thirty or three-hundred times larger than others are certainly different in terms of power structures, wealth and status stratification, kinds of neighborhoods, the nature of services to the countryside, social and economic tensions of their population, and not least, ideas of city life and that of the countryside. I don't think, as a Santa Fean, that I need belabor the point that New York City is a different kind of city than my city. In this volume, the palace of Galatas (in Buell's study) is an impressive (for him) 1 ha in size, whereas one market in Chang'an is 50 ha. The differences in these two cities is at least as significant as their shared "city-ness."

Andrew Creekmore and Kevin Fisher and the contributors to this volume, it seems to me, are mainly interested in how people lived in cities and how cities are the "products and facilitators of social life." Thus, the chapters by Creekmore, Nishimura, Fisher, Buell, Fitzsimmons, and Wynne-Jones and Fleisher on the making of the cities they study are about how neighborhoods are constructed both in top-down (by rulers or leaders) or bottom-up (by local community) processes. They cite commentators on urban structures (such as Jacobs, Lefebvre, Rapoport, and Soja) and French social theorists (such as Foucault, Latour, and de Certeau) on places as both reflecting and generating patterns of hierarchy and dominance, and refer to archaeologists such as the Smiths (Adam T., Michael, and Monica) who have insisted on the generative power and social construction of space in the study of early cities.

An alternate title for this book might have been "neighborhoods and power in early cities" since most chapters are concerned with the relation of central authorities, of different kinds, with their local communities (and the archaeological correlates of this, as in the high and low mounds discussed by Creekmore and Nishimura). Allied concerns are thus about commensality, collective identity, group cohesion, and councils of various sorts. Although cities are "products and producers of transformations" (in Fisher's words), they also can lead to "fiery destructions" (of Azoria, for example, but also of other cities), violence and disorder (in Creekmore's words), and collapses (many examples). Concern with "integration" and "cohesion" need balancing with the unstable features of urban size (even in the micro-urban examples presented here), political formations, and relations with a countryside that is "served" by cities. These services are often balanced by the resentments of those urban impositions by those in the "hinterlands" (which is itself, obviously, an urban-biased term).

In conclusion, readers of this book can see many new trends in archaeological analysis, trends that are determined to put people into ancient cities. There is a welcome turn from the formalistic study of the evolution of large sites to a concern with what happened in those sites. The contributors to this volume ask not only how did people live but also how did they understand their lives? Can we go further – with a new arsenal of studies on social memory, nostalgia, performance, and material culture? What kind of jobs did people who lived in early cities have? How did they form neighborhoods? What did they think of their political structures? How did they think of their past, and what hopes did they have for their future?

The studies in this volume offer platforms for new projects that can lead to better research into social life and change in early cities, studies that avoid essentializing "the city" and promote new and better comparative studies.

REFERENCES CITED

Dalley, Stephanie 1989 *Myths from Mesopotamia*. Oxford University Press, Oxford.

Dawdy, Shannon 2010 Clockpunk Anthropology and the Ruins of Modernity. *Current Anthropology* 51:761–793.

Glaeser, Edward 2011 *Triumph of the City*. Penguin, New York.

Pauketat, Timothy 2009 *Cahokia: America's Great City on the Mississippi*. Penguin, New York.

Renfrew, Colin 1978 Trajectory Discontinuity and Morphogenesis: The Implications of Catastrophe Theory for Archaeology. *American Antiquity* 43:203–222.

Yoffee, Norman 2009 Making Ancient Cities Plausible. *Reviews in Anthropology* 38/4:264–289.

Index